The
Home
Answer
Book

The
Home
Answer
Book

Joanna Wissinger

Editor

A STONESONG PRESS BOOK

HarperCollins*Publishers*

Excerpts from the following books are reprinted by permission of HarperCollins Publishers, Inc.: *The Car Repair Book* by Jack Gillis (page 290), *Emily Post's Etiquette,* 15th Edition, by Elizabeth L. Post (page 308), *Birnbaum's United States 1994* by Alexandra Mayes Birnbaum (page 371) and *Terry Savage's New Money Strategies for the '90s* by Terry Savage (page 401).

A Stonesong Press Book

HarperCollins books may be purchased for educational, business, or sales promotional use. For information, please write: Special Markets Department, HarperCollins Publishers, Inc., 10 East 53rd Street, New York, NY 10022.

FIRST EDITION
Designed by Jessica Shatan

Library of Congress Cataloging-in-Publication Data
Wissinger, Joanna, editor.
      The home answer book / edited by Joanna Wissinger. — 1st ed.
         p. cm.
      "A Stonesong Press book."
      Includes index.
      ISBN 0-06-270103-7
      1. Home economics. I. Title.
  TX158.W56 1995
  640—dc20   94-41952

95 96 97 98 99 ❖/RRD 10 9 8 7 6 5 4 3 2 1

Contents

----

6. Cleaning   136

Laundry Basics • Laundry Procedures • Ironing • Dry Clean Only • Stains from A-Z • Cleaning Large Items • Environmentally Safe Cleaners • Housework • Hiring a Housekeeper

7. Cooking   166

Measurements, Equivalents and Substitutions • Food Storage Basics • Food Safety Musts • A Cook's Tools • Essential Implements, Gadgets and Accessories • Herbs and Spices • Chemical Additives: Natural vs. Organic • Wine Basics

8. Clothing   187

Basic Wardrobe Planning • Updating Your Wardrobe • Going Shopping • Fabrics • Accessories • Underwear, Lingerie and Hosiery • Clothing Essentials for Men • Children's Clothing

9. Health   208

An Ounce of Prevention • You Are What You Eat • Weight Control • Eating Disorders • Health Food • Exercise • Finding a Doctor • Common Killers • Sex • Childhood Illnesses and Immunizations • Care for the Elderly • Mental Health Care • Alternative Medicine

10. First Aid   241

Lifesaving Basics • Major Injuries • Minor Injuries and Ailments

11. Owning a Car   277

Do You Really Need a Car? • Buying a New Car • Buying a Used Car • Leasing a Car • Selling Your Car (On Your Own) • Basic Maintenance: Good for Your Car and Your Wallet • Finding a Good Mechanic • Car Safety • Anti-Theft Devices • Cellular Car Phones • Bicycles

12. Etiquette and Entertaining   299

Day-to-Day Good Manners and Common Courtesy • Table Manners • Telephone Manners • Personal Communications • Writing Thank You Notes • Being a Good

Contributors

NAOMI BLACK (Etiquette and Entertaining)

FRAN DONEGAN (Real Estate: Renting, Buying and Selling a Home; Personal Finance)

ALICE FEIRING (Clothing; Cooking)

MARTHA WILHELM KESSLER (Moving)

ELISE NAKHNIKIAN (Health)

ANITA PELTONEN (Travel)

EARL P. PETERSON (Home Maintenance)

KAREN SBROCKEY (Home Organization and Storage; Owning a Car)

JANET SULLIVAN (First Aid; Legal Matters, Forms and Contracts)

DEBRA WARNER, MARY FORSELL (Pets and Gardening)

JOANNA WISSINGER (Cleaning; Home Decorating)

1

Real Estate:
Renting, Buying
and Selling
a Home

Everyone needs a place to live. Perhaps the easiest way to find a residence is to be a rental tenant. You don't have to obtain a mortgage, and the requirements for renting are usually much less stringent than for buying. If you want to buy and are in a position to do so, your choices include a single-family house, a condominium, generally known as a condo, or shares in a cooperative building, or co-op, which entitle you to live in a particular apartment in the building. But in order to own their own home, most individuals or families will have to borrow money in the form of a mortgage. This chapter provides more information on each of these possibilities, as well as advice on what to do when you want to sell your home.

Being a Tenant

Renting an apartment or house is a legal agreement between you and the landlord. Because you pay rent, you have certain rights and are entitled to specific services. The landlord owns the building and expects you to pay your rent in full and on time, and to behave in a way that protects his or her investment.

What tenants should expect from the landlord:

• A written lease that states the amount of rent and the length of time of the rental term. Leases are not mandatory, but it is to the tenant's benefit to insist on one.

• An apartment or house that is habitable, including windows and doors that work, a roof that does not leak, and a unit free of vermin and rodents.

•Standard security measures, such as locks on the doors and windows of your rental unit, and a doorman or street door that locks for apartment buildings.

•Plumbing, electrical systems and major appliances that are safe to use and in good working order.

•A heating system that is in good working order. Many cities specify an outdoor temperature at which landlord-controlled heating systems must be switched on.

•Landlord-supplied garbage removal if not provided by the city or town.

•Common areas that are clean and well-lighted.

•Prompt response to requests for repairs and maintenance.

•The address and phone number of the landlord or his representative to request repairs, register complaints and ask questions.

•Any extras promised by the landlord, such as air-conditioning or reserved parking.

•Adherence to all state and local laws governing rentals.

What landlords expect from tenants:

•Prompt payment of rent. In general, landlords want tenants to spend no more than about 30 percent of their gross monthly income on rent. In order to be certain that you can afford an apartment, they may ask for references, seek verification of employment or check with previous landlords when qualifying you as a tenant. You must pay your rent on time each month, usually by the first of the month (individual landlords may establish a grace period for tenants, or your rent may be due on some other day of the month, but these are not standard provisions).

•Strict adherence to the conditions of the lease.

•An apartment or house that is kept clean and in sanitary condition.

•Responsible use of all appliances, heating and cooling systems, and plumbing facilities.

•No damage or defacing of any part of the landlord's property.

•No changes or alterations in the apartment or house in any manner without the prior consent of the landlord.

•The right to enter the rental unit at any time. The scope of this right varies from state to state and is usually spelled out in the lease.

THE LEASE

The lease is the written contract between you as the tenant and your landlord. You can purchase standard lease forms at stationery or business-supply stores to become familiar with the terms. Your landlord will supply the official lease. It should contain:

•The exact address of the rental house or apartment.

•The name and address of the landlord.

•The names of everyone, except children, renting the unit.

•The dates the lease begins and ends.

- The amount of rent charged and a payment schedule.

- The amount of the security deposit. This can be a flat fee or an amount equal to one or two months rent. The landlord deducts the cost of repairs and maintenance from the security deposit when you move out. Some states require that the security deposit be held in an interest-earning escrow account, with the tenant receiving the accumulated interest.

Most leases contain much more than the points listed above. And most of what they contain either benefits or protects the landlord. But as a tenant you should take note of:

- Fees for late payment of rent.

- Additional charges or fees, such as a fee to use a parking garage, furniture rental, etc.

- Regulations concerning subletting. If you are forced to move before the lease expires, you may have to find a tenant to take over your lease.

- The landlord's verbal promises that are not contained in the lease, such as a promise to paint the apartment or permission to keep a cat even though the lease states that pets are not allowed. The lease should be changed to reflect the promises.

LANDLORD/TENANT RELATIONS
Many people consider this an adversarial relationship at best, but it need not be if all parties involved adhere to both the letter and the spirit of the rental agreement. As a tenant you can protect yourself in a number of ways.

Learn the local laws governing rentals. These vary widely from state to state, but they are especially important if your rent is governed by rent control or rent stabilization laws, which regulate rent increases when a lease is renewed or signed by a new tenant. Rent laws can pertain to everything from subletting to evictions to security deposits to the repair and maintenance of buildings.

Find out which state and city offices handle tenants' complaints. Discuss all complaints with your landlord first. If you are not satisfied, contact the local or state rent board; check local, county and state government listings under "Housing" or "Tenant-Landlord Relations" to find out whom to call. Document the complaint as completely as you can with photographs, copies of letters sent to the landlord and whatever other evidence you may have.

Obtain renter's insurance. Since tenants are not covered under their landlord's insurance policy, it is a good idea to obtain both personal-possession and liability insurance. When purchasing a policy, consider replacement-cost insurance rather than actual-cash-value insurance. The former will pay to replace the item with a similar one, the latter pays the cost of the original item minus depreciation. (See Chapter 15, "Personal Finance," for more information.)

Dealing with an eviction notice. Most evictions take place because the tenant failed to pay rent or broke other provisions of the lease, such as keeping a pet or failing to keep the unit clean. Legally, a landlord can start eviction proceedings the day after your rent is due or you otherwise violate your lease. However, eviction is a legal proceeding that requires a judge's order to become final. It takes time and money for the landlord to go through the whole process. Under normal circumstances, most landlords will grant a grace period of a few days, and then call or write you informally asking when they can expect the situation to be rectified. If that fails, the landlord will start eviction proceedings.

In most states eviction starts with a five-day notice from the landlord. Basically, this states that you haven't fulfilled your lease and you have five days to do so. At the end of that period the landlord can file eviction papers in county court. If your landlord is serious about the eviction, it is best to hire an attorney or consult with state or local rent boards for assistance. Appear in court on the date specified. Judges will usually grant a stay or an extension of a few weeks to give you time to pay the rent. If you are being evicted for a reason other than late payment, you will be able to argue your case before the judge. This, however, is an uncertain procedure and should be used only after other attempts to resolve differences have been exhausted.

If the situation does not change after the extension is granted, the judge will order the eviction. The sheriff's department will be charged with removing you and your belongings from the property.

If you feel you have been the victim of discrimination in housing, call the federal Department of Housing and Urban Development (HUD) at 1-800-669-9777 to file a report.

Buying a House

Residential real estate is big business. About 27 percent of the nation's wealth is derived from the financial worth of houses and residential property; new residential construction accounts for about 5 percent of the U.S. domestic national product; and about 64 percent of the nation's households own their own home.

ADVANTAGES OF HOMEOWNERSHIP

On a personal level, owning a home is often extolled as "the American dream." Though it may not be that for everyone, owning a home does have many advantages. Banks, the tax code and the marketplace offer financial incentives to home buyers that are not available to renters. Some of them include:

•Long-term mortgage loans with interest rates that are relatively low when compared to other types of loans.

•A federal tax deduction for mortgage interest. If your adjusted gross income is below $105,250 (for a married couple filing a joint return), you can deduct all of the interest on your mortgage. That means if you are in the 28 per cent tax bracket, every $1,000 of interest you pay saves you $280 in federal taxes. Because of the way payment schedules are devised, most payments during the first half of the loan term are made up of interest. Local real estate taxes are also deductible.

The tax returns of couples whose adjusted income is above $105,250 are subject to a 3 percent reduction of all of their deductions. Your deductions are also limited if you own more than one home.

•As you repay the mortgage, your *equity* (ownership rights in the property) in the house builds, increasing your personal wealth. If the value of the house also increases, your wealth grows even more.

•The ability to defer a capital gains tax on the sale of a house. When you sell your principal residence for more than you paid for it, you do not have to pay a tax on the profit if you then purchase a new house for an equal or greater amount. You must buy this new house within two years (before or after) of selling the old one.

The amount you realize from the sale of the old house equals the money you receive for it minus the expenses associated with the sale, such as commissions paid to a real estate agent and any fees you paid as the seller. You can also deduct fix-up costs, such as painting, wallpapering and any other repairs, performed within 90 days of the sale. The cost of your new house is defined as what you paid for it plus expenses such as lawyer's fees, broker's fees, title search, transfer taxes and the like.

Those who are 55 years old or older can claim an additional benefit of home-ownership. The government offers a one-time exclusion of capital gains taxes on up to $125,000 ($62,500 for married people who file separately) of profits for those who meet the age requirement. To qualify, the house you sell must have been your principal residence for three of the five years before the sale.

•Freedom. Owners can paint or decorate their homes any way they choose, as long as they comply with local zoning laws and ordinances.

•A wider selection of places to live. The number and types of houses or apartments for rent are often limited; if you want to live in a particular area or neighborhood, you may have no choice except to buy.

THE DOWNSIDE

There are some drawbacks to buying a house. For one, houses are expensive. In 1992 the median sale price of a newly built house was $107,380; for an existing house the median sale price was $91,648. Roughly 10 to 20 percent of a house's cost must be paid in cash in the form of a down payment before getting a mortgage, and there are also a number of initial fees and charges, called closing costs. Other home expenses include homeowner's insurance and maintenance costs.

Although homeowners can do what they want to a property, they are also responsible for dealing with emergencies, such as pipes that burst or furnaces that refuse to work. Renters simply call the landlord in those situations.

Being a renter gives you mobility. Renters tend to be able to pick up and move more readily than a homeowner. Finding an apartment and signing a lease is a lot less complicated than finding a house and getting a mortgage, or selling your house to buy another one.

Along the same lines, being a renter gives you more liquidity than being a homeowner. Houses require the investment of a considerable amount of money, often the majority of a family's wealth. If a need for money arises, it may be difficult to convert your home investment into cash (although the availability of home-equity loans has made this easier). If you rent, you can place your monetary assets in a more liquid investment.

In addition, out-of-pocket costs for renting are lower than those for owning a home in many parts of the country. If you want to keep your immediate housing costs relatively low, then you may want to rent rather than buy for the time being.

CONDOS AND CO-OPS

The most straightforward form of homeownership is called *fee-simple ownership*, and means a person or group of people own the property outright. They alone are responsible for its upkeep, insurance, and taxes. This is the form of ownership under which most people own their homes. *Condominiums and cooperatives (condos and co-ops)* are other forms of ownership. Superficially, there is little difference between them, but the underlying structures are very different.

If you buy a condo, you buy a living unit—an interior space—and a share in common areas. This allows you to take out a mortgage to finance your purchase of the unit and to obtain homeowner's insurance. The living units are financed and taxed individually. Control of the common areas is overseen by a condominium association, of which, as the owner of a unit, you are automatically a member. The condominium association has a set of bylaws that qualify what you are and are not allowed to do in the common areas and, sometimes, in your own apartment (you may not be able to keep a pet, for example). As an owner and member of the association, you are required to pay a monthly, quarterly or annual fee to the association, which it uses to support maintenance and repairs of the complex, insurance, fees and utilities. Payment of this fee is a requirement

of ownership. You are also required to do your own interior maintenance, although you may get help from the management association in such areas as finding a reliable contractor.

Condo ownership, like owning a home, has advantages and disadvantages. You may get the benefit of a rise in property values and the benefit of an income tax deduction, but you may have a problem selling a condominium, since they are often regarded as less desirable than houses. And since condos are multi-family dwellings, your control over your immediate environment is inevitably limited.

Unlike a condo, where you buy a unit in which to live, buying into a co-op means buying shares in a corporation that owns the project in which the unit is situated. You don't actually own the building or even your own apartment, but are a part owner of the corporation that does own it. The corporation obtains a mortgage for the property and receives a tax bill. The financial obligation—mortgage payments, taxes, maintenance and so on—is divided among the shareholder/occupants according to the number of shares they own. The loan you obtain to buy a co-op is not a mortgage (since you are not actually buying a building) but a form of personal loan. However, special tax laws apply to shareholders in a cooperative: They are allowed to deduct their share of interest payments and real estate taxes from the co-op on their individual tax returns.

A disadvantage of this arrangement is that if one shareholder defaults on payments, others are jeopardized, which is why potential shareholders are carefully screened. The corporation that runs the cooperative may also put restrictions on the sale of a unit (they have the right to approve or disapprove a potential buyer, for example) and also on subletting. The co-op form of homeownership is generally not popular except in a few areas, such as New York City and a few other large cities.

How to Find a House, Condo or Co-op

The best course is to make a list of what you want in a home. Some of the general things to consider include location, size, style, number of bedrooms and bathrooms, and commuting distance to work and schools (see "The Home Shopper's Checklist," below). Once you have an idea of what you are looking for, you can start balancing what you want with how much you can afford (see "How Large a Mortgage Can You Afford?" below).

Some sources for finding houses or other units for sale include:

Real estate listings. Every newspaper in the country has a classified section that lists houses and property for sale. A good listing will give location, the number of bedrooms, describe special features such as fireplaces, pools or a greenhouse, and give the asking price and a phone number. Some listings are from real estate brokers, but others are from people who are trying to sell the house on their own to avoid paying a broker's commission. These listings will say "For sale by owner," or FSBO for

short. The savings from not employing a broker may be passed on to the buyer, but the seller is under no obligation to do so.

Real estate brokers. Most people who sell their homes work with a licensed real estate broker. One reason is because most brokers subscribe to a multiple listing service, which is a computer network that publicizes homes for sale. So a house that is listed by one broker could end up being sold by another. The main benefit brokers provide is access to most of the houses for sale in a given area. Brokers can also explain the process of bidding on a house and drawing up a contract, which can vary slightly from area to area. For buyers, brokers also offer convenience. Each has a list of houses available for sale in the area and can show you only the houses that fit your specifications and price range.

As a buyer, however, you must be aware that unless specific arrangements are made, real estate brokers represent the home seller. The American Association of Retired Persons warns that since brokers collect their sales commissions from the seller, they are obligated to seek the highest price possible, which means they may not be able to advise the buyer during negotiations. For this reason, it is best not to discuss the top price you are willing to pay for a house with the broker.

There are exceptions to the typical broker/buyer relationship. Some brokers specialize in representing home buyers. The advantages to the buyer of working with such a broker include the advice and experience of someone who knows the local real estate market and property values. He or she might be better able than you are to spot a property's potential problems. Payment for this service will vary. Some brokers charge a flat fee, others a percentage of the house's sale price, and others collect a share of the sales commission from the seller. Be sure the payment procedure is spelled out before engaging a broker to represent you.

Builders and developers. Even in a bad construction year, hundreds of thousands of new homes are built in the United States. Some are built on speculation, meaning the builder constructs the house and then puts it on the market. Others are part of large developments where the builder offers a selection of model homes to choose from. The process is similar to buying a car in that you pick a model and then select from a list of possible options, only here the options include such things as fireplaces, air-conditioning and wall-to-wall carpeting. To find such properties, check the ads in the real estate section of the local paper.

Buying a house from the government. The federal government guarantees some mortgages. If a bank forecloses on a guar-

Brokers' Commissions

Brokers earn their living by charging a fee for selling your property. Usually the broker takes a percentage of the property's final selling price. Less frequently a flat fee is charged, regardless of how much the property sells for. Ordinarily the seller pays the broker's commission at the close of escrow (discussed later) from the money the buyer paid for the house.

Typical commission fees charged by brokers run from 4 percent to 8 percent of the selling price, with 5 and 6 percent being the most common. In more expensive properties, the commission percentage usually decreases as the price increases. For example, the broker's fee schedule may start out as 6 percent of the first $500,000 of the purchase price, 5 percent of the next $100,000, 4 percent of the next $250,000 and 3 percent of the rest.

Before signing a listing agreement, shop around and see what other brokers are charging. The percentage of the broker's commission is always negotiable; don't let anyone tell you otherwise. Any agreement between real estate brokers in an area to set a standard rate violates federal antitrust laws. If one broker refuses to bargain, find one who will. But don't opt for a low commission if the broker is not going to do much to find a buyer. Find out exactly what services the broker will be rendering and how hard he or she will work to find a buyer for you.

The following provisions of the broker's commission agreement should be included in the written listing agreement: the amount of the fee, whether it's a percentage or a flat fee, and how it is determined (normally from the actual selling price); who pays the fee (usually it's the seller); and, most importantly, when it is due. Keep in mind that unless a clause in the listing agreement states otherwise, the broker's fee usually is earned when he or she presents a person who wants to buy the property and who has the money or can qualify for a loan—someone who is "ready, willing and able" to purchase your house. Generally, the commission is payable even if the sale is never actually consummated—

for example, if you change your mind at the last minute and decide not to sell, or there is a problem with the title that causes the sale to fall through. Unless the listing agreement states otherwise, the broker is still entitled to the commission, because the broker has done what he or she agreed to do: bring you someone who wants to, and is qualified to, buy your house at an acceptable price.

Clearly, you should negotiate for a listing agreement that's to your advantage. You can, for example, provide in the listing agreement that the broker's commission is payable only if and when escrow closes. This protects you from having to pay the broker's commission if the purchase doesn't go through. At the very least, you, as a seller, should insist upon including a clause in the listing agreement stating that if the sale is not consummated because of anyone's acts other than your own, the broker does not get a commission.

From *Everybody's Guide to the Law* by Melvin M. Belli Sr. and Allen P. Wilkinson, copyright 1987, 1986. Published by Harper & Row.

anteed mortgage, the Department of Housing and Urban Development (HUD) takes title to the house and then tries to sell it. The advantage to a buyer is that HUD requires only a 3 percent down payment rather than the standard 10 to 20 percent. HUD also pays the real estate broker's commission. Local real estate brokers can tell you if any HUD houses are available in the area you wish to live.

A similar program is operated by the Resolution Trust Corporation, which was set up by the federal government to sell houses and other living units that were the property of failed savings and loan associations. These are sold at auction. Again, the advantages are a low down payment and the chance to find a real bargain. Call 1-800-782-3006 for more information.

THE HOME SHOPPER'S CHECKLIST

While house hunting, you may tour 5, 10, even 20 or more houses until you find the one you want. After visiting a few, the features of each will begin to run together in your mind. To keep them distinct, it is a good idea to make notes or even take pictures if possible. The following checklist is based on one developed by HUD. Assign a letter grade or a good, satisfactory or poor rating to each entry. Make several copies and fill out one for each house you visit.

The House:

Square footage _____

Number of bedrooms _____

Number of bathrooms_____

Layout of rooms _____

Condition of interior _____

Closets/storage space _____

Basement _____

Fireplace _____

Exterior appearance _____

Yard space _____

Patio or deck _____

Garage _____

Energy efficiency _____

Condition of windows _____

Condition of roof _____

Condition of gutters and
downspouts _____

Condition of heating/cooling
equipment _____

Condition of plumbing_____

The Neighborhood:

Condition of nearby houses
or businesses _____

Traffic _____

Noise level _____

Safety/security _____

Age mix of neighbors _____

Number of children _____

Parking _____

Zoning regulations _____

Neighborhood restrictions/
covenants _____

Fire protection _____

Police protection _____

Snow removal _____

Garbage collection _____

Schools:

Age/condition _____

Reputation _____

Quality of teachers _____

Achievement-test scores _____

Play areas _____

Curriculum _____

Class size _____

Busing distance _____

Convenience to:

Work _____

Schools _____

Supermarkets _____

Shopping _____

Child care _____

Hospitals _____

Parks _____

Restaurants/entertainment _____

Church/synagogue _____

Airports _____

Highways _____

Public transportation _____

Making an Offer

Once you've found the house you want, it's time to make an offer. The way nego- tiations are conducted varies from place to place. If you are buying an FSBO, you may be able to make an offer face to face with the owner. If a real estate bro- ker is involved, however, he or she usu- ally acts as the middleman between you and the seller. The broker may deliver your offer orally or ask for it in writing. The written offer may be stated on an initial version of the sales contract.

In either case, remember that it is tra- ditional for sellers to ask a higher price than they are actually willing to take for the house. It is also important to remember that price is only one part of the negotiation. You can also ask that such things as major appliances, rugs or even furniture be included in the sale.

THE SALES CONTRACT

The contract between buyer and seller may be known as the sales contract, the purchase agreement, the contract of purchase or the sales agreement. A typi- cal contract will contain:

• The names of the buyer and seller, and the location of the property.

• The agreed-upon price.

• The amount of the deposit or "earnest money," if any. This is usually payable at the signing of the contract and held in the real estate broker's escrow account until the closing. This amount becomes part of the down payment.

• The amount of the down payment, usu- ally 10 to 20 percent of the total cost of the house. The contract will also set a dead- line for delivering the balance of the down payment to the escrow account.

- The contract will usually place a time limit on how long the buyer has to obtain a mortgage.

- Items in the house or on the property that will be included in the sale price.

- The commission paid by the seller to the real estate broker.

Here are some provisions that you as a buyer should insist be a part of the contract:

- A statement that says the contract will be valid only after review by your attorney.

- Your right to have the house inspected by a professional house inspector. If the inspector finds something wrong, the seller can either fix it or reduce the price of the house. The contract should state that your deposit and down payment will be refunded to you if the seller refuses to do either and you decide to terminate the contract as a result.

- A listing of verbal promises made by the seller. For example, if the seller promises to complete the remodeling of the kitchen or fix a leaky roof before you move in, those statements should be part of the sales contract.

THE HOUSE INSPECTION

This is becoming an increasingly important tool for home buyers. The inspection is conducted by a professional house inspector a few days after the sales contract is signed. The inspection will cover the house's heating and cooling systems, plumbing, electrical, roof, attic, basement, foundation, visible

Do You Need a Lawyer?

The answer to this question is yes. In the past, whether a home buyer or seller was represented by legal counsel was a matter of local custom. Today, however, it is becoming the norm for both parties to have lawyers. For the buyer during a straightforward transaction, the lawyer reads the sales agreement, reviews the home-inspection report, orders the title search in some cases and reviews the loan commitment papers to make sure they follow state laws. The attorney can also help untangle snags that develop during the loan approval process and act as guide through the whole buying process. In many parts of the country, the buyer's attorney conducts the actual closing of the deal. Real estate attorneys generally charge a flat fee for their services.

insulation and the condition of walls, ceilings, doors and windows, checking for evidence of mechanical or structural problems, rot or insect damage.

Many people confuse the house inspector with the appraiser. The house inspector will not determine the value of the house, but he or she will inform you of its general condition. As a buyer, you can use this information to compel the seller to repair or replace systems or components of the house before the sale is final, or reduce the sale price.

Although it is not required, the American Society of Home Inspectors recommends that the buyers be present at the inspection. The inspector can answer questions and pass on tips on maintenance and the life expectancy of appliances and materials.

In most states, home inspectors do not need a license. Members of the American Society of Home Inspectors adhere to formal inspection guidelines and a code of ethics. To find a reputable professional, look in the Yellow Pages under "Home Inspectors" or ask your lending institution, broker or real estate attorney for a referral.

Building a House

An alternative to buying a house that already exists is to build your own home. By building we mean initiating and, perhaps, managing the construction of the building, not doing the actual work. To build a house, you will need land, a design, a contractor or builder to do the work, and financing.

BUYING LAND

Every dream house starts with a dream location. But unless you are buying an island, every piece of land is surrounded by other pieces of land. What happens on adjoining, or even nearby, property affects your property. For

Secondary Inspections

A good home inspector can point out the need for testing in addition to the standard home inspection. This is becoming increasingly important as we learn more about our environment and the dangers of some of the building products and materials used in the past. Three areas of concern are radon, asbestos and lead paint, which are not always discovered in the course of a standard inspection.

RADON

What is it?

Radon is a naturally occurring gas that is part of the radioactive decay process of uranium. The gas itself is odorless, colorless, and tasteless and is found everywhere. It becomes a problem when it finds its way into houses through cracks and crevices, then decays further into small particles that we breathe into our lungs. Once there, particles can cause lung cancer. Radon is a problem in homes because air tends to be motionless for long periods of time, particularly in areas such as basements. Outdoors, air currents dissipate radon gas, rendering it harmless. Radon can also be present in ground water.

How do I know if it is in the house?

There are a number of do-it-yourself testing kits that can tell you if your home has a radon problem. The most basic ones consist of a charcoal canister that you place in the lowest part of the house for a prescribed number of days. A testing lab analyzes the canister and sends you the results. Look for testing kits that state "Meets EPA [Environmental Protection Agency] Requirements." The lab will inform you if there is a problem. You can find radon testing kits in hardware and home stores. The kits include information on which lab to send the samples to.

How do I get rid of it?

Some radon mitigation techniques are as simple as caulking cracks in the foundation. Others are more complicated and expensive. In order to eliminate the danger from radon, deal only with EPA-certified or state-certified contractors. For more information on these techniques, call the EPA National Radon Hotline at 1-800-SOS-RADON, or the American Lung Association at 1-800-LUNG-USA.

ASBESTOS

What is it?

Asbestos is a mineral that at one time was used in a wide variety of building products. Manufacturers used it because asbestos is durable, inexpensive and fire-resistant. In recent years, however, studies of asbestos workers have shown a high incidence of cancer. Once inhaled, the microscopic fibers of asbestos can lodge in the lining of the lungs. The danger posed by lower levels of asbestos is uncertain, but experts cannot provide assurance that exposure to any level is safe.

How do I know if it is in the house?

A good home inspector can spot many products that contain

example, the site you like may get runoff from uphill neighbors after a storm. The wind could carry smells and sounds from the surrounding countryside or industries that you may find offensive. In addition, you should pick a neighborhood with similarly priced homes, good schools, low crime—all the things you take into consideration when you're thinking about buying an existing home. There is an infinite number of possible conditions to consider.

Fortunately, many problems can be mitigated by how the house is situated on the property and by certain construction methods—the province of a skillful architect. But it is important to know what you are dealing with before design and construction begin. It's best to visit the site during different times of day and under different weather conditions to obtain a true picture of the property.

Access to the property is also an important factor to consider. During construction, your builder must be able to get equipment, materials and labor to

asbestos. In homes over 20 years old, look for it in pipe insulation, the insulated jackets of furnaces, siding, flooring, patching compounds and textured paints. If you are unsure of whether or not a substance contains asbestos, your local or state environmental agency can provide a list of laboratories that can test for its presence. Do not attempt to take samples yourself until contacting the EPA or a qualified laboratory or contractor.

How do I get rid of it?
Asbestos is dangerous only when the product that contains it is damaged, crumbling or flaking, releasing the tiny, carcinogenic fibers into the air. In many cases, the best course of action is to leave the asbestos-containing material alone. A more drastic course is to encapsulate the material, and the most radical is to remove it altogether. Encapsulation and removal should be performed only by certified asbestos contractors. Removing the material incorrectly could release fibers, compounding the problem further.

The EPA offers brochures on the topic; call 1-202-475-7751.

LEAD

What is it?
Lead is a metallic element once used in making pipes and paints. Lead pipes and solders can leach lead into the water supply. The danger from paints comes when children eat flaking paint and from the dust created when leaded paint is removed from a surface. Research shows that even at low levels, lead that accumulates in the body can damage the central nervous system, the kidneys and blood cells and can cause learning disabilities. Small children, the elderly and pregnant woman are the most vulnerable to its effects.

How do I know if it is in the house?
The federal government is conducting an extensive program to eliminate lead from municipal water systems. Your local water company can provide lead levels for your area. If the house you want to buy is serviced by a well, a qualified lab can test the water.

Perhaps as many as three fourths of the homes built before 1980 contain leaded paint. A qualified lab can take a sample and test it for you. To find a lab, look in the Yellow Pages under "Testing Labs."

How do I get rid of it?
The municipal water system is responsible for removing lead from the water supply. However, it is not responsible for lead pipes or lead solders in your home that may be leaching lead into the system. Fortunately, there are filters you can install to remove lead from the water. It is also a good idea to allow the water to run for 10 or 15 seconds before using it. This flushes out water that has been standing in the pipes. For painted surfaces that contain lead, leave them alone if they are in good condition. Otherwise, the surface can be encapsulated or removed—again, by a qualified lead-abatement contractor. Call the EPA number above for more information on lead in paints. For information on eliminating lead contamination in drinking water, call the EPA at 1-800-426-4791.

and from the site easily. Other points to consider are the availability of electrical and telephone services, as well as fire and police protection. If water and sewer services are not provided by the local town, the property must be able to support a well and septic system.

Visit the local building department to learn the local zoning laws before purchasing property. Zoning laws are ordinances that regulate the growth of the area. They determine what kinds of buildings can go where, such as houses in residential areas or factories in industrial sections. They may also stipulate the size of building lots and impose certain building restrictions, such as the height of a building or the minimum distance between the property line and the building. The building department can also point out areas that are within the flood plains of rivers and streams.

HOUSE DESIGNS

There are a number of ways to obtain a design and blueprints for the house of your dreams.

Custom Designs

Both architects and house designers can create a design for you. Architects are licensed by the state and have undergone extensive academic and professional training. They are versed in both design and construction. House designers are not licensed. They may understand and have extensive experience with residential design, but they are usually restricted by law from designing public buildings.

The best way to select either an architect or house designer is to visit homes they have designed. If you like the designs, meet with the professional to see whether you feel you can work well together. Designing and building a house is a long and potentially stressful undertaking. It is important for everyone involved to get along.

You can hire a designer by the hour to develop a design and draw up the plans. Prices range from $50 to $200 an hour for this service. House designers charge less than architects. Architects can also manage the construction of the house in addition to producing the plans. Expect to pay 10 to 15 percent of the cost of the house for this service.

Plan Services

These organizations offer thousands of home designs, many of which are the work of registered architects. Each service operates differently, but the usual routine is for the buyer to select a plan from a book or magazine and then buy the blueprints. (Building plans show the layout and the dimensions of the rooms. Blueprints give the builder detailed instructions on how to construct the house.)

Blueprint prices range from $200 to $400 for the first set and $50 to $100 for additional sets. During construction the builder, building inspector and the bank will all need a set. Some plan services will work with you to customize the design. Some offer a materials list with the blueprints.

Factory-built Houses

There are a variety of styles and designs available among manufactured houses, which used to be called mobile homes; house kits, which supply lumber cut to fit and building parts; and modular houses, where whole sections of the house are delivered preassembled to the building site. In general, the less work done at the factory, the more design options are available. On the other hand, the more complete the building is when it leaves the factory, the less that must be done on site.

When considering a factory-built house, the Manufactured Housing Institute recommends that you be sure it meets local building codes. The builder should have experience with factory-built houses; the manufacturer may recommend a builder in your area. Factory-built kits do not include foundations.

WHO DOES WHAT?
Building a house requires the services of dozens of people.

Designers
The architect or house designer, as mentioned above, creates the overall design. But sometimes for structural or aesthetic reasons other design professionals become involved as well. Some projects may require the services of interior designers, kitchen/bathroom designers and structural engineers.

Contractors
The contractor or builder oversees the construction of the house. He collects bids on materials and labor, hires suppliers and labor, and deals with scheduling. The builder also arranges for building permits and inspections by the local building department.

As mentioned above, sometimes an architect acts as the builder as well as the designer. In other cases, the builder may hire the designer or the designer may be on the building company's staff. This last case is known as a design/build firm, sort of one-stop shopping for house construction.

There are two main ways builders can charge for their work. With a fixed-fee contract, the builder guarantees a price. He estimates the cost of materials, labor, price fluctuations and his own fee, and makes a bid on the project. If construction costs more than expected, he suffers; if it costs less, he gets the extra profit. In a cost-plus arrangement, the builder's fee is a percentage—usually 10 to 15 percent—of the cost of construction.

Subcontractors
These are the carpenters, plumbers, painters and other craftsmen who do the actual work. They are hired and paid by the builder and he is responsible for the quality of their work.

FINANCING
Paying for a house you build yourself is different from obtaining a mortgage on an existing home. Building your own home requires at least two financial transactions.

Banking practices vary from region to region, so be sure to check local procedures at the beginning of the process. Usually, you will need a short-term loan (also called a *bridge loan*) to cover the cost of construction, followed by a permanent mortgage that pays off the first loan and extends your payments over a longer period of time.

Many of the criteria lenders use to review mortgage applications for soon-to-be-built houses are the same as those used for existing houses. For example, you must be able to pay back the loan and you must have an equity in the property. The mortgage lender will loan you a percentage of the unbuilt house's value, usually 75 to 90 percent. This amount must cover the cost of construction. An appraiser will establish the market value of the house based on the plans you provide.

Even though you qualify for the long-term loan, the lender will not release the money until the house is built. But obtaining the long-term commitment first is essential because it will help you qualify for the short-term construction loan. Some banks will provide both loans in a package deal, but in other cases you must go to different lenders for each of the loans.

The question of financing the land can confuse the process. In many cases, it is difficult, if not impossible, to obtain a mortgage that includes both land and construction costs. One reason is that combined, these costs could be more than the market value of a house once it is built. If the lender sees no chance of getting its money back should it foreclose on the loan, it will not lend the money in the first place.

There are loans for buying land, but they are difficult to find. Even if you do finance the land purchase, the lender may require that you pay off the loan before it will issue a mortgage. Of course, if you own the land outright, it can be used as security for the loans. The best procedure is to check requirements carefully with local lenders and proceed from there.

Getting a Mortgage

Finding, applying for and waiting for approval of a mortgage can be a nerve-racking experience. But although it is a complicated process, there is an underlying logic behind the rules, regulations and customs you will encounter.

First, some terms you will be hearing when applying for a mortgage:

Adjustable-Rate Mortgage. A loan that has a variable interest rate and payment schedule. See "Mortgage Options," below, for more information.

Annual Percentage Rate (APR). This term covers the interest rate buyers apply for on the mortgage application plus other charges such as points, per diem interest and private mortgage insurance. It represents the "true cost" of the loan—the percentage rate plus other charges.

Appraisal. An expert's opinion of the market value of a house. The bank will order an appraisal of the house when a mortgage application is filed.

Assumable Mortgage. An existing mortgage that can be transferred from the current owner of a house to a new owner. The buyer assumes the obligation of the original mortgage holder.

Closing. See "Settlement."

Conventional Mortgage. A loan that has a fixed interest rate and payment schedule. See below, "Mortgage Options."

Down Payment. The amount in cash the buyer turns over to the seller when the sales contract is signed. The amount is usually held in an escrow account until the closing. The lending institution will specify the amount of down payment it requires from the buyer before approving a mortgage.

Equity. The portion of the house and property that the owner owns free and clear. It is computed by subtracting the amount of the unpaid mortgage plus any other liens on the property from the market value of the house.

Government Programs. The federal government does not make loans, but it does sponsor programs that guarantee repayment of mortgages to lenders. The Department of Veterans Affairs and the Federal Housing Administration offer a number of programs that require only small down payments. Contact local offices of the VA or FHA for more details.

Locking In. Agreeing on a specific interest rate with the lender. Borrowers may lock in a rate when they complete the loan application, or they may wait in the hope that rates will drop before the loan is approved.

Points. A point is 1 percent of the amount of the mortgage loan. Lenders charge points in addition to the interest rate to increase the yield of the loan. Points are usually paid by the buyer before or during the closing. Sometimes points are paid to lock in a specific interest rate.

Private Mortgage Insurance. This is a policy that guarantees partial repayment of a mortgage loan to a lender. Lenders usually require it with down payments of less than 20 percent. The fee is paid by the buyer.

Secondary Mortgage Market. In simplified terms, a typical mortgage goes through this process: A lender originates, or approves, the loan, then packages the mortgage with others and sells them to an organization in the secondary mortgage market; the organization then issues securities backed by the mortgages to investors. This process offers two benefits to home buyers. It forces lenders to conform to relatively standard procedures when qualifying and approving loans, and it replenishes the stock of mortgage money available.

Settlement. The conclusion or final settling of all matters relating to the sale. The mortgage, title to the property and deed are transferred to the buyer at the settlement, and most of the fees associated with a mortgage are paid. Depending on which part of the country you live in, this may be known as the closing.

Title Insurance. Protects the homeowner, or sometimes the lender, against loss if there is a defect in the title.

Title Search. This is a check of the official records to make sure the buyer is purchasing the house from the legal owner and that there are no liens or other claims on the property.

Truth-in-lending Disclosure. A statement from the lender that lists the APR, the amount financed over the life of the loan and the total of all payments (principal and interest) over the life of the loan.

MORTGAGE OPTIONS

There are scores of different types of mortgages available, but most fall into one of two broad categories: conventional fixed-rate and adjustable-rate mortgages.

The conventional mortgage has a fixed interest rate. Loans are available for 15, 20 and 30 years, and during that time, the payments and the interest rate remain constant.

The interest rate and the payments on an adjustable-rate loan change at specified intervals during the life of the loan, with six months and one, three and five years being the most common. The amount the interest rate rises or falls depends on the *index* the loan uses, which is usually an indicator of prevailing interest rates, such as U.S. Treasury securities, and the *margin*, which is a percentage agreed upon by the lender and the borrower. The lender adds the two together to come up with the new interest rate and payment amount. When the loan is scheduled to adjust again, the process is repeated.

There are many variations of the adjustable rate. A *convertible loan,* for example, starts out as an adjustable rate, but you have the option of converting to a fixed rate at some time during the life of the loan. The conversion period is usually specified, and there is often a fee for converting. A *two-step loan* begins with an interest rate slightly below fixed-rate mortgages and remains in effect for seven years; after that it adjusts to prevailing rates for the next 23 years.

Other types of loans include *balloon mortgages,* where a fixed rate is in effect for three to five years and then the rest of the loan is due. Many lenders guarantee refinancing at the end of the initial period, others do not.

HOW LARGE A MORTGAGE CAN YOU AFFORD?

Your ability to repay the mortgage will determine how much money you can borrow. Lenders judge this by figuring ratios between your income and the debt you will incur. The most common ratio is 28/36. The first number refers to the maximum percentage of gross income that you should spend on the principal and interest payments of a mortgage, along with real estate taxes and homeowner's insurance—PITI for short. To prequalify yourself, you will need some idea of local taxes and insurance rates. The second number in the ratio refers to the maximum percentage of gross income that you ought to spend on PITI combined with your other debt, such as car-loan payments and credit-card bills.

Once you know how large a payment you can afford, you can combine this with current interest rates to determine the amount of the loan you will qualify for. There are a number of mortgage amortization schedules you can purchase. Local real estate brokers and bankers can also provide the information.

WHERE TO APPLY FOR A MORTGAGE

The most common sources are savings and loan societies, savings banks and commercial banks. But there are other important sources. You will find them listed in the Yellow Pages under "Mortgages" and many advertise in the real estate sections of newspapers.

Questions to Ask When Applying for an Adjustable-Rate Mortgage

Which index is used?

What's the margin? This will vary slightly from lender to lender, but it is usually 2 to 4 percentage points.

What caps are on the loan? Most adjustables have interest-rate or payment caps. An interest-rate cap is the percentage the rate can rise or fall at each adjustment period, usually about 2 percent, and the percentage the interest rate can increase over the life of the loan, usually about 6 percent. Payment caps specify the percentage the payment can rise or fall at each adjustment period. Be wary of payment caps because they can lead to negative amortization, where your payment is not large enough to pay all of the interest on the loan. The amount not paid is added to the loan's principal.

What happens at the first adjustment? Many lenders offer low initial rates for adjustable mortgages. At the first adjustment, the rate will rise to reflect prevailing interest rates. This can be a shock, so it is best to prepare for it.

Mortgage Bankers. These are companies whose only business is writing mortgages. Some are independent while others are owned by large banks or insurance companies. They use their own funds or match borrowers with money from banks, insurance companies or pension funds.

Mortgage Brokers. They find sources of mortgage funds for borrowers.

Credit Unions. These lending institutions usually offer good rates, but only about a third of U.S. credit unions write mortgages.

Insurance Companies. Most of their mortgage money goes to large commercial and industrial buildings. Many do, however, lend to home buyers through mortgage bankers and brokers.

Home Sellers. At times, the home seller may be willing to finance at least part of the cost of the house.

APPLYING FOR A MORTGAGE

It pays to shop around when selecting a mortgage lender. Rates can vary by as much as two percentage points among local lenders. Mortgage rates and terms are advertised in real estate sections of newspapers and lenders will quote current rates over the phone. There are services (see Other Sources of Information, below), that list current rates of lenders in your area. There is usually an application fee of a few hundred dollars to apply for a mortgage.

The Application

The loan application will outline who you are and how you intend to pay for the property you want to purchase. The lender will also ask for the following:

• Sales contract

• Federal tax forms for the past two years

• W-2 forms for the past two years

• Account numbers for current checking, savings, stock and bond accounts

• The most recent three months of statements for checking, savings, stock and bond accounts

• One month of pay stubs

• Address and phone numbers of current employers

• If you currently own a home, the past 12 months of canceled checks showing timely payments of the mortgage

• If you receive a gift for the down payment, a letter stating that the gift does not need to be repaid

• If self-employed, a year-to-date profit and loss statement

The Approval Process and Commitment

Once the application is filed, the lender spends the next 30 to 60 days processing paperwork. The loan officer should be able to provide a more precise estimate of the time. During that time, the lender will:

• Order an appraisal of the house

• Verify your employment and income

• Order a credit check on you

• Order a title search (or the buyer's attorney will order one)

During this period, the lender may request additional information from you. It is in your best interests to provide the lender with whatever he needs as quickly as possible.

Most loans require *full documentation*, called *full docs* by lenders, meaning that everything stated in the application must be verified. Many lenders, however, offer *low-doc* loans, meaning that not everything need be verified. Low docs reduce paperwork for more complicated income arrangements, such as self-employed people or those who derive income from investments, partnerships and the like. The price for low-doc treatment is higher interest rates or points.

Once you are approved for the loan, the lender commits to the mortgage. Read the commitment papers carefully and make sure your lawyer receives a copy. If everything is in order, schedule the closing.

Out-of-Pocket Expenses

Here are some of the fees you can expect to pay when applying for a mortgage. Most are due at, or shortly before, the closing. Expect to pay 3 to 5 percent of the loan amount in fees and costs.

• Mortgage application fee (payable when the application is filed)

• Points

• Bank check fee

•Bank's attorney fee

•Your attorney's fee and any overnight mail, messenger and phone charges he or she incurred

•Appraisal and credit-check fees (sometimes included in the application fee)

•Private mortgage insurance premium for one year

•Hazard insurance premium for one year

•Real estate taxes that were prepaid by the previous owner

•Title search and insurance fees

•Notary fees

•Inspections

•Mortgage and deed recording fees

•Odd-day interest. The lender will require an interest payment to cover the time from the closing to the period covered by the first monthly payment. For example, if you make settlement on April 20, you will owe interest on the days from the 20th through the 30th. Incidentally, in this case your first payment is due on June 1, which will cover interest and principal charges for May.

Refinancing a Mortgage

In general, the rule of thumb is that if mortgage interest rates drop to 2 percent less than what you are currently

How to Save Money on Mortgages

Paying cash is the cheapest way to buy real estate because there are no finance charges. For example, when you pay off a $100,000, 30-year conventional loan at 9 percent interest you will have paid $189,667 in interest charges in addition to the loan's principal. But there are ways to reduce the interest payment. If you added an extra 6 percent each month to the payment for the mortgage above, which means increasing the payment by $48.28, you would save $48,259 in interest and the loan would be repaid in 23.6 rather than 30 years.

Here are some alternative mortgage plans that help save on interest.

Mortgage for a loan of $100,000 at 9%

Type of Mortgage	Monthly Payment	Total Interest Paid
30-Year Conventional	$804.63	$189,667
15-Year Mortgage	$1,014.27	$82,569
Biweekly Mortgage (where one-half payment is made every other week, 13 full payments per year, loan is paid off in 21.8 years)	$402.32, due every other week	$127,926
Growing Equity (payments increase by a set percentage each year, 3% in this example)	Start at $804.63 and rise to $1291.19 for last year of loan	$105,791 (loan is paid off in 16.7 years)

paying, it may be time to refinance. However, you must be aware that refinancing your mortgage can be just as difficult and time-consuming as obtaining one in the first place. You will have to go through many of the same steps, such as hiring a lawyer, verifying the deed and paying closing costs. You may get a few breaks on the costs—for example, if you buy title insurance from the same company, they may charge you less—but on the whole it is an expensive process. Therefore, one thing to consider is whether you will save enough on refinancing to pay for these additional closing costs within a reasonable amount of time, such as two years. If you are not planning to stay in your current house for that long, refinancing is probably not a good idea.

How to Sell a House

If you are putting your house on the market, you have two choices: listing it with a local real estate broker or acting as your own broker. Handling the sale yourself will save you the broker's commission, which can run as high as 5 or 6 percent of the sales price, but in return you will have to fulfill the duties of the broker. Here is what the broker does for the seller:

•Advises you on setting an asking price

•Advertises the sale of the house in local newspapers and multiple listing services

•Shows the house to prospective buyers

•Advises you on pre-sale maintenance and fix-ups

•Handles and guides the sales procedure that includes contracts, inspections and closing

Selling a house can be a full-time job, so make sure you have the time to devote to it. You will have to make yourself available to show it to potential buyers, which can be a time-consuming process. Buyers often want to poke around in areas you may consider private or off-limits, which can be stressful. However, asking buyers *not* to look at certain areas of the house gives them a poor impression and may put them off entirely. In addition, you will need to be careful not to let your emotional attachment to your home get in the way of making the best deal.

In addition, you may feel uncomfortable asking the screening questions about finances that most brokers ask of potential buyers.

HOME SELLER'S CHECKLIST
Here are some tips from the American Society of Home Inspectors to help make your house more attractive to potential buyers:

•Check the structure and main operating systems of the house. It may pay to have a pre-sale inspection by a professional to spot and repair major problems before they interfere with a sale. Check the foundation, roof, siding, heating and cooling systems, electrical wiring and plumbing.

•Get rid of clutter. Clean out the basement, garage and all closets. Give unneeded items to charity, hold a garage sale or put the items in storage until after the sale.

•Tone down extravagant decorating schemes. Many experts recommend repainting in a neutral color.

•Clean everything, including shampooing carpets, polishing floors and washing windows.

•In kitchens and bathrooms, fix leaky faucets and pipes and clean grout around tile, replacing caulking as needed.

•Replace all burned-out light bulbs, oil squeaky hinges, replace broken window panes, patch cracks in floors and walls, and repair any other defects.

•Outside, trim trees and shrubs and mow the lawn. Paint, if necessary, or touch up the exterior by painting the trim and front door. Keep everything neat while the house is on the market.

Here are some additional tips from a realtor:

1. When the house is being shown, turn the lights on in every room (even during the day) and open any drapes, curtains, or window shades to ensure maximum lighting. Rooms should not appear dark and gloomy.

2. If there is a fireplace, light it to provide a warm, homey and inviting atmosphere. (Of course, this won't work on hot summer days, but it's worth it during winter, spring and fall.)

3. If it is a hot summer day and the house is air-conditioned, turn the thermostat lower than normal (60 to 65 degrees). Coming in from the hot weather into a 60° room will immediately emphasize the asset of air-conditioning.

4. Brewing a pot of spice tea just before showing your home will result in a nice homey smell. If you don't have spice tea, try boiling cinnamon sticks in a pot of water.

5. Playing quiet and tasteful background music (such as a string quartet) during a showing can also help create a good atmosphere. This is especially effective if your home has an intercom system and you have it playing in every room.

6. Assist your realtor in preparing a fact sheet on your home. Since you know your home better than anyone else, you are better equipped to point out its good features.

7. Do not stay home while your realtor is showing your house to prospective buyers. Give him room to negotiate the best deal for you. Don't let your emotional attachment to your home interfere with getting the best price.

Sources of Further Information

BOOKS

The Common-Sense Mortgage. Peter G. Miller, HarperPerennial, New York, 1993.

Homing Instinct. John Connell, Warner Books, New York, 1993.

The Landlord's Handbook. Daniel Goodwin and Richard Rusdorf, Dearborn Financial Publishing, Chicago, 1989.

Landlording. Leigh Robinson, Express, El Cerrito, Calif., 1990.

Raising the Rafters. Stephen F. Collier, The Overlook Press, New York, 1993.

BOOKLETS AND PAMPHLETS

Note: For more information on pamphlets from the Consumer Information Center, or to request a copy of the Consumer Information Catalog, write:
Consumer Information Center
Pueblo, CO 81009
Or call 1-719-948-4000.

How to Buy a Manufactured Home. The Manufactured Housing Institute with the Federal Trade Commission, Consumer Information Center, Pueblo, CO 81009.

Consumer Handbook on Adjustable Rate Mortgages. Federal Reserve Board, Consumer Information Center, Pueblo, CO 81009.

A Consumer's Guide to Mortgage Lock-Ins. Federal Reserve Board, Consumer Information Center, Pueblo, CO 81009.

The Mortgage Money Guide. Federal Trade Commission, Consumer Information Center, Pueblo, CO 81009.

A Home Buyer's Vocabulary. HUD, Consumer Information Center, Pueblo, CO 81009.

A Home Of Your Own. HUD, Consumer Information Center, Pueblo, CO 81009.

Wise Home Buying. HUD, Consumer Information Center, Pueblo, CO 81009.

Marketing Tips for Home Sellers.
American Society of Home Inspectors, Consumer Information Center, Pueblo, CO 81009.

The Home Inspection and You. American Society of Home Inspectors, Consumer Information Center, Pueblo, CO 81009.

Home Buyer's and Seller's Guide to Radon. Environmental Protection Agency, Consumer Information Center, Pueblo, CO 81009.

Fair Housing: It's Your Right. HUD, Consumer Information Center, Pueblo, CO 81009.

A Home Buyer's Guide To Environmental Hazards. Various groups in the housing industry with the EPA, Consumer Information Center, Pueblo, CO 81009.

Straight Talk About Homeowner's Insurance. National Association of Professional Insurance Agents, Alexandria, VA, call 1-703-836-9340.

Insurance for Your House and Personal Possessions. New Jersey Insurance News Service, Union, NJ, 1-908-687-2828

HSH Associates
1200 Route 23
Butler, NJ 07405
1-800-UPDATES
Sells lists of current mortgage rates for thousands of lenders nationwide by county. They also offer literature for obtaining mortgages and refinancing.

2

Moving

For many Americans, moving is a way of life. According to the American Movers Conference, one out of five families moves each year. Though some families have become practiced packers, others may be overwhelmed by the thought of relocating a lifetime of belongings. But whether this is your first move or your fifteenth, careful planning can ease the pressure and ensure that your children, your household possessions, your sanity and even that rare bottle of wine arrive intact.

Selecting Your Moving Company

You should begin planning for your move and selecting a mover six to eight weeks before your actual loading date. How to select the right moving company for you? Gather information from your family, co-workers, friends and neighbors who have recently moved. Ask them the following questions:

• Were the movers on time?

• Was anything damaged during the move?

• How much did they charge?

You may also want to look in the Yellow Pages under "Moving Companies" or contact the American Movers Conference, an industry group, at 1-703-683-7410, for a list of movers who service your area. Also see "Sources of Further Information" at the end of the chapter.

The Cost of the Move

INDUSTRY REGULATIONS

Since the moving industry was deregulated in 1980, not all firms charge the same rate or offer the same services. However, all companies that move your belongings from one state to another are regulated by the Interstate Commerce Commission (ICC) and must follow certain rules. For example, once you receive an estimate, the company cannot charge you more than that estimate plus 10 percent, at the time of unloading. You must pay the balance of the charges within 30 days, but the movers can no longer hold your belongings hostage until you pay the amount in full, as they could before deregulation. If you are moving from one state to another, ask the moving company for a copy of its performance record. You may also want to check with the local Better Business Bureau.

These rules are explained in detail in a booklet produced by the ICC entitled "When You Move: Your Rights and Responsibilities," and should be available from any moving company. Also available from the ICC is a list of helpful

Should You Move Yourself?

Rental trucks are available to move everything from a single box of possessions to the contents of seven-room homes. Be aware, however, that the largest rental vans may not be available with an automatic transmission. If you need to move a large load and don't know how to drive a stick shift, you may want to rent a smaller truck with an automatic transmission and a trailer to provide additional capacity for boxes. You can also rent auto-tow bars and rooftop carriers. The busiest rental periods are Fridays and Saturdays, especially at the beginning and end of the month. Reserve a truck well in advance if you plan to move at one of these times.

To find a local rental, look in the Yellow Pages under Truck rentals or call one of the major carriers. These include U-Haul at 1-800-GO-UHAUL, Ryder Truck at 1-800-551-2030 or Hertz Truck Rental at 1-800-222-0277. Brochures are available from the large rental companies on how to pack the truck and what size vehicle to rent. Truck rental companies can also supply you—for a fee—with pads, dollies and packing supplies.

Another consideration is liability insurance, which may be purchased through most rental companies. Because of the expense involved in renting the truck, it is wise to buy insurance covering any damage to it. You may also want to buy insurance that covers damage to your belongings over the course of the move. It is important to check your homeowner's or apartment renter's policy to see if your coverage extends to damage incurred during a move. You should also be aware that your existing auto insurance, which provides coverage when you rent a car, is not likely to apply to a truck rental. Some major credit cards offer insurance for car and truck rentals charged on the card; check with the issuer to see if this is true in your case.

The price of a rental truck is usually determined by the size of the vehicle, mileage and a drop-off charge if you are not returning the vehicle to the original rental location. For this reason, it may be cheaper to rent a larger van and to make a single trip than to make several trips in a smaller truck.

You should also enlist as many friends and family members as possible to help with the move. Be sure to have your belongings packed in advance so your helpers need not wait while you put everything in boxes. Once the van is loaded, don't just drive off and expect your friends to find their own way to the new place. Give them precise directions as well as the phone number of your new home.

When all the costs are considered, you may find that moving yourself is not much cheaper than using a moving company. For small, local moves, it may be worth investigating do-it-yourself rentals, however.

tips for planning an interstate move. (See "Sources of Further Information," below). If you are moving at your company's request, find out exactly what portion of the expenses will be covered by your employer (see sidebar on relocation, below).

If you are moving within the same state, you should select a moving company licensed by the state—generally the Department of Transportation or, in some cases, the Public Utilities Commission.

Once you have compiled a list of movers, call around to inform them of your destination and the timing of your move. Here are some questions to ask in order to be able to compare them:

• Rates and charges

• Mover's liability for your belongings

• How pickup and delivery works

• What protection you have for damage claims

• Any other services the company may offer

The cost of your move is generally determined by the distance you are moving and the weight of your belongings, plus packing and any other services. Ask several companies to provide you with an estimate. This is an educated guess to help you predict your approximate moving expenses.

To help the company calculate the cost of your move, the American Movers Conference suggests you show them every single item to be moved. Go into the attic, basement, garage, and under beds and into closets. Nonbinding estimates are not final. They are the probable cost of your move. The final cost is determined by the actual weight of your belongings, or the amount of space they take up in the van, plus the distance they are transported and the amount of packing and other service provided. Movers may charge additional fees for certain conditions that exist in your present or new residence. These include charges for carrying items long distances, up or down stairs, or in and out of elevators.

ESTIMATES

Some companies may provide you with a binding estimate. This must clearly describe the shipment and all services provided. Once it has been issued, you cannot add to the shipment or change the services without invalidating a binding estimate. However, the mover cannot require you to pay any more than the cost given in a binding estimate. Though most movers offer this service free, some charge a small fee.

Before the moving industry was deregulated in 1980, the cost of a move was determined by a complex rate chart published by the ICC. Although some companies still base estimates on that chart, many movers are willing to wheel and deal to get your business. When a moving-company representative comes to your house, let him know that you plan to get quotes from other shippers as well. Make sure the written estimate breaks down the cost of the move by services. You need more than just a bottom-line total to compare movers.

Do not sign an order for service until you have obtained estimates from at least three or four companies. In addition to the binding estimate (described above), you may also be offered a *bottom-line discount estimate* or a *not-to-exceed estimate*.

The bottom-line discount guarantees you a certain percentage of discount applied to the total cost of the move. Nothing is guaranteed except the amount of the discount. The company will give you an estimate of the cost of the move, but the actual price will be based on the weight of the van, the mileage and any services provided, such as packing. The advantage of the bottom-line discount estimate is that it may be cheaper than a binding estimate if the actual weight of your belongings falls below the estimate. Under this plan, the driver will call you with the amount due after the loaded van has been weighed. Be sure to check with the company regarding its policy on rate increases that might occur after you receive your estimate but before you move.

The not-to-exceed estimate offers the benefit of the bottom-line discount combined with the peace of mind that comes with a binding estimate. Since the discount is applied to all services as well as the weight and mileage of the move, the actual amount due may be lower than the estimate. However, this program will guarantee not to exceed the estimated amount.

If, after obtaining multiple estimates, one is far below the rest, beware. Make sure the low-ball figure includes all the same services and the full amount of belongings before you grab at it. Some companies may undercut the competition, then call a few days before the move to report an "error" in the estimate. Do not simply hire the company with the lowest fee. Compare the mover's performance report with those of its competitors as well.

One way to keep a lid on costs is to reduce the amount of belongings you move. Trim the size of the load with the following approaches:

• Draft a floor plan of your new home and get rid of items that won't fit. It can be cheaper to replace certain items than to move them.

• Get rid of tools you won't need in your new locale. For instance, a lawn mower isn't necessary if your condominium fee covers lawn care. Don't move a fireplace screen and tools if your new home doesn't have a fireplace.

• Consolidate your library and investigate the cost of sending your books via the Postal Service. Shipping by book rate can be substantially cheaper than by the mover.

• Another option for shipping large parcels is by bus.

• Consider emptying planters of heavy soil and packing them with miscellaneous items. (For more information on moving with plants and animals, see below.)

• Discard record albums you no longer listen to. A hundred record albums weigh approximately 50 pounds. (See sidebar on moving sales, below.)

• Contemplate selling chandeliers, ceiling fans and light fixtures with your home.

Other potential "leave-behinds" include basketball backboards, firewood, television antennas and gas appliances if you are moving to an all-electric home.

Be aware you may have to pay an additional handling charge if you move large or bulky items, such as hot tubs, grandfather clocks, automobiles or boats. You may also have to pay an extra pickup fee if you need to collect items from your relatives' house across town, or from a do-it-yourself storage facility where you have been keeping additional household goods.

Increased competition in the moving industry has caused companies to become more creative in the programs they offer. Among the more innovative are cash-rebate programs under which the moving company will rebate a portion of your moving charges if you sell your home through a real estate agent listed with that moving company.

Other companies offer relocation services, satisfaction guarantees, free brochures, change of address packs and kits for moves involving children. Ask each company what programs are available.

FORM OF PAYMENT

Though consumers usually do not pay for services until the job is completed, moving companies are legally allowed to require you to pay the van driver before the truck is unloaded. When you arrive at your destination, be prepared to pay the van driver in cash, money order, traveler's check or cashier's check as prearranged with your mover.

Breakage claims or any disputes must be settled later.

LIABILITY

The basic mover's liability for loss or damage to your belongings, according to federal law, is limited to a maximum of 60 cents per pound per article, based on the weight of the lost or damaged item. This does not provide much coverage for small items, such as a tea set, which might be light in weight but worth a great deal of money.

In addition to this basic protection, you may opt for extra coverage, which costs more. Programs are available through your shipper that offer full-value protection (with or without a deductible) or depreciated-value protection. The former reimburses you for the full cost of replacing or repairing the damaged item. The latter reimburses you for the cost of repairing the damaged item, or pays the replacement value of an item after depreciating it for age.

High-value items such as coin collections or jewelry are often excluded from these liability programs. Check with your moving company on its policy, and be prepared to move these items yourself or to hire a specialty mover. A high-value inventory sheet should be filled out for items worth more than $100 per pound, such as antiques, cameras, computers, and TVs or VCRs. If you are packing these items yourself, you should not seal the box until the driver has a chance to inspect the articles. In the event of a claim, the settlement is limited to the value of the articles, not to exceed the declared value of the entire shipment and subject to the type of coverage you have selected. When you file a claim for loss or damage for an item on the high-value list, you will need to provide verification of ownership and proof of value, such as a receipt appraisal or sales receipt.

Inconvenience claims can be filed with the moving company when late pickup or delivery was the fault of the mover. Ask your mover to outline the company's policy regarding claims for out-of-pocket living expenses while awaiting late delivery.

Making a claim. Record any damage on the inventory sheet. You have up to nine months to file a damage claim with the company. You will be responsible for contacting the company and obtaining the correct forms. Be sure to keep the damaged items and the packing in which they were shipped as evidence to show a claims adjuster.

Arbitration

Although the American Movers Conference notes that most moves are relatively trouble-free, disputes can occur. So the AMC has developed a voluntary arbitration program for member companies to use in settling the 2 percent of moves that result in disputed loss and damage claims.

Not all moving companies take part in the program, but most of the major carriers participate. Companies that offer the program are required to tell the consumer about it before the move.

The program is limited to out-of-state moves and to disputes involving loss or damage claims. Either the customer or the moving company can request the use of arbitration, but both parties must agree to participate. An arbitrator appointed by the independent American Arbitration Association renders a decision that is legally binding on both the consumer and the moving company. There is no cost to the consumer for a standard procedure, unless an optional oral hearing is requested. The fee for that is $50.

Scheduling Your Move

Once you have selected a company, your mover will probably ask you to pick several consecutive days during which your household belongings can be loaded, and a second series of dates upon which to make delivery. If you require pickup on a special day, ask your mover about the conditions of this arrangement.

The moving company will usually be able to move your goods as planned, but delays can occur. It is best not to plan to relinquish your house until several days after the period during which the mover is scheduled to pick up your goods.

Some 45 percent of moves occur during the summer months. Some movers offer lower prices between the months of October and April. Movers are especially swamped around the first and last days of each month. If you can be flexible regarding your moving date, ask your mover what discounts may be available.

Relocation Specialists

A good source of assistance when moving to a new town can be the relocation specialist employed by your firm or by the real estate agency that handles the purchase of your new home. Moving companies may also offer relocation assistance.

Relocation specialists can provide information on your destination city, including facts on schools, climate,

HOUSEHOLD GOODS DESCRIPTIVE INVENTORY

		PAGE NO. NO. OF PAGES
CONTRACTOR OR CARRIER	AGENT	CARRIER'S REFERENCE NO.
OWNER'S GRADE OR RATING AND NAME		CONTRACT OR GBL. NO.
ORIGIN LOADING ADDRESS	CITY STATE	GOV'T. SERVICE ORDER NO.
DESTINATION		VAN NUMBER

DESCRIPTIVE SYMBOLS

CP Packed by Carrier
PBO Packed by Owner
CD Carrier Disassembled
DBO Disassembled by Owner
PB Professional Books

PP Professional Papers
PE Professional Equipment
B&W TV Black & White
C TV Color
MCU Mechanical Condition Unknown

EXCEPTION SYMBOLS

BE Bent
BR Broken
BU Burned
CH Chipped
CU Contents and Condition Unknown

D Dented
F Faded
G Gouged
L Loose
M Marred
MI Mildew

MO Motheaten
R Rubbed
RU Rusted
SC Scratched
SH Short

SO Soiled
T Torn
W Badly Worn
Z Cracked

NOTE The omission of these symbols indicates good condition except for normal wear.

LOCATION SYMBOLS

1 Arm
2 Bottom
3 Corner
4 Front
5 Left
6 Leg

7 Rear
8 Right
9 Side
10 Top
11 Veneer
12 Edge
13 Center

ITEM NO.	STG. CK./ CR. REF	ARTICLES	CONDITION AT ORIGIN	ROOM	EXCEPTIONS (IF ANY) AT DESTINATION

IMPORTANT NOTICE ⟹ BEFORE SIGNING — CHECK SHIPMENT, COUNT ITEMS AND DESCRIBE LOSS OR DAMAGE IN SPACE ON THE RIGHT ABOVE.

"WE HAVE CHECKED ALL THE ITEMS LISTED AND NUMBERED ON THIS PAGE INCLUSIVE AND ACKNOWLEDGE THAT THIS IS A TRUE AND COMPLETE LIST OF THE GOODS TENDERED AND OF THE STATE OF THE GOODS RECEIVED."

AT ORIGIN	LOADING HAULER NAME & NUMBER (Signature)	DATE	AT DESTI- NATION	DELIVERING HAULER NAME & NUMBER (Signature)	DATE
	OWNER OR AUTHORIZED AGENT (Signature)	DATE		OWNER OR AUTHORIZED AGENT (Signature)	DATE

Corporate Relocation

Each year, hundreds of thousands of employees are transferred by their companies. What can the average worker expect as part of a corporate relocation package? According to the Washington, D.C.-based Employee Relocation Council, the standard policy usually includes the following:

•Shipping of household goods, including packing, shipping, storage and unpacking.

•Temporary living expenses at the new location.

•One to two house-hunting trips for the employee and spouse.

•Coverage of normal closing costs associated with the purchase of a new home.

•Miscellaneous expenses (i.e., auto registration, appliance hookups), usually equal to one month's salary.

•Real estate sales assistance. The most common program calls for the use of a third-party purchase program under which an outside firm is used to pur-chase and resell the employee's home.

In addition, about 50 percent of firms offer some form of assistance to the employee's spouse in finding a job at the new location. Such programs usually cover the cost of an outside counseling/placement agency, but may also include resume prepara-tion, the cost of required licenses or exams, and even paid job-hunting trips. Not all companies have formal policies, so it pays to ask for help for the "trailing" spouse or live-in domestic partner.

---

shopping, medical facilities and other services. They can also assist you with information on financing and common real estate practices as well as tax information.

COUNTDOWN TO MOVING DAY (AND AFTER)
Arrangements with the moving company you have selected should be in place four to six weeks before moving day. Now you can begin the countdown (see illustration).

At 6 Weeks
•Meet with your mover to discuss all details: costs, insurance, packing, loading, delivery and claims procedures. (See "The Cost of the Move," above.)

•Begin mailing out change-of-address cards as soon as you know your new address. Magazine companies prefer at least four weeks' notice, preferably six. Notices should also be sent to friends, credit-card companies, insurance companies, accountants and other service providers.

•Make a videotape of your household belongings in case of loss or damage during the move.

At 4 Weeks
•If the mover will be doing the packing, arrange for it to be done one to two days before loading.

•If packing yourself, begin the packing process. (See "Packing," below.)

•Sort through your belongings and throw out, give away or sell things you don't want or need. (See "Moving Sales," below.)

COUNTDOWN CHECKLIST

	AT 6 WEEKS	AT 4 WEEKS	AT 3 WEEKS	AT 2 WEEKS	AT 1 WEEK	1-2 DAYS BEFORE
Meet with your mover and discuss all details: costs, insurance, packing, loading, delivery, and claims procedures.	✓					
If the mover does the packing, arrange for packing to be done one or two days before loading.		✓				
If packing yourself, begin packing.		✓				
Sort through and throw out, give away, or sell belongings you don't want or need.		✓				
If necessary, arrange for storage of your goods.		✓				
Send furniture, drapes, carpets for repair or cleaning.		✓				
Arrange for repair work on your new house.		✓				
Arrange to have appliances, utilities and telephones disconnected in your old house. Arrange utility and telephone hookup for your new house.			✓			
Make travel arrangements and hotel reservations for your trip.			✓			
Apartment dwellers — reserve elevator for pickup and/or delivery day.			✓			
Obtain medical, dental, and veterinarian records.			✓			
Organize car license, registration, and insurance records.			✓			
Obtain, fill out, and mail change-of-address cards.				✓		
Make special arrangements for transporting pets and plants.				✓		
Take care of bills, stocks, and bank accounts.				✓		
Arrange for a babysitter on moving day.					✓	
Transfer prescriptions.					✓	
Arrange for delivery services (newspapers, milk, etc.) to be discontinued.					✓	
Have mover pack your goods.						✓
Defrost and dry refrigerators and freezers to be moved.						✓
Arrange for cash/traveler's checks for trip expenses and payment to mover.						✓
If traveling by car, check your gas, tires, water, battery, oil, wipers.						✓

•If necessary, arrange for storage of your goods. If you plan on having your belongings stored for an extended period of time, consider using a do-it-yourself storage facility. This is likely to be cheaper than storage offered by your moving company and is easier to access if you need to get into your boxes.

•Send furniture, drapes and carpets for repair or cleaning. Keep them in the wrapper from the shop until you move.

•Arrange for repair work on your new home to be performed before you move in.

At 3 Weeks

•Arrange to have gas stove, gas dryer, heating gas, electrical service and telephone disconnected in your old house. Arrange utility and telephone hookups for your new house.

•Make travel arrangements and hotel reservations for your trip.

•Get a transcript of your children's school records and a letter of introduction to a new church, synagogue or other organization.

•Apartment dwellers should reserve the elevator for pickup and/or delivery day.

•Obtain copies of medical, dental and veterinarian records. Fill and transfer medical prescriptions.

•Organize car license, registration and insurance records.

•Obtain written appraisals of antique items.

At 2 Weeks

•Make special arrangements for transporting pets and plants (see below).

•Take care of bills, stocks and bank accounts. Arrange for funds to be wired when you open an account at your new location. This gives you immediate access so you won't have to wait for a check to clear before funds are available.

•Return library books and collect items that have been borrowed from you. Collect dry cleaning, shoe repairs and other belongings. Empty your locker at the health club or gym.

•Pack an old local telephone book for names and addresses.

At 1 Week

•Arrange for a babysitter (or pet sitter) on moving day.

•Arrange for home-delivery services (milk, newspaper, etc.) to be discontinued or transferred to your new address.

One to Two Days
in Advance

•Have mover pack your goods. Be specific about what should be packed, or you may find that efficient packers have carefully wrapped your kitchen garbage and kitty box complete with litter.

•Defrost and dry refrigerators and freezers to be moved.

•Arrange for cash/traveler's checks for trip expenses and payment to movers.

•Dispose of all flammable items, such as oil rags, dust mops, matches, paint, ammunition, aerosol cans and any other items that could cause an explosion or fire. Movers are not allowed to carry them.

• If traveling by car, have it serviced, or check the gas, tires, water, battery, oil and wipers yourself.

On Moving Day

• Eat a substantial breakfast.

• Confirm delivery arrangements that have been agreed upon earlier. Be available to answer questions and give directions when the movers arrive to load your belongings. Tell the mover where you or your representative can be reached. While your shipment is in transit, keep in contact with the mover's agent or central locator.

• Set aside jewelry, documents, money and especially valuable small items for which movers cannot accept responsibility.

• Strip the beds before the movers arrive, but allow the movers to take apart beds, roll up carpets and put mattresses in cartons themselves.

• Read the Bill of Lading (the contract between you and the mover) before you sign it. The inventory of your belongings should be attached. Keep a copy with you until the shipment is unpacked, all charges are paid, and any damages noted and reimbursed.

On Delivery Day

• Be available to answer questions and give movers directions regarding the placement of furniture and boxes. Under federal rules, a van driver is only required to wait two hours for you to show up at your new residence. He may then place your shipment in storage, at your cost.

• Be prepared to pay the driver before your belongings are unloaded.

• Station a family member or friend at the front door to check off box numbers and record any damage on the inventory sheet. You don't need to unpack every box, but do make a note of any carton damage on the sheet. Then if you discover later that a vase has been broken, keep the wrapping and the box it was in to show the claims adjuster. Claims should be filed as soon as possible, although you have up to nine months to make claims.

• Have a plan in mind for furniture location.

• Survey your new home for loose steps, low overhangs, and other possible causes of accidents. If you have small children, take the time to child-proof rooms: Cover outlets, secure loose cords, cover up peeling paint and splintering floorboards, and put small objects out of reach.

• Take a break with the family as soon as the major unpacking is done. Don't try to do everything as soon as you arrive.

The Next Few Days

• Call serviceperson for installation of appliances.

• Locate new doctor, dentist and veterinarian.

Tipping

There is no formal industry policy on tipping your movers. If they have been helpful and safely transported your household goods, you may want to offer them a gratuity. There is no need for a tip that's 15 or 20 percent of the bill, as in a restaurant, however. A $20 tip for the driver and $10 for each member of the crew is an acceptable amount in most parts of the country.

BILL OF LADING NO.	COMBINED UNIFORM HOUSEHOLD GOODS BILL OF LADING AND FREIGHT BILL NON-NEGOTIABLE	ORDER FOR SERVICE NO. DO NOT ALTER
DATE		
ISSUING AGENT		REFER TO THIS NUMBER IN ALL COMMUNICATIONS

RECEIVED SUBJECT TO CLASSIFICATIONS, TARIFFS, RULES AND REGULATIONS INCLUDING ALL TERMS PRINTED OR STAMPED HEREON OR ON THE REVERSE SIDE HEREOF IN EFFECT ON THE DATE OF ISSUE OF THIS BILL OF LADING

CONNECTING CARRIER

SHIPPER	CONSIGNEE
LOAD FROM C/O	DELIVER TO C/O
ADDRESS	ADDRESS
CITY CNTY STATE	CITY CNTY STATE
TEL	TEL
IN CASE OF NEED CONTACT	AGREED PICK-UP DATE / PER OF TIME
NAME	ACTUAL PICK-UP DATE
ADDRESS	AGREED DELIVERY DATE / PER OF TIME
CITY STATE	IF GUARANTEED SERVICE, PENALTY PER TARIFF IS $ PER DAY
TEL	

IF SHIPPER REQUESTS NOTICE OF CHARGES	OR IN EVENT OF DELAY	NOTIFY	ESTIMATED COST	BINDING	YES	NO

NAME	MAX AMT. REQUIRED (EST. + 10%)
ADDRESS	TO BE PAID ON DELIVERY $ BALANCE DUE IN 30 DAYS
CITY	MIN. CHARGE METHOD OF PAYMENT
TEL	BILL TO

	ORIGINAL		REWEIGH	ADDRESS
GROSS				CITY STATE
TARE				CUST. NO.
NET				TARIFF TRANS. RATE SEC. OR ITEM NO.

DRIVER NO.	VEHICLE NO.

CHARGES FOR MAT'L PACKING & UNPACKING	CONTAINERS				PACKING SCHEDULE ( )				UNPACKING SCHEDULE ( )			
	AGT / DR	QTY	RATE	CHARGE	AGT / DR	QTY	RATE	CHARGE	AGT / DR	QTY	RATE	CHARGE
DRUM-DISHPACK Not Less Than 5 Cu. Ft.												
CARTONS Less Than 3 Cu. Ft.												
3 Cu. Ft.												
4½ Cu. Ft.												
6 Cu. Ft.												
6½ Cu. Ft.												
WARDROBE CARTONS Not Less Than 10 Cu. Ft.												
MATTRESS CARTONS Not Ex. 39" x 75"												
MATTRESS CARTONS Not Ex. 54" x 75"												
MATTRESS CARTONS Exceeding 54" x 75"												
CORRUGATED CONT.												
CRATES Minimum Size												
CRATES Over Minimum Size												
	689 TOTAL				690 TOTAL				691 TOTAL			

UNLESS THE SHIPPER EXPRESSLY RELEASES THE SHIPMENT TO A VALUE OF 50 CENTS PER POUND PER ARTICLE, THE CARRIER'S MAXIMUM LIABILITY FOR LOSS AND DAMAGE SHALL BE EITHER THE LUMP SUM VALUE DECLARED BY THE SHIPPER OR AN AMOUNT EQUAL TO $1.25 FOR EACH POUND OF WEIGHT IN THE SHIPMENT WHICHEVER IS GREATER.

THE SHIPMENT WILL MOVE SUBJECT TO THE RULES AND CONDITIONS OF THE CARRIER'S TARIFF. SHIPPER HEREBY RELEASES THE ENTIRE SHIPMENT TO A VALUE NOT EXCEEDING $_____
(To be completed by person signing below)

NOTICE: THE SHIPPER SIGNING THIS CONTRACT MUST INSERT IN THE SPACE ABOVE, IN HIS OWN HANDWRITING, EITHER HIS DECLARATION OF THE ACTUAL VALUE OF THE SHIPMENT OR THE WORDS "50 CENTS PER POUND PER ARTICLE". OTHERWISE THE SHIPMENT WILL BE DEEMED RELEASED TO A MAXIMUM VALUE EQUAL TO $1.25 TIMES THE WEIGHT OF THE SHIPMENT IN POUNDS.

SHIPPER X _____
DATE

REPLACEMENT VALUE PROTECTION
Minimum value - $3.50 per pound or $15,000, whichever is greater.

☐ Option A - No Deductible
☐ Option B - $300 Deductible

THE SHIPPER SIGNING THIS CONTRACT MUST INSERT, IN THE SPACE BELOW, HIS DECLARATION OF THE RELEASED VALUE OF THE SHIPMENT. OTHERWISE, THE SHIPMENT WILL BE DEEMED RELEASED TO A VALUE EQUAL TO $3.50 TIMES THE WEIGHT IN POUNDS OR $15,000., WHICHEVER IS GREATER, SHIPPER HEREBY RELEASES THE ENTIRE SHIPMENT TO A VALUE NOT EXCEEDING $_____

SHIPPER X _____
DATE

Carrier agrees to transport the goods and effects tendered by the shipper subject to the preceding terms and conditions.

X _____
Carrier or Authorized Agent

Leave over ☐ Yes ☐ No

Agent's No.	DESCRIPTION	CODE	QUANTITY	RATE	CHARGE
	TOTAL CONTAINERS PACKING & UNPACKING				
	TRANSPORTATION MILES				
	ADD TRANSP - ORIG				
	ADD TRANSP. - DEST				
	ORIGIN TO WAREHOUSE MILES				
	WAREHOUSE TO DESTINATION MILES				
	STORAGE-IN-TRANSIT				
	WAREHOUSE HANDLING				
	EXTRA PICKUP(S)				
	EXTRA DELIVERY (IES)				
	EXTRA LABOR Men Man Hrs.				
	FLIGHT CHARGE No.				
	EXCESSIVE DISTANCE CARRY Feet				
	VALUATION				
	PIANO HANDLING				
	APPLIANCE SERVICING				
	ADVANCE CHARGE - ACCOUNT OF				

CHARGES TO BE PAID IN CASH, MONEY ORDER (OTHER THAN PERSONAL MONEY ORDER), TRAVELER'S CHECK, CASHIER'S CHECK, MADE PAYABLE TO _____ BEFORE PROPERTY IS RELINQUISHED BY CARRIER UNLESS OTHERWISE STATED. ON EMPLOYER PAID MOVES, SHIPPER IS LIABLE FOR ALL CARRIER CHARGES IF EMPLOYER FAILS TO MAKE PAYMENT AS PROMISED.

			TOTAL	
			PD. TO APPLY	
			BALANCE	

PREPAYMENT $ _____ RECEIVED BY _____ DATE _____

BALANCE $ _____ RECEIVED BY _____ DATE _____

THE ABOVE DESCRIBED SHIPMENT WAS RECEIVED IN APPARENT GOOD CONDITION EXCEPT AS NOTED ON THE INVENTORY

CONSIGNEE OR AGENT OF CONSIGNEE _____ DATE DELIVERED _____

RECEIVED FOR STORAGE IN TRANSIT AT _____

AGENCY NAME   WAREHOUSE LOCATION   BY   AGENT'S SIGNATURE   ON   DATE

- Register to vote.

- Call for newspaper delivery and other services, including garbage pickup, diapers and milk. New neighbors may be able to provide the names of vendors.

- Get new drivers' licenses and register automobiles. Change the address on any tags identifying your pets.

- Locate schools and enroll children. Accompanying children to school the first few days may ease the minds of both parents and children.

- Open new bank accounts and arrange for transfer of funds.

Packing

Some people opt to pack up part of their belongings on their own and save on the mover's packing fees. Be aware that most movers will usually not accept responsibility for broken items that they did not pack. You may elect to pack nonbreakable items yourself, and allow the mover to pack fragile items such as dishes and glassware.

Movers do sell packing materials, but these are often expensive. A good source for packing boxes is the local liquor store or supermarket. Speak to a manager in advance about obtaining cartons so that

Moving Sales

Moving costs are based on distance and weight. While you can't shorten the distance you are moving, you can reduce the weight of what you are moving by holding a moving sale to dispense with unwanted items.

Income from garage sales is generally not taxable as long as the items sell for less than the original price. But you should check with local officials to see if a permit is necessary, or if local sales tax must be collected.

The most successful sales require advance planning. Place an ad in the local shopper's guide and one in your daily paper. Post notices in nearby stores, laundromats and libraries. And tack up large, legible signs the day of the sale to lead people from major intersections to your home. Be sure to have a big sign at the site.

Clean all merchandise and arrange it in a neat, organized fashion. Mark all clothing with appropriate sizes and hang from a clothesline or rod. You may price items individually or arrange identically priced items on separate tables or in boxes. Electrical items sell better if plugged in to show customers they work.

Robert L. Berko, author of *Holding Garage Sales for Fun and Profit* (Consumer Education Research Center), suggests using catalogs from discount stores as a source for pricing. Mark most items at 20 percent to 50 percent of current retail value. Sell popcorn and soda or coffee to keep customers browsing. And be prepared to haggle. You are not just trying to make money. You are trying to lighten your moving load. Consider extending the sale an extra day with special markdowns if there is much merchandise left.

Other things to consider when planning your sale:

Decide where your customers may park and mark it accordingly.

Offer a children's table with toys and tiny grab bags, priced so children can purchase items themselves.

Borrow tables from friends, or rent them from your church or community group. Stepladders and saw horses can support plywood planks.

Cover items not for sale with old sheets.

Set aside a table for your cash box, or wear an apron with pockets for handling money. Start with at least $30 in change and $1 bills.

Make certain your homeowner's policy will cover any liability for injuries.

Keep smaller, more valuable items that could be shoplifted near your checkout table. Discourage loiterers by following them around.

Have a firm, cash-only policy.

After the sale consider donating leftover items to charitable organizations such as the Salvation Army, Goodwill or local shelters. Such donations are tax deductible.

lids will not be cut off. Office-supply stores can also be a good source for cartons, as can computer shops.

Set aside a convenient area to work and keep your packing materials in this area. It is helpful to have two sturdy tables on which to pack. One should be covered with a heavy blanket to protect the table while items are being wrapped, and the second should be used to hold items to be wrapped.

Items you'll need:

• Sturdy cartons with flaps or lids.

• White paper, tissue paper, paper toweling or blank newsprint (newspapers should only be used for cushioning material, since the ink may smudge or stain your belongings).

• Several rolls of tape 1 1/2 to 2 inches wide for sealing cartons.

• Scissors and/or a sharp knife.

• Stickers for labeling boxes.

• Felt-tip pen or marker for labeling boxes.

• Pad and pen for listing boxes as they are packed.

Moving with Pets and Plants

PETS

Most states have rules regulating the entry of pets, including dogs, cats, horses and other common pets, with the exception of tropical fish. You may want to contact the state veterinarian's office in your new capital city to determine laws regarding the entry of your pet. Most states, for example, require dogs to have a rabies inoculation.

In addition, some communities have restrictions regarding the number of pets or the stabling of horses inside city limits. Information about licensing fees and other health certificates or permits can be obtained from the city clerk or town hall.

Pets cannot be shipped in a moving van, and with few exceptions are banned from buses and trains. This limits your options to transporting pets by automobile or by air.

Pets accompanying passengers in the cabin of the plane should be put in soft or hard-sided carriers that are big enough to let them sit up comfortably. Carriers must fit under the seat. If your pets will be flying unaccompanied via air freight, you will have to make arrangements for someone to care for them after you leave and deliver them to the airport in a sturdy, hard-sided carrier. Or you may choose to ship your pet before you leave and have it cared for until you are able to collect it later. Your vet or moving company may be able to recommend a pet-handling agency that can provide these services.

The container may be of wood, metal or plastic, but must not exceed dimensions of 160 cubic inches or 100 pounds when occupied. The temperature at the origin, transfer and destination points must be between 10 and 85°F. With the exception of litters of puppies or kittens, only one pet may travel in each kennel. Shipping carriers must be large enough to allow the occupant to stand comfortably, and must have carrying handles.

If you will be shipping your pet, be sure to:

• Feed your pet no less than six hours before flight time.

• Place a label saying "Live Animal" on the container.

• Include an empty water dish in the container accessible from the outside.

• Attach feeding instructions or a notice saying "Do Not Feed."

• Attach a bag of pet food to the outside of the kennel.

If your pet will be traveling with you by car, be sure to place your new address on an identification tag before you leave. Plan frequent rest stops en route, and make sure any motel where you make reservations will allow pets. Tropical fish are best prepared for shipping by a professional. Look in the Yellow Pages under "Pet Supplies" or "Tropical Fish and Supplies" to find someone to do this. If you will be transporting the fish yourself in a car or van, drain at least half the water from the tank and cover the top with plastic wrap to pre-

Once you have gathered your supplies, start packing. It is unlikely you will have a full day just to fill cartons, so begin as soon as possible to box up out-of-season items. You may want to start in an area where goods are not in frequent use, such as the garage, attic or cellar. Other tips to consider:

•Pack on a room-to-room basis. Don't mix kitchen items with knickknacks from the living room.

•Heavier items should go in the smallest boxes. Lightweight items such as lamp shades and pillows should go in the largest containers.

•Hanging clothes should be hung in wardrobe cartons available from your mover; they cannot be moved in garment bags alone.

•Some movers will allow you to store light items in dresser drawers, while others require you to empty all drawers. Ask your mover about his policy.

•Keep all parts of things together. For example, hardware for curtain rods or shelf brackets should be placed in small plastic bags and taped to the rod or shelf to which they belong.

vent splashing. Remove filters or other items that might shift and break the glass. Put the tank inside a sturdy carton and surround it on four sides with crumpled paper.

Fish can also be taken out of the tank and packed in a plastic bag. The bag should be one-third filled with water from the aquarium and fastened tightly with a rubber band. This will ensure that there is enough air in the bag for the fish to breathe. The bag should be put in an insulated container (such as a foam picnic cooler) for transport. Open up the plastic bag every four to five hours to freshen the air.

PLANTS
Moving plants can be difficult and time-consuming. Consider giving plants to friends as remembrances, donating them to hospitals, schools or nursing homes, or offering them at a garage sale. You may want to save space and bring cuttings to grow in your new home.

However, if you are unwilling to part with certain plants, begin by determining how you will move them. Moving companies may only accept plants on short moves that require no storage. Airlines sometimes agree to ship plants, but rarely offer any special handling. Plants traveling by auto stand the best chance of survival, but should not be stored in the trunk of the car, which can reach extremes of temperature.

Plants are also subject to regulation in many states. If you will be moving between states, you may want to obtain a state-of-origin certificate that certifies your plants have been inspected by the state Department of Agriculture.

Some plants are susceptible to shock and simply may not survive the trip. Other plants should be kept at moderate temperatures, and not overwatered or kept in darkness for over one week. Here are some tips on how best to prepare your plants to survive the move:

•Two weeks before the move, plants should be allowed to become somewhat dry.

•The day before the move, water plants well and allow them to drain.

•On moving day, wrap the plants in cones of cardboard or florist's paper for protection.

•Secure plants with long limbs or branches by tying them up in the direction of growth with a soft material, like pantyhose.

•Plants should be placed upright in a high-sided container and wedged in place with crumpled paper. The box should be lined with plastic to protect against moisture.

•Temperatures should not go below 45° or above 85°.

•Once you've reached your destination, unpack the plants as soon as you can and put them in a location similar to the one in your former home. Then leave them alone for a while to recover from relocation shock.

• Build up layers in a box, with the heaviest items in the center on the bottom.

• Towels, sheets and blankets may be used for cushioning. Strive for boxes that are filled, but not over-packed.

• Fragile items should be wrapped in shredded paper or bubble wrap and placed inside a small box. These small boxes should then be placed inside a larger carton marked "Fragile."

• Once the box is sealed, label it with your name and the destination room. If you will be storing some cartons, while others will be delivered to temporary living quarters, mark the boxes to be stored with stickers of a different color.

If you choose to pack dishes and glassware yourself, you may want to purchase dishpaks—specially constructed cartons designed for china and other fragile items—along with bubble wrap and newsprint from your mover.

TIPS ON PACKING FRAGILE ITEMS

• When wrapping china and glassware, wrap each item separately in several sheets of paper.

• Larger plates, platters and other flat items should be wrapped first and placed in the bottom of the container.

• Layer cushioning material in the bottom of the box. Wrap each item of china or glassware separately, then wrap four to six items in a bundle with a double layer of newsprint.

• Place these bundles in the carton in a row on edge. Surround each bundle with crushed paper, and place several inches of crushed paper on top of the bundles to create a level space to place the next row of bundles.

• Shallow bowls should be placed on edge vertically, and large or deep bowls should be nested together and set upside down on their rims.

• Cups, cream pitchers and sugar bowls should be wrapped separately and placed upside down on the top layers. Cups and glasses can be nested inside one another after being individually wrapped. The nested glasses and cups may then be bundled to provide further protection.

• Liquor boxes with dividers can be ideal for packing glasses and cups. Line bottom and top with crumpled paper.

• Goblets and stemware should be wrapped and packed separately.

TIPS FOR WRAPPING OTHER ITEMS

• Drain air conditioners prior to moving. They do not need to be bolted down, but should remain upright in the truck.

• It is against the law to ship alcoholic beverages between two states. If you have a large wine collection, you should contact the Alcohol Beverage Control Authorities in your destination state. An appraisal is recommended prior to moving. Small collections should be moved by auto to maintain proper conditions. Transport of larger collections should be discussed with your mover.

• Appliances should be serviced by specialists prior to moving day. Refrigerators, freezers and washing machines should be unplugged, cleaned and thoroughly dried to prevent mold. Charcoal inserted in a sock can be placed in a refrigerator or

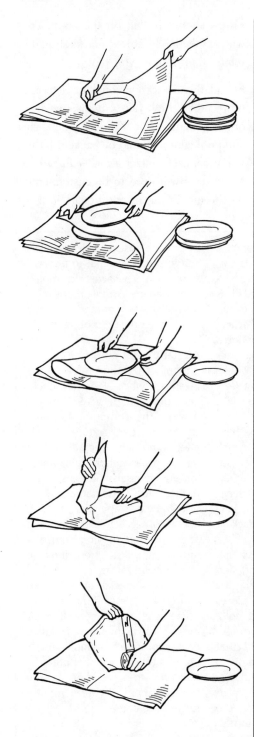

freezer to further reduce odors. Glass shelves should be removed and packed separately to prevent breakage. The tub on your washing machine should be secured as outlined in your owner's manual. Disconnect hoses and place inside the machine. Gas dryers and ranges should be disconnected by a qualified service technician before moving day.

•Bedding can be placed in clean cartons. Blankets or pillows may be stored in dresser drawers (if mover permits).

•Clock pendulums and weights should be removed and packed in a separate box. A special crate may be built for grandfather or other valuable clocks.

•Canned goods and frozen foods should be consumed before your move. Canned items are heavy and thus expensive to ship, while frozen foods can spoil in transit.

•Lightweight items may be left in desk drawers. Stuff with paper or towels to keep items from shifting in the move.

•Remove light bulbs from lamps. Wrap the cord around the base. Place cushioning material in the bottom of the box. Spread out several sheets of packing paper so that the paper is extended beyond the lamp, and roll the packing paper around the lamp to create a bundle. Several lamp bases can be packed in one large box with plenty of cushioning material in between. Shades should be wrapped in paper and placed in large boxes. While several shades can be nested together, you should pack only shades in that box.

•Remove glass trays from a microwave oven, and wrap and pack them separately. Your oven can be placed in its

Packing in the kitchen

original carton, or pad-wrapped on moving day by movers.

•Drain gasoline and oil from mowers and other power tools. Then wrap securely and pack in a large carton.

•Wrap small pictures and pack them on end in boxes with other goods. Picture frames and mirrors larger than 11 by 14 inches should be left on the walls for the mover to handle.

•Rugs should be left on the floor. They will be rolled to be stored. Tacks should be removed prior to moving day.

•Read the owner's manual to determine how other high-value items, such as organs, pianos, hot tubs, satellite dishes and pool tables, should be packed. If there is no manual, contact a dealer for advice. Most items will need to be custom-crated by the mover for an additional fee if not

Moving Your Computer

Your home computer represents an investment—whether you use it to plan your family's budget, file recipes, monitor your investments or simply to enjoy action video games. Naturally you wish to safeguard it from damage at the time of a move. With careful preplanning and proper packing, your computer can safely be transported.

BEFORE THE MOVE
If you do not have an exact record of the cost of your computer (and don't forget any accessories you've purchased to add to your system), you may wish to obtain a current retail cost of your complete system prior to selecting a protection plan from your mover. If you desire replacement cost rather than depreciated protection, many moving companies, including United Van Lines, offer full-value coverage against loss or damage.

PACKING
Your moving company is best qualified to properly pack your home computer. If you choose to pack it yourself, use the original cartons and packing material when possible. If you have discarded them, choose a sturdy box large enough to permit you to surround the computer with packing material (crumpled unprinted newsprint and plastic bubble pack are best). These materials, which can be purchased from your local moving company, will provide a cushion of protection.

The disk drive should be handled with care. This unit, which consists of several mechanized parts, is especially sensitive to jarring. Again, use a box large enough to accommodate the disk drive and plenty of packing material on all four sides.

The floppy or hard disks that contain your programming and stored data should preferably be moved with you. These pieces are sensitive to heat and cold, and warping could occur with the extreme heat or cold that can build up inside a moving van. As a precaution, you may wish to duplicate all of your stored material onto backup disks and send these to your destination via insured mail or other secure means.

The remainder of your computer—the keyboard and display screen—consists of solid-state circuitry, much like that in a television set. Place crumpled unprinted newsprint in the bottom of the box and pack as you would the other components.

AT DELIVERY
Carefully check and mark off the inventory when your household belongings are delivered.

Allow the computer to come to room temperature before attempting any operation. If it has been particularly cold, watch for any condensation, as moisture can also cause damage.

If you have any loss or damage, contact the destination agent of your moving company for assistance in preparing the proper claim forms.

For any special questions or concerns about moving your home computer, consult your moving-company representative or a computer manufacturer's representative. Proper preparation prior to a move will ensure the enjoyment of your computer for years to come.

From *Moving Your Home Computer* by United Van Lines, Inc., copyright 1985, 1987. Researched and prepared by the Bette Malone Relocation Service.

packed in advance by a third-party service. Some moving companies offer brochures explaining how to prepare these items for transit. (See "Sources of Further Information," below.)

Moving and Children

Talk with your children about moving as early as possible, taking care to accentuate the positive. Give them time to get used to the idea, and answer all their questions.

Contrary to popular belief, summer is not the best time to relocate children, since school is the primary way for children to make friends. A move made during the school year will allow your child to go directly from one social setting to another. He will be new, so his classmates, and teacher will pay special attention to him.

Infants will be the least affected by a move as long as they are comfortable and their routine is undisturbed. Younger children may react to the move by reverting to babyish actions. Help your toddler to participate in the move by packing her most treasured belongings. Reassure your child that she will not be left behind. If possible, arrange for a sitter to tend your child in your home while you pack, rather than sending the child to the sitter's home.

Older children will be concerned about fitting into a new environment, but they generally adapt quickly to a change in settings and often find new experiences exciting.

Teenagers face all sorts of challenges in changing social situations. Try to

The Moving Aid Box

Assemble a moving kit to take with you in the car or have the movers pack last and unload first. This box should contain:

•Household items: hammer, screwdrivers, pliers, an assortment of nails, masking tape, tape measure, flashlight, fuses, scissors, cleaning cloths, light bulbs, trash bags

•Kitchen items: paper plates, cups, napkins and cutlery, aluminum foil, small saucepan, serving spoons and plastic pitcher

•Snacks: canned pudding, dried fruit, dry soup mix, instant drinks

•Bath items: towels, toilet tissue, facial tissue, soap

•First-aid kit

find out in advance about sports or other groups in which your child may participate. Obtain copies of the student paper or yearbook at your child's new school, and inquire about what students wear to school in the new community. Perhaps a new co-worker's son or daughter is in the same grade and can help introduce your child around.

Involve your children as much as possible in the move.

•Assign each child age-appropriate duties, such as packing or sending out change-of-address cards.

•If possible, take them on the house-hunting trip. If you can't do this, give them as much information as possible on their new surroundings. Take pictures of your new home, the neighborhood and the new school. The local Chamber of Commerce may be able to provide additional materials.

•Children can get a sense of what lies ahead by pretending to move with dolls, boxes and wagons.

•Encourage children to exchange addresses with their friends.

•Let children decide how their new rooms are to be arranged and decorated.

Temporary Decorating Tips

Until you have a chance to unpack all your belongings and purchase new window coverings and other furnishings, here are several tips that can make a new house or apartment seem more like home.

A high priority is to set out lamps and other portable light fixtures to give your home a warm glow.

Designate one room for living and clear it of packing boxes and clutter. Furnish this temporary nest with several comfortable chairs, a table, a lamp and a few special family belongings such as photographs, plants or pictures.

Filling a house with a familiar scent can also make a barren space feel more like home. Popcorn, bacon, cinnamon toast or potpourri can add a warm touch to your house.

Sheets can be draped over curtain rods to add a touch of color until appropriate curtains or drapes can be purchased. If privacy is needed, pin sheets over rods so they can be "closed" at night and opened during the day.

Inexpensive sheer curtains can provide some privacy while allowing light to come through until heavier drapes are purchased. Curtains from your old home that are too short can be lengthened by adding ribbon trim to the bottom, or ribbon tabs on top.

Settling In

Now that you've arrived, how do you settle in to your new community? Begin by getting in touch with local organizations that specialize in welcoming newcomers. Look in the Yellow Pages under "Welcoming Services" or ask your relocation specialist for names. Encourage family members to join the scouts, YMCA, PTA, church or other community or sporting groups. Phone or visit the historical society, public library, and the tourism or visitors bureau for suggestions of things to do and places to visit.

HOUSEWARMINGS

One way to meet your neighbors and show off your new home to friends and family is to host a housewarming. This is usually an open house given by the person or couple in honor of their new home, explains Letitia Baldrige in *The Amy Vanderbilt Complete Book of Etiquette.*

Invitations to a housewarming can be extended by telephone, casual note or printed invitation. The event can be a cocktail party held in the early evening during the week, or a weekend luncheon or buffet. Usually entire families are invited, and a children's table with punch and cookies or chips is offered.

For adults, punch or mixed drinks may be served, along with hors d'oeuvres. Guests are usually expected to bring a small gift to a housewarming. These should be left in the front hallway and usually are not opened during the party.

Sources of Further Information

BOOKS, PAMPHLETS AND BROCHURES
The American Movers Conference, a national trade association of the household-goods moving industry, has several brochures available to assist consumers. "Guide to a Satisfying Move," "Moving and Children" and "Moving with Pets and Plants" may be obtained by sending a stamped, self-addressed, business-size envelope to:

    American Movers Conference
    1611 Duke St.
    Alexandria, VA 22314-3482

The Interstate Commerce Commission offers two brochures, "Helpful Tips in Planning Your Interstate Move" (available for 50 cents from the Consumer Information Center, Dept. 471Z, Pueblo, CO 81009) and "Your Rights & Responsibilities When You Move," available from your moving company.

The Consumer Education Research Center, a national nonprofit consumer group, has published a book entitled *How to Save $$$ on Your Moving Bills: Avoiding Highway Robbery* by Henry P. Constantino. For further information contact CERC at:

    350 Scotland Rd.
    Orange, NJ 07050
    Or call 1-800-USA-0121 for a credit-card order.

TOLL-FREE NUMBERS
    Bekins: 1-800-422-3334
    NorthAmerican Van Lines: 1-800-348-2111
    United Van Lines: 1-800-325-3870

3

Home

Decorating

Making a Decorating Plan

Successful home decorating involves practicality and comfort as well as good looks and style. You must discover exactly what you need, what you would like to improve and how much you can afford. You can then create a realistic budget, sort out your priorities and decide what to do.

TAKING A PERSONAL INVENTORY
To begin with, interview yourself, your spouse or partner, and your kids about practical, aesthetic and budgetary matters. Start by taking a personal inventory (from *Mary Gilliatt's New Guide to Decorating*).

Practical
• How long do you expect to stay in your present home?

• Are there now, or are there likely to be, children in the household?

• What is the maximum number of rooms you think you will need? Can these be found from existing space? Could you, for example, use roof or attic space?

• Do elderly relatives live with you, or are they frequent houseguests? Do you, for example, need extra lighting or hand-grip rails?

• Are there any pets in the household? If so, it will affect the types of finishes and surfaces used.

• Where does the family feel most comfortable eating—in the kitchen, living room, family room or dining room?

• Almost certainly some of your rooms will have multiple uses—for example, the children may do their homework in the dining room. If so, are the needs of the various users likely to conflict?

•How often do you entertain, and how? How many people do you generally entertain at once? Where do you entertain? The living room? The dining room? The kitchen?

•Are sleeping accommodations cramped for the family?

•Are the washing/bathing/toilet facilities inconvenient? Are there problems at peak times (for example, in the mornings)?

•Is your overall storage space insufficient? If so, is it capable of being expanded?

•What are the regular leisure-time activities of the members of the household? Watching TV or video, using a computer?

•Do any of the family have any specialist activities or hobbies, requiring rooms to be set aside as workrooms? Should there be rooms reserved for equipment such as the washing machine or dryer, or the freezer?

Aesthetic

•Do you and your partner share similar tastes or do you have decidedly different tastes? Have you agreed to have your own way in different rooms?

•When it comes to color schemes, do you feel quite sure of what you want? If not, are you confused and uncertain—or are you open-minded?

•With what particular colors are you happiest? Are there any colors you really dislike?

•Would you say your taste in decorating and furnishing is eclectic? Traditional? Modern? Romantic? Idiosyncratic? Minimalist? Do your views depend on the house or room in question? And what styles do you admire? Country style— from whatever country? Sophisticated townhouse? Oriental? Indoor/outdoor? American Colonial? Empire? Regency? Victorian? Neoclassical? Postmodern? Edwardian? Art Nouveau? Art Deco? 1950s retrospective?

•Do you possess any particular painting, fabric, rug or similar item that would make a good starting point for your basic color scheme?

Budgetary

•What do you feel is the maximum you can spend on your project (bearing in mind that you should always keep a contingency fund in reserve for emergencies)?

•Do you think this budget will be restrictive? Reasonable? More than adequate? Is your opinion based on research into current prices for merchandise and services, or just guesswork? (If the latter, it is essential that you research all prices *first*. You will find that almost everything is more expensive than you think.)

•If you could list (ignoring cost) the 10 luxuries that would make your home seem more attractive to you, what would they be?

•Are any members of the household good with their hands? Skillful at carpentry? Painting? This can make a big difference to the overall budget.

•Even if your budgeted plans are reasonably modest, will you have to borrow money from somewhere, such as the bank? Would it make sense, in terms of the value of the house or your desire for a better lifestyle, to be more ambitious in your plans, and arrange a large loan?

PLANNING SPACE

Drawing a plan of your living space is the foundation for a comprehensive interior design. Plans must be drawn to scale, so you will have to measure everything accurately.

Measuring works best with two people, one to hold the tape measure and the other to write down the numbers. Measure the length and the width of the room, as well as any recesses. Measure the height and width of windows and doors.

Once you have measured carefully make a plan by drawing a rough sketch and marking all the dimensions on it. Then draw a plan to scale on a sheet of graph paper. Indicate positions of electrical outlets, telephone jacks, radiators, pipes and other permanent features. Decide on a scale—1/4 to 1/2 inch to a foot is standard. If you have a lot of details, you may want to use a 1:1 scale, on a larger sheet of paper. Use a sharp pencil with hard lead to prevent smudging. Make plenty of copies of the completed plan.

Plans are an excellent means of working out a new furniture layout; you can make cutouts of your furniture and rearrange them on the plan. Also, take your plan and list of dimensions with you when you shop. If you need to make a quick decision, at least you'll have an idea of the size and scale of the piece you think might fill your empty spot; that way you're less likely to make mistakes.

LOOKING FOR INSPIRATION

Decorating plans should be influenced by the proportions and style of a house or apartment. Your home's existing elements should be used to their best advantage.

Use decorating magazines and style books to get ideas. Check out local decorating and furniture showrooms and shops for possible materials, including carpet, wallcoverings, paint colors and fabrics. Gather samples—wallpaper, upholstery fabric, paint—of the things you like. Collect these together and spread them out on a flat surface so you

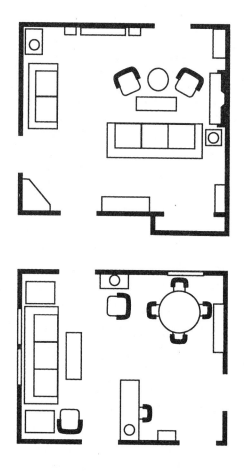

Decorating plans

can see them all at once. That way you'll know what goes together and what to eliminate.

Styles

ECLECTIC

An eclectic approach to decorating is often a necessity. People find they own objects in a variety of different styles but don't know how to put them together. Imagination and experimentation are the keys to a successful eclectic scheme. But however diverse the elements, there should be a single factor that unites them, such as color, shape or degree of formality. An overall white or cream-toned scheme is an excellent way to show off a varied group of furnishings and accessories. Wall-to-wall

Choosing Colors

Color choice is basic to your decorating scheme. Color can change the feeling of a room, making it seem larger or smaller, warmer or cooler. Colors can make a room appear cool and restful or warm and stimulating.

The best approach to color is to be analytical. When you see a color combination you like, consider carefully why you like it and how you might re-create it. Become conscious of color wherever you go.

Color affects a room's proportions. Pale colors make things appear to recede and rooms seem larger, while bright or dark tones seem to bring walls in closer. These visual effects have practical applications: A small room appears large if walls are painted in light tones or white, while a long, narrow room will assume more pleasing proportions if one of the short walls is painted a color contrasting with the other walls. A high ceiling "comes down" when painted a slightly darker tone. The reverse is true for a low ceiling—painting it white or a lighter tone of the wall color will make it

appear higher. Large pieces of furniture will appear to blend in and become much less conspicuous if covered or painted the same color as the walls; conversely, a small piece will stand out more if colored in a bright accent tone.

Reds, yellows and oranges are "warm" hues, while blues, greens and grays are "cool" colors. White and black are generally regarded as neutrals, as are beige, taupe and other variations on brown. Gray added to warm colors will make them cooler.

Colors have emotional connotations. For example, yellow, the color of the sun, is seen as lively. Green is not only the color of leaves and grass and other natural things; it also implies reliability. Blue is the color of the sky, but it's also restful and soothing, and most people choose it as their favorite color. Red is passionate and arousing, while pink is calming. Orange is also stimulating but its pastel versions, such as peach or terra cotta, are more relaxed. Think about the emotions and feeling you want to create in a room.

Choosing colors you'd like to use in a decorating scheme is one thing but putting them together is another. An effective

color scheme obeys basic rules. The conventional wisdom is that the large surfaces of a room (walls, ceiling, floors, window treatments) should be restricted to not more than three dominant colors (it's all right to use a print with more than three colors if only one or two prevail).

Traditional decorating schemes usually put the darkest tone on the floor, medium tones on walls and light tones on the ceiling. Window treatments and upholstery should contrast somewhat with walls to keep everything from blending together. Use neutral tones on large areas and bright, intense colors on smaller areas and for accessories.

Planning a color scheme for a whole house or apartment is an extension of planning for a single room. It's more complicated, of course, since you need to think about the flow from one area to another. It makes sense to envision an overall palette of colors that work well together and can be used in various proportions from room to room. Each room would seem different, but the effect of the whole would be of a pleasant overall scheme at work.

carpeting or a room-size rug can have the same effect, providing a background that ties everything together.

COUNTRY

Country furniture and furnishings cover a broad range from farmhouse antiques to contemporary pieces done in a country style. *English country* features slipcovers, often of flowered chintz, old Oriental rugs, pine furniture and casual flower arrangements. *French country* offers charming Provençal prints, checked fabrics or faded toiles. Furniture is of chestnut or pine, and chairs have caned seats and curved legs.

Small prints and checks are typical of *American country*, along with stenciled walls, painted floorcloths, braided rugs and patchwork quilts. Rocking chairs, Windsor-style settees, four-poster beds and the refined lines of Shaker furniture are among the most popular types of furnishings. *American Southwest* interiors display rough-hewn furniture, Navajo rugs, Hopi and Anasazi pottery, straw matting, and bright color combined with black in patterns inspired by Native American textiles.

Scandinavian country style, in contrast, is typified by painted wood furniture, bare floorboards, cool, clear colors, and crisp blue and white checks, seen most often on fabric but also in painted or tiled motifs.

TRADITIONAL

Simple, classical *18th-century style* is generally referred to as "traditional" style. Drop-front writing desks, wooden dining chairs with carved backs and pedestal side tables are popular furniture types that are available today in affordable reproductions. Also typical of the style is Chinoiserie—Oriental motifs and materials found in porcelain, lacquer work, faux bamboo and vivid color combinations of brilliant scarlet or emerald green contrasted with black and gilt.

Regency, or Neoclassical, style is another popular traditional style. Patterned wallpapers or painted walls are typical, as are strong colors in sophisticated combinations, such as lilac with yellow, emerald with crimson, and deep pinks and blues. Rich fabrics—watered and moiré silks, brocades and damasks—are used in elaborate curtains festooned with fringes and tassels, and adorned with decorative hardware such as brackets, finials, rings, rosettes and tiebacks. Furniture designs employ classical motifs and contrasts of light and dark woods.

PERIOD STYLES

The use of period styles doesn't require museum-quality research, but rather the employment of appropriate motifs, forms and colors. The most popular period styles are those of the 19th and early 20th centuries, such as Victorian, Art Deco and Arts and Crafts.

Victorian style features monumental sofas with overstuffed cushions and fringed and tasseled bolsters and intricate design motifs, as well as stenciled architectural ornament, available as preprinted wallpaper borders. Lace curtains, fads for Greek and Egyptian styles, and Gothic Revival motifs were all popular elements of Victorian decorating. The use of fringe, tassels, deep, rich colors and a mix of many patterns contributes to the overall look.

In the 1890s, when the elaborate Victorian styles were going out of style, a simpler look came to the fore—the *Arts and Crafts style.* Also known as *Mission, Craftsman* or *Craftsman Modern,* it employs homespun fabrics, clean, muted colors and natural materials such as stone, brick, glazed tile, copper, bronze and dark-toned woods, particularly oak. Arts and Crafts furniture is distinctive, with simple, rectilinear lines and massive proportions.

Art Nouveau, which features curvilinear, flowing motifs of stylized natural forms, also became popular around the turn of the century. Typical are richly stenciled borders or hand-printed wallpapers in deep pastels, including pink, lilac, yellow and pale green. Furniture tends to be simple, with strong silhouettes and cutout motifs of hearts or crescents.

Art Deco and Art Moderne are styles of the 1920s and 1930s. Deco furniture is geometric in form, incorporating strict angles or curvilinear motifs, with clean lines and smooth planes. The deep colors typical of the style—ultramarine, lilac, various reds—are often accented with black and silver. Fabrics combine geometric motifs, especially prisms or stepped pyramids, with floral or other naturalistic figures in bright colors.

Art Moderne furniture and accessories use many of the motifs of Art Deco but differ in terms of color, with a palette of black, shades of cream and white. Moderne pieces are sophisticated and streamlined, with an emphasis on chrome and glass. The overall look is long and low. Bleached and pickled woods, along with shaggy-pile white rugs, are also typical.

Furniture and accessories in the mainstream *Modern style,* invented in the mid-1920s, employ industrial materials and processes such as chromed or painted steel, plate glass, plastics, laminated and bent wood, and industrial coatings such as epoxy enamel on metal. In contrast to these sleek materials, the preferred upholstery is leather or ponyskin, or nubby fabrics in earth tones. Some designs substitute fabric webbing for traditional upholstery construction. Furniture design uses either straight, rectilinear shapes or abstracted, biomorphic curves. Many Modern furniture designs are available in reproduction.

CONTEMPORARY

High-tech interiors, using off-the-shelf industrial materials such as steel shelving and commercial carpeting, may seem dated now, but some elements— such as clean lines, everyday materials used in imaginative ways, and a soft color palette—can be successfully combined with other styles.

Postmodernism, as typified by Italian and American furniture of the 1980s, employs classical motifs in modern materials and jokingly refers to other eras, from the 19th century to the 1950s. Memphis furniture, designed by a group of Italian architects (the most famous of whom is Ettore Sottsass), perhaps defines the Postmodern style, using a variety of materials in a mixture of styles, often all in the same piece. The lessons learned from the eclectic mixing of the period can be applied to creating sophisticated rooms for today's relaxed, comfortable lifestyles.

Room-by-Room Essentials: The Kitchen

THE WORK TRIANGLE

The shape defined by drawing a line between the sink, stove and refrigerator is known as the work triangle. Here are the recommended dimensions, according to the National Kitchen and Bath Association:

• Each side of the work triangle should be four to seven feet long.

• There should be two feet of work space on either side of the sink.

• The dishwasher should be near the sink—next to it, preferably.

• There should be at least 18 inches of food-preparation space near the refrigerator and at least 18 inches of space on both sides of the stove.

If you can't make permanent alterations to your kitchen, you won't be able to change or improve your work triangle. But you could make the work triangle more convenient by adding a work trolley or a tall table. Be sure it is counter height (36 inches); many are not.

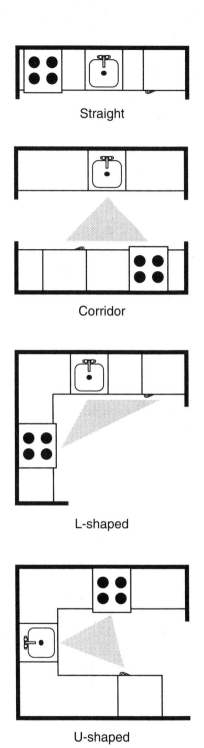

Straight

Corridor

L-shaped

U-shaped

Basic kitchen plans

RECYCLING

New laws mean that recycling now affects almost everyone. A common problem is where to put recyclable items before they go to the recycling center. If you have a deep drawer you can spare, designate it as the recycling drawer. Line it with ordinary paper bags or use plastic bags recycled from the supermarket. You can also buy a variety of ready-made bins for holding cans and glasses, or use a second wastebasket for recycling and a box for newspapers. A good housewares or hardware store should have a selection of such items.

DECORATIVE DETAILS

Although the kitchen is primarily a working area and must first of all be functional, little touches make a big difference. There are many ways to give your kitchen a new look.

•Put up new wallcovering with a scrubbable vinyl surface for easy care.

•Add a bulletin board for a cheerful effect and to keep family schedules current.

•Change the window treatments. Add a decorative valance, put glass shelves across the window to display plants or pretty bottles, repaint the woodwork around the windows to pick up a color in the new window treatment.

•The kitchen is often warmer and more humid than the rest of the house, so it's a good place for growing things. Hang potted plants from the ceiling or put them in windows.

Room-by-Room Essentials: The Bathroom

SAFETY

The bathroom can be a hazardous place for the very young and the very old. A practical approach minimizes risks.

•Both tub and floor should have a slip-resistant finish. Add stick-on nonskid strips or a rubber bathmat to the tub. Examples of slip-resistant, waterproof flooring include specially treated cork, linoleum, studded rubber tiles and slip-resist ceramic tile. Even with a slip-resistant finish, however, ceramic tile is not the safest of materials.

•Provide a place to hang a towel and bathrobe not more than 12 inches from the shower or bath. There should also be a grab bar within the tub enclosure and next to the tub. It should be at least 3/4 inch in diameter, easy to grasp, slip resistant and capable of supporting a 300-pound static load. Grab bars for a shower stall should be located just outside the entrance and within the stall, about 40 inches from the floor. Wall-hung soap dishes should be at about the same height to prevent fumbling.

•Lever door and faucet handles are easier to grasp than regular doorknobs or handles.

•Low shelves make it easier for children to reach things that belong to them (bath toys, child-safe shampoos, etc.) Young children also need a sturdy step stool in order to reach the sink.

DECORATIVE DETAILS

There are many things you can do to give your bath a quick face-lift.

•Due to high humidity, the bathroom is a great place to keep plants. You can group several small pots on the windowsill or on a tray, table or plant stand, or hang large plants from the ceiling. Choose sturdy favorites such as spider plants, aspidistra, philodendron and sansevieria.

•If you dislike the color of your tiles, paint them with yacht or marine paint. This must be done carefully, and obviously won't look the same as replacing the tile. You can also cover existing tile with plasterboard or laminate sheets, which is less expensive than retiling.

•To jazz up your walls, apply new paint or vinyl-coated wallcovering. If you choose a deep, dramatic, shiny color, it can make a small room seem larger—an effect similar to mirroring the room.

•Towels with frayed edges get a new lease on life with a border of braid, tape or fringe in a matching or contrasting color. This is fairly easy for anyone to do. You could add the same trim to curtains.

•New towels are a quick way to give a new look to the bathroom. If the wallcovering or window treatment incorporates a variety of colors, you could have several different sets of coordinating towels, or use patterned towels for a similar effect in a plain room.

Room-by-Room Essentials: The Living Room

FURNITURE PLACEMENT
Your living room should center around a focal point, such as a working fireplace, a well-designed entertainment center or a beautiful view. Group the furniture around it, using enough pieces to be flexible.

In general, try to seat six comfortably, keeping folding chairs or large floor pillows in a closet to accommodate larger gatherings. Conventional seating arrangements generally include one sofa and a pair of armchairs. In a small room, you might omit the sofa and instead have two or three very comfortable armchairs, perhaps spaced around a low coffee table. A loveseat (a small two-seater sofa) and an armchair are another possibility.

Furniture arrangement should reflect activity areas. A small room should at least have a single conversational grouping. In a larger room, you can have additional furniture groupings to reflect other activities, such as reading, watching television or even writing letters at a desk.

DECORATIVE DETAILS
Decorative objects make a room special and give it personality. Even the humblest collection, arranged with style, can add charm and interest to a room.

Small objects should always be displayed in groups, with taller items to the back. The smaller the object, the better it looks when presented in a group with other small things. One way to show off small objects is to group them according to color or material. Odd-numbered groups look better than even numbers.

Room-by-Room Essentials: The Dining Room

DINING TABLES
The most common shapes for tables are square, round, rectangular and oval. Use the number of place settings you

need to accommodate to determine the size of table required. A place setting is approximately 27 inches by 14 inches, including elbow room (add 2 inches if your dining chairs have arms). To seat six comfortably, a rectangular table should be 54 by 30 inches; to seat eight, 84 by 30. To seat four people, a round table should be 39 inches in diameter; to seat six, 52 inches, and to seat eight, 72 inches in diameter.

Most dining tables are 30 inches high. Proper seat height is about 10 to 15 inches less than table height, to fit comfortably under the table. Each chair needs approximately 3 feet of space behind it so it can be easily pulled out.

Expandable tables, with leaves, drop leaves or pull-out surfaces, are useful. However, when drop leaves are down you won't be able to seat someone on that side of the table. Two smaller tables that can be pushed together also provide more dining space for special occasions or large gatherings.

LIGHTING

You want to create a mood, not light up every nook and cranny: Lighting in the dining room should be dramatic and decorative rather than task-oriented.

•The fixture over the table should be on a dimmer switch.

•Chandeliers or other pendant lights are appropriate.

•Wall sconces or track lighting can supply additional illumination.

•A spotlight can be trained on the sideboard or focused on a special centerpiece.

Room-by-Room Essentials: Children's Rooms

SPECIAL NEEDS

Children deserve a safe environment, so make sure there are bars on the windows (vertical bars no more than five inches apart are the standard). Eliminate dangling electrical wires that a child might trip over, and cover unused electrical sockets.

The key elements of a successful child's bedroom are adequate storage space; a well-lit, convenient study/work/hobby area; and a comfortable, spacious play area, as well as someplace to sleep and perhaps space for a friend to stay overnight. Materials, finishes and furniture should be sturdy and hard-wearing.

Teenagers need privacy and a feeling that they have some control over their environment. Let them choose their own color schemes and motifs. A teenager's room might have an extra bed (for sleepover guests or for visitors to sit on), a worktable/desk/dressing table area with a chair, and plenty of storage space, along with a full-length mirror.

PLAY SPACE

School-age children should have well-defined areas for work and play. A large, well-lit tabletop or an adjustable-height desk is especially useful, if your kid likes to make things or do art projects. Even if you have a family room or basement playroom, your child also will want to play in his or her own room. Keep the furniture in the room to a minimum, or choose pieces that can be pushed out of the way, to create as much clear floor space as possible. You can also build a play loft if the ceiling height permits; 48 inches of headroom is enough for a child.

DECORATIVE DETAILS

Work out all the practical considerations—study and hobby area, play space and storage—then think about the decoration. Even if your kids choose items that seem outrageous or silly to you, remember it's their room. Bright colors and interesting textures are among the things children like best. Children's tastes change as they grow older, so try to keep the decoration flexible.

Since kids like to be able to change things around and to put up their own decorations, finish one wall as a giant bulletin board or give it a surface that can be drawn on. There are special paint finishes that will turn a wall into a giant blackboard.

Room-by-Room Essentials: The Bedroom

You spend a lot of time in the bedroom—at least one third of your life (an average person spends a third of his or her life asleep). Your bedroom is a private retreat for reading, watching TV or relaxing, as well as a place where you keep many personal possessions. There's no denying that this is one room of the house that plays a very important role in your life. Yet when it comes to decorating, the bedroom is often neglected.

LIGHTING

This is more important in a bedroom than you might think. One overhead fixture simply will not do. You need a good reading lamp, one on each side of a double or larger-size bed. Wall-hung or table lamps with switches located on the cord are easiest to reach when lying in bed. You can also buy tiny reading lights that clamp to the pages of a book, to keep from disturbing your partner if you like to stay up late and read. If your bedroom is divided into different areas (dressing area, reading area), each will need its own task lighting.

FURNITURE PLACEMENT

By far the biggest concern in decorating a bedroom is where to put the bed. You need at least 15 inches on each side of the bed for ease in making it. It will help to know standard American bed sizes, although these may vary slightly—there's nothing really standard about bed sizes:

Twin	39W × 75L
Extra-long twin	39W × 80-84L
Full/double	54W × 75-80L
Queen	60W × 80L
King	72W × 80-84L

Shopping for Furniture

The four most important factors in buying furniture are style, size, suitability, and quality. When you shop for furniture, you will discover a profusion of choices. Furniture can be divided into two style categories: contemporary and traditional. You can't go wrong with traditional designs—after all, they have survived the test of time. Adaptations may be better suited to modern lifestyles. Good modern furniture is harder to find at lower price points, but if that's what you like, it's not impossible to search it out.

Furniture is a major purchase: Shopping for it should be a practical endeavor. Visit furniture sources in your area to become familiar with what they offer. Good sources, in addition to furniture specialty stores, include design centers, auction rooms and antiques shops, and second-hand furniture stores. It's also a good idea to check out retail branches of stylish home stores such as Crate & Barrel, Ethan Allen, Room & Board, Pier One Imports, Storehouse and Workbench. Get in the habit of checking prices in furniture shops and flea markets, sales and auction rooms. When it comes time to buy, you'll know the going rate.

Furniture should be comfortable and durable or it's not worth buying. Whatever you buy, make it the best you can afford. What's on display in the

Planning a Home Office

Too often the home office is an afterthought, since most homes weren't designed as workplaces. You may be lucky enough to have an unused bedroom or study, but what if you don't? Creating an efficient work space in a multipurpose room requires a good deal of planning.

An area outside the routine course of household activities works best for a home office. Some spaces to consider are the guest bedroom, a renovated garage, attic, or basement, dressing rooms or pantries, or even a large walk-in closet. If possible, a desk shouldn't have to double as a dining table. Another basic is proper wiring for computers and other office equipment. If you use a personal computer, you need a surge protector (also called a surge suppressor), to protect your equipment from changes in current caused by lightning strikes or brownouts. The simplest way to provide this protection is to buy a unit that plugs into the outlet. A similar type of device for telephone lines—needed if you often transmit files via modem—is called a spike protector.

There are many types of office furniture available, from no-frills models with enameled tubular-steel frames to solid wood executive-style furnishings with brass hardware. Special fold-up desks, rolling file carts and desk chairs that resemble side chairs are useful for offices that must be hidden away when the work day ends.

People with back problems may want to try a Scandinavian-style kneeling chair. If you're short, get an adjustable chair with a foot rest or buy a separate foot rest. This will help you maintain the correct posture. A tall person can choose a chair with a tall back and an adjustable seat.

If you use a computer, a chair with arm rests (plus a separate wrist pad on the desk) will help prevent fatigue. A swivel chair on casters works well in a small office space, allowing you to move easily from one part of the office to another without having to get up. Printer carts and print stands make it easy to manage paper and equipment. If you work at a drafting table, which is higher than a standard desk, you will need a stool and extra storage space next to the drafting table. Some chairs adjust from drafting-table height to desk height, saving you the cost of two chairs.

Try to place your desk so that natural light enters over the opposite shoulder from your dominant hand (over the left shoulder if you are right-handed; vice-versa if you're a lefty). Putting a computer screen by a window can cause problems with glare. If glare is a problem only during certain times, use blinds or shades to block the light when necessary.

Good lighting prevents eyestrain. You should have a task light at your work station that is adjustable so you can focus it on different areas and position it so that it doesn't cast shadows on your work. If you work at a computer, even light is best, rather than just a light on the screen.

showroom is often not all you have to choose from. You can usually order the sofa or chair you prefer in a different covering or size.

UPHOLSTERED FURNITURE

A sofa and armchairs are the center-piece of most living room arrangements. Check the quality of the frame, springs, webbing and cushioning material carefully, because with upholstered furniture, you get what you pay for. A cheap sofa won't be as comfortable or durable as its twice-as-expensive equivalent. With upholstered pieces, buy from a reputable source, since it's hard to see the frame, filling and springs. You shouldn't hear creaks when you sit on the piece or try to lift it. Kiln-dried hardwood is the best material for the frame.

Eight-way hand-tied springs (tied together in eight different places) are the most durable and provide the best seat support. Wire-linked coil springs and arched sinuous springs (or S-springs) cost less and are fairly comfortable as well. Pocketed springs are the top-of-the-line choice for comfortable back cushions, while sinuous-spring backs are less expensive. Usually, if the back cushions are loose, webbing replaces springs to provide resilience. This type of construction is less expensive and is often seen in Modern designs.

High-density polyurethane foam, wrapped with down, cotton batting or synthetic fiberfill, is used for the most comfortable and long-wearing cushioning. Down is softest but costs the most, and requires frequent fluffing. Cotton

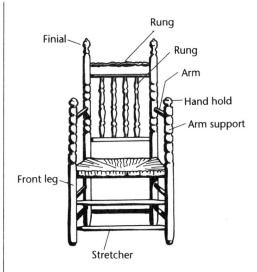

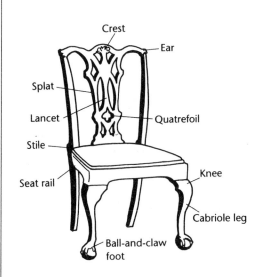

Anatomy of a chair

batting and synthetic fiberfill keep their shape better, are comfortable and give good value for money, but they are firmer than down.

Give an upholstered piece a "sit test" before you buy: Sit on it to gauge firmness and comfort, to determine if the arms and back are the right height, the seat dimensions are in proportion to your own and that there's enough support for your back.

CASE GOODS

"Case goods" is the term used in the furniture industry for all non-upholstered furniture. The term refers to tables, desks and cabinets of all types, as well as chairs, benches and settles. They can be made of metal, plastic, wood, even marble, or all of the above. The price should reflect quality of materials and workmanship.

Expensive materials used in furniture construction include domestic hardwoods such as maple, walnut, oak, pecan, cherry and birch, and tropical hardwoods such as mahogany and teak. If you buy furniture made from these woods, check to be sure they are harvested from certified sustainable sources such as plantations. Manufacturers that use wood from plantations will state that fact on the label.

Softwoods such as pine, cedar and fir are less expensive. Wood substitutes such as particle board and hardboard cost still less. Particle board (also called composite board) is usually covered with a veneer of hardwood or plastic laminate. Hardboard is often embossed with a wood-grain pattern and finished to look like real wood.

Veneer has a poor reputation, but improvements in adhesives and manufacturing techniques ensure that a piece from a reputable manufacturer should have no problems with cracking or peeling. "Solid-wood construction" means that all the exposed parts of a piece of furniture are made of solid wood. Interior parts may be of particle board or other materials.

High-quality case goods should be sturdy, well-made and stable. To check construction, look underneath. Where the legs join the top or seat of the piece, the joint should be reinforced with a corner block. When screws are used, there should be washers to protect the wood. Make sure joints are tight, as any visible gaps will cause swaying or squeaking.

Put your hands on a table or cabinet to rock it gently or sit in a chair and sway gently from side to side. There should be no wobbles or creaks. Push on the arms and back of the chair while seated; there should be no give. Feel the bottom of a tabletop or chair seat to see if surfaces are smooth.

Rap the top and sides of a chest or cabinet with your knuckles to check the construction. Thin panels will have a hollow sound, while heavy panels will sound dull. Check the back: plywood or hardwood backs are sturdier than particle board. Equal spacing around the drawer fronts is a sign of quality; there should not be more than 1/4 inch of play from side to side. Remove drawers to check for built-in guides and stops, tightly fitted joints and dust panels between each drawer slot, all signs of quality construction. Cabinet doors should hang evenly and open smoothly; hardware and hinges should be securely attached, with screws that go all the way through the panel and are anchored with a bolt and washer.

UPHOLSTERY AND SLIPCOVERS

Upholstery should be of good quality and tailored with care. Check that fabric fits smoothly, without puckers or gaps, and that pattern repeats match. The welting (cording along seams) should be neatly sewn, and there should be no puckering or loose threads. The skirt should be lined and weighted to hang straight.

Types of Fabric

Upholstery fabrics are subject to wear, so consider durability along with color and pattern. Leather and vinyl are easiest to care for. Next in terms of durability come pile fabrics such as velvet, corduroy and plush, and flat, tightly woven fabrics such as tapestries, satins, muslins and tweeds. The more tightly woven they are, the better they will wear.

Discount Furniture Sources

It's satisfying to get a great deal on something you really like. A number of mail-order outlets sell factory-fresh, name-brand furniture for up to 50 percent off the suggested retail price. They don't carry every model by every manufacturer, but it's worthwhile to check. Go to your local retailer, find out how much the piece you want costs and get the model number, finish, fabric style and size. Find out how long it will take to deliver. Then call an outlet for a price quote. Make sure to ask how much sales tax, shipping and insurance will add to the cost of the item, so you can make a direct comparison.

Once you have ordered the piece, you usually receive a confirmation by mail along with a bill for half the cost. The balance is due on delivery—which may take as long as 90 days. Only you can decide if the money you save is worth the wait for the new armchair or coffee table.

Since you're probably paying a lot of money for this item, even at a discount, make sure to find out what happens if it arrives damaged or, once it's in your living room, you decide you don't like it. Check with the Mail Order Action Line of the Direct Marketing Association (11 W. 42nd St., P.O. Box 3861, New York, NY 10163ƒ3861) and the Better Business Bureau in the town where the firm is based to see if there are any complaints on file.

Here are the names and phone numbers of a few well-regarded discount furniture retailers:

Cherry Hill Furniture
P.O. Box 7405
High Point, NC 27264
1-800-328-0933

Edgar B
P.O. Box 849
Clemmons, NC 27012
1-800-255-6589
$15.00 for catalog, plus $3 shipping and handling

Holton Furniture Co.
P.O. Box 280
Thomasville, NC 27360
1-800-334-3183

Homeway Furniture Co.
121 W. Lebanon St.
Mount Airy, NC 27030
1-800-334-9094

North Carolina Furniture Showrooms
1805 NW 38th Ave.

Lauderhill, FL 33311
1-800-227-6060
(They also have retail showrooms in many cities.)

Also take a look at what's available from mail-order catalogs. Here's a list of recommended sources (mostly Modern in inspiration):

Crate & Barrel: 1-800-323-5461 for free catalog.

Eddie Bauer Home Collection: 1-800-426-8020 for free catalog and store locations.

Ethan Allen: 1-203-743-8000 for store locations.

Leathercraft: P.O. Box 639, Conover, NC 28613, 1-800-951-3507 for catalog ($10) and video.

Pier One Imports: 1-800-447-4371 for mailing list and store locations.

Pottery Barn: 1-800-922 5507 for free catalog.

Room & Board: 1-800-486-6554 for information.

Storehouse: 1-800-869-2468 for catalog.

Workbench: 1-800-767-1710 for catalog.

While natural fibers have a nicer hand than synthetics, they are not as durable. Natural/synthetic blends make the best compromise. Nylon adds toughness. Upholstery fabrics often come treated with a soil- and stain-resistant finish.

Slipcovers

These cost about half as much as reupholstering. They can be used to cover outdated or threadbare upholstery, or to give furniture a different look and extend the life of existing upholstery.

Sturdy, washable upholstery cottons are probably the best choice, but since the cover for a large sofa probably won't fit in the washing machine, you might as well use a dry-clean-only fabric. Rayon velvet wears well and looks elegant.

Ask relatives, friends and co-workers if they have had slipcovers made and if they can recommend someone. Upholstery stores, decorating outlets and fabric stores often have a slipcover operation or can recommend an upholsterer. Major department stores with furniture departments may also do custom slipcovers. Check the Yellow Pages under "Slipcovers" or "Upholstery."

Check references and ask to see examples of finished work. A well-made slipcover should have straight seams. The stitching should be neat and the cover should fit the outline of the chair or sofa fairly closely.

Buying Used Furniture

Buying used or second-hand furniture can be a great way to get a bargain and find an unusual piece. Sources for second-hand furniture include used-furniture dealers, junk and salvage yards, charity or thrift shops, and auctions and antiques shops. Wood or metal furniture make better buys than upholstered pieces.

The rules for quality in secondhand furniture are the same as for buying new. You will have to accept some wear, but it should not affect the usefulness of the piece or be disfiguring. Don't buy pieces that need extensive repair or refinishing—unless you already have experience, chances are that you will never get around to it. On the other hand, if you're willing to spend money for professional repairs, some older pieces may still prove great buys.

Walls

Wall treatments consist of two basic types: wallpaper and paint.

Wallpaper is flexible, available in a wide range of colors, textures and patterns. It is relatively easy to install and helps to brighten up any room. Most types are easy to keep clean and last for several years.

Paint is the cheapest and quickest method of changing the appearance of a room. It comes in an infinite variety of colors, and can be applied to create various effects such as sponging, ragging and stenciling. Paint can also enhance a room with simple effects, such as picking out the molding in a different color or glazing a base color with thin coats of wash in a slightly different tone to create luminosity and depth.

MEASURING WALLS

Whatever type of wall treatment you want, you must start by estimating the area that needs to be covered. This is simple to do. First, measure around the perimeter of the room, including alcoves and jogs in the wall, then multiply by the ceiling height. This will give you the total wall area.

Estimating Wallpaper

One roll of American wallpaper covers 30 square feet; a roll of European wallpaper covers 23 square feet. In order to estimate the number of rolls you need, divide the total wall area of the room by the number of square feet in a roll. To make your estimate more precise, subtract half a roll for each window or door. Round up to the nearest whole roll. If your pattern has a repeat that must be matched, add an extra one to three rolls to make sure you don't come up short.

Estimating Paint

Depending on the surface you are painting, a quart of undercoat will cover 120 to 150 square feet. A quart of latex paint will cover about 130 to 140 square feet, depending on the finish (semigloss or matte-finish paints go a bit further), and a quart of oil-based paint covers 160 to 170 square feet; the glossier finish of oil provides slightly greater coverage.

WALLPAPER

Wallpaper varies in quality. Less expensive papers tend to be thinner and harder to hang. More costly coverings pay off in that it is usually easier for an amateur to put them up. The most expensive papers available are hand-printed designs, often reproductions of antique papers, sometimes using the original blocks. Most types of wallpapers are treated to repel moisture.

Spongeable papers are covered with a plastic film and can be washed with water; *scrubbable* papers have a thick vinyl coating and can actually be scrubbed. They are best for use in kitchens, bathrooms and laundry rooms—wherever there is a high moisture content.

Other paper-backed wallcoverings include natural fibers, such as burlap and grasscloth. These are traditionally expensive but provide a textured, neutral-toned background to create interest in a room. They can be difficult to clean and maintain, however.

Hanging Wallcoverings

The best order for papering a room is to start in the corner nearest the window and work away from the source of natural light toward the door. That way, any slight overlaps will be less likely to cast shadows and will call less attention to themselves.

Always apply wallpaper to a clean, even, dry surface. If there are a lot of cracks and irregularities, you will need to patch the wall or put up lining paper first. Here is a list of tools and equipment you will need for hanging wallpaper:

• Wallpaper paste (unless paper is prepasted)

• Pasting table, or board over sawhorses

• Plumb line (to find vertical)

- Pencil and ruler

- Stepladder

- Shears or scissors

- Paste brush, bucket, paper brush, water, sponge

PAINT

The two types of paint used in most interior applications are *latex* (water-based) and *oil-based*.

Latex paint can be cleaned up with water and dries quickly; oil-based paint must be removed with a solvent such as turpentine and takes longer to dry. It must be used with an oil-based undercoat. Both types of paint are available in various finishes, ranging from high-gloss to flat, and in a variety of colors.

Enamel paints are a type of oil-based paint that is very dense and has an extremely high gloss. They are usually applied only in small areas, on wood or metal.

You can create your own colors using artist's oil or acrylic pigments mixed with a solvent such as turpentine or water, and combined with the appropriate paint base (white oil-based paint for oils and turpentine; white latex for acrylics and water).

Preparing Surfaces

Before you paint, clear the room of furniture as much as possible. Remove lamp shades and take down curtains. Cover remaining furniture and floor with dust sheets and drop cloths.

Walls and ceilings that are in good condition need to be vacuumed or dusted before painting, then washed with a solution of detergent and water. Cracks and holes in the walls should be patched and filled, and the patches primed before painting.

Peeling paint should be stripped, then wall surface washed. Wallpaper should be removed before a wall is painted.

Techniques

Paint room surfaces in this order:

- First do the ceiling, working away from the natural light source.

- Next paint the walls, then window frames and doors.

- Finish up with moldings and picture railings. Baseboards should come last.

If you use a wide brush, a roller or a pad, apply paint in random directions, rather than up and down or back and forth. Work out from corners, which should be cut in with a smaller brush. Overlap and crisscross your strokes.

When you finish painting a section or need to get more paint, end with a light, upward stroke to eliminate marks.

Window Coverings

The way you decorate your windows will depend on several factors: style, budget and the window itself. It may have a beautiful view or look out on a brick wall, or into another person's apartment. It may get a lot of sun, or none at all. The amount of space around the window is important, too. Small windows should not be burdened with a lot of fabric, while elaborate draperies enhance tall windows.

CURTAINS AND DRAPERIES

Although the terms can be and often are used interchangeably, technically speaking draperies and curtains are not the same thing.

Draperies cover the window completely when closed and frame it when open. They can be hung from a point at the top edge of the window frame or above it, all the way up to the ceiling cornice line. They may end at any point from the sill to the floor, but they are always at least as long as the window itself.

Curtains hang closer to the window than draperies do—inside the window frame itself. If they are made of sheer material, they may be called sheers, glass curtains or sash curtains. Curtains may hang to the sill, to the bottom of the window molding or to the floor.

Draperies and curtains are often gathered or pleated in various styles, known as *headings*. Headings once were made by hand; now you can buy *heading tapes*, fabric strips with integral pockets and drawstrings which are purchased by the yard, then sewn onto the curtain or drapery material. You pull the drawstring to create the desired type of pleats or gathers.

Various types of pleats include *pinch pleats* (also called triple or French pleats), *pencil pleats, box pleats* and *goblet* (or cartridge) *pleats. Cased* or *rod-pocket headings* are gathered on the rod,

which is threaded through a casing at the top of the fabric. *Scalloped-shaped headings* may hang from metal or wooden rings or fabric tabs, which may also be used with straight headings as well.

Sheers. Sheer curtains have many uses. They can soften an unattractive view and reduce the glare of the late-afternoon sun. The best colors for sheers are white or cream, as colors tend to tint the sunlight coming through them. Suitable fabrics include tergal, voile, lightweight muslin and lace, available in easy-care synthetics.

Valances, cornices and window headings. These are a finishing note, and are useful when dealing with awkward or undistinguished windows to create the look of architectural detail when there is none. They also serve to conceal curtain hardware.

A valance is made of fabric stiffened with a backing, which may be trimmed in various ways. It is also sometimes called a *pelmet* or *lambrequin*. A *cornice* is a wood or metal heading that serves a similar function. The benefit of both of these headings is their versatility. They can be designed to echo a motif in the curtain material, for example, or they may imitate architectural motifs such as Gothic or Palladian arches.

Festoons and swags, also referred to generally as valances, are pieces of fabric carefully cut and sewn to look as though they have been draped over the top of the windows. Festoons may be single, double or triple, and have tails (also

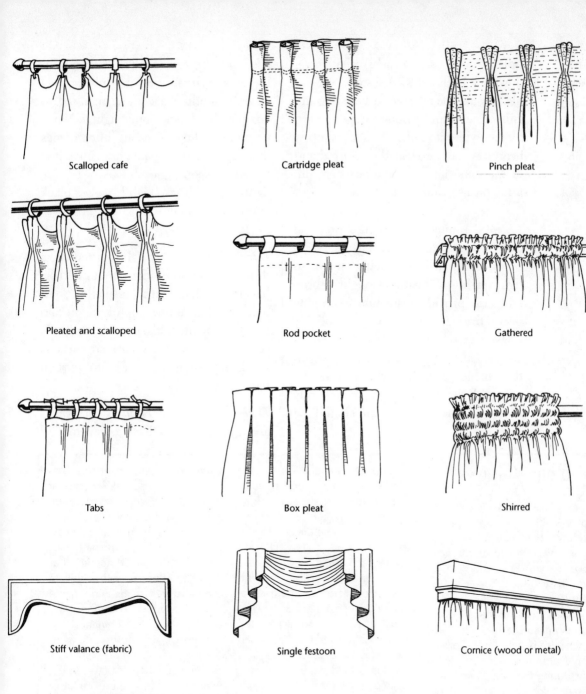

Scalloped cafe

Cartridge pleat

Pinch pleat

Pleated and scalloped

Rod pocket

Gathered

Tabs

Box pleat

Shirred

Stiff valance (fabric)

Single festoon

Cornice (wood or metal)

Triple festoon

Swags and pleats

rapery and curtain headings

called *jabots* or *cascades*) that hang down on both sides. A festoon ensemble may also be referred to as a swag and tails or swag and jabots. Swags are festoons without tails. Other, simpler headings may be pleated or shirred and of the same fabric as the curtains, but hung on a separate rod.

Linings. Linings have both a practical and decorative purpose. They serve to block out light, give better shape to lightweight or medium-weight fabric, and also provide insulation. A purely decorative curtain or drape probably doesn't need a lining unless required for shape. Curtains can also be made with detachable linings, which can be removed for washing. A traditionally lined or interlined curtain should be dry-cleaned.

Blackout linings, made of specially, tightly woven fabric with a rubbery feel and a smooth surface, are intended to completely block out light. Name notwithstanding, blackout lining comes in white, cream or pale gray. Since it is heavy, it should not be used to line lightweight fabrics. Tightly woven black cotton also works well as a light-blocking lining.

Interlining, a heavy fabric used as a third layer between the curtain and its backing, offers extra insulation and helps to change the look of the curtain by softening the folds, making the fabric seem more opulent. Interlined curtains are heavy, so make sure your curtain hardware is secure.

Decorative details. Tiebacks and trims are a simple but effective way to add

---

Problem Windows

Window treatments can solve the problem of awkwardly placed windows. Several small windows in one wall, for example, can make a room look chopped up and fussy. But they can be treated as a single unit by running a traverse rod along at ceiling height, so that a single panel or series of panels can be drawn away from the windows to let in light during the day, then closed at night for privacy. This looks much neater and serves to unify the room.

Window treatments that extend beyond the window frame and down to the floor lend importance to a small window set in the middle of a long wall, another awkward situation. Another special case that affects the style of curtains or draperies is double windows, which can be treated as one window or two. Bay or bow windows, although an architectural boon, can be difficult to curtain. You have a few choices: Drape each section of the bay separately; use short sections and special connectors to fit a traverse rod or pole around the bay; or install a curtain rod across the front to close off the bay when the curtains are drawn. Your final decision should depend on what looks best with the bay or bow's proportions.

If a window directly abuts a wall or a massive armoire or chest on one side, a pair of curtains or drapes won't fit; a solution might be a decorative shade or an asymmetrical drape. Shades are also the best choice for a recessed window set in its own alcove.

Windows with radiators beneath them also call for special treatment, since you must be careful not to block the heat. One idea is to use a shade to block the light, combined with dressy, stationary draperies that fall to the floor on either side of the radiator. A shade and a decorative window heading are another good combination, as are simple, sill-length curtains or draperies, depending on how much space there is between the window and the radiator. Window seats can be dealt with in the same fashion.

Windows that face out onto a noisy area or must be protected against extremes of heat or cold should be hung with heavy, lined draperies. Woolen, plaid or tweed fabrics create coziness.

interest to your window treatments. Flat braid or ribbon is a traditional trimming, sewn along the leading edges and bottom of the curtain. Other choices include fringe (long or short), fabric piping and ruffles.

Tiebacks can be as simple as a piece of ribbon or braid, or elaborately tailored. They may match or contrast, be ruffled or piped, padded or shaped. They don't have to be made of fabric—you can buy decorative metal hooks and rosettes to hold the curtain neatly in place. Placement is important. A tight tieback pulls the curtain back straight and creates an angle, while a looser one lets the fabric drape in a deep swag, which you can adjust to suit.

Fabrics. Colorfastness is an important consideration when choosing fabrics for curtains. Some fabrics, such as inexpensive silk, tend to fade more quickly than others when exposed to sunlight over a period of time. All fabrics will fade in the long run, which is why a lining or a separate glass curtain is a good idea.

Below is a list of fabric definitions and brief descriptions of how the fabric may best be used (adapted from *Fabric Magic*, by Melanie Paine):

Brocade. This is a heavy, rich fabric decorated with a woven, raised design of metallic thread, traditionally of silk but now available in cotton or synthetics. It is a very formal fabric and is often used for elaborate draperies.

Burlap. A coarse, loosely woven fabric of jute fibers that is best used for very simple window treatments, such as Roman shades.

Canvas. A coarse, heavy, tightly woven fabric that may be cotton, linen, synthetics or blends. Best for use as a simple shade.

Damask. Once made of silk and woven in Damascus (hence the name), this richly figured, woven fabric can be made from cotton, linen or wool. It makes for sumptuous curtains. Cotton damask is the least formal.

Gingham. A cotton fabric with a striped warp and weft that produces a checked look. The traditional color combinations are red and white or blue and white. It is considered an informal fabric.

Lace. This delicate, openwork fabric can be made from linen, cotton, silk, metallic or synthetic threads. Once woven by hand, but now mostly machine-made, lace works best in Victorian or country-style interiors.

Muslin. A plain, woven cotton available in a variety of weights, from heavy and coarse to light and nearly sheer. *Unbleached muslin* is a creamy speckled color; bleached muslin is white. An inexpensive fabric, muslin can be used effectively in large quantities for informal curtains or shades.

Organza. A stiff, sheer silk (it can be made from synthetics as well), organza is used for shades or glass panels.

Poplin. This lightweight cotton has a silky finish and a fine ribbed pattern. It can be used for a variety of window treatments.

Sailcloth. Resembles canvas and can be used in the same way.

Shirting. Usually made of cotton, this smooth, lustrous and plainly woven fabric is good for informal, unlined curtains.

Thai silk. Iridescent, slubbed silk, often dyed in bright colors, Thai silk is relatively inexpensive and informal for its category.

Velvet. With its short, plushy pile, velvet—woven from cotton or rayon—is generally used for formal or period rooms. It's also good for headings.

SHADES AND BLINDS

These may be made of paper, fabric, wood, plastic or metal. There are two types: roller shades and those controlled by a system of cords and pulleys, such as Roman or festoon shades. Blinds are made of slats, also controlled by cords and pulleys.

Plain shades cover the window simply and neatly when lowered. When raised, they practically disappear. *Roller shades* and *Roman shades* are the simplest of fabric shades. Roman shades consist of a panel of fabric lined with horizontal battens that are flat when let down and form a series of crisp pleats when pulled up. These shades are best used in streamlined or modern interiors as an unobtrusive way of making sure a window is properly dressed.

Pleated shades are made of stiffened, permanently pleated polyester, controlled by cords which run down each side. They are available ready-made in various sizes, or can be custom ordered. The main drawback to pleated shades is that they tend to sag over a period of time as the weight of the material pulls down on the pleats.

Opulent *Austrian and festoon shades* are made of shirred and ruched fabric, often trimmed with ruffles or piping. They are gathered onto a curtain heading tape to create the shirring, then ruched (pleated, fluted or gathered) with cording to form swags. An Austrian shade, sometimes called a balloon shade, is ruched only at the bottom; festoon shades are ruched all the way up. Even when fully drawn up, they will still block part of the window.

Available in standard sizes, *wooden blinds* are made of split bamboo, matchstick bamboo or wooden slats woven with string or yarn, and roll up by means of cords that run from top to bottom. They provide privacy and let light filter through.

Venetian, mini- and micro-blinds are made of slats connected by tapes, drawn up with cords. Mini-blinds and micro-blinds are Venetian-type blinds with slats only an inch or half an inch deep. *Vertical blinds* are also similar to Venetian blinds, except that the slats hang vertically instead of horizontally. All types of slatted blinds offer a tailored appearance and complete control of light, air and privacy.

MEASURING WINDOWS

You need to know the dimensions of your window before you can make or buy curtains. Measuring must be done carefully, since the effect of window

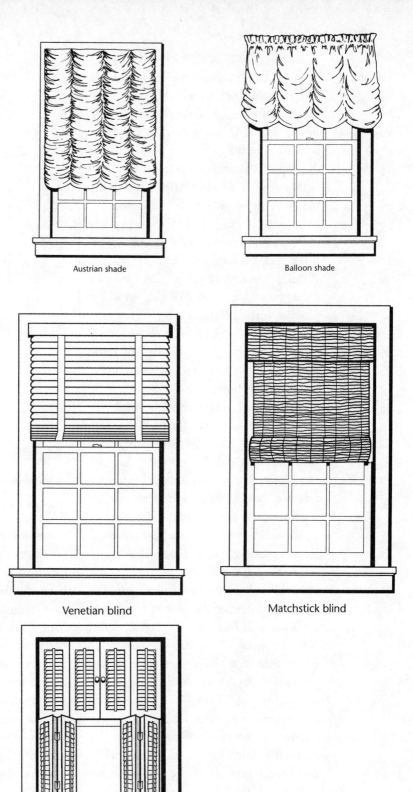

Austrian shade

Balloon shade

Roman shade

Venetian blind

Matchstick blind

Shades and blinds

Louvered shutters

treatments depends on how well they fit.

For width, measure the length of the rod or pole from which the curtain or drape will hang (A) (see illustration). If the rod is a U-shape with turnbacks, measure the full length. Then measure the top of the window frame from outside edge to outside edge (B). Next measure the inside width of the window from edge to edge (C). Depending on the type of curtain, you will use one of these measurements to calculate width. Pleated curtains require fabric two to three times the width of the window, plus at least 12 inches for hems and overlaps (overlaps are usually three or more inches deep; both sides of both panels will be hemmed, so you must multiply it by four).

If draperies will extend beyond the window frame, use the length of the rod or pole as a base for measuring; for draperies that will hang to the edge of the frame, use the width of the frame; and for curtains that will hang within the frame, use the width of the window.

For shades or blinds that are attached to the window frame, base calculations on width of the frame; for shades or blinds hung within the frame, use the width of the window. If you want curtains that will be completely clear of the window glass when drawn, add anywhere from 6 to 16 inches of fabric on both sides, depending on the type of fabric and how much room it will take up.

To determine the length of fabric needed, measure from the rod to the floor for floor-length draperies (D); from the top edge of the frame to the bottom of the sill for curtains a bit

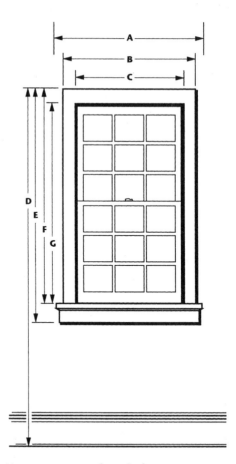

How to measure for window treatments

longer than the length of the window (E); from the top edge of the frame to the sill for sill-length curtains (F); and from the inside top of the frame to the sill for sill-length curtains that will hang inside the frame (G). To calculate the necessary amount of fabric, add a minimum of seven inches (at least three inches for headings and four inches for hems) and an additional two inches for scallop or tab headings.

To determine total yardage, divide total width needed by the width of your fabric. Multiply the result by total length needed and divide by 36 to get the total number of yards. Use a calculator and write down all numbers to ensure accuracy.

Check to make sure the finished size of ready-made curtain or drapery panels will fit your window and hardware. For example, if your curtain rod is 36 inches long, the panel should be at least 72 inches wide or wider.

Hardware

The variety of rods, poles, clips and rings may seem confusing, but among such abundance there's sure to be a type of hardware that will suit your window.

If the fixture is designed to be seen, it is frequently called a *pole*. Poles should be used with rod pocket headings, curtains hung from rings and tab headings. Many come with decorative finials.

Traverse rods are fitted with runners that allow the drapery or curtain to glide along the rod. They are made of plastic or metal (metal is sturdier) and come with a system of drawcords and pulleys. Traverse rods are attached to the wall or window frame with brackets, one at each end and one or more in between, depending on the length of the rod. Double rods or special extension brackets allow you to hang more than one set of curtains or drapes. Traverse rods can be bent to follow the curve of bay or bow windows. There is also a type designed to be bent to the curve of a Palladian window.

Hooks are used to attach pleated headings to the rod or pole. These slide into special pockets in the heading tape, then attach to the runners of a traverse rod or the rings of a pole.

Flooring

CARPETING

Wall-to-wall carpeting is a good flooring choice for many areas of the home. It is warm and soft underfoot, fairly easy to keep clean and relatively inexpensive compared to other types of flooring. It is available in many styles and at a variety of prices. Heavy, dense carpets with short pile are the most durable.

Types of Carpet

Axminster is a woven carpet with a tufted pile that may be of any height. This type of construction is used for patterned carpets.

Berber is a fleecy carpet with a low, nubby pile, often tweedy in effect.

Broadloom is a standard term describing carpets produced in widths over six feet (12 and 15 feet are the most common).

High-and-low looped carpet has a sculpted surface and is very durable.

Plush velvet carpet has an evenly cut, dense pile that is durable but shows traffic wear and footprints.

Random-sheared carpet has a pile with some high sheared strands and some low loops, giving a sculpted effect. It wears well but may flatten in high-traffic areas.

Shag carpeting has long yarns measuring anywhere from 3/4 inch to 2 inches, either sheared or looped. May mat in high-traffic areas.

Tip-sheared carpet mixes loops with cut pile, all the same length to reduce traffic wear.

Twist carpet has a looped surface of twisted yarns. Does not show traffic.

Fibers

Fibers used in carpets include *wool, nylon, polyester, polypropylene (olefin)* and *acrylic*, either alone or in blends.

•Wool. Although expensive, wool carpeting is luxurious and durable, with excellent resistance to wear. It holds colors well and is available in a wide selection of styles.

•Nylon, sold under the trade names Antron, Anso, Enkalon, Ultron and Zeftron, also is soft, wears well and is less expensive than wool. It can be treated with a stain-resistant coating that makes it easy to keep clean.

•Polyester fiber does not wear as well as wool or nylon and has poor resistance to oil-based stains. It is soft to the touch and costs less than wool or nylon. Brand names are Dacron, Fortrel and Trevira.

•Polypropylene (olefin) is not as resilient as the previously mentioned fibers, but has excellent stain resistance and wears well. Available in limited colors, it is often used for indoor/outdoor carpeting. The price range is relatively low. Brand names are Herculon, Marvess, Marquesa-Lana and Vectra.

•Acrylic fiber is not used for broadloom carpeting, but is used in area rugs; it may be cut to fit small areas, such as bathrooms. Not as resilient or wear- and stain-resistant as wool or nylon, but is very soft and comes in a wide variety of colors.

Single-Level-Loop

High-and-Low Loop

Twist

Random-Sheared

Tip-Sheared

Plush Velvet

Shag

Carpet types

WOOD FLOORS

Natural wood flooring is warm and comfortable underfoot. It may be made of hardwood, such as oak, walnut or maple, or softwood, such as pine, spruce or fir. Floorboards may be of any width, from wide to narrow, with 2 ½-inch oak strip flooring being the most common type.

Parquet floors, which are associated with the Victorian era, are made of different types of wood, light and dark, joined together in herringbone, checked and striped patterns. They are also available as 12-by-12-inch squares in more complicated patterns, such as basketweave.

All types of wooden flooring should be sealed (see Chapter 5, Home Maintenance, for more information).

SHEET VINYL AND VINYL TILE

This type of flooring is easy to install. It can be put down over almost any other type of flooring, and very little preparation is necessary. Sheet vinyl is available in rolls 6, 9 and 12 feet wide, reducing the need for seams. Some sheet vinyl has a foam backing, which makes it softer and easier on the feet.

Vinyl tiles are easier for amateurs to install than sheet vinyl. They are available in patterns that imitate ceramic or natural stone tile and come in various sizes, although 12-by-12-inch tiles are the most common. Some come with an adhesive backing and can simply be pressed into place. Whether in sheet or tile form, vinyl is relatively inexpensive, durable, easy to keep clean, waterproof and stain-resistant.

Other types of man-made hard-surface flooring include asbestos and rubber tile. Asbestos costs less than vinyl

but tends to show wear and soil more easily. Rubber needs waxing to maintain its color and is more expensive than vinyl.

TILE

Tiles come in many different forms, but almost all are hard-wearing and impervious to water and grease. Tile has the disadvantage of being cold and noisy, and hard enough so that things dropped on it tend to break. One thing to be careful of is that the subflooring in the area where you plan to lay tile is sturdy enough to bear its weight.

Types of Tile

Ceramic tiles, made from baked and glazed clay, are very hard and durable. They are available in a broad range of sizes, textures, and colors.

Quarry tiles are made from unrefined clay with a high quartz content. They come in square, rectangular or hexagonal shapes, in warm, natural tones.

Brick tiles (also called pavers) are too heavy to install above the ground floor. They come in a variety of colors, from the standard red-brown to the more unusual green, blue and purple.

Marble tiles are the most practical way to use this material in the home, since marble tends to be expensive and difficult to handle.

Like brick, *slate tile* should be used only on the ground floor of a house. Although beautiful and durable, slate is also expensive and difficult to install.

Stone flooring is unusual and beautiful. Many types of natural stone can be used for flooring, including *granite, sandstone* and *limestone*, although some types absorb stains easily.

Terrazzo tile is made of chips of granite or stone embedded in a composite base. Terrazzo is elegant and comes in many colors. It wears well and is relatively easy to install, but can be expensive.

Mosaic tiles are small (1 by 1 inch or smaller) and come in beautiful, rich colors. They may be of marble, clay or glass with a high silica content. They come mounted on a peel-off backing, making them easier to lay.

Cork tile, made of pressed and baked cork, is warm and comfortable underfoot, softer than hard-surface tile. It must be sealed for durability.

Lighting

Lighting serves two purposes, both decorative and practical. Light can be a decorating tool, enhancing other aspects of a room's decor; the right kind of lighting can even make a small room seem larger. It also serves as a nighttime replacement for the sun's light.

LIGHTING PRINCIPLES

Ambient lighting provides an overall level of light. It may be supplied by a number of different fixtures.

Task lighting illuminates specific areas; you need to install task lighting anywhere you perform an activity. Position a task light so that shadows do not fall across the page.

Utility lighting is used to illuminate potentially hazardous areas.

Accent lighting emphasizes special objects or decorative features.

TYPES OF FIXTURES

Ceiling and pendant fixtures won't suffice for all of your lighting needs, even in a small room. Even fitted with a couple of 100-watt bulbs, this type of fixture doesn't give enough illumination to be used on its own. You'll get much more use out of that wattage if you distribute it around the room. Pendant lamps are most useful over dining tables and coffee tables. A bulb with a silvered crown, to reduce glare, is best. Pendant fixtures should be 58 to 63 inches from the floor.

Downlights are high-tech ceiling fixtures (recessed or surface-mounted) that cast light on whatever is below them. They can be mounted on swivels and are especially useful for illuminating work surfaces, such as kitchen counters or desktops.

Spotlights also can be either recessed or surface-mounted. They are also available as ceiling-mounted clusters, which can be pointed in a variety of directions, mounted on a pole, or used as individual bulbs on clips or clamps that can be placed where needed.

Wall lights (also called *sconces*) are useful for ambient lighting and for setting the style of a room. They come in various designs, from traditional bracket lamps to ultramodern metal or plaster sconces and are usually used in pairs.

Table and floor lamps can provide both task lighting and ambient lighting. In terms of lampshades, translucent fabric shades diffuse light best, followed by linen, cardboard and paper. Shades should be deep enough to shield your eyes from the light source, whether you are sitting or standing. In a table lamp, there should be 39 to 40 inches between the bottom of the shade and the floor for the best effect. A floor lamp should measure 42 to 49 inches from the bottom of the shade to the floor.

Directional lamps, reading lamps or work lights should be adjustable to shed light where it is needed. For a desk lamp, the light source should be 15 inches above the work surface.

Uplights are downlights in reverse. They are easy to install because they can be plugged into a wall outlet and concealed behind furniture or in corners to create dramatic accent lighting.

Quality of light provided by various fixtures

The benefit of *track lighting* is that it provides a number of light sources from a single power source. The track mounts to the ceiling or wall and can be fitted with downlights and spots to provide lighting where needed. The tracks come in two types, open and closed. Open tracks are more flexible, but tend to accumulate dust and grease, and can be difficult to clean. Closed tracks don't have this problem, but lack the flexibility of open-track systems.

LIGHT SOURCES

The main light sources used in residences are *tungsten, halogen* and *fluorescent*. Tungsten lighting comes from familiar light bulbs, casting a warm, yellowish light. Bulbs are widely available and inexpensive, but must be replaced frequently, generate excessive heat and use energy inefficiently.

Halogen bulbs cast a cool, crisp light, whiter and brighter than standard bulbs. They are expensive and some types must be used with a transformer, which adds to the cost of the fixture. In addition, they must be used with a filter (most halogen bulbs have built-in filters) to prevent exposure to harmful ultraviolet rays.

Fluorescent bulbs and tubes use the least amount of energy, but many types emit a light that dulls the appearance of colors. Full-spectrum fluorescent tubes, which most closely resemble true sunlight, eliminate this problem. All fluorescent lamps require a special adapter if you want to use them with a dimmer.

For information on professional lighting showrooms near you, contact the American Lighting Association at 1-800-BRIGHT-IDEAS.

Displaying Decorative Items

FIREPLACE ARRANGEMENTS

A wood-burning fireplace makes a wonderful focal point for a living room. The warmth and beauty of an open fire are one benefit, but beyond that, a fireplace provides many decorating opportunities. The fireplace mantel and wall above are a traditional space to display decora-

Lighting Guidelines from the American Lighting Association			
Area	**Pendants/Ceiling Lights**	**Recessed Fixtures**	**Wall Lights**
Room under 150 sq. ft.	Three to five incandescent lamps, total 100–150 W (or 35–60 W fluorescent)	Four 75-W incandescent lamps (80 W fluorescent)	Four 50-W reflector bulbs (60–80 W fluorescent)
Room 150-250sq. ft.	Four to six incandescent lamps, total 200–300 W (or 60–80 W fluorescent)	Four 100-W incandescent lamps (120 W fluorescent) lamps	Five to eight 75-W incandescent reflector (120–160 W fluorescent)
Room over-250sq. ft.	One incandescent lamp per 125 sq. ft. for a total of 1 W (1/3 fluorescent watt) per sq.ft.	100-150 W incandescent for every 50 sq.ft. (160–200 W fluorescent)	One 75-W incandescent reflector lamp per 25 sq. ft. (160 W fluorescent)

tive objects and framed works of art. Functional items such as fireplace tools and andirons can also be considered decorative accessories. Choose them according to the style and color scheme of the living room.

PICTURES AND FRAMES

You can frame anything that's fairly flat. You can get custom frames made at a frame shop or you can clamp the piece between a sheet of glass or Plexiglas and a thin piece of board or even heavy cardboard. An art-supply store will carry all the items you need to do this and some may even cut glass to order.

If you have a collection of prints, photographs, drawings or paintings, hang them in a way that shows them at their best. If all the items are approximately the same size, it's easy to pick an appropriate frame and mat and hang them in a unified group. If the collection is varied, it is important to choose a harmonious mat shade and frame style that go with the room, rather than trying to find something that suits every item individually.

When hanging framed items, there are certain rules to follow. Don't hang

Types of bulbs: 1. General purpose tungsten bulb, 2. Tungsten striplight, 3. Parabolic aluminized reflector lamp, 4. Halogen display bulb, 5. Halogen reflector (cool beam), 6. Halogen reflector bulb, 7. Globe bulb, 8. Candle-shaped bulb, 9. Fluorescent long-life bulb, 10. Reflector bulb, 11. Fluorescent striplight, 12. Circular fluorescent tube, 13. Crown-silvered bulb, 14. U-lamp

**Displaying
decorative items**

things so that they seem crowded, nor so far apart that they look lost. Don't hang them so high that they can't seen, nor so low that people seated on a sofa or chair will bump their heads against the frame. Vertical arrangements suggest height, while horizontal arrangements will make a room or wall seem longer.

A diverse group of sizes and shapes looks best contained within an imaginary frame such as a circle, square or triangle. Experiment with arranging framed works on the floor or a table-top. Once you've arranged them to your liking, measure the distances between the items and make a sketch to scale, so you can translate the arrange-ment onto the wall.

Sources of Further Information

MANUFACTURERS AND ASSOCIATIONS

American Olean Tile Co.
1000 Cannon Ave.
Lansdale, PA 19446
1-215-855-1111

American Standard Inc.
One Centennial Plaza
P.O. Box 6820
Piscataway, NJ 08855-6820
1-908-980-3000

The Carpet and Rug Institute
P.O. Box 2048
Dalton, GA 30722-2048
1-706-278-0232
"Steps In the Right Direction, An Owners Manual For Your Carpet," $1.25.
"Carpet & Rug Care Guide," $1.
"Carpet Spot Removal Guide," $1.
"How To Choose Your Carpet and Rugs," $1.

Ceramic Tile Institute
700 N. Vigil Ave.
Los Angeles, CA 90029
1-213-660-1911

National Kitchen Cabinet Association
P.O. Box 6830
Falls Church, VA 07840
1-703-237-7580

National Paint and Coating Association
1500 Rhode Island Ave. NW
Washington, DC 20005
1-202-462-6272

National Wood Flooring Association
11046 Manchester Rd.
St. Louis, MO 63122
1-314-821 8654

BOOKS
The Complete Book of Curtains and Drapes. Lady Caroline Wrey, Overlook Press, Woodstock, N.Y., 1991.
Fabric Magic. Melanie Paine, Pantheon Books, New York, 1987.
The Furniture Buyer's Handbook. Max and Charlotte Alth, Walker and Co., New York, 1980.
House Beautiful Decorating Style. The Editors of House Beautiful, Hearst Books, New York, 1992.
Mary Gilliatt's New Guide to Decorating. Mary Gilliatt, Little Brown & Co., Boston, 1988.
The New House Book. Terence Conran, Crown Publishers, New York, 1985.
Sunset Books Home Lighting Handbook. Lane Publishing Co., Menlo Park, Calif., 1988.

4

Home Organization and Storage

Storage is an individual matter, since what you own reflects your lifestyle, values and hobbies; and how you store these items depends on where and how you live. But whether you have few possessions or many, whether you live in a three-room apartment or a three-story house, efficient storage and organization are vital to comfortable living. A cluster of cleaning supplies, a stack of CDs and a tangle of scarves all need convenient storage spots; and the same principles of smart planning apply to each.

Guidelines for Storage

The main goal of all storage and organization is to get the *maximum benefit* from the *minimum of space*. But if that were the whole story, you might hang a rack of neckties in the kitchen pantry. Items must be stored close to where you use them, so they're readily available when needed.

Integrate Storage into Overall Design and Decor

Many items, such as fine china or vintage wine, have special storage requirements in terms of light, temperature and humidity. Once these have been met, the aesthetics of a storage unit may also be a consideration. The material, style and design of a unit can affect the overall appearance of a room. Magazines in wicker baskets or rare books on polished oak shelves are part of a room's design. While this is not a consideration for all storage, it's important for those items you especially want to highlight or display.

Form Follows Traffic Patterns

Technically, every corner and every vacant wall in your home could hold a shelf, cabinet or hanging basket. But your home is not a warehouse. When planning storage space, consider traffic patterns and the need for an open, spacious feeling when deciding where *not* to store things.

As Families Change, Needs Change

As children grow, their sports equipment gets larger and heavier, and takes up more space. Kids themselves also need more space. So your basement, the perfect storage spot for miscellaneous paraphernalia, may have to become another bedroom. For best results, create storage with flexibility in mind, so that your home can change along with your family.

Do-It-Yourself or Consult the Experts?

Some challenges, such as storing children's toys and jackets, may be solved with five dollars' worth of plastic dish pans and hooks. Others, such as a built-in wall unit with glass shelving and lights to display a valued collection, may warrant expert assistance. Depending on your particular needs, architects, interior designers, contractors and closet designers are professionals who can assist you. The extent of a project—its overall impact on a room's design, the cost of materials, your own time, expertise and budget—will determine whether you need professional help.

Whatever your final decision, do some preliminary research. Do-it-yourself books, home-center stores and hardware stores provide a good foundation for starting projects on your own, or for becoming an informed client if you choose professional help.

Be Creative

Don't shy away from innovative solutions. A large linen closet may be best used as a sewing room or home office, while linens can be stored in the bedrooms where they are used.

Consider Your Family's Preferences and Habits

Homes are multi-purpose places. Take a stroll through your abode. Look at what's lying around. Consider how you actually use each room.

Your kitchen may be the center for paying bills. The living room may be your exercise space, and ironing may be done in the bedroom. If you read in the tub, you need a place for books in the bathroom.

Do a room-by-room survey (not all in the same day). Ask yourself:

- What storage areas work well here?

- What areas frustrate me?

- What items clutter up the room?

- What items constantly get carried somewhere else (and should probably be stored somewhere else)?

- What things do I need in this room which are not here?

Look for hidden possibilities—those unassuming, invisible spots under stairways, along hallway walls, in window seats, under beds—that can be transformed into useful storage. With a little ingenuity and a few materials, you can:

• Lay plywood over attic rafters to create a floor for storage.

• Enclose space under a stairway to create a closet.

• Cut into the drywall between two studs to make a shallow shelf.

• Build shelves in a wide hallway or along a stairway wall.

Consider What You Have

Analyzing the available storage space in your home is one way to tackle the challenge. Another is to take a hard look at your possessions—the junk, the gems and everything in between. Room by room, study the things that are stuffed into every corner and closet—the good, the bad and the out of style. The first question is, of course, "Do I really need this?" The most basic decision, for efficient storage, is what *not* to store.

Eliminate Clutter

All those "maybe someday" items that you've been hauling around for years—unwanted gifts, clothes that almost fit, the adorable silver box with a broken hinge—have become squatters in your home, claiming space that your favorite things could use.

Pull them out of the closet. Create separate piles for charities, second-hand stores, neighbors and friends, and the trash. Then, without regret, toss out those old shoes, clothes, toys, kitchenware, appliances, gadgets, books, magazines, jewelry, board games

Think Vertical

When organizing items for storage, packing or filing, avoid putting them in piles. Things get buried in piles. Instead use hanging folders in your file drawers; vertical hot files on your desk and for sorting mail; and shelves and grids for storing things on walls or on the backs of closet doors.

WORKSTATIONS

Set up a central station for every routine task, be it mailing, preparing breakfast, paying bills, writing letters or doing laundry. Design the station to suit the task, keeping all necessary tools within easy reach. Aim to create workstations that are easy to use, well equipped, attractive and orderly.

BE CREATIVE

Walk around your home. Are some items just taking up space or going to waste? Think of new uses for them. Use a straw basket as a planter, for example, or to display guest soap in your bathroom. Use a spare photo album for recipes or a stamp collection. Use a notebook as a travel diary. Use your imagination.

GOOD RIDDANCE

Get in the habit of dating everything, or simply circle the dates on all your purchases. Then set aside a regular time to get rid of anything out of date that isn't collectible. This organizing principle applies not only to prescriptions and perishable food items, but to travel books, calendars, old restaurant and shopping guides, books containing lots of dated material, newspapers and magazines.

GET SET

Keep sets together: clothing sets, teapot sets, games, sheets. Anything that requires another part to operate at its best should be stored with all its parts together (or very near each other).

GET HELP

Sometimes you just can't do it all by yourself. Enlist a friend to help you with a project you've been avoiding; perhaps you have a service you can offer in return. Or hire someone to do some of the work—a student or a professional, depending on the task and your budget.

and all the rest. Other people may need these things, and by getting rid of them you will make room for the things that give you pleasure and service (and, incidentally, also get a nice tax deduction).

Now, for those things you've decided to keep, ask yourself:

•How often do I use this? Daily, seasonally, occasionally, seldom?

•Is it currently stored in the room where it's used/needed?

•Is it properly stored and easily accessible?

•Does this item have special requirements in terms of light, heat or moisture?

•Is it large or unusually shaped?

•Should it be locked up or secure, kept out of reach of children and pets?

•Does it need to be in easy reach of children?

•Do I prefer it to be hidden from view?

•Do I want to display it?

•Should it be integrated into my home decor?

•How much space does it require?

•How much am I willing to spend to store it?

Room-by-Room Organization and Storage

WHAT'S COOKING IN YOUR KITCHEN?
Kitchens are usually centers of activity. Perhaps you bake or entertain frequently, or maybe the microwave is your best friend. Your kitchen may be Communication Central, with phone and answering machine, messages

---

THEY KNOW BEST
If you can't figure out how to organize something, look for a model. In other words, to organize your books, adopt the system used by a library or bookstore; for ideas on how to organize your compact disks, visit a major music store. Tour an art-supply store, a knitting store and a stationery store for good ideas that can apply to other materials as well, and consider purchasing their specialized organizational equipment.

DO THE ONE-STEP
If you think you're too busy to spend time organizing, you actually have more incentive to be organized that someone who has all the time and energy in the world to make a mess and "fix it

later." Hang up your coat in the closet immediately when you come inside, rather than (1) throwing the coat on a chair; (2) throwing the coat on the floor so you can sit on the chair; (3) taking the coat to the cleaners because it has become dirty and rumpled from being tossed around on the floor, and then (4) hanging it up in the closet. The rule is: Take a little time to do it now, or take a lot of time to do it later.

YOUR CHOICE
It's easier to learn and retain good habits than to correct bad ones. Therefore, in everything you do, make a conscious effort to learn how to do it right before plunging in. As much as is practical, think through all processes

and routines in advance. Read directions, talk to experts and don't proceed until you feel ready.

MAP IT OUT
Plan before you start. Whether you're working, shopping or traveling, almost everything takes longer if you don't envision the big picture ahead of time. Planning also prevents foul-ups. You wouldn't set off on a long trip without a map. In life, as in driving, you need to have directions but to be flexible when you run into traffic and tie-ups.

From *500 Terrific Ideas for Organizing Everything*, by Sheree Bykofsky, copyright 1992. Published by Simon & Schuster Inc.

tacked to the refrigerator and counter-top used for paying bills. However you use the kitchen, plan your storage so that the items you need are easily accessible for the jobs you do there.

Assessing Your Space

The study of ergonomics has given us useful tips on how to improve productivity, and smart design of working spaces is a vital part of that. In kitchen layout, the triangular arrangement of stove, sink and refrigerator makes it easier to coordinate food preparation, service and cleanup. Another issue is making sure the things you need for cooking are close to the stove, those needed for cleanup are by the sink, and that dishes, glasses and flatware are handy for serving and cleanup.

Work Space and Countertops

Counters and islands usually perform double duty as both work surfaces and storage places for many small items such as cooking utensils, canisters, small appliances (food processor, coffee maker, toaster) and whatever else needs to be handy.

Perhaps your counter has become too cluttered. If you need more counter/work space, some items, such as the electric can opener, coffeepot and even the microwave, can be mounted below cabinet surfaces, above the counter.

Other items, such as spices, can be wall-mounted in a neat rack near the stove. Cooking utensils can be kept on a vinyl-coated wire grid near the stove. Tiered wire baskets hung in convenient

places are ideal for miscellaneous items such as potholders and hand towels, and for root vegetables such as potatoes or onions that don't need to be refrigerated.

Work space as well as storage space can also be increased with a rolling kitchen cart. These handy, mobile items come in a variety of styles, prices and designs. Some fit under the countertop, like a cabinet. Some have a butcher-block surface that can be used as a cutting board. All have storage underneath, in the form of wire baskets, drawers, shelves and specialized compartments. Carts can be used to store items such as towels, tablecloths, cutlery, dishes, glasses, bottles of wine, cookbooks and much more.

Climbing the Walls and the Ceiling

Wire grids, attached to a wall near the stove, are handy for hanging utensils and pot holders. Depending on your overall design and space, another possibility is to suspend a rack from the ceiling to hold your pots and pans. These racks are available in a number of styles. Some are circular, others square or rectangular. They may be of wrought iron, or have a copper or chrome finish. Some are designed to hang from the wall, and incorporate shelves for cookbooks or plants as well as hooks for pots.

Smaller shelves can also be wall-mounted in unused corners, perhaps between the side of a cabinet and the adjacent wall. These triangular spaces offer ideal niches for cookbooks, plants, special glassware, outgoing mail or whatever else needs a place in your kitchen.

Shallow shelves (about 4 inches deep) can also be created between two studs in the wall by cutting into the wall surface. Such shelves (about 16 inches wide) create a cozy niche for canned goods, spices or glassware. These shelves are relatively easy to construct, although surfaces will need finishing and you must be careful not to interfere with plumbing or wiring.

Cabinets and Cupboards

Cabinets provide the bulk of kitchen storage. With the traditional models, however, much of the interior space is wasted. However, a variety of cabinet inserts and retrofitting products that have recently appeared on the market make it easy to greatly expand cabinet space. Made of vinyl-coated wire and sturdy plastic in the form of bins, baskets and open shelving, these products were created for industrial use and later adapted for homes. Now, you can get a pull-out rack to hold pot lids, a caddy that fits under the sink for cleaning supplies and a drawer insert for spices, to name just a few possibilities. Many of these products are inexpensive and can be bought at closet-organizing stores or home-supply stores. Others, for more specialized needs, can be purchased at kitchen-cabinet outlets, usually in conjunction with new cabinetry.

After throwing out what you don't need and deciding what you want to store in the space, the first step to reorganization is to measure your closet or cabinet space and get the rough dimensions of everything you want to store there. Then shop around and see what's available. A rack and a bin may both do the job, but which will work best for the items and the cabinet you have in mind? Consider several options and combinations of products. Take some home and try them out. Careful planning is the key to success.

Vertical dividers attach directly to a shelf to separate products or types of items, such as dish towels from dry goods. A rack with vertical divider slots can also be attached to the shelf and used to separate and store plates or pot lids.

Hanging Shelves

Another handy insert is a basket or bin that attaches to a shelf and hangs below it. These can be used inside the cabinet or can hang on the outside, below the lowest shelf. Racks and shallow shelves are also made for attaching to the inside of cabinet and closet doors, to hold items such as condiments, oils or small cans. Be sure there is adequate clearance for the door to close.

Before purchasing, note how the item is to be attached. If the insert screws onto the cabinet door, be sure the door is thick enough, or reinforce it, so the screws do not pass through.

There is also new hope for those deep, dark base cabinets into which serving trays, turkey roasters, and plastic pitchers can disappear indefinitely. Circular and multi-tiered racks put this dead space to good use. Customized roll-out shelves are also available for

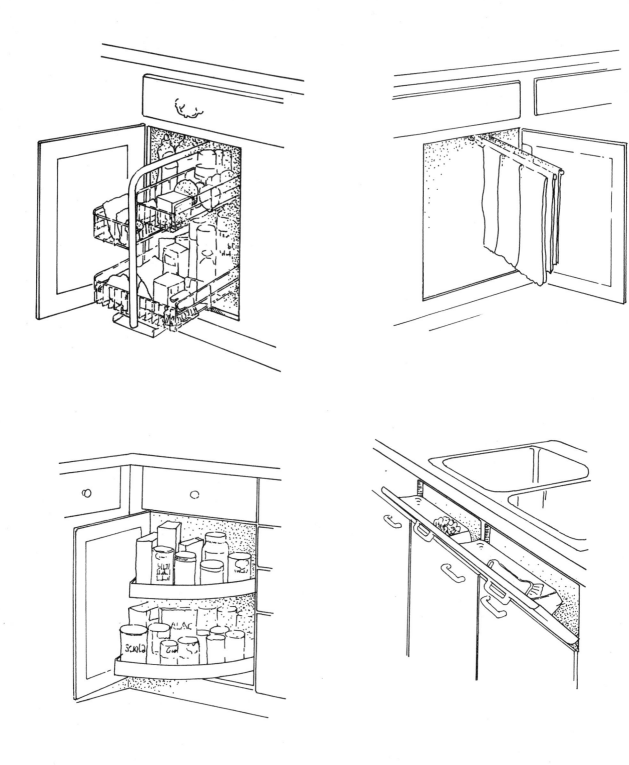

Kitchen cabinets and cupboards

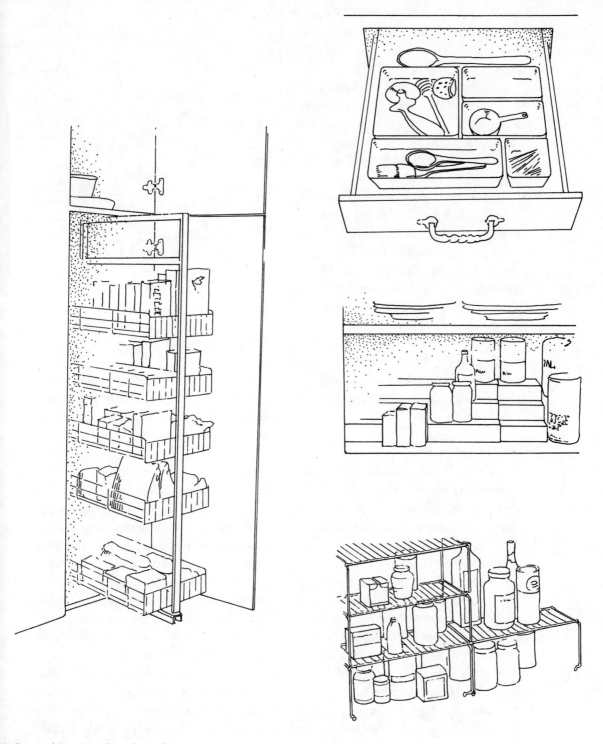

kitchen cabinets and cupboards

these hard-to-reach places. Swing-out baskets can be attached to the doors, and a lazy susan makes all items available.

All of these products work for upper cabinets as well. Lazy susans are particularly effective in corner cabinets. Replacing traditional shelving with tiered, revolving, circular shelves, they bring every item within view.

Base-cabinet shelves are traditionally difficult to access. If yours contain a jumble of pots, pans, serving bowls, baking pans, muffin tins and more, tiered, roll-out shelving may be the answer. The graduated depths make all items visible, and the roll-out design brings even the items at the very back of the lowest shelf within easy reach.

Replacing fixed shelves with adjustable shelving is another small way to make big gains in storage options and flexibility.

Don't Sink Too Low

Storage under the sink can be awkward, considering pipes and plumbing. Now there are attachments for cabinet doors, side shelves for the interior walls and wire racks that allow for clearance around pipes. Cleaning supplies can also be stored in a roll-out carry-all type basket, so each product is clearly visible and within easy reach. If you have small children, kid-proof latches are an inexpensive way to protect them from the dangerous chemicals and harmful materials stored below your sink.

Trash cans have also been modified to acknowledge sink contraptions and contortions. Some varieties pull down,

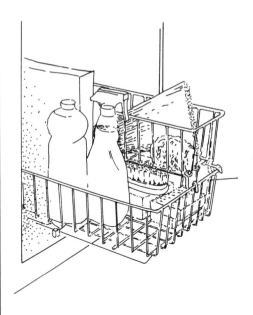

Kitchen organizers

others swing out. Measure your space, consider the obstacles and their locations, and what other items need to fit here, and choose the best product.

Recycling

Recycling plays a major role in disposal of items. One possibility, depending on your space, is to have one large plastic trash can in the pantry or laundry area, close to the kitchen, in which you temporarily stash all glass, plastic and aluminum. Keep separate bins in the laundry room, garage or outdoor shed, along with a box for newspapers, and sort the recyclable items there.

To gain space for tall, awkward items such as mops and brooms, you can remove fixed shelving from a long closet and replace it with a freestanding stack of shelves that is not as wide as the closet. Leave four to six inches on the side for tall items.

Tiered, open-wire shelving works well in a pantry or walk-in closet where you want to see and reach all items. Or you can design your own open shelves with custom shelving material sold by the foot at most hardware stores. A stack of vinyl-coated wire bins is great for storing bulky items. These bins are attached to a frame and slide out.

Double-Duty Drawers

Drawers are another bulwark of kitchen organization that have become more user-friendly. Now there are a variety of clever inserts on the market that can be trimmed to fit most stock cabinet drawers. One cutlery-drawer insert has individual knife slots as well as a cutting board. A bi-level utensil-drawer insert holds two sets of flatware. For those who prefer to have spices near the stove when cooking, a special sawtooth-style insert keeps them neat and close to hand. Most of these products are available in home and hardware stores, but the more specialized ones must be obtained through custom manufacturers.

Under-the-Counter Pull-Outs

These devices can also save precious space. A portable ironing board pull-out and even a desk surface can be incorporated into your work space. If you consider an under-the-counter pull-out, be sure there is enough room for full extension, without interrupting the traffic flow in your kitchen.

Message Centers

If your refrigerator also serves as a repository for family messages, photos, phone numbers and meeting reminders, perhaps it is time to create a more organized space for household communications.

A corner of a counter can be set apart for pens, paper and a cork board. A desk-organization tray holding paper clips, stamps, stapler, tape and envelopes may be kept in its own drawer, near the phone. A napkin holder can be used for outgoing mail.

THE BEDROOM

The master bedroom is a place for relaxation, intimacy, dressing and storage, says Stephanie Culp, in her book *Organized Closets and Storage.* For a typical family, though, life is seldom that simple. Culp sees the bedroom, like other home spaces, becoming a multipurpose room. Amid the dressers, nightstands and bed may be exercise equipment, office files, computer, television, sewing materials, books and more. On the plus side, this adds up to active, interesting lives. On the down side, it means clutter.

Bedside

The bed is the centerpiece of this room, and offers many opportunities for storage and organization. The headboard, whether simple or elaborate, provides a place for shelves, drawers, and surface storage. Closets can be built on either side of the headboard, nestling around the bed. In these can be stored blankets, pillows, books, magazines, sweaters and more.

Bedside tables may be separate or attached to the headboard. These may contain drawers for notepaper, books, magazines, tissues, sewing items and work projects, as well as a place for a lamp and the phone. At the foot of the bed, a beautiful wooden chest might serve as both storage for extra blankets, quilts, pillows and linens, and as a seat for dressing.

Under-Bed Storage

Any under-bed storage devices should not interfere with dusting or vacuuming. Roll-out drawers are included with some bed frames, or they can be bought separately. Zippered garment bags tailored to hold blankets are another good under-bed storage product.

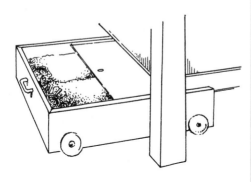

Bedroom under-bed storage

Wall Systems

Wall systems offer a stylish arrangement of open and closed shelving, drawers, cabinets, swivel shelves, fold-out desk surfaces and much more. They can hold clothing, TV, VCR, stereo system, artwork, shoes, hats, purses, luggage and whatever else you choose, beautifully and efficiently. The most extensive ones incorporate an entire closet system and eliminate the need for separate dressers. Smaller units can keep the assorted paraphernalia of your life in good order. These units can be bought ready-made or customized to your individual needs.

Handsome furniture pieces, such as an antique armoire, can also serve double duty as a storage component. With interior customizing, an armoire can hold a TV on a pull-out shelf, a file drawer for home-office work, and several drawers for sweaters, socks and underwear.

CLOSETS

"Not enough closet space" is still the primary complaint of homeowners. Many older homes and apartments have one tiny closet with a single rod and shelf in each bedroom. This results in clothes jammed together, shoes in a tumble on the floor and a closet stuffed with blankets, old sweatpants, luggage, hats and other assorted junk that you've forgotten you even owned.

Since the late 1970s, when industrial products such as wire baskets and bins and open shelving were adapted for home use, the design of closets has become a major innovation in home storage and organization. In turning an eye to closets, designers have created a new industry, closet design, with its own professional group, the National Association of Organizers. There are stores devoted solely to assisting you in making your closet a working part of your home. With a variety of products ranging from the inexpensive and ready-made to custom, closets can be tailored to your personal needs and lifestyle.

Riding Herd on Excess

Once again, in order to create maximum space for the clothing, shoes, jewelry, hats and other personal items you use on a daily basis, you must turn a cold eye on the "maybe someday" clothes that you haven't worn for many seasons, and banish these space stealers from your closet. Now you've already increased your storage capacity.

Closet Planning and Organization

•Consider everything you plan to keep in your closet. Would any of these items—luggage, for example, or extra blankets—be better stored somewhere else?

•Measure your space. Determine the depth, width and height of your closet. Count usable interior wall space and door surfaces, too.

•Make a wish list. Ideally, what would you like to see your closet hold?

•Get all these items together. Calculate whether they will fit. Make a diagram of your plan.

Consider the guidelines and average garment measurements (below) offered by Patricia Coen and Bryan Milford in their book *Closets: Designing and Organizing the Personalized Closet*. Group like items—blouses, skirts, pants—together. Allowing two inches of space between individual garments, note how wide a space each group will need.

Average Clothing Lengths

WOMEN'S

Dress	48 inches
Coat	52 inches
Skirt	35 inches
Shoes	10 inches long, 7 inches wide per pair
Folded sweater	14 inches deep, 10 inches wide

MEN'S

Suit jacket	38 inches
Coat	50 inches
Folded shirt	14 inches deep, 8 inches wide
Hat	6 inches deep, 11 inches wide

Some Helpful Architectural Guidelines

•Clothes closets should measure 24 to 32 inches wide (although some apartments and condominiums have closets 22 inches wide).

•For double-hung clothes (jackets, blouses and pants hung one above the other), hanging rods should be about 42 inches wide and 82 inches from the floor.

•To figure the amount of vertical space you need, measure your longest garment plus the hanger neck and add four inches.

Before beginning your closet plan, give some thought to the following:

Personal Preferences

Are you comfortable with shoes hanging in a bag or do you prefer a floor rack? Would you rather keep your shirts folded or on hangers?

Limitations of Your Closet

Different types of closet doors have advantages and disadvantages.

Louvered doors provide ventilation, but you cannot use the interior door surface (as you can with a hinged door) to mount racks for scarves, neckties, belts or purses. Sliding doors don't take up much space, but you can only install shelves on the outside face, which can look messy.

If you do put racks or hooks on the interior of the closet doors, be sure to allow for clearance space between the racks and your hanging items when the door is closed.

There Are Many Ways to Solve the Same Problem

A variety of products will accomplish the same result, but with different effects. Consider all the options, study the products and choose what fits your needs, preferences and budget.

It's Best to Keep Stuff Off the Floor as Much as Possible

Even when shoes are stored on the floor, there is a four- to six-inch clearance for the rack.

Are You Tall or Short?

Consider the height of the people who will use the closet when determining height of rods and shelves. Everything used on a regular basis should be within arm's reach.

Think Seasonal

Out-of-season clothing is best stored somewhere else, making closet room for in-season items.

Shelving

If you have one of those deep, dark, high closet shelves into which things disappear, there are many simple ways to make it workable. The shelf can be retrofitted with vertical vinyl-coated-wire dividers, which are easily adjustable. These will section off the space into neat compartments for items such as hats, boots and extra blankets. Another way of organizing shelves is to store items in clearly labeled, stackable plastic bins with snap-on lids. Wire baskets can also be attached to the bottom of the shelf.

Open wire shelving allows you to see all the items stored on it, as well as permitting air to circulate. These shelves

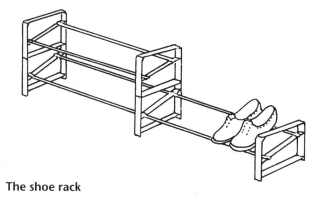

The shoe rack

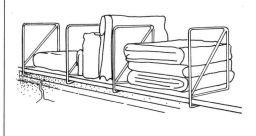

Top closet shelving

Zippered
Suit/Dress Bag

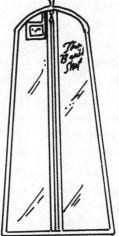

White Zippered
Gown Bag

Clear Zippered
Bell Bottom
Bridal Bag

Fabric Coat Bag

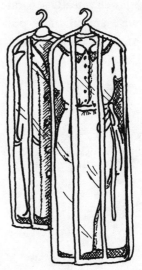

Full Length
Flap-Over Bag

Closet out-of-season clothing

are adjustable and can change height depending on items stored. Multilevel shelves keep winter hats, purses, ice skates, sweatshirts and dumbbells from getting permanently buried under an avalanche of other things.

Stackable Bins, Drawers and Pallets

With the extra space created by hanging another rod and throwing things out, you may have room for a freestanding frame with pull-out bins or baskets. These make a nice home for sweaters, underwear, socks or even belts.

An alternative to the wire system is a more permanent structure of wooden drawers or narrowly spaced pull-out pallets that hold one shirt or sweater apiece. Drawer insert dividers keep belts, scarves, socks, underwear and costume jewelry neatly separated. If you plan to use any of these pull-out systems, be sure to allow room to open and close them.

Wall Grids, Hooks and Racks

If you have space on an inside wall or door, hanging items such as your bathrobe, umbrella, purse or nightgown is a nifty choice. This keeps things off the floor and takes up less space than stackable bins or baskets.

You might select a wire grid, complete with basket or bin attachments, to hold sporting items such as a tennis racket and balls. Grids can also be fitted with V-shaped attachments ideal for shoes.

The inside of your closet door is great for holding a rack of neckties,

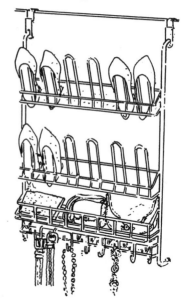

Shoe and accessory rack

Closet bins

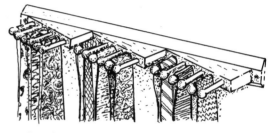

Necktie holder

belts, scarves or assorted loose items. If hooks appeal to you, choose them according to their design and use. Some hooks are attached with adhesive backing but only hold lightweight items. Others are sturdier, attach with screws and can be used for heavier items.

Hang in There

Even hangers have been revolutionized and now offer a variety of practical choices. Wire hangers, however, are not among them. Wire hangers leave ridges and they rust, causing stains. Much preferred is the nonslip vinyl variety, which is kinder to your clothing. Sweaters and knit should be hung on padded hangers. By choosing three or four different colors of hangers, you can color-code your wardrobe.

Hanger extenders allow some items, such as blouses, to hang lower than others, creating more space on the rod. Multiple-item hangers for pants or skirts offer yet another possibility for efficiency.

Garment bags are a neat option if you have lots of hanging space. Their design is versatile and their construction sturdy. They come in a variety of sizes, with clear plastic, see-through fronts. Some have canvas shelves that will hold shoes or sweaters. Others are made for long dresses, coats or suits.

Elegance also has a place in closets. Woven baskets for storage offer beauty along with practicality. They can be displayed outside the closet, holding items such as extra linens, exercise clothing or sewing needs.

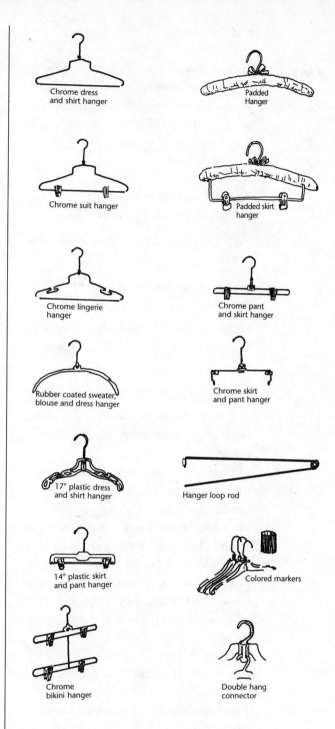

Chrome dress and shirt hanger

Padded Hanger

Chrome suit hanger

Padded skirt hanger

Chrome lingerie hanger

Chrome pant and skirt hanger

Rubber coated sweater, blouse and dress hanger

Chrome skirt and pant hanger

17" plastic dress and shirt hanger

Hanger loop rod

14" plastic skirt and pant hanger

Colored markers

Chrome bikini hanger

Double hang connector

All-purpose closet hangers

Kids' Rooms

Take a look at your child's room at its messiest. What is lying around? What is *always* lying around? Depending on your child's age, involve him or her in the organization project.

Ask Your Child the Same Questions You've Asked Yourself
• What really needs to be stored here?

• What items could be better stored elsewhere?

• What things need to be given away or thrown out?

• What do you like about how things are stored and what do you want to improve?

If your child gives input on these questions, he or she will have a vested interest in maintaining the system you create.

Kids have some unique storage needs. Young children's clothes are smaller, but clothing is only a small part of what they need organized and stored. There are stuffed animals, large and small toys, books, collections, jackets, hats, boots, sports equipment and more. And often, they want to keep it all around them, close at hand and in view.

GUIDELINES FOR CHILDREN'S STORAGE

Items Need to Be Low Enough to Be Accessible
Storage systems must be simple and easy, so that children will actually use them. One possibility is to have a long shelf for displaying favorite toys, instead of throwing them in a box.

Pick Innovative Storage Units
Brightly colored shelves (at kid's-eye level), a wheelable plastic toy box, hanging wire tiered baskets and woven baskets will keep your child's room cheerful, well-designed and neat.

Children Grow and Change Quickly
Organization and storage needs also change. Choosing flexible and adaptable systems will allow you to accommodate kids' growth, changing habits, hobbies and home needs.

Think Multiple Uses
Children's rooms are at least as multipurpose as adults' (except that their toys take up more space).

Children Need Designated Storage Space Outside Their Rooms
Each child should have specific places in the hall closet (for jackets, bats, balls, backpacks), the living room (for games, books and such), basement/garage (for bikes, skates), the bathroom (for haircare and beauty products) and anywhere else that is most appropriate for storing his or her belongings. Once again, it's important to involve kids in choosing these spaces.

If you have two children sharing the same room, a room divider that also serves as a storage unit can be built, bought or created. Two pre-built bookcases, back to back, can serve this purpose, and so can two dressers side by side, facing opposite directions. This gives both children their "own space" in more ways than one.

Children's closet organization follows the same guidelines as for adults. And the same assortment of products is workable.

STORAGE IDEAS FOR KIDS' ROOMS
•Freestanding shelves or wall shelves for books and games.

•A decorative chest at the foot of the bed for toys and extra blankets.

•Hooks on the inside of doors for jackets, hats, backpacks and sleepwear.

•A big plastic trash can for dirty laundry.

•Under-the-bed storage.

•An old hall tree cut down to kid size.

•An assortment of cigar and shoe boxes, clearly labeled, for collections and assorted stuff.

•Brightly colored plastic boxes—milk-crate types—are lightweight and can hold stuffed animals, toys and dolls.

FOR OLDER CHILDREN
•Create a work space: Make a desk with a hollow-core door and two freestanding frames of stackable bins or file cabinets.

•For paper storage, use plastic stackable desk trays, plastic vertical file holders.

Personalized peg rack

Toy box

Over-the-door organizer

- Plastic desk-accessory storage units are available for pens, paper, hobby materials.

- Install a shelf for books, radio, collections, favorite things.

- Decorative boxes and jars can hold loose pencils, pens and markers.

- Buy a rack for CD or cassette-tape storage.

- Tall closet space is needed for large items, such as hockey sticks and baseball bats.

Dining Room

If you have a separate dining area, depending on your space you may connect it functionally with the kitchen or the living room. It's important to consider the traffic flow as well as the feeling you want to create with your dining area—openness, intimacy or a formal air.

Generally, the dining room is a place to store fine china and crystal, silverware and table linens. You might also want to keep a seashell collection, a television and VCR, stereo equipment, wine storage or a full bar in your dining room, depending on your needs.

If your dining area is too open or does not have enough storage space, a room divider/storage unit may fit the bill. This unit may be floor-to-ceiling, half or three-quarter height. If it is a half-level unit dividing dining room from the kitchen, the top surface can be used for buffet service. If the divider is located between the dining and living rooms, the top can be used for decorative display, while the lower cabinets and drawers hold linens, china and glassware.

China cabinets and buffets are the traditional means of storing china, silverware and serving pieces. A wall unit is another alternative, reflecting the diversity of modern lives. In addition to holding the china, crystal and such, a wall unit may also house a TV, audiovisual equipment, board games, collections and fine art objects. This combination storage and display unit might also be wired with interior lighting to highlight prized treasures.

For showing off a collection of hand-painted dishes, one possibility is to stand them, tilted, on a grooved shelf for safekeeping and admiration.

Living Room

In the past, homes had separate rooms for the library and the parlor; and perhaps you do have a formal living room and a family room. If not, your living room probably functions as library, entertainment center, playroom and even correspondence center. Your living room storage needs may involve books, magazines, games, collections, favorite mementos, family photo albums, knitting and sewing projects, extra pillows, fireplace tools, TV, audio-visual equipment, videocassette library, CDs, toys and newspapers.

SHELVES

These are among the simplest storage devices for a living room. Whether a freestanding bookcase or a bracketed wall shelf, this practical item can also be an elegant part of the room's decor. Bookcase or wall shelving can of course also hold games, videotapes, magazines and art objects as well as books. Be sure, however, that the shelf doesn't become a catchall. One possibility for avoiding accumulated clutter is to add shelf dividers with bookends, colorful and adjustable vinyl-coated wire dividers or permanently fixed wood slats.

Placement of shelves is an important consideration. High shelving, even with the tops of door and window frames, can span one or more walls, holding books that are not frequently used or displaying mementos and collections. If your home has a fireplace or chimney, the recessed bay areas on either side are perfect spots for installing wall-hung shelving. Unused corners may provide a great niche for triangular shelves. Again, consider where the items on the shelves will be used. A bookcase holding your favorite books should be close to a comfortable chair and good lighting.

Whether you build or buy a bookcase, measure the objects you will store there, making sure the overall width of your bookcase or shelving will accommodate your widest objects. Adjustable shelves are a good idea, since books vary in height. Compartments of various sizes also lend interest to the design while separating objects. Some areas of the unit may have doors, to hide cleaning items, for example, while others may be open to display a porcelain doll or a prize conch shell.

ENTERTAINMENT CENTERS

Entertainment has many faces, depending on your technological inclinations. Whether you need to store a CD player, VCR and videocassette library, or need to find a place for your LP records and stereo system, many options are available. Wall units, whether custom-built or ready-made, offer a range of possibilities. Smaller, compact units, together with bookcases and shelves, keep the electronic equipment from dominating the room. Many units have doors that conceal the equipment when not in use and protect it from dust.

Cabinets with glass doors provide even more compact storage, with cassette and CD players and turntables neatly stacked together. However, another area is required for the attending items: CD collection, cassette tapes and LPs. These may be stored in a wall unit that also contains a TV, VCR and videocassettes. In any case, these items should all be stored as they best fit with the traffic flow and activity centers of the room.

If you are incorporating TV and audiovisual equipment into a wall unit, whether fixed or freestanding, be sure ventilation and wiring needs are adequate and that the unit is accessible to electrical outlets.

LOW-TECH OPTIONS

Tables with drawers are great for small items such as reading glasses, crossword-puzzle books, pens and a deck of cards. Some coffee tables or end tables also have lower shelves ideal for storage of a stamp collection or photo albums.

Rather than hiding these items, another approach is to show them off. Beautiful lacquered boxes set on the coffee table can hold your favorite old photos. A colorful ceramic bowl can take care of odds and ends for writing. This way, potential clutter becomes purposeful design. Woven baskets are another way to display magazines and knitting projects.

Chests and window seats offer another possibility for storing cleaning equipment, hobby supplies, firewood or extra cushions and blankets.

The Bathroom

THE VANITY

The vanity is this room's most common storage unit. Its most typical configuration is a lower cabinet crammed with a small waste basket, extra toilet paper, cleaning products and other supplies, plus drawers overflowing with beauty and grooming aids. The top surface is generally littered with everything from soap to cough medicine to hair barrettes.

Once you've thrown out the sticky messes of cosmetics, topless lotion bottles and creams gone dry, assess the possibilities from the bottom up. Lower-level cabinets can be retrofitted

Cosmetic organizers

with pull-out shelves, supply caddies or a lazy susan to keep everything in its place. A few good drawer dividers can restore sanity to your vanity. And if drawer space is plentiful, giving each family member a specific drawer definitely helps. Ceramic containers for small items such as makeup brushes and manicure equipment can be stashed in a deep drawer.

A clear plastic zippered bag does a great job of keeping cosmetics in order. Decorative baskets for soaps and hand towels and colorful cups for teeth-cleaning items can enhance your daily ablutions.

THE MEDICINE CABINET

One way to create more space is to cut shallow shelves into the area between two wall studs. This makes room for a shelf four inches deep for products used daily, and frees up space in your medicine cabinet or vanity. Again, your medicine cabinet will be much more useful if you get rid of the outdated pills and tonics, creams and sprays.

OTHER SPACE SAVERS

Wall space can provide ample storage, especially for those items such as hair dryers, curling irons and electric toothbrushes that usually end up on the countertop. A wire grid system with bins and baskets is one option. A wall-mounted vinyl pouch also works well. Some may prefer wire baskets, which can be hung below existing shelving.

Open shelving is a way to display colorful towels, plants or paperback books. There is often a handy space for

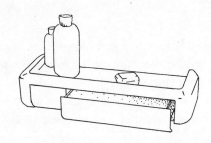

Two-drawer shelf

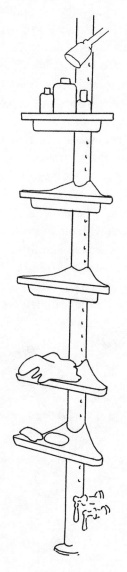

Tension-mount shower valet

such a shelf above the toilet. Or perhaps a corner provides the perfect spot for a triangular shelf. Ready-made wicker cabinets are another simple but decorative choice for storage above the toilet.

Shower and tub items including soap, shaving cream and shampoo don't have to teeter on a small window ledge or the edge of the bathtub. Shower caddies and shower towers come in many varieties and will hold a load of bottles, sponges, soapy products and rubber bathtub toys. Nylon bags are also an option for kids' toys.

Hampers aren't worth much if no one uses them. Perhaps selecting a more convenient type will catch your family's attention. One variety, built into a base cabinet, is a tip-out bin. It takes up less space than the traditional hamper and blends with the cabinet surface. Something more obvious would be a nylon bag that you hang on the back of the door. Another type slips onto a lightweight metal tubing frame.

To cope with wet towels, one possibility for a large family is a closet rod transformed into a towel rack. This spans over twice the distance of a typical towel bar, giving ample room for hanging towels. To encourage children to hang their towels, you might install hooks or a rack at their eye level, on the back of the door. Cutting into the wall between two studs can create a recess for a towel ladder—a series of rods drilled into the studs every two feet. Traditional towel bars and rings are still quite useful, of course, and they come in a variety of materials and finishes to coordinate with your decor.

Door ornaments such as wall racks, wooden pegs or brass hooks are all great solutions for loose bathrobes, nightshirts, hair ribbons and scarves.

Near the sink, attaching extra hooks, rods and rings close to the tub or shower and the mirror is a great way to keep your counter free of wet washcloths.

BEYOND BATHING

If linens are crowding your bathroom space, maybe they are best stored elsewhere—perhaps a hall closet or in the bedroom where they are used. This will give you a little extra breathing room in the bath. If extra towels are jammed into too-high shelves, you might roll them and display their colors in a wicker basket or store them in a wicker chest outside the bathroom.

Home Office or Paper-Control Center

Even if you don't run a home business, the management of your family's personal and business affairs requires organization for easy retrieval. Keeping track of softball games and civic meetings, paying bills, contacting plumbers and filing warranties all require efficient systems for scheduling and follow-through. The flow of paper in an average household—messages, school notes, letters, fliers, advertisements, bills, chore lists—can quickly become overwhelming without good organization.

Whether you have a pull-out desk in the kitchen, a card table in the bedroom or a designated home office, good storage will make your work easier.

File cabinets are the most basic element of a home office. Two- or four-drawer, letter-size metal cabinets with full suspension meet normal filing needs. (If you consistently have papers of the legal size, you may opt for a legal- rather than letter-size cabinet.) If you generate few files, you can store them in inexpensive cardboard boxes with lids (available at art-supply and office-supply stores.) Your filing space can also be incorporated into your desk; or you can create a desk using a door for the work surface and two file cabinets for supports.

Shelving for books, reference material, computer paper and floppy disks, and other necessary items need to be close to your work surface. Some ready-made computer work stations have shelf space above the surface on which the computer sits. Many of these units are also equipped with file drawers and even a drawer for small supplies, such as pens, Post-it notes and printer ribbons.

Rolling carts with slots for hanging files, or an acrylic cabinet on wheels

Wire-mesh desk accessories

that holds two full-suspension drawers, are another possibility if your space is limited and your "office" mobile.

Electronic storage has taken organization into a new plane of existence. Volumes' worth of information can be stored on disks and tomes gathered from around the world are accessible at a keystroke, without leaving your computer table. Many software programs are now available for home-management matters such as writing checks, figuring your income tax, filing recipes and keeping a daily calendar. If you own a computer, these programs provide a useful option for the homeowner who would like to eliminate boxes of canceled checks from the garage, and in general, get a better handle on the daily paper chase.

ON-DESK STORAGE

For those papers that must remain on the desk, stackable trays and vertical file slots are quite handy. Attractive brass containers or plastic divider trays work equally well for paper clips, pens, staplers and the other small paraphernalia of home work. Above the desk, a bulletin board can hold those slips of paper that would otherwise slip from mind.

Laundry/Mud Room

If you have a room designated for doing your laundry, you are indeed fortunate. In many households the washer and dryer are in the basement or near the back entry, where wet clothing is removed or recycling materials are sorted. If you have a multipurpose laundry room, organization is especially important.

Shelves above the washer and dryer should contain only detergent and laundry products. Make a space, perhaps a card table, which is just for folding clothes. A roll-out laundry caddy for hanging items should also be kept nearby.

A bench close to the entry will serve well for removing wet clothing, hats and boots, and pegs on a nearby wall will encourage family members to hang up these items. A lower rack for shoes and boots will keep them off the floor. A physical divider—perhaps an old dresser or low bookshelf—will help separate this area from the laundry and provide storage as well.

The Attic

Caution must be taken when considering attic storage. Unless well insulated, attics tend to extremes of temperature that can damage rubber and plastic items. Another hazard of attic storage is that dirt, bugs, mice and dampness can eat away at your treasures. Ease of access is another issue that must be addressed. Are the attic walls sloped? Are there stairs into the attic or a drop-down ladder?

If you must store items in the attic, pack them carefully in clean, dry boxes and label them clearly. Store the boxes off the floor on a dry shelf. Inexpensive, industrial metal shelving is an easy way to hold boxes and bins, and to assure that your attic storage will be a success.

The Basement

This is the home's most notorious catchall space. One good basement storage spot is under the stairway. Be sure the area is clean, dry and dust- and moisture-free. It's vital to plan the space. An old dresser can be placed under here, or a bookcase or metal shelving to hold appropriate items. For best results, all items should be organized and labeled. Adapt your proposed storage paraphernalia to what is best suited for this space, rather than cramming in everything that will fit. Otherwise, junk will quickly expand to fill the area.

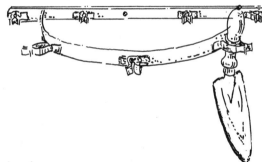

Tool rack

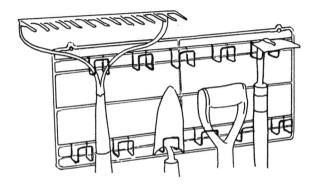

Garden tool rack

The Garage

Now that you have organized the house, don't let the garage become the last refuge for clutter. (When the car no longer fits in the garage, it's time to reorganize.)

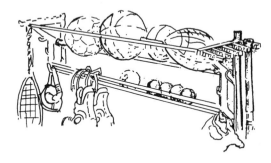

Wall-mount sports rack

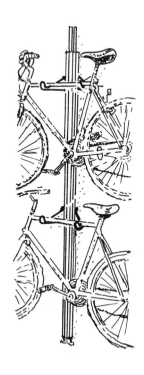

Tension-mount bike rack

Rafters and ceiling suspension are a prime way to store rarely used items such as lawn furniture, long ladders and snow shovels.

Wall mounting is another good bet. Dowels or brackets are great for holding wheelbarrows, rakes and shovels. Hoses can also be wound on a reel mounted on the wall. Heavy-duty hooks, fastened to wall studs or ceiling joists, are ideal for hanging snow tires or bicycles.

Gardening supplies should be kept together. Pots, hand tools, gardening gloves and other equipment can go on one shelf; bags of potting soil can be stored in small, covered buckets or trash cans nearby.

Hardware should be organized. Nuts, bolts, screws, nails and wire can multiply at an alarming rate if not properly tracked. Hardware stores sell storage units with 24 to 32 tiny drawers

Safe Deposit Boxes

A safe deposit box is a secure, private facility for the storage of personal or business items of value. The value may be sentimental or monetary, but one guideline is: Can this item be replaced at any cost in today's marketplace? Also consider: How often do I need access to this item?

Donna Beck, vice president of the Colorado Banking Institution, a private training company for banking employees based in Denver, offers the following suggestions of what might be stored in a safe deposit box:

Rare coins
Stamps
Jewelry
Bearer bonds
Leases
Marriage and birth certificates
Trust papers
Mortgages
Medals
Computer discs
Rare artwork
Wills

Beck also advises individuals to consider how often they need access to stored items. "A safe deposit box may not be the right place to keep a diamond ring that you wear every Friday evening to a social event," says Beck. Since banks are not open on weekends, you'd have to keep the ring at home until Monday morning.

An item's special temperature and humidity needs are another factor. Safe deposit boxes are maintained in a locked vault within the bank. During working hours, the temperature in the bank is evenly controlled. However, banks generally do not run air conditioning on weekends, so temperature conditions within the vault will fluctuate. The regional climate will also affect that of the safe deposit box.

Two keys are required to open a safe deposit box. One is held by the bank, the other by the box holder. (Only those individuals listed on the contract may use the box-holder key.) The institution's guard key prepares the lock for the box holder's key. The box holder removes the inner tin to a secure area for private viewing. Replacement of the tin is also done privately.

Contents of a safe deposit box are not insured by the bank. The box holder must have an insurance rider that covers replacement costs.

In the case of death of the box holder, access rights to the safe deposit box pass on to the survivor. However, ownership of the items contained within the safe deposit box can only be designated through a will.

The most common size of a safe deposit box is 3 by 5 by 22 inches. Some larger institutions provide boxes measuring 10 by 10 by 20 inches, or 20-by-20-inch "lockers." The largest safe deposit box is 30 by 30 by 22 inches.

Not all banks have safe deposit boxes. For those that do, prices vary depending on size, and also upon the location of the institution and the demand for boxes there.

Ask each institution that you are considering:

•What are your yearly box rental fees?

•Are there any additional fees for "excessive access" or other services?

•Is the private viewing area large enough for two to four people to use at once?

It's also helpful to visit various institutions and ask to see where the vault and the private viewing area are located.

that serve this purpose quite well. Small jars with lids, cigar boxes and coffee cans also work, if kept well organized and clearly labeled.

Hand tools can go into large, sturdy metal cabinets that are lockable and are designed to hold smaller hand and power tools. If you have only a few hand tools, a tool box will suffice. Hanging tools on pegboard is a good way to keep your tools easily accessible. Labeling each hook or painting a silhouette around each tool where it hangs will help when it's time to put tools away, especially if you have a young or inexperienced helper.

Old paint should not be stored. Rather, it should be disposed of safely, according to toxic-material disposal guidelines. Paint brushes may be hung on pegboard or stored in coffee cans, brush-side up.

Outside Storage

UNDER THE DECK OR PORCH

If you do not have a garage but do have space under a deck, porch or outside staircase, some objects may safely be stored there. It is advisable to first apply a fire-proof material to the inside surface and be sure to store only noncombustible items here. Since the area cannot be completely water-proofed, store only items that resist moisture, and for further protection, create a raised floor with plywood and blocks. Cover items with a plastic tarp.

Mini Storage Units

If you have no garage or basement for large or bulky items, you may want to consider a storage locker. These can be garagelike structures rented by the month. They are secured with a lock on the outside; sizes vary and prices vary according to size. Another, more secure option is individual lockers within a secure building. Sizes on these range from 4 by 4 feet to 10 by 10 feet. Items best stored here are furniture, large sporting equipment and other objects you do not use often or you are storing for future use.

Sources of Further Information

BOOKS

The Art of Making Houses Liveable. Peter and Susanne Stevenson, Chilton Book Co., Philadelphia, 1972.

Closets: Designing and Organizing the Personalized Closet. Patricia Coen and Bryan Milford, Grove Weidenfeld, New York, 1988.

The Closet Book. Elin Schoen, Harmony Books, New York, 1982.

The Complete Home Organizer. Maxine Ordesky, Grove Press, New York, 1993.

Creative Ideas for Household Storage. Graham Blackburn and the Editors of Consumer Reports Books, Consumers Union, Mount Vernon, N.Y., 1990.

500 Terrific Ideas for Organizing Everything. Sheree Bykofsky, Simon & Schuster, New York, 1992.

Good Housekeeping's Decorating and Do-It-Yourself. Hearst, New York, 1977.

Organized Closets and Storage. Stephanie Culp, Writer's Digest Books, Cincinnati, Ohio, 1990.

Remodeling Your Home. Sunset Books and Sunset Magazine Editors, Lane, Menlo Park, Calif., 1978.

Renovating Your Home for Maximum Profit. Dan Lieberman and Paul Hoffman, Prima, Rocklin, Calif., 1989.

Repairing and Remodeling for Home Interiors: Planning, Materials, Methods (2nd Ed.). J. Ralph Dalzell, revised by Frederick S. Merritt, McGraw-Hill, New York, 1973.

Storage: Bookshelves, Cupboards, Cabinets. Sunset Books Editors, Lane, Menlo Park, Calif., 1968).

Sunset Complete Home Storage. Sunset Books and Sunset Magazine Editors, Lane, Menlo Park, Calif., 1990.

Wall Systems and Shelving. Sunset Books Editors, Lane, Menlo Park, Calif., 1983.

Working Woman's Dream House. John Hamilton, Betterway Publications, White Hall, Va., 1989.

CATALOGS
Storage Items for the Home
Crate & Barrel, 1-800-451-8217
Hold Everything, 1-800-421-2264
Lillian Vernon, 1-800-285-5555

Storage Items for Children
Toys to Grow On, 1-800-874-4242

Storage Items for the Office
Reliable Home Office, 1-800-869-6000

Kitchen Storage
Kraftmaid, 1-800-654-3008

MANUFACTURERS
Acme Display
   1057 S. Olive St.
   Los Angeles, CA 90015
   1-800-959-5657
   1-213-749-9191

Cosmepak
   P.O. Box 1907
   Morristown, NJ 07962
   1-201-993-9140

Elfa Corp. of America
   300-3A Rte. 17 South
   Lodi, NJ 07644
   1-201-777-1554

Rubbermaid Inc.
   1147 Akron Rd.
   Wooster, OH 44691
   1-216-264-6464

5

Home Maintenance

Performing minor (and some major) repairs around the house yourself can be satisfying and rewarding, but only if you are happy with the work at the end. The key to success is preparation. Begin with a detailed checklist and proper tools to make the work go smoothly.

Making a Checklist

Before you start a project you must establish your goals. Make a checklist of what needs to be done. Ask yourself these questions:

• What tools will I need?

• How long will it take?

• Is the weather a consideration?

• Do I have the necessary skills to accomplish the project?

• What resources do I have to help me?

• Am I working with dangerous materials?

It's important to answer these questions before you get started. For example, if you don't have the right tools you won't be able to do a proper job. If you don't budget enough time for the task, you will have to rush and perhaps won't be able to complete it. To avoid this problem, estimate the time you expect to be able to complete the project in, then double it. Here's a sample checklist:

Sample Checklist
1. Project _____

2. Estimated time (multiply initial estimate by two) _____

3. Tools needed (include cleanup) _____

4. Supplies needed and expenses (many home-improvement projects are tax-deductible, so keep a list of receipts

_____

5. Make a list of steps (include prep work and cleanup) _____

6. Dangers involved (Many home repairs use chemicals or power tools that require extra care. Before you start, read instructions thoroughly. Heed all warnings. Let someone know you will be working with dangerous materials.)

_____

Essential Tools

Good tools mean good work. Even if you're not an expert home improver, you still need a tool kit to perform basic tasks.

When you are shopping for tools, hold them in your hand. Only buy those that feel good. You can buy the most expensive tool in the world but if it doesn't feel right in your hand, you won't get the full benefit from using it. Make sure the tool has a comfortable grip and is not too heavy. If it feels even the slightest bit heavy at first, imagine how it will feel after you've been wielding it for several hours.

Buy tools as you need them, rather than packaged sets. Also, purchase high-quality tools. Good tools not only encourage you to do good work, they make for a safer work environment.

Once you have your tools, take care of them. Clean them after each use and store them safely, in a tool box or a designated drawer. Tools are not toys. Keep manuals and safety instructions with your tools, so they are easy to find in the event of accident.

Here is a suggested list of basic tools:

- Pencils
- Fasteners, such as straps, clamps and vises
- Tape (masking and duct)
- Sandpaper (keep a variety of grits) and sandpaper block
- Steel wool
- Rags
- Wire brush
- Paintbrush (both roller and standard)
- Paint pails and pans
- Dustpan and brush
- Grounded extension cord (if you will need this outside make sure it is intended for that use)
- Single-edge razor blade
- Scissors
- Stepladder
- Putty knife
- Adjustable wrench
- Slip-joint pliers
- Needle-nose pliers
- Retractable ruler or tape measure
- Screwdrivers, both flat and phillips head (get a variety of point sizes)
- Curved claw hammer
- Level

- Toilet plunger
- Staple gun
- Plumb line
- Locking grip pliers
- Pipe wrench

Power tools, such as electric drills and screwdrivers, will make projects go more quickly. There are several cordless electric tools on the market, including cordless screw drivers and drills, which you may find useful. Experienced do-it-yourselfers may also want to acquire a power saw.

The Exterior

Picture your home without any kind of surface finish. Not only would it look unattractive, it would be completely vulnerable to the elements. The most popular finishes are paint (this includes staining), shingles, and aluminum or vinyl siding. Most exterior finishes last 5 to 30 years. Obviously, your home's exterior needs redoing if the paint is peeling or the shingles are falling off. There are also some other things to look for that will help you diagnose various problems.

The roof gets the greatest exposure so this area should be checked each season. The life of a roof depends on the material and the prevailing weather conditions. Asphalt shingles or rolls are the least expensive roof materials but need replacement fairly often (every 10 years). Other materials that last longer include wood shingles (which must be replaced every 25 years), wood shakes (every 50 years), standing-seam metal roofs (every 30 to 50 years), slate (every 100 years) or Spanish tile (every 100 years).

Diagnosing the problem: No matter what kind of roof you have, you will need to check periodically for breakage, wear or blistering. If your roof is lumpy, uneven or has lots of patches, check the inside of the house for water damage. If you have a pitched roof, look for a sag; this could be the result of settling or major structural problems. Also check the flashing, the thin metal plating that goes around chimneys, vents and skylights to prevent water from getting underneath the roofing in these critical areas. Rusty, loose or missing flashing could create a leak and rot structural framing.

There are several styles of siding available: aluminum, stucco, wood shingles and vinyl. Aluminum lasts approximately 30 years and usually doesn't need to be painted. Vinyl lasts about 30 years and also doesn't need to be finished. Shingles last about 50 years and can be finished with paint, stain or left in their natural state to weather to an attractive finish. Stucco also lasts about 50 years or longer and doesn't require finishing.

Check the siding periodically for worn shingles, loose sections, or worn paint.

PAINT

Paint is your home's first line of protection against the elements. Because it is constantly exposed, it tends to weather rapidly and unevenly. Professional painters know certain areas are trouble spots, and these are the first places to check to see if you need to repaint:

•Windows and sills. Sills hold water, snow and ice, and endure intense sunlight, which causes paint to blister and peel or crack.

•Eaves and soffits. Dampness causes paints to peel and also encourages mildew, which itself can cause peeling.

•Downspouts and gutters. Repeated exposure to rain and snow can cause paint to blister and flake.

•Trim. Because it gets heavy exposure, trim often shows weathering before the rest of the house and needs more frequent repainting.

Common Paint Failures

Probably the biggest contributions to exterior paint failures are sunlight, moisture and temperature fluctuations. Here is a list of the most common problems:

•Blistering. Paints, particularly oil-based formulas, can blister due to moisture behind the painted surface. Latex paint can also blister when exposed to water.

•Flaking and peeling. Blistering can lead to this. Also, changes in temperature can cause wood and other painted surfaces to expand and contract. If the paint isn't flexible, it will crack and peel away.

•Chalking. The sun's ultraviolet rays tend to deteriorate the binder of a paint. As it breaks down, the pigment is released in a powdery, chalklike form that washes away with the rain.

Blistering

Flaking and peeling

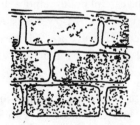

Chalking

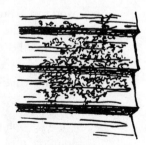

Mildew

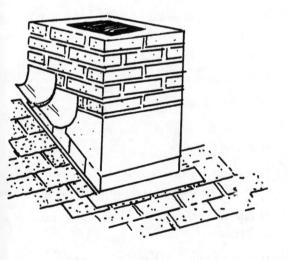

Flashing a chimney

•Mildew. This mold grows on many types of surfaces, including paint. Moist conditions encourage it—it is usually found on the damp, dark areas of the house such as the north or west side.

Solutions

Fixing any of the above problems requires elbow grease. The best way to prevent them from recurring is to prepare the surface properly before repainting.

•Previously painted wood. Remove loose, peeling or flaking paint by scraping or wire-brushing. Feather back rough edges by sanding. If there are any glossy areas, sand or wire-brush to dull the surface. Areas bare of paint should be sanded to remove surface fibers and dirt. Use a primer on this area before you paint it.

•Aluminum siding. Washing with a rented power washer—a device that uses pressurized water to take off accumulated dirt and grime—is probably the most convenient way to do it. Alternatively, try hand scrubbing, using a soft brush. If a white powdery oxidation is present, carefully remove it with steel wool, then clean off residue. If bare aluminum is exposed, spot prime before painting.

•Concrete, cinder block, brick or cement. If unpainted, these surfaces need to be cleaned by hand. A brush with coarse fibers works well, but be careful not to remove the surface of the brick itself. A power washer can also be used. Heavily pocked areas should be caulked and treated with a masonry conditioner before painting.

•If the surface is covered with hard-to-remove soot or grime, remove it with a solution of 1/3 cup powdered detergent (Tide, Fab or the equivalent) in 1 gallon of warm water; or 2/3 cup household cleaner (Soilex, Spic & Span or the equivalent) in 1 gallon of of warm water.

•Vinyl siding. Do not use a wire brush or sandpaper; either will mar the surface. Instead, power-wash the vinyl or wash it by hand with warm soapy water, then rinse and paint. You should never paint vinyl siding darker than its original color. Dark colors absorb heat, which could cause siding to warp or bend.

EXTERIOR MAINTENANCE SCHEDULE

Spring

•Recaulk joints between siding and other materials.

•Check window wells for debris.

•Check all wood surfaces for paint failure and damage.

•Nail down loose siding and trim; replace decayed sections.

•Wash vinyl, aluminum or painted-wood siding.

•Check deck or patio for loose boards, bricks or stones.

•Check roof for damaged shingles.

•Inspect flashing at chimney, dormers, vents and skylights.

•Clean gutters, downspout and leaf strainers; check for damage and paint failure.

•Evaluate roof 15 years or older for replacement.

•Clean screens and check for damage.

•Replace worn or damaged weather stripping.

Fall

•Check for bird's nests in chimneys and vents.

•Apply new caulking around windows and doors if needed.

The Interior

CARPET AND UPHOLSTERY CARE

Although no carpet or upholstery will last forever, you can add years to its life with proper care. Here are some tips to extend the life of your carpets and upholstery.

•Rearrange furniture to change traffic patterns. This promotes even wear and reduces crushing on carpet.

•Flip sofa and chair cushions and beat to remove dust buildup.

•Never pull loose yarn from carpeting. Instead, carefully snip it with scissors.

•Protect carpeting and upholstery from direct sunlight.

•Vacuum carpet at least once a week. This is especially important if you have pets. A lot of carpet wear is caused by dirt particles grinding against the fibers. Clean carpets thoroughly once or twice a year. (See Chapter 6, "Cleaning.")

WOOD FLOOR CARE

To care for your wood floor, you first need to know what kind of finish it has. There are two types of wood floor finish: penetrating seals and surface finishes.

Penetrating seals (oils) soak into the wood and harden, thus sealing out dirt and light amounts of moisture. A coating of wax will keep this floor looking its best; apply once to twice a year, depending on the amount of wear the floor receives. For wax finishes, use a dust mop and vacuum regularly. If your finish is getting dull, buff it. If buffing no longer works you might have to add more wax to that area and buff the whole floor to create an even finish.

Surface finishes include polyurethane and Swedish finishes, which form a moisture-resistant barrier protecting the floor. Surface finishes should be cleaned with a dust mop and vacuumed regularly. Periodically, mop the floor with 1/4 cup white vinegar in a quart of warm water, or a cleaning solution recommended by the manufacturer. After mopping, wipe it dry with a clean cloth or mop.

Wood flooring experts recommend that surface finishes be reapplied every five years. If you want to do it yourself, hardware and home-center stores rent sanders. There are also many books on the subject that explain the process in detail. See "Sources of Further Information," below.

Here are some "first aid" suggestions for waxed floors, which are vulnerable to spills:

•Dried milk or food stains: Gently rub spot with damp cloth. Rub dry and re-wax area.

•Stains caused by standing water: Rub spot with No. 000 steel wool and re-wax.

•Dark spots: One method is to clean the spot and surrounding area with No. 000

steel wool and a wood floor cleaner or odorless minerals. An alternative is to thoroughly wash spot with household vinegar and allow it to remain for three to four minutes. If spot remains, sand it with fine sandpaper, feathering out three to four inches into surrounding area.

There are several water-stain removers on the market. Consult your hardware store for the best one for your problem.

REFINISHING AND PAINTING FURNITURE

Refinishing or painting furniture is not only fun, but can save you money. Instead of buying a brand-new piece of furniture, you can refinish one you bought at a yard sale or found in the attic. In very little time, you will have a beautiful piece of furniture at a fraction of the cost of a new one.

Begin with a piece of furniture that needs only surface work. Here are some guidelines:

• Look for a piece that is sturdy. Test joints to make sure the paint you are about to remove is not the only thing keeping it together.

• Don't worry about the amount of paint on the piece, or the color.

• Check the height to see if it will work for your needs. Older furniture tends to be a little smaller than present-day pieces.

Paint Strippers

Most paint and varnish removers fall into one of three categories: heavy-bodied removers, general-purpose semi-paste products and liquid strippers.

Heavy-bodied removers have a thickening agent added to slow down the evaporation. These are the fastest, most effective strippers available. They'll cut through several layers of paint and dissolve tough finishes like epoxy and polyurethane. They are more expensive than other types, but do the most work for the buck. Their use requires caution: These products contain very strong chemicals and should be used only in a well-ventilated area.

General-purpose semi-paste strippers are less powerful, but will still do a good job on several layers of latex or oil-base paints, synthetic enamels and clear finishes. They don't work well on epoxy and polyurethane. Like the heavy-bodied removers, these have a thickening agent added to slow evaporation time.

Both of these types of stripper are ideal for refinishing wood floors, paneling, siding, doors and outdoor furniture. Many brands are water-rinsable. You should be careful to wipe the stripper off thoroughly or it will damage the wood.

Liquid strippers are best for removing clear finishes such as varnish, lacquer and shellac. They work more slowly than heavy-bodied and semi-paste strippers but allow more control. It might take several applications of a liquid stripper to remove latex or oil-based paints. These products evaporate quickly and because they are petroleum-based, they are highly flammable.

A fourth type of paint remover is the *powder-type strippers* designed to remove old-style paints, such as casein and milk paint. Ineffective on clear finishes, they use an alkaline substance (sodium hydroxide) to remove paint only. You mix them with water and apply the solution with a nylon brush. Powder strippers are nonflammable and emit no toxic fumes.

If you have a piece of furniture with a

Fixing Finishes

Some blemishes in finishes can be fixed relatively easily. It is generally best to try restoration or repair first. If that works, you have saved a great deal of effort; if not, you can proceed with complete stripping and refinishing.

First, clean the surface with a commercial wax remover. Choose one that will remove wax with silicones, and follow the directions on the container. Or use turpentine and very fine (00) steel wool.

Next, if you are uncertain what the finish is, test in an unobtrusive spot. Paint remover will make varnish, enamel and paint wrinkle. Alcohol will cause shellac to dissolve, then redry, and lacquer thinner will do the same to lacquer. Oil finishes lie in the wood and do not have a separate discernible surface.

Finally, identify the problem and try one or more of the following techniques, using materials appropriate for the finish. In all cases, rub, sand or polish in the direction of the wood grain. Use a sanding block or stick with abrasive papers.

DULL SURFACE, OVERALL LIGHT SCRATCHES, SCUFFING

Apply clear or colored furniture polish. Rub with 000 steel wool dipped in a 1:1 mixture of boiled linseed oil and turpentine; clean with detergent in warm water. Rub with a creamy mix of rottenstone or 3F pumice and mineral oil and a pad of soft cloth. Or use automobile polishing compound according to directions.

DEEP SCRATCHES, CHIPS

Paint in with a compatible stain, using a very fine artist's brush. Or fill with a wax, shellac or lacquer stick, available in colors to match any wood or finish. Warm a thin, flexible knife blade, such as an artist's palette knife or a kitchen fruit knife, in the flame of a propane torch, gas burner or candle (wipe off any soot). Do not overheat the blade; it can burn the filler material. Touch the stick to it and transfer the softened filler into the scratch with the blade. Fill the spot and wipe away the melted excess with the blade. When cool, sand lightly with very fine abrasive paper. Wax sticks are easiest to use, and the filler can be removed if needed. That is not possible with shellac or lacquer sticks.

DENTS

Raise a shallow dent in finished or unfinished wood by laying a thick, barely damp cloth over it and applying a moderately warm household iron or soldering iron. Steam will cause the wood fibers to swell. Remove the cloth and briefly apply cracked ice in a small plastic bag. Then smooth the area with very fine abrasive paper.

WHITE RINGS, SURFACE STAINS OR BURNS

First try a fine abrasive: cigarette ashes, plain toothpaste, rottenstone, pumice or auto polishing compound. Apply with mineral oil or lightweight household oil with a fold of soft cloth, or your fingertip in a plastic or rubber glove. Or lightly rub a shellac finish with alcohol, a lacquer finish with lacquer thinner, on a soft cloth. For deeper burns, scrape or sand away all charred material, paint or stain on any raw wood, and fill with heated stick material as described above.

CHECKING, ALLIGATORING

Checking is an overall pattern of shallow cracks; alligatoring is overall deeper cracks. It may be possible to correct them by re-amalgamating the finish—dissolving it and letting it flow to a smooth surface. For varnish, mix one part each of varnish and thinner and two parts of boiled linseed oil. Gently rub this solution over the surface with a clean cloth. With a shellac finish, flow on alcohol with a brush; with lacquer, use lacquer thinner. The surface must be horizontal to avoid runs and pooling.

With all repairs, clean the surface thoroughly when your work is done and protect it with a coat of wax.

From *The Stanley Complete Step-by-Step Book of Home Repair and Improvement,* by James A. Hufnagel, copyright 1993. Published by Simon & Schuster Inc.

clear oil, varnish, lacquer or shellac finish, you can also use a *furniture refinisher* rather than a stripper. This dissolves the finish, enabling you to lift it off with steel wool. This method is gentler on the wood patina than other strippers, and is recommended for antiques.

Strippers vary from manufacturer to manufacturer. It is important to read the instructions carefully along with all warnings. These are powerful chemicals. When opening the stripper, point the cap away from you. The best temperature to work in is between 65° and 70°. If you are working outdoors, select a spot out of the direct sun.

Apply the solution using an inexpensive paint brush. Work in sections from top to bottom, using short strokes. It's important to give the stripper enough time to work—it might take anywhere from 10 to 45 minutes for the solution to break up the finish. Even so, you may find that you need to apply the stripper more than once.

The best tool to remove sludge from a flat surface is a plastic spatula. This will prevent scratches. The wood will be soft from the stripper, so care must be taken not to damage it. To remove the sludge from moldings, legs and other curved surfaces, try No. 2 steel wool, heavy twine or thin hemp rope. Toothpicks and wood dowels of various diameters may also come in handy. Another useful tool, for soft wood such as pine, is a stiff vegetable brush.

Once you've removed the finish, take a rag soaked in mineral spirits and wipe the surface thoroughly to remove any last bits of finish, as well as dirt and grime.

DOOR AND WINDOW REPAIR

The most common problem to befall older windows and doors is swelling and warping from humidity. Modern windows and doors—those manufactured within the past 15 years or so—do not suffer from this as much, since they are precased to prevent warping.

If your door sticks, find the exact spot by pushing or pulling lightly at various parts of the closed door. The sticky area will resist your efforts. Once you've located the spot, look for wear, scratches and worn paint.

You will now have to plane the area down. Take a wood plane and gently scrap it along the area. Be careful not to take too much off—you don't want to create a gap, you just want to remove some of the resistance. If the area to be planed is on the bottom edge, you will have to remove the door. Afterward, you might find you'll need to put a sweep on the bottom to block drafts. Another method is to tape sandpaper over the sticky spot so the door will sand itself down in the course of normal use.

Windows often stick because the frame has been painted over, or humidity has caused paint to soften, forming a seal and preventing the window from opening. If this is the case, take a single-edged razor blade (you could also try using a pizza cutter) and run it along the sides. Then gently try and lift the window. Apply more pressure as needed. Keep lifting till the window comes loose. Then open and shut the window several times and remove any paint fragments that may appear. If you continue to have trouble with the window, open it and sand lightly along the inside of the track.

Another fix for a sticky window, once you've got it open, is to rub paraffin or wax on the inside of the vertical tracks. Other good lubricants are petroleum jelly or liquid silicone gel.

To hold a cracked pane in place, apply transparent liquid cement to both sides of the glass, overlapping the crack.

PEST CONTROL

Pests that invade your home can spread disease and cause physical damage. It is in your best interest to get rid of them as soon as possible.

There are a number of poisons and pesticides on the market. If you have children or pets, these might not be the best choice. If you decide to use poisons, make sure you are buying one designed for your problem. Follow the manufacturer's directions carefully and heed all warnings.

Traps can be safer than sprays. And in some cases, prevention is the best medicine.

Mice. Mice are common house pests. The best way to get rid of them is to prevent access to food. Store all food, including that packaged in cellophane and cardboard, in glass, hard plastic, or metal containers. Then clean out cupboards, including the deepest, darkest corners. Throw away nesting material such as old newspapers or clothes. Once mice are gone, seal up all entry points.

Bats. Bats roost in your attic during the day and leave the nest at night. In order to get rid of bats you must find their entry points. The best time to find these is during dusk and dawn in July and August because of the longer daylight hours. Once you've determined the entry points, you must seal them while the bats are out foraging for food. Bats can bite, so the National Association of Pest Control recommends hiring a professional. Look in the Yellow Pages under "Pest control" or "Wildlife control," or contact your local zoo for advice.

Wasps. Poison is the best approach. Buy a poison designed specifically for these insects. Best is a spray that shoots out 8 to 10 feet. Wasps can usually be found under eaves and other overhangs. Once you've found their nest, protect yourself by wearing long pants and a long-sleeved shirt. Tape cuffs and sleeves closed. Wear a hat with a bee-keeper's veil and heavy shoes and socks. Spray the poison at the nest to saturate it, then quickly go inside.

Ants and roaches. The removal of these insects has become easier and safer than in the past. The first step is to provide as little food for them as possible. Clean the kitchen after food preparation and frequently clean behind appliances or other areas where crumbs might fall. For safety's sake, buy sealed traps. Many traps today encase a poisoned bait inside a plastic disk. The roaches or ants must enter the disk to consume the poison and bring it back to the nest. There are also many sprays on the market. If you use these, follow directions carefully and keep children and pets out of the area.

INTERIOR MAINTENANCE SCHEDULE

Schedule:
• Vacuum all floors weekly.

• Care for wood floors as required. Use manufacturer's recommended method. If worn, repair according to type of floor surfacing method.

• Clean upholstery once a year in spring and shake pillows and cushions weekly.

• Check for ants, wasps in the spring and summer, and bats and other guests each season. Deal with pest problems immediately.

KITCHENS AND BATHS

Kitchen cabinets may be of solid wood or composite board surfaced with a wood veneer or plastic laminate. Whatever they are made of, they should be cleaned regularly to remove dirt and grime that builds up from cooking. Use a mixture of two parts water to one part vinegar or ammonia (don't mix them) on cabinet surfaces. A variety of spray-on cleansing products are available; check labels to see if they are safe for the finish on your cabinets.

Knobs and pulls should also be regularly cleaned and cared for. Since these get regular use you might need to tighten them as well. You will find a screw in the backside of the cabinet door or drawer. Hold the knob and turn the screw clockwise. Once it resists, stop tightening.

If drawers don't glide smoothly, remove the drawer by pulling it out as far as it will go. Lift the front end and pull it out all the way. Check the tracks and wheels for dirt and grime, then wipe clean and oil. Cabinet hinges will also accumulate dirt and grime. Clean these every six months or when they are stiff by applying some lubricating oil to the hinges.

Repairing Faucets and Toilets

Older faucets and toilets are easier to repair than newer ones because the older units have interchangeable parts between manufacturers and styles. If you know what part is broken, it is easy to replace. Fewer parts break in newer units, but the ones that do can be hard to replace. It's a matter of getting the correct part and installing it, the ease of which depends on its availability at your home-center store.

Here are some common problems and how to fix them:

• Meager flow from faucet. Unscrew the nozzle, take the washer out and inspect for wear. If it is worn, replace it. Check the aerator screen for wear. If there is no wear but just built-up soap scum, soak in water and vinegar solution to remove.

• Running toilets. The most common problem occurs because the flapper is not blocking the flush valve, so water keeps filling the tank. Check for an obstruction of some kind that prevents it from closing. Check float and chain to see if there is a tangle that prevents the flapper from closing completely. Check flapper for wear. If it looks worn, replace it. Also, check the float ball to see if it is touching the side of the tank. You may need to straighten it, or the float may have a leak. To check, unscrew it and shake it gently. If you hear water sloshing, it needs to be replaced. If none of these efforts works, call a plumber.

•Handle problems. If the toilet handle sticks or, conversely, is loose, you will need to adjust the chain and possibly clean the handle mounting nut. Use a vinegar solution to remove lime deposits. You can tighten or loosen the chain by hooking into a different hole in the handle lever, or by removing links with pliers.

•A clogged drain. The basic method is to pour hot water down the drain. Turn hot water up to highest level (approximately 160°F—it takes about two hours), then turn on hot water faucet and fill up tub or sink, leaving the drain open to dissolve soaps and grease. Be careful, or you may scald yourself. Or boil a large pot of water and pour it down the drain.

Next, try a plunger, positioning it over the drain and pushing down forcefully three times. When you remove the plunger the water should rush down. If not, repeat. If this doesn't work you can rent or buy a plumber's snake. Push the curved end

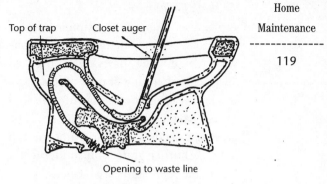

Top of trap — Closet auger — Opening to waste line

Clearing a clogged toilet

down the drain till you dislodge the blockage. Or else you can rent an auger, which is similar to a snake but longer, with teeth at the end. Powered by a hand crank, it will go farther down the drain. This should be used by professionals or an experienced person only.

If the drain continues to get clogged or you cannot unclog it yourself, call a plumber. They have professional equipment that can probe the drain and dislodge stubborn obstructions.

Testing Your Drinking Water

If you'd like to get your water tested, there are a variety of ways to do it. Several testing kits are available through home-center stores, but if you think you have a serious problem, it's best to send a sample to an EPA-certified testing lab (check your Yellow Pages under "Testing labs"). The do-it-yourself testers cover only a few of the possible problems.

A high level of calcium and magnesium means you have hard water. Not only will soaps and detergents fail to foam properly, but hard water also discolors clothes and fixtures. A rotten-egg smell is an indication of hydrogen sulfide, which is a nuisance rather than a health hazard. A tint in your water could also indicate a problem. Reddish-orange coloring is caused by iron, which could indicate rust in the pipes. A brown-gray color comes from magnesium and a green color from copper. These contaminants are a nuisance, causing laundry and other stains.

Other contaminants are more serious. Lead and mercury can damage the nervous system, and mercury also affects the kidneys. Nitrates, if absorbed by the body, restrict the circulation of oxygen. Radon causes cancer.

There are two principal ways of filtering your water: point of entry (POE) or point of use (POU).

POE equipment is installed where the water enters the house and treats it there, before it is distributed through the house. Water softeners are usually POE systems.

If you only need to treat your drinking water, you might decide on a point-of-use system. In this case, you are preventing the health risk where the water is being dispensed. Chlorination, used in POE systems, kills bacteria and viruses and controls algae. Activated carbon filters, used in both POE and POU systems, get rid of hydrogen sulfide, silt and viruses, and controls algae. Reverse-osmosis systems, also used in both POE and POU systems, push water through a series of membranes and filters to rid your home water supply of metals, coliform bacteria, hard water, sewage contamination, cesspool seepage and pesticides.

Cooking Equipment

A gas oven is one of the simplest home appliances to maintain because it has very few moving parts. The trick to keeping it operating at peak efficiency is to clean it often, before burnt food and grease have a chance to build up. The area that needs attention is not the top and the burner grates, but underneath, where the pilot lights are located.

Most gas ranges have a top that can be removed or tilted up and propped open. Before you begin, turn all knobs to the off position. After you remove the top, turn the gas off. The valve is usually located in the back of the stove. Turn the handle so it is perpendicular to the pipe; the pilot light should go out. Many newer stoves, however, have spark pilot lights. If yours is one of them, turn the gas off, then try to light the stove. It should not light but you will hear it spark or click.

The gas-burner assembly can be removed from the stove by pulling it away from the main gas line and lifting up. Soak assemblies in warm, soapy water, which will make it possible to wipe off any baked-on spills. Remove food particles from the gas passages located in the outer edge of the burner head. Rinse the unit and dry it thoroughly, then replace the burner assemblies and turn the gas back on. Light the pilot light, if your stove has one. Then turn each burner on to make sure everything works.

Electric ranges are more complicated than gas ranges. They have many connections and fuses that can break or go bad. But keeping the range properly maintained is one thing you can do to keep it functioning properly. (This also applies to gas ranges.)

Adjust the oven vents and doors. A twisted door can cause an oven to cook unevenly and use more energy. To straighten one, loosen the screws that

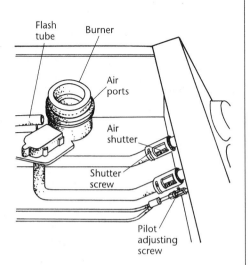

Gas range

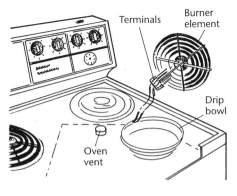

Electric range

hold the inner panel to the outer panel, gently twist the door back into shape and retighten the screws.

The oven vent is usually located under the right rear burner, inside the stove or burner. Lift the top to check the vent for blockage, which impedes air currents in the oven and causes uneven cooking.

Microwaves are easy to clean and don't need any other maintenance. Wipe the inside with a water/vinegar solution or use a cleanser suggested by the manufacturer. If your model has a rotisserie plate, pull that out and check the wheels for built-up grime and dirt. Clean as necessary.

Range hoods. There are two basic types of range hoods: those that vent to the outside and those that filter the air and recirculate it into the kitchen. Within those categories, there are pop-up or pull-up (downdraft) vents; large commercial-type hoods and smaller res-idential hoods. Most homes have the latter.

Cleaning the range hood should be done at least once a year, or more if you do a lot of cooking. First, turn off the power by unplugging the range hood or flipping the circuit that controls it. Then remove the filter. This is usually located directly under the range hood in front of the blower. Wash the filter in warm, soapy water or, if it's disposable, replace it. Clean the grill louvers with a small brush to get out built-up grease and grime. Clean the inside of the blower or fan housing. Then replace the filter.

Refrigerators
Vacuum the coils every three months. If they're underneath the refrigerator, unplug it, remove the grill and use the crevice attachment on your vacuum cleaner.

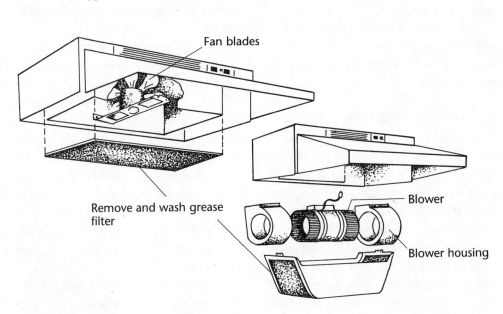

Fan blades

Remove and wash grease filter

Blower

Blower housing

Range hoods

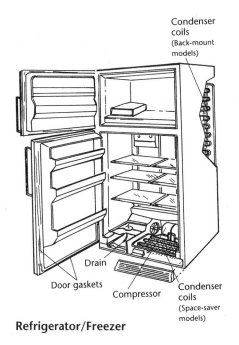

Refrigerator/Freezer

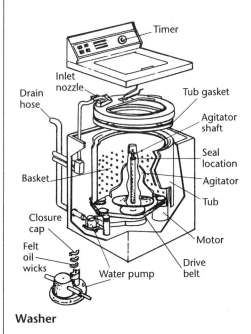

Washer

Clear the drain and occasionally pour a tablespoon of chlorine bleach, followed by a cup of water, into it. This kills algae and mold and keeps blockages from forming.

At least once a month, clean out leftover food and wipe all surfaces. Clean seals with a water/vinegar solution to remove grime.

Washers, Dryers and Dishwashers

A washing machine's biggest enemy is rust. To avoid problems, leave the lid up after use so all the water left in the machine can evaporate. To improve water flow, check to make sure the hot and cold water hoses are not kinked.

Before you perform any maintenance, unplug the unit and turn off the water. Loosen the water intake hoses at the back of the machine. Pull out the small

round washer containing the filter screens. If these show signs of wear or are badly corroded, replace them. If the screens have mineral deposits, soak them in a vinegar and water solution to remove.

The clothes dryer relies on unobstructed air flow to work properly. After every use, remove the lint from the lint catcher. Periodically check the dryer vent in the back of the machine for a buildup of lint and dust. Once a year, remove the service panel at the front and vacuum the lint catcher. Inspect the hot-air exhaust duct and hose. Repair any holes with duct tape or replace if damaged. These parts are sold by the foot, so know how long a piece you require.

The dishwasher needs lots of hot water to clean your dishes. The first

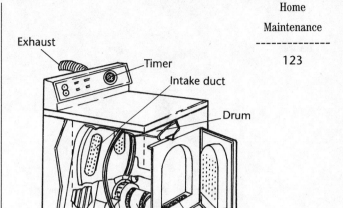

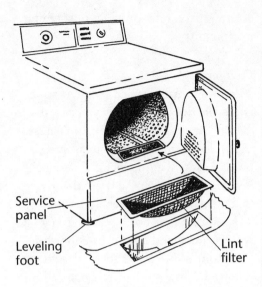

Electric clothes dryer

Clothes dryer anatomy

thing to check is the water temperature, which should be 130°. To test, turn the dishwasher on and let it fill with water, then turn it off and stick a thermometer in the water. If the temperature is too low, turn the heat up on your water heater. Also check to see if the pump screen located at the base of the unit has food particles caught in it. Check for food particles in the spray arm, and pry or poke out any blockages. Both of these should be checked every three months for optimal performance. Also check the door seals. Clean deposits of grease and soap that may have built up.

Disposals
Disposals are installed under the kitchen sink and operate on standard household current. Driven by an electric motor, the grinding mechanism

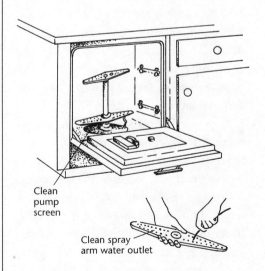

Dishwasher

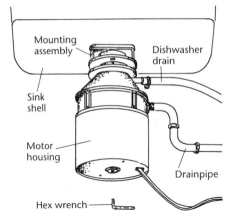

Garbage disposal

pulverizes and liquifies food waste with the aid of water from the kitchen faucet. The ground-up food is then discharged into the drain system.

There are two basic types of disposals: continuous feed, which is the most popular, and batch feed.

Continuous-feed disposals are operated by a wall switch, and can be loaded with food waste continuously while the disposal is running. The batch-feed type must first be loaded with waste then activated by inserting the sink stopper and turning it.

It is always important to run cold water when you run the disposal to help move the waste through the drain line. Additionally, fat congeals in cold water, making it easier to wash down the drain. Hot water should not be used because it can dissolve fats and grease, which may then block drain lines.

Maintenance of your disposal is fairly easy. Grinding small bones and ice is actually good for the system. For the most part, however, they are self-cleaning.

If your disposal jams up, turn it off and unplug it before attempting to clear it. Manufacturers provide unjamming instructions.

Countertop Appliances

There are many small counter appliances on the market that you may use just as often as your major appliances. These may include toasters, mixers, bread bakers, can openers, coffee makers, food processors and anything else that makes cooking easier.

Most countertop appliances come with cleaning and care instructions from the manufacturer, and these should be followed. If the appliance is plugged in, keep the cord wound up in the back of the unit to prevent accidents. Thoroughly clean around the unit and underneath it every month. These small appliances can be a breeding ground for bugs.

MAINTENANCE SCHEDULE FOR LARGE APPLIANCES

Every month:
Clean the inside of the stove.

Clean leftover food out of refrigerator and wipe surfaces.

Every three months:
Clean rotisserie plate on microwave.

Clean washing machine lines and check hose connections.

Clean refrigerator drain and vacuum coils.

Clean dishwasher spray arm and clean out pump screen.

Every six months:

Clean oven vent and beneath burners.

Check dryer vents.

Remove service panel from dryer and vacuum lint catcher.

Every year:

Adjust doors and vents on stoves.

Electrical and Mechanical Systems

MAINTAINING HEATING AND COOLING EQUIPMENT

According to the Plumbing-Heating-Cooling Information Bureau, the most important thing you can do to keep your heating and cooling equipment running at peak efficiency is to maintain it regularly. Oil-heating equipment should be tuned yearly; gas, every other year. This will typically cost you between $40 and $80. It might simply mean calling the oil or gas company after the cold season is over and having them come and tune up your equipment. It is usually cheaper at this time of year.

There are some things you can do yourself to help maintain your system. First, keep the area around the heating equipment clean. Dust, lint or sawdust can get caught in the filters and exhaust system and reduce efficiency. If you have an oil-fired unit, you should have the tank filled at the end of the season. This prevents condensation from forming in the empty tank, which can promote bacterial growth.

There is a quick test you can perform to make sure your system is operational before the first cold day of the year. Turn the thermostat up above room temperature and wait for the system to turn on. Let it run for about 15 minutes. If you notice a problem, call for service.

Clanks, Bangs and Hisses

Properly maintained heating systems should not make noise, according to the Plumbing-Heating-Cooling Information Bureau. But radiators that clank, bang or hiss are the most common heating-system problem.

Pipes that creak and tap can sound awfully bad, but the good news is that their bark is usually worse than their bite. Here are some things to check for before you call in a professional repair person.

Pipes expand and contract with cold and hot temperatures, causing creaking.

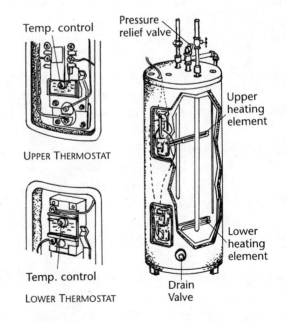

Temp. control

Pressure relief valve

UPPER THERMOSTAT

Temp. control

LOWER THERMOSTAT

Upper heating element

Lower heating element

Drain Valve

Thermostats/Waterheater

This is the result of tight-fitting fasteners, the anchors that hold the pipes to the building's frame. They won't let pipes expand, causing them to bend and release repeatedly, making a tapping or creaking sound. Loosening the fasteners or changing from metal to plastic ones will allow the pipes to move freely and stop the noises.

Other noises have a variety of causes. Baseboard heaters make gurgling, sloshing sounds, a result of air bubbles in the hydronic heating system. If the system has a valve at the end with a screw, loosen the screw. This will let out some of the air and reduce or eliminate the noise problem. If this does not work, you should call a plumber.

If your radiator is hissing, the beading valve might be open or loose. Either turn the knob and tighten it or else take a screw driver and tighten it.

Cooling Systems

There's some basic maintenance you can do yourself to get the highest efficiency out of your cooling system. Properly maintained, the system will run at peak efficiency, reducing your electric bill and keeping you more comfortable on the hottest days. Even so, your air conditioner should be serviced by a professional every two years to check the coolant levels.

The coils on an air conditioner are those metal finlike things on the back. The unit will not run well if they are dirty or clogged, so they should be checked every spring. If the fins are clogged with dirt or debris, use a vacuum cleaner to remove the material.

Another method is to spray fins with a garden hose, but if the material is packed in, soaking it might make it harder to remove. If fins are bent, use a screwdriver or putty knife to straighten, being careful not to puncture or break them.

During the hot season, filters should be checked once a month and cleaned if necessary. Dirty, clogged filters will reduce the efficiency of the system by at least 5 percent. If filters are brittle or torn, don't waste your time cleaning them. Replacements can be purchased

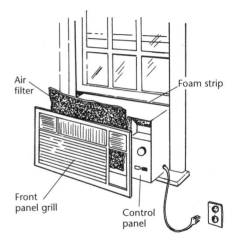

Window air conditioner

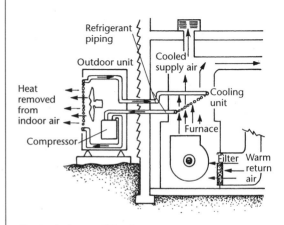

Central air-conditioning system

cheaply at a hardware or home-center store.

Check the weather stripping around the unit once a year and replace if worn. This will help keep the cool air in and the hot air out.

The air conditioner will work best if it is level to the ground, or tilted so that the exterior portion is lower than the inside portion. This allows water that has formed from condensation to drain out of the unit.

If you have a central air-conditioning system, you will need to have it professionally serviced about every two years. The manufacturer can supply a schedule. They will check the compressor and refrigerant levels for you. In the meantime, there are some things you can do to keep the system operating at peak efficiency.

Most central systems use furnace ductwork and blowers to distribute cooled air. You should change your furnace filters regularly or clean them monthly. At least once during the hot weather, clean the evaporator coils by either vacuuming them or blowing clean. (They are triangular in shape, located at the top of the unit.) Carefully straighten any bent fins.

Saving on energy can reduce your bills but it also has an important environmental impact. Energy efficiency is the first defense in reducing greenhouse gases such as carbon dioxide and methane.

Simple Tips to Save Money on Cooling
•Air conditioners perform more efficiently if they are cool, so try to keep yours in the shade. Air conditioners located on the north side of a house use 5 percent less energy than those on the south or west side. If one must be in a sunny spot, build a shade structure for it. However, the air conditioner must have good air flow; allow for about a foot of space on all sides.

•Turn the air conditioner off when you leave the house for several hours.

•Don't set thermostat to the highest setting when you first turn on the air conditioner. It will not cool the room any more quickly and wastes energy.

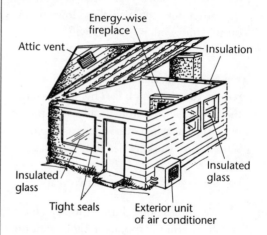

Air-conditioning insulation

•Use a timer on your room air conditioner. Set it to turn on an hour before you get home or an hour before you plan to go into the room, and to turn off after you've left the room or gone to bed.

•Use window treatments to minimize heat entering your home. A cooler room is easier to keep that way.

•Set the air conditioner's thermostat for 78°. This is the recommended energy-efficient cooling temperature.

Simple Tips to Save Money on Heating
According to the American Council for an Energy-Efficient Economy, the single most important thing you can do to save energy in is to make sure your furnaces are running efficiently. More energy is used for heating than for any other purpose in American houses.

Here is a host of other things you can do.

• Turn the thermostat down. You can cut your heating bill by at least 2 percent for every degree you do. For example, if you now pay $1,000 a year for heat with the thermostat set at 68°F, dialing down to 65° during the winter months will save you about $60.

• A setback thermostat is another way to reduce your heating bill. This will turn the thermostat back automatically at a preset time, such as when everyone is asleep or at school and work. The cost for these is between $50 and $150 and they usually pay for themselves in one to two years.

• Leave drapes open during the day, so the sun can warm the room. At night, shut the drapes to keep that warmth in.

• Insulate ductwork. Joints are the most likely place for heat loss. To check, turn the heat on and feel around the joints. If you feel heat seeping through, clean the area and seal it with duct tape.

• Seal all air leaks in the building. Common areas for drafts are doors and where electrical wires and plumbing pipes come into the house. Check weather stripping around windows and doors and replace if loose or missing.

• Caulk and weather-strip around doors, windows and entry points for electrical and plumbing lines.

Water Heaters
According to the Plumbing-Heating-Cooling Information Bureau, the main reason people call in a plumber or heating and cooling expert is that their water heater isn't working. If you encounter this problem and you don't have any experience with water heaters, it is best to call for help. However, when the technician is there, ask questions. For example, is this a problem I can fix? How did you know what the problem was? How can I fix it in the future?

That's not to say you're doomed to calling a professional every time something goes wrong. There are some things you can check for and repair yourself.

First of all, check the water heater to see if there is an external problem such as a flooded basement. If not, check the pilot light or heating element. If you don't know where this is or what kind of heating element you have, check the owner's manual, which should be attached to the back of the unit. If the problem is the heating element, follow the manufacturer's instructions on relighting it. If this does not work, call in a professional repair person.

Insulate water heaters that are 10 years old or older and water heaters in unheated rooms. It is estimated that 10 to 30 percent of the energy it takes to heat your hot water heater is used to just maintain it at a certain temperature.

Set hot water heaters at 120° for best energy use. If your hot water heater only has low, medium or high settings, use the medium one. If your dishwasher requires water at 140°, turn it up for that use and then turn it down again when the cycle is done.

ELECTRICAL SYSTEMS

Unless you're a licensed electrician, it's best to leave the maintenance and care of your home's electrical systems to the experts. But there are a few things you can do to keep things running smoothly, such as replacing worn-out plugs and switches and making sure your electric bill is correct.

Replacing plugs and switches. Plugs and switches wear out over time and need to be replaced. This is a fairly easy task.

Replace electrical plugs when the cord looks frayed or the sheathing is frayed or missing, if the prongs are bent, or if the insulation cap is cracked or missing. First, turn off the power and unplug the unit. Then cut off the damaged part with wire cutters. There are two types of cords, flat or round. You will need to replace the damaged cord with the same kind.

Once cut, the wires need to be split down the middle about two inches, separating the neutral from the hot. You will then need to expose about 3/4 inch of wire on both sides. Once this is done, pry out the plug body, then thread wires into the new shell and attach wires to screws.

Newer plugs snap or clamp onto the cord's end, and you don't need to strip it. For these varieties, pull out interior unit from end by pinching prongs and pulling, then thread cord through. Slide cord into pitch prong and squeeze shut, then feed prong back into cord shell. It does not matter which wires are attached to which screws.

Replacing a lamp switch. Unscrew set screw at base of switch. Pull off shell and insulating sleeve (the part that the light bulb goes into). Pull switch away from socket cap part that set screw is held to. Cut wires. Split about two inches. Strip 1/2 inch of insulation away. Attach wires to screws, then reassemble.

DEALING WITH EMERGENCIES

Sudden emergencies are a regrettable fact of life. The section below gives details on

Deciphering Your Electric Bill

Your electric bill includes charges for maintenance of local gas and electric lines and meters, and other costs such as meter readings. Even if you have not used any gas or electricity for a period of time you will still be billed for these services.

Your bill is based on actual meter readings (the meter may be on the exterior of your house or in your basement). If meter readers are not able to gain access to your meter, the utility company will create an average charge based on your history of usage and the time of year. You are billed on the basis of a kilowatt-hour (Kwh). One Kwh equals the energy needed to run a 100-watt light bulb for 10 hours.

Many electric bills come with usage graphs, intended to help customers conserve energy. These show your average daily electric and/or gas use for each month in the last year and often compare it to the average customer's use.

To check your bill, take the Kwh usage it lists and multiply it by the price per Kwh. Utility companies do make mistakes, so it's always a good idea to double check.

On your bill you might also find a column called Fuel Adjustment. This reflects the change in the purchase cost of fuel.

coping with small emergencies, from power outages to burst and frozen pipes, as well as how to treat the servicepeople who come to fix the problem.

What to do when the power goes out. The only thing you can do about power outages is be prepared for them. Be aware which household appliances and fixtures run on electricity. For example, if you lose your electricity, don't flush toilets. They will flush at first because a storage tank holds water, but the tank will not refill because it uses an electric pump.

Your heating system will go off during a loss of electrical power. Shut all the doors to conserve as much heat as possible. Place towels at the base of doors to unused rooms. Close curtains and shades. To prevent frozen foods from defrosting, don't open the refrigerator unless you need to.

If you have advance notice that the power might go out, fill bathtubs with water. Have candles and flashlights ready. Arrange with other members of the family to meet in one room if the power does fail. Keep bottled water on hand, along with canned food.

Changing a fuse. Changing a fuse is a simple process. If you lose power from overloading a circuit, first turn off and unplug the unit that caused the surge. Then go to your fuse box or circuit-breaker panel. This may be in the basement, garage or laundry room of a house, or in the kitchen or hallway of an apartment.

To replace a fuse without a hassle, remember to keep a flashlight and spare fuse near the box. On newer units with circuit breakers instead of fuses, an overload will cause a switch to be thrown to the "off" position, exposing a red or orange bar. In order to restore power, all you have to do is flip the switch back to the "on" position.

If you have an older unit it may be a bit more complicated. A circuit-breaker panel usually has one or more large main breakers at top. Flip them to "off" to cut power to the panel. In a fuse box, the main cartridge fuses may be mounted on blocks. To cut power, remove these blocks, also called main pullouts. If box has a lever disconnect, switch it off.

You can tell a blown fuse because it looks "burnt" in the center and a metal strip is blackened or broken. Grasp the blown fuse by its glass rim, and turn it counterclockwise. Replace the blown fuse with another one of the same amperage. The amperage will be marked on the outer rim.

Replacing a cartridge fuse. First, remove the block. Then pull out fuse with a fuse puller, a tweezerlike implement that is inside the fuse box (if yours is missing, you can replace it at a hardware store). Replace with fuse of same amperage and type.

Burst and frozen pipes. If a pipe has burst, nothing at all will come out of the faucet. If this happens the water must be turned off. Follow the pipe to a knob or valve—you will probably find one near a wall. If you're lucky, you can shut off the water to only one area of the house. If you can't locate a zone knob to turn off the water, you will have to turn off the water supply for the whole house. (You might want to fill up a few containers or the tub before you do this.) The main shutoff valve in most buildings is found in the exterior wall nearest the street. Once the water is shut off, call a plumber immediately.

If little or no water or only a hiss of air comes out of the faucet when you turn on the tap, you might have a frozen pipe rather than a burst one. The key places to check are cold areas such as the basement. Look for condensation or frost buildup on the pipes. If it is frozen, a blow dryer might solve the problem. Direct warm air at pipe.

Larger pipes will probably require professional attention. To prevent them from bursting, turn off the water supply. However, if you have hydronic heat, remember that the boiler must have a continual water supply while operating.

One way to prevent freezing is to crack open faucets in problem areas, so they emit a trickle of water. Flush unused toilets daily. If freezing is a chronic problem, the troublesome pipe should be relocated or insulated by a professional.

Dealing with Servicepeople
Servicepeople are professionals. They should be treated with respect. Be prepared to tell them all the symptoms of the problem. You might have already done this when you called for service, but information gets distorted when several people pass it along. It will be helpful if you describe the problem in detail. It might be useful to write up a list that you can refer to.

Before they start working you should have cleared the area they will be working in, removing all breakable objects. If you have pets or small children keep them out of the way. Be available for questions, but don't hover.

Replacing Appliances

Appliances are built to last for years. But they do wear out, or newer, more attractive models come on the market. According to the Association of Home Appliance Manufacturers (AHAM), when shopping for appliances, ask the dealer for the product's specification sheet, which gives information on size and power requirements. Study these carefully and note differences between one product and another.

Compare what you really need with what you are paying for. For example, if you want a refrigerator with an ice water or ice cube dispenser on the door, this will add approximately $300 to the ticket price, in addition to a loss of efficiency.

Also ask the dealer to show you the warranty. By law, they must display it or present it on request. Find out what the warranty covers: The entire product? Only certain parts? Is labor included? What period of time does it cover?

Ask the dealer for a copy of the use and care manual. It will teach you about installation and maintenance procedures for each product. Compare this with other products.

Decide on the capacity or size of the product you need. For example, if buying an air conditioner, you need to know the size of the room in order to get one that will work efficiently. All appliances today are required by law to give electrical requirements and the cost to use the system. This is described on the black and yellow "Energy Guide" sticker on the outside of the unit.

Before you buy, clearly establish the cost of delivery and installation. Ask the dealer if they service the appliance or where the closest servicing location is. Compare price in relation to convenience and service. As more features and conveniences are included, the price of the product will go up.

When shopping for appliances, also shop the dealers. If it's not a reputable store or licensed dealership, you could be taken for a ride. Here are some things to look for:

• Shop at stores that have been in business for several years and have a reputation to maintain. Concentrate on ones that specialize in appliances, where the salespeople know what they're talking about.

• Ask friends or neighbors where they purchased their appliances and if they are satisfied with the level of service they received.

• Once you've narrowed your choices down to a few stores, consider not only price, but the other amenities they offer. For example, are delivery and installation free of charge? Do they service the product?

• Compare both prices and extras to see where you can get the best deal. If a product is more expensive at one store, the price might be offset by other factors, such as free insurance, servicing, installation or delivery.

Reading warranties. When you are shopping for a new appliance, according to AHAM, you should compare warranties in the same way you compare other features. You have a legal right to inspect the warranty of a product costing more than $15. There are two types of warranties, full and limited. Under a full warranty, the manufacturer must remedy, without charge, any problem that is the result of the product's failure, not yours, if it occurs within the warranty period, as long as it is implied in the warranty. If a reasonable number of attempts to correct a problem do not succeed, you as the customer must be given the choice of a replacement or a refund. Under a limited warranty, the protection is limited to what is specifically outlined in the terms of the warranty.

Installing and hooking up new appliances. When it comes time to replace appliances, care must be taken when installing. In some cases their essential operating parts are exposed until installed.

Always, inspect the appliance when it is delivered and before you sign for it. If it was damaged in transport, you may refuse delivery. Remember, small problems can lead to big ones. Take note of how the manufacturer packed the product. This alerts you to what it considers the sensitive areas.

Read the instruction booklet before you start any installation. Also, use proper tools and adhere to local building codes. Always make sure electricity is turned off first.

When hooking up a dishwasher or washing machine, follow the manufacturer's instructions carefully. Appliances vary as to installation method and requirements.

Once connected, make sure appliance is level before you try turning it on. In a pinch, try placing a small ball on the surface and to see which way it rolls, but it is easier to use a level if you have one. Adjust the legs to make it level.

Kitchen appliances should be installed by a professional because of electrical and plumbing requirements. Make sure the area you want to install the appliance in is wide enough for it. Refrigerators, for example, should have about ½ inch clearance on the top and sides.

After installing any appliance, read the user's manual thoroughly and teach all family members the correct way to use the appliance. Any misuse will shorten its life span.

Replacing Heating and Cooling Systems

If your heating or cooling system is more than 15 years old you might want to look into replacing it. Newer equipment is about 10 percent more efficient than older equipment. For example, an oil burner is now 78 percent efficient, against 65 percent efficiency for one that is 15 years old.

Ask yourself: Does my system break down at least once a season? Do I have enough hot water? Have my bills gone up considerably? If you answer yes to any of these, contact your heating and cooling contractor for an evaluation.

Sources of Further Information

ASSOCIATIONS

Air-Conditioning & Refrigeration Institute
    4301 North Fairfax Dr., Suite 425
    Arlington, VA 22203
    1-703-524-8800
    Offers several free brochures, including "Some Matches Don't Make Sense," "Consumers Guide to Efficient Climate Control Systems," "Heat, Cool, Save Energy With a Heat Pump," "How to Humidify Your Home or Business," "Breathing Clean" and "How to Keep Your Cool and Save Cold Cash."

Aluminum Association Inc.
    900 19th St. NW, Suite 300
    Washington, DC 20006
    1-202-862-5100

American Gas Association
    1515 Wilson Blvd.
    Arlington, VA 22209
    1-703-841-8400

Association of Home Appliance Manufacturers (AHAM)
    20 North Wacker Dr.
    Chicago, IL 60606
    1-312-984-5800
    Offers several brochures, including "Microwave Oven Facts" and "Do Your Part. . . Protect Against Range Tipping,"

both free with SASE; "Comparing Room Air Conditioners: An AHAM Consumer Buying Guide," $1; "Consumers' Selection Guide to Refrigerators and Freezers," $2.

Better Heating-Cooling Council
    35 Russo Pl.
    Berkley Heights, NJ 07922
    1-908-464-8200
    Offers a variety of consumer information. Call for details.

Cedar Shake & Shingle Bureau
    515 116th Ave. NE, Suite 275
    Bellevue, WA 98004
    1-206-453-1323

The Hydronic Institute Inc.
    35 Russo Pl.
    P.O. Box 218
    Berkley Heights, NJ 07922
    1-908-464-8200
    "Selecting a Heating System" and "Home Heating Costs," $2 each.

National Wood Flooring Association
    11046 Manchester Rd.
    St. Louis, MO 63122
    1-314-821-8654
    "Easy Hardwood Floor Care," free with SASE.

National Kitchen Cabinet Association
    P.O. Box 6830
    Falls Church, VA 07840
    1-703-237-7580

National Paint and Coating Association
    1500 Rhode Island Ave. NW
    Washington, DC 20005
    1-202-462-6272

National Pest Control Association
    8100 Oak St.
    Dun Loring, VA 22027
    1-703-573-8330

Offers a 16-page booklet for $1, "The Uninvited Guests," covering the most common problems. For specific problems call the association for a list of pamphlets.

Plumbing-Heating-Cooling Information Bureau
    303 East Wacker Dr.
    Chicago, IL 60601
    1-312-372-7331

Vinyl Siding Institute
    355 Lexington Ave.
    New York, NY 10017
    1-212-351-5400
    "The Cleaning of Vinyl Siding," "What Homeowners Want to Know About Solid Vinyl Siding" and "Homes of Distinction," free with SASE.

The Paint Quality Institute
    P.O. Box 640
    Spring House, PA 19477
    1-215-923-9600
    Brochures, for $2 each, include "Don't Just Paint It! Beautify and Protect It!", "Your Guide To Home Painting" and "Advice and Ideas For Better Home Painting."

U.S. Dept. of Energy
    P.O. Box 8900
    Silver Springs, MD 20907
    1-800-523-2929

Water Quality Association
    4151 Naperville Rd.
    Lisle, IL 60532
    1-708-505-0160

MANUFACTURERS

American Olean Tile Co. (ceramic tile)
    1000 Cannon Ave.
    Lansdale, PA 19446
    1-215-855-1111

American Standard Inc. (plumbing fixtures and fittings)
    One Centennial Plaza
    P.O. Box 6820
    Piscataway, NJ 08855-6820
    1-908-980-3000

Andersen Windows Inc.
    100 Fourth Ave.
    N. Bayport, MN 55003-1096
    1-800-426-4261
    Broan Mfg. Co. (range hoods)
    P.O. Box 140
    Hartford, WI 53027
    1-800-637-1453

Combat Information Line (pest control)
    1-800-426-6228

Elkay Mfg., Co. (plumbing fixtures and fittings)
    2222 Camden Court
    Oak Brook, IL 60521
    1-800-635-7500
    Formby's Inc. (wood finishes)
    825 Crossover Lane
    Memphis, TN 38117
    Write for information.

GE Appliances
    Appliance Park
    Louisville, KY 40225
    1-800-626-2000

KitchenAid (appliances)
    701 Main St.
    St. Joseph, MI 49085
    1-800-422-1230

Kohler Co. (plumbing fixtures)
    Kohler, WI 53044
    1-800-4KOHLER

Marvin Windows and Doors
    P.O. Box 100
    Warroad, MN 56763
    1-800-346-5128

Minwax Co. Inc. (wood finishes)
    102 Chestnut Ridge Plaza
    Montvale, NJ 07645
    1-201-391-0253

BOOKS

Basic Home Wiring Illustrated. By the Editors of Sunset Books and Sunset Magazine, Lane Publishing Co., Menlo Park, Calif., 1983.

The Best Home for Less. Steve Carlson, Avon Books, New York, 1992.

500 Terrific Ideas for Home Maintenance and Repair. Jack Maguire, Simon & Schuster, New York, 1991.

Home Plumbing Projects and Repairs. Black & Decker Home Improvement Library, Cy DeCosse Inc., Minnetonka, Minn., 1990.

Popular Mechanics Home How-To: Home Repairs and Improvements. Albert Jackson and David Day, William Morrow, New York, 1989.

Popular Mechanics: Large Appliance Repair Manual. Hearst Books, New York, 1982.

6

Cleaning

Laundry Basics

Most washable clothing can be machine laundered and dried, so knowing how to use a washing machine and dryer correctly, whether it's in your own home or a commercial laundromat, makes doing the laundry easier and results in cleaner clothes.

AT HOME

Home washing machines have settings for hot, warm and cold water, permanent press, delicate and normal cycles, and varying load sizes. The benefit of these various settings is that by sorting your clothes properly (See "Laundry Procedures," below), you will be able to get the best results from doing different loads.

Home dryers have at least two temperature settings and a variety of cycles that can be set with a timer or set to sense the moisture level in clothes. The "air dry" cycle tumbles clothes dry without using heat. (See "Drying," below).

AT THE LAUNDROMAT

With a coin-operated machine you will usually have fewer choices in terms of cycles and temperatures. Since you have less control over the machine, it's even more important to separate your clothes into various loads, even if you may have to spend more money on doing several small loads rather than one big one.

Most coin-operated commercial dryers have only one temperature setting—high—so you must be careful not to overdry clothes, which creates wrinkling. Knit clothing should not even be dried in these dyers, since it might shrink. If you don't have a washer and dryer at home, in most cases it is probably safer either to hand-wash knits and delicates (see "Hand Washing," below), or place them in plastic bags after washing at a commercial laundry (the spin-dry cycle should ensure that they are damp, rather than sopping wet) and take them home to air dry.

LAUNDRY SUPPLIES

In your home, you will benefit from keeping washing supplies on hand in the laundry area. It's helpful to set up the area with shelves for supplies, a sorting table, a clothesline, a wastebasket and an ironing board, as well as a clothing rod with plenty of hangers. If more than one person has responsibility for the laundry, it might also be a good idea to have a bulletin board on which to post laundry tips and special instructions.

Other things that are useful to have on hand include a sewing kit for emergency repairs; measuring cups and spoons for adding detergents and cleaning aids; large and small dishpans and plastic pails; laundry baskets or bins, which make it easier to carry laundry, whether dirty or clean, from room to room. They can be color-coded to family members.

If you do your laundry in a laundromat, you can save time by setting up a kit of supplies to take with you. This kit should include detergent, bleach, fabric softener, a stain spray or stick, anti-static sheets and other cleaning aids. Also useful are plastic bags to hold wet items that have been washed but can't be put in the dryer.

Detergent

There are several different types and many different brands of detergents available today, including liquid or granular (also known as powder), phosphate and nonphosphate, and detergent with bleach or fabric softener added. The most traditional form, granular, is still the most widely used. Liquid detergents come next; they are useful for washing in cold water washes, in which powder detergents don't dissolves well, and for pretreating spots and stains. Those to which bleach or fabric softener have been added are among the most recent introductions. The bleach improves the overall cleanliness of your wash, as well as assisting in stain removal. Detergent with fabric softener, available in powder or liquid form, is mainly a convenience.

The type of detergent you use will affect the cleanliness of your wash. For example, in hard-water areas (above 10 grains per gallon), some nonphosphate detergents won't get clothes as clean as those that contain phosphates. In addition, some nonphosphate detergents are known to react with the minerals in hard water to leave a lintlike residue on clothing, sheets and towels, causing them to look faded and feel rough. Switching to a liquid or a phosphate granular detergent will often improve the results.

When using a detergent, follow package directions to determine the correct amount to add. However, most package directions are for an average load with average soil in water of average hardness (4 to 9 grains per gallon). If your load is heavily soiled, larger than usual, or you have hard water you should use more detergent; if washing a smaller than usual or lightly soiled load, or if you have soft water (0 to 3 grains per gallon), use less.

Bleach

Bleach comes in two types, chlorine and oxygen. Both are intended to make your colored clothes brighter, your white clothes whiter and to assist in getting rid of stains.

Chlorine bleach is the strongest type. It can make gray, dingy clothes white again, but can also fade colors. A powerful chemical, liquid chlorine bleach can also damage fabrics if applied directly. It should always be diluted. If your washing machine has a bleach dispenser, follow the instructions for use. If not, dilute the bleach in four parts water and add to wash after the agitation cycle begins.

Oxygen bleach is not as strong as chlorine bleach—it can maintain whiteness, but will not restore it—and is safe to use on all types of clothing. It may be added to your washing machine along with your detergent.

Fabric Softener

This product reduces static cling, minimizes wrinkling, and softens clothing. There are two types, those added to the rinse water and those added to the dryer.

Type of Load	Laundry Products
Regular fabrics (sturdy cottons and linens, woolens) everything washable except permanent press, delicates,	Hot/warm water: any laundry detergent Cold water: Liquid or predissolved granular detergent Chlorine or oxygen bleach Fabric softener
Permanent press/no iron items (all permanent-press and other easy-care items	Any laundry detergent Chlorine or oxygen bleach Fabric softener
Delicates (lingerie, loosely knit items, "hand-washable" items) sheer fabrics, lace-trimmed or embroidered articles,	Warm water: Any laundry detergent Cold water: Liquid or predissolved granular detergent Chlorine bleach (except for items containing Spandex) Oxygen bleach Fabric softener
Wool (machine-washable and "hand-washable" woolen items)	Liquid or predissolved granular detergent

Adapted from "Different Suds for Different Duds," The Maytag Company.

Rinse-added softeners go into the final rinse of the wash cycle. Your washing machine may have a fabric softener dispenser, which means that the softener will be added to the final rinse automatically. Follow manufacturer's instructions for use. If not, add the diluted softener per package instructions as soon as the agitation begins in the final rinse. Dryer-added fabric-softener sheets are simply added to the load at the beginning of the drying cycle. Use only one sheet per load.

See chart below for information on which types of products perform best on various loads.

Laundry Procedures

If you prepare your clothes and other items properly for washing, you can avoid problems such as shrinking, stretching, bleeding, fading, excessive lint, pilling, snags and broken zippers. Then wash the clothes according to the instructions on the care label (see "Reading the Care Label," below.)

1. First, mend any tears or snags and sew on loose buttons before washing. Empty out pockets, and do up zippers, hooks and buttons to prevent snags. To ensure that collars and cuffs of shirts get clean, turn

Laundry Tips

• You can clean the washing machine and remove mineral deposits by filling the washer with warm water and adding ½ gallon (2 liters) of white vinegar. Then put the empty machine through a wash cycle. Pour some of the solution through the fabric-softener dispenser to get that clean.

• Moisture lessens the cleaning power of powder detergents. In order to store large amounts of granular detergent properly, empty it out of its box into a container with a sealable plastic top, such as an old commercial-size ice cream bucket. Be sure to label the outside of container with contents.

• It's more efficient to add detergent and fill the machine before you add the clothes, since this spreads the detergent more evenly through the wash water. Use the time waiting for the machine to fill to sort the clothes.

• To avoid fading and bleeding of colors, test new clothes for color-fastness before you put them in the washer with your other clothes. Soak garment in water first or wash it separately.

• In order to test load size, lift the lid and keep your eye on a small item. Check to see how many times it comes to the surface in one minute. If it makes less than five appearances, the load is too large and garments will not be agitated enough to get clean.

• The optimum length of time to wash a load is about eight minutes, even though some washers have cycles that can be set for twice as long. Overwashing redeposits soil on clothing, so washing them longer won't make them any cleaner. Only frequency of washing can do that, and up to three washings may be needed to remove built-up stains completely.

• Heavily soiled items may need presoaking before being put through the wash cycle. You can do this by hand or in the

machine (a machine presoak is more effective).

By hand: Fill a pail or tub with 3 quarts (3 liters) cool water. Add a commercial presoak or 2 tablespoons (30 ml) of any type of ammonia. Add heavily soiled items or clothes with disagreeable odors. Plunge them up and down a few times (use your hands or an implement) and repeat if it seems necessary. Then wring out and wash as usual.

In the machine: Fill the washer with cold water to a level that just covers clothing. Add a commercial presoak or 1/4 cup (60 ml) ammonia and agitate for five minutes. Drain machine, then wash clothes as usual. Some machines have a presoak cycle that you can set to precede the regular wash cycle.

• In order to keep light-colored garments from becoming heavily soiled, use a spray-on fabric protector. This works well on items such as white canvas shoes or khaki raincoats.

garment inside out and button the top button. Loosely tie sashes and drawstrings. Then pretreat all spots and stains with a solid or liquid pretreat such as Spray & Wash, Shout or Stain Stick.

2. Sort garments by color. Wash white items separately to prevent dinginess. Separate colorfast items from those that might bleed. Put similar clothes together in the same load.

3. Sort similar-color garments by fabric. Separate man-made fibers from natural-fiber garments; man-made fibers can attract the oils released by natural fibers during washing. These can build up, creating noticeable stains after several washings. Garments that shed a good deal of lint (fleece or terrycloth) should also go in a separate load.

4. Sort loads by bulk. In order to get clean, clothes need enough room to agitate freely. For example, one king-size sheet, a twin sheet and a few small items of clothing make up a sufficient load for the average home washing machine.

5. Sort loads according to how dirty they are. Very soiled items, such as work clothes, should be washed together. It's best to presoak them, to keep wash water from becoming dirty (see "Laundry Tips," above, for instructions on presoaking).

6. Separate delicate items, and set them aside to do a wash using the delicate cycle, or hand wash (see "Hand Washing," below). Very delicate items, such as knitted nylon hosiery, or items such as brassieres, which have hardware that might snag, can be washed in a lingerie bag using the delicate cycle.

7. The most efficient way to wash clothes in cold or hot water using powder detergent is first to dissolve 1/4 cup (60 ml) of powder in hot water, then add 1/4 cup (60 ml) ammonia. Increase the amount of ammonia for a heavily soiled load. Add mixture to washing machine. With liquid detergent, use 2 tablespoons (3 ml) of liquid with 1/4 cup (60 ml) ammonia and pour directly into washer. *Don't add bleach when using ammonia.* Add clothes and wash as usual. Warm or hot water is more effective than cold water in cleaning heavily soiled or greasy clothes.

8. In order to remove soapy film from clothes, add 1/4 cup (60 ml) white vinegar to wash during rinse portion of cycle. Use the fabric-softener dispenser to add vinegar. You may need to add up to 1 cup (1/4 liter) of vinegar to each load, depending on the amount of soap you have used. Vinegar added to the rinse water will not cause clothes to smell.

HAND WASHING

To wash delicate garments by hand, first pretreat all spots and stains with a solid or liquid pretreat such as Spray & Wash, Shout or Stain Stick, then fill a dishpan or sink with cool water (up to 85°F; 29°C).

Add detergent and mix with water before adding clothing. Squeeze suds gently through garment without agitating. Rinse several times in cool water without wringing or twisting.

To dry knits, roll in a towel to absorb excess moisture, then lay flat (on towel or rack) to dry. Drip-dry other garments by hanging on a rust-proof hanger. Blot with a towel to remove excess moisture, but do not squeeze or wring.

Fasten zippers and top buttons on blouses, shirts and dresses. Straighten garment to hang evenly and smooth stitching on collars and seams to prevent puckering. If a garment is properly drip-dried, it will need little or no ironing.

READING THE CARE LABEL
Always check the care label on a garment and follow its instructions when laundering. Some of the most common care-label instructions and what they mean are as follows:

Hand wash: see "Hand Washing," above.

Machine wash: See "Laundry Procedures," above.

Delicate or gentle cycle: Set the washer to shorten the wash cycle time and reduce speed of agitation. Most home machines are equipped with a gentle or delicate setting that does this. Use for lingerie, sheers, laces and washable knits.

Permanent press: The permanent-press cycle on the washing machine incorporates a cool rinse before the spin-dry cycle to prevent wrinkles from setting. Always use cool-rinse setting for permanent-press fabrics.

Wash separately: Usually because garment is bulky, tends to bleed, shed or attract lint.

With like colors: Wash garment with fabrics of similar hue or intensity to prevent bleeding onto light-colored fabrics.

Warm rinse: Water should be at 90 to 110°F (32-43°C) to prevent soap residue, especially if you have hard water.

Cold rinse: Water up to 85°F (29°C) will prevent wrinkling, especially in permanent-press fabrics. The cold-rinse setting is an energy-saving tactic and is effective for most garments.

No spin/Do not spin: Remove garments from washer before start of spin cycle to prevent wrinkling and twisting out of shape. Recommended for drip-dry and knit fabrics.

Do not wring: To prevent knits from wrinkling or twisting out of shape, do not wring by hand or use mechanical wringer.

Damp-wipe only: Some extremely fragile fabrics cannot be dipped in water and must be wiped by hand with a damp cloth. This method can also be used for many fabrics labeled "Dry Clean Only."

Bleach when needed: Use chlorine or oxygen-based bleach to whiten, remove stains, or disinfect fabric.

Do not bleach: Non-colorfast fabrics or those with a flame-retardant coating may be damaged if bleach is used; it may cause colors to bleed, weaken fibers or turn whites yellow or gray.

Only nonchlorine bleach when needed: Use only oxygen bleach to whiten or remove stains. Chlorine bleach will damage fabric.

Tumble dry: It's OK to put garment in the dryer at recommended setting. If no specific setting is given, use Hot.

Medium heat: To prevent wrinkles or damage, use the Medium Heat setting, which may be labeled Permanent Press on some dryers.

Low heat: To avoid damage, wrinkles or shrinkage, use the Low Heat setting on your dryer.

Durable or permanent press: The Permanent Press setting of your dryer includes a cool-down cycle to reduce wrinkling. Use for synthetics and blends.

No heat: Use Air Dry cycle or set dryer to operate without heat to dry heat-sensitive items.

Remove promptly: To prevent wrinkling, take garments out of the dryer as soon as it finishes its cycle.

Drip-dry: Hang wet garment on rust-proof hanger or rack and let dry. Hand shape or smooth.

Line-dry: Hang wet items on clothesline to dry. Recommended for fabrics that shrink or stretch out of shape if machine-dried.

Line-dry in shade: Hang on line out of direct sunlight to avoid damage or fading.

Line-dry away from heat: Keep this garment from heat to prevent shrinkage or stiffening.

Dry flat: In order to maintain shape of garment, lay on rack or horizontal surface to dry.

Block to dry: Carefully shape garment to original proportions to prevent stretching. Let dry flat.

Iron: Garment may be pressed. If no setting is specified, it's safe to use High.

Warm iron: Set iron to Medium or to Rayon, Polyester, Silks, Blends to avoid damaging fabric.

Cool iron: Use Low or the setting for acetates, acrylics, sheer synthetics.

Do not iron: Fabrics may melt or finish may be ruined if ironed.

Iron wrong side out: Follow this instruction for fabrics with a nap or finish that might be crushed or marred by pressing (velvet, corduroy, nylon).

Steam press/steam iron: It's all right to use the steam setting on your iron, as moisture will not damage fabric.

No steam/Do not steam: Fabric could shrink or be damaged by use of steam while pressing. Crepe may shrink, metallic may tarnish and stain, or taffeta may lose lustrous finish if they come in contact with moisture.

Steam only: Hold iron on steam setting just above surface of fabric, or use portable steamer. Recommended for fabrics with nap or pile.

Iron damp: Sprinkle or spray fabric before pressing. Recommended for cotton and linen.

Use press cloth: To prevent shine or scorching, lay damp or dry cloth on top of garment before pressing.

Professionally dry-clean: Take to full-service dry cleaner, rather than bulk or coin-operated type.

Petroleum, fluorocarbon or perchlorethylene: Refers to specific type of dry-cleaning solution to be used on garment.

Leather clean: Take to dry cleaner that specializes in cleaning leather (see sidebar, "Cleaning Leather and Suede").

International Symbols
The washing symbol, an open-ended, upright box containing a wavy line, indicates washing instructions. The number 60 (for 60°C, or 150°F) means

garment may be washed in warm or hot water; 30 (86°F) means wash in cool or cold water.

The drying symbol, a box enclosing a circle, means that the garment may be tumble-dried.

The triangle symbol means that a garment may be bleached using a chlorine-based bleach.

The ironing symbol indicates ironing instructions: One dot means a cool iron, two dots a medium iron, three dots a hot iron.

A circle means that a garment may be dry-cleaned. A P within the circle specifies perchlorethylene solution; an A means any normal method; F indicates the "Solvent F" process.

An "X" through any of these symbols turns it into its opposite: *Do not* tumble dry, iron, bleach or dry-clean.

FIBERS: HOW TO LAUNDER

Always check the care label before washing or drying any garment (see above). Certain fibers, such as silk, rayon or wool, benefit from special treatment. Others, like cotton or synthetic knits, don't have to be treated as carefully.

Natural Fibers

Silk. Most silks must be dry-cleaned; some may be hand-washed. Check care label for instructions and do not wring or twist when washing.

Cotton. Most cotton fabrics are machine-washable, using a regular cycle and hot water. Dry on regular cycle and use a hot iron.

Linen. Most linen fabrics can be machine-washed using a regular cycle and warm or hot water and machine-dried on the regular cycle, finishing with a hot iron. However, since linen wrinkles easily and tends to bleed, dry-cleaning may be preferable.

Wool. Wool fabrics should be dry-cleaned unless the label says they may be washed. Knits can be hand-washed using a mild soap, then laid flat to dry.

Artificial Fibers

Acetate. Dry-cleaning is best, then finish with a cool iron.

Acrylic. Wash by hand or in the washing machine, dry on cool cycle or drip-dry, touch up with warm iron (do not press).

Modacrylic. If the fabric has a pile, dry-clean it. Some may be machine-washed (check label) using warm water, then put in dryer on cool cycle and finished with cool iron.

Nylon. Can be hand- or machine-washed. Does not need to be ironed if taken out of dryer as soon as cycle finishes.

Polyester. Wash by hand or in machine. Does not need to be ironed if removed from dryer immediately.

Rayon. Hand- or machine-wash on gentle cycle with lukewarm water, then finish with cool iron. Many rayon items are dry-clean-only.

Spandex. Wash by hand or in machine using lukewarm water. Drip-dry or machine-dry on cool cycle.

MACHINE-DRYING PROCEDURES

Do not overload dryer; this can cause wrinkles and wastes energy, since an overloaded dryer is less efficient.

Do not overdry clothes; this can cause shrinkage, wrinkling and static cling. Try to remove clothes from the dryer when they are still slightly damp, then hang on hangers or on rack to dry completely.

Shake each piece of clothing when you take it out of the washer, to loosen wrinkles before drying. Sort items into small loads according to weight of garment: Towels and jeans should be in one load, nightgowns and lingerie in another. Permanent-press and wash-and-wear clothing should be dried separately as well.

Lingerie and knits should be dried on a short cycle with low heat and removed when still damp. Knits should be dried carefully in the dryer or else air-dried, to prevent shrinkage. Vinyl, rubber and rubber-backed items can be dried in the dryer on a short cycle with no heat. Never machine-dry silk, fiberglass or wool. Bras and other items containing elastic should be dried on low heat to prevent loss of stretch.

Ironing

If you dry your clothes properly, you will find that you will have to do very little ironing. But sometimes ironing is needed. Here are some tips on the basics:

Ironing is gliding the iron across the surface of the fabric; *pressing* is applying a heated iron to fabric and then lifting it up again, without the gliding motion. Use ironing for large areas of fabric, pressing for details such as collars and cuffs. Ironing should be done with straight strokes along the grain of the fabric, as diagonal or circular strokes can cause fabric to stretch.

When ironing, try to avoid wrinkling the parts that have already been ironed, then touch up the details.

For routine ironing, it's best to begin with items requiring the steam setting, then empty the iron before using it on fabric or garments that need dry heat.

Iron shine is shininess on fabric caused by pressing too hard with a hot iron, usually on dark colors and thickly layered areas. To avoid it, use a pressing cloth or a soleplate cover, or press lightly on the wrong side of the fabric.

Don't iron stained or soiled garments, as the heat will set the stain.

Use care when pressing fabrics with a nap to avoid crushing it. It's best to put a thick towel under the fabric, then press from the wrong side.

A spray bottle of water is handy for spritzing stubborn wrinkles and creases.

Keep your iron and ironing-board cover clean. To remove starch or sizing buildup on the soleplate of your iron, pour a capful of ammonia on a damp, clean washcloth or rag, then fold in quarters. Put iron on medium heat, then stroke it over ammonia-soaked cloth, rotating it slightly to remove buildup. Unfold fabric to reveal fresh surface, and continue until iron is clean. To get rid of melted plastic, set iron at low temperature and rub with a soft cloth. If this doesn't work, use fine steel wool. To remove tough, gummy buildup, apply oven cleaner to the soleplate of the iron and let sit for five minutes and wipe with a paper towel. Repeat if necessary. Laundering should be enough to remove soil from ironing board cover.

A hand-held steamer is great for quick touch-ups, but *never* use it on a garment while someone is wearing it.

To smooth the surface or your iron and make it glide more easily, put a piece of thick brown paper on your ironing board and put a piece of wax paper over it; then slide a medium-warm iron over the wax paper.

To prevent scorch marks, do not use an iron that is too hot and never allow the iron to rest in one spot on the fabric. To remove light scorch marks, sponge with a solution of hydrogen peroxide diluted in 20 times as much water. For wool, add a few drops of ammonia. Place a clean white towel beneath the scorched area, apply solution and let it soak in for a few minutes, then place a dry towel under the area and dab with cool water to get rid of solution.

Dry Clean Only

Most items can be safely dry-cleaned unless the care label says "Do Not Dry Clean." In general, you should dry-clean dark clothes (including dark-toned prints), loosely woven fabrics, brocade, chiffon, metallic fabrics, taffeta, satin and charmeuse, as well as any garment that says "Dry Clean Only" on the care label. Because of inner construction, suits should be professionally dry-cleaned and pressed. Down garments also fare better when dry-cleaned rather than machine-washed. Fur must be dry-cleaned by a professional using the fur method, once every one or two years. Synthetic fur is cleaned using the same process.

There are three types of dry cleaning. Full-service dry cleaners provide cleaning services, pretreatment of stains, spot and stain removal, solvent cleaning, lint removal, professional pressing and often minor repairs. Clothes should be returned on hangers, enclosed in plastic bags. You pay a fee per each garment cleaned.

Dry-cleaning by bulk means that garments are priced by weight, and you pay by the pound. Services including pretreatment of stains but not spot removal or pressing. You receive each garment on a hanger, protected by a plastic bag. Keep a list of what you take to the dry cleaner, since they don't always.

Coin-operated dry-cleaning machines, often available at commercial laundromats, allow you to dry-clean your garments for yourself. You pay by the load, which can include several pieces. It's best to separate clothes into light and dark.

Cleaning Leather or Suede

Leather must be cleaned by a special leather process to keep it from shrinking, stiffening, and fading or darkening. Surface soil can be removed with a brush, or with a rag and saddle soap. Most dry cleaners will clean leather, although some have more experience than others. Fabric garments with leather trim must be cleaned by the leather process or the color of the leather will bleed onto the fabric. Leather should not be stored in a plastic bag after being cleaned or it will stiffen.

Suede can be cleaned by a specialist using the same process as leather. In order to remove surface soiling, use a wire suede brush or a dry sponge. This will also prevent the nap from flattening.

Many dry cleaners offer leather cleaning. Look in the Yellow Pages under "Leather Cleaning," or ask the store where you bought your leather garment if they can recommend a cleaner that specializes in leather and suede.

Before dry-cleaning clothing by any of the above methods, be sure to empty pockets completely. Remove buttons that could be damaged or wrap them in foil. Make simple repairs yourself, or identify them to the dry cleaner.

Stains from A to Z

The sidebar that follows, "The All-Purpose Spotting Kit," details the various stain-removal solutions that are mentioned below. Procedures are given in several steps. If a stain appears to be gone and you haven't reached the end of the suggested steps, it's generally safe to stop, with exceptions as noted. Always wash clothing as usual after stain-removing steps are completed, except as noted. For items that can't be laundered, such as carpeting, upholstery, vinyl flooring or bedding, rinse carefully with a small amount of clear, cool water (see "Cleaning Large Items," below).

Alcohol. First, sponge with cool water and if you can, soak the stain in soapy water for at least 30 minutes. If fabric or item is bleachable, soak in a solution of 2 tablespoons (30 ml) chlorine bleach to 1 quart (1 liter) water and rinse. After soaking, sponge nonbleachables with cool water, then pat dry with a towel.

For carpets, drapes and upholstery. Apply detergent solution and blot with clean damp cloth; then apply vinegar solution and blot with clean damp cloth; then ammonia solution, blotted with clean damp cloth. If needed, apply hydrogen peroxide as well. Rinse with cold water. For stain-guard-protected carpets, if the stain is from clear drinks, wine or beer, apply carpet shampoo diluted according to directions on bottle, then vinegar solution. For cocktail stains, apply carpet shampoo, then rinse with water. Allow to dry completely, then clean with dry-cleaning fluid.

Antiperspirant buildup. First, wet the stain, then apply detergent or pre-wash soil and stain remover, such as Stain Stick, Shout or Spray & Wash. Rinse, then let dry. If fabric may be bleached, soak in solution of 1/2 teaspoon oxalic acid (available from hardware store or pharmacy) in 1 cup (80 ml) hot water for one hour. Rinse, repeat soaking process twice, then rinse in solution of 1 1/2 cup (120 ml) white vinegar to 1 gallon (3 3/4 liters) water. Then wash garment with regular load. For nonbleachable fabrics, apply hydrogen peroxide or oxygen bleach to area after testing fabric for colorfastness. Let stand for 30 minutes or longer. Then rinse. If color has faded, apply solution of half ammonia, half water to restore, then rinse.

Beer. First blot with towel, then rinse in cool water. Add a few drops of white vinegar or lemon juice to 1 cup (1/4 liter) water, and rub gently into stain until solution penetrates, then rinse. Work in paste of powdered presoak and water, then wash in normal load. For carpets, drapes and upholstery: See "Alcohol," above.

Blood. If fresh, sponge area with cool water. Soak bleachable fabric in cool water for 30 minutes, then rinse. Soak in solution of 3 tablespoons (45 ml) ammonia to 1 gallon cool water for 15 minutes, then rinse. Work detergent into stain and wash in normal load. For nonbleachables, pat stain dry after sponging, then apply hydrogen peroxide and rinse. If any stain remains, sponge with oxygen bleach solution (2 tablespoon/30 ml bleach to 1 quart/1 liter water), then rinse. Make solution of 2 tablespoon (30 ml) powdered enzyme presoak to 1 gallon (3 3/4 liter) water and apply to stain, then rinse.

For dried blood, first soak in cool soapy water, changing it as necessary, then rinse and soak again in ammonia-water solution (1/4 cup/60 ml ammonia to 1 gallon/3 3/4 liter water). For bleachable fabrics, apply a paste of powdered presoak and water, then rinse and air-dry. For nonbleachables, soak fabric in solution of 1/4 cup (60 ml) salt to 2 quarts (2 liters) cool water, then rinse. Soak in ammonia solution as above. If stain remains, soak in solution of 2 to 3 tablespoons (30-45 ml) enzyme presoak in 1 gallon (3 1/4 liter) water.

For carpets, drapes and upholstery: Carefully scrape as much up off surface as you can. Apply cool detergent solution, blot with a clean damp cloth, then apply cool ammonia solution, blot and rinse. If stain remains, apply rust remover followed by 3-to-5-percent hydrogen peroxide solution. For carpets protected by stain guard: Follow the same procedure as above, but rinse with water before applying detergent and follow the ammonia solution by blotting or misting with a vinegar solution.

Butter, oil. Remove excess and blot with clean towel. Apply absorbent such as talcum powder or cornmeal and let stand for several hours. For bleachable fabrics, apply prewash stain remover (if stain is dirty as well as greasy, use glycerin or petroleum jelly for this step) and rub in with your thumbs. Then wash in hot water. Use dry-cleaning solvent if traces remain. For nonbleachable fabric, work detergent into stain, then wash fabric in warm water. If stain persists, lay fabric stain side down on a clean towel and apply dry-cleaning solvent from underside.

For carpets, drapes and upholstery: Use a commercial petroleum solvent spotter, paint thinner or dry-cleaning solution. Work all the way into the center to avoid creating a ring. Blot with clean damp cloth, apply detergent solution and rinse. For stain-guard carpets: Apply dry-cleaning solvent.

Catsup or tomato sauce. Remove excess, then blot stain with moist towel to keep it from spreading. For bleachable fabrics, apply a pre-wash stain remover, then rinse; apply again and rinse. Apply paste of powdered presoak and water, then rinse. Repeat if stain remains, and add vinegar to the final rinse. If fabric is nonbleachable, blot stain and apply absorbent such as cornmeal, talcum powder, chalk, fuller's earth or whiting, then blot again. Working from underside of fabric, work in dry-cleaning solvent with thumbs.

For carpets, drapes and upholstery: Scrape carefully and blot to remove residue. Sponge with dry-cleaning fluid. Blot with clean damp towel. If this doesn't work, sponge with solution of half vinegar, half water, then rinse. If this is ineffective, apply digestant paste, let it sit for 30 minutes, then rinse. As a last resort, bleach with hydrogen peroxide solution. For stain-guard carpets: Remove as much of the stain as possible. Clean area with carpet shampoo, blot with clean damp cloth, then mist or blot with vinegar solution. Rinse thoroughly with clear water.

Coffee, tea, hot chocolate. Blot stain with damp cloth, then pour cool water through stain. Let soak in cool water, work in detergent, then rinse. If traces remain, apply dry-cleaning solvent. Apply a paste of powdered presoak and water, wash in warm water, then pour boiling water from a height (18 to 24 inches) onto taut fabric.

For carpets, drapes and upholstery: Rub with a paste of raw egg yolk and rinse. For an old stain, apply a few drops of denatured alcohol, and rinse again. For stain-guard carpets: Apply a detergent solution, rinse, then mist or blot with vinegar solution. Let dry completely, then apply dry-cleaning solution.

Cosmetics. Blot well, then rub in dry-cleaning solvent, starting from edges and working toward the center. Wash spot with liquid detergent, rinse and let air-dry. Apply prewash stain remover, then blot, rinse and repeat application. Rinse in solution of water and a few drops of ammonia, then wash in warm water. Soak in solution of 2 to 3 tablespoons (30–45 ml) vinegar to 1 gallon (3 3/4 liter) warm water for 30 minutes.

For carpets, drapes and upholstery: Apply dry-cleaning solution, blot with clean damp cloth, then apply a detergent solution, followed by an ammonia solution and a vinegar solution, blotting in between each. Rinse with cool, clear water. For stain-guard carpets: Clean with dry-cleaning fluid, blot, then apply detergent solution or carpet shampoo. Rinse, then blot with ammonia solution, blot with clean damp cloth, then blot or mist with vinegar solution. Rinse.

Egg, meat juices, gravy. Moisten stain in cool water, then blot with towel. If fabric is bleachable, soak in cool water for 30 minutes, then work in enzyme paste made of powdered presoak and water, and wash in hot water. Soak in solution of 2 tablespoons (30 ml) enzyme presoak to 1 gallon (3 3/4 liter) water for 30 minutes For non-bleachables, soak in cool water then work in enzyme paste and wash. If traces remain, wash with soap (not detergent) and apply prewash stain remover from underside of fabric.

For carpets, drapes and upholstery: Remove as much as possible with clean, damp cloth. Apply digestant paste, leave on for 30 minutes, then rinse with warm water. If stain remains, sponge with detergent solution. Rinse, blot and allow to dry. If stain remains, sponge with dry-cleaning fluid. For stain-guard carpets: Use dry-cleaning fluid.

Fruit jams, jellies. If fresh, rinse stain in cool water and blot. Keep moist until you can soak it in cool water for at least 30 minutes. After soaking, if stain remains, work in detergent, then soak in solution of 2 to 3 tablespoons (30-45 ml) enzyme presoak to 1 gallon (3 3/4 liter) warm water, then wash in hot water. If traces persist and fabric is bleachable, force boiling water through fabric (it's best to pour it over taut fabric from 18 to 24 inches above). Repeat if necessary. For nonbleachable fabric, work in detergent, then wash in warm water and rinse well.

If fruit stain has dried, apply glycerin to loosen stain or rub with solution of half water, half alcohol, then let stand. Rinse and wash in hot water. If stain is from citrus fruit, be aware that even though it may seem to rinse out with water, heat (such as from machine-drying or pressing) will bring stain out and set it permanently, so it's best to go through entire stain-removing procedure.

For carpets, drapes and upholstery: Apply detergent solution, blot, follow with vinegar solution, then rinse thoroughly with clear water.

Fruit juice (with artificial coloring). Rinse in cool water, then blot. Soak in solution of 1/4 cup (60 ml) ammonia to 1 quart (1 liter) warm water for 5 minutes, then rinse and repeat until stain disappears. Use 1/4 cup (60 ml) vinegar in 2 quarts (2 liters) cool water for final rinse.

For carpets, drapes and upholstery: Use detergent solution, blotting frequently and making sure not to spread the stain. Repeat this procedure until a blotting towel comes up clean. Apply ammonia solution, then rinse.

Grease (car). Blot, then work in petroleum jelly and sponge with dry-cleaning solvent. Blot and apply again, then rinse well and wash in hot water. Use prewash stain remover if traces remain and wash again. (See also "Butter, oil," above.)

For carpets, drapes and upholstery: Use commercial petroleum solvent, paint thinner or dry-cleaning solution. Work all the way to the center of stain. Blot with clean towel. Apply detergent solution, and rinse. For stain-guard carpets: Use dry-cleaning fluid.

Ink (ballpoint). Spray with hairspray, blot, rub in detergent, rinse. Then saturate with rubbing alcohol and rub in with thumbs, rinse and let dry. If stain has faded, try again. If this doesn't work, apply a soil and stain remover recommended for use with permanent-press fabrics. For bleachable fabrics, you may try removing the stain with acetone or nail-polish remover. Rub in and rinse.

For carpets, drapes and upholstery: Apply dry-cleaning solution, then denatured alcohol, then apply acetone (do not use on acetate fibers, as they will dissolve). If the stain persists, use rust remover (oxalic acid). For stain-guard carpets: Use paint, oil or grease remover on a clean white cloth. Then apply dry-cleaning fluid.

Ink (felt-tip pen). Don't try to wash stain out before treating as follows: Apply acetone, dry-cleaning solvent, alcohol or prewash soil and stain remover until stain ceases to spread. Let dry, then thoroughly rub in warm glycerin. Rinse in mild ammonia and water solution, then wash. Alternatively, apply household spray-on cleanser such as Fantastik or Mr. Clean, and rub into stain. Rinse. Repeat until stain is gone, then launder in hottest water appropriate for fabric, with appropriate bleach.

For carpets, drapes and upholstery: Water-soluble inks can be cleaned with water and a detergent solution. For permanent markers, try a solution of Ditto fluid, available from office-supply stores. For stain-guard carpets: Use same procedures as for ballpoint pen. If marker label reads "permanent," apply dry-cleaning fluid. Follow with paint, oil or grease remover. Reapply dry-cleaning solution.

Milk-based stains. Sponge stain with cool water, then let soak in warm water. If fabric is bleachable, apply paste of powdered presoak and water; let sit for at least 30 minutes, then launder. If traces remain, apply prewash stain remover thoroughly, let stand for 30 minutes, then wash again. If stain persists, apply dry-cleaning solvent. If fabric cannot be bleached, first soak in cool water for 30 minutes, then work in detergent and air-dry. If any stain remains, sponge with dry-cleaning solvent.

For carpets, drapes and upholstery: Use ammonia solution or protein digester on the stain, then rinse. For stain-guard carpets: Use carpet shampoo, then blot with an ammonia solution. Blot or mist with diluted white vinegar. Weight down a pad of toweling and leave in place over the stain for several hours. Allow the carpet to dry, then clean with dry-cleaning fluid.

Mustard. Carefully scrape off as much mustard as possible without rubbing it in. For bleachable fabric, apply glycerin and let stand for 20 to 30 minutes. Work in liquid soap, let stand for 30 minutes, then wash in hot water. For

nonbleachable fabric, rinse with half alcohol/half water solution, then apply hydrogen peroxide and rinse.

For carpets, drapes, and upholstery: Apply detergent solution, blot with clean damp towel; follow with a vinegar solution. Then use rust remover or hydrogen peroxide solution if stain persists. Don't use ammonia or alkalies. For stain-guard carpets: Clean with carpet shampoo according to directions on package. Mist or blot with vinegar solution. Allow carpet to dry completely, then clean with dry-cleaning fluid.

Nail polish. Blot up excess with paper towel (from both sides of fabric). Work in acetone or nail-polish remover (if safe for fabric) from underside, pressing with white towel (paper or fabric).

For carpets, drapes, and upholstery: Apply dry-cleaning solvent to stain, then acetone or non-oily nail-polish remover. If stain remains, use detergent solution, then blot with clean damp cloth and follow with ammonia solution. Blot, then finish with vinegar solution and rinse. For stain-guard carpets: Clean with dry-cleaning fluid, then apply paint, oil or grease remover with a clean white cloth. Use dry-cleaning fluid again, if needed.

Paint, oil-based. Blot up as much as possible from both sides of fabric, using a paper towel. Keep from drying by wrapping fabric in plastic. Then sponge with dry-cleaning solvent or paint thinner and work in detergent and rinse. Soak in hot water and detergent overnight, then wash and air dry.

If paint stain is dry, rub in a heavy-duty liquid cleanser and place garment in plastic bag and leave it overnight to soften paint. Apply turpentine and blot from both sides of fabric to get rid of excess, then follow directions for removing fresh paint.

For carpets, drapes and upholstery: Apply dry-cleaning solvent directly to stain; if this doesn't work, cover the stain with towels dampened with dry-cleaning solvent or paint thinner. Leave in place for several hours to soften the paint. Blot with solvent. Apply several drops of detergent solution and work into stain. Blot with clean damp cloth, then apply an ammonia solution and rinse with warm water. For stain-guard carpets: clean with dry-cleaning solution.

Paint, water-based. Blot up excess with paper towels, then dab spot with damp sponge. Rinse sponge out and repeat. First try spot-washing with detergent and water; if that doesn't work, rub on a prewash stain remover, rinse, wash and let dry. If any trace remains, use dry-cleaning solvent.

For carpets, drapes, and upholstery: Apply detergent solution, blot with clean damp towel, then apply ammonia solution and rinse with clear water. If paint is dry, try softening it with paint or lacquer thinner (be very careful, as it may damage material), then proceed as above. For stain-guard carpets: Use carpet shampoo or detergent solution, then rinse. Dried paint can be removed using a grease, oil or paint remover, then blotted with dry-cleaning solution, followed by carpet shampoo.

Set-in stains (source unknown). For white fabrics, rub stain with paste of lemon juice and salt and let dry in sunlight. Add more paste as it dries, then rinse. If stain starts to fade, repeat paste treatment and then rinse in vinegar solution (1/2 cup/120 ml to basin of water). Soak colored fabrics in 2 cups (1/2 liter) warm or hot water mixed with 2 tablespoons (30 ml) oxygen bleach. Test fabric first. Cover with damp cloth and let sit for several hours, then rinse well.

Urine. Sponge first with cool water, then let soak. Take out of soak and rub in detergent; rinse; let dry. If color has changed, sponge with ammonia diluted with water. If stain remains, sponge with vinegar.

For carpets, drapes and upholstery: Apply detergent solution, then blot with clean damp cloth and follow with ammonia solution. Blot again. Apply vinegar solution and rinse. If stain persists, use rust remover or hydrogen peroxide (although urine may already have removed dye from fibers and caused fading). Use a deodorant if necessary. For stain-guard carpets: Rinse with water, then mist with diluted white vinegar. Blot with clean damp cloth, then use carpet shampoo.

Vomit. Sponge off with cool water. If fabric can be bleached, rub in liquid detergent and let sit for 30 minutes. Sprinkle with ammonia and rinse under the tap. Sponge with salt and water solution (1/4 cup/60 ml salt to 2 quarts/2 liters of water), and rinse. For nonbleachable fabric, work in paste of powdered presoak, and keep moist. Rinse before paste dries.

For carpets, drapes and upholstery:

First, carefully remove as much of the stain as you can. Use detergent solution. Blot with clean damp cloth, then follow with ammonia solution. Blot, apply vinegar solution and rinse. For stain-guard carpets: Apply carpet shampoo or detergent solution. Blot with clean damp cloth, then with cloth soaked in ammonia solution. Blot with clean cloth, then mist with vinegar solution. Allow to dry, then clean with dry-cleaning fluid.

Cleaning Vinyl Flooring

Be sure to blot up liquid cleaners between steps and wipe dry when done.

For most stains—including acids, alkalies, alcoholic beverages, blood, candy, catsup, cleansers, coffee, food dye, fruit and fruit juice, ink, iodine, Mercurochrome, mustard, strong soaps, vegetables and vegetable juices—simply wipe up the stain with a damp sponge, or use a cleaner recommended for your flooring. If necessary, rub with a nonabrasive cleanser such as baking soda. Then rub the area lightly with a cloth dipped in a bleach solution diluted with 10 times the amount of water.

Rubber heel marks, shoe polish, smudges and scuffs. Remove the stain, using lighter fluid, as soon as possible. Clean the area with a cleanser recommended for your flooring. If it's not a high-gloss finish, use a nonabrasive cleanser, rubbing vigorously in circles.

Lacquer, nail polish. Rub lightly with cloth dipped in lacquer thinner, then rinse.

Rust, mildew, dye, grass stains. Rub the stain lightly with a solution of bleach diluted with 10 times the amount of water, then rinse. For rust stains, follow with a solution of cream of

---

10 Cleaning Tips

1. Consider bacteria-enzyme digester.
It's the only effective way to deal with unpleasant organic messes such as urine and vomit, especially if they've seeped into absorbent materials such as carpet or upholstery. When you mix up the formula, it actually produces a live colony of beneficial bacteria that eats the stain- and odor-causing materials. It's available at pet stores and janitorial supply stores. One brand is called Outright, but there are others.

2. Disinfectant cleaner does double duty.
It cleans and disinfects at the same time. The pine cleaners available in supermarkets contain at least 20 percent pine oil. They're effective disinfectant cleaners, but you can buy other products in more concentrated form for less money at a janitorial supply store. A quaternary, or "quat," disinfectant cleaner is best and safest for most home cleaning.

3. Treat it right.
To treat a dust mop, spray it generously with Endust or a commercial dust mop oil. Roll it up like a sock and place in a plastic bag for 12 to 24 hours. This will allow the "treatment" to penetrate through the whole head and distribute it evenly so that it can catch and hold those dust bunnies.

4. Did you know?
Cold rinse water not only saves energy, but it reduces wrinkles too!

5. A laundry lesson.
If you get a pink load from a dye transfer in the laundry, don't dry it! Instead, immediately rewash with a little bleach. It may take three to five washings, but most dye bleeding will come clean, especially before the dye is set by heat drying.

6. Curtain cure-all?
You may have heard that you can toss unwashable curtains into the dryer to clean them. The tumbling and air circulation are supposed to loosen and suck soils away, but the practice is not

tartar or lemon juice, diluted in a small amount of water.

Oil paints, solvents, varnish. Blot up spill immediately. If it has dried, try to peel it up if you can. Then rub area lightly with cloth dipped in a recommended floor cleaner, and rinse.

Shellac. Rub lightly with cloth dipped in alcohol and rinse.

Urine. Clean floor with a cleaner recommended for your flooring. If stain has set, use solution of bleach diluted with 10 times as much water.

Cleaning Large Items

Sometimes you will find that you need to clean something that, because of its size, just can't be put in the washing machine. This might include wall-to-wall carpeting or room-size rugs, curtains, upholstery or pillow covers. On carpeting, for example, many of the cleaning and stain-removing techniques described above would be quite effective, except that you can't use water to flush out and remove soap, detergent or chemicals out of the weave. You can in most cases work only from one side of the fabric and therefore must be careful not to drive the stain in deeper. You have a few choices in how to clean such items:

•Hire professional carpet or upholstery cleaners. This method is the most expensive, but it can save you time (and money, if you ruin the item through your own cleaning efforts) and is recommended for heavy, all-over soiling and any spot or stain you're really not sure how to cope with.

•If you're determined to do it yourself, be prepared with plenty of white towels to blot up moisture. Also have on hand absorbents such as kitty litter, cornmeal or talcum powder for greasy stains. Scrape or

---

a cure-all. If you do it, be sure the dryer is on "air," not hot. But never use this treatment on sun-rotted drapes, which will disintegrate, plastic fabrics, which might melt, or fiberglass: Your clothes will have fiberglass slivers in them for the next 20 years or for the greatly reduced life of the dryer!

7. Dust early and often.
Dust will come off all blinds easily, even mini-blinds, if you dust them *often*. If the dust is left on, it blends with airborne oils and becomes a stubborn sticky coating that requires much more time-consuming cleaning. Dust often, using a lambswool puff duster on closed blinds.

8. Plexiglas tactics.
Before you try to clean Plexiglas, be sure to rinse it well with water. Plexiglas attracts dust, and you can be sure there will be some on the surface—rinse it away before it has a chance to be caught underneath your cleaning cloth, where it will cause scratches.

9. A clean deal.
Venetian blinds, because they have so many horizontal surfaces, are like the top of the fridge when it comes to collecting grease, dust and insect residue. They can be dusted and vacuumed in place, but for real deep cleaning they have to be taken down. Put them in the closed position and lay them in an old blanket or tarp that has been put down on a slanted or inclined surface, such as a driveway. Scrub the blinds with a soft brush and ammonia solution; then turn them over and do the other side. Rinse them with the hose, then shake them to reduce water spots. This method sure beats doing them in a tub or in place!

10. All that's not fit to blot.
Contrary to popular opinion, drying windows with newspaper will leave an ink residue that can dull the shine of the glass and even transfer to drapes. Squeegee your windows, and you won't have to dry them with anything.

From *500 Terrific Ideas for Cleaning Everything*, by Don Aslett, copyright 1991. Published by Simon & Schuster Inc.

blot up as much stain as possible from the surface of the item, being careful not to force it into the pile or filling.

•Use the least amount of liquid, whether chemical solvent or just plain water, as possible, since excess moisture may cause colors to bleed and solvents may attack the filling and lining of upholstery or carpets and cause them to disintegrate. To make up for using less, leave liquid on stain longer and rub gently to loosen stain. Be sure to blot as thoroughly as possible.

•When you've finished removing the spot and have rinsed the area for the final time, leave a pad of thick, absorbent fabric on top and weigh it down. Leave it in place until the spot is thoroughly dry.

•For quilted items, mattresses, pillows and stuffed toys, spots can usually be removed by lightly sponging with the appropriate chemical or liquid, working from the outer edges of stained area inward. Then rinse and blot thoroughly.

•Surprisingly, most pillows, including those filled with down, may be machine-washed and dried, using the gentle cycle and a low or no-heat setting.

Environmentally Safe Cleaners

Many chemicals used for day-to-day household cleansing can have a deleterious effect on the environment when used excessively. In order to do your bit to save the earth, you might want to try out some environmentally safe, non-toxic or less-toxic alternatives.

Borax. This naturally occurring mineral can be bought at most supermarkets. Mixed with liquid soap and vinegar or lemon juice and water, it makes excellent all-purpose cleanser. Can also be used with water as a scouring paste.

The All-Purpose Spotting Kit: Stain-Removal Items To Keep On Hand

TOOLS

A scraper, such as a butter knife or spatula, to remove as much of stain as possible from surface of item. For delicate fabrics, use the bowl of a spoon as a scraper.

Clean white cloths. Cotton is best.

A spray bottle

Small scrub brush or toothbrush

Nylon scouring pad

Medium-stiff brush

Dry sponge or art-gum eraser

CHEMICALS

Ammonia

Chlorine bleach

3 percent hydrogen peroxide solution

All-fabric bleach

Enzyme cleanser (powder or liquid)

All-purpose stain remover

Dry-cleaning solvent

Laundry pre-treat product, in solid or spray form

Clear dishwashing liquid

White vinegar

Absorbents (Kitty Litter, cornmeal, fuller's earth)

Denatured or isopropyl alcohol

Color remover

Glycerin

Petroleum jelly

Soap (liquid or powder)

Distilled water (if your water is hard)

Acetone

Amyl acetate (banana oil)

Citrus oil-based cleanser

Oxalic acid

Adapted from *Don Aslett's Stainbuster's Bible: The Complete Guide to Spot Removal,* by Don Aslett, copyright 1990, Penguin Books.

Poured into toilet bowl and left to sit overnight, it will get rid of ring.

White vinegar. Distilled white vinegar is cheap and has many cleaning uses. Mix half and half with water and in a spray bottle, and use it to clean and disinfect surfaces. Mix 1/2 cup (120 ml) vinegar with 2 tablespoon (30 ml) liquid soap or vegetable-based detergent and 2 gallons (6 1/2 liters) warm water to clean floors; use 3 tablespoons (45 ml) vinegar with 1/2 teaspoon (2.5 ml) soap or vegetable-based detergent and 2 cups (1/4 liter) water for windows. Mix 1/4 cup (60 ml) vinegar with 1/2 teaspoon (2.5 ml) olive oil to dust and clean furniture.

Vegetable-based detergents. These solutions use citrus oil as a base. Mix with water and vinegar to make a potent cleaning solution as above. Another recipe for an all-purpose liquid cleanser: Fill a spray bottle with 1 teaspoon (5 ml) borax, 1/2 teaspoon (2.5 ml) washing soda (available in super markets), 2 tablespoons (30 ml) lemon juice or vinegar, 1/2 teaspoon (2.5 ml) vegetable-based detergent and 2 cups (1/2 liter) hot water.

Baking soda. Can be used as a scouring powder when combined with soap or vegetable-based detergent to make a creamy paste. Use to clean oven as follows: sprinkle water on worst greasy, grimy spots, then cover spots thoroughly with baking soda. Sprinkle with water again and add another layer of baking soda. Let sit overnight, then wipe off with sponge and liquid soap. Sprinkle over rugs, leave overnight and then vacuum to remove odors. Can be added to washer as water softener.

Soap. True soap, such as Ivory or Woolite, can be combined with water, baking soda or borax, and lemon juice or vinegar to make an effective all-purpose cleanser. Can be used with water for most cleaning needs.

Salt. Pour on spots to absorb grease, leave for at least 1 hour, then vacuum.

Housework

Nobody really likes housework—but some people do put up with it better than others. It's easy to keep a clean home if you have the right tools.

CLEANING: YOUR TOOL KIT

Vacuum cleaner. Truly a must-have. It's worth it to spend the money to buy a model with a powered beater-brush head. A wet/dry vac is useful for siphoning up liquid spills. Portable, handheld vacuums (some are cordless) are convenient for quick spill cleanup but should not be your only vacuum. Useful attachments include crevice tools and broad and narrow brushes for upholstery and lampshades. Be sure to keep these clean; often, they can be washed in the dishwasher.

Mops. A sponge mop should have a replaceable sponge head. It's best to buy replacement sponges several at a time. Wet mops with cotton heads can do double duty as dust mops when dry, but can be hard to squeeze out and keep clean.

Brooms. A straw or a synthetic broom will do the job equally well. Make sure bristles are even across the bottom to pick up dirt efficiently. Whisk brooms are handy for cleaning steps and for brushing dirt off upholstery, wood chairs and lampshades. Push brooms are best for porches, basements and garages. An old-fashioned carpet sweeper can be used on small areas, and won't wake sleeping children.

Dusters. Work well on all surfaces. One with a long or telescoping handle will reach hard-to-get-spots such as picture moldings, tops of mirror frames and lighting fixtures. You may choose between feather dusters and lamb's wool. Some prefer the latter, because the natural lanolin in the fleece picks up dust like a magnet. Lamb's-wool dusters can also be cleaned with a shake.

Brushes. Useful for scrubbing and scouring a variety of surfaces. Put a toilet brush in each bathroom, along with a large, handheld tile brush for scrubbing grout clean. Toothbrushes are handy for the little jobs. All kinds of brushes can be ordered from the Fuller Brush catalog (see end of chapter for phone number).

Cloths. Cotton is best and most absorbent. White cotton diapers make great cleaning rags, as do men's knit underwear and flannel nightgowns or shirts. Old towels and dishtowels can be cut up to use as cleaning rags too. The thicker a paper towel is, the more liquid it will absorb (and the more it will cost). Reusable cleaning cloths (such as Handiwipes) are also good.

Sponges. Get a variety of sponges, large and small, for all kinds of cleaning tasks, including countertops, sinks and walls. Combination sponge/scrub pads are also very useful. They are not as abrasive as steel wool, so they can be used on nonstick and enamel surfaces. White pads are the least abrasive; green scrub pads should be used on the toughest jobs, like cleaning the oven. Replace sponges when they start to smell or shred away at the edges. You have a choice between natural and synthetic sponges. Natural sponges are softer and often more absorbent than synthetic, but fall apart faster. They are best for cleaning delicate surfaces or for picking up moisture.

Buckets. Those with double compartments—one to hold the cleaning solution, the other plain water to rinse your mop in—are probably best. You will need more than one bucket (try one in the kitchen, one in each bathroom and one in the garage for starters). You also ought to have a few different sizes, from large to small.

Rubber gloves. Wear to protect your hands from the wrinkling and drying effects of cleansers.

Squeegee. Very effective for cleaning windows and large flat areas such as shower walls.

All-purpose spray-on cleaner. Use for countertops and appliances.

Ammonia. Clear ammonia is better than scented or sudsing ammonia. Use it to cut grease, strip wax and remove all types of soil. Mix 1/2 cup (120 ml) with water to wash floors and clean windows.

Baking soda. Use as mild scouring powder and deodorant (see "Environmentally Safe Cleaners," above).

Bleach. Use it to remove mildew and stubborn stains. Try not to inhale fumes and never mix with ammonia or ammonia-based cleaners. Wear rubber gloves to protect your hands.

Scouring powder. Use heavy-duty powders for porcelain sinks and tubs, and soft-scrub cleansers for fiberglass, formica and stainless steel.

Waxes, polishes, and oil-based cleansers. Use on wood, leather, brass, silver, copper and other surfaces. Be sure to use the appropriate type of polish (check labels carefully) to avoid damaging a metal surface.

Store brooms and mops in a closet, or hang on the wall of the laundry room for easy access. A basket or container with a handle (those divided into compartments are very useful) can be used to store bottles of cleaning supplies neatly and efficiently; you can lift up the basket and carry it around to bring cleaning supplies wherever you need them. You might want to keep one such basket stocked with supplies under the sink in the kitchen and one in each bathroom. If you live in an apartment or

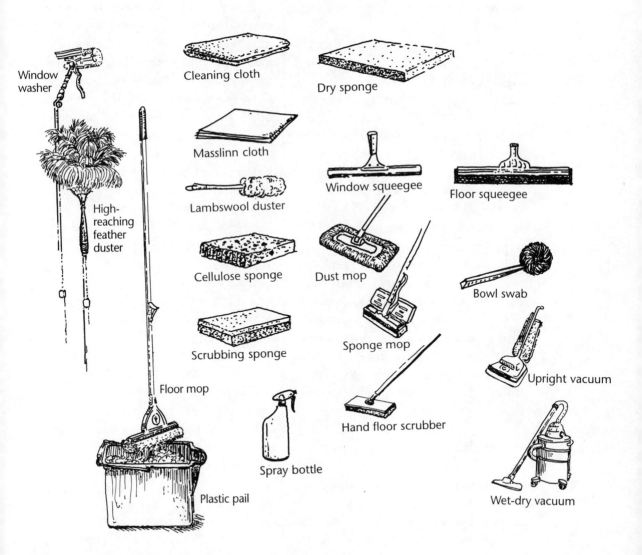

Window washer

Cleaning cloth

Dry sponge

High-reaching feather duster

Masslinn cloth

Lambswool duster

Window squeegee

Floor squeegee

Cellulose sponge

Dust mop

Bowl swab

Scrubbing sponge

Sponge mop

Floor mop

Spray bottle

Hand floor scrubber

Upright vacuum

Plastic pail

Wet-dry vacuum

Cleaning: Your household cleaning tool kit

a small house, you may want to keep everything together and carry it from place to place as needed.

DUSTING

Dusting is the first step in cleaning a room. In order to dust properly, you will need cotton dust rags; a duster (feather or lamb's-wool); a bottle of dusting spray; a whisk broom; furniture polish, and a toothbrush. Gather materials and implements together in a basket or carrier.

Check the ceiling for cobwebs. Begin dusting as high as you can reach and work down to floor level. Look for fingerprints and wipe with cleaner and rag. Dust mirror and picture frames. Check walls for marks and wipe with cleaner and rag.

Dust all horizontal surfaces. Pick up table ornaments and wipe off dust. Use your whisk broom to dust off furniture. Use the duster to dust plants. Dust tops, sides, and sills of window frames.

Don't forget to dust the telephone, bookshelves, light fixtures, lampshades, rungs of chairs and tables, fronts of tables and chests, shutters and blinds, plants, baseboards, heater vents, tops of curtains and moldings, computers, and electronic equipment such as stereos, TVs and VCRs, all of which attract dust.

VACUUMING

In order to avoid vacuuming one spot in a large room more than once, break the room down into sections and vacuum section by section. Be sure to take enough time to pick up the dirt—let the vacuum nozzle linger on each section, and move it back and forth to ensure that you pick up all the particles. Pay special attention to high-traffic areas such as hallways, doorways and around chairs and sofas.

Vacuum area rugs both top and bottom. It's a good idea to occasionally give them a shake. Clean fur rugs by working cornmeal into the pile and vacuuming it out.

Remember that it's best to vacuum or sweep hard-surface floors before you mop them. Use the floor nozzle attachment with a brush so you don't scratch the floor. Move nozzle back and forth slowly to get all the dirt. Use the small brush or crevice tool to do the baseboards and reach under radiators.

Vacuuming stairs can be a tedious task, but they must be done often, since they are a high-traffic area. It's easiest if you have a large canister-type vacuum cleaner, so you don't have to bend over so much. Start at the top and work your way down. Try to keep the vacuum cleaner below you on the steps. That way if you trip and fall you're less likely to pull it down on top of you.

In order to do a thorough job, you will have to move some furniture around. Try to move each piece as short a distance as possible. If you have to vacuum behind a large piece such as a sofa or bed, pull it out as far as you need to all at once, and move it back when you are finished.

MOPPING

Remember to vacuum first. Then, if your floor is no-wax vinyl, hardwood treated with polyurethane varnish or ceramic tile, fill one bucket with ammonia (about 1/4 to 1/2 cup) and water, the other with plain water. If you have a compartmentalized bucket, fill one section with the ammonia and the other with water. Slop the ammonia solution all over the floor with the mop. If the floor is extremely dirty, let the solution sit for a few minutes, then start mopping it back up.

Rinse the mop out in the plain water (you may need to change it a few times, depending on how dirty the floor is) and go over it again. For waxed floors, use a specialty floor cleaner. Spread a thin line of cleaner over a section of floor. Using a clean mop, spread the cleaner over the section of floor, picking up as much dirt as you can. This type of cleaner does not need to be rinsed off.

For information on cleaning appliances and polishing and cleaning wood floors, see Chapter 4, "Home Maintenance."

WASHING THE WALLS AND CEILING

Walls, whether painted, paneled or papered, should be cleaned a few times a year, particularly in kitchens and bathrooms. They accumulate grease and dust. In between washings, you can vacuum your walls, using the large brush attachment. This gets rid of dust and can be done quickly. You can also use a chemically saturated sponge, called a "dry sponge," to clean walls and get rid of dust on a regular basis. A dry sponge is also good to use on a papered wall.

Painted Walls

Use a clean, absorbent rag (terrycloth with a high cotton content is best); two buckets, one empty, one filled with warm water; all-purpose cleaner with ammonia added to cut grease, and a cellulose sponge at least 1 1/2 inches thick. If the wall you are working on is particularly greasy, add wax stripper or degreaser to the cleaning solution. Wear rubber gloves to protect your hands.

How to Dust

Venetian blinds and mini-blinds. Use a feather duster and wipe with cloth.

CDs. Wipe with soft cloth.

Computer. Wipe screen with soft cloth and screen cleanser.

Books. Dust with feather duster, wipe with soft cloth or vacuum with small brush attachment. Use soft white bread or gum eraser to remove grease spots. Rub gently, being careful not to damage the pages.

Sofas and chairs. Use your vacuum cleaner.

Framed pictures. Use cloth and glass cleanser.

Lampshades. Dust with feather duster, then finish up with brush attachment of vacuum.

LPs. Wipe with soft cloth.

Oil paintings. Dust with feather duster, then wipe with soft, *clean* cloth.

Plants. Wipe dusty leaves with a clean cloth. You can put small or medium-size plants in the tub or out in the rain for a thorough cleansing, or use a garden hose.

Radiators, baseboard heaters. Vacuum or use feather duster.

Shutters. Vacuum, then wipe with damp rag or sponge.

Stereo or CD player. Wipe with soft cloth.

Television, VCR. Wipe with soft cloth or vacuum with small brush attachment. Clean TV screen with cleanser or soap, then rinse with clean, damp rag or sponge, and buff dry with soft, clean cloth.

Telephone. Wipe with damp rag or sponge and cleaning liquid.

If you're washing all the walls of a room, move upholstered furniture out of the way and cover any wood furniture.

First, dip the sponge partway into the solution (don't saturate it). Starting at the top of the wall, spread the cleaning solution over a section (about 3 by 3 feet is easy for most people) to loosen the dirt, then go back to where you started and go over the area again with the sponge to remove dirt. After sponging, wipe the section with your clean, folded cloth. (As the surface gets dirty, refold it to expose a clean one). Then squeeze out the dirty sponge over the empty bucket. Repeat for adjacent sections. This procedure will work on walls painted with both latex and oil-based paints.

Paneling

Follow the same steps for cleaning painted walls, but use a vegetable-based detergent, such as Murphy's Oil Soap. Don't saturate the sponge with cleaning solution. When you've finished washing, buff the wall along the grain using a clean, absorbent cloth.

Ceilings

According to cleaning expert Don Aslett, it's often easier to repaint a ceiling than to wash it. But here are a few tips on keeping your ceiling clean:

•Dust it, using a dry sponge or long-handled feather duster. Stand on a step ladder and vacuum it, using the large brush attachment and extra-long hose.

•If you must wash it, take down all the ceiling fixtures first and let them soak in a basin full of cleaning solution while you work. (This applies to metal or glass fixtures only. If light shades are made of fabric, just vacuum them.) Follow the instructions given for washing walls, above.

CLEANING THE CARPET

Regular vacuuming is the best way to maintain your carpets and rugs, but every so often you will find that the carpet needs a thorough cleaning, usually referred to as "shampooing." You can do this yourself or hire professional carpet cleaners. If you do it yourself, you will have to rent the equipment and buy shampoo; it may be much simply to hire someone to do it. If your rug is an expensive antique, you should certainly go to a professional rather than trying to clean it yourself.

You can put off having to clean the entire carpet by first just cleaning the dirtiest areas, such as around furniture. Use one of the foam or powder carpet cleaners. Apply them, rub them in, wait till they dry, then vacuum them up.

If you want to go ahead and shampoo the carpet yourself, here are some tips:

•Rent or buy a machine that has rotary brushes for scrubbing and also rinses the carpet and sucks out all the dirt and suds (this is referred to as "extraction").

•Don't saturate the carpet with the shampoo or drive dirt deeper into the fibers.

•Always vacuum thoroughly *before* you shampoo.

•Make sure you don't let the cleaning solution sit too long before you extract it.

•If your carpet has a deep pile, you may need to "rake" it or sweep it after shampooing so it will dry properly.

•Protect your carpet while shampooing by putting pieces of cardboard or waxed paper under furniture legs. Loop window curtains up out of the way.

For spots in carpets, see "Stains from A to Z" and "Cleaning Large Items," above.

CLEANING UPHOLSTERY

You should vacuum all your upholstered furniture (both fabric and vinyl) regularly, using the upholstery or brush attachment. You can also remove surface dirt using a clean cloth dampened with carpet shampoo. Wipe off with a second clean, damp cloth and then wipe dry with a clean towel. This will prevent it from getting really dirty.

If your upholstery gets past the point where this type of cleaning is effective, you will have to either call in a professional upholstery cleaner (the same people who do carpets often do furniture as well) or try doing it yourself.

Wash the furniture with an upholstery cleaning solution or shampoo, then rinse it out (follow general instructions given in "Cleaning Large Items," above). Then you will need to use an upholstery extractor attachment with a carpet cleaning machine or a good wet/dry vacuum. After cleaning and extracting, rinse with clear water and extract again. Be sure not to saturate the cushions. To remove stains from upholstery, follow the instructions for carpets. (See "Stains from A to Z" and "Cleaning Large Items" for more information.)

WASHING WINDOWS

Use vertical motions on one side of the window, and wipe horizontally on the other. This way, if you are consistent, you will always be able to tell which side the streaks are on. Wash from top to bottom. For efficiency, use a long-handled, wide-blade squeegee on large windows using the steps illustrated. To make windows shine, rub them with a clean blackboard eraser.

Letting windows dry in bright sunlight can create streaks, as the cleaner dries too fast, so it's best to wash on cloudy or overcast days. If you remove the windows to wash them or you're washing storm windows, leave them to dry indoors or in a shady spot outside. Many people like to use newspapers to wash windows, then shine them with a cloth or a dry piece of newspaper. However, newspaper can leave an inky residue (see "10 Cleaning Tips." above). If you use rags instead, make sure they are clean.

Use an ammonia and water solution (1/4–1/3 cup or 60–75 ml ammonia to 1 gallon water) to clean windows, or a commercial window cleaner. Another effective cleaning solution is 1/2 cup (120 ml) ammonia, 1 cup (1/4 liter) white vinegar and 2 tablespoons (60 ml) cornstarch in a bucket of warm water.

Clean window screens with the brush attachment of your vacuum or a brush-type paint roller.

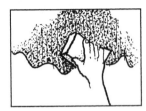

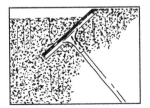

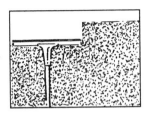

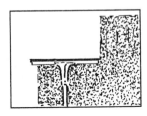

Using a squeegee: To get your windows sparkling clean use a professional squeegee. Moisten the entire glass surface with your cleaning solution–you don't have to overdo it! Positioning the squeegee diagonally, start in an upper corner and squeegee across about 1 inch from the top of the window. This will prevent any dripping that's bound to happen when using rags or paper towels. Clean the rest of the window in vertical, top-to-bottom strokes, overlapping each stroke into the clean area enough to prevent water streaks. A final horizontal stroke across the bottom will remove any remaining water puddles.

EFFICIENT CLEANING:
KEEPING CHORES TO A MINIMUM

Things to avoid. It will help you to keep your home cleaner if you avoid or replace materials that are proven dust and dirt catchers:

- Indented and embossed tile or linoleum

- Indoor-outdoor carpet

- Highly textured walls and ceilings

- Unfinished wood

- Dark colors

- Freestanding appliances

- Carpeting in kitchen, bath or dining area

Positive steps
- Get rid of as much clutter as possible. Throw out old magazines, reorganize your files at least once a year, recycle those newspapers, give away clothes you haven't worn in the past year or two.

- Make a cleaning schedule for yourself and follow it (see below for suggestions).

- Follow the old adage "A place for everything and everything in its place."

- Evaluate objects and materials in your home for ease of maintenance, accessibility, replacement cost, durability, usefulness and potential dangers. To avoid disasters, take steps to protect fragile or potentially hazardous items from accidents.

Hiring a Housekeeper

You might simply not have enough time to do the housework yourself, or be ill or injured. Rather than feel guilty about not cleaning, hire a housekeeper or maid service to do it for you.

To begin with, ask friends, co-workers and family for referrals. There are also a number of professional franchise cleaning services that charge by the hour (there is usually a minimum fee) and will send a team over to your house.

If you hire an individual, you will have to work out a relationship with him or her. Most professional cleaners do not bring their own cleaning supplies with them, so you will need to supply them. Some cleaners prefer certain types and brands over others; it's best to check with them first and buy those brands. Find out how much they charge (most charge by the hour) and tell them what you want done so they can give you an estimate. First hire them on a trial basis. If you like the job they do, and they like you, hire them permanently.

Making a Cleaning Schedule: Daily/Weekly/Monthly/Seasonal Tasks

Room	Daily	Weekly	Monthly	Seasonal
Bedroom	Make beds Put away clothing Arrange dresser top	Change bed Vacuum Dust furniture Empty trash	Organize closets and drawers Air pillows Dust lamps	Clean closets Wash blankets Wash windows Clean screens
Bathroom	Clean sink and tub Replace dirty towels Empty trash basket	Wash floor Clean toilet Wipe tile surfaces Clean mirrors	Wash shower curtain Wash walls Wash rugs Organize cabinets	Clean cabinets Wash windows Clean screens
Kitchen	Wash dishes Wipe counters Empty garbage Clean floor Clean sink	Clean range top Clean microwave Dispose of leftovers Wipe refrigerator Wash floor	Defrost and clean refrigerator/freezer Clean oven Wax floor Scrub trash can	Clean cabinets Wash stored dishes Wash windows Clean screens
Living Room	Dispose of papers Arrange magazines and ornaments	Vacuum rugs Dust, polish furniture Dust, clean lamps	Shampoo rugs Clean under furniture Clean mirrors	Clean closets Wash windows Clean screens Wash walls
Laundry	Empty pockets Pretreat stains Separate items that need mending	Sort and wash clothes Iron Dry-clean Wash bed linens Mend clothing	Wash sweaters, jackets, scarves Give away unworn clothing	Store out-of-season clothes Wash curtains, pillows, area rugs, throw pillows

If you decide to hire a service, here are some questions you should ask:

• Are your employees bonded?

• Are you insured?

• Do you guarantee your work?

• Do you provide your own cleaning supplies?

• Who will be responsible for paying the workers' social security and taxes?

It's best to use a service with bonded workers that has insurance to cover breakage or damage. Check to see if the company trains its own employees. Tell them exactly what you want done. If they are sending more than one worker, supply a room-by-room listing of tasks.

Services charge in a variety of ways. Some have an hourly rate (there is usually a minimum of two to four hours) while others charge by the task. Sometimes the hourly rate varies, depending on whether you ask for light housework or heavy-duty cleaning. Tasks like washing windows are usually charged separately.

You should fire a cleaning person for the following reasons:

• Unreliable. Shows up late, leaves early and doesn't complete assigned tasks.

• Does not clean well, even when you leave very specific instructions and supply everything needed.

• Small items and change disappear from around the house after they have been there.

Sources of Further Information

BOOKS

Is There Life After Housework? Don Aslett, Writer's Digest Books, Cincinnati, rev. ed. 1985.

Don Aslett's Stainbuster's Bible: The Complete Guide to Spot Removal. Don Aslett, Penguin Books, New York, 1990.

Too Busy to Clean?: Over 500 Tips and Techniques to Make Housecleaning Easier. Patti Barrett, Storey Communications, Pownal, Vt., 1990.

Clean Your House & Everything In It and *More Clean Your House & Everything In It.* Eugenia Chapman and Jill C. Major, Putnam, New York, 1981, 1984.

How to Clean Everything: An Encyclopedia of What to Use and How to Use It. Alma Chesnut Moore, Simon & Schuster, New York, 1980.

How to Clean Practically Anything. Monte Florman, Marjorie Florman and the editors of Consumer Reports Books, Consumers Union, Mount Vernon, N.Y., 1990.

FREE PAMPHLETS AND PUBLICATIONS

Consumer Relations, Arm & Hammer
  Division of Church & Dwight Co.
  469 North Harrison St.
  Princeton, NJ 08540
  1-800-524-1328; 1-800-624-2889 in New Jersey.

Free booklet entitled "Room to Room" explains how to use baking soda for cleaning and deodorizing around the house.

Faultless Starch/Bon Ami
   Consumer Affairs
   1025 West 8th St.
   Kansas City, MO 64101
   Write for booklets of housekeeping
tips.

Maytag Corp.
   One Dependability Square
   Newton, IA 50208
   1-515-792-7000
   Send an SASE for the pamphlets
Stain Removal, Facts of Laundry and
Commercial Laundering Procedures.
The latter two cost 25 cents each.

Don Aslett's Cleaning Center
   P.O. Box 39
   Pocatello, ID 83204
   1-208-832-6212
   Write for cleaning expert Don
Aslett's free cleaning newsletter as well
as free catalogs of professional cleaning
supplies and information and directions
for better cleaning.

Mail Order Sources of Cleaning Tools

Brookstone Hard-to-Find Tools
   1-603-924-7181
   1-800-846-3000

Fuller Brush Co.
   1-800-669-7952

Handy Helpers/The Alsto Co.
   1-800-447-0048

Professional Organizations

Association of Specialists in Cleaning
and Restoration
   10830 Annapolis Junction Rd.
   Annapolis Junction, MD 20701
   1-301-604-4411
   Represents firms that specialize in
carpet, rug and upholstery cleaning,
also restorations after flood or fire damage. Publishes information booklets
available through member firms. Call to
find firms in your area.

International Society of Cleaning
Technicians
   3028 Poplar Rd.
   Sharpsburg, GA 30277
   1-404-304-9941
   Organization representing firms spe-
cializing in carpet, upholstery and drapery cleaning, also fire and water damage
and janitorial services. Has technical
library and can supply technical bul-
letins for specific problems. Sells video
on proper cleaning techniques and how
to select a professional cleaner. Can
refer you to members in your area.

7

Cooking

When cooking, the first step is not just to have the correct ingredients, it's to have the correct amounts. Always, you'll need to measure correctly, and sometimes, you may find you need to substitute one thing for another. You must also be careful to cook food for the correct length of time to assure doneness. The following sections, illustrated by comprehensive charts, explain exactly how to do so.

Measurements, Equivalents and Substitutions

Let's end the confusion about ounces. There are two kinds.

•"Plain" ounces are a measure of weight and are equivalent to 1/16 of a pound.

•Fluid ounces are a measure of volume and are equivalent to 1/16 of a pint, or 2 tablespoons.

Since the tools you have for measuring ingredients, measuring cups and spoons, all measure volume, the ounces that most recipes call for are fluid ounces. Don't worry about weighing things unless the recipe specifies a weight.

Quantities of ingredients 1/4 cup and larger are measured in measuring cups.

•For liquids, a graduated two-cup glass or plastic measuring cup works well.

•For dry ingredients, use a cup from a set that includes 1/4-, 1/3-, 1/2- and 1-cup measures, and level with a flat blade. The only exception to the leveling rule is brown sugar, which contains a lot of moisture. Brown sugar is packed firmly. Use another cup to pack it and then scrape level.

Quantities of ingredients smaller than 1/4 cup are measured in spoons. Sets usually include teaspoon measures of 1/4, 1/2 and 1 teaspoon, and a table-spoon measure.

•For liquids, fill level. For butter, remember that one standard stick is 8 table-spoons, or 1/2 cup. Just cut it with a knife.

•For dry ingredients heap up the spoon, then scrape level.

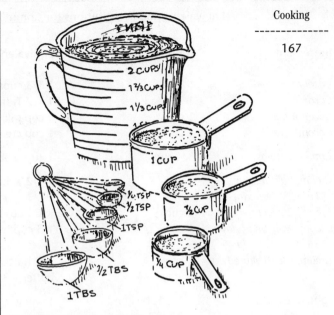

Measurements and portions

Equivalents and Substitutions for Common Ingredients

Ingredient	Amount	Equivalent/substitution
Ammonium carbonate	3/4 T. ground	1 tsp. baking soda
Arrowroot	1 1/2 tsps.	1 T. flour
as a thickener	2 tsps.	1 T. cornstarch
Baking powder (rising equivalent)	1 tsp.	1/4 tsp. baking soda + 5/8 tsp. cream of tartar; or + 1/2 cup buttermilk or yogurt; or 1/2 cup molasses)
Double-acting, SAS	1 tsp.	1 1/2 tsps. phosphate or tartrate baking powder
Bread crumbs, dry	1/4 cup	1 slice bread
Bread crumbs, soft	1/2 cup	1 slice bread
Butter	1 cup	1 cup margarine, 4/5 to 7/8 cup clarified bacon fat or drippings, 3/4 cup clarified chicken fat, 7/8 cup lard or cottonseed, corn or nut oil, solid or liquid
Buttermilk	1 cup	1 cup yogurt
Carob powder	3 T. carob powder + 2 T. water	1 ounce chocolate
Chocolate, unsweetened	1 ounce	3 T. cocoa + 1 T. butter or fat; or 3 T. carob powder + 2 T. water, 1 ounce + 4 tsps. sugar, 1 2/3 ounce semi-sweet chocolate

(Continued)

Ingredient	Amount	Equivalent/substitution
Coconut, grated	1 cup	1 1/3 cups flaked
Coconut	1 T. dried	1 1/2 T. fresh
Coconut milk	1 cup	1 cup milk
Coconut cream	1 cup	1 cup cream
Cracker crumbs	3/4 cup	1 cup bread crumbs
Cream, half-and-half, 10–12% butterfat	1 cup	1 1/2 T. butter + 7/8 cup milk, or 1/2 cup coffee cream and 1/2 cup milk
Cream, 20% butterfat	1 cup	3 T. butter + 7/8 cup milk
Cream, whipping/heavy, 36–40% butterfat	1 cup	1/3 cup butter + 3/4 cup milk
Cream, sour, cultured	1 cup	3 T. butter + 7/8 cup buttermilk or yogurt; or 3/4 cup butter + 3/4 cup cultured buttermilk or yogurt
Eggs, dried, sifted	2 1/2 T. beaten + 2 1/2 T. water	1 whole egg
Egg whites, dried, sifted	1 T. + 2 T. water	1 egg white
Egg whites, frozen	2 T. thawed	1 egg white
Egg yolks, for thickening	2 yolks	1 whole egg
Egg yolks, dried, sifted	1 1/2 T. + 1 T. water	1 egg yolk
Egg yolks, frozen	3 1/2 tsps. thawed	1 large egg yolk
Eggs, bantam	1	2/3 ounce
Flour, white	4 cups	3 1/2 cups cracked wheat
	1 cup	1 cup cornmeal, 5/8 cup potato flour, 1 cup minus 2 T. rice flour, 1 1/4 cups rye flour, 13/16 cup gluten flour
Flours, for thickening	1 T.	1 1/2 tsps. cornstarch, potato starch, rice starch or arrowroot starch, 1 T. quick-cooking tapioca, 1 T. rice flour, 1 T. waxy corn flour
Garlic	1 small clove	1/8 tsp. powder
Ginger	1 T. candied, washed of sugar, or 1 T. raw	1/8 tsp. powdered ginger
Herbs	1/3–1/2 tsp., dried	1 T. fresh
Honey	1 cup	1 1/4 cups sugar + 1/4 cup liquid
Horseradish	1 T. fresh, grated	2 T. bottled
	6 T. fresh, grated	10 T. bottled
Lemon	1	1–3 T. juice, 1–1 1/2 tsps. grated rind
	1 tsp. juice	1/2 tsp. vinegar
	1 tsp. grated rind	1/2 tsp. lemon extract
Lime	1	1 1/2–2 T. juice

Ingredient	Amount	Equivalent/substitution
Maple sugar, grated	1 T.	1 T. white granulated
Maple sugar	1/2 cup	1 cup maple syrup
Milk, whole	1 cup	1 cup water + 1 1/2 tsps. butter; or 1/2 cup evaporated milk + 1/2 cup water; or 1/4 cup dry whole milk + 7/8 cup water; or 1 cup reconstituted nonfat dry milk + 2 1/2 tsps. butter or margarine; or 1 cup soy milk or almond milk; or 1 cup fruit juice; or (in baking) 1 cup potato water
	1 quart	1 quart skim milk + 3 T. cream
Milk, to sour	1 cup	Add 1 T. vinegar or lemon juice to 1 cup milk minus 1 T., let stand 5 minutes
Tapioca	1 1/2–2 T. quick-cook	4 T. pearl, soaked
Tapioca, for thickening	1 T. quick-cook	1 T. flour
Tomatoes	1 cup packed	1/2 cup tomato juice + 1/2 cup water
Tomato juice	1 cup	1/2 cup tomato sauce + 1/2 cup water
Tomato sauce	2 cups	3/4 cup tomato paste + 1 cup water
Tomato soup	10 3/4 ounce can	1 cup tomato sauce + 1/4 cup water
Yeast, compressed	3/5 ounce cake	1 package active dry yeast
Yogurt	1 cup	1 cup buttermilk

Poultry Cooking Times

Ready-to-cook weight (lbs.)	Oven temp.	Roasting time, stuffed and unstuffed	Special instructions
Chicken			
1 1/2–2	375	3/4–1 hr.	Brush dry areas of skin occasionally with pan drippings. Cover loosely with foil.
2–2 1/2	375	1–1 1/4 hr.	
2 1/2–3	375	1 1/4–1 1/2 hrs.	
3–4	375	1 1/2–2 hrs.	
Capon			
4–7	375	1 1/2–2 hrs.	As above.

(Continued)

Ready-to-cook weight (lbs.)	Oven temp.	Roasting time, stuffed and unstuffed	Special instructions
Turkey			
6–8	325	3 1/2–4 hrs.	Cover loosely with foil. Last 45 minutes, cut band of skin or string between legs and tail; uncover and continue roasting till done. Baste if desired.
8–12	325	4–4 1/2 hrs.	
12–16	325	4 1/2–5 1/2 hrs.	
16–20	325	5 1/2–6 1/2 hrs.	
20–24	325	6 1/2–7 1/2 hrs.	
Foil-wrapped turkey			
8–10	450	2 1/4–2 1/2 hrs.	Place trussed turkey, breast up, in center of greased, wide heavy foil. Bring ends of foil up over breast; overlap fold and press up against ends of turkey. Place bird in shallow pan (no rack). Open foil last 20 minutes to brown skin.
10–12	450	2 1/2–3 hrs.	
14–16	450	3–3 1/4 hrs.	
18–20	450	3 1/4–3 1/2 hrs.	
22–24	450	3 1/2–3 3/4 hrs.	
Cornish game hen			
1–1 1/2	375	1 1/2 hrs.	Roast loosely covered for 30 minutes, then for 60 minutes uncovered or until done. If desired, occasionally baste with melted butter or a glaze the last hour.

How Much to Buy for One Serving

Chicken		*Duck*	about 1 lb.
Broiler-fryer	1/4–1/2 bird	domestic	
Capon, roaster, stewing	about 1/2 lb.		
Cornish game hens	1 bird	*Goose*	about 1 lb.
		domestic	
Turkey			
Small (5–12 lbs.)	3/4–1 lb.		
Large (12–24 lbs.)	1/2–3/4 lbs.		
Uncooked boneless roast	1/3 lb.		

Roasting Time and Temperature Chart

Cut	Approx. weight (lbs.)	Internal temp. on removal from oven	Approx. cooking time

Roast meat at constant oven temperature of 325° unless otherwise indicated.

Cut	Approx. weight (lbs.)	Internal temp. on removal from oven	Approx. cooking time
Beef			
Rib roast	4–6	140 (rare)	2 1/4–2 3/4 hrs.
		160 (medium)	2 3/4–3 1/2 hrs.
		170 (well done)	3 1/4–3 1/2 hrs.
	6–8	140 (rare)	2 1/2–3 hrs.
		160 (medium)	3–3 1/2 hrs.
		170 (well done)	3 3/4–4 hrs.
Boneless rib roast	5–7	140 (rare)	3 1/4–3 1/2 hrs.
		160 (medium)	3 3/4–4 hrs.
		170 (well done)	4 1/2–4 3/4 hrs.
Boneless rolled rump roast	4–6	150–170	2–2 1/2 hrs.
Tip roast	3 1/2–4	140–170	2–2 3/4 hrs.
Rib-eye (Delmonico) roast (roast at 350°)	4–6	140 (rare)	1 1/2–1 3/4 hrs.
		160 (medium)	1 3/4 hrs.
		170 (well done)	2 hrs.
Tenderloin roast (roast at 425°)	4–6	140 (rare)	45 minutes–1 hr.
Veal			
Leg roast	5–8	170	2 3/4–3 3/4 hrs.
Loin roast	4–6	170	2 1/2–3 hrs.
Boneless shoulder roast	4–6	170	3 1/2–3 3/4 hrs.
Fresh pork			
Loin center roast	3–5	170	2 1/2–3 hrs.
Sirloin roast	5–7	170	3 1/2–4 1/4 hrs.
Loin blade roast	3–4	170	2 1/4–2 3/4 hrs.

(continued)

Cut	Approx. weight (lbs.)	Internal temp. on removal from oven	Approx. cooking time
Fresh pork, cont.			
Boneless top loin roast	3–4	170	2 1/2–3 hrs.
Blade Boston roast	4–6	170	3–4 hrs.
Arm picnic	5–8	170	3–4 hrs.
Leg (fresh ham)	10–16	170	4 1/2–6 hrs.
Leg half (fresh ham)	5–7	170	3 1/2–4 1/2 hrs.
Smoked pork			
Ham (cook-before-eating)			
Whole	10–14	160	3 1/2–4 hrs.
Half	5–7	160	2 1/2–3 hrs.
Shank or rump portion	3–4	160	2–2 1/4 hrs.
Ham (fully cooked)			
Whole	10–14	140	2 1/2–3 hrs.
Half	5–7	140	1 3/4–2 1/4 hrs.
Whole, boneless	8–10	140	2–2 1/4 hrs.
Half, boneless	4–5	140	1 1/2–2 hrs.
Picnic shoulder (cook-before-eating)	5–8	170	3–4 hrs.
Lamb			
Leg, whole	5–7	140 (rare)	1 3/4–2 1/4 hrs.
		160 (medium)	2–3 hrs.
		170–180 (well done)	2 1/2–3 1/2 hrs.
Leg, half	3–4	160 (medium)	1 1/4–1 3/4 hrs.
Square-cut shoulder	4–6	160 (medium)	1 3/4–2 1/2 hrs.
Boneless shoulder	3–5	160 (medium)	1 3/4–3 hrs.

How Much Meat to Serve

Meat	Servings per pound
Boneless meat: ground, stew or variety meat	4–5
Cuts with little bone: beef round or ham center cuts, lamb or veal cutlets	3–4
Cuts with medium amount of bone: whole or end cuts of beef round, bone-in ham; loin, rump, rib or chuck roasts; steaks and chops	2–3
Cuts with much bone: shank, brisket, plate, spare ribs, breast of lamb or veal	1–2

Food Storage Basics

Once you've bought your food and brought it home, you must be certain to store it properly, or you will have problems with spoilage and insect infestation.

FREEZE TREATING

No matter how fastidious a housekeeper you are, bugs can get into your grains and dry goods. Their eggs, nearly microscopic, may be in the product when you buy it. You bring it home, store it tightly, but nonetheless in a few weeks, you've got bugs in the bag and can't use your flour.

The solution? If you've got a manageable quantity of something vulnerable to bugs, place it in the freezer, well wrapped, for three days. Then take it out and store it normally. The freeze treatment will kill any insects and their eggs so that as you keep the product tightly stored, it'll stay bug-free.

STORAGE TECHNIQUES

In the pantry or at room temperature:
•Frequently used flours, grains and bread crumbs. Use jars or canisters that close with a rubber seal or a very tight screw top. Canning jars are good, but not infallible. Keep checking, especially in the warm months. In the summer, consider putting little-used items in the freezer.

•Potatoes, onions and shallots keep best when stored in a cool, dark, dry place where air can circulate.

•Cans do not last forever. Check frequently for swelling and discard.

Liquid and Dry Measure, Imperial/Metric

APPROXIMATE CONVERSION

IMPERIAL	METRIC
1/4 teaspoon	1.25 milliliters
1/2 teaspoon	2.5 milliliters
1 teaspoon	5 milliliters
1 tablespoon	15 milliliters
1 fluid ounce	30 milliliters
1/4 cup	60 milliliters
1/3 cup	80 milliliters
1/2 cup	120 milliliters
1 cup	240 milliliters
1 pint (2 cups)	480 milliliters
1 quart (32 oz/4 cups)	960 milliliters
1 gallon (4 quarts)	3.84 liters
1 ounce	28 grams
1/4 pound (4 oz.)	114 grams
1 pound (16 oz.)	454 grams
2 1/5 pounds	1 kilogram

•Keep herbs and spices in tightly closed containers (small glass jars with screw-on lids are best) and store in a cool, dry, dark place. Always replace if they are more than a year old. Do not store spices near the stove.

•Paprika, cayenne pepper and caraway seeds are very vulnerable to insects. Freeze-treat them first.

In the refrigerator:
•Wheat germ, with its high oil content, should be kept in the refrigerator. Otherwise it will go rancid.

•Bread: Some say keep it in the refrigerator but refrigeration dries it out, and it can pick up refrigerator smells. Store tightly in plastic. If it will take over three days to finish, cut off what you need and store the rest in the freezer, tightly wrapped, first in aluminum foil and then in plastic.

•Nuts: Refrigerate if stored longer than two months.

•Raisins and dried fruit are best refrigerated.

In the freezer:
•Meat, if kept longer than a few days, should be frozen as soon as you get it home.

PROPER FREEZING

Freezer wrap is moisture proof and vapor proof. It is meant to protect food from the drying-out process that happens during freezing. When air is left in containers or loose packaging, it dries out the food and forms a frost. Dehydration or freezer burn occurs on all food that is not wrapped closely enough. So always wrap as tightly as possible to insure freshness.

•When freezing liquids, allow room for expansion.

•When using plastic bags for freezing, effectiveness is increased by first wrapping in freezer wrap and then bagging the item. Make sure all air is squeezed out first.

How to Tell If Food is Fresh

Meats
Beef: Bright red to deep red color. Avoid ground beef that has gray or brown patches or an off odor.

Lamb: Pinkish color, thin layer of firm white fat.

Pork: Light pink. Smoked pork will be firmer and slightly darker.

Ham: A nice rosy pink. Make sure the texture is finely grained. It should feel firm, not spongy.

Poultry
Whole birds: Plump birds with smooth clear skin free of pinfeathers and bruises. Look for a grade A inspection mark.

Fillets or pieces: As above. For skinless pieces, be sure the package is not leaking.

Fish and Seafood
Whole fish: Eyes should be clear and bright, not sunken. Gills should be bright red or pink, skin shiny and elastic and scales tightly in place.

Fillets and steaks: Should always be kept on ice. A mild smell. Make sure the fish is moist throughout.

Scallops: Should be firm and fresh in a thin cloudy liquid. They should smell sweet.

Shrimp: Moist and ripe with translucent flesh and a fresh aroma (not ammoniated). Cooked shrimp should be firm, with pink and white flesh.

Dairy and Eggs
Cheese: Always try to taste before buying. Look for pliable edges and even coloring. If the package is wet and sticky, don't buy it. Avoid cheese with dry rinds and cracked edges or ripened cheeses that smell of ammonia.

Eggs: Should be clean and fresh looking. Inspect cartons for broken or leaking eggs.

Vegetables
Look for bright color. Vegetables should be plump and crisp to the touch, dense for their size.

Artichokes: Ripe globe with large tightly closed leaves.

Asparagus: Firm, straight stalks with compact closed tips.

Green beans: Long pods that snap.

Broccoli: Firm tender stalks with small leaves. Buds should be tightly closed.

Corn: Bright green husks and plump even rows of kernels.

Potatoes: Find firm smooth ones with shallow eyes. Avoid patches of green.

Fruit
Again, look for plump, tender fruits that are dense for their size, free from mold, bruises or blemishes.

Avocados: Firm with some yield to the touch.

Melons: Should smell ripe and sweet.

Strawberries: Plump, red berries, with bright green caps.

Tomatoes: Well shaped, no scarring, firm.

Food Safety Musts

From *A Quick Consumer Guider to Safe Food Handling*, U.S. Department of Agriculture. Free from Consumer Information Service, Dept. 528Z, Pueblo, CO 81009.

•Get perishable foods into the refrigerator as quickly as possible after buying them.

•Wash raw vegetables thoroughly.

•Keep your kitchen or food preparation area clean.

•Wash your hands before preparing food.

•Keep hot foods hot and cold foods cold after they are prepared.

A Cook's Tools

KNIVES
Types of blades
Carbon. These have the advantage of holding a razor-sharp edge. But they discolor and impart an off-flavor if not wiped immediately after each use.

Stainless steel. An alloy containing chromium and nickel. No discoloration, no need to wipe after use. A disadvantage is that once the factory edge is worn, the blade will not take a new edge.

High-carbon stainless. The most expensive type of knife. Incorporates qualities of carbon and stainless steel to produce a knife that is highly corrosion-resistant, but also keeps a good edge. Sharpen often.

Basic knives
Chef's knife. Heavy and sharp for most cutting, slicing and chopping.

Utility knife. A six-to-eight-inch blade for cutting small vegetables, deboning chicken when a chef's knife is too clumsy and a paring knife too delicate.

Paring knife. Small, thin and sharp, for delicate cutting of fruits and vegetables.

Bread knife. Long serrated knife makes cutting bread easier.

Novelty knife. A small serrated one is good for slicing tomatoes and other tender-skinned vegetables and fruits. Both this and a curved grapefruit knife can be useful and are inexpensive.

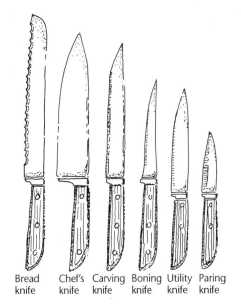

| Bread knife | Chef's knife | Carving knife | Boning knife | Utility knife | Paring knife |

A cook's tools: Knives

Shopping Tips
Pay attention to the type of blade. Look for well-balanced handles that fit nicely in your hand. Wood has the best feel, but the new molded-plastic handles are quite good and won't absorb water. Be sure to get a wooden storage rack for your knives. Your blades will not last long if they are banging around in a drawer with other implements.

Knife Sharpening
Perfectly shaped, quality knives are by far the most useful tool in the kitchen. You can easily sharpen them yourself using either a commercial gadget or the old-fashioned but reliable method with a sharpening stone. Here's how to do it the old-fashioned way:

Sharpening stones come in three grades, fine, medium and coarse. If you are faithful about your sharpening, a medium-grade stone will do. To pro-

ceed, lay the stone on a towel to prevent slippage. Gently rub a few drops of mineral oil or water into the stone. Hold the knife at 20° angle and draw the knife toward you. Repeat five times on each side. Don't push the blade into the stone. A gentle pressure is adequate. Make sure the entire blade, including tip, passes over the stone's surface. Rinse the blade under warm water and dry thoroughly.

To bring the edge to perfect sharpness you must first hone it with a sharpening rod. There are two kinds. The superior type is actually a "steel," and these come in different shaft sizes. Get one that is a few inches longer than the blade of your chef's knife. However, there are some cheap ceramic rods that are adequate if used frequently. Hone your knife with each use. Hold the device vertically. The point should rest on a damp towel or chopping board. Again at a 20° angle, starting at the heel of the blade, near your grip, draw the entire cutting edge down along the length of the steel. Make sure you get the tip.

Gadgets. There are two kinds of patent knife sharpeners. One is a gadget that regulates the knife's angle and holds it in place as you zap it in and out. The other is electric.

A word of advice from the knife-using professionals: don't ever put your fine blades through the dishwasher, as the hot water actually washes away the fine steel edge. Always wash by hand.

STOVE-TOP POTS
Choose from cast iron, aluminum, stainless steel, glass, porcelain-covered steel

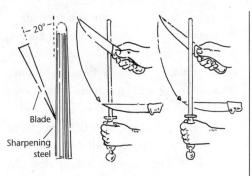

A cook's tools: Knife sharpening

or copper. Additional features include nonstick and clad. Choose a set with a range of sizes from large enough to steam corn or cook a chicken to a small melting pot for butter or sauce. A double boiler is nice for delicate sauces. A vegetable steamer is useful, but you don't need a special pot for it. Look for quality in stove-top cookware: this is something you should only have to buy once.

Safety

There have been concerns over whether various types of cookware are safe. Do scratches on a nonstick coated pan mean that you've scraped a toxic material into your sauté? Does aluminum from pots and pans leach into your food, causing health problems? Aluminum, copper, lead—all of these have been indicted. Read on for warnings in each category.

Cast iron. It's been around for 3,000 years. No health controversy here, but you must watch out for rust. Conducts heat well and cooks evenly. Porous surface needs seasoning when new (see sidebar). Moves well from stove-top to oven. *Disadvantage:* If you scrub too hard you can remove the seasoning,

although you can always re-season. *Advantage:* The iron that seeps into the food is said to be a positive additive.

Aluminum. There has been a recent scare over a link between aluminum and Alzheimer's disease. Researchers are still investigating, but according to the director of medical and scientific affairs at the Alzheimer's Association, much recent data supports the theory that brains already damaged by Alzheimer's may permit entry of abnormally high levels of aluminum. So be alert, but also realize that the coating on aluminum should prevent this.

With this in mind, aluminum pots with anodized coatings are often the choice of professionals. Heavy ones conduct heat very well.

Stainless steel. These are good if clad thickly with copper or aluminum. Don't confuse a real clad bottom with a pot that has a microfilm of copper on it—the thin film won't do a thing. Stainless steel is a long-lasting material that will resist the most ruthless scrubbing. The clad bottom will distribute heat much more evenly than a plain stainless steel pan. On aluminum-clad pans, the layer of aluminum should be at least 1/4 inch thick. On a copper-clad pot, the copper layer need not be as thick, because copper is a better conductor than aluminum (which is why copper is used to wire your home). It should measure between 1/16 and 1/8 inch, about the thickness of the cover of a hardbound book.

Copper. It's expensive and you'll have to keep it polished. But it makes for even cooking and looks impressive in your kitchen. *Disadvantage:* Copper needs to be lined with tin or aluminum to keep the metal from leaking into the food. The danger of ingested copper is well documented. It can cause nausea, vomiting and diarrhea, so be careful.

Glass. Glass is a poor conductor and as such it makes an unsatisfactory stove-top vessel. Because it cannot conduct heat efficiently, glass builds up severe hot spots.

Porcelain-covered steel. Though they often come in attractive colors, these pots, like glass, conduct heat poorly and develop hot spots that will burn your food.

Nonstick pans. *Advantages:* They're easy to clean. Omelets, pancakes, etc., need little oil—a spritz of vegetables spray will usually do. If you're trying to cut down on fat, this can help. *Disadvantages:* You'll need a set of non-metal utensils, because nonstick coatings are damaged by even the slightest contact with metal. Also, most nonstick coatings appear on thin, poor-quality cookware. If you want good cookware with nonstick, invest in heavy-gauge alu-

Seasoning a Dutch Oven or Cast-Iron Pan

To season new cast-iron cookware, first scrub it thoroughly inside and out with a dish cleanser and a steel scrubbing pad. Rinse well and towel dry. Coat the entire inside of the pan lightly with a high-smoke-point cooking oil like safflower or peanut oil. Place in a 325°F oven for one hour. When cooled, the utensil will be seasoned and ready for use.

minum with a nonstick coating. However, unlike most quality cookware, which should last a lifetime, nonstick pans generally have a limited lifetime because the coating eventually wears off.

If you don't plan to do a lot of cooking, a set of quality nonstick cookware may be a good choice. But if you do a lot of cooking, you need something that can take the punishment of repeated heating, stirring, scraping and scrubbing. The more traditional choices are better.

Health concerns over how these coatings react at high temperatures are negligible.

OVENWARE

Covered roasting pan. Great for meats and poultry. It allows juices to drain, has a removable tray for easy carving and adjustable vents on top to release steam.

Covered casserole dish or dutch oven. Something in your set of stove-top cookware might substitute for this.

Baking and oven pans. You'll probably need a variety of shapes and sizes including cookie sheets, something large and deep for dishes like lasagna and a smaller pan for recipes like cornbread or brownies. You might need cake pans or pie tins, depending on what you like to cook. If you're wondering what sizes to get, check your favorite recipes and see what they call for. Nonstick surfaces can be really useful here, as baking tends to make food stick. If you're an avid baker, double-layered bakeware can be useful to avoid burnt bottoms, especially in recipes that call for a lot of sugar or butter, both of which burn easily.

Essential Implements, Gadgets and Accessories

•Eggbeater or electric mixer

•Spatulas: one elongated and one with a nearly flat base for flipping food (if your pans are nonstick be sure your spatulas are nylon, not metal)

•Two wooden spoons, one for sweet stuff, one for strong flavors

•Slotted spoon

•Ladle

•Pot holders, two flat and two insulated oven mitts

•Aprons with bibs

•Four all-cotton dish towels

•Measuring spoons

•Measuring cups: one set of the nesting variety and one large (four-cup) glass measure for large amounts of liquid

•Mixing bowls in graduated sizes

•Hand grater—you may need this even if you have a food processor

•Large colander

•Two cutting boards, a large wooden one that can double as a cheese board and bread board, and another of acrylic for chopping onions and garlic

•Large wooden salad bowl/chopping bowl

•Strainer—to keep mesh clear, wash strainer immediately after use and brush with a toothbrush

Cooking Techniques Defined

Fry. Food is either placed in very hot oil until cooked or is cooked on a hot surface in its own fat. In deep-frying, the food is completely immersed in oil. Since oil can be heated to very high temperatures (deep-frying happens at around 375[deg]F), frying cooks the food quickly and seals in its flavors. The oil absorbed by the food in this process also carries flavors to your palate. Unfortunately, it also adds enormously to the caloric content of the food, and the standard, current medical advice is that you should reduce your consumption of food prepared in this way.

Sauté. Similar to frying but uses only a small amount of oil or fat in a hot pan. Food is stirred rapidly to expose it to the heat and avoid scorching.

Braise. Food is sautéed or seared and then cooked more slowly in liquid.

Boil. Food is placed in boiling water until cooked. Cooking under pressure, in a pressure cooker, greatly speeds up this process by raising the boiling point of the water a few degrees. Pressure cooking is the best way to cook beans.

Note: Frying, sautéing, braising and boiling are all stove-top methods that rely on heat conduction to cook the food. Heat is conducted from hot oil to the food or from hot water to the food, depending on the method used.

Roast. Meat is placed over flame or in the oven until cooked. A meat thermometer is a good way to test for doneness.

Bake. A type of convection cooking that refers to anything, except a roast, placed in the oven at an even temperature until cooked. In convection cooking, hot air circulates around the food and imparts heat to it until the food is cooked. Breads, cakes and muffins are cooked this way, and so are casseroles.

Broil. Food, often meat or fish, is cooked closely under a flame, so that the heat is imparted by radiation and not convection. The radiant energy in broiling is so intense that cooking happens very fast, and the food must be turned to cook both sides. Because of the intense radiant heat, the outside of the food cooks before the inside has had a chance to lose its moisture, so broiling is an excellent way to preserve the succulence of many foods.

•Can opener

•Vegetable peeler

•Bottle and juice-can opener

•Pepper mill

•Garlic press (jaws should be strong and tight-fitting so the cloves don't escape out the sides)

Useful Extras
•Food processor and/or blender

•Toaster oven

•Marble slab for rolling out dough

•Pounder for meat tenderizing

•Salad spinner

•Immersion blender (This is like a mobile food processor. It can be immersed directly into a pot on the stove to puree vegetables, make sauce or cream soup.)

Herbs and Spices

Strictly speaking, herbs are seasonings derived from the leafy portions of certain aromatic plants. Spices, on the other hand, are seasonings derived from portions of plants other than the leaves. They include ground seeds, beans, bark, stems and roots. The terms "herb" and "spice" are often used interchangeably.

Keep them fresh. Be sure to follow the food storage tips for herbs and spices. Spices will lose their potency during storage and will eventually become useless. The best way to test for freshness is to smell. Before putting a new spice on your shelf, close your eyes and sniff gently. Try to remember the smell. As you use your herbs and spices, sniff them occasionally and measure the scent against the scent you remember when you bought it. If the scent has lost its essential potency, replace it and discard the old stuff.

DESCRIPTIONS AND USES
The following are some of the most common uses of each spice or herb.

Allspice. Tastes of several spices (cinnamon, cloves and nutmeg) as its name suggests, but it is one berry. Whole spice is small, dark, dried berries, about the size of peppercorns. Used whole, stuffed into veal, or ground, in spice cake, apple pie.

Anise seed. Tiny, black seeds from which an oil is extracted; can also be used whole. Tastes strongly of licorice. Limited uses in some baked goods. Seeds may be sprinkled on cookies or blended in some bread recipes.

Basil. An herb from the leaves of the basil plant. Used dried and crushed or fresh. An essential ingredient in pesto and Italian seasoning. Use on tomato, fish, eggs and green salads.

Caraway seed. Tiny, brown seed. Use whole. Sprinkle into dough for rye bread, use sparingly in soups and stews.

Cardamom. Highly aromatic seeds with white shells. Use whole, steeped in tea, or ground, in certain Indian spice mixtures and in some baked goods.

Celery seed. From wild celery. Use whole in stocks, pickles and salad dressings.

Chervil. Use fresh leaves, never dried. Delicate flavor finds many uses in cheese, eggs, meats, salads, soups and stews.

Cinnamon. A spice ground from a sharply flavored bark. Use in many hot drinks, baked desserts, fruit pies. Use a dash with Italian seasonings in tomato-based sauces.

Cloves. A dark, irregularly shaped seed. Use whole in roasts and in hot beverages such as mulled wine, or ground in pumpkin pie and spice cake.

Coriander. Seeds are used whole and ground as a mild spice in marinades and soup stocks. Leaves are used fresh as a pungent herb in Mexican and Indian food, salad, soups and stews. Use ground, dried coriander in Indian spice mixtures.

Cumin. Tiny seeds. Ground cumin is an essential ingredient in many ethnic cuisines. Use in meats and chili.

Dill. Small, flat seeds are used whole, in pickling. Leaves, called "dill weed," used dried and whole or fresh in coleslaw, salad dressings, potato salad and in many soups.

Fennel. The seed is most commonly available, but fresh leaves can be used as well. Use in lentils, rice pilaf and potatoes.

Ginger. Woody, textured root with a complex flavor both sweet and hot. Used fresh, chopped or shaved, in Asian and Indian food; or dried and powdered may be used sparingly in stews and some cookies.

Mustard. Sometimes called mustard seed, the powder is actually the remainder of the seed after its oil has been extracted. Use in preparing table mustard or in salad dressings and ethnic cuisine.

Nutmeg. Large seed from the fruit of an East Indian tree. Used fresh, grated, or dry, powdered. Quite fragrant. Limited uses in desserts and hot drinks. Use in eggnog.

Oregano. Leaves are used dried or fresh. Whole dried oregano sometimes includes flowers and buds, which add a

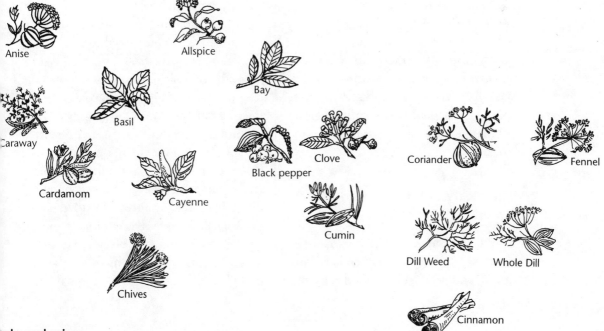

Anise

Allspice

Bay

Basil

Caraway

Cardamom

Cayenne

Black pepper

Clove

Coriander

Fennel

Cumin

Dill Weed

Whole Dill

Chives

Cinnamon

depth of flavor and aroma. Many uses in meats, sauces, poultry seasoning, vinaigrette, fish and soups. Essential ingredient in Italian seasoning.

Rosemary. Stiff, pointed leaves. Crush in palm of hand or between fingers and use sparingly to season poultry and lamb.

Saffron. Used for its yellow color, and to impart a subtle flavor. Expensive. Limited use in sparing amounts only for bouillabaisse, Spanish and Indian rice dishes.

Sage. A true American herb, mostly available dried but far superior fresh. Use to flavor turkey, goose, pork and poultry stuffing. Also use a dash in seafood soups and chowders.

Summer savory. Leaves of an annual shrub. Delicate flavor. Use in combination with sage. Also use on eggs.

Tarragon. Its chief flavor component is identical to anise. Fresh or dry leaves. Use to make flavored vinegar, or to season fish, eggs, chicken and salads.

Thyme. Leaves of any of a large variety of plants, each producing a slightly different flavor. It is sometimes sold as a powder but as such loses its potency in a matter of weeks. Use sparingly to season veal, lamb and pork, even more sparingly on poultry. Essential ingredient in poultry stuffing. Use in soups and stocks.

Chemical Additives: Natural vs. Organic

No official definition exists for "natural" as it is applied to commercially produced food products. If a food is labeled "all natural," it usually means that it contains no artificial colors or additives or chemical preservatives. Some manufacturers, however, may claim one or more natural ingredients in a product containing other, artificial ingredients. Tang, for example, claims "natural organic flavor" but contains several artificial ingredients. Read the label.

SHOPPING ORGANIC

If you shop for organic foods, ask the store owner or manager what they mean by "organic" and what kind of systems are in place to verify the exclusive use of organic farming techniques. Ask to see any certificates or affidavits with regard to growing techniques used. Sometimes an honor system is used, with farmers pledging to use certain growing techniques. More stringent and perhaps reliable systems use inspections to verify that the farmer is complying with certain standards of organic farming. "FVO," Farm Verified Organic, is one such system that is widely used.

When shopping for organic foods remember that not everything sold in the store is necessarily organic. Ask. Also, the organic fertilizer used to grow the produce may contain dangerous microorganisms. Wash thoroughly.

Finding a store that sells quality organic foods may not be easy. These stores are not usually as profitable as big chain supermarkets, so they generally don't have the resources to advertise. Look in the Yellow Pages of your local phone book under "Health Foods." You'll probably find something there, though much of what's listed may be vitamin and fitness stores that cater to body builders. If you find a store this way and it isn't to your satisfaction, ask some of its patrons if they know of anywhere else to shop. You'll often find people who shop for organic produce to be approachable and well-informed.

FOOD ADDITIVES

Food additives include any substance intentionally added to food to change it cosmetically, preserve it or even to improve its food value. Additives can be natural or artificial. Additives are commonly used as flavorings, colorings, preservatives, texture agents—including thickeners, stabilizers and emulsifiers—PH controllers, leavening and vitamins and minerals. Additives are prevalent in foods you would be better off not eating at all. This includes junk foods, artificial beverages, commercial sausage, packaged cakes and the like.

Though the mere word "additive" doesn't necessarily mean "bad for you," you should exercise some caution. There are a number of additives that are deemed perfectly safe, however. These include:

- Alginate and propylene and glycol alginate
- Alpha tocopherol
- Ascorbic acid
- Beta carotene
- Calcium (or sodium) stearyl lactylate
- Carboxymethylcelluose (CMC)
- Casein and sodium caseinate
- Citric acid and sodium citrate

- EDTA
- Erythobic acid
- Ferrous gluconate
- Fumaric acid
- Gelatin
- Glycerin
- Gums: arabic, fucelleran, ghatti, karaya, locust bean, tragacanth
- Hydrolyzed vegetable protein (HVP)
- Lactic acid
- Lactose
- Lecithin
- Mannitol
- Polysorbate 60, 65 and 80
- Sodium benzoate
- Sorbic acid and potassium sorbate
- Sorbitan monosterate
- Sorbitol
- Starch and modified starch
- Vanillin and ethyl vanillin
- Salt and sugar

Remember that this is not an inclusive list and as a frequent label reader you will become more knowledgeable about what additives are. If you wish to avoid additives as much as possible here are some tips:

- Keep your food intake varied; this will keep the kinds of additives varied.
- Eat fresh or minimally processed foods.

• Boxed and canned foods have more additives than frozen.

• Always read labels.

• Remember, "natural" doesn't necessarily mean "additive-free."

Wine Basics

Wine is a natural enhancement for food. Finding the greatest combinations, though, does take some time and some dedicated tasting. If you have to bring over a bottle of wine to a friend or choose the wine for dinner tonight, you need some hints that will get you through a wine list or help you ask the right questions at your wine store. Here's a basic primer that will equip you with enough knowledge to select a satisfactory bottle of wine.

It has become popular to order a bottle by its varietal name, i.e., calling the wine by the name of the grape. People have become hooked on Chardonnays and Cabernets. But did you know that what you call a Cabernet is one of the major grapes that make up famous Bordeaux wines, or that a Pinot Noir is the grape that fills up the bottle of the coveted Burgundy? Here are some of the grapes that are found in some popular bottles of wine:

Red
Merlot: grape of Bordeaux

Cabernet Sauvignon: grape of Bordeaux

Pinot Noir: grape of Burgundy

Syrah: grape of Côte du Rhone (also known as shiraz in Australia and sirah in California)

Tempranillo: Spanish Riojas

Sangiovese: Italian Chiantis

Nebbiolo: heavy-bodied Barolos and a host of other Italian wines

White
Pinot blanc: close relative of Chardonnay

Pinot Grigio: Italian, dry and spicy

Chardonnay: the white grape of Burgundy; popular all over the world

Sauvignon Blanc (also called fumé blanc): Loire Valley wines

Gewurztraminer: famous in Alsace, spicy and grassy in character

Riesling: German wines with sweetly dry, acid balance

Take Your Time

You probably lead a very busy life. You may have more things you need to do than time to do them. A quiet, leisurely meal may seem like a luxury when you are only on page two of your 20-page "to do" list. Gulping down breakfast while reading the newspaper, guzzling a luncheon sandwich in between phone calls and gobbling a take-out dinner while watching television may be more familiar than having a relaxed, quiet meal with friends.

There is nothing wrong with eating this way, but you pay a real price for doing so. You ignore someone very important: you.

When you eat with awareness, you become reacquainted with yourself. Here's what begins to happen:

You enjoy food more fully.

You notice how food affects you and you are less likely to overeat.

You begin to become more aware of other aspects of your inner life, including your emotional and spiritual sides.

From *Eat More, Weigh Less,* by Dean Ornish, M.D., copyright 1993. Published by HarperCollins Publishers.

Muscadet: makes a light, very dry wine, comes from region around Brittany

How to taste a wine: here are a few things you might want to notice, and look and smell for:

•Color

•Body

•Acid balance

•Fruit

•General smells, from flowers to fruit to salt to soil; let your imagination go.

•General taste

WHAT TO DRINK WITH WHAT

You say you've always heard that white wine goes with fish and red wine goes with meat? That is the popular wisdom, but there are exceptions. There is nothing wrong with a Zinfandel with salmon or a Pinot Noir with sole if this is your taste. You should remember that wine tastes different with different foods. Perfect wine and food matches should come together separately but as equals. When the two cohabit in your mouth, they should promote other wonderful tastes. Many foods do seem to go well with certain wines, but it is best to follow your own tastebuds and find your own matches. But you might start here:

•Spicy foods seem to want wines with a lot of acid or fruit to cut through the multitude of tastes.

•Rich food can stand up to big, round wines.

•Acidic foods can often take a spicy red wine.

•Italian food goes great with Italian wines.

•Red pastas go well with red wines of good acid balance.

•Salmon: heavy-bodied Burgundy, New Zealand Chardonnay or spicy red Zinfandel.

•Grilled tuna: white, red or rose with some fruit—a fruity Sauvignon Blanc, for example, or even a full-blooded Côte du Rhone.

•Oysters: Chablis or champagne.

•Barbecues: red wine with a bite, perhaps an Italian Barbera or a Zinfandel.

•Roast beef: a fine red wine of almost any kind with medium to full body.

•Asian and other spicy cusines: spicy white wine, Gewurtztraminer, Pinot Blanc, retsina. A fresh Sancerre. A spicy red, like Zinfandel.

•Hamburger: something young, fun, red and not too serious. An Italian Barbera, a young Beaujolais.

•Steaks: T-bone needs a powerful Cabernet Sauvignon or Burgundy; steak au poivre goes well with a young Rhone or Cabernet.

•Mild cheese can go with any good red or white wine. Strong cheese can completely obliterate the taste of the wine. For strong, blue-veined cheese, choose sherry or port.

•Red sauce: Chianti, Montepulciano d'Abbruzo, Barbera.

•Cream sauce: Orvieto or Italian Chardonnay.

TO LEARN MORE ABOUT WINE

You might look for adult-education seminars or ask in a local wine store whether they know of any individuals in your area who give formal sit-down tastings and seminars. There's also a lot you can do on your own. If you want a non-intimidating way to enter the oenophile world, try this: Buy two bottles of wine with dinner. Make a game of it. Taste the wine by itself and then taste it along with the food. Experiment with various recipes you might want to try or foods like pizza, oysters, Chinese takeout. Try two disparate styles of wine, thinking of the body of wine, the acidity and the fruit. Another way is to start your own circle of wine tasters. Each household of interested parties can rotate the responsibility of choosing the evening or wine tastings. This is often best done by centering the choice of wines around a particular region or a particular grape. Try not to have more than 15 people per bottle. Remember to tell people that they don't have to finish anything they don't like.

Sources of Further Information

BOOKS AND PAMPHLETS

Better Homes and Gardens New Cook Book. Meredith Corp., Des Moines, Iowa, 1974.

Calories and Weight: The USDA Pocket Guide. United States Dept. of Agriculture, Human Nutrition Information Service. Free from the Consumer Information Center, Dept. 1072, Pueblo, CO 81009.

Fish & Seafood Made Easy. U.S. Department of Commerce National Fish and Seafood Promotional Council, 1989.

Food Additives. Food and Drug Administration, in cooperation with the Food Education Foundation. Free from the Consumer Information Center, Dept. 5242, Pueblo, CO 81009.

Jane Brody's Good Food Book. Jane E. Brody, Bantam Books, New York, 1987.

The Joy of Cooking. Irma S. Rombauer and Marion Rombauer Becker, Bobbs-Merrill Co., Indianapolis/New York, 1975.

8

Clothing

Basic Wardrobe Planning

Most people have too many clothes. At the same time, they find they have nothing to wear. This seeming paradox is the result of hand-me-downs, bargain racks, hard-to-resist sales and years of never throwing out a thing. As your closet gets more and more full, everything seems to be too big or too small and to go with nothing else you own. No wonder you never have anything to wear. With a few guidelines in planning your wardrobe, less can truly be more.

You should plan your wardrobe as carefully as you decorate your home. Perhaps even more so. The way you look directly influences the way people react to you and can also affect your career. Your clothing choice signals how you feel about yourself: your confi-dence, creativity, leadership ability, intelligence and attitude. These are not trivial matters.

It is important to realize that within any budget, you can look in step with fashion. It might take more time to find quality at a lower price, but it can be done and is well worth the effort.

CLOTHING FOR OFFICE AND CAREER

Did you know that someone who is serious about their career spends between 8 and 12 percent of their household income on clothing? Clearly, if you are in the workforce, a working wardrobe is the area that needs the most thought in your closet. Though there are many rules of how and what to wear in the office, your lifestyle and personality can still be reflected in what you buy.

First, consider the kind of work you do and where you do it.

•Can you bend the rules because you are in a creative area?

•Is the code strict because of a conservative atmosphere?

•Do you need work clothes that can make the transition from day to nighttime functions?

•Do you travel often for your job?

•Do you have a lot of social obligations in your work?

A construction worker is not going to have the same clothing needs as a lawyer, and a graphic designer does not have the same constraints as an analyst on Wall Street.

Accessories are important. A tie. Socks. A big shoulder bag. A suede backpack. It is in these that you may express yourself in the workplace. If you are still developing a style of your own, rather than consulting fashion magazines consult catalogs that gear themselves toward professional women with a classic sense of style, such as J. Crew or Tweeds. Both of these push a look, and most pieces are interchangeable.

During the 168 hours in the week, a person who is employed full-time spends an average of:

•50 hours in work functions

•21 hours socializing

•68 hours sleeping

•6 hours in exercise and sports

•23 hours shopping, cleaning, reading, etc.

Whether or not you work full-time, this way of approaching your wardrobe will give you an idea of where you should put your emphasis when buying clothes. If you never go to black-tie functions, having three formal gowns in the closet, no matter what great bargains they may have been, doesn't make sense, nor does owning a tuxedo instead of renting one. Why should you have three suits instead of interchangeable separates?

Setting clothing priorities: To begin with, figure out the percentage of time during the week you spend:

•At leisure

•Working out or playing sports

•At the workplace or socializing for work

•Socializing

•Formal occasions

Now, take a look at your clothing priorities:

•Comfort

•Image

•Self-expression

•Budget

•Function

Then take a look at your wardrobe to see if your clothes-buying habits are in tune with these priorities.

The Rules

Dressing properly for business requires paying attention to a few important and widely acknowledged rules of attire.

Women's business dress:

•Dress for your professional aims. You can never go wrong with a suit or jacket and skirt.

•You cannot climb the corporate ladder wearing spike heels. Heels should not be more than two inches high and should have some width.

•When wearing boots, never allow skin to show.

•Leave the excess jewelry at home. Stay with the simple: a single accent piece, such as one bangle or a striking brooch.

•No long, killer fingernails.

•No obviously tight or sexy clothes.

•No miniskirts with heels. If you wear a short skirt, pair it with opaque or thick stockings and shoes, both in the same sober color.

•No running shoes with suits, even in the elevator.

Men's business dress:

•Always wear a suit or a jacket and tie, even if you work in the mail room.

•Navy pinstripe is always the conservative suit of choice. A brown suit shows more spark but is not as safe. Brown is fine for advertising but not for banking.

•Your socks should be long enough so that no skin shows between top of socks and pants cuff.

•No visible jewelry other than cufflinks (for dress) and wristwatch.

•No running shoes with suits, even in the elevator.

Updating Your Wardrobe

Every year you should update your wardrobe by adding a few pieces. Small additions and changes revitalize outfits. Building a wardrobe around basics is not as boring as it sounds; it is only how you wear it that can be boring. Remember that your attitude is essential. A stiff suit is suddenly made casual by wearing a T-shirt underneath (try a silk or cashmere T-shirt for more elegance, but cotton can look very spirited). A basic black suit can be jazzed up with a bright pin or a muted scarf.

Step 1: Go through what you own. Keep your function and purpose in mind and note that every item you analyze should meet these criteria:

•It fits or can be altered.

•You have worn it in the past two years.

•It works with two-thirds of your wardrobe.

•It still looks current.

How do you know if a piece is dated? By looking at the following features in relation to the current fashion:

•The length of the skirt is in proportion to its shape.

•How the armholes are set.

•It works with two-thirds of your wardrobe

•Shape of the collar and lapels.

Think of it this way: There are certain decades that had classic styling and seem to live forever. Look at the sweater set as given to the world by Chanel in the 1930s. It is still classic and in style. A fitted jacket along the lines of those worn in the forties is another classic. But the boxiness of a jacket from the early sixties might be more questionable. The wide lapels of the seventies and the long pointed collars of that decade will always look dated.

Step 2: Buy items with a long shelf life. Here are some examples:

•Sweaters in basic colors and a variety of styles, such as cardigans, V-neck pullovers and crewnecks

•Straight skirts

•Classic low-heeled pumps

•Shirtwaist dresses

•Coat dresses

•Oxford-cloth shirts

•Pinstripe shirts

•Skirts with sewn-down pleats

•Trench coats

•Pinstripe suits

•Wing-tip shoes

•White bucks

•Tweed raglan-sleeve overcoats

EASY FIXES FOR BETTER FIT AND FOR UPDATING THE LOOK OF A GARMENT

When you go through your closet or deal with secondhand clothing, some quick remodeling can give new, updated looks. Many of these you can do yourself, even if you are not skilled at sewing. A word of warning: Never cut into fabric before you are really sure. In fact don't cut unless you absolutely have to.

Here are a few easy fixes you can do yourselves with very little equipment other than a needle and thread:

•Readjust the size of shoulder pads to make the blouse or dress look like new. Here's how: Place pad on shoulder, don garment and pin it in from the outside. Then take jacket off and baste pads in.

•Shorten skirts.

•Add snaps and hooks.

•Shorten sleeves—without wrist bands.

•Move or change buttons.

•Add or remove detail, e.g., epaulets/collars and lace (see stitching illustrations).

Going Shopping

It helps to know what you want. Learn how to visualize your garment; it is out there. When you know you want a black pleated skirt, it is amazing how it jumps off the racks at you. Here are a few shopping rules:

•You should absolutely love what you buy.

• If it doesn't make you feel great you won't want to wear it and it is good money thrown out.

• The more costly a garment the greater should be its versatility. If you buy an expensive suit, be sure you can dress it up and down, and wear it as separates. It will then cost less every time you wear it!

• Don't buy a garment unless you're satisfied with these four things: fit, price, style and color.

• When you go shopping, wear something that's easy to slip in and out of. In other words, dress for undressing.

• Shop often. It's easier to find what you want at a price you like if you're not desperate.

CHOOSING YOUR COLORS

Clothing colors can make you feel warmer or cooler, larger or smaller. Many people these days have their colors analyzed so they can hit the stores with a list of their most flattering shades. This may be fun but it is not entirely necessary. If you doubt your own opinion, ask a friend whose taste you trust.

Black will always be indispensable in a modern wardrobe, but there are other options. The best advice is to base a wardrobe around three colors—two neutrals and an accent color, such as gray, black and red; white, black and red; or brown, fawn and green. All three colors should work together and all pieces for work should be interchangeable. This simple color coordination makes getting dressed in the morning much easier.

Many people insist they cannot wear certain colors, but in reality almost any person can wear any color if you wear the proper color lipstick, or a scarf around your neck to flatter your skin. Certainly any color is fine on the bottom half of the body.

QUESTIONS TO ASK IN FRONT OF THE MIRROR

• Do I feel like myself in this?

• Do I feel good in this?

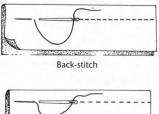

Back-stitch

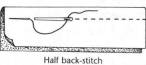

Half back-stitch

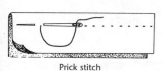

Prick stitch

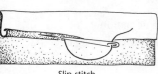

Slip-stitch

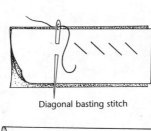

Diagonal basting stitch

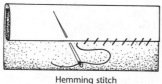

Hemming stitch

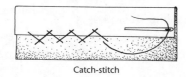

Catch-stitch

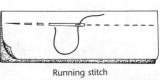

Running stitch

Even basting stitch

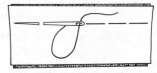

Uneven basting stitch

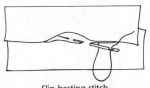

Slip basting stitch

Updating your wardrobe: Easy fixes

•Is it appropriate for the occasion?

•Does it go with many other possibilities in my closet?

•How many functions does it serve?

BASIC ITEMS

A basic wardrobe for a working woman consists of a jacket, skirt, pants, tops and accessories. Knit tops for any season are more versatile than cloth. They fit better, tuck in better, and make the transition easily from season to season as well as for different functions.

Here are some essentials:

•A black skirt with enough of a hem to shrink and grow with changing hemlines. The skirt can be either softly pleated or straight and narrow. A skirt like this is simple to dress down or dress up, depending on your choice of top.

•Two jackets, one fitted, one casual and roomy with dress-up or dress-down potential.

•Cashmere cardigan or any kind of twin set. Ultimately fashionable and versatile, it can be worn with ease and will always have a sporty elegance that works with everything.

SPOTTING QUALITY

Do you have memories of Grandmother inspecting buttonholes? It used to be a standard way to establish quality. Well, today you can still find hand-done buttonholes, but usually it will be in the couture clothing department. Most people can't afford couture, but by researching clothing in that department you can

develop an instinct for quality. Develop a feel for quality. Browse through the couture floors of a department store, look at these seams, feel the fabric. When you see it in a discount store, snap it up.

Here are some of the things you should be looking for:

•Strong patterns should match.

•Colors of dyed-to-match separates should match.

•Seams should be straight.

•Garments should be as nicely finished on the inside as on the outside.

•Stay away from decorative flaps that look like pockets but aren't. These are a sure sign of poor quality.

•Grab a handful of fabric and release it to judge the wrinkle effect.

•Pockets should be lined separately—usually with a heavy-gauge woven cotton. The inside pockets should be roomy.

•Check the outside leg seams in pants. If it's pressed flat, you're looking at fine construction.

•Check coat linings. In quality coats the hem is caught to the lining hem rather than being sewn to the coat fabric. This gives a soft, rolled finished rather than a flat one. If the coat lining hangs completely free, the coat construction is probably poor.

•Don't buy anything stitched with clear, plastic thread.

•Look for high quality horn or mother-of-pearl buttons, not plastic.

•In sleeves, sufficient amount of fabric should be pleated into the cuff, not gathered.

•Look for tight and careful stitches, with no loose ends.

•Fabric should be lush to the touch.

DISCOUNT SHOPPING

If you have time, discount places can be wonderful for saving money. Play clothes, shoes and accessories are easy to find at off-price shops, and so are lingerie, socks, stockings and underwear. Cut back where you can in these shops, and save your money for the big stuff.

Chains like Annie Sez, T.J. Maxx, Filene's Basement and Loehmann's have well-deserved reputations for designer goods at fair prices. Check to see if there are any locations near you. The big secret to shopping discount is that you have to go frequently. Get to know their stock. Stopping in weekly for a quick look can actually save hours at a later date. Go to your size, one up and one down (sometimes the merchandise is mis-sized) and run your finger down the rack, stopping at good-quality fabrics and examining your finds. This is a quick and reliable way of finding quality without having to look at each individual garment.

But beware the bright-orange-suit pitfall: Even if it is $50, it can be $50 thrown away. If you can't find what you are looking for at an off-price place, swallow hard and try the regular stores.

The Discount Maven

Sample sales are set in a warehouselike environment where manufacturers unload sample goods at a fraction of their retail price. Thousands of New York shoppers rely on their copies of Elysa Lazar's *S&B (Sales and Bargains) Report* to tell them where the bargains are. Not only does the newsletter provide a monthly calendar of exciting sample sales but also includes sales at retail, showroom, factory outlets and consignment shops and lets you know of other discount services.

Lazar has developed a solid reputation as the shopper's shopper. A large part of her busy schedule is taken up in flying around the country giving television and radio interviews, sharing her knowledge. The irony is that Lazar, who now specializes in the "the bargain," doesn't have the time to bargain-shop anymore. (See "Sources of Further Information," below, for details on how to obtain publications by Elysa Lazar). In an interview, she shared her views on outlet shopping.

Q: What kinds of discount stores are out there?

A: There are essentially two types of stores that offer discounted merchandise. These are factory outlets and discount stores, like Loehmann's and Filene's Basement. In the outlet category are the manufacturers' own factory outlets, which might be located at the factory itself, and then there are the outlet centers and villages, such as Manchester Center in Vermont and Maine's Freeport Village. These have been mushrooming around the country and all of the big designers are in the outlet business these days. Believe me, it is big business.

Q: Do outlets really offer great discounts?

A: Though the consumer can count on finding 30 to 35 percent off at these places, my rule of thumb is that it's not a deal unless it's at least 50 percent off.

Q: Are the goods the same as one can find in the department stores?

A: Some are, but many manufacturers also make clothes specifically to be sold at the outlets. And so the clothing may have the same silhouette but often the material is slightly different or the stitching a bit off; in general the quality may be of a lower grade. Be sure you ask if the garment you are interested in is the exact one available in the stores before you buy.

Q: What other things should you watch out for?

A: Much of the merchandise can be new but leftover from the previous year. Sometimes the dye lot is off. So when making a purchase at these stores, the rule is "buyer beware."

Q: What is the best time to shop the outlets?

A: The best times are around the holiday weekends, such as Fourth of July and Labor Day. Outlets often offer promotional sales on a similar schedule as the department stores. And on these sales the savings can be in the right discount category to suit my liking.

Q: What about discount stores?

A: At discount stores like Filene's Basement, Marshall's, T.J. Maxx and Loehmann's, the store buyers purchase seasonal leftovers or odd pieces or overstock that got left behind after the regular boutiques and department stores completed their orders. That's why shopping at these places can be a hit-or-miss affair. You will always find the best buys when something has gone wrong with the piece—for example, if the dye lot is slightly off. The merchandise at chains will also vary from store to store because the buyers tend to buy to suit the taste of the neighborhood. You might do well to travel to a ritzy section if you are looking for higher-quality gear.

Q: What about the shopper who is far away from good shopping? Can he or she get good deals too?

A: It is worth traveling to an affluent area to check out local resale shops or consignment shops. These are springing up all over the country and are often great dumping grounds for compulsive buyers who might only wear something once.

Q: How did you become the queen of discount?

A: My blood always was stirred by a good bargain. Friends who worked in the fashion industry let me know about sample sales and then I got the idea to list them and the *S&B Report* was born.

Q What's the best deal you ever got?

A: That's easy—it was an Armani suit at 85 percent off. It retailed for $1,000 and I got it for $150.

SHOPPING SECOND-HAND

Shopping for vintage clothing, in a store that specializes in antique clothing, can be a better deal than shopping for secondhand items at a thrift shop. Clothing was made more meticulously in the thirties, forties and fifties, and has survived the decades. These were often items that were made to last. Best finds are:

- Classic fitted jackets
- Plush cashmere sweaters
- Authentic Western shirts
- Silk nightgowns
- Formal attire
- Tuxedos

Use these pieces as accents or additions—head-to-toe vintage clothing looks eccentric.

When shopping at secondhand or antiques stores, the same rule applies as in examining your closet: Watch out for what is out of fashion and past restoration.

Every once in a while, you can find your dream outfit at a thrift shop. If this kind of find excites you, go and hunt. Feel no stigma about preworn goods. One last tip: when shopping secondhand or thrift stores, it is best to try shops in fashionable neighborhoods.

YOUR RIGHTS AS A SHOPPER

In general, if you bought something of reasonable quality and it falls apart after the first cleaning, you have a valid complaint, as long as you followed the washing instructions.

Ordering Clothes by Mail

Shopping by mail can save time, but not if you have to send the shipment back due to improper size, color or because it just doesn't look good.

Armchair shopping is not for everyone. It can be addictive, especially the TV shopping networks, which fan you into a frenzy. If you tend to be a compulsive shopper or need to stick to a budget, it's best to stay away from the television. However, there is a real old-fashioned pleasure, almost like receiving a gift, when packages come in the mail. If you order, take steps to insure satisfaction.

The same rules apply to mail-order shopping and the Home Shopping Network television programs. There are both advantages and drawbacks to each. One of the drawbacks is the limited information when ordering. To avoid disappointment you should try to acquire as much information as possible before you order.

Do not buy solely because of a picture or catchy description.

The customer-service number should be posted or easy to find in the pages of a catalog. Call and ask as many questions as you need to about a product. The order takers should be helpful. If not, don't buy from that company.

Pick dependable colors so there is no confusion between their idea of "celery" or "mushroom" and yours.

Read through the information very carefully. Make sure you understand the delivery and return policy. Ask how long it will take to get to you and how much the item will cost, including sales tax and handling charges.

Complete the order form legibly.

Keep a record of the purchase and the name of the person who took your order. Always ask for a confirmation number.

Ask family, friends and neighbors if they have ever ordered from a particular firm. You can also call your local Better Business Bureau to find out if the firm has acquired a bad reputation.

If you should run into any problems, first try to deal directly with the company by mail and then by a follow-up phone call.

In your letter of complaint, state the time and day ordered and details of the problem. Include your name, address, and day and evening phone numbers.

If your complaint is unsuccessful, contact:

Mail Order Action Line
Direct Marketing Association
11 W. 42nd St., P.O. Box 3861
New York, NY 10163-3861

Include a copy of your letter to the company and a note of when you made a follow-up call.

For additional tips about mail order and a directory of over 250 catalogs, send $3 to the above address.

Fading, shrinking, raveling and losing shape are all examples of valid complaints. Also, don't be afraid to complain about merchandise bought on sale. If you bought something "as is," that is a different story. Most reputable stores should be willing to take back a sale item for cash or store credit.

Fabrics

Angora. Soft hair of Angora goat or rabbit, used for sweaters.

Batiste. Fine, sheer linen or muslin in plain or figured weave.

Broadcloth. Densely woven fabric with soft finish in plain or twill weave.

Camel's hair. Soft, silky, felted camel wool or fabric resembling it, used for coats.

Cashmere. Very soft, downy wool from hair of Kashmir goat.

Cavalry twill. Sturdy, double twill of cotton, wool or worsted.

Challis. Soft, lightweight cotton or wool in plain weave.

Chambray. Lightweight fabric (cotton, silk or linen) with colored warp and white weft.

Charmeuse. Lightweight, drapable silk with semi-lustrous face and dull back.

Crepe. Lightweight crinkled fabric of silk, cotton or rayon.

Faille. Semi-lustrous ribbed fabric of silk, cotton, rayon or lightweight taffeta.

Gabardine. Firm woolen cloth in twill weave.

Melton. Heavy twilled wool with smooth face in solid colors.

Rep. Plain-weave fabric with prominent, rounded cording.

Seersucker. Lightweight, crinkled linen or cotton, usually striped.

Whipcord. Cotton, wool or worsted fabric with steep, diagonally ribbed surface.

Worsted. Woolen fabric with smooth, hard face and no nap.

New wools and microfibers. The "new wools" are soft, supple and are considered year-round fabrics. These garments are perfect for throwing into a valise for business travel or stuffing into a bag for the weekend. Another wonderful new fiber is microfiber. This is actually a polyester, but bears little resemblance to the polyester of old, which had no breathability and felt like plastic. Microfiber, like natural fiber, wicks moisture away from the body, allowing the body to breathe naturally. The available textures are varied: Microfiber can feel like chamoïs, washed silk, satin, taffeta or velvet.

FABRIC GUIDE TO THE SEASONS

Fall/Winter
•Wool gabardine

•Wool crepe

•Wool flannel

•Cashmere

• Alpaca

• Camel hair

Spring/Summer
• Linen

• Cotton

• Rayon

• Silk

• Blends of above

• Seersucker

In Between
• Corduroy

• Tropical-weight wool

• Silk/wool blend

• Light wool crepe

• Heavy cotton knit

Accessories

STYLES OF HANDBAGS
• Box: hard and structured

• Chanel: quilted with a chain handle

• Clutch: to be hand clutched, no handle or strap

• Envelope: long and rectangular

• Pouch: soft shape with a drawstring on the top

• Tote: like a shopping bag

Care of Handbags
• Do not overstuff

• Should not bulge

• Should be wiped with a damp cloth, and not immersed in water

• Suede should be Scotchgarded

• When not in use, stuff with paper

SHOES
Never buy cheap shoes if you can avoid it. More than any other single item, shoes can change the look of what you're wearing—they're one of the strongest fashion statements you can make without having to be a fashion victim. Shoes are truly where you can express yourself. Here are a few rules:

• They must be comfortable. Only a fashion victim will suffer corns on their toes for a look they simply must have.

• If you can buy only one pair of shoes, let it be black. Black shoes are indispensable, especially for men, since men's shoes should never be even a shade lighter than their suits. You do need to have more than one pair, however, because you should alternate shoes to preserve their working lives.

• For a day-to-day work shoe, the cap-toe is a good choice for men. A black low-heeled pump with a roundish toe works well for women. If you are concerned about how long a shoe will last, be careful not to go for trendy heels, since this is the style feature that will date the shoe. Outside the boardroom, penny loafers, brown shoes, suede shoes or shoe boots go well with jeans for both sexes.

• Did you know that feet perspire as much as half a cup of moisture in a normal day? Breathability is important. Leather shoes are recommended to allow the feet aeration. (Canvas are also all right.) Make sure you read inner labels, because some man-made materials do a convincing leather imitation on the shelf.

•Leather needs a rest after being worn. Wearing the same pair of shoes day after day will compromise longevity. Alternate pairs and store used pairs with cedar shoe trees, which will not only help maintain the shape of the shoe but also benefit the leather by slowly drawing out moisture.

•Shoes need maintenance—this means take them to your shoemaker. Do your own cleaning and polishing, but stay away from shoeshine sprays. They reduce the natural breathability of the leather and dry it out. Old-fashioned shoe polish will replenish the leather with essential oils and contribute to the long life of your shoes.

•Be a shoe tester and earn free shoes. For information contact:
Shoe Testers Association
660 Spartan Blvd. #9
Spartanburg, SC 29003
1-800-587-1719.

Underwear, Lingerie and Hosiery

Call it underwear (sounds so boring) or lingerie (much more appealing), anyway you like it, sexy or prosaic, these garments are the foundation of a woman's wardrobe. Even though these bare necessities are hidden under clothes, they influence your attitude and your comfort level, as well as the fit of your clothing.

For men, the options are simple: boxer shorts, bikinis or briefs; undershirt or T-shirt. It actually comes down to baggy underwear or tight underwear, and the most demanding decision is whether to go for silk and be frivolous or stick with cotton and be safe.

But women must choose among brassieres (underwires, soft cups, fiberfill, strapless bras, bustiers) and body shapers (girdles, corsets or panty girdles) as well as different types of panties (G-strings, thongs, briefs, boxers and bikinis). It can be tough: According to

If the Shoe Fits

1. Sizes vary among shoe brands and styles. Don't select shoes by the size marked inside. Judge the shoe by how it fits on your foot.

2. Select a shoe that conforms as nearly as possible to the shape of your foot.

3. Have your feet measured regularly. The size of your feet changes as you grow older.

4. Have both feet measured. Most people have one foot that's larger than the other. Fit to the largest foot.

5. Fit at the end of the day when your feet are largest.

6. Stand during the fitting process and check that there is adequate space (⅜ to ½ inch) for your longest toe at the end of each shoe.

7. Make sure the ball of your foot fits snugly into the widest part (ball socket) of the shoe.

8. Don't purchase shoes that feel too tight, expecting them to "stretch" to fit.

9. Your heel should fit comfortably in the shoe with a minimum amount of slippage.

10. Walk in the shoe to make sure it fits and feels right. (Fashionable shoes *can* be comfortable!)

From ``10 Points of Proper Shoe Fit,'' National Shoe Retailers Association, Prescription Footwear Association and American Orthopaedic Foot and Ankle Society.

industry statistics, 85 percent of all women wear bras that don't fit them properly.

The fabrics available include nylon, silk, rayon and cotton. The rule of thumb is: Buy natural fibers, especially for items that are worn next to the skin. It is worth the longer drying time and the price differential.

BRASSIERES

A bra can be simple or complicated, depending on the function it fulfills and the figure it is intended to fit. The various parts of a bra include the cups, which may be of various materials, and seamed or unseamed, depending on the design and purpose of the bra; the shoulder straps, which are usually adjustable and may be made of stretch or nonstretch materials; the fastening, which can be in front or in back and generally is of the hook-and-eye type; the back parts, which fasten around the wearer's back and may be thin or thick, elastic or non-elastic; the diaphragm, also known as the band, which runs beneath the cups; and the side panels, which support the bust and hold it in position.

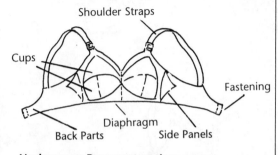

Underwear: Bra construction

Types of Bras

Seamed. These are sewed to an exact size and are available in a wide variety of styles and materials. Best for those who require firm bust support.

Unseamed. These have a smooth or molded cup, designed to be worn under body-hugging knits. Cups are molded on a form rather than sewn to fit. Available in stretch fabrics such as nylon, cotton and polyester, circular knits and tricot. Also available in support styles.

Soft Cup. Does not have an underwire.

Contour. These bras have lightweight fiberfill, giving shaping and uplift to add figure definition for women with small busts or those in between sizes.

Padded. Padding in a bra adds size and figure definition to create a well-proportioned, natural bust line.

Underwire. These bras have a thin, rigid wire (although it may also be of plastic) inserted beneath each cup, to give uplift, support and separation for those with droopy or soft bosoms. For a decollete, a half-cup underwire with fiberfill contouring is recommended.

Decollete or demi-bra. Low-cut, with side-set straps, to wear with evening clothes or revealing off-shoulder necklines.

Minimizer. A style designed for full-bosomed wearers to reduce projection of the bust and give a flatter but smooth and natural look.

Midline-long line. These bras are for those with fuller figures, to control flesh on the upper torso.

Strapless. These styles are worn under bare or strapless dresses, supporting the bust from below rather than from the shoulders. Available in contour, soft-cup or underwire styles.

Bustier (torsolette). Bustiers are corset-like garments, now a fashionable wardrobe item in such fabrics as stretch lace, satin and velvet. Torsolettes are generally longer and come with detachable garters for wearing with old-fashioned stockings.

Convertible. These bras have detachable straps that can be transformed into crisscross, lowback or halter styles.

Sport. Sports bras are designed to give comfortable support during all types of active sports, including running, aerobics and lifting weights. Cotton blends and lack of hardware protect against chafing, while nonstretch straps prevent uncomfortable bouncing. Use of polyester blends means that bras dry quickly.

Actionback. These bras, designed to give freedom of movement during sports, have V-shaped backs, with

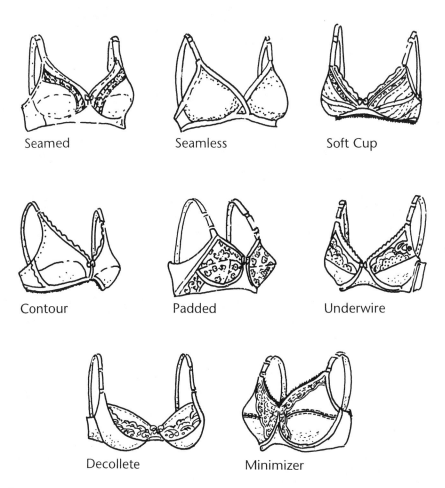

Seamed   Seamless   Soft Cup

Contour   Padded   Underwire

Decollete   Minimizer

Bra types

shoulder straps joining at the center of the back rather than the sides.

Maternity. These bras have cups that open for ease in breast feeding.

How to Fit a Bra

First of all, a good bra should be comfortable. It should not dig in at the shoulder. It should fit close to the breastbone and not stand away at the center. The cups should be ample enough to hold all of the breast tissue without creating a bulge of flesh. Bras should not ride up in back and should not be so tight that you can't slip a finger beneath the band at the base of the cups. To find out which size you wear, measure you ribcage under your breast (it's fine if you wear your own bra while you do this, but don't measure over clothing). Add five inches to this number. If you get an odd number, round up one to the even number. This is your body size. Then measure over the fullest part of the bust. The difference between the two numbers is your cup size.

A cup: 1-inch difference

B cup: 2-inch difference

C cup: 3-inch difference

D cup: 4-inch difference

Guide to bra size selection

Remember, these are general guidelines. Bra sizing varies slightly from manufacturer to manufacturer, and from style to style. You must still try on a bra to see if it fits properly. Here's how:

1. Slip bra straps over your shoulders. Grasp both sides of the bra and lean forward, easing your breasts into the cups.

2. Straighten up and without letting go of the fabric, slide both hands around to the back and hook it shut, making sure the band doesn't ride up.

3. Adjust the straps to smooth out the cup fabric. Your breasts should be supported at a comfortable level, about midway between your shoulder and elbow.

PANTIES

How many pairs do you need? This can be answered by another question: How often do you want to do the laundry? You'll find underwear, along with socks, to be the limiting factor in your laundry cycle.

Briefs: These cover the rear and stomach completely. The look is modest and functional.

Hipster: Comes to the waist, but is cut narrowly in front and sides, providing a compromise between brief and bikini.

Bikini: These have high-cut legs and low-cut waists, with fairly full coverage in the front and back. This style is the worst offender in the visible-panty-line category.

French bikini: Consists of two triangles, one in front and one in back, held together by strings around the sides. Minimal coverage.

G-string: A fabric string goes up the crease of your derriere. This style gives moderate coverage in the front and none in the back.

Thong: Like the G-string, but offers some coverage in back. Many consider it less comfortable than the G-string.

The minimal-coverage options take some getting used to. They're akin to wearing thong sandals and may be uncomfortable until you get accustomed to it. However, some women find that clothes fit better over these styles and prefer to wear them.

HOSIERY

They don't fit, they sag, they rip, they are a necessity and a luxury: pantyhose. They are expensive and fragile, but most women find they must wear them to work. The National Association of Hosiery Manufacturers gives these tips:

• Start by choosing the correct size. Always go up a size if you are between categories. Size charts are on the back of most packages of hosiery.

• Remove jewelry before you don hose, including rings, watches and bracelets.

• Check finger- and toenails for jagged edges. Keep nails short.

• Make sure hands are well-moisturized and not rough or chapped. You may even want to put on a pair of gloves for extra protection.

• Check shoes for rough spots

•Some say that storing your hose in the freezer will keep it from running, but this is just an old wives' tale—all you get is cold pantyhose.

How to Wash Socks and Hosiery

Proper washing not only keeps your hose clean, it may prolong its useful life.

•Never use hot water except on white goods.

•Do not use bleach except on white goods.

•Sheer products should never be bleached.

•Don't wash colored, striped or patterned hose with plain white items.

•Wash pantyhose by hand, with a mild detergent. After you wash them, roll them in a clean, dry towel to remove excess moisture and then hang dry. Never wring them.

•Sheer hosiery is very delicate and should be treated accordingly. If you want to wash it in the washing machine, use a lingerie bag and the delicate cycle, with warm or cool water, never hot.

Definitions of Some Hosiery Terms

Denier. This is the weight per unit length of yarn. The lower the denier, the lighter and finer the yarn and the more sheer the garment. Knit hose of high-denier yarn tend to be more durable.

Double reinforcement. These are lines of thread, usually polyester or nylon, knit into portions of the foot, usually toe and heel, to give added resistance to abrasion or stress.

Matte. Hosiery with a dull finish.

Microfiber. This is a generic term used for yarns of a filament of less than one denier. These tend to be very strong and feel wonderfully silky and soft on the skin.

Opaque. Stockings or pantyhose made of yarns which give them a heavier appearance, generally 40 denier or higher.

Clothing Essentials for Men

Most of the shopping tips above work well for both women and men, except the obvious—skirts are still not accepted for men in the workplace though they have been spotted on Paris runways! But here is some clothing advice for men only.

Some say that the most important item in a man's wardrobe is a navy blazer. It can look crisp, tailored and natty with a white shirt and tie, or it can go away for the weekend with jeans and a T-shirt. But you really have to be the navy blazer type.

The suit is the real soul of a man's wardrobe. And if you own only one, the experts agree that it should be a tropical-weight (preferably worsted) wool so that it can be worn all year round. This should probably be in navy, but black is also great because you can wear it formally as well. Gray flannel can be incredibly elegant, and so can brown, if you dare. But the navy banker's suit plays it safe.

Which shirt to wear underneath? The rule of thumb is that the tougher the fabric the more casual the garment—so keep away from Oxford cloth for formal wear. It is fine for the office, though.

Great fabrics for men's outer clothing include doeskin flannel, wool serge, cashmere, worsted, linen or blended fabrics.

THE OVERCOAT

Men often fret over what kind of coat to buy, but a raglan-sleeve tweed top coat with slash pockets is a fairly safe bet. It is roomy enough to be thrown on top of a suit, giving you plenty of mobility.

A trench coat is another possibility that will never go out of style.

Essentials for men: The overcoat

TIES

If you only need one tie in your wardrobe, buy a black knit that goes everywhere, crumples in your pocket and won't wrinkle. When shopping for ties, look for a lining and a short horizontal stitch on the back of the broad end of the tie. This keeps it from gaping and is an indication of quality. Stay away from synthetics.

MEN'S SHOES

Some basic styles for men are: 1. Monk strap, 2. Wing-tip, 3. Tassle loafer, 4. Cap toe, and 5. Lace-up Oxford.

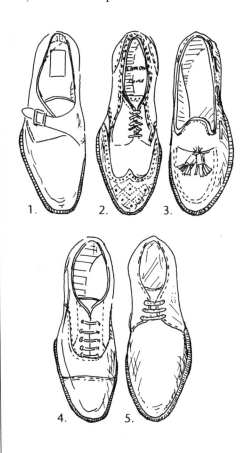

Children's Clothing

Kids grow out of things so quickly. It can be upsetting to spend large amounts of money on what will be history within a few months. Hand-me-downs and resale shops are the saving grace of children's clothing.

It's amazing how forthcoming friends and relatives are about loaning or giving away what is tucked away in their closet from their own growing children. Hand-me-downs should be received graciously, but even with plenty of them there's still a lot you will have to buy. Resale and consignment shops can be a great source for party dresses and outerwear, as well as the basics like T-shirts.

INFANCY

An infant can really spend the first five months in nothing but diapers and one piece, all-cotton body suits. These comforting garments cover all and warm the tiny feet. They come in a wide range of fabrics that run from a T-shirt look to something more fancy. It is all the same to the infant. Look for ones with snaps at the crotch for easy diapering. Always check—many European makers of adorable baby clothes neglect this important aspect of child-wear design.

Once your child begins to crawl, clothing needs to address more needs, such as knee protection, secure shoulder straps and free feet. At this point, parents tend to choose dark colors that don't show dirt and they discover sturdy overalls, which stand up to as much abuse as your child can give. (It is also a style that can prevail into adulthood.) If denim is too stiff, try cotton knit.

TODDLERHOOD

Your child is experimenting with independence now, and clothes should reflect this need. However, you still choose the clothing, not your baby, so you must imagine how your child will cope with each garment. Here is a checklist:

• Can the pants be slid on and off without adult help?

• Is the neck of the turtleneck wide and stretchy enough for your child to don it herself?

• Do shoes have Velcro instead of laces?

• Is the material flexible enough to be comfortable?

ABOUT CHILDREN'S SHOES

Before a child learns to walk, shoes are only needed for warmth, protection and dress-up. Once a toddler takes her first few steps, she needs shoes that will help her stay on her feet. Stay away from tennis shoes and shoes that will catch in carpeting, such as those with sticky rubber soles. Children's shoes should always allow for growth.

Here is a checklist for children's shoes from the American Orthopaedic Foot and Ankle Society:

• Good fit: comfortably loose when worn with soft, absorbent (mostly cotton) socks.

• Shaped like the foot, broad and spacious in the toe area.

•Shock-absorbent sole: a low wedge type is best.

•Breathable material: canvas or leather, not plastic.

Well-fitting baby shoes

Sources of Further Information

INDUSTRY ASSOCIATIONS

American Orthopaedic Foot and Ankle Society
  1-800-862-0500
  Free brochures on proper shoe fit.

Apparel Association of America
  1-703-524-1864
  Information on clothing sizes.

Cotton Incorporated World Headquarters
  1330 Avenue of the Americas
  New York, NY 10019
  1-212-586-1070
  Information on cotton.

National Association of Hosiery Manufacturers
  200 N. Sharon Amity Rd.
  Charlotte, NC 28211-3004
  1-704-365-0913
  Information on buying and caring for hosiery.

Wool Bureau
  330 Madison Ave.
  New York, NY 10017
  1-212-986-6222
  Information on wool.

BOOKS

Chic Simple: Clothes. Kim Johnson Gross and Jeff Stone, Knopf, New York, 1993.

The Clothing Care Handbook. Katherine Robinson, Ballantine Books, New York, 1985.

Dress Like a Million (On Considerably Less). Leah Feldon, Villard Books, New York, 1993.

The Image Impact: The Complete Makeover Guide. Jacqueline Thompson, ed., Bristol Books, New York, 1981.

PUBLICATIONS FROM THE LAZAR MEDIA GROUP

To order Lazar Media Group publications call or write:

112 East 36th St.
New York, NY 10016
1-212-679-5400

The S & B Report, published 10 times a year, lists sample sales in the New York metropolitan area. Get a current copy if you live in the area or plan a visit.

Museum Shop Treasures, a guide to over 200 museums offering mail-order shopping.

Shop by Mail, a "field guide," conveniently separated into categories.

The Outlet Shopper's Guide, comes with state-by-state maps and instructions.

9

Health

Staying healthy means knowing where to go for help with a physical or mental problem. But, perhaps even more importantly, it means doing all you can to stay well. Here are some tips on how to do both.

An Ounce of Prevention

Preventive health care is hardly a new idea—remember "an ounce of prevention is worth a pound of cure?"—but it's an increasingly popular one. Thanks to a recent spate of research on the causes of disease, it's clearer now than ever before that adopting the good habits below and dropping the bad ones will improve your chances of living a long and healthy life.

GOOD HABITS

Get regular exercise. "Building muscle may be the best single strategy for a longer healthy life," says *Health* magazine, "because it increases your strength, so you move around better; edges out fat, thus reducing the risk of developing a chronic disease; increases metabolism, so you burn calories faster; and fine-tunes the body's ability to use insulin, so you're at lower risk of diabetes." Regular exercise of any kind also lowers the risk of heart disease, helps relieve stress and increases your energy level. Weight-bearing exercises (these include running, walking, tennis and any other exercise in which you support your own body weight) stimulates bone growth and thus helps prevent osteoporosis, one of the major cripplers of older women. And aerobic exercise (anything that works your major muscle groups hard enough to make you sweat) can strengthen your heart, lungs and circulatory system as well as building muscle. For tips on how much exercise you need and how to work out at home, see "Exercise," below. For more on aerobic exercise and the heart, see the chart in the sidebar on "Heart Rates."

Eat right. A balanced diet includes enough vitamins, minerals, fiber, protein, fat and complex carbohydrates—but not too much of any one thing. This not only gives your body the nutrients it needs but lessens your risk of developing either of the two major killers, cancer or heart disease. For more detail, see "Nutrition," below.

Practice safe sex techniques. For more details, see "Safe Sex," later in chapter.

Manage chronic health problems. About a million Americans die every year from the effects of hypertension (high blood pressure), yet most of those early deaths could have been averted through a combination of diet, exercise and medication. The same combination can also control the symptoms and side effects of such potentially crippling conditions as hardening of the arteries, diabetes, asthma, allergies, chronic bronchitis and epilepsy.

Fasten your seat belt. More people die in traffic accidents each year than from any other single cause. Most of them would have survived if they had worn seat belts.

Relieve stress. When presented with a serious physical or emotional challenge, your brain pumps out a set of hormones that put your body on alert. This is helpful in the short term, but if it continues for weeks at a time, your body's immune system may be thrown off balance. Regular exercise helps relieve stress, which not only relaxes your muscles and mind but lowers your blood pressure and perhaps even your risk of disease. Techniques such as deep breathing, massage therapy, progressive relaxation, meditation, visualization and biofeedback can also help. For more information on massage therapy, see "Alternative Medicine," below.

Get regular medical exams and vaccinations. These include the following:

•Children need a full course of immunization shots starting at the age of two months. They should also visit a doctor and a dentist regularly. For details, see "Childhood Illnesses and Immunizations," below.

•Adults should have a complete physical, including a complete blood count and a urinalysis, every two to five years (more often if they are over 65, have a chronic illness or are at increased risk for a serious disease). They should see a dentist regularly for a tooth cleaning (every six months to a year if they have tooth or gum problems), get their blood pressure checked every other year, and get a cholesterol test every five years (more often if the count is over 200).

•People over age 50 should have an annual rectal exam to screen for blood in the stool and a sigmoidoscopy (an outpatient procedure to check the large intestine for signs of cancer) every four years.

•People who are 65 or over or whose immune system has been weakened by a chronic condition should get annual flu shots and a pneumonia shot. Six years after the first pneumonia shot, they should consider getting another.

•Women should get a PAP smear, a pelvic examination and a manual breast examination by a doctor once a year. They should also get a mammogram every year or two after a certain age, although medical opinion is divided as to when they should start. Some experts and institutions—including the American Cancer Society—say a woman should get her first (baseline) mammogram between the ages of 35 and 39, then get one mammogram every two years from ages 40 to 50. Others—including the National Cancer Institute—say a woman need not get her first mammogram before age 50. The experts all agree on one thing, though: A woman over 50 should analyze her family history and other risk factors, talk it over with her doctor and then decide whether to get tested every year or every two years.

BAD HABITS

Smoking. Quitting is probably the single best thing a smoker can do for his or her health. Lung cancer is the major preventable cause of death, and more than 80 percent of the people who get it are smokers. Smokers also are two to three times as likely as non-smokers to die from heart attacks.

Drinking. In moderation, alcohol does no harm to most people. In fact, an average of one to two drinks a day apparently cuts down on the fat that clogs arteries and causes heart attacks and heart disease. (One drink contains half an ounce of pure alcohol, the amount in a jigger of 80-proof spirits, a 12-ounce bottle of regular beer or a four- to five-ounce glass of wine.) But in excess, alcohol can weaken the heart muscle. It may also damage the liver, which increases the risk of liver cancer and cirrhosis; injure the stomach lining and small intestines, which makes it hard for the body to absorb nutrients; cause nerve and brain damage; and lead to high blood pressure or abnormal heart rhythms. What's more, drunk driving is the leading cause of traffic fatalities. Pregnant women, people taking antihistamines or other medications that interact with alcohol, and people with a personal or family history of alcoholism are advised to stay away from alcohol altogether. (For information on 12-step and other alcohol treatment programs, see "Overcoming Addiction," below.)

Overeating. Excess fat puts a strain on almost every part of your body. Not only is it hard on your back, feet, knees and other body parts, but it increases your chances of developing high blood pressure, diabetes, joint problems and heart disease or clogged arteries. For an estimation of your ideal weight range, see the chart on page 218. For information on how to lose weight healthfully, see "Weight Control," below.

Undereating. See "Eating Disorders."

You Are What You Eat

In this age of information overload, the simple pleasure of eating is in danger of becoming neither simple nor pleasurable.

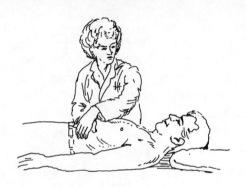

reventive care: The physical

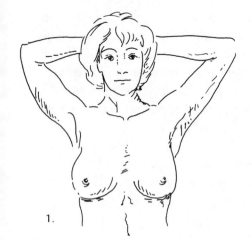

1.

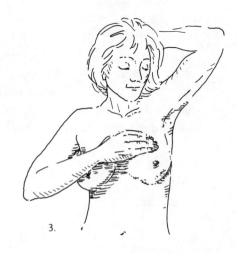

3.

2.

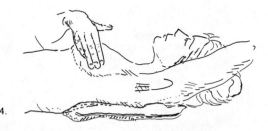

4.

east self-exam instructions: 1. Standing before a mirror, begin with your arms at your sides. Carefully examine ur breasts. Look for any dimpling, puckering or scaling. Lift your arms and interlock your fingers behind your ad, while doing this observe your breasts for any lumps, protrusions or changes in the contours.

Check for any discharge from the nipple by raising your right arm above your head and gently squeezing the pple of your right breast with your fingers. Repeat this for the left breast.

Standing, raise your right arm above your head. With your middle three fingers, gently but firmly palpate ur right breast in a circular motion. Check for lumps or thickened tissue. Repeat this for the left breast.

Lie down on a bed with a pillow under the left side of your upper back. With your middle three fingers, in cir-lar motions gently but firmly explore your left breast moving up to your armpit and across your collarbone. eck for any lumps or thickened tissue. Repeat this for the right breast.

Yet two simple facts about food remain true: too much of a good thing can be just as bad as too little, and the key to eating healthfully is eating a variety of foods.

You don't have to swear off ice cream and chocolate forever, and you don't have to include every essential nutrient in every meal. Just make sure that, over the course of an average week, you get enough of the nutrients below. You can do this by eating plenty of fresh fruits and vegetables, whole grains and calcium-rich dairy products and going easy on sugar, salt, fat, cholesterol and alcohol. (For the United States Department of Agriculture's recommendations on how to balance your diet, see the food pyramid illustration.)

ESSENTIAL NUTRIENTS
Calories
A calorie is a measure of energy—a thousand times the amount required to heat one gram of water 1°C. The calories you take in provide the energy your body needs to function.

The more active you are, the more calories you burn, but other things factor in as well. The average man uses about 2,400 calories a day, while the average woman needs only about 2,000. And muscle burns more energy than fat, so a heavily muscled person with very little fat needs more calories than an obese person who weighs the same amount. Generally speaking, though, if you want to maintain your current weight you should take in about 12 calories a day for each pound you weigh if you're extremely sedentary, about 15 calories per pound if you're somewhat active, about 20 per pound if you're moderately active and as many as 25 calories per pound if you are very

Food Guide Pyramid
A Guide to Daily Food Choices

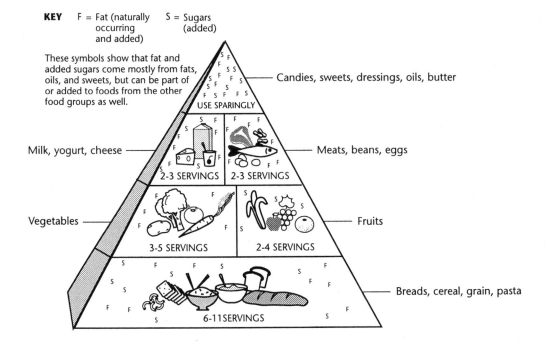

KEY F = Fat (naturally occurring and added)   S = Sugars (added)

These symbols show that fat and added sugars come mostly from fats, oils, and sweets, but can be part of or added to foods from the other food groups as well.

USE SPARINGLY — Candies, sweets, dressings, oils, butter

Milk, yogurt, cheese — 2-3 SERVINGS

Meats, beans, eggs — 2-3 SERVINGS

Vegetables — 3-5 SERVINGS

Fruits — 2-4 SERVINGS

Breads, cereal, grain, pasta — 6-11 SERVINGS

active. Take in more than that and you'll gain weight; take in less and you'll lose.

Regardless of how many calories you need, more than half should come from carbohydrates—but no more than 10 percent from sugar. Another 10 to 15 percent should come from protein, and no more—and preferably less—than 30 percent from fats. Definitions follow:

CARBOHYDRATES

Carbohydrates come in two varieties: starches and sugars. Starches (also known as complex carbohydrates) are found in corn, peas, beans, lentils, rice, nuts, seeds, potatoes, bread and whole grains. Sugars (or simple carbohydrates) are found in milk and other dairy products. Both are found in fruits and vegetables.

Starch is a good source of fiber, a natural laxative that may lessen the risk of developing hemorrhoids, diverticulosis and even colon cancer. Starchy foods also are filling and tend to be rich in vitamins or minerals and low in calories—as long as they're not smothered in calorie-rich add-ons like butter or margarine, mayonnaise, cheese or cream sauce.

Sugar as it occurs in nature—in fruit, milk and vegetables—is part of a package that contains many vitamins and minerals and relatively few calories. Unfortunately, the sugar in man-made packages, ranging from breakfast cereal to sweetened canned and dried food, adds hundreds of nutritionally useless calories to our diet (for more details, see "Sugar," below).

FAT

Fat is the main culprit in the American diet. Most of us (except children under the age of two, who need more) eat far too much fat in general and artery-clogging saturated fat in particular than is healthy. This is harmful not only because eating too much fat makes you fat, which causes its own set of problems, but because it increases your risk of stroke, heart disease and probably some types of cancer as well. In fact, saturated fat and cholesterol appear to be more strongly linked to disease and premature death than anything else we eat. Yet some fat is an essential part of a balanced diet. A tablespoon of dietary fat a day supplies the essential fatty acid your body needs, while allowing it to absorb certain essential vitamins. The trick is not eating too much fat—or the wrong kind.

Most dietary fat is made up mostly of one of three types of fatty acids: saturated, monounsaturated and polyunsaturated. Saturated fat clogs arteries, which leads to heart disease, because a diet rich in such fat tends to raise blood cholesterol. Monounsaturated and polyunsaturated fats, however, help lower cholesterol levels, as does a fourth kind of fat, the so-called omega-3 fatty acids found in some types of fish.

Animal fats are usually highly saturated, while vegetable fats—except for coconut and palm oils—are unsaturated. Most fats are a mixture of both, with the most healthful being those with the lowest percentage of saturation. The easiest rule of thumb to tell whether a fat is predominantly saturated or unsaturated is how firm it is at room temperature: The more saturated the fat, the harder it is. Thus, beef and butter fat, which are highly saturated, are solid at room temperature, while olive oil, which is 84 percent unsaturated, is liquid.

PROTEIN

Protein is one thing most Americans don't have to worry about getting enough of—in fact, most of us eat far more than we need. This would not be a problem, since the body eliminates the protein it can't use, if so much of our protein did not come from animal products (red meat, poultry, seafood, eggs, and milk and other dairy products) that are high in fat or cholesterol. We could solve the problem by eating low-fat versions of these products (skinless chicken, 1 percent or skim milk, nonfat yogurt and so forth)—or, better yet, by getting more of our protein from plants.

Protein is present in many vegetables and in fish, flour (especially whole wheat flour), cereals and grains, and legumes such as lentils, beans, soybeans, black-eyed peas, kidney beans, chickpeas, navy beans, pinto beans, split peas and lima beans. Peanuts, nuts and seeds are also excellent sources of protein, but they're rich in fat as well.

WATER

Water helps carry oxygen and nutrients to our cells, eliminate toxic waste and regulate body heat, among other vital functions. You need more of it more often than any other single nutrient: You can't survive without water for more than two or three days.

You get a lot of the fluids you need from solid foods, but you should drink six to eight eight-ounce glasses of water or other fluids each day—and more if a lot of what you're drinking is caffeinated coffee, tea or soda, as caffeine is a diuretic (a substance that makes your body eliminate extra water).

VITAMINS AND MINERALS

In order to function properly, you need 13 universally recognized vitamins and 16 minerals. (See the charts on pages 220 and 221.) It's best to get these from your food and drink, since the body absorbs nutrients more easily from food than from pills, and a balanced diet includes enough for most people. But for people who have special dietary needs, or who don't eat enough of the foods recommended by the USDA's food pyramid (see page 212), a daily multivitamin pill or calcium supplement could be the answer.

Dosing yourself with more than 100 percent of the United States Recommended Daily Allowance of any essential vitamin or mineral is never a good idea, however. Taken in excess, many have side effects—and some of those side effects are serious. Too much iron, for instance, may damage the heart, liver and pancreas. And taking too much of one vitamin or mineral may result in a shortage of another.

TOO MUCH OF A GOOD THING

It's important not to eat too much of the following things:

Cholesterol

Cholesterol is an essential chemical. It is also one of the major contributing factors to heart disease in this country, where most people eat far too much cholesterol and saturated fat, which the body converts to cholesterol.

Actually, no one over the age of six months needs to eat cholesterol at all, since the liver breaks down fats and carbohydrates to make the cholesterol your body needs. Some takes the form of high-density lipoproteins (HDLs), the "good" cholesterol that nourishes the body without harming it. But most is low-density lipoproteins (LDLs), the "bad" cholesterol that can clog arteries and cause heart disease—the kind that many Americans have far too much of.

Genetics plays a large role in determining your cholesterol count: People whose parents and grandparents have high counts are likely to have the same. But you can reduce your count by cutting cholesterol and saturated fat from your diet. Egg yolks and the fat in butter, milk, cheese and ice cream are the main dietary sources of cholesterol. For more information on saturated fats, see the section on Fat in "Essential Nutrients," above.

Strenuous exercise also helps control cholesterol, as it increases HDL and lowers LDL levels.

Sugar

We don't really need to eat sugar at all. Aside from calories, which provide energy, sugar has no nutritional value—and we could get all the energy we need from more filling, less fattening starches instead. This goes for so-called "natural" sources of sugar as well. Honey, for instance, is 99.9 percent sugar and contains only insignificant traces of vitamins and minerals.

We eat sugar because we love it—and because we love it, food manufacturers add sugar to nearly all the processed foods, sodas and juice drinks that make up the majority of what we eat and drink. All that invisible sugar adds up to more calories than we can burn off, and those extra calories get stored as fat.

To avoid eating too much sugar, check the list of ingredients before you buy any processed food. Sugar may be listed as sugar, but more often it is called syrup, honey, molasses or any of a number of names ending in "ose" (sucrose, fructose, maltose, etc.). If one of these ingredients is one of the first three things listed (ingredients are listed in order of volume, starting with the main one) or if more than one kind of sugar is listed, buy an unsweetened—or at least less sweetened—brand instead.

Another reason to avoid sweets is that they tend to give you cavities. Sticky foods are the worst, and sweet snacks are likelier to cause tooth decay than sweets eaten as part of a meal. But no sugary food need hurt your teeth if you brush within 15 minutes of eating it. If you don't have a toothbrush handy, drink a glass of water to flush out your mouth.

Salt

A combination of sodium and chloride, salt is a crucial component of the body's chemistry, regulating the balance of water outside cells and the balance of acids and bases in body fluids and cells. But we need very little—no more than 2,000 milligrams a day—and most of us consume way too much. Eating too much sodium depletes cells of needed water and potassium. Worse yet, it is linked to high blood pressure and hence to kidney disease, heart disease and strokes.

The salt we shake into food doesn't help, but the main culprit is processed food. After sugar, sodium is the leading food additive, mixed in to processed meats, baked goods, cheese and other dairy products, canned and frozen foods, fast food and virtually every other kind of processed food.

As with sugar, you can avoid excess salt. Check the labels of processed foods, and don't buy those high in sodium. (Many are available in low-sodium versions.) Keep your visits to fast food restaurants to a minimum. And when you do your own cooking, start with fresh meat and fresh or frozen vegetables and prepare them with a minimum of salt.

Saturated fat
See Fat, above, under "Essential Nutrients."

SPECIAL NUTRITIONAL NEEDS
Children under the age of two need a much greater percentage of fat in their diets than adults.

Growing children need fewer calories than adults, but pound for pound they need more protein, vitamins and minerals. This means that children can't afford to eat as many "empty" calories as adults can.

Pregnant women and women trying to get pregnant must be sure to get at least 100 percent of the USRDA of folic acid, a B vitamin. Pregnant women also need more protein, calcium, iron, phosphorus, magnesium, zinc, fluoride, sodium and iodine than usual, as well as extra doses of vitamins C, A, D and E.

Elderly people may need fewer calories than they used to, but they may need more nutrients, as they are likelier to be taking medication that interferes with the absorption of certain nutrients. (Some diuretics, for instance, deplete the body's supply of potassium.) If you are taking any daily

medication, ask your doctor if you need to counteract its effects with extra doses of a vitamin or mineral.

Vegans (vegetarians who don't eat dairy products) need to be sure they're getting calcium. They can do so by taking supplements or by eating plenty of broccoli, okra, rutabaga, legumes, dried fruits, almonds, kale, collards and other greens. They must also take care to get vitamin B_{12} (available in fortified soy milk or pills), vitamin D (in sunlight and fortified margarine), riboflavin (in various vegetables) and iodine (in iodized salt). Vegetarians who are pregnant or nursing may need vitamin or mineral supplements.

Weight Control
Quick weight-loss diets are a losing game. Diets that severely limit the kind of foods you eat may cause your body to cannibalize itself, burning muscle tissue (if your diet is low in protein) or bone (if you're not eating enough calcium) instead of fat. They may put strain on your heart or kidneys, and they may simply make you feel sick and tired.

What's more, most diets don't work. The great majority of the people who manage to lose weight put it all back within a couple of years—and all that gaining and losing is hard on the heart, whereas being just 15 or 20 pounds "overweight" won't hurt you a bit.

On the other hand, being grossly overweight isn't healthy. The accepted standard for obesity keeps changing, but it's currently believed that the most important factor is abdominal fat. To find out if you have more than is good for you, measure your waist near the navel while standing relaxed. Then measure your hips over the buttocks, where they are largest. Divide your waist measurement by your hip measurement. If the ratio is close to (.9 or higher) or more than 1, losing weight would probably help you live longer and feel better.

Part of the trick to reducing is getting more exercise (for more details, see "Exercise," below). The other part is adopting a new way of eating—one that will cause you to lose weight only gradually, but that you can stick with for the rest of your life.

Start by taking an honest look at what you're eating and drinking. If your usual diet includes a lot of sugar or fat, start taking in less. If you're not eating many fresh fruits and vegetables or whole grains, increase the amount of these in your diet. Don't try to change the way you eat overnight; give yourself time to wean yourself off old favorites and find new foods you enjoy to replace them.

Then look at when and how you eat. To reach and maintain a healthy weight, you need to eat three meals a day—but you may need to put smaller portions on your plate at meals, or eat less in between. Eat slowly, chewing each bite thoroughly, and don't reach for seconds right away. Give your stomach a chance to begin to absorb what you've already eaten—you may find that it is enough. Don't nibble endlessly while preparing meals, while watching TV or between meals—but don't go more than five hours without a meal or a healthy snack. And remember, you need to burn off 3,500 calories in order to lose a pound of fat, so cutting just 500 calories a day from your diet will allow you to lose a pound a week.

Above all, concentrate more on how you feel and less on how you look. You'll know your diet is working when you start feeling healthier, stronger and more energetic.

Eating Disorders

The two most common kinds of eating disorders are anorexia nervosa and bulimia. Both are common to adolescent girls and young women—among whom bulimia is alarmingly widespread—and all but unheard of in men and boys. People with these disorders usually suffer from low self-esteem, feelings of helplessness and an exaggerated fear of being fat. They become obsessed with food, developing secretive rituals that isolate them from other people. And they run the risk of undermining their health in many ways, some of them crippling or even fatal.

Anorexics starve themselves, eating very little when they eat at all. Many anorexics also exercise compulsively. Because their bodies react to starvation by conserving energy, their breathing, pulse and blood pressure rates drop; thyroid functions slow down; and menstrual periods stop. Their nails and hair become brittle, their skin dries, yellows and becomes covered with a soft layer of hair, and they begin to burn muscle when they have no more fat. Their low intake of calcium may lead to loss of bone density (osteoporosis), and they often suffer from anemia, swollen joints and light-headedness. Some anorexics even experience irregular heart rhythms, heart failure, brain shrinkage leading to personality changes or a dangerous level of dehydration.

Although anorexics almost always outgrow their behavior, few can be convinced to change it before they are ready. They may agree to take vital vitamin and mineral supplements, however, as these contain no calories. Anorexics whose weight drops dangerously low must sometimes be hospitalized and force-fed to keep from starving themselves to death.

Suggested Weights for Adults

The higher weights in the ranges generally apply to men, who tend to have more muscle and bone; the lower weights more often apply to women, who have less muscle and bone.

Height *Without shoes.*	Weight in Pounds *Without clothes.*	
	19 to 34 Years	*35 Years and Over*
5'0"	97–128	108–138
5'1"	101–132	111–143
5'2"	104–137	115–148
5'3"	107–141	119–152
5'4"	111–146	122–157
5'5"	114–150	126–162
5'6"	118–155	130–167
5'7"	121–160	134–172
5'8"	125–164	138–178
5'9"	129–169	142–183
5'10"	132–174	146–188
5'11"	136–179	151–194
6'0"	140–184	155–199
6'1"	144–189	159–205
6'2"	148–195	164–210
6'3"	152–200	168–216
6'4"	156–205	173–222
6'5"	160–211	177–228
6'6"	164–216	182–234[5]

Source: Derived from National Research Council 1989 (page 27).

Bulimics are often depressed, and their disorder only deepens their feelings of depression, guilt and alienation. Their lives revolve around a binge cycle: First they gorge themselves, usually on high-calorie foods (a whole bag of cookies, say, or a quart of ice cream), then they vomit or take laxatives before their bodies have absorbed any calories—or nutrients—to speak of. Bulimics who go on frequent binges may be malnourished and lethargic despite the tremendous quantities of food they take in. They may also erode the enamel on their teeth (stomach acids remain in the mouth after vomiting), dehydrate themselves or suffer from chronic diarrhea. In some cases, bulimia causes a rupture of the esophagus or stomach lining, kidney failure or a severe enough shortage of vital minerals to cause heart failure.

Extreme secrecy is a hallmark of bulimia; few bulimics will talk freely about their disorder. If you suspect that a loved one is bulimic and want to help, express your concern lovingly—and be prepared for denial. But if she agrees that she needs help, you may want to suggest that she either go to a private therapist or join a support group. For more information about eating disorders, or about support groups in your area, call the American Anorexia/Bulimia Association (AABA), at 1-212-734-1114; Anorexia Nervosa and Related Eating Disorders (ANRED), 1-503-344-1144; or National Association of Anorexia Nervosa and Associated Disorders, 1-708-831-3438. (See "Sources" for addresses).

Health Food

Just because something is called "health food" doesn't necessarily mean it's particularly good for you. And no one food or nutrient, despite faddists' claims, can cure any disease.

When it comes to food, the words "natural" and "organic" are meaningless, since the government sets virtually no limits on what these terms mean when used in food advertising. A so-called organically grown tomato may contain as much harmful residue from fertilizers or pesticides as the ordinary tomatoes at your neighborhood grocery store. Unless you have visited the place that supplies your "organic" produce and seen for yourself that its claims are legitimate, or you buy from a reputable retailer whose guarantee you trust, the only way to be sure you're not ingesting such chemicals is to thoroughly wash or peel fresh fruits and vegetables before cooking or eating them—and if you're going to do that, you may not want to pay the much higher prices for organic produce.

Cooked or otherwise processed "health foods" may not be any better for you than their mainstream counterparts, either. Such foods often have unhealthily high percentages of sugar—often in the form of molasses or honey—or saturated fats such as coconut oil. As with any processed food, read the label before buying to see what's inside, and don't pay inflated prices for something you can get cheaper in a different package.

Exercise

For some people—those who are seriously overweight, for instance, or who have weak hearts or damaged lungs—exercise may be dangerous. But if you're like most people, the only reason you don't exercise more is that you can't find the time—or so you think.

The fact is, you can build a lot of exercise into your regular routine simply by walking a mile or so instead of driving or taking a bus, or by walking up two or three flights of stairs instead of taking an elevator. Just 30 minutes a day of moderate exercise such as walking or gardening, five days a week, can improve your health—and that 30 minutes need not be done all at one stretch. And machines such as stationary bicycles let you exercise at home while watching TV. (For tips on working out at home, see "Working Out at Home," in the following sidebar.)

Finding a Doctor

The only doctor a healthy person needs is a primary-care physician. This doctor will give you regular checkups and examinations, keep track of your health history and refer you to any specialists you may need. A primary-care doctor is usually a family practitioner or internist, although children often see a pediatrician instead. Women need to find a gynecologist as well, unless their primary-care doctor is comfortable doing an annual PAP smear and pelvic and breast exam.

Don't wait until you have a medical emergency to find a doctor you're comfortable with. Start by asking friends and family members whose opinions you trust whether they have a doctor they like. Medical specialists usually know about their colleagues in different areas of medicine, so you might also ask a nurse, pharmacist or doctor you know or call the referral service at the nearest medical center. And if you have moved recently, your old doctor may be able to recommend a doctor in your new hometown.

Before scheduling an appointment, go to your library and look up the doctor in the *Directory of Medical Specialists*. Make sure the doctor got a degree from a fully accredited medical school. See whether he or she is affiliated with a hospital—being affiliated with a good hospital is no guarantee that a doctor is good, but not being affiliated with a hospital may be a red flag. Besides, any surgeons or other specialists the doctor will refer you to will be affiliated with the same hospital, so it helps if it is a good one. It's also worth noting whether the doctor did his or her residency at a widely respected hospital, as doctors usually learn more about technique during their residencies than they do in medical school.

But technique isn't everything. It's important to find someone you can trust, since you need to feel free to talk to your doctor about every aspect of

Vitamins

There are two kinds of vitamins, water soluble and fat soluble. Water-soluble vitamins must be eaten daily, since they are either used up or eliminated in urine or sweat. They are also less stable than fat-soluble vitamins and more easily destroyed by food processing and cooking.

Fat-soluble vitamins are stored in body fat, so they need not be eaten daily. Because the body does not eliminate what it can't use, however, megadoses of these vitamins—particularly A and D—can build up to toxic levels, leading to severe problems such as liver damage, deafness and nausea.

FAT-SOLUBLE VITAMINS

Vitamin A helps keeps skin, hair, teeth, bones and mucous membranes healthy. It also aids in night vision and reproduction.

Vitamin D helps build bones and teeth and helps the body to absorb calcium and phosphorus.

Vitamin E helps form red blood cells, muscles and other tissues, and keeps vitamin A and other essential fatty acids from oxidizing.

Vitamin K helps blood to clot.

WATER-SOLUBLE VITAMINS

Vitamin B_1 (thiamin) helps release energy from carbohydrates and regulate the nervous system.

Vitamin B_2 (riboflavin) helps to maintain the mucous membranes and to release energy from carbohydrates, proteins and fats.

Vitamin B_3 (niacin) helps release energy from foods; helps the nervous and digestive systems to function.

Vitamin B_5 (pantothenic acid) helps release energy from carbohydrates, proteins and fats and helps form hormones and regulate the nervous system.

Vitamin B_6 helps to metabolize proteins and fats and form red blood cells.

Vitamin B_{12} helps the nervous system to function and red blood cells to form, and helps build genetic material.

Biotin helps release energy from carbohydrates and form fatty acids.

Folacin (folic acid) helps form genetic material and red blood cells.

Vitamin C (ascorbic acid) helps form collagen, maintain capillaries, bones and teeth. It may promote resistance to colds and block formation of certain cancer-causing substances; it also prevents other vitamins from oxidizing.

Minerals

The minerals we cannot live without come in two categories:

your life that impacts your health—including your sex life and alcohol or other drug abuse. Find a doctor who listens to you and who doesn't lightly dismiss any concerns you may have. Access is also important: You need a doctor you can talk to or see when you need to. Before you make your first appointment, call the office and ask if the doctor schedules part of each day for making and receiving phone calls.

Think of your first visit as a job interview—do you want to "hire" this person as your doctor? Expect a basic physical examination and a battery of questions about your personal and family medical history. These include the types and dates of any major illnesses, surgeries and immunizations; any major medical problems your grandparents, parents and siblings have had; whether you're allergic to any drugs or other substances; and what drugs, if any, you take regularly—including vitamin supplements and other over-the-counter pills.

Pay attention to how the doctor listens to your answers, too. Did he or she let you say what you wanted to or just fire off a set of questions? Did he or she seem interested in you or eager to hustle the next patient in? Did you get satisfactory answers to your questions?

Common Killers
The bad news: There aren't many people in America who haven't either bat-

---

macrominerals and trace minerals. We need large amounts of the macrominerals (calcium, chloride, magnesium, phosphorus, potassium, sodium and sulfur), but only tiny amounts of the trace minerals (iron, zinc, selenium, manganese, molybdenum, copper, iodine, chromium and fluorine).

ESSENTIAL MINERALS
Calcium, the single most essential mineral, helps form bones and teeth and keeps bones strong. It also helps regulate nerve and muscle cells, maintains cell membranes and helps with blood clotting and absorption of Vitamin B_{12}.

Chloride helps form stomach acid, regulates the body's balance of fluids, acids and bases, and activates an enzyme in saliva.

Chromium helps the body metabolize glucose.

Copper helps with respiration and the formation of red blood cells.

Fluorine helps to form and maintain strong teeth and bones.

Iodine helps the thyroid in regulating the metabolism. It is essential for reproduction.

Iron is essential in forming several enzymes and proteins, as well as the hemoglobin in blood and the substance in the muscles that supplies oxygen to cells.

Magnesium helps to form bones, proteins and the substance in the muscles that supplies oxygen to cells, as well as helping the body to conduct nerve impulses to the muscles and adjust to the cold.

Manganese helps form bones and certain enzymes and is essential to reproduction and proper functioning of the central nervous system.

Molybdenum helps form an essential enzyme.

Phosphorus helps build bones, teeth, genetic material, cell membranes and several enzymes. It also helps release energy from carbohydrates, proteins and fats.

Potassium helps maintain the right balance of fluids and electrolytes within cells, helps transmit nerve impulses and helps release energy from carbohydrates, proteins and fats. It also helps the muscles to contract.

Selenium prevents the breakdown of fats and other body chemicals.

Sodium helps regulate the body's balance of fluids, acids and bases.

Sulfur helps form healthy skin, hair and nails.

Zinc helps in the formation of many enzymes.

Heart Rates

Even a small amount of moderate exercise is good for your health, but it takes a sustained and vigorous workout to keep your heart in shape. To give your cardiovascular system a good workout, you need to get your heart beating within 70 to 85 percent of its maximum rate (the fastest it can beat without endangering your health) for at least 20 minutes three times a week.

Taking your pulse

To do this, first warm up and then work up to the speed at which you intend to exercise. Then take your pulse. (Place two fingers of one hand on the inside of the other wrist just below the base of the thumb. Using a watch with a second hand, count the number of pulses you feel in the vein there for 15 seconds. Then multiply that number by four to get your heart rate—the number of times your heart beats per minute.)

If your heart rate is below the range given below for a person your age, start exercising harder. If it is above that range, slow down.

Age	Range
15	143–174
20	140–170
25	136–165
30	133–161
35	129–157
40	126–153
45	122–149
50	119–144
55	115–140
60	112–136
65	108–132
70	105–127
75	101–123
80	98–119
85	94–115

Working Out at Home

Working out at home is a lot cheaper than joining a gym—and much easier to fit into a busy schedule. You can do it while watching TV or listening to music and you may not have to buy a single piece of equipment. The key is finding a workout that suits you, so you'll really stick with it.

AEROBICS TAPES

If you find it hard to motivate yourself on your own, you might try working out to a videotape. Make sure the instructor is certified by the Institute for Aerobics Research, the American College of Sports Medicine or the American Council on Exercise (formerly the IDEA Foundation). His or her credentials should be listed on the video jacket. Start by renting—that way you can work your way up from an easy routine to a more strenuous one and you won't get stuck paying for a tape you hate.

A PERSONAL TRAINER

If you want personal attention and have the money, you can hire a personal trainer to tailor a nutrition and fitness program for you, check your technique and keep you motivated. Choose one who's certified by the American Council on Exercise (formerly the IDEA Foundation).

ROPE JUMPING

Jumping rope is an excellent form of aerobic exercise. Wear athletic shoes with plenty of cushioning for the balls of the feet, keep your knees slightly bent and jump on a floor with some give (wood is best; concrete is out). Warm up before you start and cool down afterward with a few minutes of walking or jogging in place.

FLOOR EXERCISES

Floor exercises such as situps and pushups are an excellent low-impact way to strengthen stomach, arm, chest and leg muscles without straining your back or knees (for examples, see illustration).

MACHINES

Rowing machines give both the legs and the upper body a good workout without straining the joints. Skiing machines also exercise both arms and legs, but are a bit trickier to operate. Stationary bicycles, treadmills and climbing machines generally provide a good aerobic workout but exercise only the leg muscles, although some bicycles and climbers work the arms as well.

Exercise at home—Note: Be sure to consult your doctor as to which exercises you should and shouldn't do. Begin exercises slowly to warm-up properly. Remember to breathe out on contractions and in on release.

Upper body

1. Back strokes. Standing up straight, rotate your arms straight over your head concentrating the motion in your shoulders (as if doing the back-stroke). Do this for a few minutes in each direction.

2. Simple push-ups. On knees and palms with the tops of your feet touching the floor, hold your upper body off the floor with your arms, keep your back straight. Bending at the elbows do 12 simple push-ups.

3. Dumbbell lifts. Lie with your back on the floor and your legs resting comfortably over the edge of a bench, low table or bed. Gripping dumbbells with your fists in and arms close to your body, slowly push straight up until elbows lock. Lower slowly to original position. Do 10 repetitions.

Stomach

Belly holds. This exercise isolates the abdominal muscles. On your back, feet together, knees bent, breathe out and hold it as you contract your stomach muscles, pulling up toward the rib cage. Hold for 2–3 seconds and release. Repeat 5–6 times.

Shoulder curls. In the same starting position, lift your head and shoulders up off the ground until you feel your abdomen contract. Hold for 5–6 seconds. Repeat 10–12 times.

Curl-ups. Remaining in the same start position, place the palms of your hands on your lower thighs. Lift your head, shoulders and upper back, keeping your lower back on the floor, and let your hands move up toward your knees. Return slowly to starting position. Repeat 10–12 times.

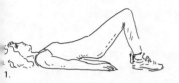

Lower body

Buttocks squeezes. On your back, feet together and knees bent, lift your hips and lower back slightly off the floor. Squeeze the buttocks for 5 seconds. Release and return to the original position. Repeat 10 times.

Side toning. On your side with your head resting on your arm, bend your lower knee keeping your top leg straight. Raise your top leg until it is even with your hip (no higher). Bend your upper knee in toward your chest and straighten it out again. Repeat this motion 10 times on both sides.

Back kicks. With your forearms on the floor out in front of you and your buttocks in the air, extend one leg out behind you with your toes touching the floor. Keeping your back straight and abdomen tight, raise and lower your leg never going above your hips. Do this 8 times on both sides.

tled cancer or heart disease themselves or been close to someone who has. AIDS is much less common, but it's spreading—and its death rate so far is 100 percent. The good news: There are steps you can take to prevent all three of these deadly diseases.

HEART DISEASE

High blood pressure, cigarette smoking, obesity and high cholesterol are the main known risk factors for heart disease, which is one of the major causes of death in this country. Although it used to be thought that it was mostly a male disease, heart disease is actually an equal-opportunity killer. But women very rarely die of it before menopause, leading researchers to suspect that estrogen may play a part in preventing heart disease.

AIDS

AIDS (acquired immune-deficiency syndrome) is a fatal disease caused by a virus called HIV (human immunodeficiency virus). The virus lies dormant for months, even years in some people. Eventually, however, it causes a breakdown in the immune system that even-

tually leads to death—usually from some disorder rarely found in people without HIV. HIV is spread when body fluids—usually semen or blood—from an HIV-infected person pass into the bloodstream of an uninfected person. The major risk factors include sharing intravenous needles and having unsafe sex with an HIV-infected person (see "Safe Sex," below). In addition, babies may get infected by HIV-positive mothers during birth or in utero. Some people also get infected from blood transfusions, although improved screening procedures have made such incidents extremely rare.

CANCER

The key to conquering any form of cancer is removing it before it has spread too far to be stopped. Some tumors grow more slowly than others and are therefore easier to catch in time, but no lump or other potential sign of cancer should be taken lightly. Skin cancer, for instance, is by far the most common type of cancer but has a relatively low death rate, as it is usually diagnosed and removed before it has spread. Skin can-

Shelf Life of Prescription Medications

Over time, exposure to moisture, oxygen, heat and light causes most drugs to lose potency. Some even decompose to produce toxic ingredients. It's best, therefore, to keep drugs somewhere other than in the bathroom, where heat and moisture make them decay faster. Some

may do best in the refrigerator, others in a kitchen cabinet (away from the heat) or on a closet shelf. If there are children in the house, keep them in a locked box or cabinet. And at least twice a year, go through them and discard the following:

Any drugs prescribed for an illness long past.

Any prescription drugs for a chronic illness if the expiration date on the label has passed.

Any over-the-counter drugs whose expiration dates have passed.

Any alcohol-based solution from which much of the alcohol has evaporated.

Any ointment or cream that has hardened or separated.

Any liquid that has discolored, become cloudy or solidified at the bottom of the container.

Any crumbly tablets or broken or melted capsules.

cer can otherwise be fatal. (For the American Cancer Society's seven warning signs of cancer, see the sidebar "The Warning Signs of Cancer," below.)

The following are the deadliest forms of cancer:

Lung

More than four out of five victims are cigarette smokers. Other risk factors include exposure to second-hand smoke, asbestos and radiation. Smokers should have checkups more frequently than other people—perhaps as often as once a year—and should quit smoking as soon as they can.

Breast

Risk factors may include a family history of breast cancer, obesity and having children late in life or not at all. Then again, breast cancer strikes many women with none of these risk factors. Eating a low-fat diet may help reduce your risk of developing breast cancer. Feeling for lumps in a monthly self-examination of your breasts, as well as scheduling an annual manual examination by a doctor and a mammogram every two years after age 40, should help you catch any lump you might develop before it spreads.

Colorectal

Risk factors for cancer of the colon (large intestine) or rectum include a family history of such cancer and eating a diet high in fat and low in fiber. People over age 50 should have an annual rectal exam to screen for blood in the stool and a sigmoidoscopy (an outpatient procedure to check the large intestine for signs of cancer) every four years. People with a family history of colon cancer should talk to their doctors about starting the exams at an earlier age and having them more often.

Sex

SAFE SEX

"Safe sex" includes any sexual activity that doesn't involve the exchange of the semen, blood or other body fluids that carry HIV, the virus that causes AIDS.

Masturbation is completely safe sex. So are massage, hugging and dry kissing (but not deep open-mouth kissing). Mutual masturbation is fairly safe—but not completely, as HIV-infected fluid can enter through any open sore or cut, even a torn cuticle. Unprotected vaginal intercourse is even riskier, especially for the woman. And unprotected anal

 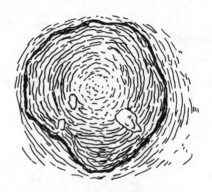

Heart disease: The progression of arteriosclerosis. Plaque builds around artery walls impairing the normal flow of blood.

intercourse is worst, as tissue often gets torn and bleeds, allowing HIV-infected semen to pass into the blood.

Even vaginal and anal intercourse, however, *can* be considered safe sex if the partners use a latex condom. The latex condom must be used properly, and in conjunction with a water-based spermicide containing nonoxynol-9 (the spermicide appears to help kill not only sperm but HIV). For a free pamphlet explaining how to use a condom, write to the Consumer Information Center, Dept. 542Z, Pueblo, CO 81009. Oral sex is also "safe" if there's a plastic barrier between genitals and mouth. This means using condoms on penises and dental dams (thin sheets of plastic that cover the genital area) on vaginas.

Even so-called safe sex is not completely safe. If you're HIV-negative, there are only two ways to be sure you won't contract HIV through sex: You can either abstain or be in a strictly monogamous relationship in which both you and your partner tested negative for the virus at least six months after your last sexual contact with anyone else. If you aren't in a monogamous relationship and don't want to be celibate, you can keep your risk of contracting the virus to a minimum by limiting the number of partners you have and by practicing safe sex every time you have sex.

SEXUALLY TRANSMITTED DISEASES

Sexually transmitted diseases, or STDs, may lead to sterility, other major complications and even death. STDs are often symptomless, but some cause painful urination, unusual genital discharge, pelvic pain or sores, blisters or warts around the genitals or mouth. Fortunately, most can be cured. The following are the most serious.

AIDS. For a discussion of AIDS, "see Common Killers," above.

Chlamydia can cause sterility in men and infertility and pelvic inflammatory disease (PID) in women. It can be cured with antibiotics.

Genital herpes may lead to cervical cancer or to miscarriage or premature delivery in pregnant women. It can be controlled with antiviral tablets.

The Warning Signs of Cancer

The great majority of tumors are benign (noncancerous) and all the warning signs of cancer may also be caused by a host of other things. But because early detection is a crucial part of battling cancer, the American Cancer Society recommends that you call your doctor immediately if you have any of the following potential warning signs of cancer:

Unusual bleeding or discharge. In women, this may include bleeding or discharge from the nipples or vaginal bleeding between periods, during pregnancy or after menopause. In both sexes, it includes rectal bleeding or blood found in feces (making them look black and tarry), urine (it may range in color from pink to brown), vomit, phlegm or saliva.

Any marked change in bowel or bladder habits.

A sore that takes more than three weeks to heal.

A change in the size or appearance of a mole, freckle or skin blemish.

A lump, swelling or thickening in a woman's breast or elsewhere in a man's or woman's body.

Nagging hoarseness or coughing or a worsening smoker's cough.

Chronic indigestion or difficulty in swallowing.

Gonorrhea may cause arthritis, heart disease, brain infections, sterility, blockage of the urethra in men and pelvic inflammatory disease in women. Most strains can be treated with antibiotics.

Hepatitis B is an inflammation of the liver that can lead to liver scarring or cancer. It almost always clears up if the patient gets plenty of rest and eats well.

Syphilis can cause blindness, paralysis, insanity, heart and blood-vessel damage and eventually death. It can be cured by antibiotics.

AVOIDING PREGNANCY

Some methods of birth control are highly effective, but none—barring celibacy—is 100 percent foolproof. Add human frailty to the equation (how many people really put more spermicide in a diaphragm before making love a second time?) and the percentages get even worse. The numbers below represent the percentage of women who get pregnant after using the device for a year. The low end of the range represents those who followed exact directions; the high end represents the typical user.

Oral contraceptives ("the Pill" and the minipill). Both forms of the birth control pill work by regulating the reproductive system with synthetic hormones, usually estrogen and progesterone. The Pill contains both synthetic estrogen and progestin (estrogen inhibits ovulation; progestin, a form of progesterone, keeps sperm from reaching an egg and stops fertilized eggs from attaching to the uterine lining), while the minipill contains just synthetic progestin. Taken correctly, either one works far better than any other form of birth control short of surgical sterilization—with the possible exception of Norplant implants (see below). They are not advised, however, for women who are at increased risk of cardiovascular disease or for anyone who has been diagnosed with breast or cervical cancer, has liver problems, smokes cigarettes and is 35 or older or suffers from severe headaches. They may cause such side effects as persistent nausea, weight gain and moodiness. Failure rate: .1 to 3 percent for the Pill; .5 to 3 percent for the minipill.

The shot. Another way of getting synthetic progestin is in the form of a Depo-Provera injection. The shots, which are given every three months in the buttock or upper arm, have the same side effects and are potentially dangerous for the same group of women as the minipill. Failure rate: .3 percent.

The condom. This thin, usually rubber sheath is rolled onto an erect penis with space left at the end to hold ejaculated sperm. Used properly and in conjunction with a spermicide (use only water-based spermicides and lubricants, as oil may weaken the latex), latex condoms are not only a highly effective form of birth control but the best way to avoid HIV infection. Failure rate: 2 to 12 percent.

The diaphragm. Users put spermicide into and around the rim of this large, flexible rubber cup, then insert it to fit around the cervix. It has no known side effects, but is somewhat inconvenient: It must be inserted no more than six hours before having sex and kept in for six to eight hours afterward, and more spermicide must be added if you have sex more than once before taking it out. Failure rate: 6 to 18 percent.

The cervical cap. Similar in concept to the diaphragm, the cervical cap is a rubber cup used in conjunction with spermicide. Smaller and firmer, it fits more tightly over the cervix, thus presumably making it harder for sperm to get through. It is also a bit easier to use, as it can be left in place for up to two days and spermicide need not be reapplied before repeated intercourse. Failure rate: 6 to 18 percent.

The intrauterine device (IUD). One of two types of T-shaped plastic devices, the Copper T and the Progestasert, the IUD is inserted in the uterus by a doctor to keep fertilized eggs from implanting. The Progestasert model also releases a slow but steady stream of a synthetic hormone that suppresses ovulation. The IUD has been linked to pelvic inflammatory disease. Although this can usually be prevented by taking a course of antibiotics immediately after insertion, IUDs are not recommended for women who have a pelvic infection or who have had PID in the past—or for those who suffer from severe menstrual cramps or heavy bleeding. Failure rate: .8 to 4 percent for the Copper T; 2 to 4 percent for the Progestasert.

Spermicide alone. Whether it comes in the form of a foam, cream, gel or suppository, spermicide used without a diaphragm or cervical cap must be inserted at least 10 minutes and no more than an hour before intercourse and must be reapplied if intercourse is repeated. This inconvenience may account for the method's high percentage of failure. Failure rate: 3 to 21 percent.

Norplant. Six very thin rods surgically inserted in a woman's arm slowly and steadily release small amounts of the hormone used in the Pill. Left in place, the implants work for five years, but they can be removed at any time and fertility is immediately restored. Women for whom the Pill is not advised should talk to their doctors about whether Norplant would be a safe alternative, as the side effects are likely to be the same. Failure rate in first year of use: .04 percent.

Natural planning (the "rhythm" method). By avoiding intercourse during a woman's fertile period, this method allows people to practice birth control without using devices, pills or surgery. Practitioners keep track of their menstrual cycles and often of tiny changes in body temperature or vaginal mucous that take place during ovulation. Because of how long sperm can stay alive in a woman's body and how long eggs are available to be fertilized (see "Getting Pregnant," below), the safest way to use this method is to abstain from intercourse for 10 days or more each month. Failure rate: 1 to 20 percent.

Surgical sterilization. In a vasectomy, the two tubes that carry sperm from a man's scrotum to his penis are clamped or severed. In a tubal ligation, the same is done to the two Fallopian tubes that carry a woman's eggs from her ovaries to her uterus. Vasectomies are cheaper, less complicated, safer to perform and somewhat more effective than tubal ligation. Both methods are highly effective—and difficult, often impossible, to reverse. They are not advised for anyone who may want to have children later, but neither has any side effects unless there are complications following surgery. Failure rate: .1 to .2 percent for vasectomy; .2 to .5 percent for tubal ligation.

Morning-after pills. A number of oral contraceptives can prevent pregnancy by bringing on early menstruation after sex, as long as the first pill is taken within three days of the unprotected intercourse. As they contain a higher dose of the hormones than other oral contraceptives, they are not advised for anyone who should not take the Pill. Failure rate: 20 to 30 percent.

Abortion. If all other methods fail, a woman may opt for an abortion. Performed by a professional in a clinic, doctor's office or hospital, abortions performed during the first three months of pregnancy have a very low risk of complications (usually infection or excessive bleeding). Second trimester abortions may be riskier, possibly involving an overnight stay in a hospital. Third trimester abortions are usually performed only if the mother's life is in danger.

GETTING PREGNANT

For many women, the question is not how to avoid getting pregnant but how to achieve it. Fertility is a problem for a growing number of couples and technology helps some of them conceive. Since the costs of infertility procedures are high and the success rates relatively low, however, it's best to give nature every chance to work before trying them.

If you're trying to get pregnant, patience is a useful virtue: A couple is not considered to have a fertility problem unless they have been unable to conceive after trying consistently for two years. Perhaps that shouldn't be surprising, considering everything that has to happen for a woman to get pregnant.

The cycle begins when she ovulates, releasing an egg from the ovaries to the uterus. This happens 14 days before the onset of her menstrual period, and for 12 to 48 hours afterward the egg remains available to be fertilized.

Sperm may stay alive within a woman's body for anywhere from two to seven days after ejaculation. This means that a woman can theoretically get pregnant by having intercourse any time from a week before she ovulates to a

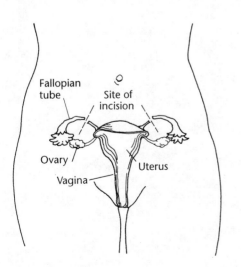

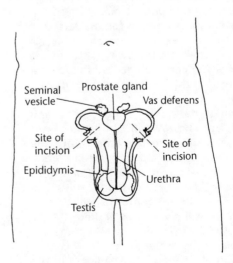

Birth control by sterilization

couple of days afterward. She's probably most fertile, however, for a period starting two days before and ending a day or two after ovulation, so she should have sex often during that period.

Women with regular menstrual cycles can estimate within a day or two when they will ovulate next. But for those who are less regular or want more precision, home ovulation kits and basal thermometers are helpful. Ovulation kits contain chemically treated strips that a woman dips into her urine for a week or so during the time of month she is likely to ovulate. The strip changes color when the hormone that triggers ovulation shows up, usually 24 to 36 hours before ovulation occurs. Basal thermometers are used to measure a woman's temperature every morning upon waking, preferably at about the same time every day. A slight drop followed by a rise in temperature indicates that she is ovulating.

If none of that works, an infertility specialist may be the answer. These doctors start by searching for a physical problem that might prevent pregnancy (perhaps a man has a low sperm count or a woman isn't ovulating regularly). If a problem is found, there may be a solution.

If blockage or other damage to the uterus, fallopian tubes or ovaries is suspected, for example, the doctor may recommend surgery. If the problem is thought to be a low sperm count, the man's sperm may be collected and concentrated in a centrifuge, then inserted high within the woman's uterus. Doctors may also suggest that the woman take medication to induce ovulation, even if she ovulates normally without it.

For couples whose infertility is of unknown origin, in vitro fertilization (IVF) or gamete intrafallopian transfer (GIFT) are possibilities. In IVF, hormone injections cause a woman to release several eggs. These are removed and fertilized in a Petri dish and up to three of the resultant embryos are then implanted in the uterus. GIFT also uses hormones

Hormones released at the start of the menstrual cycle signal the production of eggs. As the eggs grow they release the hormone estrogen, which signals the uterine lining to prepare for the fertilized egg. After about two weeks more hormones signal the egg to leave its shell and the ovary. This process is called ovulation. The egg is guided by the fimbria (the finger-like ends of the fallopian tube) to its rendevous in the tube.

Sperm swim through the cervix, into the uterus and down both fallopian tubes. Within 12–24 hours after ovulation the sperm must make contact with the egg, otherwise the egg will begin to disintegrate. The sperm must actually penetrate the coating of the egg, and has specific enzymes that enables it to do this. Once inside, an embryo forms which, over the next three days, will divide several times. At the eight-cell stage it will begin a five to seven day trip down the fallopian tube to the uterus. If all is well, the embryo will implant itself into the lining of the uterus and a fetus will begin to develop.

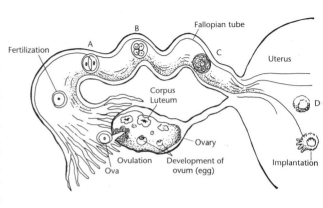

to stimulate the production of several eggs, which are removed by a doctor. The difference is that the eggs are immediately mixed with sperm and both sperm and eggs are reinjected back into the woman, allowing conception to occur in the Fallopian tubes rather than the lab. The success rate for GIFT is somewhat higher than for IVF, but both methods are expensive, emotionally taxing—especially for the women involved—and usually unsuccessful.

Childhood Illnesses and Immunizations

THE DENTIST
A child's first visit to dentist should take place at age two or two and a half. This serves two purposes: It lets the dentist ensure that the teeth are coming in all right and it gives the child an untraumatic introduction to the dentist, making him or her less likely to dread going in the future.

THE DOCTOR
Infants and toddlers need to visit a doctor at the ages of two, four, six, nine, 12, 15, 18 and 24 months. After age two, they should go every year until they are six and then every other year through adolescence. Children are usually taken to pediatricians, but family practitioners and internists are also qualified to treat them.

IMMUNIZATION
As we go through life, we build up immunities to the viruses and bacteria we are exposed to. The first time we encounter most germs, however, we are far more susceptible. Unfortunately, this can make early childhood a minefield of illnesses—especially for day-care babies, who are exposed to more germs earlier than children who stay home. But some of the most potentially serious diseases can be avoided through immunization shots. These include the following:

• A diphtheria, tetanus and pertussis (DTP) shot at two, four, six and 15 months; tetanus and diphtheria boosters every 10 years, starting at age 14 to 16.

• An oral dose of polio vaccine at two, four, 15 to 18 months and at four to six years.

• A measles, mumps and rubella (MMR) shot at 12 to 15 months and at four to six years.

• A hemophilus influenzae type b (Hib) shot at between 18 months and five years—or at two, four, six and 15 months, depending on the type of vaccine.

• A hepatitis type b (Hb) shot at birth, one and six months—or at one to two months, four months and six to 12 months, depending on the type of vaccine.

CHILDHOOD ILLNESSES
Common childhood illnesses include measles, rubella (German measles), mumps, chicken pox, colds, flu, ear infections, colic, diaper rash, meningitis and thrush. Some are life-threatening and even the mildest can escalate if left untreated. Parents soon learn from experience how to handle minor illnesses, but some things need professional care. Call a doctor immediately if your child exhibits any of the following symptoms:

• Unconsciousness or unnatural drowsiness or listlessness

• Unusually pale skin for more than a brief period of time

• Blueness around the face or lips

• Serious difficulty in breathing

• A rash that does not turn pale when you press firmly on the skin.

Care for the Elderly

When most elderly people start to need help, it is not the intensive care available in a nursing home. Instead, they simply can no longer do some simple but necessary task or they find themselves at loose ends after the death of a partner who used to take care of their needs. There are several options available for such people.

Geriatric care manager. These are specialized professionals who have graduate degrees in social work, psychology, gerontology or registered nursing. They first help a client decide what kind of help he or she needs, then help interview and hire people to do it. Care managers also stay in touch to monitor how things are working and may keep in touch with a concerned family member, supplying regular reports and addressing any concerns the family member may have. The National Association of Professional Geriatric Care Managers may have a list of geriatric care managers in your area. Write to the organization at 655 N. Alvernon Way, Suite 108, Tucson, AZ 85711, or call 1-602-881-8008.

Home health care. If all that's needed is a nurse or aide for a few hours a day, you can hire one yourself without the intervention of a care manager. Check with Medicare first—it may pay a portion of the cost.

Retirement villages. In these planned communities, residents can maintain their privacy in their own homes or apartments, yet take advantage of housekeeping services, nursing care, meals, transportation and other conveniences.

Elder cottage housing opportunities (ECHO). These prefabricated homes can be set down in the yard of a child or another family member.

Shared housing. This can mean either bringing someone into a private house or apartment or moving to a group home. For information on finding a housemate or on group shared housing, contact the National Shared Housing Resource Center, 431 Pine St., Burlington, VT 05401; 1-802-862-2727.

For some people, however, a nursing home is the best choice. These are usually people who need 24-hour nursing care because of a serious chronic disability or a recent illness or operation, so they often cannot find the right place on their own. If you are responsible for helping a friend or relative find a nursing home, start by involving the future resident as much as possible in making the decision.

Ask friends or relatives, your family doctor, hospital discharge planners or social workers which homes they recommend. If the future resident is enrolled in a group health plan, ask a plan representative which nursing homes in the area coordinate services with the plan. Or call your state's Agency on Aging (the office is probably in your state capital) and ask the ombudsman in the Office of Long-Term Care for the names of good homes in your area. If the future resident is on Medicare or Medicaid, ask for the names of homes certified to participate in the relevant program.

If a home is certified for Medicare and/or Medicaid, its performance is reviewed annually by the state. Ask to see a copy of the latest report (it must be posted at the nursing home). Also make sure that both the home's and the director's state licenses are current and on display in the home.

Visit a prospective home more than once, preferably at different times of day. Make at least one of the visits unannounced. Pay attention to the atmosphere. Is the home clean? Are the rooms and the grounds attractive? Do staff members treat residents with respect, concern and warmth? Are husbands and wives allowed to share rooms? Do residents decorate their own rooms? Notice whether residents seem alert or apathetic, whether they are dressed neatly and appropriately for the time of day and whether activities are available for interested residents.

Talk to residents by yourself, without staff members present. Ask what they think of the home and whether they will show you around. Visit private rooms, common rooms, the dining room at mealtime and outdoor areas.

Ask about the food—is it appetizing? Is it served hot? Are snacks available? Do residents who need special assistance or equipment at mealtime get what they need?

Find out, too, how good the home's medical facilities are. How many residents does each nurse or aide care for? Are licensed nurses on duty 24 hours a day? Is the confidentiality of medical records protected? How often does the home's physician visit residents? Do the physician and nursing staff meet with residents and their families to develop and review plans for treatment?

Before signing a contract, make sure it spells out the resident's rights and obligations, including safeguards and grievance procedures. The contract should also specify whether the home is certified by Medicaid and/or Medicare; spell out the daily or monthly expense of living there and the prices of items not included in that basic charge; and state the home's policy on holding a bed for a resident who leaves temporarily. If you have questions about the contract, talk them over with the nursing home's ombudsman and, if necessary, a lawyer and if you change any of the terms make sure both you and the home's representative initial the change. After signing, get a copy of the contract for yourself.

For a free pamphlet containing more details on what to look for and a checklist to help you evaluate nursing homes, write to the Consumer Information Center, Dept. 5332, Pueblo, CO 81009.

Mental Health Care

Psychological counseling can be either short- or long-term. Short-term counseling is usually sufficient for mild depression or anxiety or for someone who needs help in coping with a stressful situation. Long-term counseling or psychotherapy is usually advised for people suffering from serious and chronic problems such as severe depression, disabling phobias and other neuroses or difficulty in relationships with other people.

Finding the right mental help when you need it is as important as finding the right doctor when you're physically unwell, but it's harder to do, since people in search of a therapist are usually upset and that makes it hard to make a calm and well-reasoned choice. Yet therapy is much likelier to succeed if you find someone whose methodology and personality you're comfortable with.

First, you need to decide what kind of training you need in a therapist. Psychiatrists, who have medical training and are licensed to prescribe medication, generally handle severe mental disorders, such as severe depression or schizophrenia, that may require medication as well as lengthy treatment. Counselors who are not psychiatrists are generally psychologists or psychiatric social workers. Some have Ph.D.s in psychology, while others completed their training at the master's or undergraduate level. In general, the longer the training, the more qualified a therapist is to handle a wide range of problems. Before you schedule a visit, find out what kind of training a therapist has and whether he or she is certified by your state.

Consider seeing someone who specializes in treating problems like yours. If your problem is with a child, parent or mate, you may want to see a specialist in family or couples counseling. If the problem is sexual functioning, you may prefer a sex therapist; if it's an addic-

The Aging Process

Aging may be a natural process, but it isn't entirely inevitable. The genes you were born with play a big part in how quickly you age, but there are other factors you can control.

As at any other time of life, the two most important things you can do to maintain the strength and vitality associated with youth are to eat right and get plenty of exercise. For more information, see "You Are What You Eat" and "Exercise," above.

Some of the hardest signs of aging to slow down are the purely cosmetic ones, like the whitening and thinning of hair, the dark "liver spots" that form on the skin and the varicose veins that are especially common in women (varicose veins can be surgically removed, but this is generally recommended only if they are severe enough to cause pain). But you can minimize at least one such problem—wrinkles—by avoiding much of the behavior that causes them. Among the main culprits are smoking cigarettes, exposing yourself to direct sunlight without a sunscreen of at least SPF 15, drinking too much alcohol and gaining and losing weight repeatedly.

There's not much you can do about becoming farsighted (aside from getting bifocal glasses), losing some of your night vision, becoming slower to react to things or waking up more often and more easily during the night than you used to. But high blood pressure, which affects many men and more than half of all women over 55, can be controlled through a combination of diet and exercise and, if necessary, medication. Tooth and gum problems may be avoided—or caught before they deteriorate too far—through regular visits to the dentist. You may be able to slow down the hearing loss that is common with age, especially in the upper fre-

tion, you want a substance-abuse counselor. But if it's primarily your relationship to yourself that's off-kilter, you probably want individual or group counseling.

Once you know what kind of therapist you're looking for, ask friends, relatives or professional organizations for referrals. (For names and addresses of professional associations, see "Sources of Further Information"). Then draw up a list of questions for your first visit. You may want to know, for instance, whether he or she focuses on the past or the present, whether he or she tries to help you change your behavior or emphasizes thoughts and feelings, and how many sessions he or she expects your therapy to take. You may also want to discuss what you hope to achieve through treatment.

OVERCOMING ADDICTION

People who are addicted "need" a drug regularly—often daily. They also need to take stronger and stronger doses in order to feel its effect. Over time, these high doses may weaken the heart, liver and/or other vital organs and make it harder for the addict to function efficiently at work and in his or her personal life.

Addiction is a painfully difficult cycle to break. Perhaps the hardest part is recognizing the addiction and resolving to quit—but the work hardly stops there. To get off and stay off an addictive substance, most people need support, guidance and follow-up care from people who understand the special problems of addiction. They may get them at any of the following places:

Inpatient treatment centers
These programs, which usually last three to four weeks, give the addict a chance to clear his system of the alcohol or drugs that were poisoning it. Perhaps equally importantly, the addict trades the enabling company of the people who are part of the drinking or

---

quencies, by limiting your exposure to loud noises. And osteoporosis, a crippling thinning of the bones that can lead to curvature of the spine, broken bones and other problems, can be slowed considerably if you get the USRDA of calcium and vitamin D every day. Keeping your abdomen and back muscles strong also helps protect your spine.

Certain other diseases common among the elderly, such as diabetes and glaucoma, may be controlled through medication. Others, including cataracts and prostate problems—and, sometimes, glaucoma—can be cured by surgery if they become serious enough to warrant it. But for a few, such as Alzheimer's disease, no effective treatment has yet been found.

Depression is also a problem for many elderly people. One of the most common causes is a growing sense of isolation, as friends and mates leave or die. Another is the demoralizing fact that our society has little appreciation or use for the knowledge and skills accumulated by older people. Keeping active both mentally and socially can go a long way toward dispelling depression. Make an effort to stay in touch with old friends and make a few new ones. And find something to do—like volunteering for an organization you believe in, pursuing a hobby you enjoy or traveling to see something or someone you care about—that engages your interest.

For women who have gone through menopause (or a hysterectomy that included removal of the ovaries), there's a special pitfall in aging: The reduction of estrogen in their bodies greatly increases their risk of heart disease and may also speed the onset of osteoporosis and other disorders. Going on estrogen therapy reduces those risks—but it's not for everyone, as it may increase the risk of certain kinds of cancer as well as uterine fibroids.

using world for the support of people struggling to overcome the same addiction.

Inpatient treatment programs may be found in psychiatric hospitals, general hospitals and freestanding units. Psychiatric care may be in order if an addict has shown signs of a serious personality disorder, but nonmedical centers are the best option for the great majority of clients. Such centers are based on the idea that the addiction must be overcome through self-help, not medication.

To choose a center, start by making sure that it is accredited by the state and has a plan outlining the goals of treatment and how quickly each is expected to be reached. Make sure the center includes family members in the full course of treatment and has an aftercare program that runs for two years after a patient's release. If the center itself doesn't offer such a program, see that it makes arrangements with counselors in your area to do follow-up treatment and that the center's own counselors stay in touch with former patients.

Look for a facility where there are no more than eight patients—and preferably fewer—for every counselor. Make sure that the counselors are certified in addiction issues (some centers hire former clients, who may be empathetic but lack professional training) and the program director has been in the field for at least five years. And be sure to find out how long the staff members have been there, as a high rate of turnover almost certainly means there is an underlying problem that will affect the quality of the care provided.

Outpatient counseling
People who are functioning well at work and in their personal lives need not necessarily check into an inpatient center to overcome an addiction. Instead, they may opt for intensive outpatient individual or group therapy—or a combination of the two—with a substance-abuse counselor. For more information on choosing a counselor, see "Mental Health Care," above.

12-step programs
Another alternative to inpatient treatment, 12-step programs have helped many people. All, from Narcotics Anonymous to Overeaters Anonymous, are modeled after Alcoholics Anonymous, whose founder set up 12 stages for alcoholics to pass through while reclaiming their lives.

Not everyone can subscribe to the programs' central tenet that members must place their faith in a "higher power." Those who can, however, often transform their lives by following the 12 steps and adopting the program's philosophy of facing oneself without delusion, learning to tolerate human frailty, taking responsibility for one's own behavior and helping others. Central to the success of 12-step programs are a buddy system for new members and the frequent—and free—meetings where people struggling to overcome an addiction get the support of others who are doing the same.

Alternative Medicine

"Alternative medicine" is any method of healing other than the standard Western medicine taught in American medical schools. Most alternative medicine is neither covered by insurance plans nor sanctioned by mainstream doctors, yet many people believe they have been helped by the techniques listed below.

Acupuncture. Practiced for centuries in China, acupuncture is the art of inserting very long, thin needles into the skin at specific points to treat various problems. In the West, it was first used primarily to relieve pain, but other applications are gradually becoming more widespread.

Chiropractic. A much newer discipline than acupuncture, chiropractic was invented at the turn of this century by a self-taught healer in Iowa. Chiropractors work with the spine (and sometimes other bones and joints), using massage, sudden applications of tremendous pressure and sometimes electrical stimulation to make "adjustments," usually in a series of sessions performed over the course of months. Practitioners believe the treatments can not only relieve back pain but help cure other medical problems. Most mainstream doctors believe that, while chiropractors may help relieve some cases of back pain, their manipulations may make others worse.

Massage therapy. Massage therapy involves massaging various muscles to relieve pain and promote relaxation. Practitioners believe that this promotes

better health by improving the flow of blood and oxygen to cells throughout the body, reducing blood pressure, strengthening the immune system and stimulating the release of endorphins.

Homeopathy. Homeopathic doctors treat a variety of illnesses by prescribing extremely small amounts of natural substances that would, in larger doses, cause the patient's illness. The amount of "cure" in a homeopathic dose is so diluted that most mainstream doctors believe its cures are due to the placebo effect.

Massage therapy

Home Remedies

For serious or persistent problems, it's always best to see a doctor. But for some of life's minor problems, home remedies work just fine.

Bee stings. Mix half a teaspoon of meat tenderizer with a few drops of water and coat the sting with the mixture to stop the pain. Then gently scrape the stinger out (don't tug or pull, or it might release more venom). If you don't have any tenderizer on hand, coat the sting with mud instead and then remove the stinger.

Canker sores. Hold a wet tea bag on the sore. Not only will

the tannic acid in the tea help cure the sore, it will provide instant relief.

Colds and flu. Nothing can cure them, and the best way to get through them is what Mom always said: Drink plenty of fluids (juice or water, not alcohol), get plenty of rest, stay warm and take aspirin or aspirin substitute to reduce fever and relieve aches. If you have a sore throat, gargle with warm, salty water to relieve it and drink hot water or tea with honey and lemon to soothe it. If you have a cough, breathe in moist air, either by plugging in a humidifier, lingering in the bathroom after a hot shower or breathing in the steam from a cup of hot tea or bowl of chicken soup. Yes, chicken soup really is good for a cold.

Insomnia. Drinking a glass of warm milk just before going to bed really can help you fall asleep (the tryptophan in the milk is what does it). So can counting sheep—or any other undemanding, repetitive task that takes your mind off the fact that you can't fall asleep. Getting regular exercise and staying away from caffeine in the afternoon and evening should make falling asleep easier. If you can't sleep because you're worried about something, make a list of your worries, put it on your bedside table and make a firm promise to yourself to deal with them in the morning. If these strategies don't work, try reading a difficult or boring book.

Sources of Further Information

AGENCIES

Alcoholics Anonymous World Services
Inc.
P.O. Box 459, Grand Central Station
New York, NY 10163
1-212-870-3400
Call or write to this headquarters—or
look in your local telephone directory
under Alcoholics Anonymous—for help
with alcoholism.

American Association for Marriage and
Family Therapy
1100 17th Street NW, 10th Floor
Washington, DC 20036
1-800-374-2638
Write or call for a list of certified marriage or family therapists in your area.

American Association of Retired
Persons (AARP)
601 E St. NW
Washington, DC 20049
1-202-434-3470
Call or write for information on the
many free services and programs this
nonprofit organization provides people
50 and older in exchange for a low
annual membership fee. Several services
and programs are available for nonmem-
bers as well.

American Board of Medical
Specialties
1-800-776-CERT,
or 1-708-491-9091
Call (be persistent; the number is
usually busy) to find out if a medical
doctor is certified by any of the 24 primary medical boards.

American Council on Exercise
5820 Oberlin Dr., Suite 102
San Diego, CA 92121
1-800-529-8227,
or 1-619-535-8227
Call or write to find out if an exercise instructor or personal trainer is
certified, to get a list of certified instructors in your area or for free information on a variety of health and fitness
topics.

Centers for Disease Control
Public Inquiries
1600 Clifton Rd. NE
Atlanta, GA 30333
1-404-332-4555
Write to this federal agency for printed
health information on various topics or
call to request faxed or recorded information or to talk to a CDC expert during
standard business hours.

Consumer Information Catalog
Pueblo, CO 81009
1-719-948-4000
The federal government issues free or
low-cost pamphlets on a variety of
health issues. Write or call for a free catalog listing all the pamphlets available.

National AIDS Hotline
1-800-342-AIDS
In Spanish, 1-800-344-SIDA
For the hearing impaired,
1-800-AIDS -TTY
Information about HIV and AIDS.

National Association on Drug Abuse
Problems
355 Lexington Ave.
New York, NY 10017
1-212-986-1170

Call or write for help with a drug addiction problem.

National Council on the Aging
  409 Third St. SW
  Washington, DC 20024
  1-800-424-9046
Call or write for information on many issues of concern to the elderly.

National Health Information Center
Office of Disease Prevention and
Health Promotion
  P.O. Box 1133
  Washington, DC 20013-1133
  1-800-336-4797,
  or 1-301-565-4167
This federal office can offer a referral to any of more than 1,000 organizations that deal with specific illnesses.

National Institute of Mental Health
Information Resources and Inquiries
Branch
  5600 Fishers Lane, Room 7-103
  Rockville, MD 20857

Write for free information on mental health issues.

Planned Parenthood Federation of
America Inc.
  810 Seventh Ave.
  New York, NY 10019
  1-212-541-7800
Call or write for information on birth control.

Susan G. Komen Breast Cancer
Foundation
  1-800-I'M AWARE
Promotes public awareness of breast cancer, raises funds and sponsors mammogram vans.

THE NATIONAL INSTITUTES OF HEALTH

The NIH is a federal consortium of health institutes that conducts research and supplies public health information on various topics. For information from any of the member institutes listed below, call the appropriate phone number or write to The National Institutes of Health, Information Office/Public Inquiries, *Name of the individual institute*, Bethesda, MD 20892.

National Institute on Aging, 1-301-496-1752

National Institute of Allergy and Infectious Diseases, 1-301-496-5717

National Institute of Arthritis and Musculoskeletal and Skin Diseases, 1-301-496-8188

National Cancer Institute, 1-800-4-CANCER

National Institute of Child Health and Human Development, 1-301-496-5133

National Institute on Deafness and Other Communication Disorders, 1-301-496-7243

National Institute of Dental Research, 1-301-496-4261

National Institute of Diabetes and Digestive and Kidney Diseases, 1-301-496-3583

National Eye Institute, 1-301-496-5248

National Institute of General Medical Sciences, 1-301-496-7301

National Heart, Lung and Blood Institute, 1-301-251-1222

National Institute of Neurological Disorders and Stroke, 1-301-496-5751

The National Institute of Environmental Health Sciences has a different address than the others. For information, call 1-919-541-3345 or write to:

National Institute of Environmental Health Sciences Information Office
P.O. Box 12233
Research Triangle Park, NC 27709

10

First Aid

Lifesaving Basics

CARDIOPULMONARY RESUSCITATION (CPR) AND ARTIFICIAL RESPIRATION (MOUTH-TO-MOUTH RESUSCITATION)

In accidents or emergencies, a rescuer may encounter two very serious problems: The victim may have stopped breathing or his or her heart may have stopped. The essential lifesaving techniques of cardiopulmonary resuscitation and artificial respiration are vital in these situations.

CPR can be a lifesaving response to cardiopulmonary arrest, which is characterized by an absence of breathing and heartbeat, often—though not always—accompanied by unconsciousness. CPR is best performed by those who have received training in the technique. Courses are available through the American Red Cross; many local hospitals also offer classes.

In mouth-to-mouth resuscitation, the rescuer literally gives his own breath to the victim, pumping oxygen into the lungs until the victim can breathe on his or her own. Artificial respiration techniques can be learned in lifesaving courses, often taught at hospitals, through the American Red Cross or at your local "Y."

Before you begin CPR, you must

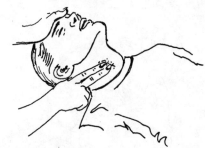

Checking for pulse

determine that the victim definitely has no pulse and is not breathing: The chest compressions involved in CPR should never be performed unless there is clearly no pulse.

Once that determination has been made, perform CPR for one minute and then call your local emergency medical service (911, in most areas). If there are others present, have someone make that call immediately while you perform CPR.

Before Beginning CPR

If the victim of cardiopulmonary arrest is an adult or older child, the American Red Cross advises:

• Check for signs of consciousness; ask the victim to respond.

• If there is no response and there are oth-

ers present, alert someone to call for emergency medical help.

• If there is no response and you are alone with the victim, begin CPR first and call after about a minute. If you haven't received training in the techniques, follow these steps for the next minute, then follow instructions on "Performing CPR," below.

• Turn the victim gently onto his or her back onto a firm surface, taking great care to support the head and neck while doing so, and move the body as a single unit.

• Kneel beside the victim, halfway between the chest and head.

• Place one hand on the victim's forehead and the other beneath the bone of the chin.

• While pushing down on the forehead, lift the chin to gently tilt the head back. If

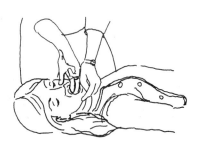

Artificial respiration

there is any indication of a head or neck injury, merely lift the chin or tilt the head back very slightly.

•Place your ear to the victim's mouth for about 5 seconds to check for breathing.

•If there is no sign of breathing, perform *Artificial respiration,* as follows:

 –Check that the mouth is clear of debris and that head is tilted back slightly.
 –Pinch the victim's nose shut, seal your lips tightly around the mouth and administer a full breath of about one and a half seconds' duration.
 –Let the victim's chest fall completely, and administer another breath in the same fashion.
 –If the victim's chest does not rise, tilt the victim's head again and deliver another breath.

 –If there is still no sign that the breath has penetrated, begin first aid for an unconscious adult whose airway is obstructed (See "The Heimlich Maneuver," below).

•While keeping one hand on the victim's forehead to keep it tilted back, place the second and third fingers of your other hand (do not use your thumb) on the victim's neck for about 10 seconds, to check for a carotid pulse. The pulse can be felt in the slight depression between the muscles on the side of the neck and the voice box.

•If you are alone with the victim, now is the time to call your local emergency medical service (911, in most areas). Alert them to the presence or absence of breathing and pulse.

•If the victim is now breathing and has a pulse, continue to monitor these functions.

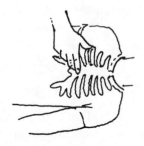

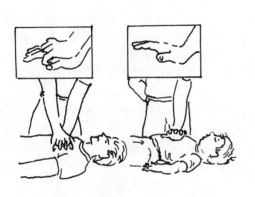

CPR

•If the victim has a pulse but is still not breathing, continue to administer one breath, one second long, every 5 seconds, in the manner described above. Check for a pulse after every 12 such breaths.

•If the victim is a child aged one to eight, the National Safety Council advises that you administer one breath every 4 seconds, and recheck for a pulse after every 15 such breaths.

Performing CPR on an Adult or Older Child

If there is no breathing and no pulse, begin CPR:

•Locate the notch in the center of the chest where the victim's ribs meet the breastbone.

•Place your middle finger on that notch, with your index finger beside it.

•Place the heel of your other hand right beside your index finger, higher on the chest, along the sternum.

•Lift your fingers from the notch and place the now-free hand directly on top of the heel of your other hand.

•Hold your fingers upward or interlace them.

•Lean over the victim, with your shoulders directly above your hands.

•Using the weight of your upper body, press forcefully down on the victim's sternum, depressing it approximately two inches.

•Remove the pressure, but keep hands in place.

•Counting aloud "One and two and three" between each downward push, compress the chest a total of 15 times, being careful to push straight down each time.

•If the victim is a child aged one to eight, administer five chest compressions at the same rate and in the same fashion, followed by one rescue breath. Continue this sequence for 10 cycles.

•Using the artificial respiration techniques described above (under "Before Performing CPR"), give two rescue breaths, and watch for a sign that the chest is rising.

•Repeat three more cycles of 15 compressions and two breaths.

•Check the pulse again, via the carotid artery.

•If pulse has been restored and victim is breathing, cease CPR efforts, but continue to monitor both pulse and breathing.

•If pulse is restored but breathing is not, administer one breath every five seconds, and continue to check pulse once a minute.

•Resume CPR if pulse stops again.

•If there is no sign of pulse or breathing, repeat the sequence of 15 compressions and two breaths until the victim has revived or medical help arrives.

•If the victim is a child aged one to eight, repeat the sequence of five compressions and one rescue breath until the victim is revived or medical help has arrived.

Performing Artificial Respiration on Infants

If the victim is an infant, Massachusetts' Beverly Hospital emergency guide advises:

•Check for signs of consciousness by shaking the baby gently and monitoring for movement or noise.

•If there is no response and others are present, alert someone to call the local emergency medical service—911 in most areas). If you are alone with the baby, begin emergency first aid as follows before calling for medical help:

•Roll the baby gently onto his or her back on a firm surface, taking care to support the baby's head and neck and moving the body as a single unit.

•Place one hand on the baby's forehead, and place the forefinger of your other hand under the bone of the chin.

•Push slightly on the forehead and gently lift the chin to tilt the baby's head back, taking care not to press on the soft tissue beneath the chin.

•Keep the baby's mouth open.

•Draw near to the baby and listen and feel for breathing, but be aware that not all chest movement can be interpreted as breathing.

•If there is no sign of breathing, keep the baby's head tilted and tightly seal your lips around the mouth and nose.

•Give two strong, full breaths of one and a half seconds' duration, pausing between each to let the chest rise and fall.

•If the chest does not rise, administer two more breaths.

•If there is still no sign of breathing, administer first aid for an infant with an obstructed airway (See "The Heimlich Maneuver," below).

•While keeping one hand on the baby's forehead to keep the head gently tilted back, place the forefinger and middle finger of the other hand on the upper arm for 10 seconds to check for a brachial pulse.

•If there is no pulse, place your ear to the baby's chest to check for a heartbeat.

•At this point, if you are alone with the baby, call your local emergency medical service (911, in most areas).

•If the baby is breathing and has a pulse at this point, continue to monitor for any change in either function.

•If the baby has a pulse but no breathing, continue to administer one rescue breath, as described above, every three seconds. Recheck pulse and breathing after every 20 breaths.

CPR For An Infant
If the baby has no breathing or pulse, begin CPR:

•Use one hand to keep the baby's head slightly tilted.

•Place the index finger of the other hand on the baby's sternum, which is generally located just below the midpoint between the nipples.

•Place the two fingers below your index finger on the sternum.

•Lift the index finger.

•Use the two fingers that remain on the chest to administer chest compressions, by pressing straight down on the sternum.

•Depress the sternum up to one inch and release, but leave your two fingers on the baby's chest, in the same position.

• Administer five such compressions, at the rate of one every three seconds.

• Deliver one rescue breath.

• Repeat the cycle of five compressions and one breath nine more times.

• Recheck breathing and pulse.

• If breathing and pulse have resumed, cease CPR and monitor both functions.

• If pulse has returned but breathing has not, continue to administer one rescue breath every three seconds.

• Recheck breathing and pulse every 20 breaths.

• If pulse stops again, resume CPR.

• If there is no breathing and no pulse, repeat cycles of five chest compressions and one rescue breath until the baby is revived or medical help arrives.

THE HEIMLICH MANEUVER
(SAVING A PERSON FROM CHOKING)
The most common incidents of choking are brought on by swallowing food that has not been chewed properly or that contains a bone, but trauma victims who suffer head or face injuries can also choke on flowing or clotted blood.

According to the American Red Cross, if a person is choking, some or all of the following symptoms will be evident:

• Grabbing the throat in distress

• Gagging

• Weak coughing, noisy breathing

• Pale and bluish complexion

• Convulsions, unconsciousness or both from lack of oxygen

• Inability to speak—this distinguishes a choking victim from a person in cardiac arrest

If the victim is an adult or a child who's old enough to talk:

1. Ask if he or she is choking.

2. Ask for permission (which can be granted with a nod) to perform first aid.

Then proceed.

Unless the victim is unusually large

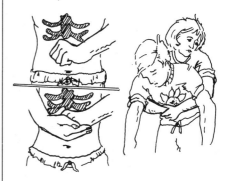

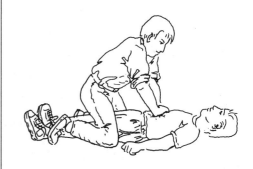

Heimlich maneuver

or is a pregnant woman, administer chest thrusts (the "Heimlich maneuver") as follows:

•Stand behind victim.

•Wrap arms around victim's waist.

•Make a fist with your dominant hand.

•Place the thumb side in the middle of the victim's abdomen, just above the navel and below the lower tip of the breastbone.

•Grasp your fist with your other hand.

•Extending your elbows, press your fist into the victim's abdomen, using quick, sharp, upward thrusts, to try to clear the airway.

•Continue performing this technique until the object is expelled.

•Seek medical help immediately even if the crisis seems to have passed; damage could have been inflicted either by the object that caused the choking or by the first aid techniques that expelled it.

If the victim loses consciousness from choking:

•Call your local emergency medical service (911, in most areas).

•Place the victim on his or her back, on a flat, firm surface.

•Clear the mouth.

•Check for breathing.

If the victim is not breathing, perform artificial breathing:

•Tilt the victim's head back, lift the chin and give two full breaths.

•Pinch the nose shut, and seal your lips tightly around the victim's mouth.

•Give two full breaths, each approximately two seconds long.

•Watch for a rising in the victim's chest after each breath is administered; wait until it falls before you resume.

•If there is no response, tilt the victim's head back further, and again administer two full breaths.

If there is still no noticeable response, proceed to abdominal thrusts:

•Straddle the victim's legs.

•Place the heel of your dominant hand against the middle of the victim's abdomen, again just above the navel with your fingers pointing toward the victim's head.

•Place your other hand on top of that hand.

•Pressing your hands inward and upward, perform 5 to 10 thrusts.

•Sweep your fingers through the victim's mouth, to see if the object has been dislodged.

•If it has been, remove it and check to see if the victim has resumed breathing.

•If the object has not been expelled, again administer two breaths, followed by another 5 to 10 thrusts.

•Continue the cycle of thrusts, checking the mouth and administering two breaths until the object is dislodged or medical help has arrived.

If the victim is unusually large or pregnant, use chest thrusts instead of abdominal thrusts, as described here.

If the victim is conscious,

•Stand behind the victim.

•Put your arms under his or her armpits.

•Make a fist with your dominant hand, and place the thumb side on the middle of the victim's breastbone.

•Grasp your fist with your other hand, and proceed with quick, sharp, repeated thrusts, inward and upward.

•Continue until the object is expelled.

•Seek medical help immediately even if the crisis seems to have passed; damage could have been inflicted either by the object that caused the choking or by the first aid that expelled it.

If the victim is unconscious and unusually large or pregnant:

•Call your local emergency medical service (911, in most areas).

•Place the victim on his or her back, on a surface that is firm and flat.

•Kneel beside the victim's chest.

•Place the heel of your dominant hand on the victim's breastbone.

•Place the heel of the other hand on top of that one, being careful to keep your fingers upward.

•Administer quick, repeated thrusts, push-

ing the heel of the bottom hand downward, and compressing the victim's chest approximately 1.5 to 2 inches.

•Sweep your fingers through the victim's mouth to see if the object has been dislodged.

•If so, remove the object and check to see if the victim is breathing.

•If the object has not been expelled, continue a sequence of thrusts, sweeping the mouth and, if necessary, performing rescue breathing (See "If victim loses consciousness," above) until the object has been cleared or medical help arrives.

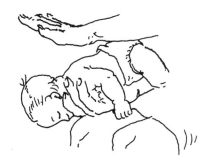

Heimlich maneuver on an unconscious infant

If the choking victim is a conscious infant, up to a year old:

•Call the local emergency medical service (911, in most areas).

•Place the child face down and tilted slightly downward, along your forearm on your nondominant hand.

•Rest your forearm on your thigh.

•Support the child's head with hand of the same arm, wrapping your thumb and index finger around the jaw.

•Using the heel of your free hand, deliver four blows to the child's back, between the shoulder blades.

•Turn the child onto his or her back.

•Rest the child on your thigh or a firm surface, again keeping the child's body at a slight downward angle.

•Place the middle and index fingers of your dominant hand below the child's breastbone.

•Administer four quick thrusts, depressing the breast area up to one inch with each one.

•Continue the sequence of back and chest thrusts, and after each sequence peer into the child's mouth to see if the object has been dislodged.

•If it has, remove it gently with your pinky finger.

•If it has not, continue the sequence of back and chest thrusts and keep checking the mouth until the object is dislodged or medical help arrives.

If the victim is an unconscious infant, up to a year old:

•Call your local emergency medical service (911, in most areas).

•Place the child on his or her back, on a flat, firm surface.

•Attempt to open the child's airway: Place one hand on the child's forehead, place the forefinger of the other hand under the firmest part of the child's chin and gently tilt the head back. Be careful not to press on the soft tissue under the chin, and not to close the child's mouth.

•Place your ear to the mouth to check for breathing.

•If the child is not breathing, tightly seal your mouth around the child's mouth and administer two breaths of approximately two seconds each in duration.

•If this is unsuccessful, try again.

•If there is still no breathing, proceed to Steps including placing the child face down through administering four quick thrusts to the breast area as described above for a conscious infant.

•After one set of chest and back thrusts, peer into the child's mouth to see if the object has been dislodged.

•If it has been, clear it from the child's mouth with your pinky finger.

•If it has not been expelled, continue the sequence of two breaths followed by four back and chest thrusts until the object is dislodged or medical help arrives.

Choking victims—especially infants—are also susceptible to seizures (see below). Should this occur, administer lifesaving techniques.

Do not interfere if a choking victim is able to cough forcefully and is still able to breathe in and out—but do be ready to step in if the condition worsens and the air exchange begins to diminish.

Do not pinch or poke at the throat, which could force the object further down the victim's airway.

Major Injuries

BLEEDING

Cases of bleeding can range from minor to life-threatening, and can be manifested internally or externally.

Internal bleeding, while obviously harder to detect, does yield clues. These include:

•Deep bruises

•Blood in vomit, stool or urine

•Blood from the vagina

•Abdominal pain or swelling, especially following physical trauma

•Weakness, confusion or lightheadedness

•Pale, cold or clammy skin

•Extreme thirst

•Rapid, weak pulse

•Shock (see "Shock," below)

If internal bleeding is even suspected, the American Medical Association advises:

•Call your local emergency medical service (911, in most areas).

•Keep the victim still, preferably lying on his or her back, unless a leg, head, spinal or neck injury is suspected and it would be dangerous to move the victim into that position.

•Maintain an open airway: While the victim is lying flat on his or her back, place one hand on the forehead, place the forefinger and middle finger of the other hand under the chin and gently tilt the victim's head back.

•Check the victim's breathing and circulation, and perform emergency lifesaving techniques if either vital sign is absent (See "Cardiopulmonary Resuscitation and Artificial Respiration," above).

•Continue to monitor for signs of shock and perform first aid if necessary (See "Shock," below).

•Examine the victim for signs of broken bones, and treat them if necessary (See "Broken Bones," below).

•If the victim begins to vomit and no head, spinal or neck injury is suspected, gently turn the victim's head to one side to maintain an open airway, sweep the vomitus from the victim's mouth with your forefinger and save it for medical personnel.

•Calm and reassure the victim, and continue to monitor vital signs until medical help arrives.

Do not give the victim anything to drink or eat.

External bleeding can range from minor wounds, which will generally clot by themselves although they still require treatment (See "Lacerations," below), to severe wounds that require direct pressure to control them.

If the bleeding is severe, the American Medical Association advises:

•Call your local emergency medical service (911, in most areas).

•Keep the victim lying down.

•Apply a compress of sterile gauze or clean cloth (such as a towel, piece of clean clothing or handkerchief) directly to the wound site, pressing firmly with the palm of your hand.

•If absolutely no compress material is available, close the wound as well as you can with your hands, and maintain pressure with your hand as well.

•Keep pressure directly on the wound.

•Unless broken bones or spinal, head or neck injuries are suspected, raise the bleeding area gently until it is higher than the rest of the body.

•If the compress is soaked through with blood, do not remove it. Place another on top.

•If the bleeding abates or stops entirely, use cloth or gauze strips to hold the compress in place.

•Continue to monitor the victim.

•Keep the victim warm, with clothing or blankets. If there are no broken bones or spinal, head or neck injury, you may also put blankets underneath the victim, especially if the ground is cold or damp.

•Remain with the victim, keeping a close watch on breathing, circulation and possible shock symptoms, until medical help arrives.

Do not give fluids to anyone who is unconscious or suffering from an abdominal injury; wet the lips with water if he or she complains of dryness.

Do not give any bleeding victim alcoholic beverages.

The AMA advises against applying a tourniquet to control bleeding, unless you have received professional training. Otherwise, apply a tourniquet only if you are in a remote area, with no medical assistance available. The recommended procedure is as follows:

•Find a strip of cloth at least two inches wide, such as a necktie, scarf, belt or length of fabric or gauze.

•Place the tourniquet on the arm or leg between the wound site and the heart.

•Wrap it twice around, and tie a knot.

•Leave it in place for a maximum of 20 minutes.

Do not tie a tourniquet too tightly; that can cause additional damage.

SHOCK

Shock can set in when a trauma to the body reduces bloodflow and limits the amount of oxygen to the body's cells. Shock is a symptom of a larger condition, such as physical injury, loss of blood, severe allergic reaction, infection, electrical accident, hypothermia or heat illness—so it is critical to treat the underlying condition as well as the shock.

According to the American Red Cross, symptoms of shock include any or all of the following:

•Dizziness

•Weakness

•Cold, clammy skin

•Unconsciousness

•Intense thirst

•Nausea and vomiting

•Chest pain or discomfort

•Shallow and/or rapid breathing

•Paleness

•Confusion or decreased alertness

•Bluish fingernails and/or lips

•Paralysis

•Numbness

If the shock victim is not suffering from a spinal, head or neck injury, the American Red Cross advises:

•Call your local emergency medical service (911, in most areas).

•Try to determine the cause of the shock, and look for medical-alert tags on the victim.

•Gently place the victim on his or her back and open the airway: Place one hand on the forehead and the forefinger of your other hand under the chin, and gently tilt the head back.

•Check breathing and circulation; perform lifesaving techniques if victim is not breathing or has no pulse (See "Cardiopulmonary Resuscitation and Artificial Respiration," above).

•Perform bleeding control, applying a compress if necessary (See "Bleeding," above).

•If he or she is breathing normally and has not suffered a spinal, head, neck or leg injury or a venomous bite, keep the victim lying on his or her back, and elevate the feet 8 to 12 inches, making use of whatever support is available (books, boxes, newspapers, etc.). If the victim has suffered a venomous bite, do not raise the site of the wound above the victim's heart; see the section on "Venomous Bites," below. If the victim has a spinal, head or neck injury, follow the bulleted steps in "Head Injuries," below.

•If the cause of the shock has been determined, administer first aid for it.

•Loosen constrictive clothing and keep the victim warm with coats, clothing or blankets; also place them beneath the body, if the ground is cold or damp.

•If the victim is vomiting or drooling, gently turn the head to one side and sweep the liquid away to keep the airway clear. Preserve any vomitus for medical personnel; it may help determine the cause of the shock.

•Continue to monitor the victim until help arrives.

If the shock victim has a possible spinal, head or neck injury, the American Red Cross advises:

•Call your local emergency medical service (911, in most areas).

•Try to determine the cause of the shock, and look for medical-alert tags on the victim.

•Open the victim's airway without moving him or her.

•Check the victim's breathing and pulse (See "Cardiopulmonary Resuscitation and Artificial Respiration," above).

•Apply compress if necessary (See "Bleeding," above).

•Administer first aid for the underlying illness or injury, if it has been determined.

•Keep the victim warm by covering him or her with coats, clothing or blankets. Do not move the victim to place anything underneath.

•If the victim begins to vomit or drool, protect the airway by gently "log-rolling" him or her onto one side, being careful to support the head and neck and move the body as a unit. This is best achieved with the help of other people.

•Continue to monitor the victim's breathing and circulation until medical help arrives.

Do not administer anything by mouth to a shock victim.

Do not apply direct heat to provide warmth.

BURNS
Treatment of burns depends largely on their severity. According to the Emergency Medical Procedures guide of Massachusetts' Beverly Hospital, the symptoms and treatment for each burn category are as follows.

First-Degree Burns
Symptoms:
•Pain

•Skin redness

•Mild swelling

Treatment:
•Apply cold, wet, clean compresses to the burn site(s), or immerse in fresh, clean, cold—but not icy or salty—water.

•Continue until pain abates—usually 10 to 15 minutes.

•Leave the burn uncovered, if possible, or cover lightly with a dry gauze pad.

•Consult a doctor if the skin does not heal within a short time.

Second-Degree Burns
Symptoms:
•Deep red skin

•Glossy skin from leaking bodily fluid

•Blistering

•Loss of skin

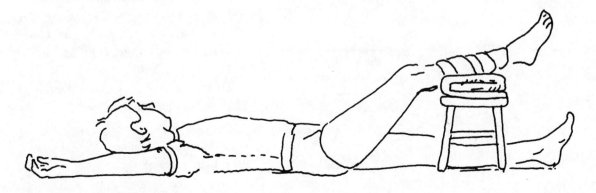

Elevating a burned limb above the heart

Treatment:

•Call your local emergency medical service (911, in most areas).

•Immerse burns in fresh, clean, cold—but not icy or salty—water or apply cold, wet, clean compresses to them.

•Gently dry the burns, being careful not to break any blisters, and cover them with clean, dry gauze or cloth.

•If the face or head are not burned, have the victim lie down. If face and head are burned, help the victim sit up.

•If arms and/or legs are burned, keep them elevated on soft pillows or rolled-up blankets.

•If the burned area is extensive, monitor victim for shock (See "Shock," above) and treat if necessary.

•Check the victim's breathing and circulation (See "Cardiopulmonary Resuscitation and Artificial Respiration," above), and administer first aid as needed.

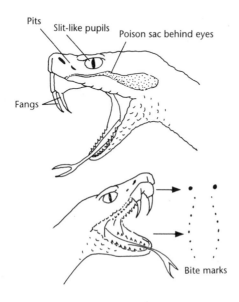

Pits
Slit-like pupils
Poison sac behind eyes
Fangs
Bite marks

•Remove any clothing and jewelry from the burn area, provided it is not sticking to the burn.

•Remain with the victim until medical help arrives.

Third-Degree Burns
Symptoms:
•Loss of all layers of skin

•Possible charring of edges of skin

Treatment:
•Call your local emergency medical service (911, in most areas).

•Cover burn lightly with clean, dry, non-breakaway material, such as sterile gauze.

•Unless it is a chemical burn—which should be flushed thoroughly with water for at least 5 minutes—do not use water to treat any third-degree burn.

•Follow the last six bulleted steps under "Treatment" for second-degree burns.

VENOMOUS SNAKE BITES
The most prevalent types of venomous snakes are pit vipers—including cottonmouths, rattlesnakes and copperheads—and coral snakes. Pit vipers are characterized by the pit between their nostrils and eyes, as well as by their triangular-shaped heads and vertical pupils. Coral snakes have black snouts and red, black and white or yellow rings.

To treat a snake bite, the American Medical Association advises:

•Call the local emergency medical service (911, in most areas).

• Try to identify the type of snake, and alert the paramedics over the phone so they can prepare an antivenin.

• Keep the victim still.

• Try to place the wound below the level of the heart.

• Check the victim's breathing and circulation (see "Cardiopulmonary Resuscitation and Artificial Respiration," above); perform lifesaving techniques if necessary.

• Wash the site of the wound to prevent further infection.

• Remove any constrictive clothing or jewelry near the bite.

• Monitor the victim for the onset of shock (see "Shock," above); treat if necessary.

• Stay with the victim until medical help arrives.

ELECTRIC SHOCK

When administering first aid for electric shock, do not touch the victim directly until the current has been turned off or the victim is clearly no longer in contact with it—or you may be electrocuted as well. Victims who have been struck by lightning, however, may be touched immediately.

Victims of electric shock may exhibit any or all of the following symptoms:

• Cardiopulmonary arrest

• Skin burns

• Respiratory failure

• Muscular pain

• Unconsciousness

• Headache

• Mouth burns

To administer first aid to a victim of electric shock, the American Red Cross advises:

• Turn off the electrical current, if it is safe to do so:

    –First, make sure you are not in or near water, including a puddle or damp area.

    –Unplug the appliance or main power switch.

• If you cannot turn off the current, try to move the victim without making direct contact:

    –Stand on a dry, insulating material such as a pile of newspapers or rubber mat.

    –Using a dry, wooden object such as a board or broomstick, separate the victim from the current. Do not use anything even remotely damp or containing metal.

    –You may also try to loop a dry rope or dry fabric length around the victim's arm or leg, and gently drag him or her away from the current.

• Call your local emergency medical service (911, in most cases).

• In the case of high-voltage current, remain at least 20 feet from the victim, and call your local emergency medical service and local power company immediately.

• Once you and the victim are clear of the current, open the victim's airway: Place the victim gently on his or her back, put one hand on the forehead and the forefinger of the other under the chin, and tilt the head back.

•Check the victim's breathing and pulse (See "Cardiopulmonary Resuscitation and Artificial Respiration," above); perform basic lifesaving techniques if necessary.

•Administer first aid for any other injuries or burns.

•Take steps to treat and prevent shock, if necessary (see "Shock," above).

•Remain with the victim until medical help arrives.

HEAD INJURIES

In the event of a head injury, keep the victim still, in the position you found him or her, unless the victim is in imminent danger and must be moved.

To administer first aid to the victim of a head injury, the American Red Cross advises:

•Call your local emergency medical service (911, in most areas) immediately.

•Try to determine what happened by asking the victim, if possible, or by questioning bystanders.

•Without moving the victim, open the airway.

•Check the victim's breathing and pulse (see "Cardiopulmonary Resuscitation and Artificial Respiration," above); administer lifesaving techniques if necessary.

•If the victim is breathing and has a pulse but is unconscious, immobilize the head and neck: place one hand on each side of the victim's head, keeping the head lined up with the spine, and prevent any movement.

•If the victim is breathing, has a pulse and is conscious, encourage him or her to lie still and try to remain calm. Try to protect the head and neck from any motion or surrounding activity.

•If the victim at any time loses consciousness or memory, even briefly, inform medical personnel when they arrive.

•Perform first aid for head injuries:

–If a fractured skull is suspected, do not apply direct pressure to any open wound and do not clean it of debris. Cover the wound site with clean, sterile dressings.

–If the head wounds are superficial and you are certain that there is no fracture, apply direct pressure to the wound sites with a clean cloth, gauze or towel. (see "Bleeding," above, and "Lacerations," below).

–If the victim begins to have seizures, cushion the head, remove any potentially dangerous objects nearby, and administer recommended first aid for seizures (see "Seizures," below).

–If a conscious victim begins to vomit, gently lean him or her forward while continuing to support the head and neck throughout, sweep away the vomitus to protect the airway, and save it for medical personnel.

–If an unconscious victim begins to vomit, place him or her in the recovery position (see "Recovery Position" under "Food Poisoning," below) while continuing to support the head and neck, sweep the vomitus away and save it for medical personnel. Moving the victim is best accomplished with the aid of others.

–Apply ice to any areas of swelling.

•Remain with the victim, and help to keep him or her immobile, until medical help arrives.

•Remember that any victim of a head injury should be observed for at least 24 hours following the trauma. If the victim falls asleep, he or she should be awakened every two or three hours during that period. In the event of unusual drowsiness, confusion, abnormal behavior, a stiff neck or vomiting, seek medical help immediately.

Do not move or pick up the victim unless it is absolutely necessary.

Do not shake the victim if he or she seems dazed.

Do not remove any object protruding from or embedded in a head wound.

Do not give the victim any alcohol.

Do not give the victim any medication, unless directed to do so by a physician.

SEIZURES (CONVULSIONS)

Triggered by a disturbance in the brain's electrical "circuitry," a seizure is a series of uncontrollable muscle movements; most seizures last anywhere from 30 seconds to about 15 minutes. According to the American Red Cross, seizures can be prompted by epilepsy, high fever, heat illness, poisoning, high blood pressure, heart disease, electric shock, choking, venomous insect bites or stings, drug or alcohol withdrawal or abuse, stroke or other brain illness, head injury or, in the case of young children and infants, violent shaking.

The symptoms may include any or all of the following:

•Localized twitching or tingling

•Blacking out

•Sharp muscle spasms

•Jerking in limbs

•Stiffening of limbs or body

Positioning an unconscious victim of convulsion or seizure

•Dizziness or confusion

•Falling

•Loss of consciousness

•Frothing at mouth or drooling

•Snorting or grunting

•Difficulty with or cessation of breathing

•Loss of bladder and/or bowel control

To treat the victim of a seizure, the American Medical Association advises:

•Look for medical-alert tags; these will provide information on pre-existing conditions, including epilepsy and allergies.

•Remain with the victim, and have someone call the local emergency service (911, in most areas) and give them as much information as possible.

•Help the victim onto his or her side, in case vomiting occurs.

•Without putting your hand in the victim's mouth, gently sweep any vomitus away from the face to aid breathing, and preserve it for medical personnel.

•Remove any objects that may cause injury to the victim during his or her involuntary movements.

•Loosen any clothing, especially around the neck.

•Monitor the victim's breathing and pulse carefully (see "Cardiopulmonary Resuscitation and Artificial Respiration," above) during recovery from the seizure; perform lifesaving techniques if necessary.

•Remain with the victim until he or she has

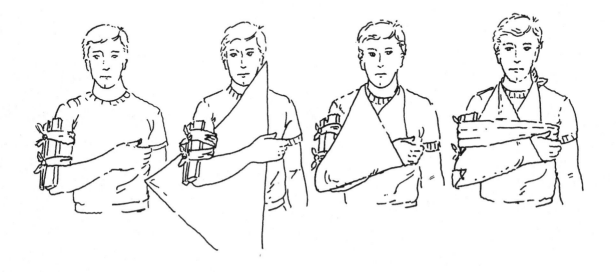

Stablizing broken bones

fully regained consciousness, and medical help has arrived.

Do not restrain the victim.

Do not move the victim unless he or she is near something that could pose a hazard.

Do not try to make the victim "come out of it"; this is impossible.

Do not administer anything by mouth until the seizure has abated and the victim is fully alert and awake.

Do not place anything between the victim's teeth during a seizure.

BROKEN BONES (FRACTURES)

The purpose of first aid in the treatment of fractures is to lessen the possibility of further injury in the time it takes for medical help to arrive.

Symptoms of a broken bone include:

•Swelling, pain, deformity or misalignment at the site of the injury

•Inability to use the injured part

•Protrusion of a broken bone through the skin

•Bruising or discoloration

•Numbness and/or loss of pulse at or near the site

•Pale, bluish skin around the wound

In open fractures, the skin as well as the bone is broken. Closed fractures are those in which the skin has not been

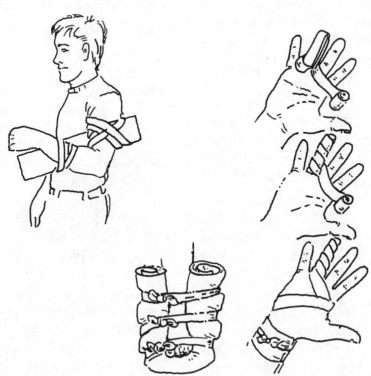

Stablizing broken bones

punctured. In the case of severe bleeding, administer first aid for that (see "Bleeding," above) before you tend to the broken bone.

For a closed fracture on an arm or leg, the American Medical Association advises:

•Call your local emergency medical service (911, in most areas).

•Unless there is imminent danger (from a fire or explosion following a car accident, for example), keep the victim—and especially the site of the injury—immobile until a splint has been applied. If the victim must be moved, use the clothes-drag technique (see "Clothes-Drag" under "Inhalation Poisoning," below). Take great care to support the head and neck, and to immobilize, cushion and support the break with your hands. This is best accomplished with the help of others and almost impossible to do alone. If you're alone, move the victim only if essential. Cradle the head with one hand and use the other to drag.

•Throughout treatment of the break, keep the victim's airway open, monitor breathing and pulse (see "Cardiopulmonary Resuscitation and Artificial Respiration," above), and check for possible shock (see "Shock," above). Administer lifesaving techniques if necessary.

•Keep the broken limb in the position in which you find it, and apply the splint to the injury in that same position.

•To apply a splint:

—Find a firm, clean material to use as the basis for support. This might be a straight stick, oar, broomstick, board, rod, pole or thick, rolled-up magazine or newspaper. The length of the splint must extend beyond the joint above the break and the joint below it.

—Place clean padding between the splint and the skin of the injury site.

—Fasten the splint with bandages or strips of cloth at at least three sites: above the joint and above the break, below the joint and below the break, and at the level of the break.

—If an ambulance or other medical help is on the way, remain with the victim, keeping him or her calm and warm until it arrives. If you have been instructed to or have no other choice, transport the victim to medical help after the fracture has been immobilized and cushioned.

Do not try to "straighten out" a break.

Do not administer anything by mouth.

Do not "test" a potentially broken bone to see if it works.

POISONING

Poisoning is one of the most preventable of first aid emergencies; it is also one in which time for preparation is ample, since you can take steps to poison-proof your home in advance.

According to the American Red Cross's tips on poison-proofing your home, all potentially poisonous substances—including medications, personal-care products, felt-tip markers, paint, insecticides, fertilizers, gasoline, lighter fluid, insulation, tobacco products, perfumes, vitamins, household solvents, cosmetics and car supplies—should be kept well out of reach of children or anyone who may not be able to understand the consequences of ingesting or inhaling them.

All such products should also be stored in their original containers, preferably in a locked cabinet, away from food and heat sources. Do not mix products, which could create potentially lethal fumes.

Fuel-burning appliances and all products that emit fumes should be used in adequately ventilated areas.

Medications should have child-proof caps and be disposed of, container and all, when they are out of date or no longer needed. While in use, they should be stored in a cool, dry, locked place—which almost never describes a typical bathroom "medicine chest."

Also, all households should have the number of the local poison-control center prominently displayed by the phone, and have syrup of ipecac and activated charcoal on hand in a first-aid kit.

To reach your state's Poison Control Center call 1-800-555-1212 before an emergency strikes, and keep the number handy.

Poison First Aid

In a poison emergency, rapid first aid is essential to keep the poison from being further absorbed into the victim's body.

Often in the case of very young children—who, according to the American Red Cross, comprise 75 percent of all poisoning cases—the victim will not know that he or she has ingested poison; being aware of the symptoms is therefore especially critical.

These may include:

- Sudden illness
- Incoherence
- Dizziness
- Headache
- Irritability
- Chills
- Increased salivation
- Fever
- Abdominal pain
- Vision disturbances
- Strange breath odor
- Paleness
- Drowsiness
- Weakness
- Unconsciousness
- Seizures
- Bluish lips
- Muscle spasms
- Chemical burns around the nose and mouth or elsewhere on the skin
- Heat palpitations
- Dry mouth
- Coughing
- Shortness of breath
- Loss of bowel or bladder control

Ingestion Poisoning

In the case of poisoning by ingestion, the culprit may be tainted food (see "Food Poisoning," below); products containing poison chemicals, such as personal-care products, household goods or car supplies; or medications taken in overdose.

Aside from signs of physical distress or lethargy, symptoms that point to ingestion poisoning include a nearby toxic substance (including solvents, auto supplies or poisonous plants), strange breath odor, stains, liquids or powder on the clothing, or burns around the face, mouth, nose or elsewhere on the skin.

Inhalation poisoning should be suspected if the victim had been working with a furnace, fire, automobile or other fuel-burning appliance, or with chemicals, especially in close, poorly ventilated quarters. The culprits are chemical fumes from such products as ammonia, carbon dioxide, carbon monoxide, gasoline, solvents or paint. If a child or impaired adult has been near such substances, however, the poison could have been ingested as well as inhaled.

Regardless of what the substance is—and whether it is ingested or inhaled—if poisoning is suspected, call your local emergency medical service (911, in most areas) and your local poison control center *immediately.* Try to identify the poison—which is crucial to knowing what method of first aid to apply—and inform the medical personnel. Meanwhile, the steps you take while waiting for help to arrive could be lifesaving.

Treatment of ingestion poisoning depends on the nature of the poison. You should *never* induce vomiting after the ingestion of petroleum-based items such as kerosene, lighter fluid, furniture polish, or corrosive products such as those containing acids, bleach, ammonia or lye (these might include household cleansers, rust removers and drain treatments).

To treat victims of such poisoning, the American Red Cross advises:

•Call your local poison control center and local emergency medical service (911, in most cases) and tell them what poison is involved and when it was ingested, the victim's symptoms and age, and how long it would take you to reach a hospital or physician.

•Check the victim's breathing and pulse (see "Cardiopulmonary Resuscitation and Artificial Respiration," above). Administer basic lifesaving techniques if either is not present.

•If the victim should at any point begin to have a seizure or convulsion, administer first aid (see "Seizures,"above).

•Keep the victim calm and warm, while continuously checking breathing and circulation and monitoring for signs of convulsions or seizures until medical help arrives.

•If the victim starts to vomit, keep his or her face down, with the head lower than the hips. Help keep the mouth and airway clear by sweeping the vomitus aside with your forefinger, and save it for medical personnel to examine.

Do not induce vomiting.

Do not give the victim any liquids.

If you have determined that the poison is non-corrosive and non-petroleum-based, the American Medical Association advises:

•Call your local poison control center and emergency medical service (911, in most areas) and inform them of what poison has been ingested and when, the victim's symptoms and age, and how long it would take you to reach a hospital or physician.

•Check the victim's breathing and pulse (see "Cardiopulmonary Resuscitation and Artificial Respiration," above). Administer lifesaving techniques if either is not present.

•If the victim is conscious, give him or her one to two cups of water.

•Induce vomiting only if medical personnel have told you to do so:

—Administer 2 tablespoons of syrup of ipecac for adults, 1 tablespoon for children. **Do not** administer syrup of ipecac to an infant under six months old.

—Follow up with one or two glasses of clear juice, such as apple or cranberry juice, or water.

—If the victim has not vomited within 30 minutes, repeat steps above.

—If victim does vomit, keep his or her face down, with the head lower than the hips. Help keep the mouth and airway clear and save the vomitus for medical personnel to examine.

—If advised to do so by emergency personnel, administer activated charcoal after the victim has vomited.

•If the victim should at any point begin to have a seizure, administer first aid (see "Seizures," above).

Inhalation Poisoning

Often in cases of inhalation poisoning, the victim must first be rescued from the site of the fumes. Before attempting to do this, *always* notify others—and instruct them to call the local emergency medical service (911, in most areas) and poison control center. The American Red Cross then advises you to proceed as follows (from *The American Red Cross First Aid and Safety Handbook*):

•Take a few deep breaths before entering, then hold your breath.

•Use protective breathing gear if possible; otherwise place a wet cloth over your mouth and nose.

•Open all windows and doors immediately to increase ventilation.

•**Do not** light any matches or candles, flip

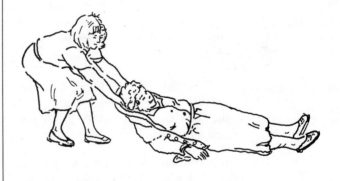

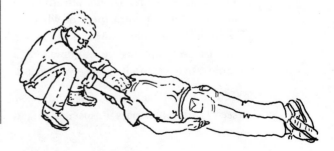

Clothes-drag technique

on any switches or in any way produce a spark or flame.

•While rescuing the victim, stay below any visible smoke or fumes in the upper part of the room, and above any that are coming from near the floor.

•Close off any fume sources, if possible.

•Remove the victim from the site, using the *clothes-drag technique*:

    —If the victim is lying sideways, place him or her face up, moving the entire body as a single unit.

    —If the victim is already face up, straighten the legs.

    —If the victim is face down, drag the victim that way.

    —Bend your knees and position yourself above the victim's head.

    —Immobilize the victim's head between your forearms and grab the clothes at the victim's shoulders. Be sure to unbutton the jacket to prevent choking.

    —Walking backwards smoothly and slowly, drag the victim to safety, using the muscles in your arms, back, legs and abdomen.

•Once you and the victim are in a safe place, call your local emergency medical service (911, in most areas) and poison control center if this has not already been done by others. Inform them of what the victim inhaled, when, how old the victim is, what the symptoms are and how long it would take to get to a hospital or physician.

•Check the victim's breathing and pulse (see "Cardiopulmonary Resuscitation and Artificial Respiration," above). Administer basic lifesaving if either or both of these is not present.

•If the victim is unconscious, place him or her in the recovery position (see "Recovery Position" under "Food Poisoning," below).

•If the victim is conscious, assist him or her in assuming the recovery position.

•Check the eyes and skin for chemical burns, and flush any afflicted areas thoroughly with cold water for 15 minutes.

•If the victim should at any point begin to have a seizure or convulsion, administer first aid (see "Seizures," above).

•If victim starts vomiting, keep his or her face down, help keep the mouth and the airway clear by sweeping the vomitus aside with your forefinger and save it for medical personnel to examine.

•Continue to monitor breathing and circulation, and remain with the victim until medical help arrives even if the crisis seems to have subsided.

In any case of ingestion or inhalation poisoning:

Do not give an unconscious victim anything orally.

Do not administer any "universal antidote"; there is no such thing.

Do not administer anything unless directed to do so by medical personnel.

Do not rely solely on the label to gauge the ingredients of a product; it may not be entirely accurate or comprehensive.

Do not wait for symptoms to develop if you have any reason to suspect poisoning; call for help and begin first aid immediately.

ALLERGIC REACTIONS

An allergic reaction—which occurs when the body perceives a usually harmless substance as a toxin—can range from the mildly irritating to the potentially fatal.

The allergens can reach the body through skin contact in the case of a plant (such as poison ivy), inhalation (pollen and other airborne allergens), ingestion (foods and medications) or insect bites and stings.

According to the American Red Cross, symptoms can include:

•Abdominal pain

•Difficulty breathing or swallowing

•Dizziness

•Flushed complexion

•Hives

•Itching

•Nausea and vomiting

•Swelling of the eyes, tongue or entire face

•Tightness in the chest

•Unconsciousness

If the reaction appears moderate and non-life-threatening—that is, if the victim is breathing normally and remains conscious, but exhibits symptoms such as itching or the development of a rash—the American Red Cross offers the following tips:

•Seek medical help regardless of the severity of the reaction; at the very least, a doctor can recommend the best over-the-counter medications.

•Help the victim to remain calm.

•Try to identify the source of the allergic reaction, and remove the victim from further contact with it.

•If a rash develops, treat the skin with calamine lotion or cool compresses.

•Observe the victim closely for signs that the reaction is worsening; be sure to report all symptoms to a doctor.

If the victim's reaction is severe from the outset or seems to be rapidly worsening:

•Call the local emergency medical service (in many areas, 911).

•Check for any emergency medical tags that denote a history of allergies; if these are present, see if the victim is carrying any emergency allergy medication; if so, help the victim to take it.

•If medical ID tags are present but medication is not, inform the emergency medical service about the tags.

•Check the victim's breathing, heartbeat and pulse; perform artificial respiration or cardiopulmonary resuscitation (see above) if necessary.

•Monitor the victim for shock (see "Shock," above), seizures and convulsions (see "Seizures," above); treat if necessary.

•Remain with and continue to monitor the victim until medical help arrives.

Do not assume that any previous allergy shots will protect the victim.

Do not place a pillow under the victim's head (this can close off a possibly already constricted airway).

Do not give the victim anything through the mouth if the victim is unconscious or having difficulty breathing.

Bee Stings
If a bee sting has caused the allergic reaction, the Children's Hospital of Philadelphia advises:

•If the reaction seems severe or is worsening, call your local emergency medical service (911, in most areas).

•Scrape the stinger from the skin with a firm, flat object such as the side of a credit card, butter knife or fingernail. **Do not** use a pair of tweezers, which could squeeze more venom from the stinger.

•Keep the victim lying down. If vomiting begins, place the victim on his or her side, and sweep the vomitus from the mouth with your forefinger.

•Apply a cold ice pack to the affected area immediately to slow the absorption of venom.

•Many allergists also recommend the use of a tourniquet in the case of a bee sting. This can help to slow the flow of blood—and therefore the absorption of the venom—through the body:

   —A tourniquet—preferably rubber, although cloth or rope may also be used—should be applied only if the

sting has just occurred, and is on either an arm or leg.

   —Apply it approximately three to four inches above the sting site, between the sting and the body. Tie firmly but not too tightly, and loosen it every five minutes until medical help arrives.

As is true in many emergency situations, preparedness is crucial. If you are planning a trip outdoors, carry a bee-sting emergency kit (available in many camping-gear stores) and learn to identify poisonous plants and shrubbery.

Other Insect Bites
Bees are not the only insects whose stings can produce virulent toxic reactions in humans. Scorpions and spiders—notably black widows, brown recluses and tarantulas—can be equally dangerous, and can generate poisonous reactions similar to bee stings.

If bitten, the American Red Cross advises:

•Call your local emergency medical service if the reaction is severe or worsening—and inform them of the bite so they can bring the necessary medication.

•Try to identify the insect, and if it can be killed safely, do so; this could help with treatment.

•Try to keep the injury below the victim's heart. Arrange the body so that the heart is higher than the injury.

•Keep the victim as still as possible.

•Check the victim's breathing; administer artificial respiration (see "Artificial Respiration," above) if necessary.

•Stay vigilant for signs of shock, such as coldness in the extremities, paleness and diminished alertness. (see "Shock," above).

•Wash the site of the bite to reduce the possibility of an infection.

•Apply cold compresses to diminish swelling and possibly slow the pace of the venom through the bloodstream.

•Remove any restrictive clothing or jewelry around the site of the wound.

•Continue to monitor and try to calm the victim until medical help arrives.

Do not apply a tourniquet.

Do not allow the victim to ingest any analgesics, including aspirin, or any stimulants or alcohol.

Victims of insect bites should also receive follow-up care from a physician, to detect and treat any infection that may develop.

Minor Injuries and Ailments

Minor injuries are injuries in which the victim is not suffering severe bleeding, is not unconscious, does not exhibit symptoms of shock and shows no signs of major infection, such as swelling or pus. This doesn't mean, however, that they don't require prompt treatment.

CUTS AND LACERATIONS
If a cut is bleeding severely, take emergency measures to control the bleeding (see "Bleeding," above).

According to the American Medical Association, medical assistance should be summoned if any of the following conditions exist:

•Bleeding is severe.

•The wound is especially deep.

•A foreign object remains embedded in the wound.

•The wound was inflicted with a dirty object.

•The victim is unsure of his or her tetanus vaccination status, or knows that it is negative.

•Any signs of infection develop: redness, swelling, tenderness or pus at the site of the laceration; fever, perspiration or nausea.

If infection is evident, do the following until help arrives:

•Keep the victim lying down.

•Elevate and immobilize the wounded area.

•Apply warm, wet compresses made of clean cloth—preferably a sterile gauze.

To treat any wound in which there is not severe bleeding, the AMA advises:

•Wash your hands thoroughly with soap and clean water.

•If wound is still bleeding, apply pressure with a clean, dry cloth—preferably a sterile gauze pad.

•When the bleeding has subsided, wash the wound thoroughly with soap and clean water, scrubbing gently to remove all dirt surrounding the wound site.

•Rinse the wound with running water, if possible.

•Pat the wound dry with a clean cloth—again, a sterile pad is best.

•Cover the wound with a sterile gauze pad and bandage.

Do not attempt to remove any foreign objects deeply embedded in the wound; this could trigger severe bleeding.

Do not apply any occlusive topical medication, ointments or "home remedies" unless medical personnel have instructed you to do so.

SCRATCHES

Although most scrapes and scratches may appear minor, they do leave the body vulnerable to infection and should be treated swiftly. Treat a scratch with the same care as you would a laceration—and if an animal has inflicted the scratch, be sure to seek prompt medical attention.

BRUISES

A bruise occurs when a blow or a fall causes blood vessels to break, resulting in discoloration and sometimes swelling (hematoma) as the blood seeps into the surrounding tissues. Initially, most bruises are blue or green, and as blood seeps away from the site during the healing process, the bruise turns brown and yellow.

To treat a bruise resulting from a blow or fall, the Emergency Medical Procedures guide of Massachusetts' Beverly Hospital advises:

•If you suspect internal bleeding, if there are symptoms of shock (see "Shock," above), if the bruise results in painful swelling, tingling or loss of sensation, if the bruise is on the genitals or is a severe head bruise (see "Head Injuries," above), call your local emergency medical service (911, in most areas). Perform emergency first aid for shock or head wounds if necessary.

•Apply a cold compress or ice pack to the area as soon as possible, to decrease the bleeding beneath the surface and the swelling.

•If the bruise is on a limb, elevate it above heart level.

•Monitor the site for increased discoloration, pain or tenderness, and watch for signs of cold, clammy skin, weakness or rapid breathing. If any of these occur, seek medical help immediately.

•Apply cold compresses periodically for approximately 48 hours after the injury, to help reduce swelling and subcutaneous bleeding.

If you are suffering from bruises for no apparent reason, seek medical help immediately. An underlying condition may be responsible.

BLACK EYES

A "black eye" is the result of direct trauma to the eye or the surrounding area and, according to the American Medical Association, it should be treated with extreme care:

•If any damage to the eye is suspected, call your local emergency medical service (911, in most areas).

•Keep the victim lying down.

•Gently apply cold, clean cloth compresses to the afflicted area to reduce swelling and help limit the bleeding from damaged blood vessels.

•Apply clean, sterile dressings to any cuts around the eye.

•Raise the victim's head and look for blood inside the iris, which can result from the seepage of blood into the area behind the cornea.

•If blood is present there, cover both of the victim's eyes with clean, sterile dressings, and be sure to alert medical personnel immediately.

Do not press on the area or rub the eye.

Do not apply a "raw steak" compress to the area; the meat contains bacteria that could cause further damage.

Do not use fluffy cotton or any other "breakaway" material on the wound.

Do not press on the area to help stop bleeding.

BLISTERS

Blisters are generally caused by clothing, shoes or sporting equipment causing friction against the skin. The most common areas afflicted are the hands, feet and backs of heels.

If the blister is small and has not opened:

•Remove the source of the irritation.

•Cover the blister with a sterile gauze pad and secure it with a bandage. If the blister

is left protected and undisturbed, the fluid contained within it will eventually be reabsorbed.

If the blister breaks:

•Cleanse the area gently with soap and clean water.

•Cover it with a sterile gauze pad and a bandage.

If the blister is large (more than an inch across) and is likely to break:

•Seek medical attention.

•Only if such assistance will not soon be available, you may try to drain the blister:

•Sterilize a needle over an open flame.

•Puncture the bottom edge of the blister gently with the needle.

•Press very gently, slowly forcing out the fluid.

•Cover the area at once with a sterile gauze pad, secured with a bandage.

Regardless of the size of the blister and whether or not it has broken, medical attention should be summoned promptly if any of the following symptoms appear:

•Red streaks leading away from the site

•Redness around the site

•Pus

SUDDEN HEADACHES

Anyone who experiences trauma to the head should receive medical attention immediately. If you have suffered a head injury, or are with someone who has, call your local emergency medical service (911, in most areas). (For more information, see "Head Injuries," above.)

A sudden, severe, debilitating headache with no obvious cause also requires immediate medical attention. Such pain could signal a stroke, meningitis, encephalitis, a tumor, a viral or sinus infection, an allergic reaction, hypertension or a delayed reaction to a previous injury. In the case of a pregnant woman, toxemia could also be the culprit.

NOSEBLEEDS

A nosebleed can be prompted by any number of things, including scratching the nose too severely, physical trauma to the nose and repeated nose blowing from allergies, colds or crying.

Any pregnant woman or elderly person who experiences a nosebleed should seek medical attention immediately. The same is also true, of course, for someone whose nosebleed is a symptom of a larger physical trauma.

For a nosebleed in which the victim is neither pregnant or elderly:

•Seek medical attention immediately if a broken nose is suspected, or if there is any other injury involved.

•If a nosebleed is the only symptom, first check to see if there is any object lodged in the nose.

•If there is an object in the nostril:

—Advise the victim not to breathe in sharply, which could cause it to travel further into the cavity.

—Gently press the unobstructed nostril closed with your index finger.

—Ask the victim to blow his or her nose.

—If the object remains lodged in the nostril, give the victim pepper to sniff, to promote a sneeze.

•If this is not effective, seek medical attention.

•If there is no object lodged in the nostril, ask the victim to sit down and lean forward with his or her mouth open, to prevent blood clots from obstructing the airway.

•Gently squeeze the sides of the nose together for approximately 15 minutes, being sure to squeeze below the bone.

•Monitor the victim during this process, to make sure that no blood is being swallowed and that he or she is breathing normally through the mouth.

•Release the pressure slowly.

•If the bleeding continues, squeeze the nose again in the same fashion for another five minutes, still checking to see that no blood is being swallowed and that the victim is breathing freely through the mouth.

•Place a cold cloth compress against the nose to help the blood vessels to constrict.

•If the victim is still bleeding, seek medical attention immediately.

Do not allow the victim to blow his or her nose until several hours after the bleeding has stopped.

Do not allow the victim to blow or touch his or her nose while you are administering treatment.

Do not allow the victim to become

involved in strenuous activity for at least 24 hours after the bleeding subsides.

Do not try to "straighten out" a nose that has suffered a blow.

FOOD POISONING

The term food poisoning is a general one; reactions to it can range from bouts of vomiting and diarrhea to the life-threatening effects of botulism.

Victims of food poisoning will often note, in hindsight, that a particular food didn't "taste right." The food may have been too old to be safely eaten, left too long at room temperature or in warm temperatures, improperly prepared or processed with potentially unsafe chemicals.

Salmonella poisoning, in which food has been contaminated by the salmonella bacteria, usually reveals itself anywhere from six to 24 hours after the food has been ingested. The most common culprits: meat, poultry, fish, milk and eggs.

Staphylococcus poisoning, sometimes known as "picnic poisoning," occurs when foods are not kept properly refrigerated. Typical suspects include mayonnaise-laden salads, poultry, meats, eggs, milk and foods filled with cream or other dairy products. Its symptoms usually become obvious two to six hours after the offending food has been ingested.

In staphylococcus or salmonella poisoning, symptoms can include any or all of the following: abdominal pain and cramping, nausea and vomiting, diarrhea, dizziness, chills, fever, headache and perspiration.

In any of these cases:

•Call your local emergency medical service (911, in most areas) immediately, even if the condition does not seem severe.

•Try to determine what was responsible for the onset of the food poisoning; keep the container for possible testing.

•Keep the victim lying down, preferably in bed.

•Keep the victim warm.

•If the victim is vomiting, keep him or her face down, sweep the vomitus from the mouth with your forefinger to keep the airway clear, and save it for medical personnel.

•Once vomiting has subsided, take measures to combat dehydration: Administer warm, mild liquids, such as broth, fruit juice, plain water or tea.

Do not take measures or administer any medication to stop the vomiting, unless instructed to do so by a doctor or emergency medical personnel. This is part of the body's effort to expel the toxin.

Botulism and **shellfish poisoning** are the most virulent strains of food poisoning; they are potentially life-threatening.

In the case of botulism, the culprit is usually smoked meat or fish, home-canned foods or honey. Very rarely a case will occur from a commercially prepared canned food. Symptoms, which usually set in 12 to 36 hours after the food has been ingested, can include:

- Muscle weakness

- Blurred or double vision

- Headache

- Difficulty in swallowing or speaking

- Unconsciousness

Shellfish poisoning manifests itself much more quickly—usually within an hour of ingestion of the tainted fish. Symptoms can include:

- Numbness that starts in the face and head and gradually spreads throughout the body

- Increased salivation

- Muscle weakness

- Paralysis

In either case, the American Red Cross advises:

- Try to identify the source of the poisoning; save any remainder of the food or container.

- Call your local emergency medical service (911, in most areas) and your local poison control center; tell them the source of the poison, and give them the food or container when they arrive.

- Also alert them to the symptoms and the age of the victim, and let them know whether the victim ingested anything after the tainted food.

- Open the victim's airway; check for breathing and circulation. (See "Cardiopulmonary Resuscitation and Artificial Respiration," above.)

- If both breathing and circulation are present and the victim is conscious, assist him or her in assuming the *recovery position*:

  –Have the victim lie face up, facing you.

  –Place the arm nearer to you at the victim's side, under the buttock.

  –Place the other arm across the chest.

  –Place the leg farther from you over the leg nearer to you, with legs crossed at the ankles.

  –Support the victim's head with your dominant hand.

  –Grab the clothing around the victim's hip area, and pull the victim toward you; the victim should gently roll over.

  –Bend the victim's top arm, to help support his or her upper body.

  –Bend the victim's top knee, to support the lower body.

  –Gently tilt back the victim's head, and make sure that the airway is open.

- If both breathing and circulation are present but the victim is unconscious, place the victim in the recovery position yourself.

- If the victim begins to have a seizure, perform emergency first aid (see "Seizures," above).

- If the victim is vomiting, make sure he or she is face down and that the airway remains clear: wrap a cloth around your fingers and clean out the victim's mouth between attacks of vomiting.

- Retain a sample of the vomitus for the medical authorities.

- Continue to monitor the victim's breathing

and circulation; perform CPR or artificial respiration if necessary.

•Wait with the victim for medical help to arrive.

Do not wait for symptoms to develop or become severe if food poisoning is suspected; summon medical help immediately.

Do not induce vomiting or give the victim anything to ingest, unless instructed to do so by medical or poison-control authorities.

Do not use any "universal antidote": there is no such thing.

Do not use any "home remedies."

Do not rely strictly on a food product's label to check the ingredients; it may not always be accurate.

HEAT-RELATED PROBLEMS
Severe heat can cause a number of problems, including dizziness, dehydration and faintness. A host of other symptoms can become increasingly severe if not treated. Such heat conditions are worst for children and the elderly. Heat-related problems are easier to prevent than treat, so keep an eye on family members who are likely to fall victim, especially during the summer months, or while on vacation in a warm climate.

Cramps
Heat cramps are prompted by dehydration through perspiration, which causes the body to lose salt. Although strenuous activity is often involved in the onset of heat cramps, anyone exposed to extremely hot weather can be a victim.

The muscles in the legs and the stomach are usually the first ones affected. Symptoms include:

•Painful spasms and cramping

•Heavy perspiration

•Possibly convulsions

If the victim is experiencing convulsions, administer first aid for that immediately (see "Seizures," above).

If there are no convulsions, only cramping and spasms at the site:

•Take the victim to a cool place, and have him or her sit quietly.

•If the victim is not vomiting, administer sips of cool salt water (use 1 teaspoon of salt per quart of water) or clear juice, at the rate of about four ounces every 15 minutes for an hour.

•If the victim at any time begins to vomit or go into convulsions or lose consciousness, stop his or her intake of any liquid and call your local emergency medical service (911, in most cases) immediately.

•If convulsions ensue, administer first aid for convulsions while you wait for medical help to arrive.

•If the victim is vomiting, make sure that he or she remains face down, and that his or her airway remains unobstructed.

•Using one finger, gently sweep the mouth free of vomitus between episodes of nausea.

•Remain with the victim and urge him or her to seek follow-up medical treatment even if all symptoms have subsided.

Heat Stroke

Heat stroke, or sunstroke, is a potentially life-threatening condition brought on by the body's inability to cool itself and regulate its temperature.

Symptoms include any or all of the following:

•Extremely high body temperature

•Dry, hot, red skin

•Small pupils

•Rapid, shallow breathing

•Confusion

•Rapid pulse

•Weakness

•Seizures

•Dark urine

•Unconsciousness

When you notice these initial symptoms, take victim's temperature. Initially, the temperature could be 105° or 106°, but even if the victim's temperature is that high, heat exhaustion or heat stroke may be the problem, especially if all other symptoms are present.

To treat heat stroke, the American Medical Association advises:

•Call your local medical emergency service (911, in most cases) immediately.

•Check the victim's breathing and circulation (see "Cardiopulmonary Resuscitation and Artificial Respiration," above), and be sure the victim's airway is clear. Also check for signs of seizures (see "Seizures," above), shock (see "Shock," above) and any injuries the victim may have suffered as a result of fainting or falling, and treat these conditions.

•If the victim is not having a seizure, is not in shock and has no injuries; is breathing and has a pulse and an unobstructed airway, proceed with treatment to lower the body temperature:

—Alert the victim as to what you are going to do before you do it.
—If you have access to a tub, remove the victim's clothing, and place him or her in a tub full of cold (but not iced) water.
—If you do not have access to a tub but a hose or a pail and water source are available, spray the victim gently with cold water, and sponge-treat bare skin—especially the neck, armpit and groin regions—with cold water or cold packs.
—Continue—while checking the victim's body temperature at very close intervals every few minutes—until the body temperature—has been brought down to 100–101° or lower.

•Once body temperature is lowered, dry the victim off and cover him or her lightly.

•Place the victim near an air conditioner or fan to continue to cool the body.

•Continue to check the victim's body temperature, which could start to rise again.

•If the victim's temperature rises, repeat the entire cooling process.

•If no water source is available, move the

victim to a cool spot or an air-conditioned car or building.

•Once the body temperature is lowered, and if the victim is breathing properly, has a pulse, is conscious and has no physical injuries, lay him or her flat, face up, and elevate the legs 8 to 12 inches.

•Continue to monitor the victim's breathing, circulation and airway, and be alert for signs of seizures or shock. Take emergency first-aid steps for these conditions if they arise.

•Remember that even if the victim's temperature is successfully brought back to normal, medical treatment is essential.

•Be aware that a heat stroke victim's temperature may start to rise again at any point up to about five hours after the initial attack. Monitor the victim's condition carefully, then repeat first aid, including calling emergency services, if necessary.

Do not administer anything by mouth, including medications, alcoholic beverages or stimulants such as coffee, tea or caffeinated soda.

Do not spray or put water on the victim if he or she is disoriented or confused.

Heat Exhaustion
Brought on by prolonged exposure to high temperatures and high humidity, heat exhaustion may manifest itself in any or all of the following ways:

•Higher-than-normal body temperature

•Nausea and vomiting

•Muscle cramps

•Dizziness

•Pale, clammy skin

•Heavy perspiration

•Extreme thirst

•Weakness

•Dilated pupils

•Unconsciousness

Heat exhaustion is a potentially serious condition—especially when it occurs in children, the elderly, pregnant women or people suffering from high blood pressure, or heart and circulatory problems.

According to *A Parent's Guide To Childhood Emergencies,* compiled by The Children's Hospital of Philadelphia, youngsters, who may not know their physical limits, are especially likely candidates for this condition, and should be monitored in extreme heat to prevent it.

The elderly are also especially susceptible to heat exhaustion because they may be less sensitive to the buildup of heat (and may not own air conditioners). The emergency medical staff at New York City's Lutheran Medical Center suggests that those with elderly friends and relatives take special note of their physical conditions during times of intense heat.

To treat the condition, the American Red Cross advises:

•Call your local emergency medical service (911, in most areas).

•Ask the victim if he or she has ever suffered from high blood pressure or heart or circulatory problems, including strokes. If the victim is a woman, ask her if she is pregnant. Give the emergency personnel a full account of the victim's current condition and medical history.

•Have the victim lie down, if possible in a room or car with an air conditioner or fan; elevate his or her feet 8 to 12 inches and loosen the clothing.

•Check the victim's breathing and pulse. If any of these vital signs are absent, proceed with basic lifesaving techniques to restore them. (see "Cardiopulmonary Resuscitation and Artificial Respiration," above). Also, monitor the victim continuously for signs of shock and seizures, and administer first aid if necessary. (see "Shock" and "Seizures," above, under "Major Injuries.")

•If the victim is breathing, has circulation and a pulse, and is not disoriented, pro-

ceed to take measures to lower his or her body temperature by placing cool, wet compresses on the forehead and body.

•Give the victim an electrolyte beverage such as Gatorade, if possible, or salt water (use a ratio of 1 quart of water per teaspoon of salt) at a rate of four ounces every 15 minutes.

•If the victim begins to vomit, discontinue fluids, sit him or her up, face down, and help to keep the airway clear by sweeping the vomitus from the mouth with your index finger between bouts of nausea.

•Stay with the victim and continue to monitor his or her condition until medical help arrives.

Do not administer salt tablets or any medications.

Do not give the victim any liquids containing caffeine or alcohol.

Sources of Further Information

BOOKS

The American Medical Association Pocket Guide To First Aid. Random House, New York, 1991.

The American Medical Association Handbook of First Aid. Stanley M. Zydlo, M.D. and James A. Hill, M.D., eds., Random House, New York, 1991.

The American Red Cross First Aid and Safety Handbook. The American Red Cross and Kathleen A. Handal, M.D., Little, Brown and Co. New York, 1992.

CPR For Infants and Children. Gerald Dworkin, Child Welfare League of America, New York, 1991.

Emergency Medical Procedures.

Patricia B. Hill, ed., Prentice Hall Press, New York, 1992.

Emergency Medical Procedures For the Outdoors. Menasha Ridge Press, Birmingham, Ala., 1992.

Emergency Medical Treatment— Children. National Safety Council, EMT Inc., New York, 1991.

Emergency Medical Treatment— Infants. National Safety Council, EMT Inc., New York, 1991.

First Aid: A Random House Personal Medical Handbook. Paula Dranov, Random House, New York, 1990.

A Parent's Guide To Childhood Emergencies. The Children's Hospital of Philadelphia, Delta Trade Paperback, New York, 1994.

11

Owning a Car

Do You Really Need a Car?

When the first automobiles billowed dust and startled horses on America's roads, many people believed the car was a passing fancy. It surely wouldn't last. Today, most Americans cannot imagine life without a car—or two or three—in the driveway. However, considering the depletion of fossil fuels and the pollution of the environment, many are beginning to feel we are entering an era when we must reexamine our car-driven lifestyles.

In large cities, public transportation—buses, subways, high-speed transit systems—provide a viable alternative to the single-occupant automobile. Car pools are another means of reducing pollution and auto-dependency. Car pool lots near bus or mass-transit entries promote sharing a ride. Most major cities are also developing intricate networks of bicycle paths to make commuting by bike a convenient alternative (see "Bicycle-Powered," below). As we approach the 21st century, we must end the auto-mated love affair and develop healthy relationships with other means of transportation.

The high cost of buying and maintaining a car causes many people to consider auto alternatives. The average cost of a new car in 1993 was $16,000, according to Jack Doo's *The Ultimate Owner's Manual.* But this is just the beginning. The U.S. Department of Transportation estimates that the average life of a car is 12 years. When you add up the ensuing costs of insurance, repair, maintenance, gas, tires and assorted fees, the average household in

1991 spent 12.3 percent of its yearly disposable income on the family car.

Thus, before you drive down to your local dealer and purchase a new car, van or truck, take a few minutes to consider whether you need one.

EVALUATING YOUR TRAVEL AND TRANSPORTATION NEEDS

Think about your travel and transportation needs. Use this checklist:

•How much and how often do you typically drive?

•How often do you take car trips of more than 500 miles?

•What others are dependent upon your providing transportation?

•Can you walk or bike to work? Is the bus convenient? Can you car pool? What other transportation is available?

Perhaps you can resolve not to drive one day per month and choose another means of transportation. This notion may seem bizarre, just as the Model T seemed strange nearly a hundred years ago.

Buying a New Car

If you decide that you do need a car, information is your most valuable tool for being a responsible owner. The following will assist you in buying and maintaining your vehicle in the most responsible way.

CHOOSING A DEALER

While you naturally want to negotiate the best price for a new car, keep in mind that other factors besides final cost are also important. Jack Doo (*The Ultimate Owner's Manual*) notes that over the long run, convenient, high-quality service is a major consideration. Doo also advises buying from a dealer who responds quickly and courteously to warranty claims—one that has a well-stocked parts department and personal service. These factors may offset some additional monetary costs.

Before you ever enter a showroom, your best investment will be time spent reading and researching cars. Talk to friends, read consumer publications and think about your real needs and preferences. Library reference such as *Consumer Reports* and *Edmund's New Car Guides* give detailed information for evaluating and pricing new cars. Car books and magazines are also valuable resources. When selecting and negotiating for a car, the informed consumer gets the best deal.

THE CAR YOU WANT

Before you enter a dealership, have a detailed description of the car you want, including options, based upon how much and how often and for what purposes you drive. Take time to define your needs and preferences for each of the following:

•Safety

•Reliability

•Quality

•Size

•Cost

- Cost of insurance

- Warranty

- Appearance/quality of drive

You will also need to consider:

- Who else will be driving the car? How many other drivers will there be?

- How often and for what purpose will the vehicle be used?

- What types of roads will you be driving on? What type of driving will you primarily be doing?

- How long do you plan to own the vehicle?

Taking the time to discover your priorities will protect you from the onslaught of high-pressure sales tactics and the urges of impulse buying. You'll avoid haggling about prices and being an easy mark.

PUMPED-UP PRICES VS. REAL COSTS

The first order of business is to learn the language of car pricing: Which numbers reflect real costs and which add up to high profits for the dealer and great expense for the buyer? Dealer costs (factory invoices) are the real numbers, which are not listed on the car window sticker. The list prices, or sticker prices, are what customers see, and what the dealer hopes you will pay. *Consumer Reports New Car Buying Guide* notes that you can get printouts for any car through their Auto Price service, to determine exactly what the dealer pays for the standard package and for each option. This service also provides lists of current cash-rebate offers, those advertised to consumers and the lesser-known ones, from factory to dealer.

Once you've obtained this information, make a list with two columns: one for the dealer's costs, one for list prices. Then, list in each column the costs for the kind of car you want (station wagon, hatchback, sports car); the make and the model you want (the "brand," such as a Honda, and the type of car, such as an Accord); the standard package you choose (the basic car); and each of the options (including air-conditioning, power steering, leather seats, tinted windows, power locks, custom floor mats). Consumer publications will help you determine:

- What is "standard" in the trim line.

- What is optional.

- What is in the packages.

- What does the base car cost the dealer.

- What do each of the optional pieces cost the dealer.

Here's an example of how this works: On a car with a list price of $15,000 with a 90 percent cost factor, the dealer's price is $13,500. The dealer hopes to make $1,500 profit on this car, but he may be quite willing to accept $300. From the dealer's point of view, both figures constitute a "reasonable profit." The main factor is what you, the buyer, are willing to pay. For high-demand vehicles, luxury models or sports models, however, there is less room for negotiation since the dealer can hold out for higher profits.

While it is not advisable to rush into the showroom waving your paperwork, you do want to be straightforward with salespeople. *Consumer Reports New Car Buying Guide* advises showing your figures and asking the salesperson to add the lowest markup the dealership is willing to accept to the bottom of the dealer's price column. Let the salesperson know you are still comparison shopping. Do not allow yourself to be pressured to buy on the spot or to leave a deposit. If the salesperson quotes a low price that is later rejected by the dealership manager, this is an unethical operation. Take your business elsewhere.

AVOIDING LAST-MINUTE ADD-ONS AND EXTRAS

Last-minute markups can eliminate the benefits of an hour's hard-won bargaining. "Conveyance fees," a last-minute item the salesperson may throw in, is a fee for processing paperwork. This is often negotiable. An extended warranty is an expensive add-on, generally *not* recommended by consumer car experts. Extended warranties often duplicate standard coverage. Sometimes the additional markup appears on the sticker only as initials. The initials may appear in one of three ways:

ADM	Additional dealer markup
ADP	Additional dealer profit
AMV	Additional market value

They all mean the same thing: dealer profit. And profit is almost always negotiable.

THE BEST TIME TO BUY

It used to be true that new cars came out only once a year, in October. Consumers could get a good deal on last year's models at that time and salespeople were in high gear to sell the new vehicles. Now new cars are introduced year-round, but some times of the year are still better than others. Smart car buyers will take advantage of these times.

James R. Ross, a former car salesman, offers these valuable tips in *How to Buy a Car*:

There are seasonal times that are to a consumer's advantage. The Christmas holidays are a good time to buy, since people are spending on other things and car sales are slow. Salespeople are willing to negotiate in order to "move" some cars. Do not, however, say that the car is a Christmas gift, or you will lose the advantage of a nonchalant negotiating position.

Summer is also a good time to buy. It is midyear and salespeople assume the public is spending its money on vacations. February is a slow month; salespeople are waiting for the spring rush.

Ross also advises potential buyers to watch the papers. If a dealer is having many big sales, it means overall business is slow. This is a good time to negotiate a good deal. Do not be fooled, however, by deals that sound too good to be true. They are. These come-on ads concern very specific cars that the dealer wants to move. They are meant to get you into the showroom and don't mean that other models will be available for equally enticing discounts. Do not be distracted from your own agenda.

TRADE-INS VS. PRIVATE SALES

Buying a new car and selling your old one are two separate transactions, yet salespeople almost always immediately ask, "Are you trading in your old car?" Say, "No." You can always change your mind, and it is to your advantage to keep the purchasing of a new car separate from trading in and financing. Even if you plan to do all three with the same dealer, handle the transactions separately. This will allow you to negotiate the best price on a new car and to receive the most money for your old one because it will be easier to keep track.

Selling your old car privately takes more time and energy, but is generally more profitable than selling it to the dealer. (See "Selling Your Car on Your Own," below.)

FINANCING A NEW CAR

Again, this is something you want to investigate before you enter a dealership. If you plan to obtain a loan to pay for the car, call various banks, savings and loans, and credit unions. Compare their loan options. The most important factor is getting the lowest annual percentage rate (APR). Most institutions have a 48-month repayment plan. Some offer 60 months, but this is at a higher rate, since default is greater the longer the repayment period.

When you buy a new car, the salesperson always asks if you need financing. Usually, these deals are not as good as those you can get on your own. Often, publicized low interest rates from the dealer have a catch. They may apply only to cars the dealer wants to

sell, or they may be for fairly short-term loans. Be sure you are clear on the details and exclusions before choosing dealer financing, make sure you have done thorough comparison shopping with banks, savings and loans, and credit unions. However, for marginal borrowers—those who have a weak credit history—the automakers' credit subsidiaries are a viable option, since they are more flexible in approving loans.

If you do choose dealer financing, read the contract carefully before signing. If you object to something, ask for the contract to be reworded. Insist that it state that you can void the agreement if something goes wrong—if the car is not delivered by the specified date, for example. Be sure that the manager or general manager of the dealership signs the contract. It may not be legally binding if only the salesperson signs.

If you want to pay cash for your new car, consider the interest rate. If rates are lower for a car loan than the sum you can earn on your money invested, the car loan is advantageous. Some buyers consider home equity loans to finance cars. Again, thoroughly consider whether this is the best choice, considering interest rates, your other options and the fact that your home will become the collateral for the car payments. If you fail to make the payments, you could lose your home.

THE EXTENDED WARRANTY

A warranty comes with a new car. It is included in the original price. An extended warranty is an addition to the standard warranty coverage. It doesn't go into effect until the other warranty expires.

An extended warranty can cost from $200 to $1,000 and offer service for three to five years. Extended warranties are generally not recommended by consumer experts as necessary or cost-efficient. However, if you do buy one, make sure it is backed by the automaker.

Buying a Used Car

When shopping for a used car, pricing books are essential. These resources give the average prices that might rea- sonably be paid for vehicles of various makes, models and years, with and without options. The prices given should not be considered absolute, but they do provide a valuable foundation for pricing a used car.

Most libraries have at least one of these helpful resources:

•NADA Official Used Car Guide, a monthly publication produced by the National Automobile Dealers Association

•Automobile Red Book, eight issues per year, Maclean Hunter Market Reports Inc.

•Kelley Blue Book Used Car Price Manual, bimonthly, Kelley Blue Book Co.

Auto Service Contracts

An auto service contract is not the same as a warranty. It's intended to cover repairs not included in the warranty and also to provide coverage after your warranty expires. However, auto service contracts often unnecessarily duplicate standard warranty coverage, and they cost from $200 to $1,000. For new cars the warranty generally covers repairs for one year or 12,000 miles. Even many used cars come with a warranty.

Some 50 percent of new-car buyers purchase an auto service contract, according to Jack Gillis in *The Car Book,* and he asserts that it is "one of the most expensive options you can buy and generally, a poor value." Service contracts are a major source of profit for many dealers.

Gillis advises car owners to "deposit the money you'd spend on the service contract in a savings account." If you do believe you need the extra protection, contact an insurance company, such as GEICO. Their service contracts can be obtained at about half the cost of the dealer's contract.

Before you buy a service contract, test drive it on the following criteria:

Compare the terms and details with those of your warranty coverage.

Consider the reputation and longevity of the company offering the contract. (If they go out of business, you're out of luck.)

What exactly does the contract cover (and not cover) and for how long?

If you sell the car, does the contract transfer to the new owner? With what costs and stipulations?

How will the repair bills be paid? (Must you pay initially and wait to be reimbursed?)

Is there a deductible expense? Per visit? Per repair?

Who is liable to perform or pay for repairs: the car manufacturer, the dealer or an independent company?

What if the liable party goes out of business? (A backup plan should be specified.)

Is the contract underwritten by an insurance company?

Also note whether you are responsible for routine maintenance such as oil changes and tuneups. If this is required and you do not have records of such, the contract may be null and void.

If problems occur with a service contract, you may seek assistance and information from local and state consumer protection agencies, the state insurance commissioner or attorney general, and/or the Federal Trade Commission (FTC). For further information, write for the free *Facts for Consumers* brochure to: "Auto Service Contracts," the Federal Trade Commission, Washington, DC 20580.

The price guides are just that—*guides,* not absolute dictates about a car's value. The fair value of a car can vary considerably, depending on certain factors such as mileage. The average car is driven 10,000 to 15,000 miles a year. A car with over 50,000 miles on the clock is not considered a low-mileage vehicle and depreciates more quickly.

According to Jack Doo, high mileage is not necessarily a bad sign. A car driven mainly for commuting with 60,000 easy highway miles is the equivalent of 30,000 miles' driving on average roads. A car with low mileage may have been used for short trips and city driving, which are much harder on the engine than longer journeys, because short trips do not allow the engine to warm up enough to burn off internal corrosive condensation. Short-trip vehicles will have a rear muffler that is rusting or burned out or has been prematurely replaced. The muffler reveals the effects of corrosive condensation. Thus, a high-mileage car may be in better condition than its low-mileage counterpart.

But how can you know if this high-mileage vehicle you're considering is a rugged, sound vehicle or a wheezing old geezer on its last legs? In *The Used Car Book,* Jack Gillis advises having the car inspected by a mechanic. The places Gillis considers best are local AAA inspection centers, since they are not affiliated with repair facilities. If the seller will not allow you to take the car for a mechanic's inspection, don't buy it.

While most mechanics follow a standard procedure for inspection, be sure the following areas are included:

•Engine compression

•Brakes (for condition of disk or drum, pads and lines)

•Front wheel bearings and suspension

•Frame (for rust, breaks and signs of welding)

•Exhaust (muffler system)

•Cooling system

•Electrical and electronic systems (such as ignition, fuel injection, battery, starter and computerized parts)

•Transmission

Ask also if the mechanic will road-test the car for you. Then, get an estimate for any repairs deemed necessary.

If a used-car dealer steers you toward a particular mechanic for an inspection, beware. You may be taken for a ride. Some mechanics and dealers have a dishonest but profitable arrangement, whereby the cars check out "just fine" in exchange for future repair referrals.

USED CARS: SAFETY FIRST

Safety features have gradually been refined over the years as drivers have become more conscious of the hazards of driving and manufacturers have responded to consumer needs. However, older cars may not have some of the features we have come to take for granted, so be sure to check the car over for safety items even before you have it inspected.

Look for:

•Recessed knobs and controls (to avoid injury in case of accident).

•Padding on steering wheel hub, dashboard, sun visor and roof supports, to protect against injury.

•Doors free of sharp and protruding objects.

•Adjustable head rests, or non-adjustable ones that are high enough for the center of the head rest to be just above the center of your head.

•Fuel tank located forward or above the rear axle to prevent leakage in rear-end collision.

•Good visibility: vision free of obstructions when the driver turns her head in either direction.

•Right side rear-view mirror.

•Good brake lights and, preferably, one centrally mounted rear brake light (required on all cars after 1986; very helpful in preventing rear-end collision).

•Safety belts that are convenient and easy to use. Be sure they pull out and retract correctly.

•Back seat belts with harness.

ODOMETER FRAUD

Another important check is for odometer fraud. If the owner wants to conceal the fact of high mileage, he may turn back the odometer. Federal law makes this illegal. Not even a car's owner is permitted to turn back the odometer, or even to disconnect it except for necessary repairs. Even though it is a federal crime, odometer fraud is quite common.

The Used Car Book, by Jack Gillis, recommends some simple, basic checks to determine whether the odometer has been tampered with:

•Check wear on foot pedals. If the odometer reads less than 20,000 miles, the pedal shouldn't show extra wear.

•Check ignition lock. If it's heavily scratched or the shine is gone, and mileage is less than 20,000, assume the odometer has been changed.

•If the dashboard has scratch marks or missing screws, or if the numbers on the odometer don't line up correctly, this indicates fraud.

•Study the car title carefully. All numbers should be clear and easy to read, including the VIN (vehicle identification number), which should match the one on the dashboard, and the mileage, if your state requires this to be recorded on the car title.

WHAT TO LOOK FOR

A used car can be a money-saving venture or a financial nightmare, depending on your preparation and know-how. There are several main sources for buying used cars: a private party, a used-car dealer and a new car dealer. Each has advantages and disadvantages.

If you plan to buy from an individual, a stranger whose ad you answer, prepare a list of questions and ask to see the repair receipts:

Find out the following:

•Has the car ever been in an accident?

•Was it ever painted?

•Are you the original owner? If not, can you give me the name and phone number of the original one?

•How many miles are on the car? Is the odometer correct? Was it ever broken or replaced?

• Has the car been used mostly for city or highway driving?

• How often was the oil changed and basic maintenance performed?

• Where has the vehicle been serviced?

• How many miles will it travel before oil must be added?

• Is it normally parked in a garage?

• Why are you selling the car?

The answers to these questions will give you a good basis for judging the condition and worthiness of the vehicle. For most private sales there is no warranty; the car is generally sold "as is." However you can negotiate a contract. It must be in writing. You can also have the car's warranty, or extended warranty, transferred to your name, for a fee.

If you want to buy from a used-car dealer, find one that is established in the community. Look for a clean lot and a good car service area. Call the Better Business Bureau to see about complaints. Ask the dealer for references from satisfied buyers and call these people. Unlike new car dealers who also sell used cars, used-car lots have no major service areas. They can steam clean engines and clean car interiors and tires, but cannot do major repairs. Jack Doo (*The Ultimate Owner's Manual*) believes the disadvantages of buying from a used-car dealer far outweigh the advantages. Still, they do have to comply with state and federal regulations for safety, brakes, lights and emissions. The FTC also requires used-car dealers to put a "buyer's guide" sticker in the window of every used car, truck or van, informing customers of the vehicle's known limitations and problems.

New car dealerships also sell used cars. They have mainly good-condition, near-new vehicles gained from trade-ins. (They sell the poor quality trade-ins to used-car dealerships.) For purposes of service and repair, look for used cars of the same brand as the new ones sold at the dealership. New car dealerships have the advantages of having a good service department on the premises. They can offer a warranty with the used vehicle.

New car dealerships also sell a small number of nearly new rental-return vehicles, used by major car-rental agencies, and leased cars. These are low-mileage current-year models with documented service records. They are available for thousands of dollars less than a new car. Rental cars generally sell their own used cars in their own lots, so contact large rental agencies to find out when and where they sell off cars from their fleets. New car dealers generally sell these cars as "program cars."

Executive cars are another money-saving way to get a nearly new used car. These vehicles have been driven by automaker executives and factory representatives. They have documented service records and cost a good deal less than a new car. These are available at new car dealerships affiliated with the automaker in question; call to find out if a local dealership handles such cars, which are also known as "program cars."

Leasing a Car

If you. . .

• Don't want to make a large down payment

• Want to keep your monthly payments low

• Like to drive an expensive car and have the same monthly payment as if financing a less expensive one

• Like to change cars often and drive new cars

• Drive less than 15,000 miles a year

. . . Leasing rather than buying a car may be the best option for you.

Leasing a car is like renting a house. You do not have the responsibilities of ownership and the monthly lease payment is about $100 to $200 less than the loan payment on a similar car.

Lease agreements are generally made for periods ranging from 24 to 60 months. If you decide to, you can buy the car at the end of the lease, for its residual value.

The FTC offers a free *Consumer Guide to Vehicle Leasing* brochure (write to Public Reference, Federal Trade Commission, Washington DC 20580).

"Lemon" Laws

Cars are generally well made, but occasionally, a "lemon" is produced. A lemon, legally speaking, is a vehicle that has inherent flaws that cannot be fixed, even after repeated repair attempts. Laws vary from state to state, but generally a car is classified as a lemon if the same problem cannot be corrected in four or more repair attempts, or the vehicle has been out of service for more than a total of 30 days.

If you've purchased a lemon, you may be entitled to a refund or a replacement vehicle, but some important steps must be followed.

First, file a formal complaint with the maker. If you do not receive a satisfactory response, you may need to take the problem to a third-party consumer appeals board. Some major ones are the Ford and Chrysler consumer appeal boards, AUTOCAP and AUTOLINE. The findings of these boards are binding on automakers but not on the car owner, who can reject recommendations and file suit against the maker.

Your best insurance policy, if you fear you've purchased a lemon, is to keep receipts and records of all repairs and problems. Make notes of all phone calls to dealers, mechanics and others regarding the car. Include names and addresses.

Further information may be obtained from:

Aid for Lemon Owners
2177 West Ten Mile Rd., Suite 210
Southfield, MI 48075
The Center for Auto Safety
2001 South Street NW, Suite 410
Washington DC 20009

Selling Your Car (On Your Own)

If you are buying a new car, you might decide to sell your car on your own instead of trading it in. Owner-generated sales generally bring a better price, but you will also have to take the time to get the car ready, advertise it, answer phone calls and show it.

If selling the car on your own appeals to you, follow Steve Marsh's advice in *How to Sell Your Vehicle Yourself*. First, determine the fair market value of your car. One good source is the loan department of your bank. Ask for the "Blue Book" value on the make, model and year of your car. You can also call the Department of Revenue/Division of Motor Vehicles in your state. They will give you the average price that a car such as yours is selling for in your area.

Newspaper and auto magazines offer reliable pricing standards as well.

Check the classified ads to get a range of what people are asking for cars like yours. You might also visit dealerships to see how they've priced used cars similar to yours. Always price your car a little higher than the price you are willing to take. This gives you room for negotiation.

HOW TO MAKE YOUR CAR A GOOD DEAL
When a car is sold "as is," the implication is that much work is needed and the price will be low. Although Jack Gillis advises not to do major repairs before selling your car, he does recommend basic cleanup and preparation. Go the extra mile to show your car in its best light.

•Replace spark plugs.

•Change the oil and oil fitter.

•Check the points, plugs, condenser and air filter.

•Tighten all loose nuts and bolts.

•Replace worn tires with inexpensive used tires.

•Have an emissions test done.

•Clean the car's exterior, including windows and chrome, and remove bumper stickers and decals.

•Clean the interior: Vacuum and spray with air freshener and clean the inside of windows and trunk.

•Advertise your car in the newspaper or even on a bulletin board at work. Park the car where it is likely to be seen. Put à "For Sale" sign in the car window. (Note: this is illegal in some areas.)

•Keep a file handy of the repairs done and the basic maintenance and service dates, to show prospective buyers.

Basic Maintenance: Good for Your Car and Your Wallet

By spending about 15 minutes each month making the following basic checks, advises Jack Gillis in *The Car Book,* you will save hundreds of dollars in repairs and increase the life of your car.

Check the coolant.
It's in a plastic reservoir next to the radiator with marks that say "Full Hot" and "Full Cold." If the coolant level is below the "Full Cold" mark, add water to bring it up. Or you can add antifreeze in cold weather for extra protection.

If the car is hot, don't ever open the radiator cap. Pressure and heat escaping can cause severe burns. Wait till the car cools down.

Check the brakes.
A very simple test will alert you to brake problems. If your car has power brakes, have the engine running for the test. Push the brake pedal down and hold it. It should stop firmly about halfway to the floor and stay there. If the stop is mushy or the pedal keeps moving slowly to the floor, you need some brake work. Checking the brake fluid on most new cars is also very easy. Check your owner's manual for the fluid reservoir's location. Add fluid only to the level indicated.

Check the oil.
First, turn off the engine. Find the oil dipstick under the hood. If the car has been

running, be careful; the dipstick will be hot. Pull the dipstick out, clean it off, reinsert it and pull it out again. Notice the oil level. "Full" and "Add" are marked on the end of the stick. If the oil level is between the two marks, you are OK. If it is below "Add," add enough oil to reach the "Full" line.

To add oil, remove the cap at the top of the engine. You may have to add more than one quart.

Changing your oil regularly—every 3,000 miles—is the single most important way to protect your engine. You should change the oil filter whenever you change the oil.

Check transmission fluid.

An automatic transmission is complicated and very expensive to replace. Checking your transmission fluid level can prevent costly repair, and it's a simple operation. First, find the transmission fluid dipstick. (It's usually at the back of the engine, and looks like the oil dipstick but smaller.) The engine should be warmed up and running. If fluid is below the "Add" line, pour in one pint at a time. (Your owner's manual will tell you the correct type of transmission fluid for your car.) Do not overfill the reservoir.

Note the fluid's color. It should be bright cherry red. If it's a darker, reddish brown, the fluid needs changing. If it is very dark and has a burnt smell, your transmission may be damaged. Take it to a specialist.

Keep the tires inflated.

Improper inflation is the major cause of premature tire failure. Check your tire pressure at least once a month. The side of the tire is stamped with the maximum pressure of the most fuel-efficient inflation. Buy a good tire gauge, since the one at a service station is not generally reliable.

Check your power steering fluid.

If your car has power steering, this also requires fluid. Checking the fluid will prevent major repair bills. The power steering fluid reservoir is connected by a belt to the engine. Unscrew the cap and look into the reservoir. There will be markings inside. Some cars have a little dipstick built into the cap. Replace fluid to the indicated marking if it is low.

Keep drive belts taut.

A loose drive belt in your engine can lead to electrical problems, cooling problems, even air-conditioning problems. To check the belt tension, push down on the middle of each drive belt. It should feel tight. If you can push down more than half an inch, the belt needs tightening.

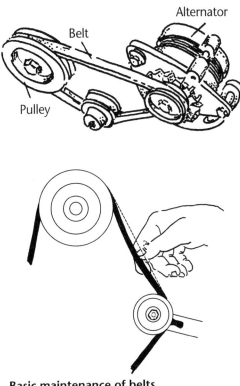

Basic maintenance of belts

Check the battery.

If your battery has caps on top, lift each one off and check that the fluid comes to the bottom of the filler neck. If it doesn't, add water. (Distilled water is recommended.) If the outside temperature is very low, add water only if you plan to drive immediately. Otherwise, the newly added water can freeze and damage your battery. Look for corrosion around the connections. This can prevent electrical circuits from being completed, leading you to assume your perfectly good battery is dead.

If the cables are corroded, remove them and clean with fine sandpaper or steel wool. The inside of the connection and the battery posts should be shiny when you put the cables back on.

Change the air filter.

This is probably the easiest item to maintain. Simply look at it. If it looks dirty, change it. If you're not sure how clean it should be, you can do a simple test. Start the car and let the engine warm up, then put the car in park or neutral, put on the emergency brake and let the engine idle. Open the filter lid and remove the air filter. if the engine begins to run faster, you need a new filter.

How to Pay Less for Auto Insurance

Auto insurance is a major, constant expenditure in maintaining a vehicle. Still, there are many ways to reduce your payments. Cost is not a fixed matter, but varies depending on the insurance company, agent or broker. It pays to shop around and ask questions.

Some cost benefits may be beyond your control or desires. For example, the lowest insurance rates go to rural communities, the highest to major cities, where traffic is fast and dense. Also, "high-profile" cars, which are expensive to repair and favorite targets for thieves, have higher insurance premiums.

Aside from issues of personal preference and need, the following information can save you hundreds of dollars a year on your auto insurance premium.

First of all, get the lowest overall premium quote. Then ask the agent what sort of discounts the company offers. You may qualify for a combination of the following, reducing your costs anywhere from 5 to 25 percent:

Auto and homeowner insurance coverage with the same company

Multi-car insurance with the same company

Good-driver renewal: no at-fault accident for three years to six years; no moving violations for three years

Mature driver (over 50, retirees only) with no unmarried drivers under 25 in the household

Automatic safety belts and air bags

Anti-theft devices

Anti-lock brakes

Student driver; good grades; driver's training

Student away at school (must live more than 100 miles from family home)

Low annual mileage driven

Nonsmoker, nondrinker

Woman over 30, sole driver

Car pool

Farm-use vehicle

You can change your policy to take advantage of discounts at any time. You can also reduce your premium by taking a higher deductible ($500 to $1,000) on collision and comprehensive coverage. If you have an older car, this makes sense. If the car is worth less than $1,000 you could drop collision and comprehensive coverage altogether.

Also, eliminate duplicate medical coverage. If you have adequate health insurance, you may be paying for duplicate medical coverage on the auto policy in terms of Personal Injury Protection (PIP).

Keep in mind that prices alone do not make a good insurer. Reliable, efficient service is a vital component.

For further information, contact the National Insurance Consumer Help-line at 1-800-942-4242, or write for the free brochure *Nine Ways to Lower Your Auto Insurance Costs* from the Insurance Information Institute, 110 William St., New York, NY 10038.

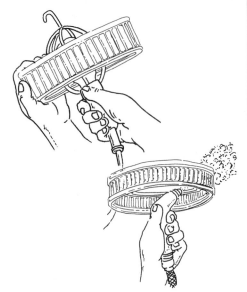

Check the filters with a lamp. You can then clean a filter with a jet of air.

Finding a Good Mechanic

An honest, capable mechanic is worth much more than his or her weight in motor oil. Jack Gillis (*The Car Book*) gives the following suggestions for finding the right person for your car.*

Ask friends and acquaintances who have similar cars. Word of mouth is a good way of getting names initially. Also, if you're considering a prominent shop, check its reputation with people you know, or ask for references from the shop.

When you need major repairs, always get several estimates. Don't necessarily go for the lowest price, or the highest.

*From The Car Repair Book, *by Jack Gillis with Tom Kelly and Amy Burch, Cheryl Denenberg, Alisa Feingold, Seth Krevat and Julie Beth Wright, copyright 1991. Published by HarperPerennial, a Division of HarperCollins Publishers.*

One mechanic may be cutting corners, the other overcharging.

A mechanic's certification is not a guarantee of competence, but it is an assurance of experience. Notice whether the shop has certificates on the walls, such as one from the National Institute for Automotive Service Excellence, an organization that offers training in eight areas of repair.

Show interest in the problem and ask about the repair (but don't pretend to be an expert if you don't understand what's wrong).

If the mechanic has done a good job, express your satisfaction. Ask for that mechanic the next time. He or she will get to know your car.

MONEY-SAVING TIPS FROM A MECHANIC
Jack Gillis in *The Car Book* recommends:

•Read your owner's manual. Performing basic maintenance yourself can eliminate expensive trips to the shop.

•Some repairs are preventative rather than corrective. If a trustworthy mechanic suggests extra work, it may save money down the road.

•There is no direct correlation between price and quality of work.

•Don't expect too much too quickly. No mechanic can fix in three hours what has resulted from three years of neglect.

•Before you pay for major repair work, take the car for a test drive. This simple act can prevent a lot of trouble later. If the problem still exists, it's easiest to verify it right on the spot rather than after you've driven home.

Car Safety

Using a car to get from place to place is convenient and in many areas, your only transportation option, but car accidents are a major source of injury and death in this country. Even if you are a careful, experienced driver, it's best to take precautions. Below are some suggestions for ensuring safety for both you and your passengers. In addition, car theft is on the rise, especially in urban areas. Read "Anti-theft Devices" and "Car Alarms" for information on how to keep your car from being stolen.

Driving Tips

In addition to regular maintenance and initial break in, the way you drive can affect the life of your car. Practicing the following tips can substantially extend your car's life.

1. Never ride with your foot on the brake, and always remember to release your parking brake. Use the same foot on the accelerator and the brake to avoid being a two-footed driver. Also, avoid sudden stops, as heavy use of the brakes will dramatically shorten their life.

2. Do not crank your starter motor for over 15 seconds at a time. Continual cranking causes the starter motor to overheat and shortens its life.

3. Your owner's manual will have recommendations for severe driving conditions. You may be surprised that "severe" driving is not long distances at high speeds but stop-and-go, around-town driving. Short trips, combined with rapid acceleration, are hard work for your car.

   A car driven primarily on the highway is more likely to be in top condition than one with half the mileage that has been driven only around town. If you regularly drive in stop-and-go conditions, treat your car to a freeway trip for at least 15 minutes a week.

4. If you regularly carry heavy loads (in your trunk or trailer) and other drivers signal that your high beams are on, you may need heavy-duty shock absorbers to keep your car at the proper level.

5. Start your engine before you turn on the lights or other electrical items to direct all of your battery's starting power to the starter.

6. Do not use the temporary spare tire longer than is absolutely necessary. These smaller tires put an extra strain on your suspension system and can throw your car out of alignment.

7. Avoid letting the engine idle with the transmission in gear. Put the car in neutral and use the emergency brake, or shift into park.

8. Don't shift your automatic transmission into gear if the engine is running at high speed. A hard clunk when you shift means you're either giving too much gas or your engine is idling too high. A quick tap on the gas pedal can slow down your idle.

9. With manual transmission, always push the clutch pedal fully to the floor when shifting. Also, try to keep your hand off the shift lever while driving. If you stop at a light for more than 30 seconds, put the transmission in neutral, and take your foot off the clutch to avoid overheating. Avoid using the clutch to hold you on a hill. Keeping the pedal slightly depressed increases the wear on your clutch and shortens its life. Even with an automatic transmission, don't hold the car on a hill by slightly accelerating.

   Check your owner's manual for the proper speed for shifting manual transmissions. Using the wrong gear increases fuel consumption and strains the engine.

10. Don't adjust your driving habits to compensate for changes in the way your car handles. For example, don't start pumping the brakes harder if they get softer, and don't over correct the steering if the car pulls in one direction. Have the problems checked out; your car is telling you something.

11. Try to avoid short trips, which are expensive because they usually involve a cold vehicle. For the first mile or two, a cold vehicle gets just 30 to 40 percent of the mileage that it gets when fully warm. After an engine runs for 10 to 15 minutes without interruption, it is usually fully warmed up.

    In addition to being inefficient, short trips generate the most wear and tear on your engine.

AIR BAGS

Clarence Ditlow, president of the Center for Auto Safety, estimates that air bags will "prevent at least half the fatalities and half the serious injuries" that would otherwise occur in passenger cars. Peter Spencer, in *Consumers' Research,* also notes that by 1994, 90 percent of new cars had air bags as standard equipment on the driver's side, and many have them on the front-seat passenger side as well.

Air bags, hidden in the steering wheel hub, inflate with a harmless nitrogen gas to protect the driver from impact with the steering column and windshield in the event of a crash. Air bags tested by General Motors in 10,000 cars (1974-76) did indeed result in half the fatalities of cars without air bags. However, reliance on air bags alone is not advised. Drivers must use them in conjunction with all other safe driving techniques, seat belts and child safety seats.

Air bags are safe, even if they inflate accidentally, because they deploy and then deflate in fractions of a second. Designed to billow only in frontal impacts equivalent to hitting a solid wall at 10 or more miles per hour, the bag will not inflate if you go over bumps, potholes or hit something at low speed. Even slamming on the brakes will not trigger inflation, unless you hit something.

Air bags require no maintenance and will last the life of your car. Some manufacturers do recommend inspections every several years.

CHILD SAFETY SEATS

Each year, according to the National Safe Kids Campaign, 1,700 children are killed and 10 times that number are injured in motor vehicle crashes. Until a child weighs at least 70 pounds, a seat belt alone will not protect him.

Child safety seats come in three different types, depending on a child's age and weight. Be sure to get the one that is designed for your child and be sure it is installed correctly. One of the most common installation errors is incorrectly routing of the car's safety belt through the car seat frame. This greatly reduces the effectiveness of the child safety seat in an accident. Read the installation instructions carefully.

Other Important Tips

•The center position of the back seat is the safest place for a child safety seat, regardless of the child's age and weight.

•Check the seat's safety harness and the car's seat belt regularly to ensure a tight, secure fit.

•Be sure the car seat you buy meets Federal Motor Vehicle Safety Standard No. 213, established after 1981. This will be indicated on the label.

Child safety seats are specifically designed for each of three groups:

•Infants under 20 pounds; these seats are installed to face the rear of the vehicle.

•Infants and toddlers up to 40 pounds, in seats installed to face the front of the vehicle.

•Booster seat for children weighing between 40 and 60 pounds.

For older children who weigh between 60 and 70 pounds, use your own judgment, based on the child's overall size, to determine whether a seat belt provides proper restraint or whether your child should stay in a safety seat until he or she weighs more than 70 pounds. Be sure to choose the seat and procedure most appropriate for your child.

In choosing a model within the correct category, convenience and appearance preferences need to be weighed against safety considerations. For example, the five-point harness strap is often difficult to buckle and adjust, but it is also the safest.

Pay attention to design features. Exposed metal buckles or parts may burn your child in the hot sun. Child safety seat models with the sides extended out do block the child's side view but protect his or her head in a side-impact crash.

Some adults mistakenly think that holding a child will protect him or her from harm. This is not true, and does not replace the protection of a properly installed child safety seat. It is also dangerous to use an infant seat in the front seat of a car that has a passenger side air bag. This can cause the child neck injuries in an accident.

In 1991, approximately 1.8 million safety seats were recalled. Most recalls were due to minor problems, but some involved car seats with features that could cause great damage in an accident. For further information about recalled products, contact the National Highway Traffic Safety Administration

A child safety seat

hot line, 1-800-424-9393. Have the name of your car seat ready, along with the manufacturer, model name, model number and date of manufacture.

For general information about child safety seats, write to the National Safe Kids Campaign, 111 Michigan Ave. NW, Washington, DC 20010.

SAFE DRIVING FOR ALL SEASONS

An extra few cautious seconds is all it takes to save a life. Simple, sensible practices go a long way to ensuring safety for both drivers and pedestrians. As a driver, make sure you can see out the windows. Keep them clean. When buying a car, choose a vehicle with good visibility, front, rear and sideways.

Emergency safety items kept in the trunk can be lifesaving on a snowy night in an isolated area. Good items to have are a blanket, shovel, chains, flashlight, flares, gloves, rags, paper towels, window cleaner and extra motor oil.

Driving in bad weather requires not only extra alertness, but also specific techniques. According to *The Ultimate Car Owner's Manual,* more fatal accidents occur in conditions of heavy rain than snow, because speeds are higher in rain. The wet surface causes hydroplaning at high speeds and drivers lose control.

When driving in slippery conditions, Chris Vaughn, former Colorado ice-driving instructor, advises all drivers to:

•Use controls smoothly.

•Avoid rough use of the accelerator, brakes or steering.

•Avoid locking the wheels under braking.

•Avoid spinning the tires under acceleration.

Richard A. "Doc" Whitworth, General Motors' Traffic Safety Manager also notes (in "Smart Ideas for Safer Driving," *Prevention,* November, 1992) that "many people are confused by the old rule which is to steer in the direction of the skid... No one can figure out which way the car is skidding! A better rule is this: in a skid, ease off the gas and steer in the direction you want to go. Use the front of the car as a guide."

Many insurance companies give discounts for adults over 50 who take defensive-driving courses. Courses are a good, easy way to brush upon on safe driving tips last heard at the age of 16.

Anti-Theft Devices

Car theft is on the rise, according to the Consumer Electronics Group. Every 20 seconds a car is stolen; 15.6 percent of all thefts are of car parts and accessories such as cassette and CD players, CB radios and cellular phones. A professional thief doesn't need much time to steal a car—in fact, less than a minute.

Japanese cars are the most frequently stolen, according to the *Ultimate Owner's Manual,* because they have less finely discriminated and precise door and ignition locks. A filed-down key from another Japanese car will open a locked door and operate the ignition.

As for American and other makes, a "Slim Jim" slipped between the window and door can open nearly any model. A professional car thief can also easily remove the ignition switch with an autobody sliding hammer. The car is then "hot-wired" and driven off. Even an expensive alarm system cannot completely prevent theft. The car can simply be towed away.

However, there are also many simple ways to protect your car. Since a quarter of all cars are stolen for joy rides, if yours is not an easy mark, thieves may go elsewhere.

BASIC PREVENTATIVE TIPS
•Always lock your car, take the keys and roll up the windows tightly when you leave it parked anywhere.

•Park in a locked garage whenever possible.

•Replace standard door locks with an anti-theft unit that defies bent-coat-hanger entry.

•Don't hide spare keys in the car. Thieves know to look under bumpers and fenders for hidden keys, especially in magnetic boxes.

•Place alarm stickers on the windows. The stickers alone can deter crime.

•Get an inexpensive ignition-kill switch or starter disabler (available from a distributor of car-alarm systems), which prevents your car from being hot-wired.

•Install a hardened steel rod (available from auto-parts stores) that locks onto the steering wheel and makes the car undriveable.

CAR ALARM SYSTEMS

A car alarm system is an effective way to protect your vehicle and its contents. Regardless of type, the presence of an alarm system deters a great percentage of car thieves. Insurance companies validate alarm systems' effectiveness by giving discounts of 5 to 25 percent for authorized systems properly installed.

Kinds of Alarms

The Electronic Industries Association provides a free pamphlet that gives basic information about types of alarms.

•A blinking light on the dash or the doors lets thieves know you have set an alarm.

•An electronic hood lock stops thieves who try to disable your alarm by disconnecting your battery cables.

•Vibration sensors (which fill your car with ultrasonic sound waves) sound an alarm when a thief hits the car window with a hard object, tries to open the hood or attempts to tow the car away.

•A field-disturbance sensor (also known as a proximity alarm) shields an open convertible or truck cargo bed with an invisible microwave field. An alarm sounds if the field is broken.

•An ignition cut-off switch prevents the car from starting.

•Homing devices, the most recent type of security device, allow police to pick up and follow signals from your stolen car.

Remote arming and disarming systems are also available. They let you open car windows and trunk, turn on lights and unlock car doors from outside the car. Remote control can also be used as a panic button, if you see someone trying to break into your car.

The electronic homing devices, which range from $500 to $1,800, are considered the most effective systems since they enable recovery of your stolen vehicle. However, any alarm will deter a great number of thieves. The most important deterrent with any system is proper installation and proper use.

Cellular Car Phones

As the price of car phones falls dramatically, more and more drivers can be seen carrying on conversations alone in their cars, with a phone to the ear. Cellular phones are a convenience and, in the case of illness or accidents, a beneficial safety device. Police and fire operations have benefited from citizens' cellular car phones. Since 911 is a free number to call, drivers frequently call to report crimes, drunk drivers and fires.

But cellular phones also cause problems and can be a hazardous driving distraction. Recently there's been a great increase in the number of car accidents involving cellular phones. The AAA Foundation for Traffic Safety survey reports that some distractions occur when a driver places a call and carries on a simple conversation; this slows down driver reaction time and decreases alertness. Drivers over 50 years old are the group at greatest risk for distraction while using a car phone. The AAA recommends making complex calls only when your vehicle is not in motion.

The initial cost of a car phone is now less than $300. Additional monthly fees range from $29 to $50, and air time ranges from 30 to 50 cents per minute.

Phones with an automatic answering

Earth-Friendly Car Considerations

Air pollution, destruction of the ozone layer, overflowing landfills and finite natural resources are very real problems today, and the car has a definite, negative impact in all these areas.

If you own a car, truck or van, you can take steps that will not only increase the life of your car, but will also lessen its detrimental impact on the environment. As Jack Doo recommends in *The Ultimate Owner's Manual*, "Drive only when necessary and car pool when you must drive. Take public transit, walk or bicycle."

Other earth-friendly acts include keeping your car in good working condition.

Auto emissions are an area of much concern, especially in urban areas where cars produce as much as 90 percent of total carbon monoxide emissions and more than 50 percent of the total ozone pollution.

Auto emissions testing is required in many states to regulate these amounts. Getting your car tuned up at least once a year insures that the engine burns gas more efficiently, lowering emissions. Buying fuel-efficient vehicles and using new low-emission-formula gasolines are conscientious choices.

Repair leaking air conditioners, which emit freon, an ozone-damaging gas. If you are considering a new car with air conditioning, choose one that has a non-CFC (chlorofluorocarbon) refrigerant. Most cars use ozone-depleting R-12 as a refrigerant for air conditioning. However, under the 1990 U.S. Clean Air Act, the government requires terminating production of this CFC. By Jan. 1, 1996, manufacturers must replace R-12 with non-CFC alternatives.

Tire care promotes fuel economy. Major tire makers have developed "green tires" that feature less rolling resistance and better fuel economy. You can also use less fuel by keeping tires properly inflated. Cold weather reduces tires' inflation pressure more quickly than warm weather, so check tires more often in winter and add air as needed.

Dispose of waste products. Changing the car's oil every three months keeps it running more efficiently, but what do you do with all that used oil? Americans who change their own oil throw away 180 million gallons of recoverable oil every year, according to the Environmental Protection Agency. If this oil is recycled, one gallon yields 2.5 quarts of lubricating oil—a 63 percent recovery rate. Recycling can save the U.S. thousands of barrels of oil a day.

Many automotive centers now recycle used oil. If you take your old oil to an automotive center, ask how they dispose of it. Contact your local or state government used-oil recycling program for other recycling locations. If your area does not have an oil recycling program, you can start one. Call the EPA's Superfund Hotline at 1-800-424-9346, or write U.S. Environmental Protection Agency, Office of Solid Waste, 401 M St. SW, Washington, DC 20460.

Antifreeze also requires special handling. Never pour it down a drain. It is recyclable. Contact your local environmental authority, a car-care center or the department of sanitation for locations.

Batteries contain toxic substances: sulfuric acid and lead. Do not put your old battery in the garbage. Take it to a recycler. Look in the phone book under "Scrap Metals."

feature are the least distracting, since you don't have to lift a receiver to talk. These units have a microphone mounted on or near the sun visor and external speaker jacks, allowing the driver to keep both hands on the wheel while taking a call.

Bicycles

Bicycles are not just for children. Over the past 20 years, a bicycle boom has occurred in this country, and adults are riding bikes for recreation, travel and even for commuting to work. Most major cities now sponsor a "Bike to Work Week," encouraging commuters to use two wheels instead of four to get to the office.

If you are considering alternatives to your automobile, a bike can provide invigorating exercise along with environmentally sound transportation.

Glen's New Complete Bicycle Manual describes the following types of bikes for adults:

The one-speed "tank" or cruiser bike is the most basic. It is a heavy bike with no gears, best used for easy, flat, short-distance riding. (Cost: between $60 and $200.)

Utility bikes have three speeds and moderately wide tires. The gears give a slightly wider range of riding possibilities than the cruiser.

Lightweight multi-speed bikes have dropped handlebars and narrow tires. This group is divided into *"sport" bikes,* with a short wheel base for quick maneuvering, and *"touring" bikes,* with longer wheel bases and lower gears for comfort. The price range is $100 to $1,500.

All-terrain or "mountain" bikes combine the durability of the cruiser with sporty performance and easy hill climbing. These bikes are lightweight and may have from 10 to 21 speeds. These cost from $150 to $1,500.

When shopping for a bike, consider some of the same issues as when buying a car: how much and what type of riding you'll be doing and the kinds of terrain you'll ride over. Service is also an important component in choosing the right place to buy. Discount and department stores may have cheaper prices, but without the service provided by a good bike shop.

Every bicyclist needs some very basic accessories to insure safe and comfortable riding. The most fundamental are: U-lock, water bottle, helmet (with optional mirror), handlebar bag, tool kit, tire pump and biking gloves. For night riding you'll also need reflectors on the bike and a light. Reflective clothing also increases your visibility to motorists. Other accessories that allow for longer trips and riding in a variety of weather conditions are rain gear, bike bags and riding shorts.

Many major cities now have an intricate network of bicycle paths that allow riders to travel easily throughout the city. Maps of routes are available at bicycle shops and, often, from the city parks and recreation department.

As is true with cars, alert, defensive riding is the best way to avoid accidents. In fact, most bicycle accidents are due to riders not obeying traffic and safety rules. Ride with the traffic, not against it, and always signal for turns.

Sources of Further Information

BOOKS

The Car Book. Jack Gillis, Harper Perennial, New York, 1992.

Consumer's Guide Used Car Book (1993 Edition). Publications International Ltd., Illinois, 1993.

Glenn's New Complete Bicycle Manual. Clarence W. Coles and Harold T. Glenn, Crown Publishers, New York, 1987.

How to Buy A Car. James R. Ross, St. Martin's Paperbacks, New York, 1992.

How to Sell Your Vehicle Yourself. Steve Marsh, Littleton, Colo., 1993.

New Car Buying Guide (1993 Edition). Consumer Reports Book Editors and Bill Hartford, Consumer Reports Books, Yonkers, N.Y., 1993.

The Ultimate Owner's Manual (1993 Edition). Jack Doo, Edmund Publications Corp., New York, 1992.

The Used Car Book. Jack Gillis, Harper Perennial, New York, 1992.

PAMPHLETS

All pamphlets listed below are available through the Consumer Information Catalog, Pueblo, CO 81002. Write for a free copy of the catalog.

All About Auto Electronic Products. Washington, D.C.: Consumer Electronics Group, 1992.

"Auto Service Contracts," Facts for Consumers. Washington, D.C.: Federal Trade Commission, 1991.

Buying a Used Car. Washington, D.C.: Federal Trade Commission, 1990.

Consumer Tire Guide. Washington, D.C.: Tire Industry Safety Council, 1990.

Gas Mileage Guides. Washington, D.C.: Department of Energy/Environmental Protection Agency, 1994.

How to Find Your Way Under the Hood & Around the Car. Washington, D.C.: Department of Commerce, 1993.

New Car Buying Guide. Washington, D.C.: Federal Trade Commission, 1992.

Nine Ways to Lower Your Auto Insurance Costs. Washington, D.C.: U.S. Office of Consumer Affairs, 1990.

Recycling Used Oil. Washington, D.C.: Consumer Protection Agency, 1990.

What You Should Know About Your Auto Emissions Warranty. Washington, D.C.: Environmental Protection Agency, 1988.

Your Car (Or Truck) and the Environment. Washington, D.C.: Environmental Protection Agency, 1993.

12

Etiquette
and
Entertaining

As more and more children are brought up in families where mealtimes mean eating fast food in front of the television, the classic manners of Emily Post and Amy Vanderbilt are being lost. And it's not just table manners that are suffering. Fewer people write letters, whether it's a note to express congratulations or condolences or an invitation to a party. The telephone rules supreme, which necessitates its own set of courtesies.

The section below provides a basic guideline with answers to some of the more common problems and questions people have about etiquette. It is by no means a thorough dissection of how to behave. To learn etiquette by the book, consult the more traditional *Emily Post's Etiquette* (15th edition, compiled by her granddaughter-in-law Elizabeth Post) or Letitia Baldrige's *Complete Guide to the New Manners for the '90s,* which takes into account the changing mores of our times—drugs, sex and if not rock and roll, loud music. Like this chapter, both books emphasize, however, that basic good manners require nothing more than a kind heart, thoughtfulness and common sense.

Day-to-day Good Manners and Common Courtesy

The most basic guideline to good manners is to be considerate of other people, whether it's opening a door for someone laden with packages or telling an acquaintance you're sorry that you've forgotten his name. A gracious person will, in response, appreciate the gesture or the honesty.

Rules came into play, however, to help show deference and to remind us all to think of others.

RULES FOR INTRODUCTIONS

Picture yourself at a party where you're speaking to one friend and an acquaintance comes up to greet you. You know that it's polite to introduce the two, but whose name do you mention first? Who should be introduced to whom? The rules are really very simple. And if you do forget them, just try your best. If you think your friends will get along and want to engage them in conversation, include a flattering description of each person, one that will initiate a dialogue between the two (for instance, "John is the best tour guide in New York. I'm sure he'd be happy to give you some hints on where to find the most interesting architecture in the city during your stay," or "Barbara just came back from Eastern Europe.")

Use the guidelines below in everyday interactions. If you find you'll be in the company of a government, military or church official, however, call the appropriate local office for specifics (see "Sources of Further Information," at the end of this chapter). Also, the customs of our country may be alien to a visitor from another country, so if you want to be sure you won't offend, contact the embassy or the United Nations (see "Sources of Further Information"). In most cases, however, the rules below should serve you for a lifetime of introductions.

•Introduce a man to a woman.

•Introduce a young person to an older person.

•Introduce a less important person to a more important person ("important" here means a member of the clergy, a politician or a diplomat).

•Introduce a non-family member to a family member.

State the name of the woman, the older person, the official or the non-family member first to make it easier to remember. If you do this, phrase the introduction, "Mrs. Gordon, I'd like you to meet Mr. Hodosh," or "Mr. Hodosh, I'd like to introduce you to Mrs. Gordon." It may be easier to understand with a few more examples. For instance, "Governor Lieber, I'd like you to meet my husband, John Hart," or "Ms. Bachman, may I introduce Mr. Lewis." You can also use other phrases such as "Abby, this is my son, Harrison Hart. Harrison, this is Abby Mills." Or "Professor Mufson, my colleague, Carolyn Johnson." Or "Amanda, have you met my niece Susannah Haden?"

In general, keep the following in mind:

•Don't phrase your introduction as a command. ("Mr. James, meet my son Alex.")

•Use first and last names in most informal situations. They should not be used, however, when introducing a young and old person, or a person of superior rank in business, or a business client. Here, you should use a courtesy title (Miss, Mr., Mrs. or Ms.) and the person's last name.

•Introduce yourself by using your full name, saying for example, "Hello, I'm

Naomi Black." The person to whom you are speaking should introduce himself in return.

• The host and hostess should rise when a woman who has not been introduced enters the room. Other men in the vicinity should also rise.

• A woman should rise if she plans to shake hands with someone or wants to continue the conversation.

• Both men and women should rise for a very old or very prominent person.

Forgot someone's name? Introduce them any way you can as best you can. If a mistake is made, apologize and maintain your sense of humor whenever possible. "I'm not good at names either. Don't worry about it at all" might be a fitting response for a mis-introduction after you've made the correction. Acknowledgment of the error is better than pretending it didn't happen.

HOW TO ADDRESS PEOPLE

Men, in general, should be addressed verbally as "Mr." followed by their last name. A woman can choose to use the title "Ms.," which means her marital status is not revealed. "Ms." is not to be used interchangeably with "Mrs." Some people still prefer to use "Miss" if a woman is unmarried and "Ms." only if she is married. This defeats the purpose of the term, however. The woman's choice, whatever it is, should be respected. This is also true if she opts to use her maiden name after marriage. If this is the case, address her in introductions and in correspondence with her maiden name and not as Mrs. John Hart. (For example, Ms. Amanda Peters and Mr. John Hart.)

Use the sources at the end of the chapter to find out how to address politicians and members of the military. In day-do-day conversation, the courtesies listed below should provide you with all the information you need to be polite.

• A widow will often retain her husband's name, as in Mrs. John Hart.

• Both men and women should be addressed as "Dr." if that is their earned title.

• Do not use "Sir" or "Madam" if you are speaking to a peer.

• Address a commissioned Army or Air Force officer by his rank. In the Navy this is true only for officers holding the rank of Lieutenant Commander on up. "Officers below that rank are called 'Mr.' in conversation but are introduced and referred to by their titles," notes Elizabeth Post.

• Although there are many different kinds of admirals, colonels, lieutenants, etc., when you're speaking to them, use only the title above, except when introducing the person. In an introduction, you would mention their full rank.

• Clergymen are addressed by their appropriate titles:

–Catholic priest—Father

–Catholic archbishop—Your Excellency

–Catholic monsignor—Monsignor

–Catholic or Protestant bishop—Bishop

–Protestant clergy—Pastor, Reverend or a more specific title of their choosing

–Jewish rabbi—Rabbi

HOW TO BEHAVE IN PUBLIC

Let common courtesy—and common sense—be your guide. A woman who waits for a heavily burdened man to open the door for her is not displaying common courtesy, no matter what rules of chivalry once governed the land. A man who insists on giving a pregnant woman a seat when she says she'd rather stand is not helping at all; the offer should be made, and a refusal, if there is one, should be taken graciously.

The "rules" for proper behavior in public are arbitrary. Those listed below come from the etiquette experts, notably Elizabeth Post and Letitia Baldrige. Add on to the list as you come across examples of how you'd like to see people behave.

• Be prompt. (And if you're delayed, call to let the person know when he can expect you.)

• If you prefer not to greet someone with a kiss, immediately offer them your hand, then take a step back.

• Wave hello if you see a friend in a crowded place. Don't shout across the room. (Shouting in public is never a good idea unless you're shouting a warning.)

• With a nod to the old order of chivalry, a man should open a car door for a woman if it makes safety sense and if it's a special occasion. Otherwise, a woman should not feel offended if she has to open the door herself.

• Men generally should allow women to precede them through a door (although men should be alert to a woman's sense of equality).

• In an elevator, whoever is closest to the door should go in first and hold the Door Open button.

• Anyone young and healthy should offer a seat to an older, infirm, mobility-impaired person or pregnant woman on a bus or in a room with limited seating.

• Smokers should heed No Smoking signs and put out their cigarettes in the nearest ashtray or sand receptacle, not on the street or the floor. In other areas, it's polite to ask if anyone minds a lit cigarette.

• Use litter cans to discard your trash. If none is available, ask where you can find one, just as you would for a water fountain or a telephone.

• Be polite to strangers and those in the service industries.

• Holding hands in public is a wonderful way to display affection. Necking, or snogging as the British say, is not.

• Respect people's privacy. Do not butt in on overheard conversations.

• Don't talk at the movies, the theater, a lecture or a concert.

Table Manners

Good table manners are becoming harder to instill in children, especially those who are left to eat alone in front of the television. Learning rules to use only when you eat out or dine with guests defeats the idea of manners that come naturally. So teach children from the earliest how to sit still and eat properly. Reward them by allowing them to excuse themselves from the table once they've finished. (Forcing them to sit with the adults through an entire meal often invites disaster.)

A child will learn from an adult, so teach through example.

THE BASICS

The first and foremost "rule" is to relax. Dining, even at breakfast, should be a pleasure, never rushed or interrupted, if possible. Remember that a good conversation is as important to a meal as are good manners. Below are a few basics to keep in mind while enjoying your repast:

• Place the napkin on your lap (don't snap it open), and if you get up, put it loosely to the left of your plate.

• Keep your elbows close to your body while eating; don't rest them on the table.

• Sit up fairly straight. Lean slightly forward while eating, but don't slouch forward. Don't tip your chair back or throw your arms akimbo.

• Wait for your hostess to begin eating if it's a small dinner party; otherwise, begin after the first few guests are served.

• Take reasonable portions. You can always ask for seconds.

• Cut off small portions to chew. (And don't cut everything at once.) Don't stuff your mouth.

• Keep your mouth closed while eating.

• Put the utensils down and finish chewing before you take a drink.

• Break bread with your fingers into pieces that are large enough for a few bites.

• Transfer a pat or knife full of butter to your bread plate before buttering the bread.

• Move your soup spoon toward the back of the soup dish as you eat. Tip the bowl away from you as necessary. Leave the spoon in the soup bowl or, if it's a soup cup, on the saucer.

• If you're a picky eater, help yourself to at least small portions of the food. Eat what you can without drawing attention to your dislikes.

• Wet your fingers only in a finger bowl; don't wash your hands in it.

• Don't push your plate away from you when you're done.

• Wait until your hostess gets up before you rise.

SILVERWARE

Silverware can be placed on the table in the order of use or in order of size. The more acceptable setting—in order of use (see illustration)—requires that the silver on the outside, or farthest from your plate, will be set for the first course; the next course will make use of the utensil set next closest, etc.

Settings look more symmetrical when the silverware is placed in order of largest to smallest. This is a more contemporary approach to table settings.

Watch your host if you're not sure how the table's set. If you're unused to formal settings, it can be easy to make a mistake. Don't worry. Just continue to eat with the utensil you've chosen;

that's much better than putting the soiled silver back on the tablecloth. Rest your knife and fork beside each other on the right side of the plate when you are just pausing in your meal; a trained waiter will know not to take your plate away yet.

When you're finished, leave the utensils resting on your plate beside other from top left to bottom right. The knife blade faces the fork, which should be placed prongs down. However, if you're only using a fork, place it in the same position but with the prongs up.

AMERICAN VS. EUROPEAN
EATING STYLES
Right-handed Americans hold their fork in their right hand to eat and switch it to their left hand when cutting with a knife. Right-handed Europeans cut their food in the same way, and instead of switching, they move the fork to their mouth with the utensil still in their left hand. (See illustration.) Don't turn the fork over. Keep the movement from plate to mouth uncomplicated and graceful.

Telephone Manners

Speak in a well-modulated voice and hold the receiver close to your mouth so the person on the other end can hear you without picking up extraneous noise. Lower the television or the stereo if it is on in the background.

Most people agree that a phone can be an intrusion. If this is the case, consider getting an answering machine. In any case, never show annoyance on the phone if someone is calling at a bad time. Rather, graciously give the caller a time when you will be free.

American vs. European eating styles

Formal dinner service

Mrs. Hahn

Everyday dinner service

Silverware placement

ANSWERING THE PHONE

When you pick up the phone, the easiest—and best—greeting is simply to say "Hello." You don't have to state your name (and in these days you shouldn't, just to be on the safe side). If someone calls you and rudely asks "Who's this?" either ask to whom he'd like to speak or apologize, state that you don't recognize his voice and ask, "Who is this, please?"

On the other hand, if the person says hello and requests to speak to someone in your household, it is perfectly fine to ask who is calling.

In general, try to answer the phone within four or five rings. Once you've answered it, focus your attention on the phone call. Don't let small matters intervene. Things arise, however, and if something should interrupt your conversation, explain to the caller that you'll return his call in a few minutes. Don't forget! If you say you'll call him right back or at a specified time, do so. Keep a pad and pen near the phone so you can jot down the whatever details are necessary to return the call.

MAKING PHONE CALLS

Remember that a phone call can be seen as an intrusion or as a welcome and thoughtful message. Keep this in mind, especially when you're telephoning someone you don't know well. Make your calls between the hours of 9 A.M. and 9 P.M. and try to avoid telephoning during dinnertime (unless, of course, the person tells you that another time is best). If you think you may be calling at a bad time, ask if there's a better time to call back, and remember to call back at that time. Let the phone ring at least half a dozen times. This gives the person time to interrupt whatever he's doing.

When making a call, if you reach the person you want and you recognize his voice, say hello and identify yourself. If you reach someone else, state your name, then ask for the person you'd like to speak to. Don't ask "Who's this?" when you reach someone on the other end of the line.

IN GENERAL

Be as polite on the phone as you would be if you were speaking in person. Some people have gotten into the habit of washing the dishes or watching television while on the phone; this diminishes the call.

•Never eat or chew gum while on the phone.

•It's a good idea to return phone calls within two days, preferably on the same day.

•It's handy to have a notepad and a pencil by the phone for messages. Ask for the caller's name (if necessary, request that he spell it out) and phone number (if long distance, the area code too). Remember to include who the message is for and the time of the call.

•Guests do arrive when you're on the phone. When this happens, tell the person on the phone that you'd like to call them back, explaining that someone has dropped in.

•Traditionally, the caller is the person to

end the phone call. However, if the call seems never ending and you must get off, firmly state that you're late for an appointment or whatever pressing engagement lies ahead.

•To refuse a telemarketing call, say "No, thank you. I'm not interested." In addition, you may ask that your name be removed from whatever list it's on.

•When a child is home alone, he should say that the adult requested "is busy right now" if he doesn't recognize the caller's voice or name.

NEW TECHNOLOGY
We'll all look back on the day when the notion of telephone manners seems as quaint as formal stationery. Computers, electronic mail and cyberspace will change our views drastically about what the phone can do and how we relate to it. In the meantime, the most common questions about the new technology have to do with answering machines and Call Waiting.

Answering Machines
Using an answering machine is considered quite acceptable, "the modern equivalent of a butler," according to etiquette expert Judith Martin. Compose a staid, brief message for callers. Include the number being called and instructions on how to leave a message. Musical interludes and lengthy instructions are not necessary and may be considered discourteous.

Call Waiting
Although Call Waiting is an option that is becoming increasingly popular, many people consider it impolite to allow others to interrupt a phone call. If you take a call and are expecting another, important phone call, tell whoever it is that you may have to take another call ("I'm so glad you called, but I may have to respond to Call Waiting. I'm waiting for _____ to call"). That allows the caller to make the choice to stay on the line or not.

OBSCENE CALLS
Keep calm. If you receive an obscene, abusive or silent phone call, New York Telephone recommends that you press the number 6 button and hold it down for a moment before saying, "Operator, this is the call I want to check for the police." This action should discourage the caller. Hang up immediately and write down the exact time and date of the call.

If the calls continue, keep a record. Phone companies will want you to wait a number of days before reporting the calls to the police. For example in New York, they ask you to wait four days. You must be willing to press charges to instigate an investigation. (They don't investigate silent calls on answering machines.)

After four days, contact your local police department, file a complaint of aggravated harassment and get a case number. With the case number in hand, call the telephone company again (ask for the Annoyance Bureau or for the department that handles obscene calls). While procedures may vary from region to region, the idea is the same: Let the person know you will be contacting the police, keep careful records of the time and date of the calls, and get in touch with your local telephone company.

Personal Communications

ANSWERING PERSONAL QUESTIONS

People ask the strangest questions, from "When are you going to have a baby?" to "How old are you?" Although you may be tempted to supply a forthright answer, you may be just as tempted to say, "It's none of your business." Resist the latter; it's a rude response. However, you can gently persuade your friends from prying by any number of kind diversions. The next stage is a firm "I'm sorry, but that's a private matter and I'd rather not talk about it."

COMMUNICATING ABOUT
LIFE CHANGES

Sometimes the unpleasant happens: You lose a job, get a divorce, fall ill for an extended period of time, etc. You probably want to tell a few friends the details, but for most people a brief acknowledgment of your change of circumstance is enough. How do you fend off offensive queries and prying remarks? Try using the phrase above. And for those people you do want to let know, how do you mention it without ushering in a host of unwanted questions? Tell them that it's not something you want to discuss in detail, but that you value their friendship and want them to know what the situation is. As in most situations that call for tact, rely on honesty and trust in the relationship.

It is inappropriate to send out printed cards notifying people of a divorce; even worse are form letters. Elizabeth Post suggests writing a personal note on one's Christmas cards in combination with alerting your friend to your new address ("As you can see, Bob and I were, unfortunately, divorced last August. Hope to hear from you at my new address.") Judith Martin recommends simplicity in the form of "unembellished statements."

As a rule, don't send out formal announcements of any major change in your life. That includes engagements, pregnancies and deaths. Many people now send out creative change-of-address notices, but even these are more sincerely welcomed if they are personal.

Writing Thank You Notes

A letter or a note to say thank you is one of the nicest ways to tell someone that you're thinking of them and of their thoughtfulness. In this day of telephones, electronic mail and faxes, a handwritten note becomes even more of a gesture. Although you can always include a thank you in some other communication, a personal letter written in ink truly shows the recipient that you are taking the time to say "thank you."

Susannah Catherine Wright

Personal stationery for Thank you notes

DIDN'T RECEIVE A THANK YOU?
It happens all the time. A bride forgot one person on her list. A child never got around to writing to grandma. The presents were sent through the mail. What is the gift giver to do? How can he find out, courteously, whether or not the gift was received?

The only proper thing to do is write and inquire: "Should I assume the gift was lost?" or "Since I haven't heard from you, I assume the gift never found its way to you."

Being a Good Neighbor

Do unto others as you would have them do unto you. The Golden Rule is just as appropriate today as it ever has been, especially as we crowd in on one another in cities across the country. Wherever you happen to live, courtesy should be the first rule when dealing with neighbors, even problematic ones.

DEALING WITH ETHNIC SLURS AND UNKIND OPINIONS
Ethnic jokes and generalizations cause the perpetuation of stereotypes. They don't have a place in anyone's company. Don't feel pressured to go along with what's being said. "It's important not to let a situation go by," says Ellen Bettman, head of A World of Difference Institute, a part of the Anti-Defamation League. "But there's no formula," says Bettmann. "You don't have to jump on the person right away. You can give him space to save face. In a social context [as opposed to a meeting] suspend judgment and assume good will. Ask for clarification. You may have misunderstood because of your own sensitivity to the subject."

When Thank You Letters Are Necessary

Dinner parties: Obligatory only if you are a guest of honor. Otherwise, always appreciated but not necessary if you have thanked your hostess when leaving.

Overnight visits: Thank you notes are obligatory except in the case of close friends or relatives whom you see frequently. Then, a telephone call would serve the purpose.

Birthday, anniversary, Christmas and other gifts: Always, when you have not thanked the donor in person. Here again, a phone call to a very close friend or rela-tive is sufficient. It is never wrong to send a note in addition to your verbal thanks.

Shower gifts: You must write a thank you note if the donor was not at the shower or you did not extend verbal thanks. Many women like to add a written note to their verbal thanks, but it is not necessary.

Gifts to a sick person: Notes to out-of-towners and calls or notes to close friends are obligatory as soon as the patient feels well enough.

For notes of condolence: Thank yous should be sent for all notes of condolence except for printed cards with no personal message.

For congratulatory cards or gifts: All personal messages must be acknowledged. Form letters from firms need not be acknowledged.

Wedding gifts: Thank you notes are obligatory—even though verbal thanks have been given. All wedding gifts must be acknowledged within three months, but preferably as the gifts arrive.

When a hostess receives a gift after visitors have left: Even though the gift is a thank you itself, the hostess must thank her visitors, especially if the gift has arrived by mail, so that the visitor will know it has been received.

From *Emily Post's Etiquette,* 15th Edition. Elizabeth Post, copyright 1992, HarperCollins Publishers.

If you do want to confront the person at the time, start your sentence with how you feel ("I'm offended. . .," or "I'm hurt. . ." or "I'm surprised to hear you say that. . ."). Starting your sentence with "You" is an attack that closes doors. So is an edict. You're not out for retribution; you want to try to teach the offender that jokes and slurs keep stereotypes and other misinformation alive.

But do say something—even if it competes with your sense of courtesy (making people feel welcome or being respectful of elders).

How to Treat Disabled People

When addressing anyone who is physically disabled, deaf or blind, recognize that they usually wish not to be categorized. Therefore, avoid using collective nouns—the blind, the deaf, etc.—when introducing them.

HOW TO HELP A PERSON WHO IS BLIND
It's very easy to hesitate instead of helping someone. It's just as easy to be too helpful when the assistance isn't needed. To help sighted people learn how they can assist people who are blind, the American Foundation for the Blind (AFB) has produced a brochure entitled "What do You Do When You See a Blind Person?" This list has been adapted from that and from another AFB handout called "Sensitivity to Blindness and Visual Impairments: Etiquette for Hoteliers," which was put together by the AFB's Americans with Disabilities Act Consulting Group.

• If you see a blind person who seems to need help, offer your services. Identify yourself and let him know you're talking to him. Otherwise, he might never know.

• If he accepts your offer, let him take your arm. He can follow the motion of your body. Never push or pull a person with a visual disability.

• It's OK to use words such as "see" and "look."

• Speak directly to a person who is blind, not through a third party.

• Don't be tempted to pet or feed a dog guide. The dog should never be distracted from his duty.

• When you're leaving a person who is blind, let him know that's what you're doing. Don't leave him stranded.

Being a good neighbor when speaking to blind people

COMMUNICATING WITH SOMEONE WHO IS HEARING-IMPAIRED
The National Association of the Deaf with the help of Thelma Edwards, RN, has compiled a few tips (adapted below) for communicating with people who are deaf or hearing-impaired. Ms.

Edwards is the creator of a disability-awareness program called Be Aware and Care.

•Before speaking to a person who is deaf, look directly at him and ask him how he communicates. If he doesn't respond, try writing your question out. Some hearing-impaired people read lips, others use pen and paper, while others may use a sign and gesture language.

•Don't confuse speaking ability with intelligence. A person who is hearing-impaired may not be able to speak well, but that has nothing to do with his intelligence or education.

•Feel free to communicate using a variety of gestures and facial expressions, including nodding your head for "yes," shrugging your shoulders to say "I don't know" or displaying anger, fear, joy, etc. through your face.

•Refrain from using the term "mute" for a person who is hearing-impaired.

•Don't turn away from a deaf person while you are speaking to him.

•Try to avoid shouting and using overexaggerated mouth or facial expressions. If the person can't hear you, try decreasing the distance between the two of you.

•Reword a phrase if the person is having trouble reading your lips. Some words are easier to "read" than others.

HELPING SOMEONE WHO IS MOBILITY-IMPAIRED

Normally, you'd offer to lend a hand to someone who seems to be having trouble. Do the same for someone who has a mobility impairment. Many people who are impaired are very self-sufficient and would rather get along on their own, but they still are happy to receive an offer of help. One person writes, "I think an offer of assistance is appropriate any time another person appears to be having some difficulty. I almost always appreciate an offer of help, whether or not I accept it." In return, accept their wishes graciously.

In addition, Chalda Maloff and Susan Macduff Wood, authors of *Business and Social Etiquette with Disabled People* (see "Sources of Further Information," below), recommend the following:

•Act without asking only when there appears to be an immediate physical danger. Even then, proceed with caution.

•Listen to the person with the impairment; get instructions from him before acting.

•Follow through with whatever needs to be done.

•Open doors and hold them open as the person approaches.

•Hold elevator doors open and ask the person with the impairment if he'd like a certain button pressed.

•Always ask before pushing someone in a wheelchair. Push slowly, and be sure to let the wheelchair user know when you plan to release the chair.

•When you extend an invitation to a wheelchair user, it's thoughtful to call the restaurant, theater or other destination in advance and ask if there are any barriers. Better yet, check out the place yourself.

Parking places, stairs and rest rooms are the three most common trouble spots.

•Try to seat yourself at eye level when conversing with someone who is in a wheelchair.

•When cooking dinner for someone who is mobility-impaired, ask in advance if there are certain foods to be avoided.

•If your children ask questions, answer them honestly.

As far as introductions are concerned, introduce yourself as you would to anyone else even if that person's right hand is missing or impaired. According to Elizabeth Post, a person who is disabled will usually appreciate the display of inclusion and simply say, "Please forgive me if I don't shake hands, but I'm very glad to meet you."

Coping with Other People's Children

Parents should be training their children from the very start to respect and be kind to other people, and to respect their property. Unfortunately, as a child grows, it's only too apparent that some lack manners. Sometimes this can be chalked up to youthful rambunctiousness and overlooked. At other times, however, you may feel it is necessary to say something.

Try speaking to the parents first, if you don't have a relationship with the child. Or, simply say, "Please quiet down. You should not be running in these corridors," or whatever statement is appropriate. You are an authority fig-

ure and your word, if firmly stated, should be heeded. It is inappropriate, however, to lecture another's child; that is the parents' responsibility.

ETIQUETTE BASICS FOR A GROWING CHILD

Letitia Baldrige, former chief of staff for First Lady Jacqueline Kennedy, recommends that by age 10 a child should understand the ideas behind certain manners, including the concepts of deference, kindness to others, respect, privacy and safety. With these in mind, Ms. Baldrige has published a list of basic rules of behavior.

A child should. . .
•Stand and greet an adult who comes in from outside of the house.

•Develop good table manners.

•Stand by his chair at the dining table until all the adults are seated.

•Pass food first to guests, then to parents, before serving himself.

•Wait until an adult has begun eating before beginning his own meal.

•Wait until a person pauses in conversation before speaking (never interrupt).

•Protect and be kind to younger siblings.

•Feel comfortable with and know how to talk to an adult.

•Refrain from making a lot of noise in public places.

•Refrain from yelling in the house.

•Respect elders at all times.

•Respect people's privacy.

•Answer when spoken to.

•Respect people's homes, including his own. Learn to do chores cheerfully.

•Know how to use the telephone properly, including how to take messages.

•Keep his room neat.

•Develop good bathroom manners.

•Play music at low volume.

•Learn to wait in line and not to push ahead of others.

•Learn to become a good host.

•Say "excuse me" if he brushes against someone inadvertently.

•Write thank you notes after receiving gifts or being welcomed into someone's home for dinner.

•Be punctual.

•Respect the driver of a car.

•Respect the environment around him.

•Learn the rules of safety concerning crossing streets, riding a bicycle and playing sports in public areas.

•Be kind to animals.

Visiting a Friend's Home

Whether you're staying for an evening or a weekend, a guest should above all be gracious, flexible and, if it comes naturally, conversationally adept. Use good humor and a positive attitude to comfort a host if something goes wrong and to cheer the host if everything is going well. Bring a present: a bottle of wine, champagne or sparkling cider are never

wrong. For longer stays, maybe your host would like a game, a book, something tasty (that doesn't spoil) from a gourmet food store or something to be used around the house that you noticed was lacking the last time you visited. Make sure to thank your host promptly—by phone the next day for a dinner or lunch, by letter within a day or two of a weekend visit.

Treat your host's house with respect. A few things to remember for dinner and weekend guests follow:

•Put the toilet seat and lid down.

•Use hand towels, if provided, but don't fold it back up to make it look fresh.

•Make use of coasters. If none are available and the furniture is nice, ask. The host may have forgotten to put them out.

•Offer to help with last-minute preparations or clearing the table. If your host declines your offer, don't press.

•Should something break or be stained, apologize. If possible, replace the item promptly.

•Use a calling card number or reverse the charges, if you must make a long-distance call.

WEEKEND HOUSEGUESTS
You'll most likely be invited again if you and your host are on the same wavelength about how the days are organized (or not organized, if that's someone's preference). Don't plan to spend every minute with your host; pack a book, crossword puzzle or jogging shoes to keep yourself occupied during

"private time." Speak to your host about any plans you may have or wish to make—visiting another friend, sightseeing, bringing work, etc. This will give both of you a better idea of how to plan the time.

Offer to help out with a meal, either by bringing something in advance, making something while there, taking care of ordering a delivery or making a reservation for a dinner out. Do this before you visit, so your host can decide if it fits in with his plans.

In general, don't arrive early. Be specific about when you will arrive and when you plan to depart. Call if you're held up on the road and will be late. Don't overstay your welcome or ruin it by arriving with an overloaded car that you plan to unpack all over the host's house.

Most people know to bring a small present for the host, but if the household contains children, get something simple for them as well.

Keep to your host's schedule for meals and bedtime, unless you've discussed other plans. If you get up early or like to sleep late, talk to your host about what will make both of you comfortable in the morning. Very early risers or midnight snackers may even want to bring simple provisions from home. One guest even brings her own hotwater heater for coffee and a can of evaporated milk.

Other tips:

•Make your bed. On the day you're departing, ask where to leave the bed linens.

•Clean up after yourself in the bathroom.

•Don't leave your toiletries in the bathroom if you're sharing it, and don't hog the hot water.

•Last but not least, leave your pet at home unless your host specifically invites you to bring it along.

Going to Church, Synagogue or Temple

Every religion dictates its own rules about proper dress and behavior within the doors of its house of worship. No matter what the accepted practices are, you can be at your most gracious by being respectful and reverent.

APPROPRIATE DRESS

Dress conservatively. Jackets for men and dresses, skirts or nice pants for women are suitable.

In Catholic churches, although women no longer have to wear a head covering, it is still considered proper to wear a hat or a scarf. Men, however, should never don a hat in church. Older women may still wear gloves but now take them off inside.

Hats, called yarmulkes, are provided by synagogues for all men in attendance. Wearing a yarmulke is a matter of custom, while wearing a prayer shawl is a commandment. Therefore, non-Jewish visitors may want to don a yarmulke out of respect, but they should not put on a prayer shawl. Only in Orthodox and in some Conservative temples do women follow the custom of covering their heads.

SOCIALIZING

Catching up on gossip may be appropriate for outside a church, temple or mosque, but if you carry on a conversation at length inside during the service, it can distract other worshipers. Catching someone's eye or saying hello is fine, as is talking after the service.

PARTICIPATING IN THE SERVICE

No one expects you to know the customs of a religion that is not your own. And in visiting a house of worship, the best behavior often comes from following the lead of others around you (standing, kneeling, bowing the head, etc.). If you do not feel comfortable kneeling, crossing yourself and so on, don't feel pressured to follow another's example; simply bow your head and look respectful. If an offering plate is passed when you are visiting a house of worship, add something to the plate as a courtesy.

Gifts and Giving

Giving a gift to a friend sends a message that lasts for quite some time, especially if the present reflects the recipient's personality and even more so if the gift comes as a surprise. When you do send presents, make sure the address is correct and that you've included a card or enclosure with your full name on it. Take time to wrap it beautifully, but don't put it in another store's box, because the person who receives it may try to return it.

Use the birthstone chart for birthdays if you want to get a gem or even to choose

Birthstones for Every Month

January: Garnet or zircon

February: Amethyst

March: Aquamarine, bloodstone or jasper

April: Diamond

May: Emerald

June: Pearl

July: Ruby

August: Sardonyx, peridot or carnelian

September: Sapphire

October: Opal or zircon

November: Topaz

December: Turquoise or lapis lazuli

a color theme for a party. For other gift-giving occasions, refer to the following sections: "Visiting a Friend's Home," "Weekend Houseguests," "Engagement Announcements and Parties," "Bridal Showers," "Wedding Gifts," "Baby Showers," "Choosing Godparents," "Bar and Bat Mitzvahs" and "Anniversary Parties."

WHEN CASH IS AN APPROPRIATE GIFT

Elizabeth Post writes, "Although in most circumstances I consider gifts of 'pure' money in poor taste, a 50th anniversary can be an exception." She also notes that teenagers and senior citizens often appreciate cash—or a gift certificate—instead of a chosen gift. Some people still choose to give cash. At large parties, recipients may choose to open the gift envelopes after the guests have gone. The intimacy of a smaller party provides a better background for opening the envelopes with other gifts. Immediate thanks, as for any other present, are appropriate, but never mention the amount given.

If a check or cash is received as a wedding present, let your friend know how you intend to spend it. It will seem more personal.

TIPPING GUIDELINES

Many people rely on tips as a supplement to their salaries. Yet service is not always up to par. Tip well if the person in question has been friendly and competent. If he is rude or inept, decrease the amount of the tip. Leave no tip only if the service has been very bad, in which case you may want to bring the problem to the attention of the manager. Also, don't be caught without change. Plan for tipping in advance.

The guidelines below reflect the current rates for services in a large city. You may wish to pay slightly less when dining or staying in a small town.

Take note if you are being served or helped by the owner of an establishment. It is acceptable to ask one of the other employees if the owner accepts tips (they often don't).

Restaurant:
•Wait staff: 20 percent of the bill, not including taxes (and not including wines, if there is a sommelier). If you're also leaving a tip for the captain, tip the waiter 15 percent.

•Sommelier: 10 to 20 percent of the cost of the wines to the sommelier, in cash (minimum $5).

•Captain: 5 percent of the bill.

•Washroom attendant: 50 cents or $1.

•Maitre d'hotel: $10 only if you visit the restaurant regularly and have requested a particularly good table for a special occasion (otherwise, most restaurateurs say tipping for a good table does not do any good).

•Coat check: $1 per coat.

•Doorman: $2 for hailing a taxi, more if it's raining.

•Valet parking: $2 upon departure, more if it's raining.

Taxi:
•Driver: Approximately 20 percent of the total, including night charges, although some people round up or down to the closest 50 cents.

Hotel:
•Doorman: $1 to $2 on arrival if you have luggage and $2 if he hails a taxi; more if the weather's bad.

•Bellman: $1 per bag (minimum $2) and $2 to $5 if he provides you with any special services.

•Room service: 15 to 20 percent of the bill, not including taxes (minimum $2).

•Concierge: $5 to $25 if he has gone out of his way to be helpful (at the end of your stay).

•Maid: $2 to $4 per night (use the higher figure if more than two people are staying in the room). Give it to her in person or put in it in an envelope addressed "For the Maid" and leave it with the desk clerk.

•Valet or laundry: $1 to $3 if you're in the room when it's delivered.

Hairdressing salon or barber:
•Hair stylist: 15 to 20 percent of the cost of the cut.

•Colorist: 15 to 20 percent of the cost of the tinting.

•Shampooer: $2.

•Manicurist: 15 percent of the cost of the manicure ($2 minimum).

•Specialists: 15 percent of the cost for facials, waxing, etc.

Delivery services:
•Fast food: 10 to 15 percent of the bill, depending on the weather and the physical size of the order.

•Groceries: $2 (although some people tip $1 per bag).

•Department store: $5 to $10, only if the delivery men are unpacking and setting up your purchase.

Airports:
•Porters: $1 per bag

Tipping in Other Countries
Although in some countries such as China—and some places in Japan—leaving a tip is an insult, giving someone a monetary "thank you" in Europe is considered absolutely proper. The notion of tipping supposedly came from 16th-century England, where customers helped themselves to a drink and left coins "to insure promptitude."

If you're not sure of a country's customs, Jerry Newfield, owner of Tip Computers International, recommends calling the U.S. Embassy or your concierge. Use the chart below as a starting point, and "when in doubt, always err on the side of generosity," says Newfield.

No matter where you are, examine the bill to see if service has been included. A quick rundown by country may help.

Austrian restaurants often add 10 percent to the bill; add the extra 5 percent as a courtesy. *In England,* the most expensive dining establishments may add a full service charge to the bill, requiring no extra tip; this is not the case in less expensive restaurants, where a 10 to 15 percent tip is standard. *Most restaurants in France* add a 15 percent service charge (the check will say *service compris*), but knowledgeable tippers add an extra 5 to 7 percent to the bill for the wait staff. *Service charges in Germany* usually add a 10 to 15 percent bite to the bill; you can tell because the bill will have *bedienung* written on it. Rather than leaving an extra percentage, simply round out the bill to the nearest mark or two.

Italian cafes and restaurants almost always include a service charge (*servizio compreso*) of 10 to 18 percent; it's considered proper to leave a 5 to 8 percent tip for the waiter in addition. *In Spain,* a 10 percent tip for the waiter is normal. *The Swiss* automatically add a 15 percent charge on cafe and restaurant bills (and on taxi rides), so not leaving a tip is OK. If you're dining at a more expensive restaurant, though, you should consider leaving an extra 5 to 10 percent for the staff.

Tipping in Europe and Japan

Refer to the text for specific information about which countries tend to add a service charge to the restaurant bill. The tipping suggestions included here are for standard practices. Also note that the descriptive tags in the first column ("per bag," "per night," etc.) apply to all the figures in that row.*

Note: AS=Austrian schilling, £=pound, p=pence, F=franc, L.=lira, pta(s)=peseta(s), SFr=Swiss franc, ¥=yen

	Austria	England	France	Italy*
Hotel				
Bellhop	5AS per bag	50p	10F	—
Chambermaid	10AS per night	£1	10F	2,000 L.
Room service	20AS per meal	—	10F	1,500 L. if not included
Taxi	10% of fare	15%	10–15%	10%
Porter/Skycap	10–15AS	£5	5–10F per bag	—
Restaurant				
Waiter	5% of meal	10–15% 5–7%,	12–15% if not included	5%
Bartender	10% of drinks	none, in pubs	—	200 L.
Washroom attendant	5AS		5F	—
Other				
Theater usher	—	—	1–2F	—
Checkroom attendant	— —		1F	1,000 L.
Wine steward	—	—	10% of the wine bill	5,000 to 10,000 L.

	Spain	Switzerland	Japan
Hotel			
Bellhop	50–100 ptas	1SFr	none
Chambermaid	100 ptas per day	2SFr	none
Room service	125 ptas per meal	—	none
Taxi	5–10%	none	none
Porter/Skycap	60 ptas	1SFr per bag	¥200–300
Restaurant			
Waiter	10%	5–10%	—
Bartender	—	1–2SFr	none
Washroom attendant	—	1SFr	—
Other			
Theater usher	—	2SFr	—

*The lire is the most changeable of currencies in this chart. The suggestions above are for an exchange rate of approximately 1,500 lire to the dollar.

Tipping in Japan differs from tipping in Europe, although the rules seem to be changing each year. Generally, you won't have to tip. Taxi drivers don't expect it, nor do hotel workers, bartenders or beauty salon attendants. You should, however, tip airport porters about ¥200 per bag, and if you're traveling with a car and driver, you will be expected to tip about ¥1,000 per day.

Invitations and Replies

People do take advantage of others, especially when it comes to invitations to parties or dinners that sound wonderfully enticing. No matter how extraordinary the event, don't be tempted to ask for an invitation. Wait to be invited. And if you aren't extended an invitation, be gracious to the host and hope you'll be asked to the next occasion.

Similarly, never ask to bring friends, especially to a small party. If it's appropriate, simply explain that you have friends visiting and that you'll have to decline the invitation. An accommodating host often may extend the invitation to your friends (don't expect this, however, if it's a sit-down dinner or small reception).

ISSUING FORMAL INVITATIONS
Many formal invitations are beautifully engraved on traditional white or off-white cards, but an invitation to a formal lunch or dinner can also be handwritten on white or off-white paper. Both, following the custom of formality, should be worded in the third person (as in the illustration).

To assume that guests know how to dress is a mistake. Specify "black tie" in the lower right-hand corner of the invitation to differentiate that from an event that calls for a business suit.

Punctuate the invitation only within a line, never at the end of a line, except for "RSVP," which normally appears in the lower left-hand corner of the card. State the time in old form: "half past seven o'clock" not "seven thirty." Include the

Mr. and Mrs. John Jacob Bower
INVITATIONAL LINE
request the pleasure of your company
REQUEST LINE
for cocktails and dinner
EVENT LINE
Thursday, the fifteenth of June
DATE LINE
at seven o'clock
TIME LINE
2126 Lazy Lane
LOCATION LINE
Houston, Texas
CITY AND STATE LINE
favour of a reply is requested
REPLY REQUEST LINE

You are cordially invited
REQUEST LINE
for cocktails and dinner
EVENT LINE
on Thursday, June 15th
DATE LINE
at 7 o'clock
TIME LINE
2126 Lazy Lane
LOCATION LINE
Houston, Texas
CITY AND STATE LINE
Louise and Jack Bower
INVITATIONAL LINE
Please reply
(713) 555-1212
REPLY REQUEST LINE

Formal invitations

return address on the back flap of the envelope or under the RSVP. A response card may also be used (see illustration), although some people find them irritatingly impersonal. If you do choose to enclose a response card, it is thoughtful—and now almost standard—to also include a self-addressed, stamped envelope.

Send out the invitations at least two weeks in advance.

Besides dinners and luncheons, formal events range from graduation parties and benefit dances to anniversary parties, receptions to meet prominent members of the community and weddings (for weddings, see "Engagements and Weddings," below).

RESPONDING TO FORMAL INVITATIONS

To reply to a formal invitation, handwrite a note or letter, unless a telephone number is printed with the RSVP.

Typewritten or electronic mail just doesn't do justice to the occasion. Be sure to write out the hosts' full names when addressing the reply. Spelling out all abbreviations is also in keeping with the tradition of formal invitations.

Use the invitation as a guide for your response. If the invitation is written in the third person, reply in the third person (see illustration). Of course, if you are especially close to the host and wish to explain your absence, a personal note on formal stationery is also appropriate. It is also possible for one spouse to accept and the other to decline an invitation. If there is more than one host, be sure to write the names of each after "the kind invitation of." The envelope, however, should be addressed to the first name on the list or to the host whose name appears by the RSVP.

Send your answer as soon as possible, and once you make the commit-

Mr. Matthew Bota

☐ accepts

☐ regrets

Friday, January second
Columbus Country Club

M_____

will_____attend

Friday, January second

Mr. and Mrs. Peter Alan Epstein
accept with pleasure
Mr. and Mrs. Christopher Robert DeAngelis'
kind invitation
for Saturday, the sixth of May

Mr. and Mrs. Peter Alan Epstein
sincerely regret that
their absence from the city
prevents them from accepting
the kind invitation of
Mr. and Mrs. Christopher Robert DeAngelis
for Saturday, the sixth of May

Response cards

ment to go, don't cancel for a more interesting invitation. If you must cancel, call the host immediately so that he may invite someone in your stead or adjust the expected number of guests for the caterer.

ISSUING AND RESPONDING TO INFORMAL INVITATIONS

The telephone has all but replaced the note for invitations to informal parties. A hand-written invitation, however, "is certainly never incorrect," states Elizabeth Post. Fill-in invitations, whether from Tiffany's or the local card store, provide a full range of possibilities from staid, elegantly bordered dinner invitations to brightly colored, fanciful baby shower invitations. Using a little imagination, you can even create your own.

RSVPs call for a reply, even if you can't attend. Some invitations will state "Regrets only." If that's the case, call or write if you're unable to make the date.

Call if the host has included a telephone number; otherwise, send a quick note on a correspondence card, a postcard or your stationery. A simple, "We're looking forward to dinner with you on July 22 at 8:00" or "We'd love to come to lunch on December 26 at 3:00." Be sure to include your thanks and sign your name.

If you receive a semiformal fill-in invitation written in the third person, respond with an informal note as mentioned above.

With no RSVP on the invitation, there's no need to contact the host, although it's a nice gesture to confirm or decline in advance.

Entertaining at Home

HOW TO BE A GOOD HOST

The easiest way to be a good host is to plan ahead. Use the sidebar "Plan Your Party Well" to figure out which details pertain to your party, whether it's a sit-down dinner or a cocktails and a trea-

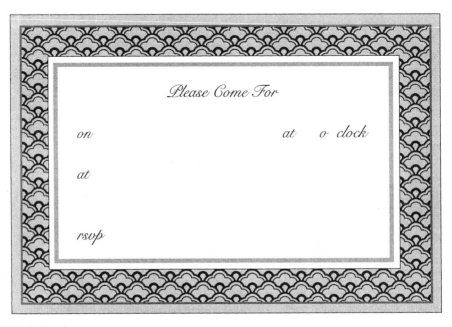

A fill-in invitation

sure hunt. Relax before the guests arrive, even if you can spare only 15 minutes.

On the off chance that guests drop in and you're caught without being able to prepare in advance, be flexible and adapt to the circumstances. Raid your refrigerator or call in for food to be delivered, if that's possible. If you know your guests well enough to welcome a spontaneous visit, they should also be ready for whatever comes their way. Most people, however, should not drop in on friends unless it's been established beforehand that it's appropriate to do so.

Whatever type of party you'll be giving, you'll want to make sure that the guests are mixed and matched well. Try to establish what your guests have in common when you make your introductions. A tidbit of information can

Plan Your Party Well

IN ADVANCE

Call calligrapher, typesetters or engraver for invitations and other party necessities, or buy them.

Send out invitations or telephone guests.

Make shopping list.

Place food orders with mail order, caterer or takeout business.

Reserve rental equipment, plan shopping trips or confirm that borrowed items will be available.

Test any electrical equipment you may need to rent, buy or borrow.

Plan centerpiece and other decor and furniture arrangement. Plan entertainment.

FIVE TO SEVEN DAYS AHEAD

Shop for party items, frozen foods, canned goods and ingredients to make dishes in advance.

Prepare whatever dishes possible this far in advance.

Check liquor/drinks supply and frequently used items, and add whatever is necessary to the shopping list.

Order flowers.

Buy candles or other decor items.

Make sure table linens are cleaned and pressed.

Select your party clothes and launder or dry-clean them, if necessary.

THREE TO FOUR DAYS AHEAD

Polish silver; clean seldom-used dishes.

Make sure glassware is not dusty or streaked.

Do major house-cleaning tasks.

Confirm all hired help.

Confirm all equipment to be brought in.

Make any food that can be frozen or will keep until the day of the party.

TWO DAYS AHEAD

Clean house.

Make the seating plan.

Confirm flower delivery.

Prepare whatever dishes you can at this stage.

Buy ice.

Make sure you have all the ingredients you need on hand except for those that should be purchased at the last minute.

THE DAY BEFORE

Finish as much of the cooking as possible.

Rearrange furniture where necessary.

Prepare room for guests' coats.

Set out umbrella stand.

Set out fresh towels and soap.

Neatly write out or type instructions for catering and serving help.

Prepare sound system and select music.

Set up bar.

Iron linen, if it hasn't been done.

Set table.

Arrange all other dishes and flatware in order of use.

Have coffee and tea service ready.

THE DAY OF THE PARTY

Recheck supplies of anything that may have been consumed.

Refrigerate white wine and other things to be chilled.

TWO HOURS AHEAD

Arrange the flowers and final decor.

Make room for dirty dishes.

Empty garbage.

Get dressed.

JUST BEFORE THE PARTY

Set out cheeses or nonperishable snacks. Open red wine and mix first batch of cocktails or juices.

Relax and get ready for a good time!

become a lively discussion after you've excused yourself. If someone seems left unattended, engage him in conversation and gently lead him to another guest with whom you think he shares a mutual interest.

Periodically ask your guests if they'd like another drink or a glass of something else. Always provide nonalcoholic drinks such as seltzer, soda, diet soda, juice or sparkling cider. Once everyone is seated, don't delay picking up your fork or telling your guests to go ahead and begin.

If a disaster strikes, take it upon yourself to set the mood. Behave calmly, as if disasters were a part of daily life. It's easy if you're the brunt of the misfortune. However, when a guest is involved in the calamity, do your best to comfort him with gentle humor and a positive attitude. Don't call attention to what happened. Simply help out discreetly.

POLITE WAYS TO END A PARTY

You may not think you're ending the party by leaving early, but if done indiscreetly, one guest's departure can inadvertently be a signal for all the other guests to leave. So take your leave prudently. You don't want to signal to other guests that it's time to depart: That's the host's responsibility. Look for the host and say goodbye quietly, telling how him enjoyable the party was.

When the host is ready to end the party, put away the food and liquor. If friends do not get the message, gently tell them that the hour is late or, if it's an early party, that you have made plans with another couple to meet them and must get ready to go.

DEALING WITH DRUNKEN OR UNRULY GUESTS

According to one of the instructors at the National Bartender School in New York City, if you must intervene with a drunken guest, sit him down, tell him to relax and calm down, and offer him anything but alcohol. "Don't offer him coffee either, you don't want him to have lots of energy." You must be firm; ask him to leave and make sure he gets into a taxi or a car with another driver. Basically, there aren't any nice ways of asking someone to leave if they don't want to go. If the guest insists on staying, suggest that he go to another room, away from the majority of party guests. You want to avoid a confrontation.

Edith Gilbert's Advice to Wedding Guests

Edith Gilbert is the author of *The Complete Wedding Planner: Helpful Choices for the Bride and Groom* (Warner Books). She also writes a column called "It's Customary" for the Petaskie News in Petaskie, Michigan. She encourages everyone to relax and have a good time at a wedding while respecting the solemnity of the occasion. Her guidelines for guests are as follows:

Respond to the invitation promptly.

Send the present to the bride's home (or other address, as noted) in advance of the wedding.

Don't bring any guests or children with you unless they're invited. Don't assume. If you have any questions, ask.

Keep your conversation short in the receiving line, with a simple greeting or words of future happiness.

Dress properly. Men and women should dress as a couple (not one in jeans, the other in a cocktail outfit).

Refrain from taking flash pictures.

Engagements and Weddings

Weddings and engagements are times of joy to be shared with those you love and cherish. While whole books have been written about planning weddings, we've chosen to highlight some of the questions that guests have about responding to invitations, giving parties and presents, and choosing the right clothes. See "Wedding Thanks" for tips on sending out thank you notes.

For more information about weddings in general and specific, look for books in your local library or bookstore. Possibilities are Edith Gilbert's *The Complete Wedding Planner: Helpful Choices for the Bride and Groom* and *Bride's Book of Etiquette* by Cele Lalli. Look through a few books before you choose a planner; some are more conservative than others. One or two now include African-American traditions as well as customs of a few other cultures. Rites and rituals differ from ethnic group to ethnic group; to follow a custom, call the couple's church or a close friend for advice.

ENGAGEMENT ANNOUNCEMENTS AND PARTIES

Telling close friends and family is easy. A telephone call or a nice, handwritten note is always welcome. Many couples, however, choose to announce their engagement formally, either at a party or through a newspaper announcement (not by way of formal, engraved cards). Informally, the choices are limited only by the couple's imagination.

Parents, grandparents, aunts, uncles, even close friends can host an engagement party. There are no set rules; the spirit is what's important. Although bridal showers are more common, if there's to be a long time between the engagement and the marriage, a party is a wonderful way of bringing people together. Surprise parties, where the guests don't know the reason for the fete, can be great fun.

If you attend an engagement party or read of a friend's happy news in the paper, don't feel obligated to buy the bride or groom a present. You will be sending them a wedding gift soon enough. Godparents, very close friends and members of the bride's and groom's family may get something to welcome the spouse-to-be to the family or to share the joy of the occasion. Typical gift selections include bed or table linen, jewelry or something small in sterling.

BRIDAL SHOWERS

Traditionally, the bridal shower was given for a woman by women. Men were not welcome. That notion may still be the case for some showers, but just as likely, a wedding shower will now be for both the bride and the groom and will be attended by friends of both. Showers are basically small parties designed to "shower" the bride with presents that may or may not be related to a theme: kitchen (knives, electronic gadgets, etc.), bathroom (towels, guest soaps, etc.), lingerie (at an all-female shower) and so on. The guest of honor opens the gifts as part of the party's entertainment.

Presents should not be elaborate,

because you'll be buying a wedding present shortly. However, a few friends can pitch in for a more expensive present, which may be appreciated more by the couple. Bring the gift in person; don't have a store deliver it.

The bride-to-be usually attends a shower given by close friends, with family members present. (The bride-to-be's mother and sister customarily do not host the party.) She then may go to a shower hosted by work mates or friends from a group—a reading group, an exercise class, a charity, etc. The event can be a cocktail party, a tea or a lunch, usually held about a month before the wedding. To make life easier for all involved and to avoid imposing on a friend to attend more than one or two showers, the bride normally writes up a guest list for each shower after the host has informed her of the number of people to be invited.

Don't be surprised by some of the quaint customs that have been perpetuated at female-only bridal showers. One of the more traditional activities involves threading the bows and ribbons from the gifts onto a round paper plate or piece of cardboard. By the end of the party, the plate is covered with brightly colored furbelows. The bride can then use this as her bouquet at her rehearsal.

WEDDING GIFTS

Choosing a wedding present can be delightfully easy if the couple shares the same interests and tastes or abysmally difficult if the two have unique predilections. Wedding presents should ideally be bought and delivered before the wedding date.

The gifts normally go to the bride's home or to her mother's house. If the delivery predates the wedding, address the gift to the bride; otherwise, label it for "Mr. and Mrs." Some guests may choose to bring the presents to the wedding reception, but this may be a burden to the couple.

Typical presents include practical or ornamental items for the dining room or kitchen, decorative art, luggage for the honeymoon, picture frames, fine wine, even gift certificates to the couple's favorite book or gourmet store or tickets to the theater, if they have already set up a household together.

The bride and groom may have "registered" at a store; if so, take advantage of this, especially if you don't know the couple well and aren't sure what to get them. The registry, sometimes computerized, is a list of what the couple would like. It often itemizes china, silverware, bed and table linens, and other household necessities, ranging from inexpensive objects to expensive silver or crystal.

Some stores offer monogramming. You can pay in advance for the service and let the couple choose whether to have the present engraved or not. (They may also elect to return the present if it's not personalized.)

To give or not to give money is often the question. Some cultures deem this perfectly acceptable. Others do not. Ask, to be sure. The amount will vary depending how close you are to the bride or groom. Checks, bonds, and shares of stock are equally welcome.

If a bride exchanges the wedding present you've given her, accept the fact graciously.

WEDDING INVITATIONS AND ANNOUNCEMENTS

Invitations

A wedding invitation should reflect the nature of the ceremony. For instance, if the bride and groom have chosen to exchange vows underwater in scuba gear, a formal, engraved invitation may not be the most fitting choice. Alternatively, if the wedding is held in the evening at a house of worship and formal attire is requested, an informal letter with a quote from a philosopher is inappropriate.

A small wedding party allows the bride and groom the opportunity to write out their own invitation. The traditional invitation, however, is engraved, printed by thermography or written out by a professional calligrapher. The wording is fairly standard, but there are a number of variations depending on whether one or both of the parents are divorced or deceased, whether the couple chooses to send out the invitations, whether it's a second wedding and so on. There are a number of possibilities for enclosures, also. For more information, consult *Emily Post's Etiquette* by Elizabeth Post, *Letitia Baldrige's Complete Guide to the New Manners for the 90's* or *Crane's Blue Book of Stationery* by Steven Feinberg.

Responding to an invitation now usually means returning a response card promptly. The most formal response to a wedding invitation is still a handwritten note centered on formal stationery. The wording is simply: "Mr. and Mrs. Harrison Hart accept with pleasure Mr. and Mrs. Joshua Franklin's kind invitation for Saturday, the thirteenth of March." The regret also takes the form of third person as shown.

No matter what form, the invitation should be addressed only to those who are invited. Children receive their own invitation if they are to be included.

Announcements

Announcements are what they appear to be: a formal message from the bride and groom letting their friends and acquaintances know of their union. If you receive an announcement, you're not obligated to send a present although it's a nice gesture to do so.

The wedding couple sends announcements to friends who live far away or to those not invited to the wedding. Announcements are also a handy way to notify alumni magazines and business associates. An "At Home" card (see illustration) usually accompanies the announcement. This informs friends if the couple has a new address and whether the bride has kept her maiden name. A wedding invitation may also include an "At Home" card.

At home
Dorothy Wendell Bower
Edward Warren Sanders
1435 Second Avenue
New York City, New York 10011
212-555-1546

An At Home card

PROPER WEDDING ATTIRE

The chart "Dress for Wedding Guests" details what guests should wear at different types of weddings. Use it as a guide. The veil and gloves, although proper, are not as common today as they once were.

In general, guests should "dress as they would for almost any other social event held at the same hour and season," writes Cele Lalli in *Bride's Book of Etiquette.* Wedding trends do come and go, and if you happen to be invited to a wedding during the New York Marathon or on a mountaintop, obviously the chart will not make sense. Guests invited to a garden wedding may also choose to dress more creatively (a vintage light-colored jacket, for instance, or a shorts suit for a woman).

If a wedding is black tie, it will usually be written on the invitation. Men should wear a tuxedo or dinner jacket and matching or black trousers, a cummerbund or waistcoat, formal shirt and bow tie.

Women guests should refrain from wearing white, the traditional color of most wedding dresses, so as not to take attention away from the bride. That goes for loud colors and hats as well.

Other Celebrations

All over the world, rites of passage continue to be celebrated with a long list of rules to follow. In the melting pot that is the United States, we commemorate all sorts of significant days in a person's life. Below are some of the most common. The suggestions that follow are for people who are unfamiliar with what to expect.

Dress for Wedding Guests

This list, taken from *Emily Post's Etiquette,* outlines proper, conservative choices for wedding attire whether day or evening.

Occasion	Women Guests	Men Guests
Most formal daytime	Street-length cocktail or afternoon dresses (colors preferred to black and white), gloves; hat optional	Dark suits; conservative shirts and ties
Most formal evening	Depending on local custom, long or short dresses; if long, veil or ornament, otherwise optional; gloves	If women wear long dresses, tuxedos; if short dresses, dark suits
Semiformal daytime	Short afternoon or cocktail dress; hat optional for church	Dark suits
Semiformal evening	Cocktail dresses, gloves, hat for church optional	Dark suits
Informal daytime	Afternoon dresses, gloves, hat optional for church	Dark suits; light trousers and dark blazers in summer
Informal evening	Afternoon or cocktail dresses, gloves, hat optional for church	Dark suits

BABY SHOWERS

The imminent arrival of a first child is cloaked with nervous but happy anticipation. A baby shower gathers together the mother-to-be's closest friends and family and helps to ease the way into motherhood both financially and emotionally.

Most showers call for bringing simple gifts, although the expectant mother may provide a close friend with a list of needed items. With a list, the well-wishers have the choice of pitching in for a more expensive present or getting a less costly one on their own.

Times have changed and both men and women can be included in a baby shower, especially if it's given by office friends. The cost of showers given by co-workers is often split among all those attending.

A shower is equally welcome for the mother-to-be of an adopted child. If you're organizing the event, be sure to include the baby's clothing size.

BIRTH ANNOUNCEMENT

When the expectant parents go to the hospital, the father-to-be usually has a list of close family and friends to call after the arrival of the baby. This should not preclude sending anyone a more formal announcement of the baby's birth.

It's a joyous occasion, one that does not rule out odd behavior: fathers going up to strangers and proclaiming the news or renting billboards to tell the world. The most gracious announcements, however, are uncomplicated, straightforward notes sent through the mail. Card shops offer a variety as do stationers and stores such as Tiffany, Saks Fifth Avenue and Neiman-Marcus.

Some of the more classic announcements feature a pale blue or pink border, an engraved message in a serif typeface in black and a smaller card with the baby's name on it attached to the larger card by a tiny bow. Other common announcements include a photo of the baby (or baby and mother or parents), a copy of the baby's footprint; or an illustration. Sending word in a Christmas card is another nice way to bring the message into friends' homes.

The message should contain:

•The baby's full name

•His or her birthdate

•Parents' names

The parents' address, the baby's weight at birth and the exact time of the birth are all optional, as is the birthplace (the hospital, for instance, or the name of the country if the baby was born overseas).

As with any note of this sort, a personal message makes the announcement that much nicer.

For those receiving announcements, contact the parents right away with a letter or a phone call or a gift. Receipt of an announcement should be thought of as nothing more than a note to share joyous news; it is not a call for gifts.

CHRISTENING OR BRIT INVITATIONS

The invitations for a christening are most often communicated by phone.

Strictly, guests who live out of town should receive a written note, but christening invitations should be warm and informal and exceptions to this are always made. You can even jot the details (occasion, date, time and place) on the birth announcement.

The Jewish *brit* (or *briss* or *b'rit milah*), the ceremony that welcomes a male child into the world, is held eight days after he is born. "Brit" means covenant; "milah" refers to the circumcision. It is at the brit that the child will be named and then circumcised.

Phoned invitations are best because of the short time between birth and the ritual. Parents may also send out informal invitations to a few friends for a girl's naming ceremony held at a Reform synagogue usually on the Saturday closest to the girl's day of birth.

Choosing Godparents

Parents should talk to their child's potential godparents before the christening date is decided upon—even before the child is born, if desired. Although it's always nice to speak to your friends in person about such an enjoyable issue, a phone call or telegram sometimes is more practical and just as nice for those receiving the good news. It should be obvious, but it isn't: Ask only close friends or family members to serve as godparents.

The role of a godparent traditionally has been to educate the child in the ways of the parents' religion and to extend the child's family if it is small. But today parents are stretching the rules and asking friends of other faiths to be their baby's godparents; this is usually done because the parents respect their friend's values and wish these to be passed on to their child. (The Catholic Church, however, forbids Catholics from being godparents to a child of another faith.)

The godparents' obligations usually include sending the child a gift on his christening day, at each birthday and at Christmas. They do not assume responsibility for the child if something should happen to his parents; the parents will select a guardian for that. (Sometimes it will be the same person, but the parents should discuss this with the guardian-to-be and give them plenty of leeway to decline the request.) Nor does a godparent have to provide for his godchild financially.

Officially, the godparents should also be present at the christening if at all possible. If not, choose someone to go in your stead and send a note to the minister informing him of your decision.

BAR AND BAT MITZVAH

When a boy reaches the age of 13, he is recognized as an adult in the Jewish temple. The coming-of-age ritual is called a *bar mitzvah*. Its female counterpart, the *bat mitzvah*, is practiced in some Reform and Conservative congregations. A few Orthodox congregations have adopted a nonreligious ceremony called a *bat Torah*, which allows a girl to study and be rewarded with a celebration like those of her Reform and Conservative counterparts. The boy's ceremony varies from the more informal Reform services to the very traditional

Orthodox services. The common element requires that the child read from the Torah, the Old Testament and the Haftarah, a book that complements and expands upon one of the themes from the Bible. Afterward, the parents give a reception, which these days in some communities comes second only to the child's wedding. It is considered impolite to attend the reception and not the service.

Do not be surprised if you receive an elaborate invitation. Receptions can be formal or informal, and invitations and dress go hand in hand with that decision. Dress as you would for a religious service or a wedding (if there is to be a black-tie reception, it will be noted on the invitation). Some parents go to extremes, but it is not necessary to follow in kind. A gift, however, is expected if you attend the ceremony. In some communities, it is acceptable to give cash or a check; if you have any question, ask the parents. Send the present directly to the child's home, not to the synagogue.

ANNIVERSARY PARTIES

Every year is a good year to celebrate an admirable marriage, and what better way to do it than with an anniversary party? The most common anniversary parties, however, are held on the benchmark years: the 5th, 10th, 25th and 50th.

For the first few benchmarks, plan a party as usual, remembering to toast the happy couple (the couple may even plan the party themselves). But for the latter two events, something a little

more special is called for—specifically, a receiving line and a "wedding" cake. Below are a few tips:

• Anyone can plan an anniversary party.

• Celebrate on the anniversary itself or on the Saturday closest to the actual date.

• Invitations—from phone calls to engraved notes—depend on the formality of the party.

• Hold it at home, at a restaurant, club or even a resort.

• Consider re-creating the wedding menu, complete with cake.

• Toast the couple with champagne or punch.

• Decorate with silver for the 25th and gold for the 50th anniversary.

1945 ～～ 1995

Mr. and Mrs. Blair Farley
Mr. and Mrs. Glenn Roberts
request the pleasure of your company
at a dinner in honour of
the Fiftieth Wedding Anniversary of
Mr. and Mrs. Derek Farley
Saturday, the seventeenth of October
at half after seven o' clock
The Saddle and Cycle Club
Chicago, Illinois

R.s.v.p.
209 East Lake Shore Drive
Chicago, Illinois 60611   No gifts, please

Anniversary party invitation

•Older couples may not appreciate a surprise.

•Seat the couple in a convenient spot if they are infirm or tire easily.

The invitations can say "No gifts, please." Otherwise, open the presents after everyone has eaten. Assign someone to take care of making a list of gifts sent by people not at the party; these friends should be thanked right away. A written thank you is optional for gifts that are opened at the party if the giver was thanked in person.

Loss and Grieving

CONDOLENCE CALLS AND NOTES

Losing a loved one is a shattering experience. No matter how stoic the person surviving the loss may be, grief is there. Be sensitive to a person's needs. Some prefer to talk about the death, while others yearn to be distracted. If you're a close enough friend, don't attempt to be a mind reader, ask what will help. If you're not that close to the person who has suffered a loss, don't fret over helping. He will make it known if there is something that you can do. Also, keep in mind that minimizing the loss doesn't usually help. A person needs a time to grieve, so much so that some religions even prescribe a period of mourning.

As soon as you hear of someone's death, send a note of condolence to the survivors. Don't worry over what to say, just be sincere. Concentrate on recalling

Traditional and Contemporary Anniversary Presents

Year	Traditional	Contemporary
1.	Paper	Plastics or clocks
2.	Cotton	China
3.	Leather	Crystal or glass
4.	Linen	Electrical appliances
5.	Wood	Silverware
6.	Iron	Wood
7.	Copper or wool	Desk sets
8.	Bronze	Linens or lace
9.	Pottery	Leather
10.	Tin or aluminum	Diamond jewelry
11.	Steel	Jewelry or accessories
12.	Silk	Pearls or colored gems
13.	Lace	Textiles or furs
14.	Ivory	Gold jewelry
15.	Crystal or glass	Watches
20.	China	Platinum
25.	Silver	Silver
30.	Pearls	Diamonds
35.	Coral or jade	Jade
40.	Rubies	Rubies
45.	Sapphires	Sapphires
50.	Gold	Gold
55.	Emeralds	Emeralds
60.	Diamonds	Diamonds

good memories of the person who has passed away and on how that person has affected your life. Don't be afraid to mention a light or humorous event. Keep the note brief and heartfelt. Offer your assistance if you really can help out.

Always hand write a letter of condolence, and if you choose to use a store-bought card, be sure to add a personal note. Mailgrams, telegrams, flowers, food, donations to a charity and, if the deceased is Catholic, mass cards may also be sent.

Address the correspondence to the person you know best and extend your condolences to the more immediate family member who you don't know as well.

NOTIFYING FRIENDS AND RELATIVES
OF A DEATH

Letitia Baldrige recommends that "someone should immediately shoulder the responsibility of ensuring that the bereaved family members are being helped." This person—a relative or close friend of the deceased—will have many duties, usually including organizing the funeral arrangements. He or she will also coordinate making phone calls to other family members, to the deceased's place of employment and to the lawyer. He or she may even ask you to call other family members or friends. So don't be offended if the bereaved spouse or child does not call you directly, and don't feel left out if that person does not wish to speak to you. As a friend, you should make it known

that you're there to help, whether it's bringing over food or making arrangements for small children.

The coordinator (or other person) will also be called upon to send in a notice to the local newspaper. This is a paid announcement that should be written up before the phone call to the paper is made. If the person has gained prominence in the community, a reporter may call and ask for information. Letitia Baldrige, in her book *Letitia Baldrige's Complete Guide to the New Manners for the 90's,* has listed what an obituary might contain:

•Name and address of the person

•Date and place of death

•Cause of death

•Name of spouse

•City of birth

•Name of company or place of work and title

•Education, including both earned and honorary degrees

•Military service, if applicable

•Corporate directorships

•Major awards received, if any

•Titles of published works, films or plays; names of museums where the deceased's art is exhibited; or major theaters or concert halls where he or she may have performed

•Names of survivors and their relationship to the deceased

• Details of the funeral services or a note saying, "Funeral private"

One example that follows these guidelines:

Brown, Henry. On April 15, 1993, age 64. Beloved husband of Zelda, devoted father of Peter, of New York City, and Philip, of Los Angeles. Distinguished scholar and professor of English and Russian. A memorial service will be held on Friday, April 17, at 1 P.M. at the K. Ashe Funeral Home, 333 Beech Ave. In lieu of flowers, donations may be sent to the newly founded Henry Brown Scholarship Fund, c/o the university.

Including the person's age and cause of death are optional, as are the listings of his titles, degrees and work. If a married woman is mentioned— either the deceased or the deceased's sister or daughter—be sure to include her given and maiden names as well as her married one. Daughters precede sons.

ATTENDING FUNERALS AND MEMORIAL SERVICES

Customs vary among religions and ethnic groups, so we've noted a few general customs that are most common in the United States. General respect and courtesy are more important than knowing specific religious details.

Friends and acquaintances may visit the funeral home within specified hours, making sure to sign the guest register formally—that is, Mr. and Mrs. Gordon Smith or Ms. Veronica Stein. The family will keep certain hours; you may wish to greet them or not, depending on your closeness to them. If you do see them, you do not have to send a condolence card. A visit may be as short as 10 minutes or so, time enough to greet the family and pay respects to the deceased. An open coffin suggests that guests pass by, but this is entirely up to the you.

Tradition once dictated that mourners must wear black; this is no longer the case, but restrained colors and fashions are called for. Smoking, laughing and boisterous behavior is usually discouraged. If you happen to meet a friend, greet them as you usually would. Keep your conversation at a low level or chat in an unobtrusive part of the funeral home.

At a church service, sit toward the middle or the back unless you're part of the family's intimate circle.

A memorial service takes the place of a funeral if the deceased is cremated, buried far from home or has no remains to be honored. It can be held at a funeral home, a private home or anywhere that has meaning for the bereaved relatives. The family may wish to include friends' eulogies in the service (they will most often ask in advance) or ask that well wishers contribute their memories to a family scrapbook put out solely for the occasion. A receiving line is optional.

Sources of Further Information

USEFUL ADDRESSES

American Rental Association
   1900 19th St.
   Moline, IL 61265
   1-309-764-2475
Publishes a free 16-page pamphlet called "Rent a Successful Party" and the "Wedding and Reception Planner," a checklist for the bride-to-be.

American Formalwear Association
   111 East Wacker Dr., Suite 600
   Chicago, IL 60601
   1-312-644-6610
Produces a pamphlet called "Your Formalwear Guide." For a free copy send a stamped, self-addressed No. 10 envelope.

The National Bartenders School
   164-01 Northern Blvd.
   Flushing, NY 11358
   1-800-BARTEND
Gives tips on how to mix drinks. Call them if you're interested in getting a more formal education on back-of-the-bar techniques.

The Hilton at Short Hills
   41 JFK Parkway
   Short Hills, NJ 07078
   1-201-379-0100, ext. 7971
If you live in the New York metropolitan area, you might want to inquire about the etiquette classes given for children 5 to 12 at the Hilton at Short Hills.

American Foundation for the Blind
   15 West 16th St.

New York, NY 10011
1-212-620-2000;
TDD 212-620-2158
This organization has six regional centers around the country and a toll-free hot line: 1-800-AFBLIND (232-5463). They can provide guidelines for professionals and a catalog of books and gifts for the blind.

A World of Difference Institute
   Anti-Defamation League
   14 Conant Rd.
   Hanover, NH 03755
The institute conducts sensitivity workshops and teacher training on college campuses, at law enforcement agencies and in general seminars. For information contact Ellen Bettmann.

Elizabeth Post answers etiquette questions in her column in *Good Housekeeping* magazine. Write to her there at 959 Eighth Ave, New York, NY 10019 or in care of her publisher at HarperCollins (Attn: Elizabeth Post), 10 East 53rd St., New York, NY 10022.

Edith Gilbert, author of *The Complete Wedding Planner: Helpful Choices for the Bride and Groom* (Warner Books) also writes a column called "It's Customary" for the Petaskie News in Petaskie, Mich. Her book is available at most major bookstores.

L'ecole des Ingenues, headed by Anne Oliver, designs etiquette seminars and teaches etiquette courses on many different levels (private classes to corporate workshops to high school and college-focused classes). Ms. Oliver is also the author of Finishing Touches

(Bantam, 1990). To purchase a copy, send a check for $25 to:

Anne Oliver
440 Kenbrook Dr. NW
Atlanta, GA 30327
1-404-843-864

Etiquette International
Protocol/Business Etiquette
Consultants
254 East 68th St., Suite 18A
New York, NY 10021
1-212-628-7209

To learn the finer points of business etiquette, call Hilka Klinkenberg, president of the company and the author of *At Ease Professionally,* Chicago: Bonus Books, 1992.

If you expect to be doing business in Washington and have questions about titles and relative importance of officials, call the Department of State, Office of Protocol, Ceremonial Section, 1-202-647-1735.

The Social List of Washington, D.C. (also called "The Green Book") and *Social Precedence in Washington* (Thomas J. Murray, 10335 Kensington Pkwy., Kensington, MD 20895) are considered standards for doing business in Washington. Write to:

Thomas J. Murray
10335 Kensington Pkwy.
Kensington, MD 20895.

Call the governor's or mayor's office of a state or city for questions about regional protocol.

Call the appropriate embassy in Washington or the United Nations Office

of Protocol (1-212-963-7176) if you will be entertaining an official or a businessman from a foreign country and have questions regarding etiquette, especially terms of address and introductions. For those who entertain foreign guests frequently, consider getting a list of information agencies from the Public Inquiries Unit of the U.N. Ask for the list entitled "Sources of Information on United Nations Member States." Write:

Dept. of Public Information
United Nations Headquarters
New York, NY 10017

BOOKS

Bride's Book of Etiquette, 6th edition. Bride's Magazine Staff, Putnam, New York, 1989.

Business and Social Etiquette with Disabled People: A Guide to Getting Along with Persons Who Have Impairments of Mobility, Vision, Hearing or Speech. Chalda Maloff and Susan Macduff Wood, Charles C. Thomas Publisher, New York, 1988.

Crane's Blue Book of Stationery: The Styles and Etiquette of Letters, Notes and Invitations. Steven L. Feinberg, ed., Doubleday, New York, 1989.

Emily Post's Etiquette, 15th edition. Elizabeth L. Post, HarperCollins Publishers, New York, 1992.

Fielding's Europe 1993. Joseph and Judith Raff, Fielding Travel Books, William Morrow, New York, 1993.

Fodor's Affordable Europe '93. Paula Rackow, ed., Fodor's Travel

Publications, New York, 1993.

Fodor's Japan '93. Paula Consolo, ed., Fodor's Travel Publications, New York, 1993.

Letitia Baldrige's Complete Guide to the New Manners for the '90s. Letitia Baldrige, Rawson Associates, New York, 1990.

Miss Manners' (R) Guide for the Turn-of-the-Millennium. Judith Martin, Pharos Books, New York, 1989.

Tiffany's Table Manner for Teenagers, Walter Hoving, Random House, New York, 1989.

13

Pets and Gardening

Dogs

Dogs are a favorite pet, both in the city and in the country. They come in a variety of breeds and are relatively easy to care for.

CHOOSING A DOG

Like styles of clothing or cars, dog breeds go in and out of fashion. Don't base your decision on the latest trends. Choose a dog best suited for your lifestyle. Many breeds require more exercise and training than owners have time for. The result: behavioral problems ranging from destructiveness to biting. Ask breeders and trainers how much training the breed typically needs, about behavior around children and how much the dog sheds and barks.

Some breeds are especially prone to certain health or behavioral problems, such as deafness in Dalmatians or hip dysplasia in large breeds like Rottweilers or German shepherds. Therefore, owners must choose a breeder who mates his dogs carefully. A rule of thumb: the careful breeder will screen you carefully as a potential owner.

SPAYING AND NEUTERING

Dogs and cats that are not purebreds destined for a show career should be spayed or neutered at about six months for health and behavioral benefits. This is the standard wisdom of numerous national and local humane societies, vets and pet publications. Sterilizing reduces the risks of breast and uterine cancer for a female pet and testicular cancer in males. Equally important: You're not contributing to the pet overpopulation problem.

FLEAS AND TICKS

In areas where fleas are a problem, owners must treat their homes as well as their pets with flea-control powders and sprays. Those containing insect growth regulators (methoprene or hydroprene, for example) are considered effective indoors; pyrethrin products are among those considered effective on the pet.

Take care to reach under furniture and on baseboards, where fleas hatch.

A nontoxic alternative for carpeted areas: Sprinkle a powdered desiccant such as diatomaceous earth (you will find it at nurseries or garden centers) on carpets and under furniture. Vacuum, and wash pets' bedding frequently.

In regions where ticks are common, owners must check dogs after each outdoor outing to be sure they have not picked up ticks. Owners must run their hands over a shorthaired dog or comb

What Can Your Dog Expect from You?

Many factors go into the selection of a dog. First ask yourself what kind of dog will fit with your lifestyle. Consider four important points: how much you can afford to spend on a dog; where you live; whether you have children; and how much time you will devote to your pet. If you have reserved a small sum for the purchase of a dog, it might be wise to choose a random-bred shelter dog or one of the less expensive purebreds. Keep in mind that dogs are generally priced according to rarity and popularity. Remember, too, that the purchase price of a dog is just the initial outlay; you must be willing and able to pay for veterinary bills, dog food and many miscellaneous items for the life of your dog.

Where you live will determine the amount and kind of exercise you can give your dog. Is your home in the city, the suburbs or the country? Do you divide your time between two residences? Do you have a fenced-in yard or live in a fifth-floor walkup? Dogs that can be paper trained—such as any

of the toys, or even some small breeds like the dachshund—might be a good choice for owners who are away for much of the day or do not care to walk their dogs late at night. If you live in the country, you can more easily give a proper home to one of the larger sporting dogs, such as the Irish setter or the pointer, or a working dog, like a Great Dane or mastiff, all of which require a prodigious amount of real exercise.

Do you have children, or are you planning to have children? If so, you should rule out selecting many of the miniature or toy breeds. These dogs are generally not pleased with the rough-and-tumble play of children. But many other, more robust, breeds—including the retrievers and terriers—thrive on the activity that living with children provides.

Large dogs—especially working dogs—were bred to protect their owners' property. These animals are powerful and intelligent, but they need firm training and a great deal of exercise. Their natural instincts can be a liability if they are not given proper direction. To live in harmony with such a dog, an owner must be assertive, confident and experienced. On the other hand,

small breeds often make excellent watchdogs—possibly even the best watchdogs of all.

Dogs with a full coat, such as the English sheepdog, require extensive grooming to maintain their appearance. Double-coated dogs, such as the Siberian husky, Rough Collie, and chow chow, shed far more than other breeds; this factor must be taken into consideration if you want to love your dog as much in April as you did in December. Shedding can be a constant annoyance, and there has been more than one dog banned from the house because of its unmanageable coat. But no dog grows its long, thick coat as a surprise. There is no excuse for being unprepared for the length of a dog's coat, or for being unwilling to spend time maintaining it. If someone in your family has allergies, it would be wise to choose a breed that does not shed, such as the poodle or schnauzer. (It is dog dander, rather than dog hair, that causes allergies; only shed hair has dander.)

From *Harper's Illustrated Handbook of Dogs, Health Care Section* by Robert W. Kirk, DVM, edited by Roger Caras. Published 1985 by HarperPerennial, A Division of HarperCollins Publishers.

through a longhaired dog to be sure they have not picked up ticks. Remove the tick with a pair of tweezers. Always wash your hands with soap and water after removing ticks.

FOOD

Except for the cheapest generic brands, all commercial dog and cat foods offer complete nutrition without harming pets' health. Premium foods have the advantage of producing fewer and more compact stools. Dogs do not require a variety of foods or flavors. Obese dogs suffer health problems, so feed only the amount suggested on the dog food label, and keep treats to a minimum.

GROOMING

Dogs may be bathed as often as once a week if they become soiled or have picked up fleas. Otherwise, bathing frequency depends on the breed; those with curly or thick coats, such as poodles, may need daily brushing and monthly bathing; smooth-coated dogs, such as the beagle, may be bathed only when necessary. Use a dog shampoo or an alkaline human shampoo; do not use other liquid soaps without first consulting your veterinarian.

Brush longhaired breeds such as the Maltese every other day to prevent mats. Check dogs' ears weekly; they may need cleaning about once a month. Put a small amount of mineral oil or a commercial pet ear cleaner on cloth to clean the outer folds of the ear; do not enter ear passages. Check toenails every two weeks and trim them if necessary. Some shorthaired dogs shed more than longhaired breeds and their sharp hairs can be harder to clean off furniture. The amount of shedding rather than fur length determines how much a dog aggravates allergies.

If a dog scoots its bottom along the ground, it may need to have its anal sacs emptied; this can be done at the vet's office or by a skilled groomer.

Giving medication

HOUSEBREAKING

Give your dog a chance to eliminate first thing in the morning, after each meal and just before bedtime. Look for signs that your dog has to go—he may sniff the ground or other likely targets or walk around in circles.

Scold your pet if you catch it in the act; then take it to the proper spot immediately. Verbally praise the pet with great enthusiasm when it goes in the proper spot.

"Accidents" should be cleaned up with a white-vinegar solution or a commercial odor neutralizer (available in pet shops or janitorial supply stores). Do not use ammonia or products that contain ammonia—the odor reminds

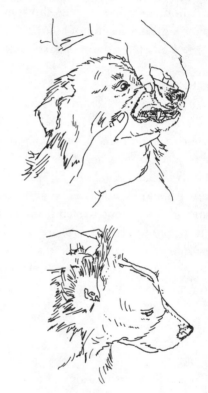

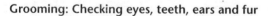

Grooming: Checking eyes, teeth, ears and fur

Training your dog

dogs of urine and may encourage them to use the same spot again.

Many trainers recommend crates to housebreak puppies or adult dogs. During training, the dog stays in the crate except when it's time to go outside or on paper inside to eliminate. The principle: a dog will not soil its own den. "Wire crates provide more air circulation; plastic pet traveling crates offer a greater feeling of security," says *Dogs USA* editor Connie Jankowski.

KENNELS

When choosing a kennel to board your dog, arrange to visit it a week before your vacation date. A kennel should be free of odor, flies and fleas and should be disinfected regularly. Sleeping quarters should be clean, dry and roomy enough for the dog to stand, stretch and turn around. Exercise space and time should be provided. To find a kennel in your area, ask your vet or friends for a recommendation, or look in the Yellow Pages, where they will be listed under "Dog Kennels."

HOME DECORATING

To avoid the frustrations of a pet-worn home, choose furniture, flooring and drapes that can withstand staining and snagging.

•Choose fabrics with a tight weave that a pet can't hook its claws into.

•Decor should be in a midrange of colors—not too dark, not too light. Choose patterns that help disguise pet hair, such as tweed types or other nubby textures that include a mixture of colors.

•To slow the constant wear from a pet's sofa snoozes, have extra cushion covers made to fit like a fitted sheet. Or cover one area with an afghan or towel and train the pet to sleep there.

HOLIDAY HAZARDS

Halloween trick or treaters and July Fourth fireworks can frighten dogs into running away, biting or destructive behavior. During loud, confusing times, confine dogs in a quiet closed room or garage.

To avoid Christmas dangers:

•Keep holiday candy out of reach. Chocolate is the third major cause of dog poisoning: overconsumption can kill a dog, according to the National Animal Poison Control Center.

•Cut off access to the Christmas tree. Place ornaments out of the dog's reach and secure the extra wire ties.

•Poinsettia is not as dangerous as once reputed—just irritating. Mistletoe, however, can be fatal if a pet eats as few as three berries or leaves.

OTHER HAZARDS

To keep dogs away from household cleaners, try baby-safe latches on cabinets. Rodent poisons, snail baits and antifreeze are common poisons consumed by dogs. So are some types of medicine: Never give a dog or other pet human medications without consulting your vet.

If you suspect poisoning, bring the product container to your vet to assist the diagnosis. Be cautious when using flea and tick killers; contact a vet if you see slobbering, tremors or depression after treatment with an insecticide.

Cats

Cats are popular with apartment dwellers but also like to roam outside, catching, killing and eating small rodents and occasional birds. Cats are beloved for their soft fur and their soothing purr when contented.

CHOOSING A CAT

First, decide if you want a purebred or a mixed breed. If you buy a purebred, choose your breeder carefully; ask for recommendations from a breeder's club, for example. Ask a breeder what steps he or she takes to make sure the kittens are free of genetic problems.

If you choose a mixed breed, whether at an animal shelter or from a neighbor or friend, be sure a kitten is at least eight weeks old before you take it from its mother. It should be alert and free of signs of illness, such as runny eyes. A kitten that has been handled frequently is more likely to be confident and affectionate with people. You might also consider adopting one of the many affectionate, attractive adult cats available at shelters.

HEALTH PROBLEMS

Feline Leukemia. Feline leukemia afflicts as many as 5 percent of the nation's cats, and about a third develop symptoms and can die within six months. The disease is easily transmitted between cats by licking, biting and

What Is Your Ideal Cat?

Think carefully about your lifestyle before choosing a pet. Sit down and list the qualities that your ideal pet would have. Then look for that ideal pet. In general, if you want an active cat, think in terms of a shorthair; if your ideal is a quiet, well-mannered cat, consider the longhairs.

For an elderly person, the gentle presence of a Persian or Himalayan might be far preferable to the noisy activity of a Siamese. A retired person might find the required daily grooming a pleasant way to pass the time. On the other hand, a busy, career-oriented couple probably would not want a cat that requires much extra care, and might do well with an independent, easygoing breed like the American Shorthair rather than a demanding cat like the Burmese, which may resent being left alone.

A family with young children should avoid a cat that is either high-strung or shy. A high-strung cat might strike out at the children during rough play; a shy cat might spend its time hiding under the bed, much to the children's frustration. Look for a calm, bold, friendly animal. If possible, let the children interact with it before you bring it home to see whether they like one another.

Older children can have marvelous fun with a smart, lively cat such as a Siamese, Abyssinian or Somali; people say they can teach these cats to walk on a leash and shake hands. A homebound single person probably would enjoy a sensitive, eager-to-please cat such as the curly-coated Cornish Rex or the tailless Manx, both of which would become extremely devoted to their owners. Those who entertain often might want an elegant, exotic cat they can proudly present to their friends. Many of the rarer breeds fit this description, including the svelte Oriental Shorthair, which resembles the Siamese yet comes in a wide array of stunning colors.

A final note about lifestyle: If you are away from home a great deal yet want a cat, why not consider getting two? That way the cats will have each other for companionship and are less likely to become destructive out of sheer boredom. Whatever type of cat you select, you will discover that given the care and love it needs, a cat can make a wonderful pet and devoted companion.

From *Harper's Illustrated Handbook of Cats, Health Care Section* by Robert W. Kirk, DVM, edited by Roger Caras. Published 1985 by HarperPerennial, A Division of HarperCollins Publishers.

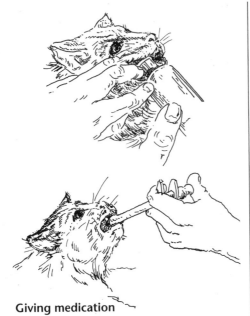

Giving medication

Grooming

even sneezing. Be sure to have your cat vaccinated as part of its regular one-year checkup.

Obesity. Obesity is a common health problem for cats, particularly indoor cats. Cats show obesity in their stomachs, first noticeable when the skin starts to hang down in the groin area. Owners may reduce the amount of food their cats eat, or a vet may recommend a prescription food. To encourage a cat to exercise more, try a fishing-pole type cat exercise toy, sold at pet stores.

GROOMING

Longhaired cats must be groomed daily to avoid mats and help prevent hairballs. Small wire slicker brushes (sold at pet stores) may be used on shorthaired cats, but a grooming comb is needed for a longhaired cat. With proper grooming, many cats never need a bath. They may need a bath as part of a flea treatment or if soiled by diarrhea or sticky dirt.

Cats should have their claws trimmed regularly. A toenail clipper designed for humans works fine. Press on the pad beneath the claw to make the claw extend; clip off only the claw's sharp tip.

PREVENTING DAMAGE TO FURNISHINGS

Cats need to scratch off the dead, outer layer of their claws. To accommodate them, owners should put out scratching posts—one more than the number of cats in the household. Rub the post with catnip and tie toys to the top to entice the cat to use it. Cats prefer a rough, sisal-type material. If the post is carpeted, try dragging a slicker brush through the nap to break it in for the cat. Avoid quilted bed covers, which cats can destroy with their claws.

Never hit a cat. If they scratch furnishings, try deterrents such as spraying the cats with a water pistol or squirt bottle filled with plain water.

TREATING LITTER BOX PROBLEMS

When a cat stops using its litter box, have the cat examined for a medical problem such as a urinary tract infection. If your cat has a medical problem, have it treated, then clean all the areas the cat has soiled with a commercial odor neutralizer.

If the cat is spraying for territorial reasons, owners will find evidence on vertical surfaces such as curtains, walls or stereo speakers. The problem could be anything from someone new in the house to a cat outside.

If the cat is squatting and urinating, the evidence will be on the horizontal surfaces. The problem: usually the litter box setup.

Possible solutions: Clean the box more frequently with a mild chlorine bleach solution (one part bleach to 20 parts water); do not use harsh-smelling chemical cleaners. Be sure you have at least one litter box for each cat in the house; or find a litter with a different texture or odor.

SAFETY CONSIDERATIONS

Never use a grooming or other product formulated for dogs on a cat. Don't let your cat play with strings, tinsel or other playthings that he could swallow. Some household plants, including many ivies, asparagus ferns and philodendron, are toxic; don't let your cat eat them. You can satisfy a cat's urge to nibble on green things by planting a pot of grass and keeping it by your cat's food dishes.

Apartment dwellers should set up a protective barrier along patios or open windows to prevent their cats from jumping or falling out.

If you do not want your cat to attack birds, tie three bells on its collar and keep it inside mornings and evenings when birds are most active.

MOVING

Cats are creatures of habit who can be made tense by changes such as a new pet, a new baby, a stranger in the house or moving. When you move:

•Keep the cat indoors at least two weeks before allowing it to roam the new neighborhood.

•Give the cat a name tag with the new phone number and address.

•Try to set things up as much like the old house as possible, with familiar bowls and blankets.

•Don't punish the cat if he forgets to use the litter box, scratches the furniture or acts aggressively. He should calm down within a few weeks.

Birds

CHOOSING A BIRD

Pet birds vary widely in everything from size, color and speaking ability to rarity and price. Before buying a bird as a pet, educate yourself by reading books and magazines and try to attend local bird club meetings and bird shows.

Beginners should consider getting a small bird that is easy to care for. Parakeets, cockatiels, lovebirds and conures are often recommended as a "first bird" because they are relatively inexpensive and have the ability to speak. With larger birds, consider such factors as noise; macaws, for example, can be considerably more raucous than African gray parrots.

Whatever bird you decide to buy, deal only with reputable breeders, pet stores or specialty bird stores.

BEHAVIOR TIPS

Do not set up a parrot's perch higher than your own head, because in the wild, a high perch symbolizes power.

Most parrots scream in the morning or when you get home from work, just as they scream in the jungle when their mates go foraging. Say hello straight away and give it food.

Birds respond to affection. Praise them. If you are starting with a baby, handle it gently and often. Stroke the bird all over with two fingers.

TALKING BIRDS

African gray and Amazon parrots are considered the best talkers, followed by macaws, cockatiels, mynas and some smaller parrots.

No matter what the breed, though, some birds never learn to talk. Choose a bird that appears alert and interested in is surroundings.

Young birds, especially hand-raised ones, are more likely to talk than older birds. For smaller breeds, begin training at four to six months; with larger breeds, begin training between 6 and 12 months.

One bird is easier to teach than two, because the two birds are more likely to talk to each other than to pick up your language.

Shower the bird with attention, starting slowly with timid birds. Birds that feel comfortable around you are more likely to talk. Training may be more difficult if you first teach your bird to whistle.

FEEDING

Many owners malnourish their pets by providing only bird seed, but seed should comprise at most 20 percent of a bird's diet. The other 80 percent should consist of a combination of proteins such as cheese or cooked lean meat; fresh fruits and vegetables; and carbohydrates such as dry cereals, uncooked oatmeal and granola. Most birds require a dietary supplement such as a powdered vitamin marketed specifically for birds as well. Never feed avocado, raw milk or chocolate to birds.

HEALTH CARE

Because birds tend to hide symptoms of illness, owners should be aware of their bird's appetite and behavior when healthy, and consult an avian vet quickly when they notice changes. Look for symptoms such as discharge from eyes or nostrils; closing eyes; droopy wings; inactivity or sneezing.

Clean perches frequently with soap and water and sandpaper. Cage bottoms should be changed daily and cages completely scrubbed at least once a month with products available at pet stores.

Many bird experts recommend that pet birds, particularly larger birds, have

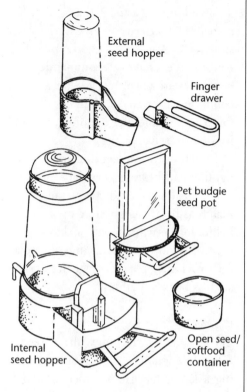

External
seed hopper

Finger
drawer

Pet budgie
seed pot

Internal
seed hopper

Open seed/
softfood
container

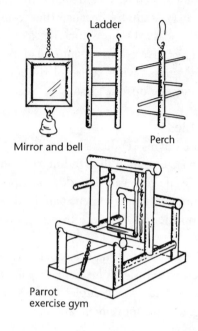

Ladder

Mirror and bell

Perch

Parrot
exercise gym

Feeders

both wings clipped by a vet. Nails need periodic trimming.

Feather picking, in which a bird pulls out its own feathers with its beak, is a common problem caused by medical problems or stress. Have the bird examined and try to relieve stress; move the bird's cage to a quieter spot, for example. Offer bird toys (available at pet stores) to prevent boredom.

HOUSEHOLD HAZARDS

Pet birds should only be allowed free when the owner is present. Exploring birds may chew items containing lead, such as costume jewelry, wine bottle wrappings or drapery weights. They can

Keep your bird entertained

also poison or injure themselves chewing plants, electrical cords or carpet.

Be careful when using Teflon-coated pans. If they burn or overheat, the fume can quickly harm or kill a bird. Cigarette or other smoke can cause illness.

CAGE LOCATION

Birds need sunlight, but must have an area of shade to avoid becoming too warm. Don't put a bird in front of a glass window during hot weather; the glass acts like a magnifying glass and birds can't stand the heat. Mild drafts are not especially harmful to healthy birds, but birds should be kept away from air conditioners, heating and ventilation outflows.

Sometime birds accidentally fly into sliding glass doors because they don't see the glass. Options include keeping windows covered, using antique glass, a heavy glass with a rippled effect, appliques or opaque glass.

Reptiles

Before buying reptiles such as snakes or iguanas, consider their adult size and decide if you can handle the space requirements and expense of feeding. Set up their cage before bringing them home.

Possible signs that a snake is ill include a refusal to feed, regurgitation, abnormal feces, incomplete skin shedding, erratic movement and abnormal behavior.

Children should never be left alone with constricting snakes, regardless how apparently docile the snake may seem.

CHOOSING A SNAKE

To avoid buying a snake that is ill or has parasites, it is crucial to choose a pet store or breeder with a good reputation. Among the snakes recommended for beginners are corn, rat, gopher and the common garter snake. The corn snake, for example, tolerates handling well and is not aggressive.

In setting up a cage for any reptile, lighting and heating—crucial to the animal's health—should be arranged to match as nearly as possible the animal's habits in the wild. Small snakes can be kept in small glass terrariums, but plan on providing a larger cage for snakes such as boas or pythons.

IGUANAS

Set up a glass terrarium with a screened top as the iguana's cage. Consider buying a larger terrarium to accommodate the iguana's growth to as long as six or seven feet.

Reptiles and fish as pet choices: Clockwise: snake, iguana, lizard and frog

Heating lights should be set outside the cage to avoid thermal burns.

When first taken home, iguanas are reluctant to eat. Try tempting them with brightly colored fruit such as papaya, guava, tomatoes, grapes or melon; or try edible flowers like hibiscus, dandelion, geranium, carnations or roses.

TURTLES AND TORTOISES

To keep a turtle or tortoise healthy, owners must duplicate the creature's original habitat, whether tropical, desert or aquatic. Proper diet and temperature are the most crucial elements for a healthy pet. A poor diet can cause eye infections, respiratory and other ailments.

Depending on breed, a turtle or tortoise diet can include anything from fruits and vegetables to a dog chow.

Fish

Partly clean a fish tank once a week by siphoning off about 20 percent of the water and bottom debris. Clean tank completely once a month.

Do not overfeed fish. Overfeeding can create too much organic material in the tank, which creates deadly levels of ammonia.

Protect a new fish from the shock of rapid temperature change, Place the fish, still in its own water bag, in the tank until the bagged water reaches the same temperature as the tank water.

Saltwater or reef fish can be both more expensive and more complicated to keep than freshwater fish. Many require extremely specialized diets. They also take longer to adapt to their new tanks. Among good choices of saltwater fish for beginners are damsel fish, trigger fish, lion fish and cardinal fish. For more information, consult some of the excellent aquarium publications, such as *Aquarium Fish* magazine.

Small Pets

Small pets include rodents such as rabbits, hamsters and guinea pigs, which are often chosen as a child's first pet. However, some hamsters have a fierce temperament not suitable to children. Whatever pet you choose, your child should be carefully supervised at first and taught to handle the animal gently.

The best place to buy a small pet is at a reputable pet store or by contacting local breeders through pet clubs.

General tips: Do not line cages with cedar shavings, which can emit toxic fumes when wet. Keep food in an airtight container to avoid staleness. Keep bowls clean and provide a constant supply of clean, fresh water.

Reptiles and fish as pet choices: Turtle

RABBITS

Rabbits are more sociable and intelligent than their reputation suggests and many rabbit lovers believe that they should be kept in the house rather than in a backyard hutch. Some considerations:

•Rabbits chew electrical, telephone, computer and other cables, so cover the cables with plastic tubing from the hardware store. Also, never give your rabbit amoxycillin; this antibiotic prescribed for humans, dogs and cats is deadly to rabbits. Be sure your rabbit is safe at all times from strange or stray dogs, which could attack or kill your pet.

•Feed your rabbit a handful of alfalfa hay daily to prevent hairballs. Avoid sugar treats.

•Trim a rabbit's nails every six to eight weeks. Ask your vet to do it or do it yourself; use a nail clipper and trim just before the point where the blood vessel is visible within the nail.

•Keep a longhaired rabbit's hair trimmed to an inch or less.

•Rabbits like to play with simple toys, such as a toilet paper roll, a rolled-oats box with ends cut off, a wire ball with bell inside (made for cats) or straw baskets.

HAMSTERS

Hamsters are nocturnal animals that should not be startled or handled roughly. Some have a temperament unsuited to small children.

Hamsters can eat boxed, processed hamster food or food made for laboratory rats, available in bags or in bulk at some pet and feed stores. Otherwise, feed them a balanced diet of whole-grain breads, dry, whole-grain cereals such as rolled oats and even uncooked pasta, supplemented by fruits and vegetables.

Hamsters sometimes stop eating if their teeth become overgrown. Owners should provide balsa wood, available at pet stores or feed stores, so hamsters can wear their teeth down. Hamsters should be housed one per cage.

Small pet choices: Rabbits or guinea pigs

GUINEA PIGS

Guinea pigs have small, thin feet, so choose a cage with a solid, not a wire, floor.

Because they need a special diet—18 percent protein and 125 milligrams of vitamin C daily—guinea pigs need food pellets designed especially for them, not the type for rabbits. The safest treats are lettuce or fresh fruit. Do not feed them unshelled sunflower seeds or dried fruits, as this might cause them to choke.

RATS AND MICE

Fairly easy to care for, rats and mice require a gnaw-proof cage, terrarium or screen-topped aquarium that is kept away from direct sun or drafts. Also provide sleeping boxes, made from nontoxic household containers such as jars or oatmeal cartons, an exercise wheel and a wooden gnawing block to hone teeth. Pine shavings can be used for bedding.

Laboratory pellets and a grain mixture, available at pet shops, make the best diet, complemented by greens, fresh fruit and vegetables and whole-wheat bread.

GERBILS

Gerbils are amiable and make excellent pets for children. They are very active, much more so than hamsters, and enjoy a running wheel and chewing anything made of cardboard, especially toilet paper rolls, which they can demolish in a few minutes. They are sociable and can be housed together.

A red discharge from a gerbil's eye is often normal, but check the cage if you see a bloody nose. Gerbils should not have a cage with sharp edges they might push their noses against.

Horses

CHOOSING A HORSE

Though many beginners want their first horse to be a young one, horse experts say it is safer to begin with a horse that's at least nine years old: A mature horse is more likely to tolerate mistakes in handling, such as jerking motions or yanking on the headstall or bit. Before buying a horse, have a veterinarian examine him to be assured there is no chronic lameness or other health problems. In some cases, you may be able to lease the horse for a period in order to get to know it before you decide to buy.

PROPER FACILITIES

Stables should have a good source of natural light, by skylight or window. Stalls should be draft free but offer good ventilation. To prevent boredom and the resulting bad habits, such as chewing equipment left within reach or kicking the stall, the horse should have a good view of the stable and of other horses.

Cuts and abrasions are a frequent problem, and horses are prone to hurt themselves, so be aware of any loose bars, wires or other potential dangers in the stable.

BEDDING

Good choices are dry oat, wheat or barley straw. If you use sawdust, which has a deodorizing effect, you must clean the stable more often. Not only will damp sawdust clog drains, it can also ball up in a horse's feet and is unhealthy for the hooves. Stalls should be cleaned at least daily to avoid health hazards such as allergic reactions, hoof infections or cracking and, in winter, slipping on the wet surface.

FEEDING

A horse needs a supply of fresh water at all times. Small amounts of food given frequently are preferable to one or two large amounts a day. In establishing a new diet, allow the horse to adjust by making changes gradually. Don't give large amounts of grain or fresh grass as a treat if your horse isn't used to it.

HEALTH

For healthy hooves, keep the stable clean and dry and clean hooves daily. Have the farrier (horse shoer) trim the hooves every four to six weeks, more often for growing horses.

Horses should be dewormed at least every two months and vaccinated twice a year by a vet; at minimum, they must be vaccinated for tetanus.

Horses' teeth should be checked at least annually; they can grow too long and cause digestive problems.

A horse's mental and physical well-

Exercise your horse regularly   **Check your horse's teeth annually**

being depends on adequate exercise—at least an hour a day. Don't exercise your horse more than he's used to on weekends if he's not kept in shape during the week.

Call your vet if you notice signs of illness such as loss of appetite; lethargy or agitation; runny nose or eyes; rough, dull coat, or other changes in the horse's appearance and demeanor.

Finding a Good Vet

New puppies, kittens and other animals should be examined by a vet who will check the animal's health and vaccinate it if necessary.

Older animals should be seen at least once a year, and when they show any symptoms of illness or sudden behavioral problems that could be linked to a medical condition.

Tap a network to help you find the best vet.

Ask friends, co-workers and neighbors who their vets are. Ask if they are happy with their pet's treatment; inquire about the vet's willingness to explain procedures and the attitude of the vet's staff.

Contact experts in your area—dog or cat breeders, for example, or members of the local snake or bird club. Such enthusiasts are familiar with the vets most qualified to treat your animal, and are usually happy to help with referrals.

If you have moved and left behind a trusted vet, ask him or her for a recommendation.

To screen your new vet:
Check with the regional veterinary association. They can tell you if a vet is a member and has already been screened, and where he or she went to school.

Before scheduling an appointment, call and ask what the vet's policies are on matters of concern to you.

Be sure the vet is familiar with your type of animal. Some small-animal vets are interested in dogs primarily. Increasingly, owners can find vets that specialize in only cats, or only in more exotic species.

As with any doctor, you should feel comfortable with your vet and with the cleanliness of the office. You should feel free to ask questions about your pet's health. Your vet should not add treatments or vaccinations to your bill without consulting you.

If the vet you're comfortable with is some distance from you, be willing to drive, but find out if there is a 24-hour veterinary emergency clinic near you.

How about a ferret?

Exotic Pets

Whether your favorite exotic animal is a pot-bellied pig or a piranha, you'll need to do more research and groundwork than for old Rover. Some considerations:

Is it legal? Check city, county and state laws. Laws on keeping pets such as monkeys, pot-bellied pigs, miniature horses, wildcats, large snakes, ferrets and other animals vary, usually because of health, safety or zoning regulations.

Care and feeding: Dog and cat owners can confidently buy fully balanced pet foods at the supermarket. But exotic pets often receive imbalanced diets that can result in serious illness, because owners either do not know about or cannot find suitable nutrition.

Do not rely on advice from a pet store. Consult vets, specialty magazines and local hobbyists for advice. Clubs can provide invaluable resources and advice on care, feeding and housing.

Gardening

A well-planned yard featuring a flower or vegetable garden will benefit your household in many ways. Landscaping can add considerable value to your property and the garden provides food and flowers for a fraction of the price of buying them at the store—not to mention gorgeous seasonal displays of color.

The National Garden Bureau (NGB) recommends that beginning gardeners should:

•Start small, with a plot no larger than 10 by 10 feet.

•Raise a few varieties of easy-to-grow vegetables or flowers that can be grown from seed in the garden, rather than begun indoors as seedlings.

•Locate the garden near a water source.

•Select a garden site based on the light requirements of the plants that will be grown. Most flowers and vegetables need a very sunny spot.

The American Association of Nurserymen (AAN) recommends that you keep the following garden tools on hand: rake, spade, watering can, hose, leak-free sprinkler, wheelbarrow and gloves. Handy extras include trowels, a hoe, pruning shears, pruning saw, lopping shears and bulb planter.

PREPARING A BED

According to the NGB, you can prepare a garden bed for planting at any time of year. But fall is the recommended time, even if you will be sowing seeds in spring, because the sooner you begin enriching the soil, the better off it will be by planting season. Here are the suggested steps:

•Determine what type of soil you have (clay, loam, or sand) with this simple test: Moisten a bit of soil, take a handful and rub a bit between your thumb and forefinger, attempting to form a "snake." If the soil doesn't clump together at all, it's fairly sandy. If you can make a little snake, it's loamy (ideal for planting). If the snake is fairly long, the soil has a high clay content.

Clay soil tends to hold too much water and is too soggy. In this case, add sand or a combination of peat moss and sand to improve the texture. Water passes too quickly through **sandy soil**; you will need to add peat moss or organic matter (such as compost) to retain water.

•If the snake test proves inconclusive, try this drainage test: Dig a hole in your garden bed with a flat bottom about a foot wide by a few inches deep. Fill it with water. Ideally, the hole should drain in six to eight hours. If the water runs out in two or three hours, you probably have a sandy soil. If so, add peat moss or organic matter as above. If it takes longer than 10 hours, there's too much clay, and deep planting holes with drainage tiles at the bottom are recommended.

•Test the soil for nutrient content with a soil-test kit. Your local county extension agent (check your phone book's blue pages under "County Government") can tell you where to go for such a test and how much it will cost, and provide tips on how to interpret the results. Most plants thrive in slightly acid to neutral soils (ph 6.0 to 7.0). Soils in moist climates are generally acid, while those in dry climates tend to be alkaline.

•The NGB recommends regularly using a combination of organic and inorganic fertilizers to provide the soil's most important nutrients: nitrogen, phosphorous and potassium. Go to your local garden shop or nursery to obtain the appropriate nutrients. Based on your soil tests for drainage and nutrients, add materials to soil using a hoe or spade.

•At the same time, thoroughly turn over the soil and loosen clumps with the hoe or spade. Avoid working the earth when very moist. If you can squeeze water out of a handful of soil, it's too wet. Wait until it dries somewhat.

SOWING SEEDS

The NGB recommends these four easy steps for planting seeds:

•Dig a straight furrow with a hoe parallel to one edge of the bed.

•Sprinkle the seeds from the packet. A good rule of thumb is to plant small seeds by tossing handfuls into the furrow. Plant large seeds in groups of two in the bottom of the furrow, spaced according to package directions.

•Lightly tap the soil back over the seeds with the back of the hoe to ensure seeds are held in soil. Follow with a gentle watering, and continue to maintain a moist soil until seeds germinate, after which you should follow the instructions under "Maintaining the Garden" (below).

•After they have sprouted, thin seedlings to correct spacing, as indicated on seed package.

MAINTAINING THE GARDEN

To keep your garden in top form, keep the following points in mind.

•The average garden generally needs between 1/2 and 1 1/2 inches of water weekly. Both the AAN and NGB recommend less frequent but thorough watering during morning or late-afternoon hours. To determine if your garden or yard needs watering, check the soil at six inches—it should be moist. If so, it doesn't need watering.

•Weed regularly, as these unwanted plants compete with cultivated types for water. It's best to eradicate weeds while they're young and easy to pull out. The task is considerably easier after a rainfall.

•Mulch to control weeds, conserve water and maintain an even soil temperature, which protects plants during weather extremes. Use organic mulches such as straw, peat moss and compost or inorganic mulches such as black plastic and aluminum foil.

FLOWERS

Annuals are plants that complete their life cycles within one growing season. Many annuals self-sow, but they usually need to be replanted every year—which gives the gardener the advantage of starting afresh each season. Biennials are flowers that require two seasons to complete their life cycles, though some bloom from seed their first year and are thus treated as annuals. Perennials reappear year after year and die back to dormant roots during the winter. Depending on where you live—and your hardiness zone—some perennials are treated like biennials and even annuals. For these reasons, the flowers recommended in this section may not all technically be annuals but will be treated as such. Flowers (and all plants) are also classified as hardy, half-hardy and tender, according to their ability to withstand cold. Half-hardy and tender annuals can be sown where they are to grow only after danger of frost is past.

To grow annuals, follow instructions as given under "Preparing a Bed." Plant in spring.

Perennials

Perennials respond well to both spring and fall planting, though most Northerners opt for spring because soil is easier to handle. To decide when to plant a particular perennial, check gardening catalogs to see when it's available or stop in at your local nursery.

When grown from seed, some perennials do not grow true to the characteristics of the parent plants, so the easiest way to raise them is by buying potted perennials from a garden center. To plant and maintain them, follow these steps:

•Water the ground thoroughly. Dig a hole a bit larger than the pot. Add compost to the hole to spur new plant growth.

•Turn over the pot and tap it lightly. If the root ball does not give easily, turn it right side up, insert a knife and work it gently around the edges, as if you're removing a cake from a pan. Then turn the pot over again and tap plant out.

•Set the root ball in the hole with its top just beneath the surface of the soil. It should be a neat fit, so you do not have to add additional soil.

•Water immediately. Add a little fertilizer if you wish. Continue watering daily for about two weeks; skip a day or two if it rains. After the plants are established, only water as much as specified under "Maintaining the Garden."

•In order to remain healthy throughout their long lifetimes, perennials need to be divided every two to four years. After several years' growth (conditions vary from plant to plant), if a perennial plant begins to spread and crowd out neighboring plants, or simply begins to look unhealthy (for example, if its leaves are undersized) it probably needs to be dug up and divided. Division rejuvenates the plant and is done before or after flowering. Most gardeners divide spring or summer bloomers in late summer to early fall and late bloomers the following spring. To divide, push two spading forks into the plant's crown and then pull the handles away from each other to detach the roots. Then pull the clump apart and replant young root stocks.

HERBS

An herb garden can be composed of mixed annual and perennial beds. The perennials—such as thyme, lavender, peppermint and rosemary—can go in first, followed by such easy-to-grow annuals as basil, parsley, dill and calendula (also known as "pot marigold") as filler, perhaps all arranged around a simple focal point such as a sun dial or shrub.

The following are important points to keep in mind:

•Most herbs thrive with at leave five hours of sun daily in a well-drained soil.

•Herbs that tolerate shade include monkshood, angelica, chervil, feverfew, foxglove, sorrel, mint and wintergreen.

•Especially if it is to be a culinary herb garden, locate your herb garden as close to the house as possible, so that when you're cooking you can easily run out and cut herbs.

•Don't treat herbs with conventional fertilizer—you don't want to produce luxurious, overly leafy plants, but vigorous, compact plants, rich in essential oils. Instead, in late winter or early spring apply garden compost, manure, wood ashes or medium-grade bonemeal.

•Harvest leaves and flowers in the morning just after the dew has evaporated from the plants. Flowers should be harvested just at the point when they are beginning to open.

VEGETABLES

Prepare your vegetable garden as described under "Preparing a Bed" and keep these particulars in mind as you proceed:

•Pay special attention to the results of the soil test, especially if the garden is near a driveway, road or in a new development where previous land use is a mystery. Heavy metals, such as lead, could lurk in the soil and contaminate your vegetable plants.

•Vegetable gardens need at least six hours of direct, unfiltered sunlight. Plant tall varieties where they will not shade smaller crops.

•The NGB recommends growing such high-yielding and easy-to-grow varieties as lettuce, summer squash and carrots. Other best bets are cabbage, beans, tomatoes and radishes. Maximize the space by training pole beans, peas and vine crops (cucumbers, squash and melons) on trellises.

•Rotate the vegetable garden each year. Different vegetables take diverse nutrients from the soil at varying depths and rotation enables them to draw on varying nutrient reserves.

Easy-Care Annuals

The following annuals are especially easy to grow and provide a range of garden color.

Amaranthus caudatus (love lies bleeding): not fussy about soil; red

Calendula officinalis (calendula): long blooming season; self-sows; orange

Cleome spinosa (spider flower): self-sows; rosy violet

Centaurea cyanus (cornflower): needs little thinning; blue

Cosmos (cosmos): long blooming season; yellow disk with pink, red and white petals

Euphorbia marginata (snow-on-the-mountain): showy white flower bracts (lower part of flower)

Gomphrena globosa (globe amaranth): long blooming season; white, orange, red and pink

Impatiens balsamina (balsam): white, scarlet, salmon, yellow, purple

Lobularia maritima (sweet alyssum): long blooming season; self-sows; white, lilac

Nicotiana grandiflora (flowering tobacco): self-sows; white

Petunia hybrida (petunia): self-sows; long blooming season; white, pink, blue, red

Phlox drummondii (phlox): long blooming season; white, purple and range of other colors

Tagetes spp. (marigold): yellow, orange, red

Tropaeolum majus (nasturtium): long blooming season; self-sows; yellow, red

Verbena hortensis (verbena): long blooming season; white, yellow, pink, red

Zinnia angustifolia (zinnia); yellow, orange, red

• The United States Department of Agriculture recommends early spring planting for very hardy plants such as broccoli, cabbage, lettuce, onions, peas, potatoes, spinach and turnips. Plant them four to six weeks before the first frost-free date in your area (approximately two to three weeks after the last freeze, at just about the time that oak trees begin to leaf out).

• Less hardy plants (snap beans, okra, sweet corn and tomato) should be planted on or around the frost-free date.

• Summer planting is good for such heat-tolerant plants as beans (all types), chard, New Zealand spinach, squash and sweet corn.

• Vegetables for late summer or fall planting include beets, kale, collard, lettuce, mustard, spinach and turnips.

Bulbs Through the Seasons

Bulbs are a special type of perennial plant with modified budding structures and a longer dormancy period. They are among the most popular of the perennials and among the first plants to bloom in spring and the last to bloom in autumn.

Spring-blooming bulbs need winter chilling in order to bloom the following year, and should be planted in fall—anytime from September through December, as long as the garden soil isn't frozen and can still be worked. Daffodils, crocuses, tulips, hyacinths, Dutch iris and scilla are all spring bloomers.

Plant spring-blooming bulbs twice as deep as the bulb is long. In areas with severe winters, you could add about four inches of mulch on top for protection.

Summer-flowering bulbs are planted between the very last frost date and the end of May. Examples are gladioli, Persian buttercups, begonias, dahlias and summer hyacinth. With the exception of lilies, they are all frost sensitive and must be dug up and kept indoors in winter.

Plant summer-blooming bulbs at specific depths according to their needs, not based on the size of the bulb. Examples are the tuberous begonia, which should be covered with ½ to ¾ inch soil; the gladiolus, which is planted at 2 ¾ inches; and lilies, which should be planted at least 8 inches deep. Check with your local nursery for specifics.

The Netherlands Flower Bulb Information Center recommends that when purchasing bulbs, remember that the larger the bulb, the bigger the blossoms. Do not select soft, mushy, moldy or heavily bruised bulbs. Don't be alarmed, however, if a bulb's outer papery, onionlike skin is loose or torn. This doesn't damage the bulb and may actually speed root growth.

**Bulbs and
the heights of their flowers**

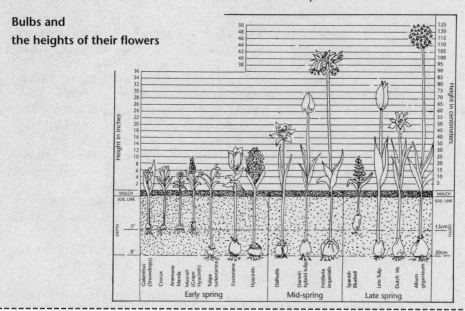

BASIC LANDSCAPING

To be visually pleasing and useful, your property should have some order to it. The following are the basic steps of successful landscaping:

•If you've recently moved to an already landscaped property, observe one growing season before making any changes and keep a notebook on flower blooming periods, autumn foliage and the like.

•Draw up a list of all the amenities you desire—such as gardens, paths, children's play area and pool—and then translate those ideas to paper, creating bubbles scaled to the relative size of different areas.

•When making plant selections, opt for a variety of shapes and sizes and visualize the entire landscape as a painting. The landscaper's general formula is to place trees and larger plants in the background, medium-size plants in the main yard area and smaller, decorative plants in the foreground near the house.

•Play up views by framing them with plants. You can also lead the eye to a view with a walkway.

•Draw the eye to different areas of the yard with focal points, such as specimen trees, sundials and fountains.

SUCCESSFUL LANDSCAPING STRATEGIES

Once you've established how your yard should generally look, carefully consider how to deal with potential problems before making plant purchases and undertaking the final design.

•For an easy-to-manage landscape, select disease-resistant, drought-tolerant plants,

says the AAN. Suggested plantings are hens and chickens (*Sempervivum*), dusty miller (*Artemisia stelleriana*), sun moss (*Portulaca grandiflora*), wallflower (*Cheiranthus cheiri*), sedums (*Sedum* species), hardy cacti (*Opuntia* species) and junipers (*Juniperus*).

•If you don't have time for weekly mowing, consider making your lawn smaller. Replace the edges with drought-tolerant shrubs, groundcover or flower beds, or create an area with naturalistic plantings that will attract wildlife. Among the United States Soil Conversation Service "wild" landscaping plant choices are "Roselow" sargent crabapple (*Malus sargenti*), "Midwest" Manchurian crabapple (*Malus baccata* var. *mandshurica*), elderberry (*Sambucus canadensis*), "Gobbler" sawtooth oak (*Quercus acutissima*) and flowering dogwood (*Cornus florida*).

•Hedges not only provide privacy but also act as windbreaks to shield more delicate garden plants. The Soil Conservation Service suggests such fast-growing evergreen hedge plants as Northern white cedar (*Thuja occidentalis*), mountain laurel (*Kalmia latifolia*), white pine (*Pinus strobus*) and hemlock (*Tsuga canadensis*).

•If the site is too flat (which can make it look smaller), create the illusion of spaciousness and changing levels by raising garden beds and framing them with bricks. Plantings around the background perimeter also create the illusion of depth.

•The Soil Conservation Service also recommends low-maintenance shrubs and vines for controlling erosion on hilly sites. Suggested plantings include periwinkle (*Vinca major*), pachysandra (*Pachysandra terminalis*), English ivy (*Hedera helix*), lily-turf (*Liriope spicata*) and Western swordfern (*Polystichum munitum*).

•For more complex problems, such as a poorly draining lawn or a very steep site, contact either the AAN or the American Society of Landscape Architects (ASLA) to get a professional designer's help. Before hiring a landscape architect, ask for references and photographs of previous jobs. Draw up a written agreement that details specifics, such as budget, schedule and date of completion.

PLANTING TREES AND SHRUBS

Trees are available at your garden center in three forms: container-grown, bare root and balled-and-burlapped (called B&B). There are advantages to planting trees in either spring or fall, depending on the type of plant. Bare-root trees have already been transplanted and therefore must be planted when dormant, preferably in spring before budbreak. With healthy container-grown and B&B trees, new roots will grow throughout the cool growing season until the soil temperature reaches 40[deg]F at the root zone. When you plant in the fall, therefore, the plant has more time to make roots in its new home before new shoot growth occurs. There are certain plants that do not respond well to fall planting, however, such as magnolias and the stone fruits, including cherries, peaches and apricots. So check with your local nurseryman.

The AAN outlines these simple steps for tree planting; additional recommendations are from the International Society of Arboriculture (ISA).

•Make sure your chosen tree grows in your hardiness zone.

•Check maximum height and spreading distance of tree so that it will not outgrow its planting space. If width information is unavailable for a particular species, the ISA recommends that you figure on planting the tree a distance of half its height from houses or other structures.

•The same considerations apply to shrubs. Space them half their spreading distance away from one another. Hedge shrubs growing to about four feet high should be spaced a foot and a half apart, while ones that are even taller will probably require distances of three or four feet between them.

•Your planting hole should be two to three times wider than, and about the same depth as, the root ball. Dig the planting hole deeply enough so that the plant is at, or slightly above, the same depth that it was in the nursery field. (You can tell what point this is by a stain on the trunk, indicating which part of the trunk was above the ground). If you dig it any deeper, the roots could suffocate.

As you dig your planting hole, leave a slight mound at the bottom. Container-grown and B&B plants should be set on top of the mound, while the roots of bare-root plants should be spread around the mound. When planting a bare-root tree, gently place the roots in the hole and be sure not to twist or tangle them in your planting site. When planting a B&B tree, if it is encased in real (cloth) burlap, leave the cloth in place; if the "burlap" is plastic, gently remove it at this time.

•The ISA suggests pruning sparingly at this point, cutting off broken roots just

Landscaping Pays Off

According to statistics compiled by the American Association of Nurserymen (AAN):

Landscaping adds between 7 and 14 percent to a home's value and can speed a home's sale by an average of five to six weeks.

Plants control runoff, slow erosion and allow water to be absorbed by the soil.

Fully grown trees are often appraised at $1,000 to $10,000 apiece.

Trees muffle street noise by as much as 50 percent. A full acre of trees removes about 13 tons of dust and potentially harmful gases from the air each year, while releasing oxygen.

Landscaping can reduce air-conditioning costs by up to 50 percent. Furthermore, the Environmental Protection Agency (EPA) has concluded that simply shading an air conditioner with trees or shrubs can save up to 10 percent in annual costs. The EPA recommends planting deciduous trees on the west-facing side of your house and conifers on the east-facing side. The result is cooling shade in summertime and insulating warmth in winter.

before the break and pruning any broken branches on the tree.

•Gently refill the hole with soil, firming down the soil as you go—but not stamping down with your feet. Remove any burlap that's still visible; for container trees, break off the rim of the plastic container that is showing.

•Water the tree. The ISA recommends keeping the soil moist, but not too damp, by watering once a week or more depending on rainfall. You'll know it's time to water when the soil is dry four inches below the surface. Around mid-fall, slowly taper off your watering schedule, resuming in spring.

•Fertilize in the fall if you wish, but only with fertilizers containing phosphorous and potassium, and only a small amount of nitrogen. The ISA strongly warns against applying a high-nitrogen fertilizer at planting time, as it could burn the roots.

•The ISA recommends mulching with organic matter (leaf litter, pine straw, shredded bark and twigs, peat moss and wood chips) at the base of the tree at this time, creating a two- to four-inch layer to protect roots through the winter.

Lawns

For a great-looking lawn that won't demand constant maintenance, follow these simple tips from the Professional Lawn Care Association of America (PLCAA).

GRASS CHOICE
The most low-maintenance seed mixtures tend to be of fescue, bluegrass and perennial ryegrass. They are generally resistant to disease and drought and can tolerate shade. Consult with your local garden center for the grass mixes that thrive in your area.

SEED VS. SOD

The decision to grow from sod or seed is largely a budgetary one. It's cheaper to go with seed, but with sod the results are quicker. Also, newly planted seed washes away easily from hilly areas; therefore, steep sites are better off sodded.

Seeding: You can plant seed in spring after danger of frost has passed or in fall, generally around mid-September. Because grass seed is so fine, it's best to plant on a day without wind following these steps:

•Correct soil problems with regard to clay or sandiness as described previously (see "Preparing a Bed"). If the ground is very rocky, you may need to add topsoil.

•Fertilize planting area with any good blend intended for lawns available at your local nursery or garden center (there are several organic fertilizers on the market).

•Rake soil.

•Distribute half of seed over planting area, walking in one direction. Scatter other half of seed over the same area, walking in the opposite direction, crisscross style. Firm soil with hoe. Water.

•Keep soil moist until germination—generally within two weeks.

Sodding: You can sod a lawn in spring or fall, though spring is the optimum time (professionals recommend the first two weeks of May) because there tends to be a greater amount of rain. However, a lawn can be sodded whenever the ground isn't frozen, as long as it is kept moist. It needs about an inch of water every three or four days, whether through natural rainfall or by watering.

•Strip area to be planted of all vegetation; renting a sod stripper for this job will make your work a lot easier.

•Correct soil problems as described in the first two steps under "Seeding," above.

•Roll out sod in a row, in end-to-end fashion with long sides touching.

•Roll out the next row alongside the first, but don't exactly match up the pieces along the short ends–stagger them a bit; this will stabilize the area.

•Firm sod, preferably with a lawn roller, which you can rent from a garden center.

•Keep newly sodded lawn moist.

MOWING

The PLCAA recommends the following lawn mowing procedures:

•Mow only when the grass is dry.

•Make sure your mower blade is sharp; never remove more than one third of the lawn height in order not to shock the lawn's root system.

•Recycle grass clippings by detaching your lawn mower's collection bag and allowing the cut grass to remain on the lawn. This not only alleviates the current landfill problem but also returns nutrients to the soil. Many newer lawn mowers have mulching attachments that help speed the natural decomposition process.

Houseplants

A sunny windowsill is an ideal location for growing houseplants. No less than five hours of direct sunlight a day are essential for such blossoming plants as amaryllis, geraniums, gardenia and astilbe. These will do best in a window facing south or southwest; alternatively, they fare well in a window with eastern light. In south-facing locations in summer, you might want to move the plants a few inches back from the window and even add a gauzy curtain at the peak hours of sunlight to shield them.

Only foliage plants such as ferns, coleus, aspidistra, ivy and palms should receive northern light. Since they need only about three hours of sunlight daily, they'll also do quite well in an eastern location.

The following are tips for year-round houseplant care:

Tree-Buying Tips

With container-grown trees, roots should be well developed, but not to the extent that they are visible around the surface of the container or protruding from the drainage holes.

With B&B trees, look for a firm, compact root ball.

With bare-root trees, check to see there are several well-developed roots radiating from the central root.

With all trees, look for straight, upright trunks and a pleasing, well-balanced overall shape.

Seasonal Garden Schedule

SPRING
Apply fertilizer to garden beds—don't overfertilize; simply follow instructions on product label.

Plant summer-flowering bulbs, annuals, perennials and hardy vegetables.

Plant bare-root trees.

Divide or transplant fall-blooming perennials.

Replant perennials that were upheaved from the ground by frost.

Begin watering whenever soil feels dry at three or four inches down, says the AAN. Too much watering encourages shallow roots.

Start weeding.

Start a compost heap to recycle organic materials: cut grass, chopped leaves and even remains from your meals, such as fruits and vegetables (do not include meats).

Prune shrubby herbs such as rosemary, lavender, sage and santolina.

SUMMER
Bring houseplants outside if you wish, making sure not to overwhelm them with too much sun or wind.

Mulch the garden with organic matter such as cocoa hulls, buckwheat hulls, chopped leaves, wood chips or grass clippings to prevent weed growth.

Establish a lawn-mowing schedule.

Continue weeding and watering.

Plant summer and autumn vegetables.

FALL
Add spent plants to the compost pile.

Divide spring- and summer-blooming perennials.

Prepare soil for spring and fall planting. Plant spring-blooming bulbs and perennials.

Plant B&B and container-grown trees.

WINTER
Surround dormant garden plants with burlap, dark plastic or old sheets to keep them warm.

Spread a layer of organic material—chopped leaves, grass clippings and wood chips—around the roots of all plants to protect from cold.

Prune established trees (if the temperature is above 20°F) to get rid of dead branches and promote regrowth, says the AAN.

•To bring humidity into the room in winter, fill bowls with water and set atop radiator; mist foliage frequently.

•Avoid exposing houseplants to sudden drafts.

•Water only when the plant needs it (you can check this simply by feeling the soil). If the soil cakes when rubbed between your fingers, water until it runs out the drainage holes. During the dormant period after flowering, give the plants less water.

•Every time you water, give the plants a quarter turn so that they grow evenly.

•Treat your houseplants to liquid fertilizer every few months—but not after flowering, when the plant goes into dormancy.

•In general, most plants begin a renewed season of growth in late spring, and this is the best time for repotting. Use a good potting mixture and make sure the new container can accommodate new root growth.

•After repotting, houseplants usually do best when given a little summer air. If you put your houseplants outside, remember that unglazed clay pots are porous and water can quickly evaporate from them in summer sun. Plastic containers don't "breathe" and are therefore a better choice. If you don't like the look of plastic containers, camouflage them inside a larger container of your choice.

Sources of Further Information (Pets)

ORGANIZATIONS

American Boarding Kennels
Association
   1-719-591-1113

American Fancy Rat and Mouse
Association
   Call 1-714-892-7523 for information on a group in your area.

American Federation of Aviculture
   P.O. Box 56218
   Phoenix, AZ 85079
   1-602-484-0931
   For bird lovers.

American Federation of
Herpetoculturists
   P.O. Box 300067
   Escondido, CA 92030-0067
   Dedicated to the dissemination of information on reptiles and amphibians. Write for information on membership.

American Humane Association
   1-800-842-4637
   The American Kennel Club
   51 Madison Ave.
   New York, NY 10010
   1-212-696-8266

American Society for the Prevention of Cruelty to Animals (ASPCA)
   441 East 92nd St.
   New York, NY 10128
   1-212- 876-7700

American Veterinary Medical
Association
   1101 Vermont Ave. NW, Suite 710
   Washington, DC 20005-3521
   1-202-789-0007

The California Turtle and Tortoise
Club
   P.O. Box 7300
   Van Nuys, CA 91409-7300
   Send an SASE for information on care and feeding of your turtle or tortoise.

The Cat Fanciers' Association Inc.
918 Millard Court West
Daytona Beach, FL 32117
1-904-258-7199
Call or write for information on cat breeders.

House Rabbit Society
1615 Encinal Ave.
Alameda, CA 94501
1-415-521-4631

Has branches around the country; call or write to find one near you.

Humane Society of the United States (HSUS)
5430 Grosvenor Lane, Suite 100
Bethesda, MD 20814
1-301-571-8989

Pet Information Bureau
1-800-553-PETS

Sources of Further Information (Gardening)

BOOKS

All About Trees. Barbara Ferguson, ed., Ortho Books, San Remo, Calif., 1982.

The American Horticultural Society Encyclopedia of Garden Plants. Christopher Brickell, ed., Macmillan, New York, 1989.

The Beautiful Food Garden: Creative Landscaping with Vegetables, Herbs, Fruits and Flowers. Kate Rogers Gessert, Storey Communications/Garden Way Publishing, Pownall, Vt., 1987.

Foliage Plants for Decorating Indoors. Virginia F., and George A. Elbert, Timber Press, Portland, Ore., 1989. (Available from Timber Press, 9999 SW Wilshire, Portland, OR 97225; 1-800-327-5680.)

Gardeners' Questions Answered. National Gardening Association with Dr. Stefan Buczacki, Villard Books, New York, 1987.

The Garden Primer. Barbara Damrosch, Workman Books, New York, 1988.

Hortus Third. Liberty Hyde Bailey, Macmillan, New York, 1987.

Rodale's Landscape Problem Solver. Jeff and Liz Ball, Rodale Press, Emmaus, Pa., 1989.

Shortcuts for Accenting Your Garden: Over 500 Easy and Inexpensive Tips. Marianne Binetti, Storey Communications/Garden Way Publishing, Pownall, Vt.,1993.

Successful Perennial Gardening: A Practical Guide. Lewis Hill and Nancy Hill, Storey Communications/Garden Way Publishing, Pownall, Vt., 1993.

Taylor's Encyclopedia of Gardening. 4th edition, Norman Taylor, ed., Houghton Mifflin, Boston, 1976.

PERIODICALS

Fine Gardening
63 South Main St.
P.O. Box 5506
Newtown, CT 06470
Discusses all aspects of ornamental gardening.

Flower & Gardening
700 West 47th St., Suite 300
Kansas City, MO 64112
General-interest gardening topics with Midwestern focus.

Harrowsmith
Ferry Road
Charlotte, VT 05445
Country lifestyle magazine with articles on fruit and vegetable growing in the Northeast U.S. and cold climates.

House Plant Magazine
Route 1, Box 271-2
Elkins, WV 26241-9742
Organic Gardening

Rodale Press
30 Minor St.
Emmaus, PA 18098-0099
Covers all aspects of chemical-free gardening.

Pacific Horticulture
Pacific Horticultural Association
P.O. Box 485
Berkeley, CA 94701
Focuses specifically on growing conditions and plants of the West Coast.
Southern Living
P.O. Box 523
Birmingham, AL 35201
Southern lifestyle magazine which features excellent gardening articles.

ORGANIZATIONS

American Association of Nurserymen
1250 I Street NW, Suite 500
Washington, DC 20005
1-202-789-2900
1-202-789-1893 (fax)
Trade association; write for information and gardening/landscaping brochures.

American Society of Consulting Arborists
700 Canterbury Rd.
Clearwater, FL 34624
Professional organization; write for information.

American Society of Landscape Architects
4401 Connecticut Ave. NW
Fifth Floor
Washington, DC 20008-2302
1-202-686-2752
Professional organization; write for information and literature on selecting a landscape architect.

Home Orchard Society
P.O Box 230192
Tigard, OR 97281-0192
1-503-630-3392
Aids home gardeners in growing and propagating fruit trees; quarterly newsletter and handbooks available; call or write for membership.

International Society of Arboriculture
P.O. Box GG
Savoy, IL 61874
1-217-355-9411
Nonprofit organization supporting tree-care research around the world and dedicated to the care and preservation of ornamental trees; call or write for tree-care pamphlets "New Tree Planting" and "Mature Tree Care" (both 1991).

Indoor Garden Society of America
128 West 58th St.
New York, NY 10019
Indoor gardening association dedicated to exchange of information among members through newsletter; write for membership.

National Garden Bureau
1311 Butterfield Rd., Suite 310
Downers Grove, IL 60515
1-708-963-0770
1-708-963-8864 (fax)

Nonprofit educational service offers information to media. Brochures include "The Gardener's First Garden," NGB Press Service Sheet, October 1983, and "Today's Garden," NGB Press Service Sheet, September 1993.

Netherlands Flower Bulb Information Center
    426 Henry St.
    Brooklyn, NY 11231-3009
    1-718-596-5400
    1-718-596-4917 (fax)
    Provides brochures on growing spring- and summer/fall-flowering bulbs, as well as forcing bulbs indoors in winter, including "Ask Me. . . About Spring Bulbs," "Ask Me. . . About Summer Bulbs" and "Colourful and Fragrant Accents in Your Home."

Professional Lawn Care Association of America
    1000 Johnson Ferry Rd.
    Marietta, GA 30068
    1-404-977-5222
    Sells booklet titled "Grasscycling: Community Action Plan," and offers free brochures with tips on lawn care.

BOOKLETS AND BROCHURES
The following USDA, Soil Conservation Service and EPA publications are available from:

U.S. Government Printing Office
    Washington, D.C. 20402
    1-202-783-3238
    Agricultural Research Service and Extension Service. Fassuliotis, George, and Ricardo E. Gomez, reviewers. "Growing Vegetables in the Home Garden," Home and Garden Bulletin No. 202, 1986.

Environmental Protection Agency, "Cooling Our Communities: A Guidebook on Tree Planting and Light-Colored Surfaces," Jan. 1992.
    United States Department of Agriculture, "Mulches for Your Garden," Home & Garden Bulletin No. 185.
    USDA Soil Conservation Service, Lorenz, David G. et al., "Conservation Plants," Program Aid 1154, Feb. 1991.

SOURCES FOR SEEDS
Member companies and sources for All America Selections of top-rated seeds are as follows (M indicates mail-order seed catalog; P, seed packets offered in retail store; R, retail store operated by company offering seed):

Advance Seed Co.
    Box 488
    Fulton, KY 42041
    P

Applewood Seed Co.
    5380 Vivian St.
    Arvada, CO 80002
    M,P

W. Atlee Burpee Co.
    300 Park Ave.
    Warminster, PA 18974
    M,P,R

Henry Field Seed. Co.
    415 N. Burnett
    Shenandoah, IA 51602
    M

Garden Trends Inc.
    P.O. Box 22960
    Rochester, NY 14692
    M

Gurney's Seed & Nursery
110 Capital
Yankton, SD 57079
M,R

Chas. C. Hart Seed Co.
304 Main St.
Wethersfield, CT 06109
P

Johnny's Selected Seeds
RFD 1, Box 2580
Albion, ME 04910
M,R

J.W. Jung Seed Co.
335 South High St.
Randolph, WI 53957
M,R

Lake Valley Seed Inc.
5741 Arapahoe Ave., No. 4
Boulder, CO 80303
P

Chas. H. Lilly Co.
7737 N.E. Killingsworth St.
Portland, OR 97218
P

Earl May Seed & Nursery
208 North Elm St.
Shenandoah, IA 51603
P,R

Michael-Leonard Inc.
13367 E. Route 17
Grant Park, IL 60940
P

Nichols Garden Nursery
1190 North Pacific Highway
Albany, OR 97321
M

NK Lawn & Garden
7500 Olson Memorial Highway
Golden Valley, MN 55427
P

The Page Seed Co.
P.O. Box 158
Greene, NY 13778
P

Geo. W. Park Seed Co.
P.O. Box 31
Greenwood, SC 29647
M,R

Porter & Son, Seedsmen
P.O. Box 104
Stephenville, TX 76401
M,R

Rocky Mountain Seed Co.
P.O. Box 5204
Denver, CO 80217
M,R

Shepherd's Garden Seeds
6116 Highway 9
Felton, CA 95018
M,P

Otis S. Twilley Seed Co.
P.O. Box 65
Trevose, PA 19053
M

Wetsel Seed Co.
P.O. Box 791
Harrisonburg, VA 22801
M,P,R

14

Travel

Planning Your Trip

When you are planning to go away, whether it's a spur-of-the-moment junket or a long-awaited dream vacation, the options in terms of types of tours, fares and places to stay can seem overwhelming. Below are listed the various methods of planning a trip.

WITH A TRAVEL AGENT

A lot of people assume that you will have to pay more money if you make plans through a travel agent.

This is incorrect. In fact, because agents have on-line and other professional channels of access to a huge range of pricing and tourism information, a travel agent should in theory be able to find you a very good deal for your money. You have to make only one phone call in most cases, and the agent should do the rest. In addition, it is the airlines that pay agents a commission, not you, the traveler. (Occasionally, agents will charge for communications if they have had to make many long-distance calls, faxes or telexes in order to complete your arrangements.) There are, as in any industry, however, careless travel agents, and for this reason–or simply because you like to oversee arrangements personally and have the time to do so–you may choose to do the footwork yourself. Get a recommendation from friends, if possible, about agents they have used in the past with success.

If you are going to work with an agent, there are several things you should look for, starting with affiliations. There are five major affiliations a travel agent/agency should have:

• The Air Traffic Conference of America (ATC)

• The International Air Transport Association (IATA)

• The Trans-Atlantic Passenger Steamship Conference (TAPSC)

• The Trans-Pacific Passenger Steamship Conference (TPPSC)

• The Rail Travel Promotion Agency (RTPA)

You should also look for membership in the American Society of Travel Agents, which indicates that the agency has been in existence for more than three years. In addition, you might see the acronym CTA after agents' names, indicating that the agent has attended training courses with the Institute of Certified Travel Agents.

These affiliations ensure that agents are knowledgeable and qualified to dispense up-to-the-minute information, plus reservations and tickets.

When you call an agent, ask him or her about any documentation you might need for your particular trip. Even though this information is not difficult to find elsewhere, the travel agent is usually well-acquainted with such requirements and it will streamline your planning if you use the travel agent as a single source. Agents will have in many cases visited the destinations themselves, or have a colleague who has, and here, too, they can be a good resource for car rental arrangements, restaurant recommendations and pointers on other local diversions.

If you want a specialized tour, call a specialized agency. Some focus on a certain country or group of countries. Others specialize in tour types, such as eco-tourism or art tours. Ads in your local newspaper or in the national dailies will give you some idea of what's available; some travel guides also recommend specialized agencies. Recommendations from friends or colleagues are probably the best way to go, however, for only they can give you a real measure of the quality of service received from an agent. Lacking such recommendations, check with your local Chamber of Commerce or Better Business Bureau.

Here are some of the various tour types that travel agents may offer:

Independent Tour. This is not a contradiction in terms. In this case, a tour simply means that logistics and accommodations have been planned for in advance, in a unique arrangement made for you in agreement with a travel agent. Independent tours can be as precisely or loosely planned as you wish.

Group Tour. There are two types of group tours. One is where you have a chosen collection of people you want to travel with and the agent will design a tour for that group. The other is where you join a group of people you don't know, all going to the same destination for the same period of time. Done via a travel wholesaler, either type of group travel arrangement should give you a better price than more individual plans because groups are usually offered discounts.

Escorted Tour. As the name implies, an escorted tour comes with the services of a guide. Such tours are usually set up for a group with special interests or special needs, or for travel in less accessible parts of the world where language or other expertise is needed. Escorted tours almost always include advance transport and accommodations as well—and usually cost more.

Package Tour. Such tours give purchasers a fixed set of transport and accommodation arrangements and hence are most likely your cheapest option. You are neither in a group nor escorted; you will, however, have a limited choice of accommodations and/or dates of travel. The limitations placed on the customer account for the fact that package travel is usually the least expensive way to get to and stay at a given destination.

ON YOUR OWN

Some trips may not require calling a travel agent, or you may enjoy the feeling of creating your own itinerary. Travel guides can provide much of the necessary information, while on-line electronic databases can provide much of the same information available to travel agents. If you are willing to take the time to explore these a little, you can even make your own reservations. See "On-line Sources," below, for details.

EXTRA AID: THE TRAVEL GUIDES

If you don't want to depend solely on personal recommendations, buy or borrow from your library the most recent travel guides on your destination and ask the agent to book you any hotel which sounds appealing and meets your budget requirements. Also, travel guides can give you a feel for a place, and help you decide what you do and don't need to worry about in advance: Is there a legendary restaurant you hope to eat at, which requires reservations well in advance? Then do book ahead, with your agent's help if necessary. Is there a plethora of bookstores with good, reasonably-priced English-language selections? Then don't tote a paperback library with you; buy on location.

Choosing the Best Travel Guides

There are currently dozens of travel guides to choose from for most major destinations, and these days even the more obscure destinations are likely to be covered in some guide. Most major newspapers now have travel sections, and there are dozens of magazine titles dedicated to all varieties of travel. There are travel books, too, which describe countries in terms of cultural and historical background. Although they are not expressly meant for travelers, they can be invaluable in giving you an idea of what you will experience in the country in terms of environment and atmosphere, local traditions, and possible areas worth exploring on a special excursion.

Travel Guide Series. Many publishers put out travel guides in series, covering various countries or destinations. Each series has its own character, and inevitably you will find that some suit you better than others. The list below will give you an idea of the slant each of these well-known guides takes.

The Lonely Planet series is aimed at low-budget travelers willing to risk it off the beaten track. The series began as guidebooks to exotic destinations in Africa, Asia and South America, but the editors are now adding books on more "conventional" places, including the United States and Western Europe. Publisher: The Lonely Planet.

The Real Guide series bills itself as "the guides for the '90s." Publisher: Prentice Hall.

The *Let's Go* series, put together by the Harvard Student Agencies, is researched by college students and targeted to the young, low-budget traveler who is not looking for luxury. Publisher: St. Martin's Press.

The *Frommer's Guides* series comes in different versions, including family-oriented books and those intended for the budget traveler. Publisher: Frommer Books/Prentice Hall.

The *Birnbaum's Travel Guides* series is very detailed. Its special sections include "Diversions," a selective guide to events and interests, and "Directions," which suggests routes for touring by car. Publisher: HarperCollins.

Fielding's guides also come in various versions for family and budget travel. Publisher: William Morrow.

Fodor's guides cover not only the standard destinations, but also a new series of alternative guides concentrating on special interests, such as sports or history. Publisher: Fodor's Travel Publications.

Bantam Travel Guides pride themselves on having good maps, including color atlases. Guides to foreign countries include chapters on the local language and specialized information for the business traveler. Some country guides are available in pocket-size "Quick & Easy" versions. Publisher: Bantam Books.

Access Guides, developed by an architect, are upscale but budget-conscious. Their design is unique—the text is color coded and arranged in the sequence of a suggested walking or driving tour through a specific area. Publisher: HarperCollins.

There are a number of more specialized travel handbooks you might want to try out.

For special needs:
Access to the World, by Louise Weiss, Owl Books, Henry Holt & Co.

Travel for the Disabled, Helen Hecker RN, Twin Peaks Press.

Traveling Like Everyone Else (A Practical Guide for Disabled Travelers), by J. Freedman and S. Gersten, Adama Books.

Women:
The Confident Traveler, A Complete Travel Guide for the Business Woman, by Shirley Escott Davis with illustrations by Dolores Popp, Shiro Publishers.

The Real Guide: Women Travel (part of the *Real Guides* series from Prentice-Hall Publishers).

Safety:
The Safe Travel Book, by Peter Savage, Lexington Books (Macmillan).

Seniors:
Travel Easy, published by the American Association of Retired People (AARP).

Unbelievably Good Deals That You Absolutely Can't Get Unless You're Over 50, by Joan Rattner Heilman, Contemporary Books.

Free and very cheap travel:
Volunteer Vacations, by Bill McMillon. Chicago Review Press.

On-line Sources

There are many ways to hook yourself into the travel business on-line, and even make your own reservations, if you have a personal computer with a modem. You can get a lot of information, including flight schedules, hotel and automobile rentals, and restaurant ratings, quickly via computer on-line

Older Travelers

Special discounts and more free time are just two factors that have given older travelers a chance to see the world at affordable prices. Many travel suppliers offer senior discounts—sometimes only to members of certain senior citizen organizations, which provide other benefits. Prepare your itinerary with one eye on your own physical condition and the other on a map, and remember that it's easy to overdo when traveling.

PUBLICATIONS
The Mature Traveler, GEM Publishing Group, P.O. Box 50820, Reno, NV 89513-0820; 1-702-786-7419.

The Senior Citizen's Guide to Budget Travel in the US and Canada, by Paige Palmer, Pilot Books, 103 Cooper St., Babylon, NY 11702; 1-516-422-2225.

Take a Camel to Lunch and Other Adventures for Mature Travelers, by Nancy O'Connell, Bristol Publishing Enterprises, P.O. Box 1737, San Leandro, CA 94577; 1-800-346-4889 or 1-510-895-4461 in California.

Travel Tips for Older Americans, Publication No. 044-000-02270-2; Superintendent of Documents, U.S. Government Printing Office, P.O. Box 371954, Pittsburgh, PA 15250-7954; 1-202-783-3238.

Unbelievably Good Deals & Great Adventures That You Absolutely Can't Get Unless You're Over 50, by Joan Rattner Heilman, Contemporary Books, 180 N. Michigan Ave., Chicago, IL 60601; 1-312-782-9181.

ORGANIZATIONS
American Association of Retired Persons (AARP), 601 E St. NW, Washington, DC 20049; 1-202-434-2277.

Golden Companions, P.O. Box 754, Pullman, WA 99163-0754; 1-208-858-2183.

Mature Outlook, Customer Service Center, 6001 N. Clark St., Chicago, IL 60660; 1-800-336-6330.

National Council of Senior Citizens, 1331 F St. NW, Washington, DC 20004; 1-202-347-8800.

PACKAGE TOUR OPERATORS
Elderhostel, P.O. Box 1959, Wakefield, MA 01880-5959; 1-617-426-7788.

Evergreen Travel Service, 4114 198th St. SW, Suite 13, Lynnwood, WA 98036-6742; 1-800-435-2288 or 1-206-776-1184.

Gadabout Tours, 700 E. Tahquitz Canyon Way, Palm Springs, CA 92262; 1-800-952-5068 or 1-619-325-5556.

Grand Circle Travel, 347 Congress St., Boston, MA 02210; 1-800-221-2610 or 1-617-350-7500.

Grandtravel, 6900 Wisconsin Ave., Suite 706, Chevy Chase, MD 20815; 1-800-247-7651 or 1-301-986-0790.

Interhostel, UNH Division of Continuing Education, 6 Garrison Ave., Durham, NH 03824; 1-800-733-9753 or 1-603-862-1147.

Ridgebrook Travel, 104 Wilmont Rd., Deerfield, IL 60015; 1-800-962-0060 or 1-708-374-0088.

Saga International Holidays, 222 Berkeley St., Boston, MA 02116; 1-800-342-0273 or 1-617-262-2262.

networks, such as CompuServe, American Online and Prodigy, and some systems let you act virtually as your own travel agent. Most on-line networks allow subscribers access via a series of pull-down menus that offer prompts. If there are extra charges for their use, a message to this effect appears on screen.

Following are a few electronic resources, but keep in mind that the list of on-line services expands daily; a public library with good on-line resources should be able to guide you to any new ones. In addition, many on-line services support travel bulletin boards, which allow you to post questions about various destinations and methods of getting there. You can also search their libraries for files related to such topics.

RESERVATIONS

The Official Airline Guide (OAG) Electronic Edition Travel Service.
Networks: AT&T Easylink, CompuServe, DIALOG, Dow Jones, Genie; or anyone with a PC and a modem can subscribe directly to OAG by calling 1-800-323-3537 (information and orders). There is a $25 hookup fee, and subscribers also pay a per minute charge of 47 cents peak hours, 17 cents off peak.

You can make reservations and arrange ticket purchase with a major credit card on-line with this system. It offers detailed information on 1.5 million flights the world over; the schedule is updated weekly. It also lists airfares for more than half a million North American destinations on all licensed carriers; fares are updated every day. (Aircraft model number, number of stops and meals are some of the

details provided.) The OAG Electronic Edition also publishes information on hotels.

EAASY SABRE
Networks: America OnLine, CompuServe, Prodigy

Data on flights, fares, car rentals and hotels presented in Windows or Terminal Emulation format; you can make flight and hotel reservations. The service includes The Travel Profile, which allows subscriber to save ticketing information.

INFORMATION SOURCES

International Travel Warning Service
Network: CompuServe
This electronic newsletter lists information on international health and travel conditions as issued by the State Department, World Health Organization and the Centers for Disease Control. It also lists passport, visa and vaccination requirements for most countries. Updated monthly.

The Traveler's Corner
Network: America Online
This information service offers profiles of U.S. and international destinations, the opportunity to order more detailed travel reports and data on a variety of exotic destinations, including a destination of the month.

SOFTWARE
Taxi, by News Electronic Data Inc.
The Zagat travel and leisure group now sells a software program to guide you through a number of American cities via maps, restaurant and hotel reviews, and other practical information. The program can locate city addresses, create and print custom maps and tell you how to get to

selected destinations. It's available as a PC disk or on CD-ROM. Call 1-800-Hey-Taxi for information.

Print Sources for Consumer Travel Information

One of the best print sources of information for the general user is the *Consumer Reports Travel Letter,* published monthly. Each issue carries a cumulative index so you can look up any subject the newsletter has ever covered. Available at most libraries. (See "Sources of Further Information" for details on how to subscribe). Its companion book, published yearly, is *The Consumer Reports Travel Buying Guide* (Consumer Reports Books, a division of the Consumers Union, Yonkers, NY 10703). This annual is updated yearly and can be found in most libraries. It goes into great detail on many issues of concern for the average airline passenger including, among others, tips on finding the best deals, trip insurance and travelers' consumer rights in the event of baggage damage or overbooked or canceled flights. It includes many useful telephone numbers and addresses as well.

Saving Money on Travel

There are numerous travel clubs and associations in existence today. They cater to all tastes, needs and interests, and many can get you privileged information, discounts or both.

If your destination is overseas, seek out the nearest branch of the country's national tourist board (embassies and consulates will tell you where to find them) and tell them what you want, whether it is a list of bed-and-breakfast associations or sports vacation resorts.

In North America, ask your travel agent for travel club recommendations or go to the library and seek out the various consumer travel publications and the classified travel ads of some magazines. Certain on-line subscriber networks, such as CompuServe, also have travel clubs.

Professional and retiree organizations (AARP and the National Retired Teachers' Association, for example) also extend information and member bonuses.

TRAVEL DISCOUNTS
You will almost always get a better deal on travel if you travel off season. In most parts of the world, summer is high season—unless it's a question of ski resorts, or special events that bring in the crowds at specific times of year (such as Mardi Gras in New Orleans). Local tourist boards are the best reference in helping you determine when and when not to go somewhere. Naturally, you want to reach your destination when it's at its best. However, you may want to avoid the peak travel time so that the crowds won't overwhelm you.

Note: If you are traveling to the southern hemisphere, remember that the seasons are six months' different than in the northern hemisphere (e.g., summer in Australia is December through March).

FREQUENT FLYER BONUSES

Now that most airlines have programs to award frequent customers "free miles" toward future travel, people who are in the air a lot can get free trips with some regularity. The awards and bonuses vary with each airline. Call those airlines that travel the routes you use most. Sometimes your business travel miles can be used for free personal travel; this depends on your company's policy.

There is one monthly publication that can help you sort out the plethora of programs on offer. Aimed at the active air traveler, *The Frequent Flyer* can be ordered by calling the Official Airlines Guide (OAG) at 1-800-323-3537; cost is $24 per year. The OAG itself lists up to 100,000 flights in the U.S., Canada and Mexico, including connections; it's available for $86 a year and can be ordered by calling the same number. Subscribers get a subscription to *The Frequent Flyer* as a bonus. There are three other versions of the OAG available, for Latin America, Europe and the Pacific-Asia market.

Many of the airlines' programs let you accrue free travel miles when you rent from certain car rental companies or stay at designated hotels. In addition, several credit cards automatically give you bonus miles based on dollars spent on regular credit card purchases. You may request the information from your credit card company, but usually such programs are advertised in leaflets sent with the monthly statement.

FLY-DRIVE PACKAGES

These arrangements combining land and air travel are one good way to package together most of the peskier logistics of travel and save some money at the same time. Both airlines and travel agents offer them. Many airlines will sponsor you for a discounted car rental at destination, and some include accommodation deals, too. Local newspapers are a good source of the fly-drive packages currently on offer from your area. In-flight magazines also list car rental companies with complementary programs; most airlines have a chosen fly-drive partner (for example Delta Airlines' partner in the United States is Alamo). Upon presentation of your boarding pass from the partner airline at the car rental desk, you will be given whatever discount applies in that location. Rates vary enormously depending on city and season, so check with car rental agencies before you go; their toll-free numbers are listed below.

HOTEL DEALS

A large number of vacationers like to travel in the summer, especially those with children to consider. Luckily for them, there are a good number of hotel discounts to be had in North America and Europe in the summer. This is because this is the season when business travel, many hotels' mainstay, drops off. Several chains, such as the Hotel Intercontinental, cut rates by as much as 50 percent in summer (and children under 14 stay free) in North America, and Hilton International cuts its European rates in the summer through September 30, with children sharing parents' rooms at no charge.

Another way to get travel discounts is

through membership in such nationwide organizations as the American Automobile Association (AAA), which in addition to travel discounts offers members such important services as free maps, route advice and emergency road service. The AAA's travel benefits extend throughout the United States, whether you are driving your own car or renting. The association is also affiliated with automobile clubs in Canada and many European countries, so that you may enjoy similar security on the road while abroad. Some foreign auto clubs offer fully reciprocal services to AAA members, and others offer partial services. Since there is great variation from one foreign auto club to the next, AAA members should call their own AAA club for details.

Service in the U.S. military can also qualify you for discounts, as can affiliation with the AARP (see above).

Traveling with Children

Children can be difficult to travel with, but parents know that their trip wouldn't be the same without the little ones along. Some families prefer to pack all the kids in the car and set off on the highway; others travel frequently by air to far-flung destinations. Below is information on traveling with children, including information on taking children on the plane, suggestions for family activities to enrich your trip and a rundown of specialized guides on the topic.

Some countries and some airlines now require that parents show separate passports for all children, even for children under five (check with the U.S. Passport Office for up-to-date information; numbers and addresses are listed later in this chapter).

TRAVELING BY AIR

Costs for children to fly vary, but at most times the cheapest way for a child to travel, whether accompanied or not, is on the same Supersaver fare basis that is least expensive for most adults. Nonrefundable, paid 14 days in advance and including a stay over a Saturday night, a Supersaver usually costs about one third the full coach-class fare. Where child discounts are available, they are usually calculated as a percentage of adult fares—for example, 50 percent of the regular full coach fare. This usually works out to be more expensive than Supersavers, since full coach fares can be three to four times the Supersaver ticket price.

However, children's discounts may be in effect only on certain routes and/or on a seasonal basis. Summer is when the most child fare super-bargains are offered, since business travel is slack then. The discounts usually apply to children 2 to 11 years old; children 12 and over pay adult fares.

Children under the age of two who sit in their parents' laps usually fly for free on domestic flights, and for 10 percent of full coach airfare on international flights. However, a reserved seat for an under-two-year-old will cost the going adult or child fare.

No advance reservations are required for lap-traveling children. A second child under two traveling with one adult will usually be charged the 2–11-year-olds' fare, although this pricing policy can vary. (Note: Charter and other tour operators often do not offer discounts for children.) In many cases, a child without a reserved seat will be permitted to take a free seat if the plane is not full and the parent has an approved child-safety seat—a children's car seat that has been approved by the Federal Aviation Authority (check for the FAA label on the seat's underside). Approved child-safety seats are a must on most airlines for most younger children; check your airline for age limits. Some airlines provide bassinets for infants on request, but parents must check availability ahead of time.

HOTELS

The age limitations for hotel charges for children vary widely (anywhere from 0 to 50 percent) depending on the children's age and the country you are traveling to. Keep in mind, too, that some hotels don't allow children at all. Call the hotel, your travel agent or the national tourist board of the country you are visiting to find out the general rules. (If you are staying at a hotel that's a member of an international chain, see the list of toll-free numbers in this chapter.)

FAMILY ACTIVITIES

There are a lot of common-sense ways to keep a trip with a child on the happy side, but keep in mind that when traveling, you will never be in a predictable or controlled environment. Add into this formula of uncertainty the fact that you may be spending long periods of time in close quarters with large numbers of strangers, and it makes sense to be well-armed for situations where children are bored, restless, jet-lagged, upset by changes in their routine or just plain homesick.

There are some general rules that will save most situations short of genuine disasters. First of all, try to introduce any strange innovations—especially to very young children—as play. If travel is an adventure for you, it should be doubly so for a child companion. For example, in countries where you might need to drape their beds in mosquito netting, you could pretend you are making a tent or castle for them. You also may have to pull a few swift ones to get your child to eat foods he or she isn't used to, like pretending you are the taste testers for Bird's Eye deciding whether or not the food you are eating is good enough to bring home, mass produce, freeze and sell from every supermarket's freezer case.

For children old enough to hold one, give them their own camera and notebook so they can document the trip. A majority of children will get very involved in such activities; urge them to keep a log of photos, or a diary of the places visited and their feelings and impressions of them. Or urge them to write letters to good friends or relatives telling about the trip; if there are no postcards to be had, most hotels provide airmail stationery, and some children will enjoy buying and possibly collecting foreign stamps.

Give older children small pouches on strings or pouch-type money belts that can hold passports, money and other useful small items. Make sure older children memorize the name and address of the hotel you're staying at; for children of all ages, you might want to put this information, along with parents' names, in their pouches. (If you will be staying in a foreign place any great length of time, it might be a good idea for everyone's peace of mind to register at your home country's embassy or consulate, for extra security.)

You might want to let younger children carry some small favorite toys or games, a disposable camera, crayons and scrap paper along with sunglasses, sunblock and a small carton of juice.

GUIDES TO TRAVELING WITH CHILDREN

There are now a host of books devoted exclusively to travel with children, giving information on everything from comparisons of child car seats to the top 10 destinations for families with children.

Numerous guides concentrate solely on destinations for family travel, such as Disney theme parks, national parks and nature reserves. Several more general guides for travelers with children cover everything from safety tips and first aid to on-the-go entertainment suggestions. Among them:

Are We There Yet? (Travel Games for Kids), by Richard Salter, Prince Paperbacks, New York, 1991.

Families on the Go, a catalog of travel and activity books for parents and kids; from Families on the Go, 1259 El Camino Rd., Menlo Park, CA 94025.

Kids on Board (Travel to 10 Major U.S. Cities), by Ken and Marilyn Wilson, Warner Books, New York, 1989.

When Children Must Travel Alone

Most airlines require that an unaccompanied child be at least five years old to travel, whether on a domestic or international flight.

Unaccompanied children five to seven years old can only travel under the following conditions:

If the flight is nonstop or "direct," which means no change of planes is involved if there is a stop.

The child's parent or guardian must inform the airline of the child's age when making the reservation. When taking the reservation, the airline will record the name, address and phone number of the adult(s) who will escort the child at both ends of the trip; the adults will need identification, so ask the airline you are dealing with what I.D. they will accept.

The previously named parent or guardian must accompany the child to the gate, and a previously named parent or guardian must also pick up the child at the destination.

Unaccompanied children 8 to 11 years old travel under the same conditions, but are in addition allowed to travel on flight routings that require a change of plane. Most airlines require that an employee escort eight- and nine-year-olds between planes, but this is optional for children 10 and 11. Typically, airlines charge $25 for any passenger requiring an airline employee's accompaniment for a change of plane. (Elderly, ill or otherwise disabled passengers might find this service useful, too.)

On most airlines, unaccompanied children 12 to 17 years old are treated as adult passengers.

Most of the same rules apply for unaccompanied children traveling internationally, but remember that any child being sent overseas alone must have his or her own passport. In addition, since adults must escort 5- to 11-year-olds to their departure gates, they must request a gate pass in order to be allowed to take the child through security and immigration checkpoints; non-passenger adults should request this pass at the check-in desk.

Traveling With Children and Enjoying It, by Arlene Kay Butler, Globe Pequot Press, Chester, Conn., 1991.

Also, many general travel guides include thorough sections on travel with children, and selecting one of these may save you the expense of buying a second book.

Travel with Your Pet

There are several crucial things to consider before taking a pet on a trip away from home. The first is whether it is really necessary. By the time you get the cat or dog carrier, immunizations (if going abroad) and airline tickets (see below for the cost of flying pets), it may be cheaper and healthier for your pet to stay home. Strict quarantines are the rule for European and some other countries, with a six-month incarceration period for Britain and up to four months for Scandinavia.

Quarantines aside, traveling with animals to foreign countries is cumbersome. There are different immunization rules for each country, and a series of shots can cost a fair amount of money and take a good deal of time, especially if booster shots are required for an animal whose shots have become outdated. If you are going to bring your pet abroad, call the consulate or embassy of the countries of destination (consulates of all nations are in New York City, Chicago, Los Angeles and other major U.S. cities; embassies are in Washington, D.C.) and get a detailed—written, if possible—list of the documents you will need to show upon arrival with your pet.

FLYING WITH ANIMALS

The airlines will require proof of an exam for your pet 10 days or less before travel overseas, and a written record of vaccinations plus a Certificate of Good Health from the vet.

Pets are generally allowed to travel on planes (one or two per passenger cabin only; the rest must travel underneath in a heated, depressurized cargo area, so reserve far ahead if you want the passenger cabin space).

On domestic flights, a typical charge is $50 per pet whether it travels in the cabin or in cargo. On international flights each pet costs $85, which is the charge for each item of excess baggage. On overseas trips, airlines charge 1 percent of first-class airfare for every kilo (2.2 pounds) of the pet's weight plus carrier weight.

Carrier kennels have to fit under the seat, and the standard acceptable size, as it is for carry-on bags, is 21 inches in length, 16 inches in width and 8 inches in height. Anything larger must fly in the depressurized, temperature-controlled cargo area.

GROUND TRANSPORTATION

The rules vary for other forms of transport. Trains, buses and some limo services refuse to carry pets. If it's a question of any of these forms of transport in another country, contact the nearest consulate or embassy of the country concerned. Whatever form of transport you are considering, try a test run to see if motion sickness or extreme hyperactivity or anxiety result. If so, your vet may be able to prescribe anti-nausea pills or tranquilizers.

Also keep in mind that many hotels do not allow pets. Call in advance to check.

PETS WHO STAY BEHIND

If you decide your pet is going to stay home, you'll have to plan ahead to leave it with a qualified kennel (far ahead if you are traveling at peak season). Your best bet is usually with the animal's regular veterinarian, or a kennel the veterinarian recommends. Another option is to leave it with friends who are equipped to take care of it. You will have to determine your options according to your economic situation and your pet's disposition—some fare very badly at kennels, others are known to destroy friends' houses. Still others suffer from loneliness if only visited once a day while alone at your home.

One book designed specifically for those traveling with animals is *Travel With Your Pet,* by P. Weideger (Gaines Dog Research Center, P.O. Box 1007, Kankakee, IL 60901). Your veterinarian may have brochures or other advice on the subject.

Travel Insurance and Trip Cancellation

Since most travel involves some degree of uncertainty and risk, prospective travelers should consider the different varieties of travel-related insurance

available and decide which, if any, are needed. Policies can cover some or all of these: canceled trips, trip interruption, unforeseen costs related to emergencies that take place during trips, and lost or damaged baggage.

The widest range of options will be available to those who contact insurers well ahead of time; for last-minute purchasers, however, there are travel insurance sales points at some airports, or else airline ticket agents can refer you to a telephone number you can call from your point of departure. Credit card holders should first check with their credit card companies, whose policies often include certain types of automatic travel coverage when you pay for travel with their card.

When deciding whether or not to buy coverage that ensures you will get your money back in case of a canceled trip, you should first find out what returns you are entitled to. Some tickets (usually the more expensive) already allow for healthy refunds; the cheaper the ticket, the more likely there are to be restrictions, charges for changes and a no-money-back policy for cancellations. If a large, nonrefundable deposit or full payment at booking is required for your ticket, cancellation insurance is probably worthwhile.

Operator failure—where a travel agent, company or airline goes out of business or defaults—is another eventuality you may want to defend against. When considering operator-failure insurance, be certain to read between the lines to see that the policy does not offer bankruptcy insurance only; some companies that go out of business never file for bankruptcy, they simply fade away. In this case, your insurance would be useless.

If your travel agent doesn't have an insurance program to offer you, below are some general travel insurers listed by the *Consumer Reports Travel Buying Guide*. You should be able to find a package as narrow (baggage only) or broad-ranging as you like. Most offer cancellation, health or comprehensive plans (comprehensive plans usually cover baggage losses or damage, trip cancellation and accidents). For overseas travel, some typical comprehensive packages had provisions to reimburse passengers for cancellation, delay, medical emergency treatment costs and medical emergency treatment costs plus emergency transport costs.

The cost for this comprehensive overseas package varies according to the length of your trip and destination. (You will not be covered if you go to a country on the insurer's exception list, which usually excludes countries at war or countries with a proven record of kidnappings or terrorist attacks.) Several of these comprehensive coverage plans for a 9-to-15 day trip overseas cost under $100. A typical plan's compensations include $1,000 for cancellation, $500 for delay (minimum length varies; check policy), $10,000 for emergency medical treatment and $50,000 for treatment plus emergency transport. Among the companies to call are:

•Access America Inc., 1-800-424-3391

•Carefree Travel Insurance, 1-800-323-3149 or 1-516-294-0220

•Travel Assistance International, 1-800-821-2828 or 1-202-331-1609

•Travel Guard International/Gold, 1-800-634-0644 or 1-715-345-0505; fax 1-715-345-0525.

Traveler's First-Aid Checklist

You can ask a travel agent, official national tourist board or embassy to provide you with sources of the most up-to-date-health precautions for each country you intend to visit. Make these inquiries well in advance, because some shots and preventative medications need to be taken care of well ahead of arrival at your destination in order to be effective.

Malaria is probably one of the easiest infectious diseases to catch while traveling; make sure to get the pills if you are traveling in a malaria-ridden area. Also, if any insect bite seems abnormal, seek medical help; insects carry a great deal of disease, especially in the tropics. In this era of AIDs, some people may want to carry empty, sterilized syringes in case of the need for an emergency injection abroad. However, getting permission to buy them can be difficult; consult your physician.

If you are traveling with children, be sure to let the family doctor know and ask about any precautions you should take. Even a change in drinking water can sometimes make younger travelers very sick.

Ask an embassy or local authority about the quality of the drinking water. Bottled water is widely sold in most places, so it would be rare that you would need to carry liquids long distances. If you think there is a good reason not to drink even the bottled water, bottled sodas or juices are another option. In hotter climates, always carry a flask for water, and drink a lot of it; dehydration can cause headaches and real illness, in the form of sunstroke or worse.

If you will be traveling in remote areas or in non-Western countries for long periods, you may want to carry as many of the following as you can. For urban destinations or places closer to home, carry only those things that are helpful preventatives or would be crucial in treating a serious injury if help is not immediately available.

•Adapters for electrical items, to adapt both plug shapes and the actual current.

•Antiseptics and first aid cream.

•Bandages, an assortment: one roll of ace (support) type, one roll of gauze and some smaller Band-Aids. Remember to bring the tape or clips that go with the heavier-duty bandages and gauze.

•Condoms

•Diarrhea remedy

•Mosquito repellent and mosquito bite balm

•Pocket knife, preferably with small scissor

•Protective clothing to prevent overexposure to elements, whether extremely hot or cold. Good sunglasses with UVA filter can help avert or lessen snow blindness and sunstroke. Remember to layer your clothes in conditions of extreme cold, and

it's a good idea to always bring a waterproof cape or raincoat.

•Shaver

•Styptic pencil (men)

•Sunburn and burn salve

•Sun block

•Tampons

•Water flask

•Water treatment tablets (if you will be drinking from clean but nontreated water sources, such as slow-moving streams, lakes, etc.). If you are in a part of the world where the water is undrinkable because of dangerous bacteria, these tablets will not help; buy bottled drinks.

As at home, you will have to use common sense in the event of any first-aid emergency, but do factor in the extra time it may take to get help due to distances and possible communication problems. Before longer and more rugged trips, a first-aid course would be a good idea. Many community organizations, such as local YMCAs and YWCAs, give such courses at reasonable cost.

The New York Times, in a July 1993 article on emergency medical transport insurance for travelers, listed several "travel-assistance" organizations that are in the business of providing customers with information and, in some cases, actual aid in the event of medical emergencies during travel. These assistance companies, most of which also have medical consultants available to answer questions via telephone and employees who speak foreign languages, are:

•International SOS Assistance, 1-800-523-8930

•Travmed/Medex, 1-800-732-5309

•USAssist, 1-800-756-5900

•Travel Assistance International, 1-800-821-2828.

The companies listed offer subscribers not only information in the event of a health emergency during travel but also may have partner plans with underwriters who provide compensation for ambulance and evacuation costs, medical expenses and trip cancellations caused by health emergencies. They usually provide toll-free telephone numbers. Also, check to see if your credit card company offers a so-called "enhancement plan" that gives you access to a telephone link to a travel assistance group; many do.

Note that compensation for medical emergencies during travel may be restricted for pre-existing conditions. For example, some plans require that the condition has not recurred within 60 to 90 days before departure. Those with pre-existing conditions must research the specifics. The companies listed above also deal with medical travel emergency plans.

If you have access to CompuServe, see "On-line Sources," above, for information on the International Travel Warning Service, a database with vast quantities of useful information about travel health and safety.

Car Rentals (Toll-Free Numbers)

To rent a car, you must in all cases have a valid driver's license, and many companies require that drivers give a cash deposit or their credit card number as a guarantee against the car's return. Do be aware, too, that when you sign out a car, rental companies usually "run" your card and hold $500 or more against your credit card account as a kind of guarantee deposit that you will return the car. (This is canceled upon return of a car when less than the amount held has been spent.) Since this means some people may hit their credit limit at the beginning of their trip, it's wise to bring a second or third credit card along to cover your travel expenses.

Several major credit cards that once automatically paid for some types of insurance each time card holder rented a car have now dropped that coverage, so be sure to check your specific card's coverage. Consult the literature you received along with your credit card when it was issued to you. Or contact a customer service representative to find out what kind of car rental insurance, if any, is covered.

Senior citizens note: Some car rental agencies in Europe will not rent to people more than 70 years old, citing insurance risk. Double-check before you go, particularly if you are headed to Ireland, where car rentals are also notoriously expensive. Conversely, many rental companies require drivers to be at least 21, 23, 25 or even 30 years old (depending on model rented), citing the high cost of insurance for very young drivers. Call around to check age limitations.

National 800 numbers for major rental companies are:

Alamo	1-800-327-9633
Avis	1-800-331-1212
Budget	1-800-527-0700
Dollar Rent A Car	1-800-800-4000
Hertz	1-800-654-3131
National	1-800-CAR-RENT
Sears Rent A Car	1-800-527-0770
Thrifty Rent A Car	1-800-367-2277

If you want to find out about renting from these agencies overseas, call the above numbers and ask for further information.

Major Hotel Chains
(Toll-Free Numbers)

The range of accommodation quality, services and settings for hotels varies so greatly that you should get information by requesting brochures in advance. Prices for rooms vary throughout the year (see "Travel Discounts," above), so be sure to ask what the best rates are for the season and days of the week you are interested in. Remember to find out about air/hotel packages, too.

Most travel guides give excellent details on hotels and are worth consulting in advance to help you do some comparison shopping, especially if you are looking for something small or out-of-the ordinary. A profusion of books,

for example, specialize in bed-and-breakfast accommodation only. The toll-free numbers for some of the major North American-based hotel chains with overseas members are:

Best Western	1-800-528-1234
Hilton	1-800-445-8667
Holiday Inn	1-800-Holiday
Hotels of the World	1-800—223-6800
Howard Johnson	1-800-654-2000
Hyatt	1-800-228-9000
Marriott	1-800-228-9290
Ramada Inn	1-800-2Ramada
Red Lion	1-800-547-8010

Major Airlines
(Toll-Free Numbers)

Below is a list of general information and reservations numbers for airlines that serve some of the more popular destinations inside the U.S. and abroad.

AerLingus	1-800-223-6537
Aeromexico	1-800-237-6639
Air Canada	1-800-422-6232
Alaska Airlines	1-800-426 0333
Alitalia	1-800-223-5730
American Airlines	1-800-433-7300
British Airways	1-800-247-9297
Continental Airlines	1-800-525-0280

Delta Airlines	1-800-221-1212
Eastern Airlines	1-800-Eastern
Iberia Airlines	1-800-221-9741
Japan Airlines	1-800-525-3663
Lufthansa	1-800-645-3880
Northwest Airlines	1-800-225-2525 (domestic); 1-800-447-4747 (overseas)
Qantas Airlines	1-800-227-4500
Scandinavian Airlines (SAS)	1-800-221-2350
Swissair	1-800-221-4750
US Air	1-800-428-4322

Traveling by Train

Passenger train routes still cover much of North America, and travel by rail can be cheaper and more relaxing than plane or car travel, depending on your time and budget allowances. Business and leisure travelers, and passengers old and young, will appreciate the opportunity a train provides to stretch the legs and, usually, to spread out a bit more than is possible on planes. You might also seize the opportunity to sleep comfortably, in a reserved berth or reclining seat, if long-distance travel is involved. When you call to make a reservation, inquire as to whether there are different classes of travel available, and what the cost and comfort differentials are. Some routes have several classes available while others have only one uniform class.

For fares, schedules, and reservations in the United States, call Amtrak, 1-800-872-7245. For rail travel in Canada, call Via, 1-800-561-9181.

If you plan to travel by rail outside North America, you should contact the National Tourist Board (see passport section of this chapter on where to find the number) of the country or countries you plan to visit and ask them about their rail system. Many nations offer nonresidents special discounted train passes for an unlimited number of trips in a fixed period of time. The Eurail system for Europe has long been a favorite with foreign visitors, especially those who plan to see several countries in one trip. However, in recent years, many individual European countries have dropped out of the system, so it is nowhere near as comprehensive as it was before the 1990s.

For Eurail Pass information, call Rail Pass Express, 1-800-551-1977 (9 A.M. to 8 P.M. weekdays Eastern Standard Time, and 9 A.M. to 3 P.M. Saturdays).

Travel Abroad

For U.S. citizens, travel outside the country is not only exciting, it can be very educational. But before you leave, make sure your passport is in order and all your travel documents, including a visa if necessary, are up-to-date.

HOW TO APPLY FOR A NEW PASSPORT

Under normal circumstances you should allow up to two months for processing of passports. The easiest way to apply is through your local post office. The official application form, number DSP-11, is available at U.S. post offices or U.S. embassies abroad. The items you need to have a passport processed are:

Proof of citizenship.

•This can be a certified copy of a birth certificate, if you were born in the U.S.; naturalization documents, for citizens who were born outside the U.S.; an expired passport issued not more than 12 years ago, or a valid U.S. passport issued when applicant was under 16.

Proof of identification.

•Acceptable I.D. includes a valid driver's license or an affidavit from an identifying witness.

•Two (identical) photos, black and white or color.

•They must have been taken within the last six months and measure 2 by 2 inches, with your head centered and occupying 1 to 1 3/8 inches of vertical space.

Fees.

•The total cost at press time was $65 ($55 basic fee plus $10 administration fee) for all applicants 18 or over, and $40 total for those under 18. It is advisable for parents to get passports even for small children. The back of the application lists acceptable forms of payment.

Present all of the appropriate documentation to the postal clerk. You should receive your passport in six to eight weeks. In the case of more urgent travel, passports can be prepared in about 10 days and sometimes less; ask the post office clerk about how to get a rush passport done; he or she should give you the name of an agency or passport office that can help.

Passports are valid for either 5 or 10 years.

RENEWING A PASSPORT

To get a new passport if you already have a valid passport that will expire soon, you must supply your current passport, if it is no more than 12 years old and was issued in your correct, current name. The passport must also have been issued *after* your 16th birthday. Reissuance documents can be presented to a post office clerk using the same application form as for a new passport. If you don't have your old passport, bring the same I.D. as for a first-time passport (see above).

PASSPORT OFFICES IN THE U.S.

JFK Building
  Government Center, Room E123
  Boston, MA 02203
  1-617-565-3940

Kluczynski Federal Office Building
  230 S. Dearborn, Suite 380
  Chicago, IL 60604
  1-312-353-5426

New Federal Building
  300 Ala Moana Blvd., Room C
  1-80006
  Honolulu, HI 96850
  1-808-546-2130

1 Allen Center
  500 Dallas St.
  Houston, TX 77002
  1-713-229-3607

Federal Bldg.
 11000 Wilshire Blvd., Room 13100
 West Los Angeles, CA 90024
 1-213-209-7070

Federal Office Bldg.
 51 SW 1st Ave., 16th floor
 Miami, FL 33130
 1-305-536-5395

Postal Service Bldg.
 701 Loyola Ave., Room T-12005
 New Orleans, LA 70113
 1-504-589-6728

630 5th Ave., Room 270
 New York, NY 10111
 1-212-541-7700

Federal Office Bldg.
 600 Arch St., Room 4426
 Philadelphia, PA 19106
 1-215-597-7480

525 Market St., Suite 200
 San Francisco, CA 94105
 1-415-974-7972

Federal Office Bldg.
 915 2nd Ave., Room 992
 Seattle, WA 98174
 1-206-220-7788

1 Landmark Square
 Broad and Atlantic Streets
 Stamford, CT 06901
 1-203-325-3538

1425 K St. NW
 Washington, DC 20524
 1-202-523-1355

If you want travel information about foreign countries before you go abroad, you might want to contact the U.S. offices of their national tourist boards.

Travel magazines, such as *Travel & Leisure, Condé Nast Traveller* and the Sunday travel sections of most major newspapers, often carry listings, or you can try contacting the embassy (located in Washington, D.C.) or consulate (in New York and other major cities) for tourist information. Your travel agent is another possible source. Note that some groups of countries, such as the Scandinavian countries, pool their services in one office.

National tourist boards can also give you information as to whether or not you need a visa to be admitted as a tourist or businessperson. If not, they can give you the number of the visa section of their embassy in the United States. The U.S. Department of State also publishes a pamphlet, "Foreign Entry Requirements," that gives this information. It is available from the Consumer Information Center (see "Sources of Further Information," below).

Travel databases also offer passport information (see "On-line Sources," above).

DEALING WITH LANGUAGES

Ideally, we would all like to be able to speak the language of the foreign countries we most want to visit; but for most people this simply is not the case. If you have a trip planned for the fairly distant future, you might want to check out a local college, adult education program or cultural institution of the foreign country you are traveling to and enroll in a course. Otherwise, a trip to the local library or bookstore for some phrasebooks and/or language-learning audio or video cassettes will yield some benefits.

However, native speakers of English are lucky in terms of travel and communication, because English is the most widely spoken language in the world—not as a mother tongue, but as a second language. German and French still serve as major second languages in some parts of Eastern Europe, Africa and the Middle East, but English is the second language of choice in a vast number of countries today, especially for the younger generations.

Nonetheless, no matter where you are going and what the purpose of your journey is, common courtesy dictates that a traveler know at least the basic words of politeness. Not only is it polite to be able to say "please" and "thank you" in the language of the country you are visiting, but it may give the windfall benefit of better service and a richer travel experience overall. If you are traveling to areas unaccustomed to Westerners or have a work-related task you must perform, contact the U.S. embassy in that country and ask about hiring an interpreter.

If while making advance arrangements for a trip you need to deal directly with a non-English speaker over the phone, try AT&T's Language Line service either from the U.S. or abroad. The range of languages is extensive, and the cost is $3.50 per minute. To access the service from the U.S., call 1-800-628-8486. From outside the U.S., the service is available via the AT&T USA Direct number for the country you are in. For further information on this service call 1-408-648-5871 in the U.S.; at your request, operators will give you the access number from the country you are visiting, or send you the list of all extant USA Direct access numbers.

Otherwise, you may want to call AT&T, MCI or Sprint—the three major U.S. phone-service companies—in advance of your trip and find out the number you would dial from overseas to get an English-speaking operator to assist on your calls home while abroad.

AT&T   1-800-525-6152

MCI   1-800-444-3333

Sprint 1-800-877-4646

Air Travel Comfort Tips

No one has yet claimed mastery of the art of air travel without some discomfort, but there are a few things you can do to stave off the worst effects of air travel, even in a crowded economy cabin on a long-haul flight.

The most crucial point is not to let yourself become dehydrated. The cabin air is very dry, and even a moderate-length flight can dry out your skin, lips and nasal passages. Bring travel-sized (i.e., small) containers of skin moisturizer and lip and nose ointments to compensate. Also, drink a lot of water (non-alcoholic beverages such as spring water are free on most airlines now), remembering to avoid those sparkling waters that contain salt. Intake of salty food should also be limited. In addition, alcohol consumption increases dehydration, so it helps to avoid drinking a lot of liquor the day before and also during a flight.

Get the meal you want: In order to ensure that your dietary needs are met while flying, you must contact the airline you are traveling on at least 48 hours in advance to request special meals. Most long-distance flights will have a variety of meals available in addition to the standard fare offered to all passengers who have not specified a choice. Choices usually include vegetarian, low-salt and sugar-free meals, and a variety of meals made to comply with several religions' dietary restrictions. Meal requests can also be made while making reservations.

Use those hours to rest: To ensure your peace and quiet while on board, bring along several items. A sleeping mask helps block out the strong light that comes in the windows or from overhead lights. Earplugs can also help you rest on board; they block out enough noise so that you can sleep, but not so much that you won't hear very loud noises. Many veteran air travelers also use a small inflatable neck pillow that supports the neck while you sleep. These items can also be a help when you arrive at your destination; many travelers find themselves in noisy hotels. With jet lag to fight, a sleeping mask may help you take a nap during daylight hours so you can catch up on lost sleep.

Travel in good health: For passengers prone to nasal or sinus congestion, antihistamines or nasal sprays may be advisable. For the best results, they should be swallowed or applied 10 to 15 minutes before boarding. Some travelers might want to get a prescription for sleeping tablets in order to sleep under the sometimes stressful or disruptive conditions imposed by travel. In addition, there are several over-the-counter airsickness products available; in a crunch, flight attendants may be able to provide these and other over-the-counter medications like aspirin, but if you want to be certain or want a specific brand name, carry your own. Many larger airports have shops that sell these products.

Passengers with certain types of ear congestion, inflammation or infection might want to consider postponing travel; if you have a serious ear problem, consult a doctor as some ear conditions can actually be worsened by airplane travel. The same logic should be applied to any chronic or severe health condition or physical discomfort. Seek your doctor's advice.

Dress for comfort: You can dress to look good, but make sure you also dress for comfort, which means loose, layered clothing. Although blankets and pillows are usually distributed, cabins may be very cold, or very hot and dry. You can add or remove layers to compensate. Shoes with a little room to spare are a good idea, too, since most air passengers' feet swell a bit.

Bonus tip: If a flight is full in economy class but has some spare places in business and first class, the airline may, at its discretion, "bump up" a couple of passengers to a higher class at no extra charge. Although purchasers of expensive first- and business- class tickets may basically wear what they want on a plane, the better-dressed economy-class passengers are often the ones to get bumped up (sometimes, however, bump-ups are done based merely on luck of the draw). If you think there is a chance this could happen on your flight, dress for the part: no jeans.

Pick a seat: Specific seat assignments may be requested from most airlines at the time your reservations are made; larger passengers may want to request aisle seats. And remember that the best way to ensure you will keep that chosen seat is to show up at the airport on time. Ask reservation assistants or travel agents what this margin should be; the amount of time you should arrive in advance varies depending on destination, airline, airport and many other factors. Passengers requiring assistance boarding or traveling with small children are always requested to board first.

Avoid extra waiting: Air travel can involve a lot of waiting and idle time. To avoid extra waiting, call the airline a few hours before your flight to check that it is scheduled to depart on time. Often, delays or cancellations are recorded many hours in advance, allowing you to revise the time you need to arrive at the airport. Delays and cancellations can also come at the last minute, though. To help get through any wait, and also the flight itself, bring reading material, games or a light, portable project you can work on in your lap or on those tiny airline trays.

Taking Care of the Home Front and Other Safety Tips

Whether you are traveling for business or pleasure, your next trip away from home can be made easier and less expensive with a little informed planning. One of the things people forget about when they leave home is home. It can happen easily when you are caught up in anticipating a vacation or preparing for a business trip. Yet it is crucial that you give as much thought to the place you are leaving as the one you are going to.

•If possible, give your spare key to someone you trust who has the time to look in on your place. If anything appears out of order, that person should call the police.

•Cancel all newspaper subscriptions. Uncollected newspapers on the doormat or in the hallway are a blatant announcement that a house or apartment is unoccupied, and any burglars casing the area will see them as an invitation. (Note: Some newspapers credit subscribers for undelivered newspapers.)

•Have your mail held by your local post office (you must sign a form at the post office for this service), or have a family member or trusted friend pick it up daily, again to avoid the appearance of a deserted house.

•If you live in an apartment building, let the superintendent or landlord know you will be gone and, if appropriate, give him/her a key. That way, if there is any kind of urgent maintenance problem—flooding, for example—the super can get in and save your home from further damage. Some tenants may not feel comfortable about giving the key to super or landlord. In this case, give it to someone you trust, and then give that person's name to your building super or landlord, as well as your contact number during your trip.

•Think twice before you drive your own car to the airport. Vandalism and burglaries in airport lots are common. Public transport options are usually good to most major airports, and even private car services have become relatively cheap in this highly competitive field. If you do choose to drive, park in an area that is well-lit at night and as close to terminals or a cashier's booth as possible. (Remember, too, that an empty garage back at home is another invitation to potential burglars.)

Sources of Further Information

PUBLICATIONS

Bottom Line/Personal
Subscription Center
P.O. Box 58446
Boulder, CO, 80322
A general consumer interest monthly newsletter with information on doing business, including travel tips, investment advice, etc.

The Consumer Reports Travel Letter
Subscription Department
P.O. Box 51366
Boulder, CO 80321-1366
1-800-234-1970
Consumer Reports Travel Buying Guide, published yearly by the Consumers Union, Yonkers, NY 10703; also available in bookstores and libraries.

Travel Easy (The Practical Travel Guide for People Over 50), Rosalind Massow for the American Association of Retired Persons, Scott, Foresman and Co., Glenview, Ill., 1985.

Many free booklets on travel opportunities can be ordered from the U.S. Consumer Information Center. Write Consumer Information Catalog, Pueblo, CO. 81002 for a free copy of the catalog. Among the publications are the following:

Access Travel: Airports outlines facilities at the world's major airports with an eye toward the concerns of the disabled and elderly traveler.

New Horizons for the Air Traveler with a Disability describes required airport facilities for the disabled and gives suggestions for planning your trip.

Foreign Entry Requirements lists addresses of embassies and consulates where you can obtain information about visas and special requirements for visiting that country.

Passports: Applying for Them the Easy Way gives details on how, when and where to get a passport, including information on fees.

Discover America: A Listing of State and Territorial Travel Offices of the United States gives information on where and how to order free vacation information.

A Guide to Your National Forests; Lesser-Known Areas of the National Park System; National Park System Map and Guide and *National Trails System Map and Guide* explain opportunities for visiting historically significant or scenic sites within the United States park system.

15

Personal
Finance

Managing Your Money

It's ironic that we spend much of the early parts of our lives preparing for our adult careers, yet devote very little time or effort to learning how to deal with the monetary rewards of that career. Money needs to be managed whether it is earned by a factory worker, inherited by an heiress or comes in the form of stock options for the CEO of a Fortune 500 company. If it isn't, it can be easily wasted or frittered away. It's even possible to outright lose some of your hard-earned cash without realizing it by making bad investment decisions or just not making the right one.

There are hundreds of books on personal finances, but money management for most of us involves taking care of the cash we spend now and the money we save or invest for later use. Today we need money for such things as paying the rent, buying food and putting gas in the car. Tomorrow we may need money to pay for a child's college education, to buy a cabin in the woods or to enjoy a comfortable retirement. The trick to managing your money is finding a way to accomplish all of those goals.

Net Worth

The first step to gaining control of your finances is to figure out just what your net worth is by listing your assets, which are the things you own, and your liabilities, which is what you owe others. It's a good idea to determine your net worth periodically because the results will give you a firm idea of how you are doing financially.

In addition, such things as college aid are often based on a family's net worth, and some lenders require a net worth statement for mortgages and other large loans. You can also use periodic reviews to adjust investment strategies.

The tables below are based on those provided by the American Association of Retired Persons in cooperation with the Federal Trade Commission. Simply list the amounts for each item. If you are married, make three columns: one for yourself, one for your spouse and a third that totals the two. Once you've completed the list, subtract the liabilities from the assets to find your total net worth.

Assets	Yourself	Spouse	Total
Checking accounts			
Savings accounts			
Brokerage accounts			
Money-market accounts			
Certificates of deposit			
IRA accounts			
Keogh or 401K accounts			
Other retirement accounts			
Pension funds			
Life insurance cash values			
Annuities			
Bonds			
Stocks			
Mutual funds			
Other securities			
Home			
Other real estate			
Personal property			
Total assets			

Liabilities	Yourself	Spouse	Total
Home mortgage			
Other mortgages			
Automobile loans			
Credit card balances			
Installment accounts			
Other money borrowed			
Income taxes			
Real estate taxes			
Alimony			
Other liabilities			
Total liabilities			
Total assets			
Subtract liabilities from assets			
Net worth			

This exercise is a first step in determining your financial picture. Knowing your net worth will help you figure out a budget. Use it as a starting point for day-to-day money management or as a guide to investment strategies. For example: If you discover that your net worth is negative, you know that you need to take steps to rectify this, such as concentrating on paying off credit-card debt. On the other hand, you may find you're worth more than you think and can be more aggressive in developing a long-range plan for large expenses such as retirement or paying for your children's college education.

Cash Flow

Your net worth will provide the big picture of your finances, but to track the day-to-day activities of earning and spending money you will need a cash flow statement. The statement can help you develop a budget because it will tell you how much you currently spend and where you need to cut back. It's common to find that you are spending more money than you thought on some items. It's good to learn this because you can use the information to adjust your spending habits, such as cutting back unnecessary items and saving more for the future. A cash flow statement is divided into income and expenses.

Income	Yourself	Spouse	Total
Salary/wages	_____	_____	_____
Interest/dividends	_____	_____	_____
Social Security (current distributions)	_____	_____	_____
Retirement plans (current distributions)	_____	_____	_____
Other investments	_____	_____	_____
Total income	_____	_____	_____
Expenses	_____	_____	_____
Savings	_____	_____	_____
Income taxes	_____	_____	_____
Real estate taxes	_____	_____	_____
Insurance (health, life, homeowner's, car, others)	_____	_____	_____
Mortgage or rent payments	_____	_____	_____
Utilities	_____	_____	_____
Auto loans	_____	_____	_____
Credit card debts	_____	_____	_____
Other debt payments	_____	_____	_____
Transportation	_____	_____	_____
Food	_____	_____	_____
Restaurants	_____	_____	_____
Entertainment	_____	_____	_____
Holiday expenses	_____	_____	_____
Gifts	_____	_____	_____
Education	_____	_____	_____
Clothing	_____	_____	_____
Personal items	_____	_____	_____
Other	_____	_____	_____
Miscellaneous	_____	_____	_____
Total expenses	_____	_____	_____

Once you have determined your actual cash flow, use the information to take short-term action in the areas where you might be able to cut back and save.

Types of Banks

In the old days, differences among financial institutions were well defined. Businesses and individuals with large accounts dealt with commercial banks; most other people had accounts with savings and loans, savings banks or credit unions. But deregulation in the 1980s changed all that. Today, most financial institutions can provide a full range of services.

Savings banks and savings and loans. These tend to be small institutions that serve a particular area. Many believe that service is more personal than one would receive from a large bank. Generally, fees charged for checking and other services are lower than those of commercial banks. Savings accounts are usually insured up to $100,000 by the Federal Deposit Insurance Corporation (FDIC).

Commercial banks. These institutions offer a full range of banking services. They tend to be large and have numerous branches, with many operating on a global scale. Deposits are insured by the FDIC up to the same limit.

Credit unions. These are nonprofit organizations that are owned by its members. They offer savings plans, checking accounts and loans, and some even offer home mortgages. Deposits are insured up to $100,000 by the National Credit Union Association. All members of a credit union usually have a common bond, such as a place of employment, union affiliation or membership in a fraternal organization.

Brokerage firms. These companies offer investment services that may include checking and money-market accounts. Many require large minimum balances.

TYPES OF ACCOUNTS
Here are some of the different types of accounts available at banks:

Savings Accounts
Passbook accounts. These are the most basic savings accounts. Your record of deposits and withdrawals is entered in a small ledger (the passbook) that remains in your possession. The bank teller will compute the interest either quarterly or annually.

Statement accounts. These are similar to passbook accounts except your business is recorded on a monthly or quarterly statement. Be sure to save all deposit and withdrawal receipts to compare against the statement.

Money-market accounts. These accounts usually pay more interest than passbook and statement accounts, and you may be able to write a limited number of checks on the account. However, most banks require a minimum deposit.

Certificates of deposit (CDs). These are savings instruments that last a specific length of time, which can range from one month to five years. They require a minimum investment and offer higher interest rates than other types of accounts.

Generally, the longer it takes the certificate to mature the higher the interest rate it pays. The drawback is you must pay a penalty if you withdraw your money early. When a certificate matures, you either invest your money elsewhere or reinvest (called roll over) in a similar certificate. The current market conditions may cause the interest rate to be higher or lower than the original certificate. Bank-issued certificates of deposit are insured up to $100,000 by the FDIC.

Checking Accounts

Regular checking. In its most basic form, a checking account charges you a monthly fee, a fee for each check or a combination of the two. Your money does not earn interest.

NOW accounts. The initials stand for "negotiable orders of withdrawal." These are checking accounts that earn interest on the balance in the account. Many banks require a minimum balance be kept in the account at all times. If you drop below the minimum, you will be charged maintenance and check fees.

CHOOSING A BANK

All banks offer the same basic services: savings accounts and checking accounts (they also offer credit cards and a variety of loans, but more on those later). The problem is, each bank has its own twist on these services. For example, one may offer consistently high interest rates on savings, but charge high fees for checking. Another may offer good interest and free checking, but once your balance drops below a set minimum they start piling on the charges.

The goal is to find the bank, or banks, that best suits your needs. Here are some questions to ask yourself when looking for a bank.

How Are Interest Rates Computed?

There are two things to find out here: whether the interest on savings accounts is simple or compound, and what method the banks uses to figure interest. With simple interest you earn a simple percentage of your investment. For example, a $1,000 one-year CD at 8 percent earns $80 in simple interest for a yield of $1,080. With compound interest, you earn interest on the original investment and the interest itself. For example, here's what happens if the same CD has interest compounded quarterly:

Original Investment	Yield
$1,000	$1,000
1st quarter add 2%	$1,020
2nd quarter add 2%	$1,040.40
3rd quarter add 2%	$1,061.21
4th quarter add 2%	$1,082.43

The $82.43 you earn on the original investment is actually a yield of about 8.24 percent.

CDs have a specific life span, but other types of savings plans have indefinite lengths. Your balance in these plans will rise and fall as you make deposits and withdrawals. Banks use one of three methods to determine interest.

1. Day of deposit to day of withdrawal: Your money earns interest the whole time it is in the bank. It is the best method for you, the depositor.

2. Average daily balance: The bank pays interest on the average balance for a given period, such as a quarter.

3. Lowest balance: The bank pays interest on only the lowest amount on deposit during the period.

Does the Bank Offer Direct Deposit?

Direct deposit of pay and Social Security checks is a convenient way to get money into your accounts without going to the bank. Your employer, if he participates in the program, arranges an electronic transfer of your pay into your account. Rather than receiving a paycheck, you get a receipt of the transfer. The government will do the same for Social Security checks.

Does the Bank Have ATMs?

Most banks have automated teller machines (ATMs), and most let you make deposits, withdrawals and payments free of charge at any time of the day or night. However, many charge a fee if you use the card at another bank's ATM. Many retailers now let you use a bank card to pay for purchases. The cost of the items is deducted directly from your checking or savings account.

Does the Bank Have Overdraft Protection?

This protects you if you mistakenly write a check when there are insufficient funds in your account.

Is the Bank Conveniently Located?

Are the bank's branches convenient to where you live and work, and are the people there pleasant? This is more important than it may seem. In his book *Still the Only Investment Guide You'll Ever Need,* Andrew Tobias writes that all banks offer pretty much the same services when it comes to insured, liquid accounts, such as savings, money-market and NOW accounts. Sure, one bank may pay a higher interest rate today, but chances are it won't be in the top position for long. And even if it is, rates for similar accounts usually vary by only 1/2 to 1 percentage point from bank to bank. One percent of $10,000 is $100 before taxes. Is it worth the time and effort necessary to keep moving your money around and follow the highest rate for $100, less taxes? If it is, fine. But if it isn't, finding a conveniently located bank that you are comfortable with becomes an important criterion in making your decision.

Other Investments

Savings, interest-earning checking accounts, money-market accounts and certificates of deposit are only some of the investment options open to you. You can also put your money in stocks, bonds and mutual funds.

STOCKS

When you buy a company's stock, you buy a piece of the company. It's possible to make money in two ways: The company pays its shareholders (those who own its stock) dividends, which come from the company's profits; and you can sell the stock for a higher price than you paid for it. Of course, neither one of these scenarios is guaranteed. The company may decide not to pay dividends or its dividends may be lower than expected; and the price of the stock could drop while you own it.

There are over 34,000 publicly traded companies. Investors pick stocks based on their goals. If the investor wants to generate short-term income, he or she will pick a stock that is likely to pay high dividends. If they have long-term goals, they may pick one whose price is likely to rise in the future.

Investors buy and sell stocks through brokerage firms. Full-service brokers offer investment advice as well as a way to trade stocks. Discount brokers act as your buying and selling agent only, but their fees are usually less than those of a full-service broker.

BONDS

These are issued by corporations, state and local governments, the federal government and even government agencies. When you buy a bond you make a loan to whomever issued the bond. Bonds have an interest rate, which is how you make your money, and a set period of time until maturity.

You can buy bonds when they are issued and hold them until they mature. Or you can buy and sell bonds between the issue and maturity dates. In this case, the price of the bond will fluctuate with the market. Government bonds include Treasury Notes and Bonds, which have terms of 1 to 30 years and are sold in amounts of $1,000 and up; Treasury Bills, which last from 13 to 52 weeks and are sold in lots of $10,000;

and U.S. Savings Bonds, which are sold for as little as $25.

Corporate bonds are sold through brokers. U.S. Treasury Notes and Bonds can also be purchased directly from commercial banks and any Federal Reserve Bank. Savings bonds can be purchased from banks or through a payroll savings plan offered by your employer.

MUTUAL FUNDS

These are collections of stocks, bonds or whatever the investments happen to be. A fund will have a stated goal, such as investing in small companies, in government-backed bonds or in companies that are environmentally conscious.

Mutual funds offer many advantages over buying single stocks or bonds. For one, the funds are managed by professionals who can adjust the mix of stocks or bonds to accommodate market conditions. For another, your money is spread over a variety of investments, so a single company in trouble will have only a slight impact over the entire fund. And finally, you can invest in some funds for as little as $500, although many funds have higher minimum investments. When considering a fund take into account its costs, which include sales charges (called the load; a fund that does not charge an initial sales charge is called a "no load"), fees to administer the fund, the risk involved and the long-term past performance of the fund.

Remember, mutual funds are not guaranteed; your original investment can shrink rather than grow.

You can buy shares of a mutual fund directly from the fund. They all have toll-free phone lines that allow you to order a prospectus, which is a description of the fund and a list of its investments, and an application. Check the financial pages of newspapers for fund advertisements. In addition, all the personal-finance magazines publish at least one issue a year that examines the funds available. These ratings usually include the phone number of the fund.

Developing a Financial Plan

Personal financial plans are based on meeting financial goals. To develop your plan, first set your goals, then compute your net worth and develop a day-to-day budget to meet those goals. Obviously, it is not as simple as that and there are a lot of options to consider. Here are some of those options.

SHORT-TERM NEEDS
The goal here is to prepare for the unexpected: loss of a job, sudden illness or some other large expense. To be ready, have three to six months of income in a safe (which means insured), liquid (which means you can withdraw the money quickly) account.

LONG-TERM GOALS
These, of course, will vary from individual to individual, but two of the most common are saving for a child's or children's education and saving for retirement.

The cost of a college education rises every year. Some estimates say that one year at a private college or university could cost $32,000 by the year 2000. To meet these costs it is important to begin a savings plan early and to contribute to it on a regular basis. The goal is to have the investment grow and mature when the bills for tuition, books and housing come due. As with meeting any long-term goal, it is important to minimize the taxes you need to pay on the investment.

One strategy is to purchase U.S. Savings Bonds. All savings bonds are free of state and local taxes, and if you use the bonds to pay college costs they are also free of federal taxes. There are income restrictions and the tax exclusion applies only to bonds used to pay tuition and fees, not books and housing expenses. The federal government publishes a booklet, "U.S. Savings Bonds for Education," that explains the program.

Saving for retirement has changed drastically in the last few years. No longer is it enough to rely on a company pension and Social Security. Today many people find it necessary to take a more active role in planning for their retirement years. Here are some of the options open to you in saving for your retirement.

Social Security
Everyone has a general idea of how Social Security works. The government deducts money from your paycheck, then when you turn 65, you receive income back from the government. The income you receive is based on an average of your 35 highest salary years. Few people, however, know what their retirement benefit will be. You

can get an estimate by contacting a Social Security office or calling 1-800-772-1213 for "A Request for Earnings and Benefit Estimate Statement" (form SSA-7004).

Plans offered by your employer

Most large companies, those with over 250 employees, offer some sort of pension plans to their employees. Basically, an employer contributes money to an account in the employee's name. At retirement, the employee takes the money in a lump sum or receives regular payments.

Another way your company can help with retirement is with a 401(k) plan. You save money in two ways with this type of plan: You contribute to the plan, but your contributions remain untaxed until you with-draw the money. For example, if you contribute $5,000 on a $45,000 salary you pay income tax on only $40,000. In addition, the money you earn on the investment is also tax deferred until you withdraw it. Some companies will match all or part of your contribution.

However, 401(k) plans are not guaranteed. These plans can invest in stocks, bonds, money-market funds and guaranteed investment contracts (offered by insurance companies) or a combination of investments.

Plans you set up yourself

Individual Retirement Accounts (IRAs) allow you to invest money that accumulates tax free until you withdraw it at retirement. There are limitations, how-

Picking a Professional Financial Planner

A financial planner helps you manage your money to reach your financial goals. The industry is not regulated, so it is important to be cautious when choosing a planner. Some planners charge a flat fee for their advice, others are paid a commission by the marketers of the investment products they sell. The American Association of Retired Persons and the Federal Trade Commission recommend you ask planners you are considering the following questions.

1. What are your credentials to practice financial planning?

Specialized training is important in this field. Look for qualifications such as Certified Financial Planner (CFP) and Chartered Financial Consultant (ChFC).

2. Are you registered with the Securities and Exchange Commission or with a state agency?

Anyone who gives advice on securities or the stock market should be registered with the SEC or a state agency that deals with investment advisers.

3. How would you prepare my financial plan?

Each plan should be tailored to the individual the plan is for. A good adviser will discuss your current financial situation, your financial history and long-term goals with you.

4. How many companies do you represent?

Someone who deals with only one or two companies is probably a broker or salesperson for those companies. A good adviser will offer you a wide range of options for your financial needs.

5. Whom will I work with?

It is important to work with someone who is familiar with your account. If considering a large firm, ask how the various experts the firm employs will coordinate about your account.

6. How do you keep up with the latest financial developments?

Staying abreast of financial developments is important in a planner. Members of the Institute of Certified Financial Planners are required to complete 30 hours of continuing education every year.

7. How will my financial plan be evaluated and updated?

The plan should adjust to changes in your life and financial circumstances, and to changes in the economic climate and tax laws. Inquire about the frequency and cost of periodic reviews.

ever. For example, there is a $2,000 annual cap, the original contribution can only be taken by those who do not have a pension plan where they work and there are income limitations as well. Congress is forever tinkering with IRA plans and the rules governing them are likely to change. For up-to-date information, go to the bank or mutual fund where you plan to open an account, ask your accountant or check with the IRS.

Another option is a tax-deferred annuity. In this type of plan you invest with an insurance company either with a lump-sum payment or with periodic payments. The earnings are tax free until retirement. Annuities are complicated to set up and there are many options to consider. For more information write to the U.S. government's Consumer Information Center for "Building Your Future with Annuities: A Consumer's Guide."

Plans for the self-employed

Simplified Employee Pension Plans and Keogh Plans allow those who are self-employed to plan for retirement. Each allows you to contribute up to $30,000 in tax-deductible contributions per year. The earnings are tax deferred. There are restrictions on each type of plan, which are offered by banks, mutual funds and brokerage firms. Find out more about these plans from IRS publication 560, "Retirement Plans for the Self-Employed."

Credit Reports

When you apply for a loan or a credit card, the bank expects two things: one, that you pay back the amount you borrowed, called the principal; and, two,

that you pay a finance charge for the use of the money. To determine if you can fulfill that obligation, the bank will order a credit report from one of the national credit-reporting bureaus. The report is a summary of your financial dealings. It tells the bank how you have handled loans in the past and your current amount of debt.

It is a good idea to check your credit report occasionally, especially before applying for a large loan, such as a mortgage. The bureaus do make mistakes and the lenders reporting on your credit can also make mistakes. (See sidebar for addresses of the three largest national credit bureaus.) When dealing with a credit-reporting agency under the Fair Credit Reporting Act, your rights include:

•If you are turned down for credit, insurance or employment (some employers do check credit reports), you must be told the name and address of the credit-reporting agency.

•If you are turned down for credit, insurance or employment because of information in a credit report, you are entitled to a free report. Otherwise, you may be charged a fee for a report.

•You have the right to have disputed information investigated. If the information is found to be incorrect or it cannot be verified, it must be removed from the record. If a change is made, you can request that the new report be sent to anyone who has denied you credit. If the matter is not resolved, you can have a brief statement placed in your file.

•You are also entitled to be told who has received a credit report on you within the past six months, or two years if a report was furnished for employment purposes.

•You can ensure that adverse information is removed after seven years; 10 years for bankruptcy.

READING YOUR CREDIT REPORT

When you order a report, the credit-reporting agency will send you instruc-tions for deciphering the information. Here are some of the highlights the report will contain:

•The names of the financial institutions that subscribe to the credit bureau and with which you have credit accounts. The report also lists closed accounts.

•The types of loans or credit cards and their terms.

Credit Strategy No. 1: Get a Copy of Your Credit Report

There are three national credit bureaus: TRW Credit Services, Trans Union Credit and Equifax. If you've ever borrowed money, received a credit card, purchased a home or applied for life insurance, the odds are that one or more of these credit bureaus has a file on you. Each of these bureaus has a file on nearly 200 million Americans. Their computers accept information about your payment habits from all of the major companies with which you do business.

Credit bureaus do not deny credit or issue credit ratings. They merely report your payment history to business subscribers, who then make their own credit decisions based on your credit report. It's your right to see what's in your credit report, and you should check it for errors every year. You can contact the major credit bureaus at the following addresses:

Trans Union Credit
Trans Union National Consumer Disclosure Center

25249 Country Club Blvd.
P.O. Box 7000
North Olmstead, OH 44070

TRW Credit Services
TRW Consumer Assistance Center
P.O. Box 2350
Chatsworth, CA 91313

Equifax
Equifax Information Service Center
P.O. Box 740241
Atlanta, GA 30374

Include your name (and any variations of your name that you use), your address and your Social Security number, and sign the request personally. If you've recently been turned down for credit, there is no charge for getting a copy of your report.

WHAT'S IN YOUR CREDIT REPORT?

Your credit report tracks payment history of any purchase you made using credit. Whether you make extended payments on credit or you always pay your bills in full every month, your payment record is reported to the credit bureau. The printed report uses a series of codes to identify your payment habits, but the credit bureau is required to give you a clear explanation of its reporting terminology. If a lender has recently inquired about your credit, that inquiry will be noted on your credit report.

Your credit record does *not* include information about your salary or wages, your bank accounts or your assets. However, if you apply for a large insurance policy or mortgage, the lender can request an "investigative" report, which could contain the above information as well as information gathered from business associates and neighbors about your personal living habits. (In 1992, Equifax signed an agreement limiting investigative reporting questions.)

Although the three major credit bureaus do have overlap files on many people, the information in each company's file may be different. To check thoroughly on your credit, you should contact the three major agencies and read each report.

From *Terry Savage's New Money Strategies for the 90s*, by Terry Savage, copyright 1993. Published by HarperBusiness, a Division of HarperCollins Publishers.

•The original amounts you borrowed and the credit limits for all credit cards.

•Outstanding balances and current monthly payments.

•A record of your payment history, including note of 30-, 60-, 90- and 180-day past-due payments.

•Information that is part of the public record, including judgments against you, bankruptcies and liens on your property.

Obtaining Credit

There are many different types of loans, but they all fall into two broad categories: secured and unsecured. A secured loan is one where the borrower puts up collateral as a guarantee that the loan will be repaid, such as with a car loan. If the borrower fails to make the payments, the bank or finance company can repossess the car. An unsecured loan is one where no collateral is involved and the money is lent on the borrower's promise that he or she will repay. Credit cards and revolving lines of credit are examples of unsecured loans.

Banks, credit unions and finance companies all lend money. Insurance companies will also lend money on certain types of insurance policies. Each organization has its own routine for qualifying potential borrowers, but in general all will require:

•Verification of employment. You may be asked to supply recent pay stubs and the address and phone number of your place of business.

•A list of checking, savings and investment accounts.

•A list of outstanding debt.

•A credit report from a credit-reporting bureau.

•In some cases, references.

Here are some of the terms you will encounter when applying for credit:

Annual Percentage Rate. Usually referred to as the APR, this is the true cost of the loan. It combines the annual interest rate and the cost of fees and charges that may be associated with the loan. For example, such items as application fees and charges for credit reports make up part of the APR.

Fixed and Variable Interest Rates. A fixed interest rate remains constant, as do your payments, over the life of the loan. A variable rate changes to reflect market conditions. As the interest rate changes, so do your payments.

Installment Loans. This is the basic form of loan. The lender gives you a lump sum of cash that you repay with interest over time. Car loans are typically installment loans.

Personal Lines of Credit. With this type of loan you qualify to borrow a specific amount of money, but the money stays in the bank until you need it. You can access the line of credit by writing special checks that the bank provides. The bank charges interest only on the amount you use. Once you've repaid the amount you borrowed, you can use the money again without applying for another loan. A credit card is a form of a line of credit.

Special Lines of Credit. A Home Equity Line of Credit is one example of this type of credit line. The credit limit is based on the equity you have in your house. Lenders figure the amount you can borrow by taking a percentage, say 75 percent, of the appraised value of your house and subtracting the balance of the existing mortgage. This tells lenders how much equity you have in the house, but lenders also consider your ability to pay when setting a credit limit. The interest paid on a home equity line is tax deductible. Since the line is secured by your home, failure to make the payments could mean loss of your home.

CREDIT CARDS

They are everywhere, yet no two are alike. In fact, some of the pieces of plastic in our wallets aren't even true credit cards. Visa, Mastercard and Discover are credit cards. You borrow money with the option of repaying principal and interest in monthly installments. American Express, Diners Club and Carte Blanche are travel and entertainment cards. You must repay your balance in full each month.

And then there are hybrids. For example, the American Express gold card is tied to a line of credit at a bank. You can pay the balance by tapping into the line, which you repay in monthly installments. Charge cards are issued by retailers and oil companies and are usu-ally only honored by the company that issues them.

Many credit cards offer cash advances, so you can get cash using your credit card. This feature can be useful in emergencies, such as when traveling. It is not a great deal financially, however; usually you will be charged a fee (generally a percentage of the advance), as well as a higher interest rate. You can procure these advances through any commercial bank, although some credit cards also issue checks or provide you with an ID number (a Personal Identification Number, or PIN) so you can use ATMs to obtain cash.

Visa and Mastercard offer their cards through banks and credit unions. A Visa card issued by one bank may be totally different from a Visa card from another bank. Companies like American Express and Discover offer their cards directly to you. When shopping for a credit card, compare one with another by looking at what they charge and what they offer. Examine the following:

Interest rates

There will be an annual interest rate and a periodic rate. This last is the rate the lender applies to outstanding balances in a billing period. For example, the periodic rate for an annual 12 percent interest rate is 1 percent. In one month you will owe 1 percent of your outstanding balance. The actual dollar amount you pay each billing period is called the finance charge and will be indicated on your statement each time you receive it.

Fees

Some cards charge an annual fee, others do not. Other fees include charges for cash advances, late payments and when you exceed your credit limit.

Grace periods

Some lenders begin applying finance charges as soon as you make a purchase. Others, however, do not impose finance charges until the first payment is due. If you pay off the entire purchase before the due date, there are no finance charges.

How finance charges are computed

Lenders use one of three methods to decide how much you owe them:

Adjusted balance method. In each billing period, the lender subtracts your payment from the beginning balance and computes the interest charge on the rest. You will pay less interest with this method.

Average daily balance. The lender computes a daily average of the money you owe. He then adds the averages together and divides them by the number of days in the cycle. This is the most common method used.

Previous balance. The lender computes the finance charge on the amount you owe at the end of the previous billing cycle. Payments you make during the current cycle are not taken into account until the next cycle of billing. This is usually the most expensive method for you.

Other incentives

Although lenders advertise the extras their cards offer, it is more important to select cards based on their cost to you. But if you've done your homework and nar-rowed your decision to a few cards, examine the incentives some cards offer:

Travel insurance. Many cards offer free insurance when you pay for your tickets for transportation with their card. In some cases, you can increase coverage with a small charge.

Additional cards. Family members can receive credit cards on your account. Some companies offer the cards free, others charge for them.

Shopping discounts. With some cards, the lender offers shopping discounts when you use the card. For example, a car company may apply a percentage of your purchases to the purchase of a new car.

Extended warranties. These extend the manufacturer's warranty. Some even replace lost or stolen goods when purchased with the card.

Collision insurance. This is used in place of high-priced collision coverage charged by car rental agencies.

Credit Card Protections

You have certain rights when it comes to using credit cards. They are:

Prompt credit of payments. The lender must credit your account the day it receives your payment. Follow the lender's instructions when making payments to avoid delays.

Refunds of credit balances. When you return or cancel merchandise that you paid for with a credit card, you can keep the credit on your account or request a refund from the lender if you have already paid the card issuer.

Protection against lost or stolen

cards. If you report the card lost or stolen before it is used, you cannot be held responsible for any unauthorized use. If the card is used before you report it stolen or lost, you will be liable for up to $50 per card. It is a good idea to keep a list of credit card account numbers and phone numbers in a safe place in case you need to report them missing.

Quick resolution of billing errors. If a billing mistake is made on your credit card bill, notify the issuer in writing. You have 60 days to do so. Save your purchase receipts to compare against the credit card bill. The lender will investigate and either correct the error or explain why the original bill is correct. The card issuer will provide you with information on requesting a billing-error investigation. Some even print instructions on each bill they send you.

Help with disputes involving defective merchandise or services. If you

---

Tips on Living with Credit Cards

Credit cards are a convenient way to pay for purchases, but misusing them carries financial consequences. Here are some points to keep in mind when handling credit cards, according to Gerri Detweiler, executive director of Bankcard Holders of America.

Too much credit can be bad. Although it may sound as if the reverse were true, having too many cards can be a reason for being rejected for an auto loan or mortgage. Obviously, if you already owe a lot of money, banks will not lend you more. But even if your balance is zero on many cards, lenders become cautious because of the potential for overextending yourself. It's best to keep two cards and cancel the rest.

Don't automatically accept a bigger credit limit. Again, lenders don't like it when loan applicants have too much credit available. Some lenders add up credit limits rather than actual debt.

You don't have to provide personal information when paying with a credit card. Some merchants ask for your address and phone number to expand their own mailing lists or to sell the lists to direct mail marketers.

Never give your card number to anyone unless you are buying something. Beware of anyone calling and asking for your card number to verify you won a prize.

Destroy all carbons to keep your card number out of the hands of dishonest people.

How to Deal with Your Debts

One of the biggest dangers of using credit cards and loans to pay for purchases is overextending your financial resources—owing more than you can comfortably afford to pay. This can lead to bad credit ratings and repossession of collateral, or your wages could be garnisheed to pay your bills or you might be forced to declare bankruptcy. If you are in financial trouble, there are a number of steps you can take and people and organizations you can turn to for help.

Creditors. The banks that lend you money do not want you to default on your loans or credit cards. If you alert them to a problem, they may be willing to revise your payment schedule so that you have smaller payments stretched out over a longer period of time. It is in their interest to do this because it helps them get their money back, and they can charge you interest over an extended period.

Credit counselors. There are many companies that claim they can clear up all of your debts. Be careful when selecting one. Sometimes the fees are extremely high for little or no service. An alternative step may be to contact a low-cost, non-profit counseling service. Some are operated by universities, credit unions and military bases. Check with a bank or your local consumer protection office for referrals to a low-cost credit-counseling service. The National Foundation for Consumer Credit is a nationwide nonprofit organization that can help you develop a repayment plan and realistic budget. Call 1-800-388-2227 for information.

have a dispute over merchandise or services you purchased with a credit card and cannot resolve it with the merchant, you can withhold payment from the credit card issuer. The amount must exceed $50 and the purchase must have been made within 100 miles of your home or billing address. The card company will investigate your complaint and decide if payment is necessary.

Insurance

Insurance plays an important part in everyone's financial plan. Without it, property loss due to fire or some other catastrophe, or the serious illness or death of a wage earner, could leave a family penniless. We will look at three different types of insurance: homeowner's, health and life. But first here are some general terms you should be familiar with.

Agent. This is the person who sells insurance policies. Some agents work for only one company. Others, called independent agents, offer policies from a number of companies.

Claim. This is your request for payment from an insurance company.

Deductible. This is the amount you agree to pay before the insurance company begins paying on a policy. For example, if you have $1,000 worth of damage to your home and a deductible of $500, the insurance company will pay only $500. Generally, the higher the deductible, the lower the premium you pay.

Endorsement. This is an attachment to a policy that changes the policy's original terms.

Insurance Department. Each state has rules governing the insurance industry. Your state agency may be able to provide free information; look in the blue pages of the phone book under "Insurance Department" for a number. The department usually handles consumer complaints about insurance companies.

Premium. This is the annual amount you pay for insurance coverage.

HOMEOWNER'S INSURANCE

If you have ever purchased a house, you know that one of the things you must bring to the settlement table is a homeowner's insurance policy. The financial institution that holds the mortgage will usually require a policy that at least equals the amount of the mortgage. But there are other factors you should consider too. Policies differ from one another and you should read yours carefully, but the standard policy usually covers:

• The house and any separate structure on the property, such as a garage or tool shed.

• Your furniture and other personal possessions. The amount covered is usually 50 percent of the amount of insurance on the building.

• Your liability if someone is injured while on your property.

Here are some points that are worth inquiring about:

Cost to rebuild. Though your bank may require a policy only in the amount of the mortgage, that amount may not be enough to cover the cost of rebuilding your home should it be destroyed. In fact, if the house is insured for less than 80 percent of its replacement value, then even partial losses may not be fully reimbursed. Discuss this with your agent.

Replacement cost coverage. On a typical policy the insurance company will pay the actual cash value of a loss, which means the cost of the item minus depreciation. Replacement cost coverage is the actual cost to replace an item with a similar item at current prices. This type of coverage may be available on the structure as well as personal possessions. There are restrictions and your premium will increase with replacement cost coverage.

Limits on personal possessions. A standard policy insures such items as jewelry, silverware, furs, art and collectibles up to a certain limit. If the pol-icy does not cover your possessions adequately, consider adding a floater, which is extra coverage added to your policy.

LIFE INSURANCE

Life insurance is one of those things that a lot of us don't care to think about. Ignoring it, however, could lead to severe financial consequences in the future. Here are the basic types of plans available:

Term Insurance. With this type you are covered for a specific amount of money for a specific length of time, usually one, five or 10 years. If you die during that period and the premiums are paid, your beneficiaries receive the value of the policy. This is the least expensive type of insurance you can buy. However, premiums increase as you get older. Some policies allow you to convert to a permanent policy, which is described below.

Whole Life Insurance. This is also called straight life or permanent life.

Filing a Homeowner's Insurance Claim

One of the things that can make filing an insurance claim easier is to have a complete inventory of your possessions. The inventory should contain a description of the item, the price and the date you purchased it. Back up the list with photographs and purchase receipts. The Insurance Information Institute can provide a form to help you fill out the inventory.

Here is a claim-filing checklist based on information from the Society of Chartered Property and Casualty Underwriters and the Insurance Information Institute.

Report a burglary or theft to the police.

If someone is injured on your property seek medical attention immediately.

Phone your insurance agent or company representative as soon as possible. Some policies have time limits for filing claims.

Follow up your phone call with a written report.

For property claims, do not alter the condition of the house until it has been inspected by a claims adjuster. However, you should make temporary repairs to prevent further damage.

Make a list of the damaged items.

Keep a record of any repairs you make and submit them to the insurance company.

Keep a record of living expenses if you must find other accommodations until repairs are made to your home.

Discuss any complaints you have with your agent or adjuster. Check your policy to see what appeal steps it outlines.

These types of policies have a fixed death benefit and a fixed premium. Part of your premium goes toward insurance coverage and part toward a tax-deferred cash reserve in your name, which is invested by the insurance company. If you cancel the policy, you receive its cash value.

Universal Life Insurance. This is similar to whole life insurance, but universal life offers more flexibility. The policies are structured to allow you to change both the premiums, as long as they are above a fixed minimum, and the death benefits over the life of the policy. Unlike whole life policies your premiums go first to cover the cost of insurance, with the amount left over going to a cash reserve.

Variable Life Insurance. This is similar to the other two except you direct how the cash reserve will be invested. Usually, the insurance company will offer a selection of mutual funds for you to choose from.

HEALTH INSURANCE
Health insurance provides coverage when you are sick or have an accident. The least expensive type of health insurance is provided through a group of some sort, such as your employer, a professional association or a union. Since the insurer provides coverage for everyone in the group, expenses can be kept lower than if each individual in the group purchased a separate policy. You can, however, purchase a policy as an individual.

Policies vary widely. Here are the most common types of coverage:

How Much Insurance Do You Need?

There really isn't an easy answer to this question. Life insurance covers immediate needs, such as burial costs, and long-term needs, such as helping to fund a child's education. Begin by finding your net worth and computing a budget. Then consider your circumstances. For example, if you have young children, you may want to provide for them through college. If you have children who are already in college and about to enter the job market, it may not be necessary to have a large insurance policy. Whatever you decide be sure to adjust your policy or policies to reflect changes in the economic climate and your family's life.

Hospital-Surgical Policies. These cover conditions that require you to be in a hospital for treatment. Some policies require a deductible, others do not.

Major Medical. This type of policy pays the bills for treatment in and out of hospitals. In its simplest form, it is designed to help with costs where more basic policies leave off.

Comprehensive Policies. There are variations but, in general, these policies cover medical expenses in and out of the hospital. A common type requires a deductible for expenses outside of the hospital while paying full or nearly full costs for expenses incurred in a hospital.

Excess Major Medical or Catastrophic Policies. These are designed for people who may not have sufficient coverage with other policies. They have very high deductibles, which could be as high as $15,000, and limits.

Long-Term Care. These policies cover the costs of custodial care in a nursing home or at home.

Disability Income Insurance. These policies provide replacement income if you are unable to work because of illness or accident. Generally, the policy will pay a percentage of your income for a specific amount of time.

Buying Health Insurance

There are many different types of health insurance policies available, and many employers now offer their employees options from among different types of plans. Here are some points to consider:

What's covered:
•Inpatient hospital services

•Outpatient surgery

•Physician visits while in the hospital

•Office visits

•Nursing care

•Medical tests and X-rays

•Prescription drugs

•Drug- and alcohol-abuse treatment

•Psychiatric and mental health care

•Rehabilitation facility care

•Physical therapy

•Hospice care

•Maternity care

•Chiropractic care

•Preventative care

•Well-baby care

•Dental care

Premiums. It pays to shop around and compare premiums and levels of insurance.

Deductibles. The cost of your insurance premiums will be reduced if you raise the deductible on the policy.

Co-insurance. After you reach your deductible, the insurance company will pay part of the bill and you will pay the rest, with an 80/20 split—you pay the 20 percent—being the most common. This will continue until you reach an out-of-pocket limit, after which the insurance company pays the full bill. Most policies have a maximum benefit they will pay.

Fee-for-service vs. managed care. In the past, you went to your doctor, paid for his services and filed a claim with the insurance company. This procedure is called fee-for-service care. A relatively new way to obtain medical services is through a managed-care program, with Health Maintenance Organizations (HMOs) being the most common. With this type, a group of doctors, hospitals, nurses and other health care professionals provide medical services to the people who enroll in the group. When you become part of the group you pick from a list of professionals. Or you may go to a specific location and see the professionals available at that time.

Some medical plans offer a combination of fee-for-service and managed care. One variation is the Preferred Provider Organization, where a group of professionals agree to be part of the plan. If you choose to use a doctor not registered in the plan, you will pay more of your own money for services.

Taxes

Federal tax laws and regulations are extremely complicated. But it is possible for most of us to save the necessary documents and prepare our own income tax returns. Some of the most important forms include:

Form W-4. Our income tax system is a pay-as-you-go system. In other words, the government expects to receive your tax payments throughout the year. If you have a full-time job, you will fill out a W-4 form to determine how much of your pay is withheld in taxes. Your employer then sends your taxes to the government. The W-4 form has a worksheet to help you figure the amount that should be withheld.

1040-ES. This is an estimated tax form. If not enough money is withheld from your pay because you earn extra income or if you are self-employed, this form, which you file quarterly, estimates the amount of tax you owe. You send an estimated tax payment with the form.

Form W-2. Your employer should send this form to you every January. It lists all the federal taxes you paid during year as well as state and local taxes that were withheld from your pay. Check it carefully and file it with your tax return.

Dealing with the IRS

Keeping Records. All deductions from income that you claim on your return should be verified with receipts and canceled checks. Appointment and travel logs are also important. Get IRS publications 17, "Record Keeping" and 526, "How to Report," for more information.

It is also important to keep your records for some time after you have filed. Here are some guidelines:

Tax returns should be kept at least six years.

Records of income and expenses should be held at least three years, because that is how long the IRS has to audit your return. However, they have six years if you underreported your income by 25 percent or more. And if you simply don't file returns they have forever to audit you.

Records that cover real estate improvements and the cost of selling your house should be held for at least seven years after you sell the house.

Responding to an audit. The IRS examines or audits a number of tax returns every year. Publication 1, "Your Rights As a Taxpayer" and Publication 556, "Examination of Returns, Appeal Rights and Claims for Refund," spell out your rights as a citizen. There are different types of audits.

In an examination by mail, the IRS informs you that you made an error on your return. Or they may request certain records to clarify the return. This is the most common form of audit. If the matter cannot be resolved by mail, you can request an interview.

The examination by interview is the one everyone dreads. Basically, you meet with an IRS representative to discuss certain parts of your return. The IRS will tell you which records to bring to the interview and they will explain your rights under IRS regulations. If you don't agree with the IRS's findings you can appeal the decision to the IRS appeals office. If the matter still isn't resolved to your satisfaction, you can appeal to the court system.

Form 1040. This is the master form you complete when you file your tax return. Filling one out could require you to file additional forms and schedules. 1040EZ and 1040A are shorter versions of 1040 for less complicated returns. The Internal Revenue Service (IRS) sends tax packages complete with the most often-used forms and preprinted mailing labels every year. If you don't receive one you can get forms at banks, post offices or regional IRS offices. Or you can call 1-800-829-3676 to order forms and instruction booklets, including Publication 910, which is a catalog of the free services and publications the IRS offers.

Sources of Further Information

BOOKS

Still the Only Investment Guide You'll Ever Need. Andrew Tobias, Bantam, New York, 1987.

The Wall Street Journal. Guide to Understanding Personal Finance. Kenneth M. Morris and Alan M. Siegel, Lightbulb Press, distributed by Prentice Hall Professional Publishing, New York, 1992.

BOOKLETS AND PAMPHLETS

The booklets listed below are available from the Consumer Information Center, Pueblo, CO 81002. Write for a free copy of the Consumer Information Catalog.

Facts About Financial Planners, American Association of Retired Persons and the Federal Trade Commission, 1990.

Investors' Bill of Rights, Commodity Futures Trading Commission, U.S. Postal Service and The National Futures Association, 1987.

Building Your Future with Annuities: A Consumer's Guide, Fidelity Investments and U.S. Department of Agriculture.

Federal Credit Unions, National Credit Union Association, 1992.

Staying Independent: Planning for Financial Independence in Later Life, The U.S. Department of Agriculture and American Express, 1990.

Investment Swindles: How they Work and How to Avoid Them, National Futures Association and Commodity Futures Trading Commission, 1987.

Fair Credit Reporting Act, Federal Deposit Insurance Corporation, 1987.

Protecting Your Privacy, U.S. Office of Consumer Affairs and American Express, 1990.

Several brochures detail how to check your credit file and medical records, handle telephone sales and have your name removed from mailing lists. They are also available from the Consumer Information Center, Pueblo, CO 81002.

Information About Marketable Treasury Securities (Bills, Notes and Bonds), Department of the Treasury, 1993.

Facts for Consumers: Solving Credit Problems, Federal Trade Commission and Office of Consumer Protection, 1992.

Facts for Consumers: Choosing and Using Credit Cards, Federal Trade Commission and Office of Consumer Protection, 1991.

The Savings Bonds Questions and Answer Book, Department of the Treasury, 1994.

Internal Revenue Service publications are available by calling 1-800-TAX FORM or from your local IRS office (check the blue pages of your phone book to find one in your area).

Your Rights as a Taxpayer, IRS Publication 1.

Examination of Returns, Appeal Rights and Claims for Refund, IRS Publication 556.

ORGANIZATIONS

Insurance Information Institute
110 William St.
New York, NY 10038
1-212-669-9200
Publishes *Here Today Gone Tomorrow: Renters and Homeowners Insurance*; *Taking Inventory: A guide to preparing an inventory of your personal possessions*; *How to File an Insurance Claim* and *Insurance for Your House and Personal Possessions: Deciding How Much You Need.*

National Association of Professional Insurance Agents
400 N. Washington St.
Alexandria, VA 22314-9980
1-703-836-9340
Publishes *Straight Talk About Homeowners Insurance.*

American Council of Life Insurance
1001 Pennsylvania Ave. NW
Washington, DC 20004-2599
Publishes *A Consumer's Guide to Life Insurance.*

Health Insurance Association of America
1025 Connecticut Ave. NW
Washington, DC 20036-3998
Publishes *The Consumer's Guide to Health Insurance.*

National Consumer Insurance Hotline
1-800-942-4242
For complaints or questions about insurance.

16

Legal Matters, Forms and Contracts

Into every life a few legal transactions must fall. Some, but not all, require you to hire a lawyer. One of the most common, one that you might not even think of as a legal transaction, is the purchase of an item.

Bills of Sale

A bill of sale, whether for a can of corn or a convertible, serves as evidence of the transfer of title from one party to another. For a major purchase, the bill of sale should contain a detailed description of the item (in the case of a car, boat or other vehicle, this includes color, make, model, registration numbers, etc.), date of transfer from seller to buyer and signatures of both parties.

A bill of sale does not, however, instill the buyer with any specific set of rights. To establish these, a sales contract is necessary. When making a major purchase, be sure to secure a sales contract, signed by both you and the seller.

Not all sales contracts are created equal. No matter how much you want a particular item, resist the urge to "sign on the bottom line" until you know exactly what is in the contract you are signing. In its publication *Everyday Contracts: Protecting Your Rights,* HALT, a Washington, D.C.-based public-interest group, suggests the following tips before you sign any contract, including a sales agreement:

•Get all of the terms of the agreement in writing. In other words, don't "shake on" anything or rely on anything being "written in later." The content of the written agreement you sign is your only protection.

•Don't sign anything unless you're absolutely sure. Make certain that you read and understand everything in the contract—don't merely listen to a salesperson describe what's in it. Ask questions, and if you have doubts, take the contract home and read it over with someone you trust or who is knowledgeable or experienced in the subject.

•Change the language to fit the terms, if necessary. Make sure that all the terms you are agreeing to are in the contract, and that none of the terms you are not agreeing to are still there. Don't let a salesman tell you a clause is irrelevant or "not really binding." If you sign it, you're agreeing to it.

•Fill in the blanks. Never sign a contract that has any blank spaces left; they must all be either filled in or crossed out.

•Make sure you understand the payment schedule. This includes knowing the full amount you owe including interest, delivery and other charges, how much each payment is and how often each is due, and what the consequences of late or missed payments are.

•Keep a copy of the contract. This is your proof that an agreement has been made. Keep it in a safe place.

•Consider adding a mediation or arbitration clause to the contract. This provision means that if problems arise during the course of the agreement that cannot be successfully resolved between you and the other party, you both agree to take the dispute to an arbitrator or mediator, which can be a much less costly solution than cross-filing lawsuits.

HALT also points to two types of consumer-protection laws that are designed to ward off the "hard sell." The "cooling-off" rule, which is enforced by the Federal Trade Commission, applies to any sales contract that meets all of the following criteria:

•It is not made at the seller's usual place of business (this applies to such vendors as door-to-door salespeople).

•It is not made by mail or telephone (although there are other laws that govern these purchases).

•It is for more than $25.

•It is not for real estate, insurance or securities (again, other regulations cover these sales).

•It is not for emergency home repairs.

"Plain language laws" are also on the books in many states to protect consumers. These require that all consumer contracts be written in clear, understandable, non-technical language.

Wills

Many people are under the mistaken impression that spouses, children or other family members automatically inherit everything left behind by those who die *intestate,* or without wills. This is not the case in most states. Call local or state probate court; if they can't answer your questions to your satisfaction consult a lawyer.

The laws of intestacy of each individual state determine the distribution of any assets that were solely owned by the decedent. In many cases, the estate is liquidated in probate court and divided among family members. This could mean, for example, that assets would be divided equally among the spouse and children of a married decedent with a family, or the wife, parents, brothers, sisters and possibly even nieces and nephews of a married, childless decedent. In many cases, the probate court can also order the sale of the home of those left behind, if it was owned by the decedent alone.

Suffice it to say that the monetary and emotional costs of settling an estate for which there is no will are usually considerably higher than those for which there is one.

WHEN TO WRITE YOUR WILL

Anyone of legal age who has amassed any funds, property or possessions should have a will. When to write it? As soon as possible. The thought of your own mortality may be unpleasant—but the thought of everything you've worked hard for coming under the control of the courts after you've gone is even more so.

Writing your will is only the first step in estate planning, however. You should review the document at least every two to three years—sooner if your economic status changes considerably—with your financial, tax or legal advisor, and make updates as necessary.

WHERE TO STORE YOUR WILL

Once you have drawn up a will, you must take care to store the original in a place that is both secure and accessible to you and, upon your death, to your executor.

For many people, a safe-deposit box seems the most logical choice—but in some states, laws dictate that these be sealed until state tax authorities can review their contents, which would leave the will out of your executor's reach until such a review is completed. Most states, however, do allow a safe-deposit box to be searched after the death of the owner, to determine if the original will is inside.

What are your alternatives? Most state probate courts, some county clerk's offices and many law firms will store your will for a nominal fee. You can also keep your will in your office or home, in a safe, water- and fireproof container with other vital papers. Be sure that the executor of your will and any key family members know the location of the box. The best way to do this: Make a clear, detailed written record specifying the location of all important documents and other relevant material, and make sure that people know where it is. Give a copy to each person in question, or keep it in your desk, where it will be easy to find. Such a record can help to streamline the entire estate process for the executor of your will and others you leave behind.

PROBATE

Assets that are left in a will must go through the probate process—although in many states, estates that are valued at less than a certain amount or left by one spouse to another are either exempt from probate or subject to a very informal procedure.

Probate is the legal process that involves filing the decedent's will, identifying and accounting assets, paying debts and death taxes, and distributing the remainder as dictated in the terms of the will.

The purpose of probate is to allow a court to have temporary supervision over the management of an individual's estate, to protect it from possible fraud or abuse and to guarantee that those who are legally entitled to the estate are provided for.

The entire process generally takes anywhere from six months to a year, and is managed by the will's executor and an attorney whom he or she hires; a will can include a suggestion about which attorney to retain, but the suggestion is not legally binding on the executor.

The principal duties of the executor are as follows:

•Locate the will.

•Carry out any funeral or burial requests specified in the will.

•Submit the will to probate court, with proof that this is the original and only will.

•Obtain from the court "letters testamentary" (official authority) to act as executor.

•Get a federal tax identification number for the estate and notify the Internal Revenue Service of the executor's identity.

•Obtain access to the decedent's safe-deposit box (which is permissible in most states) and record the contents.

•Collect the net proceeds of the decedent's outstanding assets, such as veteran's or Social Security benefits, rent and utility deposits, life insurance, pensions or other retirement funds, bank accounts, etc.

•Inventory all of the decedent's personal property and assemble all relevant documents, and have the property appraised for actual value.

•Carry out the decedent's instructions concerning business or investment interests.

•Determine and collect any debts owed to the decedent.

•Set aside property that is probate-exempt and distribute it to the beneficiaries.

•Tend to changes in titles owned jointly by the decedent and another person.

•Publish or in some other way give appropriate notice to the decedent's creditors to allow them to make claims to the estate.

•Pay off the decedent's debts, including funeral and estate-administration expenses.

•Represent the estate in court against any legal action, such as contesting of the will.

•Gather the beneficiaries and distribute the remainder of the estate in accordance with the dictates of the will.

•Give the court a "final accounting" of services, including detailed records of receipts and payments.

•Obtain a "formal discharge" from the court after all duties have been performed.

Both the attorney and the executor receive their fees from the estate. Fees vary from state to state, and in many states they are calculated on either a percentage of the estate's "gross" worth (before debts are factored in) or its "net" worth (after debts).

Attorneys' fees must be approved by the probate court—so if the fee seems unreasonably high, the executor or a beneficiary should file a formal, written objection.

If you are planning your own estate and considering the financial consequences of probate, you may wish to protect certain assets—especially a big-ticket item such as a home—from the process. Attorney Denis Clifford, author of *Nolo's Simple Will Book*, suggests that you investigate such probate-avoidance devices as:

•Living trusts, in which you, as the "trustor" of the property, name a successor trustee who will take over the management of the property upon your death, and pass it on to your designated trust beneficiaries.

•Joint tenancy, a type of shared property ownership in which the surviving owner automatically inherits your share of the property at the time of your death.

•Retirement plans such as IRAs and Keoghs, which allow you to name a beneficiary to receive any remaining funds upon your death.

•Life insurance, in which you designate a specific beneficiary.

•Gifts, which in the broad legal sense include any property given freely from one living person to another, with no commercial intent.

•Informal bank trusts, in which you as "trustor" open an account in trust for a specific beneficiary, who gains control of the funds only upon your death.

If you wish to protect any of your assets from the probate process, consult with your attorney or financial adviser about the above options and other available methods.

Living Wills

A "living will," also referred to as a directive to physicians, is in the technical sense not a will at all, since its provisions are carried out while the signatory is still alive. A living will directs medical personnel to withhold or withdraw "heroic measures" or life-support equipment if you are suffering from a terminal, irreversible illness and death is imminent.

Many states still do not recognize the validity of such documents. Issues of desired/undesired medical care may be better settled through the use of an instrument known as durable power of attorney (see below), which is recognized in all states.

If you do wish to write a living will, check first to make sure that they are recognized by the laws of your state. Then obtain a living will form from your state's department of health, and carefully review the requirements for filling it out correctly. If you are unclear about anything, ask questions.

The book *Write Your Own Living Will* by Bradley E. Smith advises that you then do the following:

•Find two witnesses and a notary who meet your state's requirements, and fill out the living will form in their presence.

• When you enter your name, print or type it as you commonly use it, as it appears on bank records or tax returns.

• In the presence of and with the guidance of the notary, sign your form and have your witnesses sign it.

• Make copies of your executed living will form and your checklist of medical intervention (see next section), and distribute them to your physician and anyone else you deem necessary.

• Complete a living will record noting the execution date, names and addresses of notary and witnesses, location of the original document, names of those with copies, and dates for two- and four-year reviews and a five-year re-execution.

• If you want to change your form in any way, make sure your witnesses and a notary are present.

Living wills govern which life-sustaining procedures should or should not be used in the event that you become terminally ill and death is imminent. The determination of terminal illness and probable imminent death are made by your attending physician—but the definition of what qualifies as "life-sustaining equipment" is much more vague. The following, from *Write Your Own Living Will*, is a checklist of medical interventions that you should discuss with your physician, who can explain them in detail. The list of medical interventions that you choose should be kept in your medical file, along with a copy of your living will:

• Pain medication: narcotics and other drugs administered to reduce pain.

• Antibiotic treatment: the use of drugs to fight bacterial infection.

• Blood transfusions.

• Simple diagnostic tests: blood tests, Xrays, etc.

• Invasive diagnostic tests: more complex tests requiring cutting of the skin or insertion of an instrument (cardiac catheterization, etc).

• Chemotherapy: treatment of cancer with drugs, which may have substantial side effects.

• Kidney dialysis: mechanical removal of waste from blood.

• Minor surgery: minor operative procedures.

• Major surgery: more difficult and potentially dangerous procedures.

• Organ transplantation: replacement of a diseased organ with the organ of another person.

• Mechanically assisted breathing: may require the insertion of a tube into the windpipe.

• Cardiopulmonary resuscitation (CPR): techniques for stimulating a stopped heart.

• Artificial nutrition and hydration: intravenous feeding, nasogastric intubation (nourishment from a tube from the nose to the stomach) and gastronomy (nourishment through a tube surgically implanted in the stomach).

It is critical to periodically review your living will—at least once every two years—to determine if you need to update it for such reasons as a change in your health or advances in medical science. It is advisable to re-execute the document every five years, with a notary as a witness. (This is simply a matter of (re-reading and re-signing it.) You can also revoke your living will at any time.

Durable Power of Attorney (Caregiver Letters)

When drawing up your last will and testament, you may also want to take the time to prepare for the possibility that you could become physically or mentally incapacitated, and unable to tend to your own medical or financial affairs.

The document that addresses this issue is called a durable power of attorney, in which you appoint someone else, your "attorney in fact," to handle your financial affairs and make and manage your health care decisions in the event that you can no longer do so. The document does not take effect until that time.

Durable power of attorney grants enormous powers to your "attorney in fact," who can sign checks and contracts, deposit and withdraw funds, make business and health-care decisions, enter safe-deposit boxes, transfer, buy or sell property and make gifts on your behalf. He or she can also carry out your specified wishes concerning the use or refusal of extraordinary life-sustaining equipment, including life-support mechanisms.

Some people opt to name two attorneys in fact, which increases the paperwork, since both must sign all documents, but may reduce the risk involved.

If you have no such document and you become incapacitated, a representative, known as a conservator or guardian, will likely be appointed by the probate court. In this public and often expensive process, the probate court notifies family members and often other interested parties, and after meeting with them makes a decision that may or may not coincide with what you would have wished. So if you want to ensure that your specific wishes are carried out, make sure that they are written down and entrust them to someone with durable power of attorney. Some states would honor a simple written request.

Lease Agreements

Most residential leases have standard "boilerplate" language—but you still must read it carefully. Also remember that some clauses, such as those concerning pets, may be negotiable. If you and your landlord do agree to any changes, make sure that they are in writing and that the clauses they are replacing are removed, or crossed out and initialed by you and your landlord.

•Many leases, for example, contain clauses that effectively allow the landlord to postpone your move-in date if the apartment isn't ready on time, or if the previous tenant has failed to vacate. Some states have already outlawed such clauses—but most have not. If this clause pops up in your lease, negotiate an arrangement that covers you in the event the apartment is not available as soon as the lease takes effect. Replace this language with the original clause in the lease, and have the change initialed.

•Your lease will probably also contain a clause in which you agree that the apartment is in proper condition. If you and your landlord have agreed to any upgrades or repairs, make sure they are completed before you sign your lease. If there is damage to the apartment that you are willing to live with, or if your landlord has agreed to make repairs after you move in, make sure this is noted in writing and initialed in the lease, and that the "proper condition" language is omitted or struck out and initialed; otherwise, you may be held liable for damage that existed before you ever saw the place.

•Many people are also tripped up by the "access to the apartment" clause, which generally allows the landlord to make repairs or show the apartment as a sample to prospective tenants. This clause should contain specific language about the hours your landlord can enter your apartment and how much notice you must be given. If such specifics are not in your lease, see to it that they are written in and initialed, and that more general language is removed or crossed out and initialed.

•Also look for clauses regarding late fees: Many states have laws governing when they can kick in and how high they can be.

•Clauses that oblige you to follow the landlord's "rules and regulations" can be tricky as well. Ask for a written copy of any such rules before you sign your lease.

•Never assume that any utilities are part of the package; take careful note of what's paid for by the landlord and what isn't, and factor this into your monthly budget.

•Certain clauses should raise red flags not because they are onerous but because they are outright illegal. A landlord cannot, for example, demand that you "sign away" your right to hold him or her legally responsible for any property damage or personal injury that stems from his or her negligence; your right to sufficient notice to vacate the premises; your right to heat and hot water if they are provided by your lease; or your right not to be forced to pay your landlord's attorney's fees in the event of a legal dispute with you.

Even if an illegal clause in your lease is voided by the courts, however, the lease itself will in most cases remain legally valid.

If your lease contains any language you do not understand, don't ask your landlord to explain it: Ask an attorney or real estate professional who is not associated with your landlord to go over the lease with you before you sign.

"Open" Rental Agreements (Oral Agreements)

An "open" rental agreement, or one that does not involve a lease, gives you, as a tenant, much more freedom than a written agreement—but far fewer, if any, rights. Such a pact is considered legal if the agreed-upon term is short enough (in most states, up to one year).

Typically in such an agreement, you

and the landlord come to terms on an apartment, amount of rent, payment schedule, date of occupancy—and little or nothing else. You have virtually no practical recourse if the landlord fails to have the apartment ready by the scheduled move-in date, fails to perform agreed-upon repair work—or fails to inform you that a heavy-metal band practices next door and a tap-dancing troupe lives upstairs.

While you have the freedom to bolt on short notice (usually a month or so), the landlord can boot you—or boost your rent—just as quickly. In short, most legal experts agree that an oral rental agreement is not worth the paper it's written on.

Owner/Contractor Agreements

If they are not approached with care, "improvements" to your home can result in a greatly diminished quality of life. Stories of contractor nightmares are legion—but fortunately so are the ways to avoid them.

First, determine whether you want to act as your own general contractor and hire independents to work for you, or whether it's wiser to hire a general contractor to manage the whole job. It is usually best to serve as your own general contractor only if the job is simple and not especially time-consuming.

According to the how-to manual *Everyday Contracts: Protecting Your Rights,* the responsibilities of the general contractor are:

•Buying supplies.

•Obtaining permits, which are always required when structural work is involved or a home's basic living area is being changed.

•Making sure renovations meet code requirements.

•Hiring and paying subcontractors.

•Supervising the work.

Make sure that your contractor agreement contains the following:

•A release of lien, which means that independent contractors, subcontractors and suppliers cannot place a mechanics' lien on your property if the general contractor fails to pay them.

•A specific deadline for completion of each phase of the project.

•A "time is of the essence" clause for specific aspects of the project, which compensates you for damages if, for example, the windows are not completed before blizzard season sets in.

•A date of "substantial completion" by which the owner of the property can once again use or occupy the site of the work, and a provision for compensation if the date is not met.

•A detailed description of all work to be completed, including references to documents such as drawings and specifications.

•A total price, including taxes and ancillary fees.

•A requirement that the contractor give you a receipt for all labor and materials you pay for.

•A precise payment schedule detailing specific amounts and time increments.

•A provision guaranteeing that "corrective work" of any job that does not meet specifications, and a specific date by which the work will be carried out.

•A clause giving the owner the right of inspection, supervision and approval.

•A provision stating that the general contractor is solely responsible for the hiring, supervision and payment of subcontractors.

•A clause stating that the contractor is solely responsible for providing all materials and equipment, and related warranties, for the work to be performed; and is also responsible for any injuries to persons or property during performance of the work.

•A warranty clause covering all equipment and materials.

•A clause permitting the owner to make revisions, deletions or additions within the scope of the project, for which written adjustments in price would then be made.

•A termination provision allowing the owner to end the contract with a specified amount of notice, should the contractor default in the performance of the job.

•A clause mandating the contractor to keep the work space free of accumulated garbage and other waste materials, and to clean the entire site upon completion of work.

•A requirement that the contractor take special care to protect the work site and materials from inclement weather, and that the contractor not use any materials during inclement weather unless appropriate precautions are taken.

When setting a budget for home improvements, determine exactly what you want done and where, and give specific plans to contractors as you gather estimates. If you are obtaining a home-improvement loan, tack on a "cushion" of about 20 percent more than you determine the job will cost, so you are not in danger, for example, of running out of funds when you have half a roof.

When choosing among contractors:

•Check their licenses and references.

•Speak with their former customers.

•Inquire about their bond and trade-association memberships.

•Find out about their insurance coverage.

•Ask about warranty coverage.

Above all, do not make a hasty decision: It is one you will literally have to live with for a long time.

Small Claims Court

Cases that involve less than a certain amount of money—in most states, about $1,500 or $2,000—are settled in small claims court. These cases involve money damages only, and are strictly for noncorporate claimants. Corporations can be sued in small claims court, but they cannot sue others.

Cases generally involve such issues as botched repairs, damages from dry cleaning or other services, defective merchandise and nonpayment for services.

If you believe you have a case, go to

your local small claims court, fill out the necessary paperwork and pay a small filing fee. A certified letter will then be mailed to the defendant, and a time (usually in the evening) will be set for the claim to be heard. If you will not be able to make it to court at that time, you can request an alternative time.

If damaged merchandise is the issue, bring with you as proof of its value an itemized bill or invoice, which is receipted or marked paid; or two itemized estimates of what it would cost to fix or replace the item. You are also free to call witnesses and, of course, to be represented by an attorney; most small claims plaintiffs, however, opt to represent themselves.

Cases are heard by either a judge or an arbitrator, who is a volunteer attorney. Judges are bound by the rules of evidence, so there are tighter restrictions on admissible testimony. Hearsay is not acceptable, for example. Also, a judge's decision can be appealed. If the two parties agree to go before an arbitrator, all testimony will be heard, but the final decision will be binding and cannot be appealed.

If your hearing is before a judge, find out which judge will be presiding over your case; if the proceedings are open to the public, sit in on one of the judge's sessions to determine his or her general style and demeanor, and which approaches seem to work best (and worst).

Attorney Stephen Christianson, author of *100 Ways to Avoid Common Pitfalls Without A Lawyer,* suggests that on the day of your hearing, you:

• Dress conservatively.

• Remain calm throughout the proceedings.

• Never raise your voice or use foul language.

• Avoid getting into arguments with the opposition and his or her counsel or representatives.

• Address the judge respectfully, as Your Honor.

Attorney Michael Connors, a partner at Connors & Sullivan in New York City, adds:

• Arrive on time—preferably early. Never assume a court calendar will be running behind schedule; the day of your hearing is the day it won't be.

• Tell your whole story from the beginning. Try to remember that the judge or arbitrator knows nothing about your case prior to your arrival.

• Stick to the point. Most judges have to hear 10 to 12 cases in a single session.

If the judgment has gone in your favor and you are having trouble getting paid, take your complaint to the city marshall or sheriff's office, which will follow up on it. There is usually a small filing fee involved.

When to Hire a Lawyer

Any time a significant amount of money is on the line or you are involved in proceedings that require court clerks, you should be represented by counsel, who can navigate the system much better than you can on your own. Handling a case badly on your own can ultimately be far more expensive and time-consuming than handling it right the first time with a lawyer.

To find a lawyer, ask your friends and family first; find out if someone who had a similar case was satisfied with results. Or call local bar or legal associations to find out which lawyers in the area handle cases of your type. As always, check out an attorney's background, education and licensing; see if he or she will let you talk to other clients.

Sources of Further Information

BOOKS

CCH Estate Planning Guide. Commerce Clearing House Inc., Chicago, 1992.

Collect Your Court Judgment. Gini Graham Scott, Stephen Goldfarb and Lisa Goldoftas, Nolo Press, Berkeley, Calif., 1991.

The Complete Book of Wills and Estates. Alexander Bove Jr., Holt and Co., New York, 1989.

Everyday Contracts. Theresa Meehan, George Milko and Kay Ostberg, HALT Inc., Washington, D.C., 1989.

Everyday Legal Forms. Irving Sloan, Oceana Group, Dobbs Ferry, N.Y., 1991.

How To Handle Your Own Contracts. Christopher Neubert and Jack Withiam Jr., Sterling Publishing, New York, 1991.

How To Probate an Estate. Julia Nissley, Nolo Press, Berkeley, Calif., 1991.

Instant Legal Forms. Ralph Troisi, Tab Books, Blue Ridge Summit, Pa., 1993.

Law Dictionary. H.C. Black, West Publishing, St. Paul, Minn., 1992.

The Legal Forms Kit. Homestead Publishing, Torrance, Calif., 1992.

Nolo's Simple Will Book. Denis Clifford, Nolo Press, Berkeley, Calif., 1991.

100 Ways to Avoid Legal Pitfalls Without a Lawyer. Stephen Christianson, Citadel Press, New York, 1993.

Plan Your Estate With a Living Trust. Denis Clifford, Nolo Press, Berkeley, Calif., 1989.

The Power of Attorney Book. Denis Clifford, Nolo Press, Berkeley, Calif., 1991.

Simple Contracts for Personal Use. Stephen Elias, Nolo Press, Berkeley, Calif., 1990.

Tenant's Rights. Myron Moskovitz and Ralph Warner, Nolo Press, Berkeley, Calif., 1991.

What You Should Know About Contracts. Robert Farmer, Simon and Schuster Inc., New York, 1992.

Write Your Own Living Will. Bradley E. Smith, Crown Publishing, New York, 1991.

Writing Your Will. Holmes F. Crouch, Robert Erdmann Publishing, Escondido, Calif., 1991.

You Can't Take It With You. David C. Larsen, Vintage/Random House, New York, 1988.

Your Will and Estate Planning. Fred Tillman and Susan Parker, Houghton Mifflin, New York, 1990.

ORGANIZATIONS

American Bar Association
    1800 M Street NW
    Washington, DC
    1-202-331-2200

Legal Services Corp.
    750 First Street NE
    Washington, DC
    1-202-336-8800

U.S. GOVERNMENT

Department of Housing and Urban Development
    451 Seventh St. SW
    Washington, DC 20410
    For federal-housing issues.

Federal Trade Commission
    Sixth and Pennsylvania Aves. NW
    Washington, DC 20580
    For federal credit-law information.

Federal Reserve
    20th and C Sts. NW
    Washington, DC 20551
    For federal banking-law information.

A number of useful free or low-cost pamphlets are available from the Consumer Information Center. Write Consumer Information Catalog, Pueblo, CO 81002 for a free copy of the catalog.

Index
